T0213873

Lecture Notes in Computer Science   10040

Commenced Publication in 1973
Founding and Former Series Editors:
Gerhard Goos, Juris Hartmanis, and Jan van Leeuwen

More information about this series at http://www.springer.com/series/7409

Xingming Sun · Alex Liu
Han-Chieh Chao · Elisa Bertino (Eds.)

Cloud Computing and Security

Second International Conference, ICCCS 2016
Nanjing, China, July 29–31, 2016
Revised Selected Papers, Part II

 Springer

Editors
Xingming Sun
University of Information Science and
  Technology
Nanjing
China

Alex Liu
Michigan State University
East Lansing, MI
USA

Han-Chieh Chao
National Dong Hwa University
Shoufeng
Taiwan

Elisa Bertino
Purdue University
West Lafayette, IN
USA

ISSN 0302-9743   ISSN 1611-3349 (electronic)
Lecture Notes in Computer Science
ISBN 978-3-319-48673-4   ISBN 978-3-319-48674-1   (eBook)
DOI 10.1007/978-3-319-48674-1

Library of Congress Control Number: 2016955502

LNCS Sublibrary: SL3 – Information Systems and Applications, incl. Internet/Web, and HCI

Printed on acid-free paper

This Springer imprint is published by Springer Nature
The registered company is Springer International Publishing AG
The registered company address is: Gewerbestrasse 11, 6330 Cham, Switzerland

Preface

This volume contains the papers presented at ICCCS 2016: the Second International Conference on Cloud Computing and Security held during July 29–31, 2016, in Nanjing, China. The conference was hosted by the College of Computer and Software at the Nanjing University of Information Science and Technology, who provided the wonderful facilities and material support. We made use of the excellent EasyChair submission and reviewing software.

The aim of this conference is to provide an international forum for the latest results from research, development, and applications in the field of cloud computing and information security. This year we received more than 270 submissions from 15 countries and regions, including USA, UK, France, Australia, Ireland, South Korea, South Africa, India, Iraq, Kazakhstan, Indonesia, Vietnam, Ghana, China, and Taiwan. Each submission was allocated to three Program Committee (PC) members and each paper received on average of three reviews. The committee decided to accept 97 papers.

The program also included ten distinguished talks: "A Bacteria-Inspired Solution for 5G Mobile Communication" by Prof. Han-Chieh Chao, National Dong Hwa University, Taiwan; "Flow-Net Accountable Logging and Applications" by Dr. Yang Xiao, University of Alabama, USA; "Security and Privacy in Cloud Computing: Challenges and Opportunities" by Prof. Yang Xiang, Deakin University, Australia; "Internet of Vehicles: When Cloud Computing Meets Intelligent Transport Systems" by Prof. Yan Zhang, Simula Research Laboratory and University of Oslo, Norway; "Children's Privacy Protection Engine for Smart Anthropomorphic Toys" by Prof. Patrick C. K. Hung, University of Ontario Institute of Technology (UOIT), Canada; "Bioinformatics and Cloud Computing" by Dr. Zemin Ning, Wellcome Trust Sanger Institute, UK; "Towards Smart and Secure Connected Health" by Dr. Honggang Wang, University of Massachusetts Dartmouth, USA; "Semantic Searchover Encrypted Cloud Data" by Dr. Zhangjie Fu, Nanjing University of Information Science and Technology, China; "Coverless Information Hiding Method Based on the Text Big Data" by Dr. Xianyi Chen, Nanjing University of Information Science and Technology, China.

We would like to extend our sincere thanks to all authors who submitted papers to ICCCS 2016, and all PC members. It was a truly great experience to work with such talented and hard-working researchers. We also appreciate the external reviewers for assisting the PC members in their particular areas of expertise. Finally, we would like to thank all attendees for their active participation and the organizing team who nicely managed this conference. We look forward to seeing you again at next year's ICCCS.

July 2016

Xingming Sun
Alex Liu
Han-Chieh Chao
Elisa Bertino

Organization

General Chairs

Xingming Sun	Nanjing University of Information Science and Technology, China
Alex Liu	Michigan State University, USA
Han-Chieh Chao	National Dong Hwa University, Taiwan
Elisa Bertino	University of Purdue, USA

Technical Program Committee Chairs

Chin-Feng Lai	National Chung Cheng University, Taiwan
Yang Xiao	University of Alabama, USA
Yun Q. Shi	New Jersey Institute of Technology, USA
Jian Shen	Nanjing University of Information Science and Technology, China

Technical Program Committee

Saeed Arif	University of Algeria, Algeria
Zhifeng Bao	Royal Melbourne Institute of Technology University, Australia
Hanhua Chen	Huazhong University of Science and Technology, China
Jie Chen	East China Normal University, China
Xiaofeng Chen	Xidian University, China
Ilyong Chung	Chosun University, South Korea
Jintai Ding	University of Cincinnati, USA
Zhangjie Fu	Nanjing University of Information Science and Technology, China
Jinguang Han	Nanjing University of Finance and Economics, China
Mohammad Mehedi Hassan	King Saud University, Saudi Arabia
Debiao He	Wuhan University, China
Wien Hong	Nanfang College of Sun Yat-Sen University, China
Qiong Huang	South China Agricultural University, China
Xinyi Huang	Fujian Normal University, China
Yongfeng Huang	Tsinghua University, China
Zhiqiu Huang	Nanjing University of Aeronautics and Astronautics, China
Patrick C.K. Hung	University of Ontario Institute of Technology, Canada
Hai Jin	Huazhong University of Science and Technology, China
Sam Tak Wu Kwong	City University of Hong Kong, SAR China

Mingwu Zhang	Hubei University of Technology, China
Wei Zhang	Nanjing University of Posts and Telecommunications, China
Xinpeng Zhang	University of Science and Technology of China, China
Yan Zhang	Simula Research Laboratory, Norway
Yao Zhao	Beijing Jiaotong University, China

Organizing Committee Chairs

Chih-Hsien Hsia	Chinese Culture University, Taiwan
Yingtao Jiang	University of Nevada at Las Vegas, USA
Eric Wong	University of Texas at Dallas, USA
Zhangjie Fu	Nanjing University of Information Science and Technology, China

Organizing Committee

Xianyi Chen	Nanjing University of Information Science and Technology, China
Zhiguo Qu	Nanjing University of Information Science and Technology, China
Zhaoqing Pan	Nanjing University of Information Science and Technology, China
Yan Kong	Nanjing University of Information Science and Technology, China
Zhili Zhou	Nanjing University of Information Science and Technology, China
Baowei Wang	Nanjing University of Information Science and Technology, China
Zhihua Xia	Nanjing University of Information Science and Technology, China

Contents – Part II

Multimedia Applications

Multimedia Security and Forensics

Contents – Part I

Cloud Computing

Cloud Security

IOT Applications

A Lifetime-Aware Network Maintenance Method for Wireless Sensor Networks

Long Cheng[1,2(✉)], Yan Wang[1,2], Hao Chu[1], and Qilin Wan[2]

[1] School of Information Science and Engineering,
Northeastern University, Shenyang 110819, China
[2] Department of Computer and Communication Engineering,
Northeastern University, Qinhuangdao 066004, China
chenglong8501@gmail.com

Abstract. Wireless sensor networks (WSNs) own large quantities of small, inexpensive sensor nodes over a region of interest. The sensor nodes are randomly deployed in the region. WSNs may suffer coverage problem due to death of the nodes. It may reduce the coverage quality. In this paper, the network maintenance problem is investigated. We firstly introduce the network health indicator model using the sensing probability model and energy consumption model. And then the holes determination problem is converted into the optimization problem, so we employ the Fuzzy C-Mean method to identify the network holes. Finally, network repair method is proposed to maintenance the network. Simulation results show that the proposed method could effectively improve the lifetime of network and sensing quality.

Keywords: Wireless sensor networks · Network maintenance · Lifetime · Sensing probability · Network hole

1 Introduction

Wireless sensor networks (WSNs) consist of hundreds of sensor nodes which compose of micro-processor, memory, sensors and battery [1, 2]. WSNs have attracted many attentions due to their various application areas such as healthy monitoring, remote surveillance and target tracking. The sensor nodes are randomly deployed in the monitor field. The node measures the physical signal and sends it to sink node through the multi-hop communication. The sensor node is powered by the battery, so the energy consumption is the key problem for WSNs. If the energy is exhausted, the sensor node will dead and loss the sensing functions. It will lead to the coverage hole and decrease the Quality of Service (QoS) of WSNs. Therefore the network lifetime is a key indicator for WSNs [3].

The network needs maintenance (or repair) when the coverage hole appear. Some recent works have investigated the network maintenance problem. In [4], a method to repair network partitioning by using a mobile node is proposed. In this method, a degree of connectivity with neighbors is firstly used. Then the mobile node finds the position where to deploy a new node to restore the network connectivity. In [5], the proposed network repair scheme consists of a regular repair and an instant repair schemes. The regular repair scheme is to periodically refresh the network to keep it in a good shape.

© Springer International Publishing AG 2016
X. Sun et al. (Eds.): ICCCS 2016, Part II, LNCS 10040, pp. 3–13, 2016.
DOI: 10.1007/978-3-319-48674-1_1

The instant repair scheme is triggered when a router identifies that the ink to its parent is broken. A distributed k-connectivity repair algorithm [6] that interacts with a mobile robot is proposed. This algorithm could determine the almost-minimum number of additional sensor nodes to augment an existing network. In [7], an efficient distributed coverage holes repair algorithms are proposed in the post deployment scenario. This method considers limited mobility of the nodes and can select the mobile nodes based on their degree of coverage overlapping. It could minimize the coverage overlapping and maximize the percentage of coverage holes. A least-movement topology repair scheme which is a distributed network recovery method is presented in [8]. This scheme relies on the local view of a node about the network and strives to relocate the least number of nodes. It could reduce the total travelled distance and communication complexity. A level set method based coverage holes detection algorithm [9] is proposed for hybrid sensor network. The network repair problem is converted into data segmentation problem. This algorithm could estimate the number of holes and the size of the holes. It could leverage mobility to optimize the coverage quality and movement distance.

The above methods focus on the degree of connectivity. But they do not consider the residual energy of sensor node. The sensor node which owns lower residual energy may run out the energy in a relatively short period. In [10], the network maintenance problem is formulated as a semi-definite programming optimization problem. And the weighted minimum power routing algorithm to increase the network lifetime due to the efficient utilization of the deployed new nodes. Finally, an adaptive network mainte-nance algorithm is proposed based on the established network health indicator. A chain based relocation approach [11] is proposed to relocate a minimum number of redundant sensors from their initial positions within the region of interest. In order to balance the energy consumption among the sensor nodes, an average energy consumption model is used in selection of the redundant nodes. A novel tracking method and repairing algorithm are proposed for maintaining the coverage quality of WSNs [12]. The pro-posed repairing algorithm could establish an efficient route with low overhead in terms of lower consumption. Therefore, it could maintain the coverage quality while the required energy consumption could significantly reduce. In our previous work [13], COST_MAX_MIN and COST_MAX_AVG algorithms are proposed to improve the coverage quality and decrease the maintenance cost. The computational complexity of COST_MAX_MIN algorithm is relatively lower than COST_MAX_AVG. But the maintenance period of COST_MAX_MIN is also lower.

In this paper, we investigate the network maintenance problem for wireless sensor networks. The network holes determination algorithm is firstly proposed to determine the area of candidate nodes. And the network holes repair method is presented. The proposed maintenance method owns lower computational complexity. This method considers the residual energy of sensor nodes. Therefore, it could improve the coverage quality and prolong the lifetime of network.

The remaining parts of this paper are organized as follows. Section 2 introduces the system model which consists of sensing model, energy consumption model and established network health indicator. Section 3 illustrates the proposed network holes determination and repair algorithms. Section 4 depicts the simulation experiments. The conclusion of this paper is presented in Sect. 5.

2 System Model

In this section, we present the sensing model and energy consumption model of the sensor node. And the network health indicator is established using the sensing model and energy consumption model. It is used to indicate the area that need repair. The scenario we consider is as follows: N beacon nodes are randomly placed in the field, K signal sources are generated randomly. The location of nodes is known by themselves. And the base station knows their location information.

2.1 Sensing Model

The measurement of i-th sensor node as follows:

$$y_i = \begin{cases} \sum_{k=1}^{N} \frac{\beta_k}{d_{ik}^{\gamma/2}} + n_i, H_1 \\ n_i, H_0 \end{cases} \tag{1}$$

where, y_i is the received signal, and n_i is the white Gaussian noise. H_1 is the target present hypothesis and H_0 is the target absent hypothesis, d_{ij} is the distance between target i and sensor j, β_k is energy of k-th source, γ is the scale.

The probability density function of y_i under H_1 and H_0 conditions as follows:

$$P(y_i|H_1) = \frac{1}{\sqrt{2\pi\sigma^2}} \exp\left\{ -\frac{1}{2\sigma^2} \left(y_i - \sum_{k=1}^{N} \frac{\beta_k}{d^{\gamma/2}} \right)^2 \right\} \tag{2}$$

$$P(y_i|H_0) = \frac{1}{\sqrt{2\pi\sigma^2}} \exp\left\{ -\frac{y_i^2}{2\sigma^2} \right\} \tag{3}$$

According to Neyman-Pearson criterion [14], Eqs. (2) and (3), we can obtain:

$$L_i(y_i) = \frac{P(y_i|H_1)}{P(y_i|H_0)} = \exp\left\{ \frac{1}{2\sigma^2} \left(2y_i \sum_{k=1}^{N} \frac{\beta_k}{d^{\gamma/2}} - \left(\sum_{k=1}^{N} \frac{\beta_k}{d^{\gamma/2}} \right)^2 \right) \right\} \underset{H_0}{\overset{H_1}{\gtrless}} \omega \tag{4}$$

where, ω is the decision threshold.

According to Eq. (5), we can obtain:

$$\frac{1}{2\sigma^2} \left(2y_i \sum_{k=1}^{N} \frac{\beta_k}{d^{\gamma/2}} - \left(\sum_{k=1}^{N} \frac{\beta_k}{d^{\gamma/2}} \right)^2 \right) \underset{H_0}{\overset{H_1}{\gtrless}} \ln \omega \tag{5}$$

$$\underbrace{y_i \sum_{k=1}^{N} \frac{\beta_k}{d^{\gamma/2}}}_{h} \underset{H_0}{\overset{H_1}{\gtrless}} \underbrace{\sigma^2 \ln \omega + \frac{1}{2} \left(\sum_{k=1}^{N} \frac{\beta_k}{d^{\gamma/2}} \right)^2}_{k} \tag{6}$$

According to Eq. (2), the above equation can be converted as

$$
\begin{cases}
H_0 : h \sim N\left(0, \sigma^2 \left(\sum_{k=1}^{N} \frac{\beta_k}{d^{\gamma/2}}\right)^2\right) \\
H_1 : h \sim N\left(\left(\sum_{k=1}^{N} \frac{\beta_k}{d^{\gamma/2}}\right)^2, \sigma^2 \left(\sum_{k=1}^{N} \frac{\beta_k}{d^{\gamma/2}}\right)^2\right)
\end{cases}
\tag{7}
$$

We set $\mu_1 = \left(\sum_{k=1}^{N} \frac{\beta_k}{d^{\gamma/2}}\right)^2$, $\sigma_1^2 = \sigma^2 \left(\sum_{k=1}^{N} \frac{\beta_k}{d^{\gamma/2}}\right)^2$

Therefore, the false alarm rate is

$$
P_F = P(h > k|H_0) = 1 - \Phi\left(\frac{k}{\sigma_1}\right)
\tag{8}
$$

where, $\Phi(\bullet)$ is the cumulative distribution function of standard normal distribution, i.e. $\Phi(x) = \int_{-\infty}^{x} \frac{1}{\sqrt{2\pi}} \exp\left(-\frac{y^2}{2}\right) dy$.

The detection probability of sensor node is

$$
P_D = P(h > k|H_1) = 1 - \Phi\left(\frac{k - \mu_1}{\sigma_1}\right)
\tag{9}
$$

According to Eqs. (9) and (10), we can obtain:

$$
\begin{cases}
\frac{k}{\sigma_1} = \Phi^{-1}(1 - \alpha) \\
\frac{\mu_1}{\sigma_1} = \frac{1}{\sigma} \sum_{k=1}^{N} \frac{\beta_k}{d^{\gamma/2}}
\end{cases}
\tag{10}
$$

where α is the false alarm rate.

The sensing model is

$$
p_D = 1 - \Phi\left(\Phi^{-1}(1 - \alpha) - \sum_{k=1}^{N} \frac{\beta_k}{\sigma} d^{-\gamma/2}\right)
\tag{11}
$$

2.2 Energy Consumption Model

The residual energy of sensor nodes is the key indicator for the lifetime of WSNs. In this section, we present the energy consumption model to predict the lifetime of sensor nodes. The energy consumption in transmission per packet is

$$
E_{tx}(l,d) = l \times E_{ele} + l \times d^2 \times E_{amp}
\tag{12}
$$

where, E_{ele} is the energy consumed by non-transmitted device which include frequency synthesizer, mixers, and filters. E_{amp} is the energy consumed by transmitter. l is the length of data packet, and d is the transmission range.

The energy consumption in transmitting and receiving packet is

$$E_{1hop}(l,d) = E_{tx}(l,d) + E_{rx}(l) = l\left(E_{ele} + d^2 E_{amp} + E_{rx}\right) \tag{13}$$

The WSNs employ the CSMA/CA protocol. Therefore, the rate of packet success transmission can be denoted as

$$P_{success} = N \cdot P_r \left[1 - \sum_{i=1}^{r} P_i\right]^{N-1} \tag{14}$$

where, P_i is the transmission probability of i-th slot being selected, N denote the number of contenders.

So the expectation of energy consumption in one hop communication can be expressed as:

$$E_{CSMA} = E_{1hop}(l,d) + (1/P_{success} - 1)E_{busy} \tag{15}$$

2.3 Network Health Indicator

In this section, we establish the network health indicator using the sensing model and energy consumption model. We divide the 2D monitoring field. The network health indicator at grid point (i, j) is given by:

$$C(i,j) = P_D(i,j) + E(i,j) \tag{16}$$

where, $P_D(i,j) = 1 - \prod_{k=1}^{K}\left(1 - p_{ijk}\right)$ is the joint sensing probability of the grid point (i, j) in the sensing radius. $E(i,j) = \sum_{n=1}^{N_s} w_{ijn}\left(1 - E_{CSMA}^{ijn}\right)$ is the prediction of energy consumption, $w_{ijn} = \dfrac{1/E_n^{res}}{\sum\limits_{n=1}^{N_s} 1/E_n^{res}}$ is the weight of each node, N_s is the number of neighbor nodes.

Figure 1 shows the sensing probability, energy distribution and network health indicator. It can be observed that the network hole existing in the network.

3 Network Holes Determination and Repair Algorithms

In this section, we present the proposed methods which consist of two steps. Firstly, the network holes determination algorithm is proposed to identify the positions of holes. Secondly, the holes repair algorithm is investigated to maintenance the network.

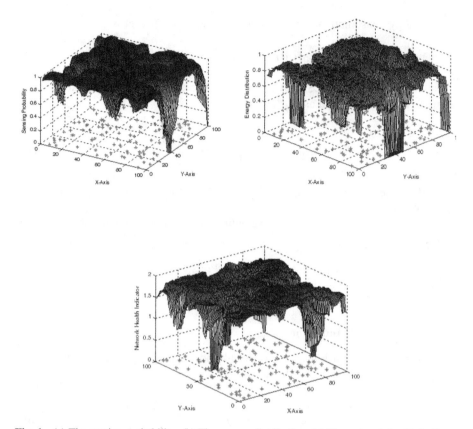

Fig. 1. (a) The sensing probability, (b) The energy distribution, (c) The network health indicator

3.1 Network Holes Determination Algorithm

As shown in Fig. 1(c), the value of network health indicator is less 2. So we firstly convert this figure into the gray image. Then we employ the Fuzzy C-mean (FCM) algorithm to identify the network holes. The holes determination problem is converted into optimization problem. The objective function of optimization is

$$\min J(U, V) = \sum_{i=1}^{c} \sum_{j=1}^{n} \left(u_{ij}\right)^{m} \left(z_{ij}\right)^{2}$$

$$s.t. \sum_{i=1}^{c} u_{ij} = 1, 0 \leq \sum_{j=1}^{n} u_{ij} \leq n \tag{17}$$

where, $1 < m < \infty$, n is the number of grid points, u_{ij} is the degree of membership of grid point j for i-th class. z_{ij} is the Euclidean distance between grid point j and cluster center i.

The steps of the FCM partitioning algorithm are

Step 1. Initialization. We set iteration error ε, $m = 2$, and the classification matrix is initialized in a random way.

Step 2. Computing the cluster center using the following equation:

$$v_i = \frac{\sum_{j=1}^{n} u_{ij}^m x_j}{\sum_{j=1}^{n} u_{ij}^m} \tag{18}$$

where, x_j is the value of grid point j.

Step 3. Update the degree of membership using the following equation:

$$u_{ij} = \left(\sum_{j=1}^{c} \frac{\|x_j - v_i\|}{\|x_j - v_j\|} \right)^{-\frac{1}{m-1}} \tag{19}$$

Step 4. Identify termination conditions: If $\|U^{(s+1)} - U^{(s)}\| \leq \varepsilon$, stop iteration; else goto step 2.

Step 5. Deblurring. The maximum membership criterion is employed to remove fuzziness. The grid point is classified into the satisfied U_i, and $u_{ij} = \max\{u_{qj}\}$, $q = 1, 2, \ldots, c$.

Step 6. If x_j belongs to U_i, x_j will remain unchanged; else $x_j = 0$.

The grid points belong to U_i is in the network holes.

3.2   Network Holes Repair Algorithm

The grid points belong to the networks holes construct the candidate position matrix M. We redeploy the new node on the candidate position to repair the network. The selection scheme as follows.

1. Initialization. Set the number of redeployed nodes $R_n = 0$.
2. Compute the network health indicator of the candidate position. Find the minimum value of network health indicator in the matrix M.
3. Deploy a new node on the selected position in Step 2 and $R_n = R_n + 1$.
4. If the number of redeployed nodes or the average network health indicator achieves the requirement, then stop deploying the node; else goto step 2.

4   Simulation Experiment and Results

In this section, we verify validity and feasibility of the proposed algorithms using the simulation experiments. In the initialization, 100 nodes are randomly deployed in the field of size 100×100. The residual energy of each node is different from 0 to 3000 J.

Table 1. The parameters for the sensing and energy consumption models

Parameters	Values	Parameters	Values
α	0.97	E_{rx}	11.13
σ	1	E_{amp}	3.63
β_k	200	E_{ele}	2.1
$P_{success}$	0.9	l	200
E_{busy}	26	–	–

We compare the proposed method with random redeployment (Rnd) and uniform redeployment (Unif) schemes. The values of the parameters in the sensing and energy consumption models are shown in Table 1.

Figure 2 shows the sensing probability, energy distribution and network health indicator after repairing when the number of redeployment nodes is 80. It can be seen that the network holes no longer exist. So the proposed method could effectively repair the network holes.

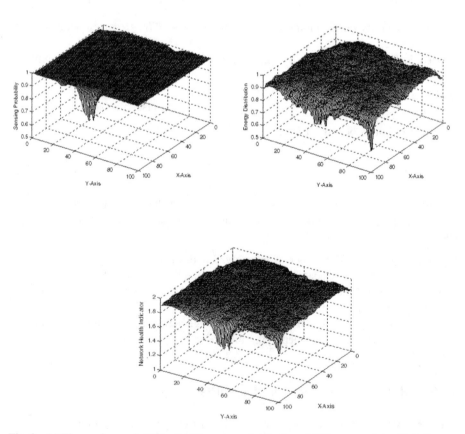

Fig. 2. (a) The sensing probability, (b) The energy distribution, (c) The network health indicator

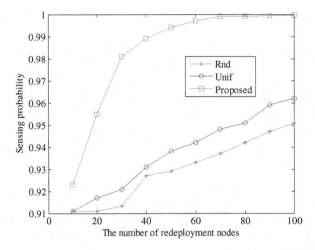

Fig. 3. The number of redeployment nodes versus sensing probability

Figure 3 shows the sensing probability of the three methods under different numbers of redeployment nodes. It can be observed that the sensing probability of the three methods increases with the number of redeployment nodes increases. The Rnd method owns the worst performance. The proposed method has the best performance when compared with other methods.

Figure 4 indicates the lifetime of the network versus the numbers of redeployment nodes. We can see that the proposed method could prolong the network lifetime significantly. And the larger number of redeployment nodes is, the longer lifetime of network achieved.

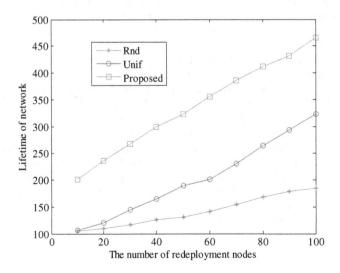

Fig. 4. The number of redeployment nodes versus the network lifetime

5   Conclusions

In this paper, we have addressed the problems of the network maintenance for wireless sensor network. The Neyman-Pearson criterion is used to establish the sensing model. And the node energy consumption model is introduced. The network health indicator is established using the sensing model and energy consumption model. The FCM based network holes determination algorithm is proposed to identify the holes. Then the network holes repair algorithm is investigated to maintenance the network. Simulation results show that the proposed method could repair the network sensing holes and prolong the lifetime of network.

Acknowledge. This work was supported by the National Natural Science Foundation of China under Grant No. 61403068 and No. 61501100; Natural Science Foundation of Hebei Province under Grant No. F2015501097 and F2016501080; Scientific Research Fund of Hebei Provincial Education Department under Grant No. Z2014078; NEUQ internal funding under Grant No. XNB201509 and XNB201510.

References

1. Guo, P., Wang, J., Li, B., Lee, S.: A variable threshold-value authentication architecture for wireless mesh networks. J. Internet Technol. **15**(6), 929–936 (2014)
2. Shen, J., Tan, H., Wang, J., Wang, J., Lee, S.: A novel routing protocol providing good transmission reliability in underwater sensor networks. J. Internet Technol. **16**(1), 171–178 (2015)
3. Xie, S., Wang, Y.: Construction of tree network with limited delivery latency in homogeneous wireless sensor networks. Wireless Pers. Commun. **78**(1), 231–246 (2014)
4. Dini, G., Pelagatti, M., Savino, I.M.: Repairing network partitions in wireless sensor networks. In: Proceedings of the IEEE International Conference on Mobile Adhoc and Sensor Systems Conference, pp. 1–5. IEEE (2007)
5. Pan, M., Tseng, Y.: A lightweight network repair scheme for data collection applications in Zigbee WSNs. IEEE Commun. Lett. **13**(9), 649–651 (2009)
6. Bredin, J.L., Demaine, E.D., Hajiahjayi, M.T., Rus, D.: Deploying sensor networks with guaranteed fault tolerance. IEEE/ACM Trans. Netw. **18**(1), 216–228 (2010)
7. Sahoo, P., Liao, W.: HORA: a distributed coverage hole repair algorithm for wireless sensor networks. IEEE Trans. Mobile Comput. **14**(7), 1397–1410 (2015)
8. Abbasi, A.A., Younis, M.F., Baroudi, U.A.: A least-movement topology repair algorithm for partitioned wireless sensor-actor networks. Int. J. Sens. Netw. **11**(4), 250–262 (2012)
9. Yu, X., Wu, C., Chen, D., Hu, N.: Level set based coverage holes detection and holes healing scheme in hybrid sensor network. Int. J. Distrib. Sens. Netw. **2013**, 1–9 (2013)
10. Ibrahim, A.S., Seddik, K.G., Liu, K.J.R.: Connectivity-aware network maintenance and repair via relays deployment. IEEE Trans. Wireless Commun. **8**(1), 356–366 (2009)
11. Korbi, I.E., Zeadally, S.: Energy-aware sensor node relocation in mobile sensor networks. Ad Hoc Netw. **16**, 247–265 (2014)

12. Chang, C., Lin, C., Yu, G., Kuo, C.: An energy-efficient hole-healing mechanism for wireless sensor networks with obstacles. Wireless Commun. Mob. Comput. **13**(4), 377–392 (2013)
13. Wu, C., Cheng, L., Zhang, Y.: Node redeployment for effective prolong maintenance period in wireless sensor networks. IEICE Trans. Commun. **E95B**(10), 3179–3186 (2012)
14. Xiang, M., Zhao, J.W.: On the performance of distributed Neyman-Pearson detection systems. IEEE Trans. Syst. Man Cybern. Part A **31**(1), 78–83 (2001)

An Efficient Task Assignment Mechanism for Crowdsensing Systems

Zhuan Shi[1], He Huang[1,3], Yu-E Sun[2,3(✉)], Xiaocan Wu[1], Fanzhang Li[1], and Miaomiao Tian[3]

[1] School of Computer Science and Technology, Soochow University, Suzhou, China
[2] School of Urban Rail Transportation, Soochow University, Suzhou, China
sunye12@suda.edu.cn
[3] Suzhou Institute for Advanced Study,
University of Science and Technology of China, Suzhou, China

Abstract. Crowdsensing has attracted more and more attention in recent years, which can help companies or data demanders to collect large amounts of data efficiently and cheaply. In a crowdsensing system, the sensing tasks are divided into many small sub-tasks that can be easily accomplished by smartphone users, and the companies take advantage of the data collected by all the smartphone users to improve the quality of their services. Efficient task assignment mechanism design is very critical for crowdsensing under some realistic constraints. However, existing studies on task assignment issue are still have many limitations, such as most of them are failed to consider the time budget of smartphone users. Therefore, this work studies the optimal task assignment problem in crowdsensing systems, which can maximize the task completion rate with consideration of the time budget of users. We also prove that the optimal task assignment problem is NP-hard, thus we adopt the linear relaxation and greedy techniques to design a near-optimal crowdsensing task assignment mechanism. We also empirically evaluate our mechanism and show that the proposed task assignment mechanism is efficient.

Keywords: Crowdsensing · Task assignment · Time budget · Approximation algorithm design

1 Introduction

In recent years, with the advent of emerging wireless technologies (*e.g.* 4/5G, Femtocell, Offloading) and micro-embedded sensors (such as digital compass, camera, accelerometer, GPS, proximity sensor, gyroscope, and *etc.*), smartphones and the some other intelligent mobile devices are becoming the crucial central computing devices in our daily lives [2,12,14]. Meanwhile, the storage capacities and computing capabilities of the smart devices are getting powerful [10]. Thus, the smartphone not only serves as the common communication and computing device, but it also acts as an information collection and programmable device nowadays. With the increasing number of smartphone users,

© Springer International Publishing AG 2016
X. Sun et al. (Eds.): ICCCS 2016, Part II, LNCS 10040, pp. 14–24, 2016.
DOI: 10.1007/978-3-319-48674-1_2

crowdsensing (*a.k.a* mobile phone sensing, mobile crowd sensing, participatory sensing) applications have been emerging as a promising paradigm which takes advantage of the smartphones to collect the ubiquitous environment data efficiently and cheaply. Comparing with the traditional static and artificial data collecting methods, the sensed data collected from smartphones also far beyond the scale of traditional ones.

Crowdsensing system borrows from the original idea of crowdsourcing, which is regarded as a distributed problem-solving and business production model. To reduce the production costs, a crowdsourcing system (*e.g.* Amazon Turk) often introduces a large amount of volunteers to solve a complex problem by offering some of them with bonus [7,21]. Thus, crowdsensing systems can leverage the power of large crowd to complete the large-scale sensing tasks at a lower cost [6]. Considering of the full potential of crowdsensing, many researchers have proposed numerous crowdsensing systems. For instance, literature [17] proposed a crowdsourcing system, named VTrack, for estimating the travel time in urban area to relieve the traffic delay with the built-in GPS. Kumar Rana *et al.* [16] implements a Ear-Phone system for urban noise mapping, which can monitor the environmental noise pollution in urban areas through crowdsourcing data collection.

Many existing studies assume that the volunteers are willing to upload their sensed data to the task demanders without any reward. Unfortunately, due to the limitation of battery and CPU resources, most of the smartphone users are not willing to participate in crowdsensing tasks without payment [8,20]. Therefore, task allocation issue is playing an important role in mechanism design. There have been large amount of efforts in researching the task allocation problem for the crowdsensing systems [1,6,9,22,23]. However, most of the existing studies did not consider the time budget of smartphone users. In practice, the smartphone users may not always available during each round of task assignment. Different users may have different time budget for crowdsensing tasks according to their schedules. We can only assign tasks which can be finished by users within their time budgets. Moreover, most of the existing studies restrict that we can only assign no more than one task to each user in each round, which makes the task assignment mechanisms are not very efficient. Only [6] assumes that each user has a time budget, which corresponds to a traveling distance budget. However, the distance budget is not always equal to the time budget. For example, the time budget of one user is 1 h and his moving speed is 5 km/h, which does not mean that this user is willing to achieve the tasks within 5 km. In a more realistic scenario, most of the users only want to achieve the tasks nearby. To ensure this, users in [6] need to set their distance budgets to small values, which will decrease the performance of the task assignment mechanism. To deal with the above challenges, more practical and efficient crowdsensing task assignment mechanisms are needed.

This work is focused on an efficient task assignment mechanism design for mobile sensing systems, which can maximize the task completion rate with consideration of time budget of the smartphone users. We define the task completion rate as the ratio of the number of tasks that are assigned to users and the total number of tasks supplied by platform. In general, the more tasks are finished by users, the more improvement of the quality of service supplied by the platform we can get. Thus, to design an efficient task assignment mechanism that maximizes the task completion rate can help to improve the service performance. To make our model more efficient, we also allow the platform assign multiple tasks to users in each round of assignment. However, it is a hard work to design an efficient mechanism under our crowdsensing system model. We can prove that the optimal task assignment problem studied in this work is NP-hard. To tackle this NP-hardness, we use LP (*a.k.a* linear programming) relaxation and greedy techniques to design a near-optimal task assignment algorithm. The main contributions of this work can be summarized as follows:

- To the best of our knowledge, we are the first to study crowdsensing task assignment mechanism which assumes that each user has a time budget and aims at maximizing the task completion rate.
- We design a near-optimal task assignment algorithm, which based on LP relaxation and greedy techniques.

2   Problem Model

In this section, we will introduce the crowdsensing system model and the optimal task assignment problem we studied in this paper.

2.1   Crowdsensing System Model

We study a mobile sensing system, which is composed of a mobile sensing platform and a set of smartphone users. In our model, the platform will assign the sensing tasks to the smartphone users, and the users will be paid accordingly after finishing their tasks. For instance, if some application providers are willing to draw the noise map of a city, the sensing platform will assign the tasks of collecting noise to the smartphone users. Each selected user need to collect noise data from a certain number of monitoring points and submit the sensing data to the platform. In this work, we assume that each task can only be assigned to one user, and leave the case that one task can be accomplished by multiple users as our further work.

Our task assignment mechanism runs periodically. In each round, we assume that there exist m tasks in the platform, which are in the set $T = \{t_1, t_2, t_3, ..., t_m\}$. Each task $t_j(j \in [1, m])$ can be denoted as $t_j = \{L_j, d_j\}$, where L_j is the location of t_j and d_j is the detailed description of t_j. After reading the description of tasks, there are n smartphone users want to join in the tasks. We use $U = \{u_1, u_2, u_3, ..., u_n\}$ to denote the set of smartphone users. Each user $u_i \in U$ will submit the sensing plan to the platform. The sensing plan of each u_i can be described as $s_i = \{L_i, r_i, time\_budget_i, b_i\}$, where L_i is the geographical location of u_i, r_i is the acting radius of u_i, $time\_budget_i$ is the upper bound of u_i's working time duration, and b_i is the per-unit time bid of u_i for completing the tasks. Usually, people only want to do the tasks nearby. Thus, we assume that each user only wants to do the tasks that are located in the circle within the geographical location L_i as the center and r_i as the radius. Moreover, we also consider the time budget of each user, which is not considered in most of the previous studies. Thus, the total working time of u_i is defined as the time consuming for achieving all the tasks that assigned to u_i, which should not exceed $time\_budget_i$.

2.2   The Optimal Task Assignment Problem

In general, the more tasks are accomplished, the better performance of the crowd-sensing system can get. Therefore, in this work, maximizing the accomplished tasks is the optimal object during the task assignment procedure. The so-called optimal task assignment problem is aiming at maximizing the number of the tasks accomplished, which can be represented as $\max \sum_{t_j \in T} x_j$. Here, $x_j = 1$ denotes that t_j is assigned to user, and $x_j = 0$ means that t_j is not assigned to any smartphone user. To assign tasks to users optimally, we first introduce a variable $c_{i,j}$ to indicate whether t_j is within u_i's activity range. If t_j is within u_i's activity range, t_j can be assigned to u_i and we set $c_{i,j} = 1$; otherwise, t_j cannot be assigned to u_i and we set $c_{i,j} = 0$. Further, we use a binary variable $x_{i,j} = \{0, 1\}$ to denote whether t_j is assigned to user u_i or not. According to the constraints mentioned above, we can conclude that $x_{i,j}$ should be no more than $c_{i,j}$ (i.e. $x_{i,j} \leq c_{i,j}$). From the relationship between x_j and $x_{i,j}$, its easy to get that $x_j = \sum_{u_i \in U} x_{i,j}$.

Then, we use $time_{i,j}$ to denote the consumption time that u_i requires to achieve the task t_j. Note that $time_{i,j}$ includes the time of u_i arrives to the required location of t_j from L_i, the required time to accomplish t_j, and the time return to L_i from t_j. In our model, we assume that each user has a time budget. Thus, we will ensure that all the tasks that assigned to u_i satisfies $\sum_{t_j \in T} x_{i,j} time_{i,j} \leq time\_budget_i$ in the proposed task assignment mechanism. Since $\sum_{t_j \in T} x_{i,j} time_{i,j}$ is the upper bound of time for u_i to finish all the tasks that assigned to it, the time budget of each user will not be violated.

Finally, we use p_i to represent the payment of u_i after the smartphone user i accomplishes all the assigned tasks. In this work, we assume that $p_i = \sum_{t_j \in T} x_{i,j} time_{i,j}$. We further assume that the platform has a general budget constraint B in terms of the task assignment plan, so the total payment of users can not exceed B, which should satisfy the constraint $\sum_{u_i \in U} p_i \leq B$.

According to the analysis above, the optimal task assignment problem studied in this work can be described as an integer problem (IP(1)):

$$\max \quad g(x) = \sum_{t_j \in T} x_j,$$

subject to

$$\begin{cases} x_{i,j} \leq c_{i,j}, \forall i, \forall j \\ x_j = \sum_{u_i \in U} x_{i,j}, \forall j \\ \sum_{t_j \in T} x_{i,j} time_{i,j} \leq time\_budget_i, \forall i \\ \sum_{u_i \in U} (b_i \cdot \sum_{t_j \in T} x_{i,j} time_{i,j}) \leq B \\ x_j = \{0,1\}, \forall j \\ x_{i,j} = \{0,1\}, \forall i, \forall j \end{cases}$$

We can prove that the proposed IP(1) is NP-hard.

Theorem 1: The optimal task assignment problem studied in this paper is NP-hard.

Proof: Consider a simple situation where there is only one user. In this case, the problem we studied can be viewed as a 0–1 knapsack problem, where the time that the user consumes to accomplish tasks can be viewed as the weight of goods in 0–1 knapsack problem, the volume of the knapsack is the time budget of this user and the value of goods in 0–1 knapsack problem are all equal to one unit in our problem. Since the 0–1 knapsack problem is a typical NP-hard problem, the optimal task assignment problem studied in this paper is NP-hard.

As is known to all, there exists a PTAS (Polynomial-time approximation scheme) mechanism based on dynamic programming to solve the 0–1 knapsack problem. However, this mechanism can only be used in the case that there is one user. For the case that there exist multiple users, we need to design other mechanism to solve the NP-hard problem we studied in this paper.

3 Approximation Task Assignment Mechanism

To tackle this NP-hardness we studied, we adopt the linear programming (LP) relaxation technique to design a near optimal task assignment mechanism in this section. In the following, we will give the details of the proposed mechanism.

3.1 The Relaxation of IP(1)

We first relax IP(1) to linear programming LP(2) by replacing $x_{i,j} = \{0,1\}$ with $0 \leq x_{i,j} \leq 1$, and replace $x_j = \{0,1\}$ with $0 \leq x_j \leq 1$. Then, the optimal task assignment problem is reformulated as the following relaxed LP problem (LP(2)):

$$\max \quad g(x) = \sum_{t_j \in T} x_j,$$

subject to

$$
\begin{cases}
x_{i,j} \leq c_{i,j}, \forall i, \forall j \\
x_j = \sum_{u_i \in U} x_{i,j}, \forall j \\
\sum_{t_j \in T} x_{i,j} time_{i,j} \leq time\_budget_i, \forall i \\
\sum_{u_i \in U} (b_i \cdot \sum_{t_j \in T} x_{i,j} time_{i,j}) \leq B \\
0 \leq x_j \leq 1, \forall j \\
0 \leq x_{i,j} \leq 1, \forall i, \forall j
\end{cases}
$$

The relaxed problem LP(2) has a polynomial number of variables and constraints, thus it can be solved optimally in polynomial time. Assume that the optimal solution of LP(2) is O_{LP}, the optimal solution of IP(1) is O_{IP} and F_{IP} is a feasible solution of IP(1). Obviously, we can get O_{LP} in polynomial time by solving LP(2) optimally. However, either $x_{i,j}$ or x_j should be equal to 0 or 1 in the task assignment model, which means a value between 0 to 1 is meaningless. Thus, O_{LP} is often not a feasible solution of IP(1). To solve this problem, we need to design a mechanism to convert the O_{LP} to a feasible solution of IP(1).

3.2 A Near-Optimal Solution for the Optimal Task Assignment Problem

To convert O_{LP} to a feasible solution of IP(1), we need to select the allocation relationships which satisfy $0 < x_{i,j} < 1$ in O_{LP}, and set them equal to 1. In this work, we propose a greedy-like mechanism, which is described in Algorithm 1.

During the process of assigning the tasks, the platform applies Algorithm 1. Before applying it, we have already had the optimal solution of linear programming O_{LP}, the set of users sensing plans S, the set of tasks T released by the platform, the budget constraint B of the platform. First, we introduce a variable B', whose original value is $B' = 0$, to represent the actual payment of the platform. We introduce a variable t'_i for each user u_i, whose original value $t'_i = 0$, to represent u_i's actual working time. At the beginning, we sort all the $x_{i,j} \in O_{LP}$ in descending order. When $x_{i,j}$ was scanned, we decide first whether t_j has been assigned to users, then whether the actual working time that u_i consumed is within the upper time limit $time\_budget_i$ if we assign t_j to u_i, and finally whether the actual payment of the platform is no more than the budget constraint B if we assign t_j to u_i. If the above three conditions are all met at the same time, we will assign t_j to u_i, which means sets $x^f_{i,j} = 1$ and updates the value of B' and t'_i. Otherwise, we set $x^f_{i,j} = 0$. Then we decide the next one $x_{i,j}$ in the ordered list. We repeat the process again and again until all the $x^f_{i,j}$ has been decided. At last, we output the set $F_{IP} = \{x^f_{i,j}\}_{u_i \in U, t_j \in T}$. The value correspondent to the set F_{IP} is the final result of our winner determination mechanism.

Algorithm 1. Approximation task assignment mechanism

Input: the optimal solution of LP(2): O_{LP}, the sensing plan of users $S = \{s_i\}_{i \leq n}$, the set of tasks T, the budget B;

Output: the feasible solution of IP(1): F_{IP};

1: Set $B' = 0$;
2: **for** each $t_i \in T$ **do**
3:     Set $x'_j = 0$;
4: **for** each $s_i \in S$ **do**
5:     Set $time'_i = 0$;
6: Sort all the $x_{i,j} \in O_{LP}$ in descending order;
7: **for** each $x_{i,j}$ in the sorted list **do**
8:     **if** $x'_j < 1$ **then**
9:         **if** $time'_i + time_{i,j} \leq time\_budget_i$ **then**
10:            **if** $B' + b_i time_{i,j} \leq B$ **then**
11:                Set $x^f_{i,j} = 1$;
12:                Set $x'_j = 1$;
13:                Set $B' = B' + b_i * time_{i,j}$;
14:                Set $time'_i = time'_i + time_{i,j}$;
15:     **if** $x_{i,j} < 1$ **then**
16:         Set $x^f_{i,j} = 0$;
17: **return** $F_{IP} = \{x^f_{i,j}\}_{u_i \in U, t_j \in T}$;

---

4   Simulation Results and Analysis

In this section, we will provide the results of simulation experiment of the proposed algorithm, thus to analyze and verify its practical performances. Since the target of our mechanism is to maximize the task completion rate, we will give the formal definition first.

Task completion rate: We define the task completion rate as the ratio between the number of tasks that assigned to users and the total number of tasks that supplied by the platform (*i.e.* $\eta = \sum_{t_j \in T} x_j / n$).

In the simulation, we assume that the tasks and users are located in a $200 * 200$ area. In our model, we assume that $time_{i,j}$ includes the time of u_i reaches t_j from L_i, to accomplish t_j, and return to L_i from t_j. Thus, we set that the completion time that u_i accomplish t_j is (which does not include the time that users consume to reach t_j and return to L_i from t_j) uniformly distributed in the range of $[1/3, 1/2]$, and the moving speed of users are uniformly distributed in the range of $[40, 50]$. Suppose for each user in the set, the working time, radius and per unit time bid are uniformly distributed in the range of $[6, 8]$, $[25, 35]$ and $[35, 50]$ respectively. Finally, all the results are the average value of data from 2000 independent experiments. Meanwhile, in order to testify the stability of the algorithm, we respectively conduct our experiments in uniform distribution and hot spot distribution according to the distribution of the users.

Uniform distribution model: In this model, all the geographical location of tasks and users are uniformly distributed in a $200 * 200$ area.

Hot spot distribution model: In this model, the geographical location of tasks are uniformly distributed in a $200 * 200$ area, the geographical location of 90% users are uniformly distributed in a $16 * 16$ square hot spot area, and 10% users are located uniformly in other area.

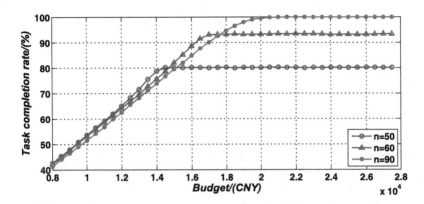

Fig. 1. The relationship between the task completion rate and the budget constraint under uniform distribution

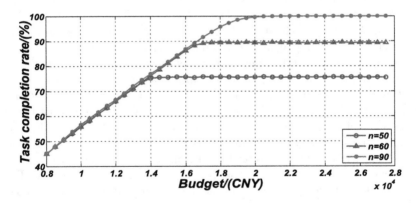

Fig. 2. The relationship between the task completion rate and the budget constraint under hot spot distribution

Figures 1 and 2 show the relationship between task completion rates and the budget constraint of the platform when the number of users is 50, 60, and 90 in uniform and hot spot distribution. Apparently, with the budget constraint increasing, the task completion rate first increase and then level off. This is mainly because the platform has no enough money to pay the users who are willing to do the tasks when the budget constraint is relatively low. Thus, larger budget means the platform can assign more tasks to users in this case, the number of the accomplished tasks increase with the increasing of the budget constraint. Due to each user has a time budget, the platform only can assign limit tasks to each user. Thus, the task completion rate will not increase with the budget constraint when there are no user can be assign more tasks, and the task completion rate curve will level off. Obviously, more user can do more tasks when the budget is larger enough, thus the task completion rates should increase with the increasing number of the users, which is confirmed by Figs. 1 and 2.

5 Related Work

In recent years, many state-of-art studies on crowdsensing systems have been proposed [3,4,11,15–19]. For example, [16] and [17] are making effort on road traffic monitoring. In [4], the authors proposed a crowdsensing based street holes detection system by letting users share vibration and location information captured by smartphones.

Task assignment mechanism is critical in crowdsensing system design, which determines whether a crowdsensing system can achieve good service quality. Recent years, the optimal crowdsensing task assignment problem has been widely studied and many efficient mechanisms have been proposed. For instance, Zhao *et al.* designed an online mechanism for tasks allocation with consideration of budget constraint [22]. In [5], Feng *et al.* proposed two allocation mechanisms for mobile crowdsensing system in two different scenarios with consideration of uncertain arrivals of tasks, strategic behaviors. In [23], Zhao *et al.* proposed two fair energy-efficient approximation algorithms for allocating tasks optimally in crowdsensing systems. In [13], an allocation mechanism based on all-pay auctions is studied, which aims at attracting more users' participation while maximizing the organizer's profit. In [1], the authors proposed an online model to efficiently decide the most appropriate set of users to achieve the incoming tasks. Many tasks of the crowdsensing systems are location dependent, thus the users need to spend a certain amount of time to travel around when they finish the tasks. In practice, many users only have limited times to achieve the tasks. However, the time budget of users is only considered in [6]. Even in [6], the authors viewed the time budget of users as distance budget, which is not very reasonable. Thus, we will solve this challenge in this work and propose an efficient task assignment mechanism.

6 Conclusion

In this paper, we propose a near-optimal crowdsensing task assignment mechanism, that consider the time budget of users, support assigning multi-tasks to each user in each round of assignment and maximizes the task completion rate. Compared with the existing studies, the crowdsensing system model studied in this paper is more practical and efficient. The detailed experimental results show that our task assignment mechanism has good performance.

Acknowledgements. This work is partially supported by National Natural Science Foundation of China (NSFC) under Grant No. 61572342, No. 61303206, No. 61672369, Natural Science Foundation of Jiangsu Province under Grant No. BK20151240 and No. BK20161258, China Postdoctoral Science Foundation under Grant No. 2015M580470 and No. 2016M591920. Project Funded by the Priority Academic Program Development of Jiangsu Higher Education Institutions (PAPD), and Jiangsu Collaborative Innovation Center on Atmospheric Environment and Equipment Technology (CICAEET). Any opinions, findings, conclusions, or recommendations expressed in this paper are those of author(s) and do not necessarily reflect the views of the funding agencies (NSFC).

References

1. Boutsis, I., Kalogeraki, V.: On task assignment for real-time reliable crowdsourcing. In: IEEE ICDCS 2014, pp. 1–10 (2014)
2. Chatzimilioudis, G., Konstantinidis, A., Laoudias, C., Zeinalipour-Yazti, D.: Crowdsourcing with smartphones. IEEE Internet Comput. **16**(5), 36–44 (2012)
3. Chon, Y., Lane, N.D., Li, F., Cha, H., Zhao, F.: Automatically characterizing places with opportunistic crowdsensing using smartphones. In: Proceedings of the 2012 ACM Conference on Ubiquitous Computing (Ubicomp 2012), pp. 481–490 (2012)
4. Eriksson, J., Girod, L., Hull, B., Newton, R., Madden, S., Balakrishnan, H.: The pothole patrol: using a mobile sensor network for road surface monitoring. In: ACM MobiSys 2008, pp. 29–39 (2008)
5. Feng, Z., Zhu, Y., Zhang, Q., Zhu, H., Yu, J., Cao, J., Ni, L.M.: Towards truthful mechanisms for mobile crowdsourcing with dynamic smartphones. In: IEEE ICDCS 2014, pp. 11–20 (2014)
6. He, S., Shin, D.-H., Zhang, J., Chen, J.: Toward optimal allocation of location dependent tasks in crowdsensing. In: IEEE INFOCOM 2014, pp. 745–753 (2014)
7. Howe, J.: Crowdsourcing: How the Power of the Crowd is Driving the Future of Business. Random House, New York (2008)
8. Huang, H., Sun, Y.-E., Li, X.-Y., Chen, S., Xiao, M., Huang, L.: Truthful auction mechanisms with performance guarantee in secondary spectrum markets. IEEE Trans. Mob. Comput. **14**(6), 1315–1329 (2015)
9. Jin, H., Su, L., Chen, D., Nahrstedt, K., Xu, J.: Quality of information aware incentive mechanisms for mobile crowd sensing systems. In: ACM MobiHoc 2015, pp. 167–176 (2015)
10. Kanhere, S.S.: Participatory sensing: crowdsourcing data from mobile smartphones in urban spaces. In: Hota, C., Srimani, P.K. (eds.) ICDCIT 2013. LNCS, vol. 7753, pp. 19–26. Springer, Heidelberg (2013). doi:10.1007/978-3-642-36071-8_2
11. Koukoumidis, E., Peh, L.-S., Martonosi, M.R.: Signalguru: leveraging mobile phones for collaborative traffic signal schedule advisory. In: Proceedings of the 9th International Conference on Mobile Systems, Applications, and Services (MobiSys 2011), pp. 127–140 (2011)
12. Lane, N.D., Miluzzo, E., Lu, H., Peebles, D., Choudhury, T., Campbell, A.T.: A survey of mobile phone sensing. IEEE Commun. Mag. **48**(9), 140–150 (2010)
13. Luo, T., Tan, H.-P., Xia, L.: Profit-maximizing incentive for participatory sensing. In: IEEE INFOCOM 2014, pp. 127–135 (2014)

14. Ma, T., Zhou, J., Tang, M., Tian, Y., Al-Dhelaan, A., Al-Rodhaan, M., Lee, S.: Social network and tag sources based augmenting collaborative recommender system. IEICE Trans. Inf. Syst. **98**(4), 902–910 (2015)
15. Rai, A., Chintalapudi, K., Padmanabhan, V.N., Sen, R.: Zee: zero-effort crowdsourcing for indoor localization. In Proceedings of the 18th Annual International Conference on Mobile Computing and Networking (MobiCom 2012), pp. 293–304 (2012)
16. Rana, R.K., Chou, C.T., Kanhere, S.S., Bulusu, N., Hu, W.: Ear-phone: an end-to-end participatory urban noise mapping system. In: ACM/IEEE IPSN 2010, pp. 105–116 (2010)
17. Thiagarajan, A., Ravindranath, L., LaCurts, K., Madden, S., Balakrishnan, H., Toledo, S., Eriksson, J.: Vtrack: accurate, energy-aware road traffic delay estimation using mobile phones. In: ACM Sensys 2009, pp. 85–98 (2009)
18. Xu, W., Huang, H., Sun, Y.-E., Li, F., Zhu, Y., Zhang, S.: DATA: a double auction based task assignment mechanism in crowdsourcing systems. In: 8th International ICST Conference on Communications and Networking in China (CHINACOM 2013), pp. 172–177 (2013)
19. Yan, T., Kumar, V., Ganesan, D.: Crowdsearch: exploiting crowds for accurate real-time image search on mobile phones. In: MobiSys 2010, pp. 77–90 (2010)
20. Yang, D., Xue, G., Fang, X., Tang, J.: Crowdsourcing to smartphones: incentive mechanism design for mobile phone sensing. In: ACM Mobicom 2012, pp. 173–184 (2012)
21. Yuen, M.-C., King, I., Leung, K.-S.: A survey of crowdsourcing systems. In: IEEE Third International Conference on Privacy, Security, Risk and Trust (PASSAT 2011) and IEEE Third Inernational Conference on Social Computing (SocialCom 2011), pp. 766–773 (2011)
22. Zhao, D., Li, X.-Y., Ma, H.: How to crowdsource tasks truthfully without sacrificing utility: online incentive mechanisms with budget constraint. In: IEEE INFOCOM 2014, pp. 1213–1221 (2014)
23. Zhao, Q., Zhu, Y., Zhu, H., Cao, J., Xue, G., Li, B.: Fair energy-efficient sensing task allocation in participatory sensing with smartphones. In: IEEE INFOCOM 2014, pp. 1366–1374 (2014)

FPAP: Fast Pre-distribution Authentication Protocol for V2I

Wei Guo, Yining Liu$^{(\boxtimes)}$, and Jing Wang

Guangxi Key Laboratory of Trusted Software,
Guilin University of Electronic Technology,
Guilin 541004, Guangxi, China
ynliu@guet.edu.cn

Abstract. The authentication between the vehicle and the infrastructure is a vital issue for Vehicular Ad Hoc Networks (VANET), which guarantees to verify the user's identity and avoids the private information leakage. In this paper, a fast authentication protocol is proposed using the group communication and proactive authentication, in which the authentication is achieved by the symmetric encryption. Therefore, it is more efficient. Moreover, the trade-off between the anonymity and accountability is well.

Keywords: VANET · Fast authentication · Group communication · Anonymity · Privacy

1 Introduction

With the development of wireless technology, the vehicular Ad Hoc Networks (VANET) has been gradually applied to the driverless car. In order to communicate with the other vehicles or the road side unit (RSU), every vehicle is equipped with the on-board unit (OBU) that is a wireless device based on dedicated short-range communication (DSRC) [1]. In the VANET, the job of RSU is to transport vehicle's message to the server, which authenticates the legal devices, accesses to the internet and records the account of the commercial services. In addition, the communication model includes vehicle-to-vehicle (V2V) communication and vehicle-to-infrastructure (V2I) communication.

In V2V model, the vehicles directly connect to each other and share the running state with the wireless channel to help the driver control the vehicle. For example, in the heavy fog, the vehicles equipped with the OBU can tell the driver how far the oncoming vehicle is before him.

V2I model is similar to the mobile network in which the vehicle connects to the server for the Internet services and RSU is viewed as the wireless router [2–4] between the server and vehicle. The main goal of V2I is to download the data from the Internet, including maps, traffic data, and multimedia files. Compared with the mobile network model, V2I has a high mobility and packet loss rate. For those reasons, some technical standards, such as IEEE 802.11 and IEEE 1609 [5], are designed.

Since the channel of VANET is open, the secure communication protocol is necessary to prevent the message eavesdropping, forging and tampering. For example, the

© Springer International Publishing AG 2016
X. Sun et al. (Eds.): ICCCS 2016, Part II, LNCS 10040, pp. 25–36, 2016.
DOI: 10.1007/978-3-319-48674-1_3

trace of a vehicle is the private information, which the attacker can overhear with the private identity or public key. Therefore, it is necessary to design a secure V2I communication model. There are many kinds of literature to address this issue. In 2004, a proactive key distribution and pre-authentication scheme [6] was proposed. In 2014, Zhu et al. proposed an efficient authentication protocol [7] based on group signature between vehicle and RSU, which is pointed that RSU is not adequate to verify each vehicle's identity when too many vehicles drive in its service range and then proposed a proxy authentication scheme [8]. In 2016, Hassan Artail et al. [9] came up with an idea that using a pseudonym to achieve anonymity of vehicle, which makes the attacker cannot track the vehicle. There are also many articles [10–14] using asymmetric cryptography to achieve the authentication between the vehicle and RSU. The works in [15, 16] use symmetric cryptography to replace the asymmetric technique to accelerate the speed of the authentication.

In this paper, we propose a fast pre-authentication scheme between the vehicle and RSU. The server can predict the RSUs that the vehicle will pass by, and pre-distribute the group key to the vehicle and RSUs using Shamir's secret sharing. The main contributions include:

Firstly, we design a fast authentication protocol for the V2I based on group communication, which predicts the vehicle' track and applies the Shamir's secret sharing to distributing the group key to the RSU for authentication. Since the Shamir's secret sharing, the key is involved in all members of the group.

Secondly, a pseudonym is employed to protect the real identity of the vehicle. Nevertheless, the anonymity and accountability point in two different ends of the lever. Thus, in order to ensure the vehicle cannot reject the action that it had done, our paper designs a nice balance between them.

The rest of the paper is organized as follows. Section 2 introduces the related works and analyzes their advantages. Section 3 is about Communication model, threat model and design goals. Section 4 is the detail description of our FPAP. The performance analysis is presented in Sect. 5. Finally, the conclusion of our protocol is presented in the Sect. 6.

2 Related Works

The vehicle in VANET has more high mobility than mobile communication networks. The faster the vehicle, the less the communication time between the vehicle and RSU. In this short period, RSU authenticates the vehicle and provides the Internet service to it. Thus, the authentication efficiency is vital. Many kinds of research aim to reduce the computation cost, we will introduce three outstanding related schemes as follows:

2.1 HMAC and Group Networks

To reduce the authentication delay, two methods are proposed in [7]. The first method is to replace the certificate revocation list (CRL) with the hash message authentication code (HMAC). In the asymmetric scheme, it's difficult to control the valid duration of the certificate. In order to solve this problem, researchers proposed CRL scheme, similar to a blacklist, to revoke the certificate. In the beginning, the certification authority (CA) verifies the vehicle's identity and issues a license to it. When the license of vehicle is timeout, its identity will be added into the blacklist. Then RSU will refuse to provide the Internet service for the vehicle as long as its identity is on that list. The scheme [7] uses HMAC to replace the CRL scheme. HMAC is just a hash value of the functions, like MD5, SHA2 and SHA3 et al. We compare the time-consumption between hash function and RSA signature verification algorithm; we find the former is two orders of magnitude more rapid than the latter.

The second method is dividing the networks into several groups. Each group can be viewed as a group network, and contains only one vehicle and a few RSUs. This way decreases the storage burden of the RSU, and it needn't store all vehicles' information. By combining the HMAC and divide-and-conquer method, the scheme can verify 600 messages per second [7].

2.2 Proxy-Based Authentication Scheme for V2I

Since spending much time in the calculation of asymmetric cryptography, RSU is not adequate to authenticate all vehicles in its range. So, a proxy-based authentication scheme was proposed in [8], which makes a vehicle as a proxy role to reduce the computational burden of RSU. From Fig. 1, firstly, RSU selects a vehicle in its range as a proxy. Secondly, the proxy vehicle verifies other vehicles (A, B, C), which directly or indirectly communicate with the proxy. This scheme [8] can reduce 88 % computational burden and increase the authentication range of the RSU in the meantime.

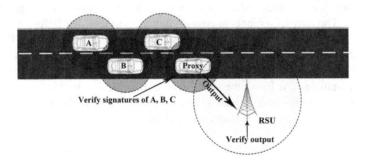

Fig. 1. Proxy-based authentication scheme

2.3 One-Time Pad Used for the Authentication

The one-time pad is an uncrackable encryption technique used for the secure communication, and both sides negotiate a session key for the latter secure communication. In which the session key is used only once. Since the encryption key and the decryption key are the same, one-time pad is viewed as a symmetric key.

Li and Liu [15] proposed a lightweight identity authentication protocol (LIAP) based on the one-time pad, which consists of three phases: the initial phase, the fast handover authentication phase, the renewal phase. In the initial phase, a one-time pad is generated by the involvement of OBU, RSU, and server. Then, the server will give a list including RSU that a vehicle may pass by and distribute that one-time pad to it using proactive key distribution and pro-authentication technique. After the vehicle leaving the first RSU and encountering a new one, an authentic process will happen again. The new RSU can use the one-time pad to fast authenticate the vehicle. The fast authentication depends on the one-time pad that is pre-distribute in the new RSU.

The uncrackable premise of the one-time pad is based on the correct usage. However, there are some flaws in it. In 2015, its shortcoming [17] is analyzed that cannot resist the parallel session attack that the attacker can forge the other's certification to pass authentication of RSU and get the access to Internet successfully.

In this paper, a fast pre-distribution authentication protocol (FPAP) is proposed based on symmetric cryptography and group network [18, 19], which not only inherits the merits from the previous, but also achieve a lower construction computation burden, a more fast authentication, the non-repudiation and the anonymity.

3 Models

The communication model, threat model and our design goals are introduced in the following.

3.1 Communication Model

The provider of VANET deploys RSUs along the road. The duty of the RSU is to provide the wireless communication to the vehicle and to connect to the server on a cable channel. The duty of server is to control the access to Internet. Before the Internet service, the prime thing is to achieve the mutual authentication between RSU and vehicle, that is, only the legal users can access the Internet service. To reduce the number of RSU, multi-hop is used in the system model. For the example, the Fig. 2, there are two vehicles (A, B) on the road. Vehicle B is driving in RSU service range, but A is not. In this situation, A can still connected to the RSU by the multi-hop: A sends a packet to RSU, which is routed through B.

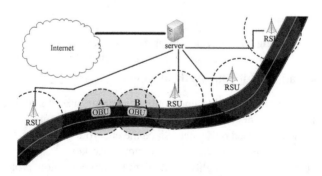

Fig. 2. Communication model

3.2 Threat Model

The attacker tries to overhear the user's private message and get the track of the user. In this paper, we employ the threat model proposed by Raya and Hubaux [20]. There are three pairs as follows:

- Global or Local: This dimension is about the activity range of attacker. If it is global, the attacker can collect the communication information from total networks of vehicle.
- Active or Passive: The main works of the passive attack is to monitor and collect the vehicle, but the active attacker is to attempt to attack the target vehicle.
- Internal or External: This dimension classifies the attacker according to whether he is the member of the communication model. For example, in the V2I model, if the RSU is an attacker, he is viewed as an internal attacker.

We suppose that infrastructures, such as RSU and server, are credible. In addition, we also suppose that the attacker attempts to attack the vehicle. In order to guarantee the confidentiality of our protocol, we suppose the activity range of attacker is global, so our threat model is Global Active External (GAE) model. In GAE, an attacker can collect all messages in the communication model.

3.3 Design Goals

In this threat model, our proposed fast authentication protocol aims to achieve the following goals:

- Confidentiality: Confidentiality guarantees that the secure information communication over the open channel between vehicle and RSU, and nobody can get other user's private data.
- Fast Authentication: In order to guarantee the security of the high-speed vehicle, the authentication computation should be fast and efficient.
- Practical Anonymity: Balance the anonymity and accountability. Anonymity guarantees the driver's privacy, and accountability assures that the authority can trace the vehicle according to the law.

4 FPAP Using Shamir's Secret Sharing

This paper proposes an efficient V2I authentication protocol between RSU and vehicle using the authenticated group key transfer protocol [21] to establish a group communication. In the classic method, the trusted key generation center selects the group key and translates it to all members of the group. Before transferring the group key to a member, the server encrypts the key under its public key. However, our protocol relies on Shamir's secret sharing to assign the group key. There are two advantages:

Firstly, the pubic key manager is simplified. The assignment of group key is only signed under the server's private key and isn't involved in the member's public key.

Secondly, the group key is more random and isn't only manipulated by the server. The key is generated under each member's involvement.

In this section, the Shamir's Secret Sharing (Shamir's SS) and our protocol are fully described as follows:

4.1   Shamir's Secret Sharing

Shamir's SS is based on Lagrange interpolating polynomial over Galois field $GF(p)$, and the confidential data D can be hidden in it. If the degrees of the polynomial are $k - 1$, the attacker cannot recover the D unless k polynomial solutions have been obtained. Shamir's SS is divided into two algorithms: secret share algorithm and secret reconstruct algorithm.

Secret share algorithm uses a polynomial $f(x)$ to hide D. The description in detail is as follows:

- $f(x) = a_{k-1}x^{k-1} + \ldots + a_1x + a_0$ *(mod p)* is picked, where $a_0 = D$ and $a_i(i = 1, 2, 3, \ldots, k - 1)$ are random numbers over $GF(p)$.
- n shares are calculated, $D_i = f(X_i)(i = 1, \ldots, n)$, where X_i is the random number over $GF(p)$.
- $D_i(i = 1, \ldots, n)$ are shared to the corresponding group members.

Secret reconstruct algorithm aims to recover D. The description in detail is as follows:

- k polynomial solutions are collected.
- D is reconstructed as $D = f(0) = \sum_{i \in A} D_i B_i = \sum_{D_i B_i} D_i \left(\prod_{j \in A - \{i\}} \frac{x_j}{x_j - x_i} \right) (mod\ p)$, where set $A = \{i_1, \ldots, i_k\} \subseteq \{1, 2, \ldots, n\}$ and B_i are Lagrange coefficients.

4.2   The Proposed Protocol

In our protocol, the group members are a vehicle, the server and some RSUs that the vehicle may pass by. When the vehicle encounters an RSU for the first time, the group key will be negotiated among all the group members. Each member of the group shares the key to authenticate each other with it. That is to say, the vehicle and RSUs can apply the group key to complete the mutual authentication. This method only employs the symmetric encryption and has a low computational burden. As a result, this protocol can reduce the delay of the authentication between RSU and vehicle. There are three phases of our protocol: the initialization, the key negotiation, and the fast handover.

Phase 1. Initialization
In this phase, the server's public key (PK) is distributed and stored in the tamper-resistant device of vehicle or RSU. Meanwhile, the vehicle registers to the server by submitting a password (PWD) stored in the vehicle's tamper-resistant device. That information can update every year against the brute-force attack. The PWD is used

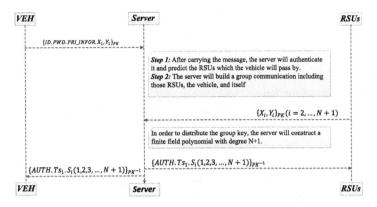

Fig. 3. Key negotiation phase

to establish the secure channel with the server. Before sending a secret message to the server, a vehicle or RSU will apply the PK to encrypt it. As a result, only the server can recover it which can prevent the message from eavesdropping.

Phase 2. Key negotiation
When the vehicle drives into the range of an RSU, the RSU checks whether the related group key has been stored in its memory. If yes, the protocol jumps to the fast handover phase directly; otherwise, the key negotiation will be triggered. After getting the key, the vehicle and RSU can use it to authenticate each other. Meanwhile, in the proactive key distribution and pro-authentication scheme, the server distributes the K to each member of the group. The Fig. 3 shows the negotiation among the group which containing three steps: the establishment of group, the negotiation of group key and the distribution of the key.

Step 1. Establishment of Group
The server predicts the vehicle's trace and selects RSUs that the vehicle may pass by in the future. At the beginning, a vehicle will send $\{ID.PWD.PRI\_INFO.X_1, Y_1\}_{PK}$ to the server, where *ID* and *PWD* prove that the vehicle is a legal register; *PRI_INFO* is the private information and (X_1, Y_1) is the random point generated by the vehicle. The server applies the *PRI_INFO* to foretell the trace of the vehicle. Besides, the server has a position map of RSUs, so it will pick some RSUs on the trace from them. If N RSUs are selected, there will be $N + 2$ members of a group: the picked RSUs ($R_i (i = 0, 1, 2, ..., N - 1)$), the server and the vehicle (VEH).

Step 2. Negotiation of Group Key
Every group member generates a random point, and there are $N + 2$ points in total: $(X_i, Y_i)(i = 0, 1, 2, ..., N + 1)$, where (X_0, Y_0) is generated by the server and vehicle, (X_1, Y_1) has been received by the server in *Step 1* and $(X_i, Y_i)(i = 2, 3, 4..., N + 1)$ correspond to the N RSUs which use PK to encrypt all $(X_i, Y_i)(i = 2, 3, 4..., N + 1)$, and then transform them to the server.

After receiving all $N + 2$ polynomial points including its own, the server calculates a finite filed polynomial $f(x)$ with degree $N + 1$ which goes through all those points.

$$f(x) = a_{N+1}x^{N+1} + \ldots + a_1x + a_0 \qquad (\mathrm{mod}\ p)$$

Since all solutions are random, all coefficients are random, too. As a result, a_0 is used as the group key.

Step 3. Distribution of the Key

Now, the random number a_0 has been assigned to the group key (K) by the server. After that, the server distributes the K to all members of the group as follows:

- According to Shamir's SS, $f(x)$ divides the secret K into $N + 1$ shares: $S_i = f(m_i)$ ($i = 1, 2, 3, \ldots, N + 1$) where $m_i(i = 1, 2, 3, \ldots, N + 1)$ are random numbers over $GF(p)$. Meanwhile, the server calculates a hash value: $AUTH = hash(K, Ts_1, S_1, S_2, S_3, \ldots, S_{N+1})$ that be used for the authentication, where Ts_1 is the timestamp of *AUTH*.
- The server structures a packet: $\{AUTH.Ts_1.S_i(i = 1, 2, 3, \ldots, N + 1)\}$. Before sending to the vehicle and RSU, the packet is signed with the server's private key (PK^{-1}).
- The members of the group can verify the source of packet and get $N + 1$ polynomial shares. In the addition, each member has generated a random share in the *Step 2*. Totally, each members have $N + 2$ shares, and then can restructure the group key (K') according to the Shamir's secret reconstruct algorithm. Then each member calculates a hash value: $hash(K', Ts_1, S_1, S_2, S_3, \ldots, S_{N+1})$ and checks whether it equals to the *AUTH* which he received. If yes, the authentication succeeds, otherwise the authentication fails. After above three steps, all members can share the same group key. The vehicle and RSU can apply it to authenticate each and build a secure channel.

Phase 3. Fast Handover

In this phase, the vehicle is assigned a pseudonym, $PID_{veh} = AUTH$, which is used to hide its real identity, and the memory of RSU will store it with the group key as a tuple: $\{PID_{veh}.K\}$. The vehicle and RSU can apply the tuple to fast authenticate each other. The Fig. 4 visualizes this phase:

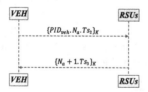

Fig. 4. Fast handover phase

- The vehicle sends RSU a challenge message: $\{PID_{veh}.N_a.Ts_2\}$ where PID_{veh} is the pseudonym, N_a is a random number and Ts_2 is a time stamp. Before sending RSU the message, the vehicle will use the K to encrypt it.

- RSU decrypts the message and gets the pseudonym: PID'_{VEH}. After that, RSU will verify whether it equal to the one on the database. If equality, RSU returns the $N_a + 1$ and Ts_3 to the vehicle, otherwise the authentication is failed. And the returned message is still encrypted by the K, too.
- After receiving $\{N_a + 1\}'$, the vehicle checks whether it equals to $N_a + 1$. If yes, the authentication finish, otherwise it is failed.

After the authentication finish, the vehicle and RSU will use the K to build a secure channel.

5 Analyses

In this section, we will analysis our FPAP from three aspects: the confidentiality, the fast authentication, the practical anonymity. In addition, our protocol is formally analyzed based on the BAN logic model [22] and its security is verified.

5.1 Confidentiality

We have assumed that the attacker is Eve and that the threat model is Global Active External (GAE) model in Sect. 3.3. Thus, Eve can overheat all messages in the communication which are showed in the Figs. 3 and 4.

Scenario. Even if Eve collects all messages, he still cannot recover the group key.

Proof. Not obtaining the private key of the server and the group key, Eve cannot get the data in the M.1, M.2, M.5 and M.6. Since M.3 and M.4 signed by the public key of the server, Eve can learn its context: $AUTH$ and $S_i(1, 2, 3, ..., N + 1)$. In our protocol, the group key is hidden in a finite filed polynomial of $N + 1$ degrees. According to the Shamir's secret share model, the group key cannot be recovered unless collecting $N + 2$ secret shares. However, Eve only has $N + 1$ shares, that is to say, our protocol is confidential.

5.2 Fast Authentication

We assume that there are 100 RSUs between the position A and position B. A vehicle drives from P_1 to P_2, and the server assigns n RSUs into a group in the key negotiate phase. The n can be 10, 20 or 30, which stand for that there are 10, 20 or 30 RSUs in a group communication respectively.

Moreover, we assume the vehicle will pass by all the predicted RSUs. If there are n RSUs in the group, one key negotiation process and $n - 1$ fast handover processes happen in our protocol. The key negotiation phase firstly negotiates the group key between the vehicle and RSUs and then authenticates each other with it. From Fig. 3, in the Sect. 4, the main time of key negotiation phase is taken on two asymmetric encryption and decryption processes. Besides, in the fast handover, the vehicle and RSUs only need to authenticate each other with the group key. From Fig. 4, in the

Sect. 4, the main time of fast handover phase is taken on two symmetric encryption and decryption process, which has a low computational burden. For a better explanation, an execution time of authentication is evaluated on Banana PI M1, which is equipped with an A20 ARM Cortex™-A7 Dual-Core processor at 1.0 GHz and a 1 GB DDR3 memory. In addition, the time of classic authentication [10–14] also is simulated in the same platform. In our experiment, the asymmetric algorithm is the ECC-secp160r1, the ECC of ASN recommended parameters. The symmetric algorithm is AES256. In the Fig. 5, the classic protocol and FPAP under different number of RSUs in the group are compared.

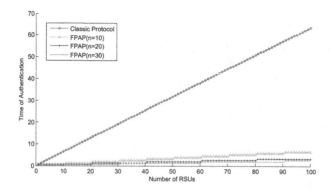

Fig. 5. Comparison time between classic and FPAP protocol

In the highway, the speed of the vehicle is 120 km per hour. In the key negotiation phase, the authentication is achieved within the distance of 21.193 m. While in the fast handover phase, it is finished within the distance of 0.0053 m. A long distance is needed in the former, but there, fortunately, exists only once in a group. Moreover, it can be employed at the origin of the highway where the vehicle has a lower speed.

5.3   Practical Anonymity

The pseudonym PID_{veh} replaces the real identity for preventing the vehicle's location information. PID_{veh} is a hash value of $(K, Ts_1, S_1, S_2, S_3, ..., S_{N+1})$ which is viewed as a random number. In addition, PID_{veh} will change once in a while, and its valid time is controlled by the server. Based on those, the attacker cannot get the location information. For example, the employer deploys a radio monitoring equipment in the company's car park for eavesdropping the employee's leaving time. However, the device only can eavesdrop PID_{veh} and cannot connect it with employee's real identity.

The complete anonymity clashes with the repudiation: the illegal vehicle can refuse to admit its action. In order to solve this problem, the database of the server will store the tuple: $\{PID_{veh}.ID\}$. Thus, if the police have the illegal vehicle's pseudonym, it can find its real identity in the server.

6 Conclusions

In this paper, we have proposed an authentication protocol between vehicle and RSU: fast pre-distribute authentication protocol in the V2I. It is based on the group communication and pre-distribute the group key to the group members. In addition, our protocol is practical anonymity that a great trade-off between the anonymity and accountability. Moreover, when using the multi-hop network between the vehicle and RSU, our FPAP can increase the service range and save the expense of the RSU's deployment.

Acknowledgements. Project supported by the Natural Science Foundation of China (No. 61363069, 61301166), Innovation Project of Guangxi Graduate Education (No. YCSZ2015149), Innovation Project of GUET Graduate Education (No. 2016YJCX44).

References

1. Jiang, D., Taliwal, V., Meier, A., et al.: Design of 5.9 GHz DSRC-based vehicular safety communication. IEEE Wirel. Commun. **13**(5), 36–43 (2006)
2. Wen, X., Shao, L., Xue, Y., Fang, W.: A rapid learning algorithm for vehicle classification. Inf. Sci. **295**(1), 395–406 (2015)
3. Ma, T., Zhou, J., Tang, M., Tian, Y., Al-Dhelaan, A., Al-Rodhaan, M., Lee, S.: Social network and tag sources based augmenting collaborative recommender system. IEICE transactions on Information and Systems **E98-D**(4), 902–910 (2015)
4. Shen, J., Tan, H., Wang, J., Wang, J., Lee, S.: A novel routing protocol providing good transmission reliability in underwater sensor networks. J. Internet Technol. **16**(1), 171–178 (2015)
5. Jiang, D., Delgrossi, L.: IEEE 802.11 p: towards an international standard for wireless access in vehicular environments. In: Proceedings of the VTC, pp. 2036–2040. IEEE (2008)
6. Mishra, A., Shin, M.H., Petroni, N.L., et al.: Proactive key distribution using neighbor graphs. IEEE Wirel. Commun. **11**(1), 26–36 (2004)
7. Zhu, X., Jiang, S., Wang, L., et al.: Efficient privacy-preserving authentication for vehicular ad hoc networks. IEEE Trans. Veh. Technol. **63**(2), 907–919 (2014)
8. Liu, Y., Wang, L., Chen, H.H.: Message authentication using proxy vehicles in vehicular Ad Hoc networks. IEEE Trans. Veh. Technol. **64**(8), 3697–3710 (2015)
9. Artail, H., Abbani, N.: A pseudonym management system to achieve anonymity in vehicular Ad hoc networks. IEEE Trans. Dependable Secure Comput. **13**(1), 106–119 (2016)
10. Weerasinghe, H., Fu, H.: ESAP: efficient and scalable authentication protocol with conditional privacy for secure vehicular communications. In: Proceedings of the GC Workshops, pp. 1729–1734. IEEE (2010)
11. Calandriello, G., Papadimitratos, P., Hubaux, J.P., et al.: Efficient and robust pseudonymous authentication in VANET. In: Proceedings of the Fourth ACM International Workshop on Vehicular ad hoc Networks, pp. 19–28. ACM (2007)
12. Studer, A., Bai, F., Bellur, B., et al.: Flexible, extensible, and efficient VANET authentication. J. Commun. Netw. **11**(6), 574–588 (2009)
13. Zhang, C., Lin, X., Lu, R., et al.: An efficient message authentication scheme for vehicular communications. IEEE Trans. Veh. Technol. **57**(6), 3357–3368 (2008)

14. Zhang, C., Lu, R., Lin, X., Ho, P., Shen, X.: An efficient identity-based batch verification scheme for vehicular sensor networks. In: Proceedings of the INFOCOM, pp. 246–250. IEEE (2008)
15. Li, J.-S., Liu, K.-H.: A lightweight identity authentication protocol for vehicular networks. Telecommun. Syst. **53**(4), 425–438 (2013)
16. Lyu, C., Gu, D., Zeng, Y., et al.: PBA: prediction-based authentication for vehicle-to-vehicle communications. IEEE Trans. Dependable Secure Comput. **13**(1), 71–83 (2016)
17. Jia, X.-D., Chang, Y.-F., Chang, C.-C., et al.: A critique of a lightweight identity authentication protocol for vehicular networks. J. Inf. Hiding Multimedia Signal Process. **6**(2), 183–188 (2015)
18. Harn, L., Lin, C.: Authenticated group key transfer protocol based on secret sharing. Trans. Comput. **59**(6), 842–846 (2010)
19. Liu, Y., Cheng, C., Cao, J., et al.: An improved authenticated group key transfer protocol based on secret sharing. IEEE Trans. Comput. **62**(11), 2335–2336 (2013)
20. Raya, M., Hubaux, J.-P.: Securing vehicular ad hoc networks. J. Comput. Secur. **15**(1), 39–68 (2007)
21. Shamir, A.: How to share a secret. Commun. ACM **22**(11), 612–613 (1979)
22. Burrows, M., Martin, A., Needham, R.M.: A logic of authentication. Proc. R. Soc. Lond. A **426**(1871), 233–271 (1989)

CACA-UAN: A Context-Aware Communication Approach Based on the Underwater Acoustic Sensor Network

Qi Liu[1,2(✉)], Xuedong Chen[2,3], Xiaodong Liu[4], and Nigel Linge[5]

[1] Jiangsu Collaborative Innovation Center of Atmospheric Environment and Equipment Technology (CICAEET), Nanjing University of Information Science and Technology, Nanjing 210044, China
qi.liu@nuist.edu.cn
[2] School of Computer and Software, Nanjing University of Information Science and Technology, Nanjing 210044, China
1554667161@qq.com
[3] Jiangsu Engineering Centre of Network Monitoring, Nanjing University of Information Science and Technology, Nanjing 210044, China
[4] School of Computing, Edinburgh Napier University, 10 Colinton Road Edinburgh EH10 5DT, UK
[5] The University of Salford, Salford, Greater Manchester M5 4WT, UK

Abstract. Underwater acoustic sensor networks (UANs) have emerged as a promising technology which can be applied in many areas such as military and civil in recent years. Among these applications, the communication between the devices is crucial for providing the better service to the users. To facilitate the communication, effective communication approaches need to be developed, however, underwater communication may pose more challenges than terrestrial communication due to the unique characteristics of underwater acoustic channel, such as the high latency and the low bandwidth. In this paper, the context-aware technology is introduced to the design of the communication approach, and the context-aware communication approach for the UAN (CACA-UAN) is proposed which consists of an ontology-based context-aware modeling approach for the UAN, context-aware device association and context-aware communication mechanism to improve the overall performance of the underwater communication system. We have demonstrated that the proposed CACA-UAN can reduce the transmission latency and jitter of communication, and increase the efficiency and reliability of the underwater communication system.

Keywords: Context-aware · Underwater acoustic sensor network · Context communication

1 Introduction

Recently, with the development of the terrestrial wireless sensor network (WSN) and the precision electronic equipment, the technology of deploying the sensor nodes

© Springer International Publishing AG 2016
X. Sun et al. (Eds.): ICCCS 2016, Part II, LNCS 10040, pp. 37–47, 2016.
DOI: 10.1007/978-3-319-48674-1_4

under the water has gradually matured and make communication between the underwater nodes have become feasible. The underwater acoustic sensor network (UAN) is as a new and emerging field, which has attracted the attention of many scholars and has extensive application prospects in marine environment monitoring & data acquisition, underwater exploration, disaster prevention, seismic monitoring, assist navigation and etc. Compared with the traditional terrestrial WSN [1], the UAN has the following characteristic: high cost of deploying the nodes under the water, the acoustic wave as the communication medium, sparse deploying and the mobility of the whole network. Many researchers have developed advanced communication solutions for the terrestrial WSN [2], but these solutions cannot be used for the UAN directly, because of the unique characteristics of the underwater acoustic sensor networks which bring many challenges in designing the communication technology and therefore require to design the new protocols to carry out the efficient and reliable communication. Note that it is essential to focus on the high delay and low bandwidth of the communication for many designers.

In underwater acoustic sensor network, the sensor nodes cooperate with each other for their common purpose to guarantee the overall performance of the communication network. First, each node senses the surrounding information, and then communicates with its neighbors in order to share the sensed data between the sensor nodes or communicates directly with the autonomous underwater vehicle (so-called AUV), which collect and aggregate the sensed data from the normal nodes. In this paper, the context-aware [3] is used as a means of sharing information between all kinds of nodes which include normal nodes and AUV instead of directly communication.

The term "context-aware", as a central feature of ubiquitous networks and pervasive computing system, was introduced by Schilit in the 1994 [4, 5] and then has been developed greatly in the computer science where context-aware can be used for sensing and reacting based on the context. The main goal of context aware is to provide the service to the users according to surrounding information about time, location and etc., which can be termed as context. In the current world, the context-aware has combined with many areas of intelligent application and developed many context-aware system based on the context to service the society. The context-aware system mainly include the following aspects: the acquisition of context, the processing of context and the application of context, among which the acquisition of context is most important. Therefore, it is necessary to construct context modeling for managing context information which are representing, storing and retrieving context for the whole environment. However, general context modeling approaches are lacked, only for the specific environment. In the paper, we first propose an ontology-based context modeling approach which is used for UAN to represent and storage the context information, and then introduce how to exploit the context information [6] in designing the communication approach.

The rest of this article is organized as follows. First, the development of the communication technology and challenges is discussed in Sect. 2, then we present the proposed context-aware CACA-UAN, including an ontology-based context modeling approach, context-aware device association, and context-aware communication mechanism in Sect. 3. Next in Sect. 4, the simulation and performance evaluations on CACA-UAN are given. Finally, we conclude the paper and discuss future works in Sect. 5.

2   Related Work and Challenges

The underwater sensor networks have been greatly developed in the military and civil areas and simultaneously enable a broad range of applications, including tracking, navigating and monitoring. For enhancing the service quality of these applications, reliable and efficient communication technologies can be developed to supporting the data transmission. However, the fundamental concern about communication is the communication medium, and three mediums which are radio frequency (RF), optical wave and acoustic wave can be used in communication. In fact, the transmission of the RF under the water is different from the air, and result in high attenuation and shorting the transmission distance. If RF propagates at the longer distance through conductive salty water [7], but only at the ultra-low frequencies (30–300 Hz), and at the cost of large antennae and high transmission power. Although the signal of optical wave communication under the water cannot decay, are affected greatly by the scattering and refraction of the optical. Therefore, the RF and optical wave are both not suitable for underwater communication and the acoustic wave is used as a proper communication medium.

The acoustic communication is as the most general and widely used underwater communication technology currently [8] due to the low loss of the sound in water, but many characteristics of acoustic communication cannot be ignored, such as limited bandwidth, high delay and time-varied multipath and fading, therefore many new, efficient and reliable communication protocols which are applied to underwater acoustic communication require to be designed, but many design challenges remained, which are

- High propagation delay on underwater acoustic communication due to the low transmission speed of sound under the water and is five orders of magnitude higher than the radio frequency and reduce the throughput of communication system [7];
- The limited and low available bandwidth due to strict constraints;
- Underwater acoustic channel is seriously affected by multipath and attenuation, and high bit error;
- The battery power is limited, and usually cannot be charged;
- These sensor nodes which are deployed under the water are prone to failure due to the harsh underwater environment.

Communication approaches for UAN have been widely explored by many scholars, and which include new emerging approaches and the improvement of original methods, related to bottom-up-layer communication system architecture which consists of five layers: physical layer, data link layer, network layer, transport layer and application layer. In the paper, we primarily focus on reviewing the MAC protocols for UAN. MAC protocols can be categorized into two types: contention-based and schedule-based [9]. For the contention-based protocols, such as Carrier Sense Multiple Access/Collision Avoidance (CSMA/CA), each sensor have to compete for a channel to achieve a chance to transmission. However, the collisions and retransmission of packet occur in the competition, and result in increasing the energy consumption. Slotted FAMA [10] is a CSMA-based MAC protocol, which combines the carrier sensing and a dialogue to relieve collision. Before data transmission, the source node sends a control packet to the receiver to avoid the receiver receiving at the same time. Although the packet collisions are decreased, the transmissions of multiple control packets can lead to low system throughput. The schedule-based protocol such as Code-Division Multiple Access (CDMA), Time-Division Multiple Access (TDMA) and Frequency-Division Multiple Access (FDMA), which divide the channel into code, time and frequency slots respectively, and then assign these slots to each node. Therefore, these nodes have to work in their own slot, or keep asleep. In this mode, the packet collision can be avoided and the energy consumption can be reduced. However, the existing schedule-based MAC solutions are primarily concentration on CDMA, and the CDMA is considered to be a promising technique in the underwater communication due to the unique characteristics of underwater channel. The FDMA is unsuitable for the UAN, and is restricted by the narrow bandwidth, while the limited bandwidth and variable delay make TDMA difficult to realize a precise synchronization and require the large overhead. UW-MAC [11] is a distributed CDMA-based MAC scheme, and is the first protocol of leveraging the CDMA properties to implement multiple access to the scare bandwidth under the water [2], which achieves a trade-off among high throughput, low delay and energy consumption by the means of incorporating the optimal transmit power and code length.

Although existing communication approaches are useful to address the low communication bandwidth and high access delay, still to be improved and developed so as to provide better underwater communication service to the user. For UANs, reliable and efficient communication technologies [12, 13] are crucial to be developed to implement data transmissions and improve the overall performance of the communication system. In this paper, we propose CACA-UAN, a context-aware communication approach for underwater acoustic sensor network which includes an ontology-based context modeling approach, context-aware device association, and context-aware communication mechanism, and we mainly focus on how to apply context awareness to the underwater communications, and exploit context information to improve the performance in term of delay and jitter.

3   Context-Aware Communication Approach

In Sect. 3, CACA-UAN is proposed which consists of a context-aware modeling approach, context-aware device association and context-aware communication mechanism, details are provided in following subsection.

3.1   CACA-UAN Overview

To tackle the challenges mentioned earlier in underwater communication, the CACA-UAN is proposed, which incorporates the context-aware with the existing underwater communication technology and applies context awareness to the overall design of the communication system, such as context-aware communication association and context-aware data transmission. CACA-UAN primarily focus on designing new medium access control layers functions on the environment of the underwater acoustic channel, and to improve the performance of the existing communication system.

3.2   Context-Aware and Context Information

Context is the any information that can be used to highlight the situation of an entity, and the entity is a person, a place or an object, based on the definition of Dey [14], and the context aware system means to provide service to the user and improve the overall system performance simultaneously by exploiting the context information. For the communication system, the new designed protocol should have the capacity of sensing context information of the surround environment, and with the context information to provide service to the upper layer. To facilitate the context information interaction of the communication system, including the context information collecting and the context information sharing, an appropriate context modeling approach is essential for the UAN.

Although there are many existing context modeling schemes, such as the synonym [15], five interrogatives [16], objective and cognitive [17] and etc., but are only targeted at the particular environment, and the common context modeling approaches are lacked. Therefore, in the paper, we propose an ontology-based context modeling approach for the UAN.

In our context modeling approach, the hierarchy and index scheme is used, where all context information that are related to the underwater acoustic communication, are classified into several context levels based on a certain rule (e.g., service, energy and location), and each context information is assigned a unique identifier to ensure the context information special in all defined context. The root ID of the hierarchical structure is the service type ID which the device provide, and then the context information tree is extended by the means of horizontal or vertical. For example, as shown in Fig. 1, the simple model is presented.

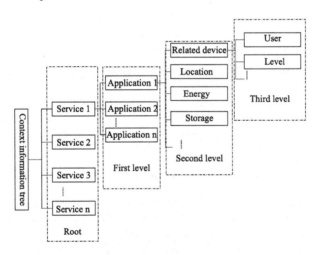

Fig. 1. The context information tree

The context information may contain the following components: the service context and identifier to represent the categories of the service which the device can provide (e.g., the temperature acquisition), the application context and identifier to represent the classification of application and which service belongs to (e.g., application ID), the application-particular context and identifier to represent the characteristic of application or the device (e.g., location, energy or storage), and some device-related context to represent the inherent attribute of the device (e.g., level). The Fig. 2 shows that the context information and identifier of application 1 which belongs to the service 1 where the index of the context information is assigned by the dotted format between the two associated context ID, such as the service ID is 1, the application ID is 1.1, the ID of the energy is 1.1.3, and the level ID is 1.1.1.2.

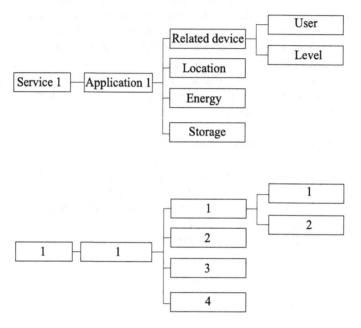

Fig. 2. The context information of the service type 1 on application 1

As mentioned earlier, context information can be used for the communication association and data transmission. The new proposed context model approach which is based on the hierarchy and index scheme are useful and effective to the CACA-UAN.

3.3 Context–Aware Communication Association

Basically, the communication is a process of interaction on the associated devices, however, the communication association need to establish before communication. The context-aware communication association essentially means to establish a virtual connection between the two devices based on the specified context information. In our CACA-UAN, the idea of third-party handshake protocol is exploit to establish a reliable association, and the communication association period is divided into three phases, which are service discovery, connection establishment and connection termination, and are introduced in detail in the following section.

The Context-Aware Service Discovery. The initial phase is the service discovery before the communication association, which is triggered when a new device adds into the network and need to initialize or a signal of the service discovery that comes from the next phase. The goal of the context-aware service discovery is to exploit the related context information to find the surround devices which are desired to a device and is prepared for the next phase.

At the procedure, each device plays a double role, which is to discover the surround service-desired devices or to be discovered as the desired service device by the surround devices, and can be converted from the "to discover" to the "to be discovered" on the certain condition.

The proposed context-aware service discovery in the paper consists of the following three stages: 1. device searching for the same desired service; 2. the selection of leader between the devices on the same service; 3. the AUV adds into the network. The device first enter the stage of the device searching actively, and search the surrounding service-desired devices based on the service context information by checking the beacon broad-casted of the other devices. If these desired devices are discovered, the cluster is formed in accordance with the same service, and then the second stage begins. If not discovered for a certain time, the device can convert to the passive discovery. On the second stage, the cluster header of each cluster is selected on the basic of the location context and energy context, and the selection of the cluster header needs to keep a balance the signal strength and the energy. The cluster header can manage the context information of the other devices in the cluster and coordinates the communication of the devices between the inter-clusters or the intra-cluster. For the devices of each cluster, they can discover the service-desired device with the cluster header, and each device obtains a device-device list which is formed by the desired devices. The third stage initializes only at the need of the AUV which is applied to receive the data from the devices. When the AUV adds into the network, since the communication range of AUV is higher than the devices, AUV broadcasts a beacon to the all clusters for the desired service, the cluster header checks the beacon, and select the desired devices context to form an AUV-device list, finally the list is transmitted to the AUV by the cluster header.

On the period the service discovery, the service context and the location context information are exploited to form clusters and select the cluster header of each cluster. As mentioned before, the context identified is effective for device discovery. To discover the devices fast, the matching method is used, where the device checks the beacon broadcasted by other devices, if the service context ID of the beacon matches the service ID of the desired-service device, the following application ID, location ID and etc. are need to be checked according to the sequence, if the service context ID is not matched, the device immediately stops the procedure, and not to check the all context information ID.

Context-Aware Connection Establishment. The context-aware connection estab-lishment is the second phase of the communication association, and at the phase, the device-device list is exploited between devices and the AUV-device list between the devices and the AUV which is obtained from the service discovery.

In the each cluster, the cluster header manages the context information of other devices, and the devices can obtain the device-device list with the assistant of the cluster header. The each device selects the most appropriate device from the device-device list based on the certain standard such as the communication traffic, link status and so on. The device then send a request to the device which is the final selected, the connection is established between the two devices until the response form that device is received.

For the AUV, the AUV-device list is received, and AUV sends an association request to the all devices from the list. Upon the association response from the device is received by the AUV, the connection is established between the device and the AUV.

At the phase, if the context information of the device has changed, the context-aware association update procedure can be triggered and the change should be informed to the device on the association. The device which context information is changed sends an update request to the device which is on the same association, and the request contains the changed context information and identifier. Device on the other side updates the association information upon receiving the request, and then sends an update success-fully response to the device. If the energy of the device is inadequate or the device is broken due to the harsh environment, the cluster header of which cluster the device located can report the failure information of the faulty device to the AUV, and then AUV sends the failure device identifier and corresponding error context to the user, to facilitate the fault addressed in time.

Context-Aware Connection Termination. The connection termination is the final phase of the communication, if a device want to terminate the communication connec-tion with the other device due to the inadequate energy or broken of the device, the context-aware disconnection procedure is initialized, and disconnect the connection between the two devices based on the identifier of the service and device. In the device movement, if a device moves out of the communication range of the other device, the disconnection procedure is also invoked. Although the association of the two devices are disconnected, the association context information are stored by the two devices for a period of time. At this time, if the device is backed to the communication range, the connection is re-established by the stored association context. For the AUV, if the AUV receives a command from the user which is requested to return or the AUV has gathered the information from the device of the network and need to report to the user, the disconnection procedure is called until the new command coming, and re-establishing connection.

4   Simulation and Performance Evaluation

In this section, we simulate the CACA-UAN on Aqua-Sim which is a discrete-event cluster simulator developed on the basic of NS2 and has attracted many attention from the networking research, and the performance of CACA-UAN is evaluated and analyzed.

We set an area of 100 m × 100 m × 100 m, and the simulation time is set to 500 s to implement the simulation, the delay of each packet transmitted and the jitter of communication is analyzed. Since our CACA-UAN mainly focuses on acquiring new functions on the MAC layer, the two MAC protocols of ALOHA and UWAN are selected as a reference to our CACA-UAN in the paper for simplifying the experiment. As shown in Fig. 3, the delay of the each generated packet transmitted is presented. It is easy to see that our proposed CACA-UAN has played a better performance than other two protocols and the delay of each packet transmitted is lower than other two protocols due to the efficiency of exploiting the context information in communication, and in the same simulation time, the number of the packets generated of the UWAN is less than the ALOHA and our solutions. For the communication system, especially for the underwater sensor network which is high-delay and low-bandwidth network, it is crucial to decreasing the delay of the communication, our proposed CACA-UAN which applies the context information into the communication between the devices can reduce the latency of packet transmitted on the communication, and can maintains the efficiency of the underwater communication.

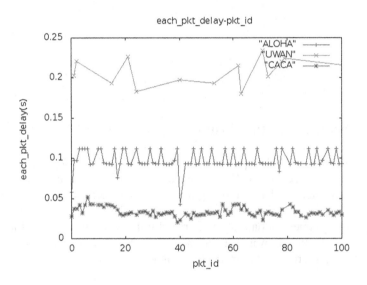

Fig. 3. The delay of each generated packet

The Fig. 4 shows the jitter of communication system, and our proposed CACA-UAN has the minimum jitter and the tendency of the jitter is more smooth compared with the ALOHA and UWAN, however the jitter of the ALOHA is maximum between the three protocols, although the delay of the packet transmitted in ALOHA is lower than the UWAN. Therefore, this can be explained that the CACA-UAN is more reliable than other two protocols in the communication, while the reliability is the other characteristic of communication system which needs to be maintained, and the probability of collision that the packet occurs in the data transmission can be decreased due the smooth and low jitter rate. The context-aware is integrated into the communication system, and can improve the reliability of the communication system in the data transmission.

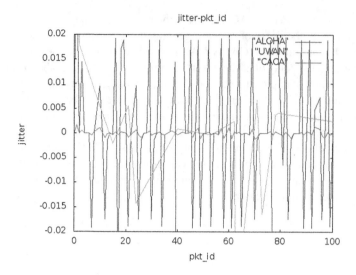

Fig. 4. The jitter of communication system

5 Conclusion and Future Work

In the paper, the CACA-UAN is proposed which consists of an ontology-based context-aware modeling approach for the UAN, context-aware device association and context-aware communication mechanism to improve the overall performance of the communication system. With the simulation experiment, the improvement of performance of the underwater communication system is proved in terms of the delay and jitter, and also indicates that context-aware can enhance the performance of the communication system and have a broad prospect in the design of the underwater communication system.

However, the research on the integration of context-aware and underwater communication is not attract much attention presently, the new and better communication approaches in the environment of underwater need to be developed to improve the communication performance.

In the future, we intend to utilize context-aware technology and context information to improve the existing MAC schemes for the underwater acoustic sensor network, or implement new context-aware MAC protocol to improve the underwater acoustic communication.

Acknowledgements. This work is supported by the NSFC (61300238, 61300237, 61232016, 1405254, 61373133), Marie Curie Fellowship (701697-CAR-MSCA-IFEF-ST), Basic Research Programs (Natural Science Foundation) of Jiangsu Province (BK20131004) and the PAPD fund.

References

1. Ping, G., Jin, W., Bing, L., Sungyoung, L.: A variable threshold-value authentication architecture for wireless mesh networks. J. Internet Technol. **15**(6), 929–936 (2014)
2. Pompili, D., Akyildiz, L.F.: Overview of networking protocols for underwater wireless communications. IEEE Commun. Mag. **47**(1), 97–102 (2009)
3. Misra, S., Das, S.N., Obaidat, M.S.: Context-aware quality of service in wireless sensor networks. IEEE Commun. Mag. **52**(6), 16–23 (2014)
4. Schilit, B.N., Adams, N., Want, R.: Context-aware computing applications. In: Proceedings of IEEE Workshop on Mobile Computing Systems and Applications (WMCSA 1994), pp. 85–90 (1994)
5. Schilit, B.N., Theimer, M.M.: Disseminating active map information to mobile hosts. IEEE Network **8**(5), 22–32 (1995)
6. Qing, L., Hongkun, L., Russell, P., Zhuo, C., Chonggang, W.: CA-P2P: context-aware proximity-based peer-to-peer wireless communications. IEEE Commun. Mag. **52**(6), 32–41 (2014)
7. Akyildiz, I.F., Pompili, D., Melodia, T.: State of the art in protocol research for underwater acoustic sensor networks. In: Proceedings of ACM International Workshop on Under-Water Networks (2006)
8. Lanbo, L., Shengli, Z., Jun-Hong, C.: Prospects and problems of wireless communication for underwater sensor networks. Wireless Commun. Mob. Comput. **8**(8), 977–994 (2008)
9. Bin, L., Zhisheng, Y., Changwen, C.: MAC protocol in wireless body networks for e-health: challenges and a context aware design. IEEE Wirel. Commun. **20**(4), 64–72 (2013)
10. Molins, M., Stojanovic, M.: Slotted FAMA: a MAC protocol for underwater acoustic networks. In: Proceedings of MTS/IEEE OCEANS, Boston, pp. 1–7 (2006)
11. Pompili, D., Melodia, T., Akyildiz, I.F.: A CDMA-Based medium access control for underwater acoustic sensor networks. IEEE Trans. Wireless Commun. **8**(4), 1899–1909 (2009)
12. Jian, S., Haowen, T., Jin, W., Jinwei, W., Sungyoung, L.: A novel routing protocol providing good transmission reliability in underwater sensor networks. J. Internet Technol. **16**(1), 171–178 (2015)
13. Shengdong, X., Yuxiang, W.: Construction of tree network with limited delivery latency in homogeneous wireless sensor networks. Wireless Pers. Commun. **78**(1), 231–246 (2014)
14. Abowd, G.D., Dey, A.K., Brown, P.J., Davies, N., Smith, M., Steggles, P.: Towards a better understanding of context and context-awareness. In: Gellersen, H.-W. (ed.) HUC 1999. LNCS, vol. 1707, pp. 304–307. Springer, Heidelberg (1999)
15. Rodden, T., Chervest, K., Davies, N., Dix, A.: Exploiting context in HCI design for mobile systems. In: Proceedings of Workshop on Human Computer Interaction with Mobile Devices (1998)
16. Abowd, G.D., Mynatt, E.D.: Charting past, present, and future research in ubiquitous computing. ACM Trans. Computer-Human Interact. **7**(1), 29–58 (2000)
17. Mei, L., Easterbrook, S.: Capturing and modeling human cognition for context-aware software. In: Proceedings of International Conference for Research on Computational Models and Computation- Based Theories of Human Behavior (2009)

Combating TNTL: Non-Technical Loss Fraud Targeting Time-Based Pricing in Smart Grid

Wenlin Han and Yang Xiao[✉]

Department of Computer Science, The University of Alabama,
342 H.M. Comer, Box 870290, Tuscaloosa, AL 35487-0290, USA
whan2@crimson.ua.edu, yangxiao@ieee.org

Abstract. Electricity theft is the main form of Non-Technical Loss (NTL) fraud in the traditional power grid. In Smart Grid, NTL frauds co-occur with various attacks and have more variants. Time-based Pricing (TBP) is an attracting feature of Smart Grid, which supports real-time pricing and billing. However, adversaries could utilize TBP to commit NTL frauds, and we name them as TNTL frauds. Different from NTL frauds which "steal" electricity, TNTL frauds "steal" time. Thus, existing schemes cannot detect them. In this paper, we summarize four attack models of TNTL frauds and analyze various attacks in Smart Grid. We eliminate attacks that do not relate to TNTL frauds and propose countermeasures for those related attacks to prevent TNTL frauds.

Keywords: Smart grid security · Smart meter · Non-Technical Loss fraud · Time-based pricing · AMI

1   Introduction

Electricity theft is the main form of Non-Technical Loss (NTL) fraud [10,18,20] in the traditional power grid, including physically slowing down a meter or getting free electricity via a bypass [6]. In Smart Grid, NTL frauds co-occur with various attacks [7], such as man-in-the-middle (MIM) attack, data injection, etc. For example, an adversary could intercept communication between a smart meter and the head-end system and alters the total amount of the electricity consumption contained in a message [13].

The main reason that the utility urges to get rid of NTL frauds is due to the tremendous economy loss. NTL frauds count for $6 bn loss in the U.S. every year [14]. In the top 50 emerging market countries including China, India, Indonesia, etc., an annual loss of $58.7 bn is due to NTL frauds, and these countries will invest $168 bn in combating NTL frauds and enhancing the reliability of Smart Grid [3].

Time-based Pricing (TBP) is an attracting feature of Smart Grid, which supports real-time pricing and billing. In other words, the price of electricity is different at a different time in Smart Grid. However, adversaries could utilize TBP to commit NTL frauds, and we name them as TNTL frauds. The main

© Springer International Publishing AG 2016
X. Sun et al. (Eds.): ICCCS 2016, Part II, LNCS 10040, pp. 48–57, 2016.
DOI: 10.1007/978-3-319-48674-1_5

feature of the traditional NTL frauds is that the amount of the billing electricity is always smaller than the amount that consumed, no matter what methods are used to commit the NTL frauds [9]. Thus, existing NTL frauds detectors are designed based on this features, no matter what mechanisms they employ, e.g. load profile analysis [4,12,15], Intrusion Detection Systems (IDS) [5,11], comparison-based analysis [8,16,17,19], etc.

However, TNTL frauds do not have this feature, and thus, existing NTL frauds detectors cannot deal with them. Instead of manipulating the "amount" of the electricity, adversaries target the "time" of the electricity. The utility could still lose money although it does not lose electricity. Adversaries could alter the billing time to drag a peak-time billing to non-peak-time, and thus pay less for it. Adversaries could attack time synchronization systems to force packets drop, and thus delay the billing.

In this paper, we study TNTL frauds and summarize four attack models. We analyze various attacks in Smart Grid eliminating attacks that do not relate to TNTL frauds and propose countermeasures for those related attacks. The main contributions of this paper include:

- We newly identify a potential NTL fraud, namely TNTL, in Smart Grid;
- We introduce four attack models of TNTL frauds and analyze various related attacks;
- We propose countermeasures to deal with TNTL frauds in Smart Grid.

The rest of the paper is organized as follows: In Sect. 2, we introduce the background of Advanced Metering Infrastructure (AMI), four attack models, and attack tree of TNTL fraud. We discuss related attacks and propose countermeasures for them in Sect. 3. We conclude the paper in Sect. 4.

2   AMI and TNTL Fraud

In this section, we will introduce the features, attack models, and attack tree of TNTL fraud.

2.1   AMI Overview

AMI is an integrated metering system employed in Smart Grid. As shown in Fig. 1, a smart meter is installed in each household. It connects to home appliances via a Home Area Network (HAN). A collector is employed to connect several smart meters forming a Neighbourhood Area Network (NAN) [18,20]. These collectors are connected to the head end of AMI via Wide Area Network (WAN). The main function of AMI is to read smart meters automatically and to send pricing and control information from the utility. The communication protocol of AMI employed in United State is ANSI C12 serials, including ANSI C12.18, 19, 21 and 22 [2].

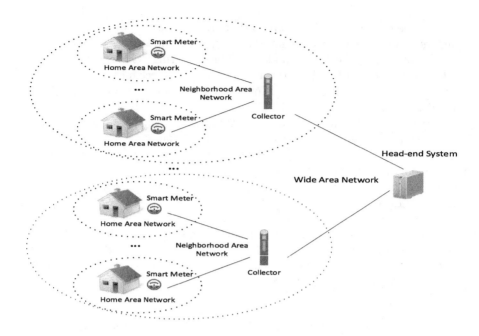

Fig. 1. The conceptual framework of AMI.

2.2   Attack Model

In the traditional NTL frauds, the billing amount of electricity is less than the amount that supplied, after eliminating technical loss, which causes economical loss to the company. A customer may slow down his (her) meter on purpose to steal electricity. An adversary may alter metering data, and change the amount of billed electricity to be smaller. Although there are many ways to commit an NTL fraud, there is one thing in common that the billed amount of electricity is smaller than the amount supplied.

Different from the traditional NTL frauds, the billing amount of electricity remains intact in TNTL frauds. An adversary gains illegal benefit by altering time-related information. As shown in Figs. 2, 3, 4, and 5, these are four typical attack models of TNTL frauds. Fig. 2 shows the load profile of a typical user from 6:00 PM to 12:00 PM. The meter data is sent to the head end every 15 min. The pricing strategy is Time-Of-Use pricing (TOU), where the usage in peak time, 7:00 PM to 10:00 PM, is charged 1.5 times, and the usage in other time segments is charged at a flat rate. If the billing time was altered, in some ways that we will introduce in the following section, the bill will change as well.

An adversary could move the billing time a little forward by adjusting the logical time, altering time information in messages, or various other attacks. As shown in Fig. 2, if the billing time was moved 1 s forward at 7:00 PM, what will happen? Although the billing time is only one second forward, the AMI system collects metering data every 15 min, and therefore, the amount of electricity

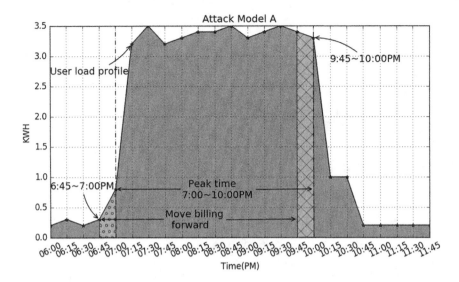

Fig. 2. Attack model A of TNTL fraud: move time window forward.

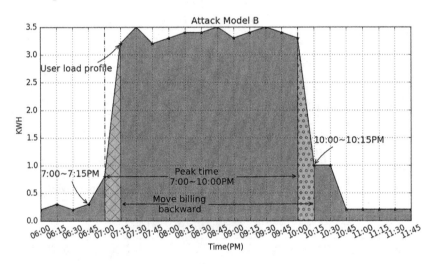

Fig. 3. Attack model B of TNTL fraud: move time window backward.

consumed from 6:45 PM to 9:45 PM will be charged 1.5 times. The average electricity rate in the U.S. is 12 cents per kilowatt-hour, and the average monthly household electricity bill in the U.S. is about \$110 [1]. If we use this rate to calculate, the user pays \$4.5 less in 30 days, which is over 2 % of the monthly bill. Thus, this slight move may cause 2 % loss to the utility annually. Accordingly, an adversary could disrupt the local clock resulting in billing window shift right, as shown in Fig. 3.

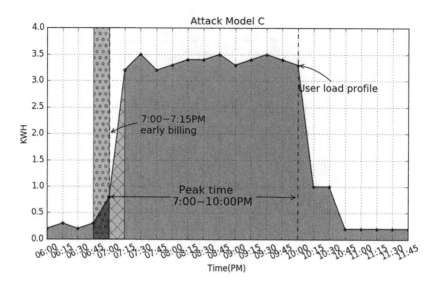

Fig. 4. Attack model C of TNTL fraud: early billing.

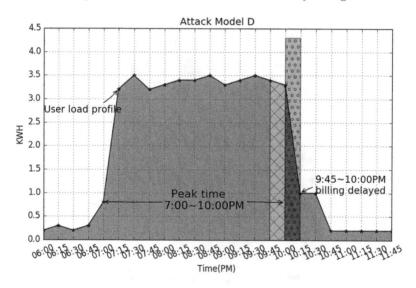

Fig. 5. Attack model D of TNTL fraud: delayed billing.

2.3 Attack Tree

We study various attacks in Smart Grid and propose an attack tree for TNTL fraud, as shown in Fig. 6.

There are two general ways to commit a TNTL fraud, to tamper smart meters and to intrude networks. A smart meter has embedded firmware to control its operations and it stores a large range of data, including encryption key, password,

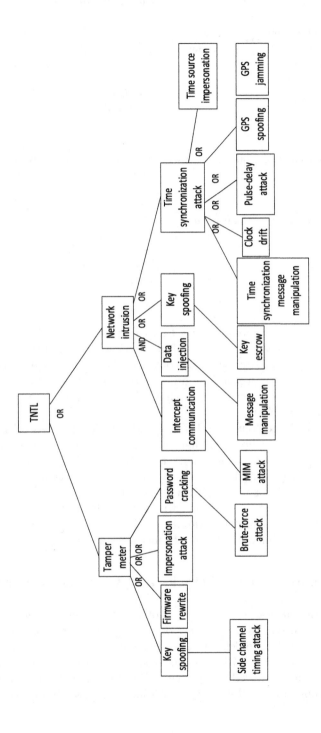

Fig. 6. The attack tree of TNTL fraud. "AND" means the left subtree should co-occur to commit a TNTL fraud. "OR" means the left or the right subtree is the prerequisite of a TNTL fraud.

Table 1. Summary of attack models and countermeasures

Attack model	Main method	Category	Related attacks	Countermeasure
A	alter local time/clock	tamper meter	firmware rewrite, key spoofing, password cracking, impersonation attack	tamper-resistant smart meter
B				
C	alter message	intrude network	message manipulation, key spoofing, MIM attack	secure key management
D	drop packet	disturb time synchronization	TSMM, Pulse-delay, TSI, Clock drift, GPS spoofing, GPS jamming	secure time synchronization

tariffs for TBP, logs, etc. It extends meter tampering from physical methods to various other ways. Also, the adversaries of meter tampering are not limited to inside customers. A smart meter could be controlled by outside adversaries. We study various ways of smart meter tampering, and identify four attacks related to TNTL, including firmware rewrite, side channel timing attack, impersonation attack, and password cracking.

Another general way to commit a TNTL fraud is to intrude networks. Messages exchanged between a home appliance and a smart meter, between two smart meters, between a smart meter and a collector, or between a collector and the head-end device, could be utilized by an adversary to commit a TNTL fraud. After studying various network attacks, we identify some attacks related to TNTL, including message manipulation attack, pulse-delay attack, etc., which will be introduced in the following section in details.

We summarize attack models and countermeasures in Table 1.

3   Time Synchronization Attacks and Countermeasures

Time synchronization attack in AMI is a class of attacks targeting time synchronization systems to de-synchronize devices or disturb normal timing processes, including GPS spoofing, pulse-delay attack, etc. We analyze various time synchronization attacks in Smart Grid and find that some of these attacks could cause TNTL frauds including GPS spoofing, GPS jamming, time synchronization message manipulation, pulse-delay, time source impersonation, and clock drift.

Table 2. Various time synchronization attacks related to TNTL fraud

Time synchronization attack	Description	Networks	How relates to TNTL?	Countermeasure
GPS spoofing	falsify GPS signal	AMI, WAN	de-synchronization, packet drop, delayed billing, wrong billing time	notify the device with correct time
GPS jamming	interfere GPS signal	AMI, WAN	de-synchronization, packet drop, delayed billing, wrong billing time	correct billing information and resend
Time synchronization message manipulation	alter time synchronization messages	AMI, HAN, NAN, WAN	de-synchronization, packet drop, delayed billing, wrong billing time	message authentication
Pulse-delay	relay time synchronization messages	AMI, HAN, NAN, WAN	de-synchronization, packet drop, delayed billing, wrong billing time	end-to-end delay threshold
Time source impersonation	impersonate time source	AMI, HAN, NAN, WAN	de-synchronization, packet drop, delayed billing, wrong billing time	end-to-end authentication
Clock drift	clock runs slower	AMI, HAN, NAN, WAN	de-synchronization, packet drop, delayed billing, wrong billing time	time compensation

We summarize time synchronization attacks that could be utilized by TNTL frauds in Table 2. Some other time synchronization attacks are affecting the functionalities of networks such as Zigbee, PLC, Homeplug, etc. However, these networks convey information for communication and control, not for billing. Thus, these attacks do not relate to TNTL frauds. For example, ASN attack and node identity attack [21], they de-synchronize devices in Zigbee networks. However, they do not affect the billing processes. Therefore, they do not relate to TNTL frauds.

4   Conclusion

In this paper, we introduced a potential fraud, TNTL fraud, in Smart Grid. We summarized four typical attack models of TNTL fraud and generated an attack tree to demonstrate various attacks related to TNTL fraud. We discussed related time synchronization attacks and proposed countermeasures. As a future work, we will further study how to secure smart meter and key management to prevent TNTL frauds.

Acknowledgement. This work was supported in part by the National Nature Science Foundation of China under the Grant 61374200, and the National Science Foundation (NSF) under Grant CNS-1059265.

References

1. The price of electricity in your state (2011). http://www.npr.org/sections/money/2011/10/27/141766341/the-price-of-electricity-in-your-state
2. ANSI C12.19-2012 (2012). https://www.nema.org/Standards/Complimentary Documents/C12-19-2012-Contents-and-Scope.pdf
3. Emerging markets smart grid: Outlook 2015, December 2014. http://www.northeast-group.com/reports/Brochure-Emerging%20Markets%20Smart%20Grid-Outlook%202015-Northeast%20Group.pdf
4. Costa, B.C., Alberto, B.L.A., Portela, A.M., Maduro, W., Eler, E.O.: Fraud detection in electric power distribution networks using an ann-based knowledge-discover process. Int. J. Artif. Intell. Appl. (IJAIA) 4(6), 11–23 (2013)
5. Gao, J., Liu, J., Rajan, B., Nori, R., Fu, B., Xiao, Y., Liang, W., Chen, C.L.P.: SCADA communication and security issues. Secur. Commun. Netw. Secur. Comm. 7(1), 175–194 (2014)
6. Han, W., Xiao, Y.: NFD: a practical scheme to detect non-technical loss fraud in smart grid. In: Proceedings of the 50th International Conference on Communications (ICC 2014), pp. 605–609, June 2014
7. Han, W., Xiao, Y.: IP^{2}DM for V2G networks in smart grid. In: Proceedings of the 50th International Conference on Communications (ICC 2015), pp. 782–787, June 2015
8. Han, W., Xiao, Y.: CNFD: A Novel Scheme to Detect Colluded Non-technical Loss Fraud in Smart Grid. In: Yang, Q., Yu, W., Challal, Y. (eds.) WASA 2016. LNCS, vol. 9798, pp. 47–55. Springer, Heidelberg (2016). doi:10.1007/978-3-319-42836-9_5
9. Han, W., Xiao, Y.: FNFD: a fast scheme to detect and verify non-technical loss fraud in smart grid. In: International Workshop on Traffic Measurements for Cybersecurity (WTMC 2016), Xi'an, China, pp. 24–34, 30 May 2016. doi:10.1145/2903185.2903188
10. Han, W., Xiao, Y.: Non-technical loss fraud in advanced metering infrastructure in smart grid. In: The 2nd International Conference on Cloud Computing and Security (ICCCS 2016), Part II. LNCS, vol. 10040 (2016). doi:10.1007/978-3-319-48674-1_15
11. Han, W., Xiong, W., Xiao, Y., Ellabidy, M., Vasilakos, A.V., Xiong, N.: A class of non-statistical traffic anomaly detection in complex network systems. In: Proceedings of the 32nd International Conference on Distributed Computing Systems Workshops (ICDCSW 2012), pp. 640–646, June 2012
12. Lin, C., Chen, S., Kuo, C., Chen, J.: Non-cooperative game model applied to an advanced metering infrastructure for non-technical loss screening in micro-distribution systems. IEEE Trans. Smart Grid 5(5), 2468–2469 (2014)
13. Liu, J., Xiao, Y., Li, S., Liang, W., Chen, C.L.P.: Cyber security and privacy issues in smart grids. IEEE Commun. Surv. Tutorials 14(4), pp. 981–997 (2012). Fourth Quarter
14. McDaniel, P., Smith, S.W.: Security and privacy challenges in the smart grid. IEEE Secur. Priv. 7(3), 75–77 (2009)
15. Werley, E., Angelos, S., Saavedra, O.R., Cortés, O.A.C., Souza, A.: Detection and identification of abnormalities in customer consumptions in power distribution systems. IEEE Trans. Power Delivery 26(4), 2436–2442 (2011)
16. Xia, X., Liang, W., Xiao, Y., Zheng, M.: BCGI: a fast approach to detect malicious meters in neighborhood area smart grid. In: Proceedings of the 50th International Conference on Communications (ICC 2015), pp. 7228–7233, June 2015

17. Xia, X., Liang, W., Xiao, Y., Zheng, M., Xiao, Z.: Difference-comparison-based approach for malicious meter inspection in neighborhood area smart grids. In: Proceedings of the 50th International Conference on Communications (ICC 2015), pp. 802–807, June 2015
18. Xiao, Z., Xiao, Y., Du, D.: Building accountable smart grids in neighborhood area networks. In: Proceedings of the IEEE Global Telecommunications Conference 2011 (GLOBECOM 2011), pp. 1–5, December 2011
19. Xiao, Z., Xiao, Y., Du, D.: Exploring malicious meter inspection in neighborhood area smart grids. IEEE Trans. Smart Grid $4(1)$, 214–226 (2013)
20. Xiao, Z., Xiao, Y., Du, D.: Non-repudiation in neighborhood area networks for smart grid. IEEE Commun. Mag. $51(1)$, 18–26 (2013)
21. Yang, W., Wang, Q., Qi, Y., Sun, S.: Time synchronization attacks in ieee802.15.4e networks. In: Proceedings of the 2014 International Conference Identification, Information and Knowledge in the Internet of Things (IIKI 2014), pp. 166–169, October 2014

Social Influence Analysis Based on Modeling Interactions in Dynamic Social Networks: A Case Study

Liwei Huang[1], Yutao Ma[2(✉)], and Yanbo Liu[1]

[1] Beijing Institute of Remote Sensing, Beijing 100854, China
huangliwei.1985@gmail.com, liuyanbonudt@163.com
[2] State Key Laboratory of Software Engineering,
Wuhan University, Wuhan 430072, China
ytma@whu.edu.cn

Abstract. Interactions occur across social networks, and modeling interactions in dynamic social networks is a challenging research problem that has broad applications. By combining topology in mathematics with field theory in physics, topology potential, which sets up a virtual field via a topology space to reflect individual activities, local effects and preferential attachments in different interactions, has been proposed to model mutual effects between individuals on social networks. In this paper, we take into consideration not only the information of topology structure and content but also two factors, namely, individual mass and interaction strength. From the perspective of smooth evolution of social networks, we propose a method based on dynamic topology potential, which captures the correlations between different changing snapshots of a social network and can be used to model interactions dynamically, so as to quantify the effects of interactions between individuals on dynamic social networks. Finally, we utilize the dynamic topology potential method for user influence analysis, especially for influential user identification, and the experiment conducted on a real-world data set from AMiner demonstrates the feasibility and effectiveness of our method in terms of a measure for network robustness.

Keywords: Interaction · Dynamic topology potential · Influential user identification · Network robustness

1 Introduction

Because social networking services become the most popular platform for interaction, communication, and collaboration between friends, in recent years they have attracted great interest for a variety of social processes, such as information processing, distributed search [1], and the diffusion of social influence. Different types of content of these services, such as text, messaging, and tags, change over time, leading to dynamic dyadic or one-way interconnectivities among various users. In such cases, any individuals or ties between them can be added to or deleted from a social network rapidly, as a result of which the network topology evolves over time. Moreover, due to complex interactions between nodes (viz. users) in such social networks, the intrinsic attributes

© Springer International Publishing AG 2016
X. Sun et al. (Eds.): ICCCS 2016, Part II, LNCS 10040, pp. 58–70, 2016.
DOI: 10.1007/978-3-319-48674-1_6

of both nodes and links may also change. Hence, the social network perspective offers a promising way to analyze the structure and dynamics of social groups on the Internet.

Nowadays, it has been recognized that social networks can be modeled more naturally from a dynamic perspective [2], which has aroused enormous interest in the field of managing and mining dynamic social networks. Frequent interactions often result in a similarity in user behavior or user preferences. Then, online communities composed of individuals who act in a similar manner or share similar interest will emerge. To better understand the nature of such dynamic social networks' evolution, it is necessary to explore social interactions that can be observed through the properties of relationships between individuals in both the virtual and real worlds. However, compared with social relationships or ties, many forms of social interactions are transient in nature and occur over a relatively short period.

Generally speaking, user interactions in dynamic social networks are important and could be deemed to be a key factor to the dynamics of such social networks [3, 4]. Although considerable progress has been made in social networks research, to the best of our knowledge, there are few studies in modeling such interactions in dynamic social networks. For this challenging problem, Jiang et al. [5] argued that it was difficult to model the characteristics of local interactions (rather than global interactions within a network) among users and to quantify the effects of such interactions on the whole network. For example, there are some essential characteristics to consider when individuals interact with others on dynamic social networks, such as individual activity, local effect, and preferential attachment.

By combining topology in mathematics with field theory in physics, Hu et al. [6] proposed a new concept termed *topology potential*. It sets up a virtual field via a topology space to reflect the above three characteristics of social interactions. However, the studies based on topology potential can only analyze static interactions between individuals. In this paper, we extend the concept from an evolutionary perspective and present an approach based on *dynamic topology potential* to describe the dynamic effects of social interactions. Compared with the previous work [6], our work takes into consideration the evolutionary smoothness of dynamic social networks using their continuous snapshots. Besides, we also show an important application of the approach, i.e., important node modeling and identification in dynamic social networks, to validate its feasibility and effectiveness in terms of a recently proposed measure of network robustness.

The remainder of this paper is organized as follows. In Sect. 2, we present an overview of the related work for social influence analysis. The preliminaries to our work are introduced in Sect. 3. Section 4 introduces our approach based on dynamic topology potential in detail, and Sect. 5 discusses the results of the experiment conducted on a real-world data set from AMiner[1] (formerly known as ArnetMiner). Finally, Sect. 6 concludes this paper and proposes our future work.

---

[1] https://aminer.org/.

2 Related Work

2.1 Statistical Analysis on Social Interactions

Statistical analysis is the easiest way to understand user interactions in social networks, which has been deemed as a significant task in the field of social science. Golder *et al.* [7] studied the rhythms of social interactions between college students on Facebook and found some interesting regular patterns. For example, although Facebook users often have a large number of declared friends, they contact only a small number of people. Wilson *et al.* [8] analyzed interaction graphs which were derived from Facebook user traces, and they found some different properties that have not been shown in traditional social networks, for example, significantly lower levels of the small-world property and fewer super-nodes that have extremely high degrees. Viswanath *et al.* [9] investigated the evolution of activities between users on Facebook. Although the links in such an activity network changed rapidly over time, many graph-theoretic properties of the network remained unchanged.

Macskassy *et al.* [10] explored the characteristics of user interactions on Twitter, and they found that roughly half of the users spent a substantial amount of time interacting, whereas 40 % of the users did not seem to have active interactions. Moreover, the vast majority of interactions involved only two people despite the public nature of these tweets. Yan *et al.* [11] analyzed Micro-blog user behavior and found that the exponent of the distribution of Micro-blogs has a negative correlation with the degree of each user. They then proposed a human dynamics model based on social networks to simulate the practical situations.

Overall, the above studies focused on analyzing topological properties of famous online social networks like Facebook, Twitter, and Micro-blog, while ignoring the content and scope of interactions [12, 13]. So, there is a growing recognition that a more nuanced understanding of social interactions requires an analysis of the semantic content of communication in addition to topology structure. For example, Shriver *et al.* [14] conducted an experiment to test whether users' online content-generation activities were co-determined with their social ties, and they found that economically significant effects were able to generate positive feedback that facilitated local network effects in content generation. Interestingly, similar findings were reported in [15] by Zeng *et al.* However, to the best of our knowledge, there are seldom effective research studies on modeling the effects of interactions among individuals in dynamic social networks with quantitative methods, except for the prior work [6].

2.2 Influential User Identification

Considering the applications of behavior analysis in online social networks, influential user identification is one of the most enduring topics in this field [16]. In general, it is always converted to the problem of node importance ranking in social networks. As you know, there are various measures for node importance, such as degree, betweenness, closeness, and PageRank value, but different measures with distinct viewpoints may obtain different results. In recent years, social influence has been considered to be an indicator for measuring the importance of nodes in static and dynamic social networks [17, 18]. For example, Wang *et al.* [19] used a time-dependent factor graph model to find influential nodes in dynamic social networks, and the experimental results on three data sets showed that their approaches were able to efficiently infer the dynamic social influence.

Recently, several researchers began to attach importance to modeling social interactions when they analyzed influential users in dynamic social networks. For example, Sun *et al.* [20] presented a regional user interaction model to analyze and understand the interaction between users in a local region, according to the finding that there exists influence transfer effect during the process of user interactions in online social networks such as SINA Weibo. Yet despite all that, the work is still at the initial stage of research studies, implying that there is plenty of room for improvement.

3 Preliminaries to Topology Potential

Inspired by the idea of field theory in physics, the concept of *topology potential* (field), which is a virtual field constructed in a given topology space, was proposed in [6]. If any node of a network in the topology space is viewed as a particle, it generates a virtual field around itself and certain forces acting upon other nodes within the field. The strength of such forces is directly proportional to the values of the node's intrinsic attributes such as mass and is inversely proportional to the distance from the node. The interactions among all of nodes in the topology space then form a field of topology potential over the network.

As an interpretation of non-contact interaction between nodes in any networks, topology potential can characterize the aforementioned characteristics, namely, individual activity, local effect, and preferential attachment [6, 21]. First, due to various intrinsic attributes and behavior, individuals on social networks exhibit different characteristics of activities in their interactions. Second, it is more likely that an individual interacts with other individuals who are similar to him/her, suggesting the characteristic of preference attachment. Third, the strength of such an interaction effect is determined by the distance between two individuals, i.e., the closer the distance, the greater the effect would be. This indicates the characteristic of local effect.

Next, we present the definitions of pairwise potential and topology potential [6].

Definition 1. *Pairwise potential* is defined as the potential at any node produced by another node in a network, and it reflects the influence of one node on another node. Given a network $G = (V, E)$, where V is the set of nodes and E is the set of edges. For $v_i, v_j \in V(v_i \neq v_j)$, let $\varphi(j \to i)$ be the pairwise potential at any node v_i produced by v_j.

Definition 2. *Topology potential* is defined according to the differential position of each node in a network, and it reflects the capacity with which one node influences other nodes within a certain range. A node's topology potential equals the sum of the pairwise potential generated from the node onto all of the other nodes in the network.

For real social networks, it has long been recognized that interaction effects between nodes will rapidly decrease with an increase in the distance between them, according to *Six degrees of Separation* (also known as small-world effect) [22]. As you know, Gaussian potential functions have clear mathematical properties and can describe the potential distribution of short-range fields, which satisfies $\int K(x)dx = 1$ and $\int xK(x)dx = 0$ (where $K(x)$ is a unit potential function). Hence, we use a Gaussian potential function to describe such interaction effects.

Definition 3. *Gaussian-type pairwise potential* generated from v_j onto v_i is defined as

$$\varphi(j \rightarrow i) = m_j \times e^{-\left(\frac{d_{j \rightarrow i}}{\sigma}\right)^2}, \tag{1}$$

where m_j is the mass of node v_j, $d_{j \rightarrow i}$ is the Euclidian distance between nodes v_j and v_i, and σ is a self-defined factor which adjusts the influence range of visual fields around a given node.

Definition 4. *Gaussian-type topology potential* at node v_i is defined as

$$\varphi(v_i) = \sum_{j=1}^{n} \varphi(j \rightarrow i)(j \neq i), \tag{2}$$

where n is the number of nodes in a network.

As shown in the definition of topology potential, there is a positive correlation between the influence range of each node and the factor σ. When $0 < \sigma < D$ (viz. the diameter of a network), the interactions among nodes in the network are different, and the values of the topology potential at different nodes vary. Thus, the factor should be optimized to make the value of the topology potential at each node as diverse as possible to minimize the uncertainty of the network. As is known, Shannon entropy is a useful measure of uncertainty in an information system [23]. Hence, we define *potential entropy* based on Shannon entropy, and then optimize the factor for topology potential in terms of potential entropy.

Definition 5. *Potential entropy* is defined as

$$H(V) = \sum_{i=1}^{n} P(v_i)I(v_i) = \sum_{i=1}^{n} P(v_i) \ln\left(\frac{1}{P(v_i)}\right) = -\sum_{i=1}^{n} P(v_i) \ln(P(v_i)), \tag{3}$$

where $P(v_i) = \frac{\varphi(v_i)}{\sum_{i=1}^{n} \varphi(v_i)}$ $(\sum P(v_i) = 1)$.

Definition 6. *Optimization function for potential entropy* is defined as

$$minH = max \sum_{i=1}^{n} P(v_i) \ln(P(v_i)), \sigma > 0. \tag{4}$$

4   Dynamic Topology Potential Method

4.1   Topology Distance

As mentioned above, the distance between two points is measured by the Euclidian distance [6], but such a distance does not exist in a virtual network topology space. In this paper, we replace the Euclidean distance with the topology distance between two nodes in a network. However, traditional metrics such as hops or the shortest path length, which have been widely used in social network analysis, are insufficient to characterize the interactions on different paths between nodes. According to cognitive physics [24] and shunt-wound circuit theory in electricity, we redefine the topology distance as follows.

Definition 7. If there exists a set of nodes $P = \{v_j, v_k,\ldots, v_l, v_i\}$ and none of the nodes appears repeatedly in P, P is considered as a *reachable path* between nodes v_j and v_i.

Suppose that nodes v_i and v_j are mapped to two electric potentials U_i and U_j in a shunt-wound circuit, K reachable paths between them can be mapped to K branches in the circuit. Then, the resistance of each branch can be represented as a function of reachable path lengths, and the topology distance between v_j and v_i $(d_{j \to i})$ is calculated by mapping inversely the equivalent resistance R_e between U_i and U_j, defined as follows.

$$\sum_{k \in S_{ij}} \frac{1}{R_k} = \frac{1}{R_e}, \tag{5}$$

where S_{ij} denotes the set of all reachable paths between v_j and v_i.

4.2   Dynamic Topology Potential

For dynamic social networks, a widely used approach is the two-step approach proposed in [25], in which static analysis is applied first to each snapshot of a social network with time stamps, and the follow-up work is then conducted to interpret dynamic properties of the network. Because data in the real world is often noisy, such a two-step approach often results in unwarranted and unstable topology potential values for nodes in a social network. Moreover, the optimization of the factor σ could be highly sensitive to the changes in a network, even if only a few nodes and edges are added to or deleted from the network. Obviously, due to an independent parameter optimization for each snapshot, we have no incentive to maintain such temporal contiguity between the topology potential values of nodes.

Indeed, we have to make a first-order Markov assumption. In other words, the topology potential value for a node at a given time should be close to its value at the most recent time. To acquire smooth network evolution, we add a temporal regularization term, which ensures a topology potential sequence to be smooth across different snapshots in terms of potential entropy, and the new objective function is denoted as F. Thus, with this regularization, the problem can be formulated as

$$\min(F(\sigma)) = \min\left\{\left[-\sum_{i=1}^{n^t}\frac{\varphi(v_i)^t}{\sum_{i=1}^{n^t}\varphi(v_i)^t}\ln\left(\frac{\varphi(v_i)^t}{\sum_{i=1}^{n^t}\varphi(v_i)^t}\right)\right] + \frac{\lambda^t}{2}\sum_{i=1}^{n^t}\left\|\left(\varphi(v_i)^t-\varphi(v_i)^{t-1}\right)\right\|_F^2\right\}, \quad (6)$$

where n^t is the number of nodes in a network at time t, $\varphi(v_i)^t$ represents the topology potential at node v_i at time t, and σ^t denotes the influence factor at time t. Note that various optimization methods, such as the gradient decent method, can be applied to find a local minimum value.

4.3   Algorithm for Influential User Identification

In dynamic social networks, we have to face a basic but very difficult challenge: which users are more influential? In this paper, we measure the influence of a node in a social network with different snapshots in terms of dynamic topology potential. That is, the topology potential value of a node reflects the degree of a node's influence on other nodes. Generally speaking, there are two main steps to discover influential users in a dynamic social network based on dynamic topology potential.

First, we determine the optimal factor σ for each snapshot of the network in question to evaluate each node's topology potential value. Here, a stochastic gradient decent method is used to optimize the influence factor. Second, for each snapshot, we sort the nodes with the topology potential values in descending order. The algorithm for node influence ranking is summarized in Fig. 1.

Algorithm 1. Node influence ranking in dynamic social networks

---

Input: A network $G^t = (V^t, E^t)$ at time t, where $|V^t| = n^t$ and $|E^t| = m^t$, the learning rate η, and the topology potential sequence in the recent snapshot $\{\varphi(v_i)^{t-1}\}$

Output: A list of top-k nodes

Step 1: Calculate the optimal value of the factor at time t

1. Initialize σ^t

2. **Repeat**

3.   Calculate the gradients of σ^t and λ^t, described as below
$$\frac{\partial(F(\sigma^t))}{\partial\sigma^t}, \quad \frac{\partial(F(\lambda^t))}{\partial\lambda^t}$$

4.   Update the parameters σ^t and λ^t with the learning rate η, described as follows
$$\sigma^t \leftarrow \sigma^t - \eta \cdot \frac{\partial(F(\sigma^t))}{\partial\sigma^t}$$
$$\lambda^t \leftarrow \lambda^t - \eta \cdot \frac{\partial(F(\lambda^t))}{\partial\lambda^t}$$

5. **Until** convergence

Step 2: Calculate the updated topology potential value of each node according to σ^t

6. $\varphi(v_i)^t = \sum_{j=1}^{n^t}\varphi(j \rightarrow i)^t = \sum_{j=1}^{n^t}m_j^t \times e^{-\left(\frac{d_{j\rightarrow i}^t}{\sigma^t}\right)^2}$

7. Sort the nodes in descending order

8. **Return** top-k nodes

Fig. 1.   An algorithm for node influence ranking in dynamic social networks

5   Case Study

5.1   Data Collection

Our data set used in this paper is collected from the academic researcher social network AMiner, which is provided by Tang *et al.* [26]. Although the data set contains 1,632,442 articles and 1,036,990 authors, we only choose the articles published between 2001 and 2010. In this refined data set, each time slice lasts two years. Note that only the authors who have published at least five papers in each 2-year period are considered in our experiment, because the goal of this paper is to identify those influential users, namely those top scholars in computer science.

5.2   Network Construction

According to the selected authors' papers published in each 2-year period, we construct the corresponding co-author network in each time slice, where a node represents an author and an edge indicates the co-authorship between the selected authors. The mass of a node in such networks is defined as the total number of papers published by the corresponding author in a time slice. For those five networks to be discussed, there are a total number of 5,028 nodes, and the numbers of edges are 14,526, 16,933, 18,845, 18,416, and 14,593, respectively.

Considering the application scenario of our method, our experiment takes into consideration the strength of the interactions between authors which is defined according to their cooperative behavior, even if they have established co-authorships. In particular, there exists an interaction between two authors if they co-authored one paper in any 2-year period. According to the prior study [27], in this paper the strength of such interactions between authors i and j at time t is defined as

$$w_{ij} = \sum_T (\tau)^{t-T} (\tau \in (0, 1)), \tag{7}$$

where T is the time that a given paper is published and τ is a decay factor. The smaller the value of τ, the influence of interaction behavior on the strength of interactions decays more quickly. In this experiment, τ is empirically set to 0.8 according to the experimental data.

Then, five weighted networks derived from the original co-author networks are created for our experiment.

5.3   Measures for Node Importance

As is known, there are many measures to address the issue of important nodes discovery in a network, e.g., node degree, betweenness, closeness, the PageRank value, and so on. Many state-of-the-art methods proposed in computer science utilize the above concepts and measures in network science, and they have achieved good results [16]. To show the effectiveness of our method based on dynamic topology potential, we compare it with five typical measures, including weighted degree, weighted closeness, weighted betweenness, weighted PageRank [28], and semi-local centrality measure [29]. The first four measures are the corresponding extensions of degree, closeness, betweenness, and PageRank for weighted networks, respectively. Because the last measure [29] is designed only for un-weighted networks, in this paper we extend it to weighted networks. The local centrality $C_L(v)$ of node v is defined as

$$C_L(v) = \sum_{u \in \Gamma(v)} Q(u), \tag{8}$$

$$Q(u) = \sum_{w \in \Gamma(u)} N(w), \tag{9}$$

where $\Gamma()$ is the set of the nearest neighbors of a given node and $N(w)$ is the sum of the nearest distances between node w and the nearest as well as the next-nearest neighbors of w.

5.4 Evaluation Measure

Actually, it is very difficult to achieve an objective and generally recognized criterion to evaluate the rankings generated by different approaches. From the viewpoint of robustness analysis or vulnerability analysis, Schneider *et al.* [30] recently proposed a new measure for robustness to compare the advantages and disadvantages of different methods. An essential assumption is that the functions and structure of a network will be greatly affected when those important nodes are removed [31]. After those important nodes are removed from the network in question, this measure can quantify the proportion of the nodes that belong to the largest component of the network to the total number of nodes in the network, which is defined as [30]

$$R = \frac{1}{n} \sum_{Q=1}^{n} s(Q), \tag{10}$$

where $s(Q)$ represents the ratio of the remaining nodes in the largest connected component after a fraction q of the most connected nodes (viz. $Q = qn$ nodes) are removed from the network.

5.5 Experimental Results

According to the five weighted networks under discussion, we identify the top ten authors in each 2-year period with the method based on dynamic topology potential and list them in Table 1. Because Professor Jiawei Han is ranked number one in all of five 2-year periods, there is no doubt that he is the most remarkable scholar in this field in the period of 2001–2010, followed by Professor Philip S. Yu who wins four runner-ups and one third-place.

As shown in Table 2, the performance of our approach is, on average, better than those of the five methods. Moreover, compared with the best one among the five methods, namely weighted PageRank, the evaluation measure of our approach is

Table 1. The top ten authors in different periods

Rank	2001–2002	2003–2004	2005–2006	2007–2008	2009–2010
1	Jiawei Han	Jiawei Han	Jiawei Han	Jiawei Han	Jiawei Han
2	Mahmut T. Kandemir	Philip S. Yu	Philip S. Yu	Philip S. Yu	Philip S. Yu
3	Philip S. Yu	Mahmut T. Kandemir	Thomas S. Huang	Mario Piattini	WeiWang
4	Hongjiang Zhang	Erik D. Demaine	Erik D. Demaine	Erik D. Demaine	Mario Piattini
5	Erik D. Demaine	Hongjiang Zhang	Mario Piattini	Thomas S. Huang	Erik D. Demaine
6	Thomas S. Huang	Mario Piattini	Mahmut T. Kandemir	Wen Gao	Thomas S. Huang
7	Elisa Bertino	Thomas S. Huang	Hongjiang Zhang	Mahmut T. Kandemir	Wen Gao
8	Luca Benini	Elisa Bertino	Wen Gao	WeiWang	Mahmut T. Kandemir
9	Diego Calvanese	Luca Benini	WeiWang	Hongjiang Zhang	Lei Zhang
10	Mario Piattini	Wen Gao	Luca Benini	Lei Zhang	Luca Benini

Table 2. Comparison of different methods in terms of the measure of robustness

Method	2001–2002	2003–2004	2005–2006	2007–2008	2009–2010	Average
Weighted degree	4.79e−3	3.22e−3	3.14e−3	0.95e−3	5.35e−3	3.49e−3
Weighted closeness	2.92e−3	4.01e−3	2.36e−3	3.33e−3	2.14e−3	2.95e−3
Weighted betweenness	3.33e−3	2.05e−3	2.12e−3	3.36e−3	4.27e−3	3.03e−3
Weighted PageRank	0.92e−3	1.87e−3	3.48e−3	1.22e−3	3.03e−3	2.10e−3
Weighted local centrality	1.22e−3	2.53e−3	2.45e−3	2.12e−3	2.67e−3	2.24e−3
Our method	1.56e−3	1.25e−3	2.09e−3	0.87e−3	1.82e−3	1.52e−3

increased by up to 27.62 %. Note that the decimal number in each cell of the table indicates the value of the evaluation measure when all nodes ranked by the method in question are removed from the corresponding network in a given time period.

6   Conclusion and Future Work

Interactions exist widely in social networks. Because of the instantaneity of social interactions and the dynamics of social networks, modeling interactions in dynamic social networks becomes a challenging problem. To model the mutual effect of interactions, in this paper we consider not only the topology structure of a network but also the content within it. Individual mass and interaction strength are introduced to traditional social networks in a novel way. Considering the smooth evolution of social networks, we further propose a novel approach based on dynamic topology potential which extends topology potential in a dynamic perspective. In this paper, we use the dynamic topology potential method for user influence analysis, and the experiment conducted on the data set collected from AMiner demonstrates the feasibility and effectiveness of our method.

There are still a number of open problems to be addressed in our future research on modeling interactions in dynamic social networks. First, the model of a snapshot graph separates time into discrete time slices according to a predefined time interval. Unfortunately, it is rather difficult for users to define a reasonable time interval; as a result, an approach is needed to automatically configure the proper time interval or even to define different time intervals according to the extent of network evolution. Second, our method is only used to explain the observed data from a case study to date. To extend the capability of our approach, predicting future interactions between individuals and the related emerging social communities in the wireless mobile network environment [32] is one of the future directions for our research.

Acknowledgement. We greatly appreciate Professor Deyi Li's constructive comments and useful suggestions as well as anonymous reviewers' professional comments, which help us to improve the quality and readability of our paper.

This work is supported by the National Basic Research Program (973 Program) of China (Grant No. 2014CB340401) and the National Natural Science Foundation of China (Grant Nos. 61272111, 61273213, and 61305055).

References

1. Xia, Z., Wang, X., Sun, X., et al.: a secure and dynamic multi-keyword ranked search scheme over encrypted cloud data. IEEE Trans. Parallel Distrib. Syst. **27**, 340–352 (2016)
2. Berger-Wolf, T.Y., Saia, J.: A framework for analysis of dynamic social networks. In: 12th ACM SIGKDD International Conference on Knowledge Discovery and Data Mining, pp. 523–528. ACM Press, New York (2006)
3. Benevenuto, F., Rodrigues, T., Cha, M., et al.: Characterizing user behavior in online social networks. In: 9th ACM SIGCOMM Internet Measurement Conference, pp. 49–62. ACM Press, New York (2009)
4. Christakis, N.A., Fowler, J.H.: Social contagion theory: examining dynamic social networks and human behavior. Stat. Med. **32**, 556–577 (2013)
5. Jiang, J., Wilson, C., Wang, X., et al.: Understanding latent interactions in online social networks. ACM Trans. Web **7**, 18 (2013)

6. Hu, J., Han, Y., Hu, J.: Topological potential: modeling node importance with activity and local effect in complex networks. In: 2nd International Conference on Computer Modeling and Simulation, vol. 2, pp. 411–415. IEEE Computer Society Press, New York (2010)
7. Golder, S.A., Wilkinson, D.M., Huberman, B.A.: Rhythms of social interaction: messaging within a massive online network. CoRR, abs/cs/0611137 (2006)
8. Wilson, C., Boe, B., Sala, A., et al.: User interactions in social networks and their implications. In: 4th ACM European Conference on Computer systems, pp. 205–218. ACM Press, New York (2009)
9. Viswanath, B., Mislove, A., Cha, M., et al.: On the evolution of user interaction in Facebook. In: 2nd ACM Workshop on Online Social Networks, pp. 37–42. ACM Press, New York (2009)
10. Macskassy, S.A.: On the study of social interactions in Twitter. In: 6th International AAAI Conference on Weblogs and Social Media, pp. 226–233. AAAI Press, Palo Alto (2012)
11. Yan, Q., Wu, L., Zheng, L.: Social network based microblog user behavior analysis. Phys. A **392**, 1712–1723 (2013)
12. Wilson, C., Sala, A., Puttaswamy, K., et al.: Beyond social graphs: user interactions in online social networks and their implications. ACM Trans. Web **6**, 17 (2012)
13. Musial, K., Kazienko, P.: Social networks on the Internet. WWW **16**, 31–72 (2013)
14. Shriver, S.K., Nair, H.S., Hofstetter, R.: Social ties and user-generated content: evidence from an online social network. Manage. Sci. **59**, 1425–1443 (2013)
15. Zeng, X., Wei, L.: Social ties and user content generation: evidence from flickr. Inf. Syst. Res. **24**, 71–87 (2012)
16. Rabade, R., Mishra, N., Sharma, S.: Survey of influential user identification techniques in online social networks. In: Thampi, S.M., Abraham, A., Pal, S.K., Rodriguez, J.M.C. (eds.) ISI 2014. Advances in Intelligent Systems and Computing, vol. 235, pp. 359–370. Springer, Heidelberg (2014)
17. Ghosh, R., Lerman, K.: Predicting Influential Users in Online Social Networks. CoRR, abs/1005.4882 (2010)
18. Aral, S., Walker, D.: Identifying influential and susceptible members of social network. Science **337**, 337–341 (2012)
19. Wang, C., Tang, J., Sun, J., et al.: Dynamic social influence analysis through time-dependent factor graphs. In: 2011 International Conference on Advances in Social Networks Analysis and Mining, pp. 239–246. IEEE Computer Society Press, New York (2011)
20. Sun, Q., Wang, N., Zhou, Y., et al.: Modeling for user interaction by influence transfer effect in online social networks. In: 39th Conference on Local Computer Networks, pp. 486–489. IEEE Computer Society Press, New York (2014)
21. Han, Y., Li, D., Wang, T.: Identifying different community members in complex networks based on topology potential. Front. Comput. Sci. Chi. **5**, 87–99 (2011)
22. Newman, M., Barabsi, A.-L., Watts, D.J.: The Structure and Dynamics of Networks. Princeton University Press, Princeton (2006)
23. Shannon, C.E.: A mathematical theory of communication. Bell Syst. Tech. J. **27**, 379–423 (1948)
24. Li, D., Du, Y.: Artificial Intelligence with Uncertainty. Chapman & Hall/CRC, London (2007)
25. Lin, Y.-R., Chi, Y., Zhu, S., et al.: Analyzing communities and their evolutions in dynamic social networks. ACM Trans. Knowl. Discov. Data **3**, 8 (2009)
26. Tang, W., Zhuang, H., Tang, J.: Learning to infer social ties in large networks. In: Gunopulos, D., Hofmann, T., Malerba, D., Vazirgiannis, M. (eds.) ECML PKDD 2011, Part III. LNCS, vol. 6913, pp. 381–397. Springer, Heidelberg (2011)

27. Tang, J., Wu, S., Sun, J.: Confluence: conformity influence in large social networks. In: 19th ACM SIGKDD International Conference on Knowledge Discovery and Data Mining, pp. 347–355. ACM Press, New York (2013)
28. Xing, W., Ghorbani, A.: Weighted pagerank algorithm. In: 2nd Annual Conference on Communication Networks and Services Research, pp. 305–314. IEEE Computer Society Press, New York (2004)
29. Chen, D., Lü, L., Shang, M.S., et al.: Identifying influential nodes in complex networks. Phys. A 391, 1777–1787 (2012)
30. Schneider, C.M., Moreira, A.A., Andrade, J.S., et al.: Mitigation of malicious attacks on networks. Proc. Natl. Acad. Sci. U.S.A. 108, 3838–3841 (2011)
31. Iyer, S., Killingback, T., Sundaram, B., et al.: Attack robustness and centrality of complex networks. PLoS ONE 8, e59613 (2013)
32. Guo, P., Wang, J., Li, B., et al.: A variable threshold-value authentication architecture for wireless mesh networks. J. Internet Technol. 15, 929–936 (2014)

Automated Vulnerability Modeling and Verification for Penetration Testing Using Petri Nets

Junchao Luan[1], Jian Wang[1], and Mingfu Xue[1,2(✉)]

[1] College of Computer Science and Technology,
Nanjing University of Aeronautics and Astronautics, Nanjing 211106, China
{luanjunchao,wangjian,mingfu.xue}@nuaa.edu.cn
[2] Information Technology Research Base of Civil Aviation Administration of China,
Civil Aviation University of China, Tianjin 300300, China

Abstract. With the increase of network size, there are more and more potential vulnerabilities, which makes it difficult to conduct penetration testing in multihost networks. Attack graph is a useful tool for penetration testing to analyze the relevance of vulnerabilities between hosts and provides a visual view for attack path planning. However, previous works on attack graph generation are inefficient and not applicable to practical penetration testing process. In this paper, we propose an automated vulnerability modeling and verification approach for penetration testing, which generates attack graph efficiently and can be applied to attack process. Petri net is adopted for vulnerability modeling and attack graph synthesis. We implement a prototype system named Automatic Penetration Testing System to verify our method. The system is tested in real networks and the experiment results show the efficiency of our approach.

Keywords: Vulnerability modeling · Vulnerability verification · Attack graph · Penetration testing · Petri net

1 Introduction

At present, the network environment [1] has become more and more complex which makes conducting penetration testing difficult. A valuable penetration test requires a detailed analysis of threats and potential attackers. However, considering relevance between vulnerabilities and network size, it usually takes penetration testers much time to plan attack path and launch attacks to verify the existence of vulnerabilities, which largely depends on professional experience of testers.

Attack graph is introduced into penetrating testing to analyse vulnerability relevance and determine attack path. It can be derived from network topology and vulnerability information. Under the guidance of attack graph, testers can launch the process of penetration testing efficiently.

© Springer International Publishing AG 2016
X. Sun et al. (Eds.): ICCCS 2016, Part II, LNCS 10040, pp. 71–82, 2016.
DOI: 10.1007/978-3-319-48674-1_7

Phillips and Swiler put forward the concept of attack graphs in 1998 [2]. It considers the physical network topology [3,4] and the set of attacks. However, attack graphs are constructed manually and there are match problems from the templates to configuration and attack profile. J.P. McDermott proposed modeling of penetration testing as a Petri net [5], which has the ability to use discovered transitions to connect subnets.

Automatic technique for generating attack graphs was proposed by Sheyner in 2002 [6]. The technique was based on symbolic model checking algorithms and constructed attack graphs automatically and efficiently. However, when applied to moderate-sized networks, Sheyner's tool encountered a significant exponential explosion problem. The problem is solved by Xinming Ou [7], who proposed logical attack graphs to directly illustrate logical dependencies among attack goals and configuration information. Since then, many attack graph models [8,9] came up to deal with large-scale networks. But these models are not quite applicable in practical scenarios because they generate full attack graph which are not necessary for penetration testing. Xue Qiu proposed automatic generation algorithm of penetration graph in penetration testing [10]. The algorithm reduces redundant information effectively by optimizing the network topology before generating the penetration graph.

Vulnerability analysis methods usually follow attack graph generation. S. Jha put forward two formal analysis of attack graphs in 2002 [11]. MulVAL [12] was developed by Xinming Ou to analyze multistage vulnerability. Sushil Jajodia also implemented a tool to analyse network vulnerability [13]. Based on vulnerability analysis, risk evaluation [14,15] and security hardening schemes [16–18]are proposed to help improve network security. Kotenko introduced computation of different security metrics after attack graph construction to evaluate network security [14]. Steven Noel presented an efficient exploit-dependency representation in computing network hardening measures to reduce total cost [16].

The complexity of previous attack graph generation algorithm grows rapidly with the increase of network size and they are not incorporated with practical penetration testing process. In order to solve these problems, this paper proposes a vulnerability modeling and verification approach and implements an automatic penetrating testing system. Experiment results show the effectiveness and efficiency in practical penetration testing scenarios. The contributions of this paper are:

1. We propose an efficient attack graph generation algorithm adaptable for penetration testing. We adapt traditional single vulnerability exploit model for penetration testing and put forward the concept of network attack path to reduce the number of atomic exploits.
2. We present vulnerability verification method. The method can conduct vulnerability attacks along with the attack paths generated from attack graph and confirm existence and severity of vulnerabilities.
3. We implement an automatic penetration testing system named APTS. The system outputs successful attack paths and vulnerability severity evaluation based on penetration testing results.

The remainder of this paper is organized as follows. Section 2 depicts vulnerability modeling for penetration testing. In Sect. 3, we present verification method of vulnerability based on attack graph. Section 4 shows the experiment and results analysis. Finally, we conclude in Sect. 5.

2 Vulnerability Modeling for Penetration Testing

2.1 Penetration Testing Environment Description Language

To support automatic vulnerability modeling and verification, we introduce penetration testing environment description language (PTEDL) based on [10]. PTEDL gives definitions of elements including network information, vulnerability information and host information abstractly.

Definition 1. *Network information refers to the network environment of penetration testing, which can be denoted as follows:*

$$Network\_Info ::= \langle NetworkID, Range, Access \rangle \tag{1}$$

NetworkID is a unique identifier for the network in penetration testing environment; Range refers to the ip range of the network; Access refers to a set of reachable networks from current network.

Definition 2. *Vulnerability information represents the defect information of a vulnerable host, whose definition is as follows:*

$$Vuln\_Info ::= \langle VulnID, VulnType, VulnOrigPriv, VulnGainPriv \rangle \tag{2}$$

VulnID is a unique identifier for each vulnerability organized by CVE; VulnType refers to the exploit pattern, locally or remotely; VulnOrigPriv represents the least privilege capable for an attacker to launch the vulnerability exploit; VulnGainPriv is the privilege an attacker obtain after a successful vulnerability exploit.

Definition 3. *Host information is the information about the node in penetration testing environment which has potential security problems. It can be denoted as follows:*

$$Host\_Info ::= \langle HostID, IPAddress, NetworkID, Vuln\_List \rangle \tag{3}$$

HostID is a unique identifier for each host; IPAddress is the ip address of the host; NetworkID is the network identifier; Vuln_List is a set of Vuln_Info, each of which contains vulnerability information.

2.2 Single Vulnerability Exploit Model

This paper simplifies the single vulnerability exploit model (SVEM) [19] to make it suitable for penetration testing. The formal definition of SVEM is as follows:

Definition 4. *Single vulnerability exploit model (SVEM) is a pure Petri net, which can be denoted as follows:*

$$SVEM ::= \langle P_{pre} \bigcup P_{con}, t; F \rangle \qquad (4)$$

In SVEM, P_{pre} is a set of input places, each of which denotes one of conditions before attack behaviour takes place; t is a set of transitions, which denote vulnerability exploit behaviour; P_{con} is a set of output places, which denote results of successful vulnerability exploit; F refers to the flow relation from P_{pre} to t and from t to P_{con}, i.e., $F = ((P_{pre} \times t) \bigcup (t \times P_{con}))$.

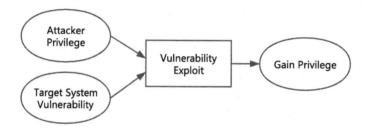

Fig. 1. Single vulnerability exploit model

Figure 1 illustrates the SVEM. As shown in Fig. 1, attacker privilege and vulnerability of target system are reserved , and attack reachability as well as service activeness are removed compared with atomic attack model in [19], which are not quite necessary in penetration testing.

2.3 Attack Graph Generation

The generation of attack graph is an important step for the whole penetration testing process. The time complexity of attack graph generation algorithm largely decides whether penetration testing is efficient. Attack graph generation is usually divided into two steps: firstly, build single vulnerability exploit models; secondly, construct attack graph using dependencies among SVEMs. Before we build single exploit models, we propose the concept of network attack path as follows, by which we can reduce the number of SVEMs to improve efficiency.

Definition 5. *Network attack path(NAP) is a sequence of NetworkID, in which any two nonadjacent networks are unaccessible. NAP can be denoted as follows:*

$$NAP ::= NetworkID_1, NetworkID_2, \ldots, NetworkID_n \qquad (5)$$

NAP demonstrates $NetworkID_n$ can be reached from $NetworkID_1$ through some intermediate networks.

Assumption 1. *Network attack path monotonicity.*
Network attack path is monotone, i.e., the same NetworkID in the NAP won't appear twice.

Assumption 1 shows that an attacker won't backtrack to the previous network, which is true of most penetration testing situations. Based on Assumption 1, we propose network attack path generation algorithm.

Algorithm 1. Network Attack Path Generation

Input: $startNet, endNet, Network\_List$
Output: $NetSequence$
1: **function** $GetNetPath(startNet, endNet, Network\_List, NetSequence = \emptyset)$
2:     $NetSequence.Append(startNet)$
3:     **if** $startNet \equiv endNet$ **then return** $NetSequence$ **end if**
4:     $NetworkIDs \leftarrow FindAccessNetworksByID(Network\_List, startNet)$
5:     **for each** $node \in NetworkIDs$ **do**
6:         **if** $node \notin NetSequence$ **then**
7:             $NetSequence \leftarrow GetNetPath(node, endNet, NetSequence)$
8:             **if** $NetSequence \not\equiv \emptyset$ **then return** $NetSequence$ **end if**
9:         **end if**
10:     **end for**
11:     **return** $\emptyset$
12: **end function**

Algorithm 1 describes the network attack path generation process. $startNet$ and $endNet$ refers to $NetworkID$ of initial network and target network respectively. $NetSequence$ is an empty sequence at the beginning, and then networks reachable from $startNet$ is traversed. Line 5 takes every network accessible from $startNet$ as initial network and loops until the initial network is equal to target network. Line 6 confirms that each $NetworkID$ is unique in final $NetSequence$.

Assumption 2. *No interactions between hosts in the same network.*
Once an attacker holds the privilege of a host in a network, it usually means he controls the whole network.

Assumption 2 demonstrates it's not necessary to launch attacks from a host controlled by an attacker to other hosts in the same network. With these assumptions, the attack graph can be constructed easily. Firstly, we give the definition of attack graph model as follows:

Definition 6. *Attack graph model (AGM) is a Petri net system, which can be denoted as*

$$AGM ::= \langle P_{init} \bigcup P_{rea}, T; E, P_{init} \rangle \tag{6}$$

P_{init} is a set of initial places of the whole penetration attack graph; P_{rea} is a set of reachable places from places in P_{init} through transitions; T represents a set of transitions in SVEM; E is flow relation, which satisfies $E \subset ((P_{pre} \bigcup P_{rea}) \times T) \bigcup (T \times P_{rea})$.

Algorithm 2. Attack Graph Generation

Input: $HostInfo\_List, NAP$
Output: AGM
1: $P_{init} \leftarrow \{Root(HostInfo\_List.Attacker)\}$
2: $P_{rea} \leftarrow \emptyset, E \leftarrow \emptyset, T \leftarrow \emptyset, i \leftarrow 0, length \leftarrow len(NAP)$
3: $AGM \leftarrow \langle P_{init} \bigcup P_{rea}, T; E, P_{init} \rangle$
4: **while** $i < length - 1$ **do**
5:     $attackers \leftarrow FindHostsByNetworkID(NAP[i])$
6:     $targets \leftarrow FindHostsByNetworkID(NAP[i+1])$
7:     **for each** $attacker \in attackers$ **do**
8:         **for each** $target \in targets$ **do**
9:             $vuln\_List \leftarrow FindHostByID(target).Vuln\_List$
10:             **for each** $vuln\_Info \in vuln\_List$ **do**
11:                 $P_{init}.Append(VulExist(target + vuln\_Info.VulnID))$
12:                 $SVEM \leftarrow ConstructSVEM(attacker, target, vuln\_Info.VulnID,$
    $vuln\_Info.VulnOrigPriv, vuln\_Info.VulnGainPriv)$
13:                 $AGM.Append(SVEM)$
14:             **end for**
15:         **end for**
16:     **end for**
17: **end while**
18: **return** AGM

Algorithm 2 depicts the process of attack graph generation. Line 1 to line 3 initializes variables: P_{init} is set to a set which only includes the place of *Root* privilege of attacker; P_{rea}, E, T are set to empty; AGM is initialized to $\langle P_{init} \bigcup P_{rea}, T; E, P \rangle$. Line 4 starts a loop to traverse network attack path. Line 5 and line 6 search all hosts in neighbouring networks respectively. Line 7 to line 16 is a three-level iteration and it constructs single vulnerability exploit model between two hosts in the adjacent network of NAP, and appends the $SVEM$ to AGM. Line 18 returns the AGM finally. We can see the maximum time complexity of Algorithm 2 is $\Theta(n^2/m)$ (n, m is the number of hosts and networks respectively) when the hosts is distributed throughout different networks, compared with $\Theta(n^3)$ of MulVAL [12].

3   Verification of Vulnerability Based on Attack Graph

3.1   Attack Path Generation

To verify existence of vulnerabilities in AGM, attack path is necessary for penetration testers to launch attacks. The definition of attack path is as follows.

Definition 7. *Attack Path is a transition firing sequence, which can be denoted as*

$$AP ::= t_0, t_1, \ldots, t_n \qquad (7)$$

t_0 *is the initial transition of the attack path, whose source host is the initial attacker;* t_n *is the final transition of the attack path, whose target host is the target of the whole penetration testing; the latter transition depends on the success of former transition.*

Algorithm 3. Attack Graph Model to Attack Path(AGMtoAP)

Input: AGM, s, e
Output: APs
 1: $APs \leftarrow \emptyset$
 2: $Graph \leftarrow ConvertAGMtoDiGraph(AGM)$
 3: **if** $HasPath(Graph, s, e)$ **then**
 4:    $APs \leftarrow FindAllSimplePaths(Graph, s, e)$
 5: **end if**
 6: **return** APs

As shown in Algorithm 3, attack graph model is converted to attack paths. s and e are places of root privilege of attacker host and target host respectively. Algorithm 3 first initializes APs to a empty set and then converts AGM to a directed graph, which can be solved with graph theory easily. Next, it judges if there is a path from s to e and if exists, function $FindAllSimplePaths$ is called and returns APs. All possible attack paths useful in real attack process will be obtained in this way.

3.2   Attack Process Automation

With above work, automatic attack path planning has finished. To achieve automatic attack process, Metasploit Framework (MSF), a well-known open-source penetration testing framework, is introduced. MSF integrates a lot of vulnerability exploit scripts in exploit module and some other scripts of great use in penetration testing.

The whole attack process is divided into four steps:

1. fetch a transition from provided attack path in order; if empty, return true;
2. obtain exploit-related information such as source host, target host, exploit script path of current transition;
3. add the router to the network of target host via last session into routing tables if there is no direct path from initial attacker to target host;
4. run the exploit script and get new session with target host. If fails, return false; otherwise, go to step 1.

3.3   Vulnerability and Attack Path Evaluation

There may be several successful attack paths after attack process and each attack path can be evaluated by time. The faster attack path means bigger risks and it should be cut off at a higher priority.

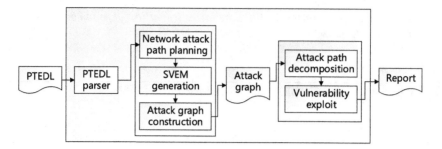

Fig. 2. The structure of APTS

The existence of vulnerabilities are proved by successful exploits and the severity of vulnerabilities are evaluated by the number of times they appear in successful attack paths. We consider the more times a vulnerability appears in successful attack paths, the more severe it is. The vulnerability and attack path evaluation approach provides reference for network managers to fix vulnerable defects at the lowest cost.

3.4 Automatic Penetration Testing System Implementation

Based on vulnerability modeling and verification approach, we implement a prototype system named APTS for automatic penetration testing. Figure 2 illustrates the structure of APTS.

The system takes penetration testing environment information in PTEDL format as input and outputs a report on successful attack paths and existing vulnerabilities as well as vulnerability severity evaluation. APTS includes three parts: PTEDL parser module, attack graph construction module and penetration attack module. PTEDL parser is responsible for extracting valid information from input and transfers it to attack graph construction module. Attack graph construction module contains three submodules which cooperate to generate attack graph. Penetration attack module conducts attacks according to attack graph and generate the penetration testing report.

4 Experiment and Results Analysis

To validate vulnerability modeling and verification approach, we build a typical penetration testing environment. The topology of the experiment is as shown in Fig. 3. The firewall divides the whole network into three networks: Outer, DMZ and Internal. The access control rules of firewall are as follows: network Outer and DMZ can access each other, as well as network DMZ and Internal; the access is forbidden between Outer and Internal. Table 1 shows the detailed configuration and vulnerability information about the experiment environment.

The attack graph constructed by APTS is shown in Fig. 4. The attack graph contains all possible paths from H0_ROOT to H3_ROOT.

Finally, APTS reports five successful attack paths as follows.

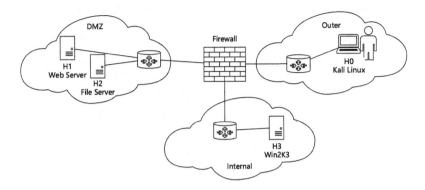

Fig. 3. The topology of the experiment networks

Table 1. Host configuration and vulnerability information

HostID	IPAddress	VulnID	VulnType	VulnOrigPriv	VulnGainPriv
H0	192.168.10.128/24	None	None	None	None
H1	172.16.100.130/24	CVE-2007-5423	Remote	Root	User
		CVE-2015-7857	Remote	Root	User
H2	172.16.100.128/24	CVE-2007-2447	Remote	Root	Root
		CVE-2004-2687	Remote	Root	User
		CVE-2009-1185	Local	User	Root
H3	10.10.10.128/24	CVE-2008-4250	Remote	Root	Root
		CVE-2011-0406	Remote	User	Root
		CVE-2009-1979	Remote	User	Root

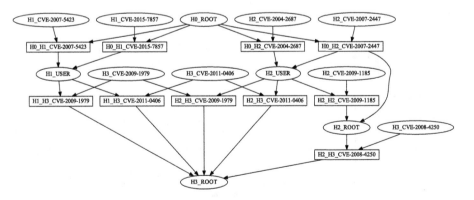

Fig. 4. Attack graph generated by APTS

Table 2. Average attack time

Attack path	Average time (s)
p1	12.3546
p2	9.7245
p3	8.6592
p4	7.7689
p5	6.4421

Table 3. Vulnerability severity

Vulnerability	Severity rank
H2_CVE-2004-2687	3
H1_CVE-2015-7857	2
H3_CVE-2011-0406	2
H3_CVE-2009-1979	2
H2_CVE-2009-1185	1
H3_CVE-2008-4250	1

p1. H0_H2_CVE-2004-2687, H2_H2_CVE-2009-1185, H2_H3_CVE-2008-4250
p2. H0_H2_CVE-2004-2687, H2_H3_CVE-2011-0406
p3. H0_H2_CVE-2004-2687, H2_H3_CVE-2009-1979
p4. H0_H1_CVE-2015-7857, H1_H3_CVE-2011-0406
p5. H0_H1_CVE-2015-7857, H2_H3_CVE-2009-1979

The system launches attacks along each successful attack path 10 times and calculates the average time. Table 2 shows the average time of each attack path. From Table 2, it's clear that $p5$ is the fastest attack path of the five paths, which only needs 6.4421 s to gain the root privilege of H3. $p1$ is the slowest path largely because it takes advantage of three vulnerabilities instead of two and much time is spent on waiting for the response of target host. Evaluation of vulnerability severity is shown in Table 3. The value of severity rank of each vulnerability is the times it appears in $p1 - p5$. We can see from the results that CVE-2004-2687 in $H2$ is the most risky vulnerability and should be fixed first.

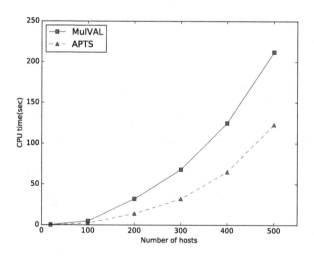

Fig. 5. Attack graph generation CPU time compared to MulVAL

In addition, we compare our attack graph generator with MulVAL by running both tools in the same network environment, in which all hosts are fully connected and each host has a vulnerability. MulVAL is a logic-based network security analyzer proposed by Xinming Ou which can generate partial attack graph by setting a target. The tests are performed on a Intel Core i3 CPU, 2 GB RAM, Debian 4.3 LINUX operating system. As shown in Fig. 5, with the increase of network scale, the CPU time of both attack graph generation methods grows rapidly and it's clear that the CPU time of MulVAL grows faster than our tool.

5   Conclusion

This paper proposes an automatic vulnerability modeling and verification approach for penetration testing. Attack graph is introduced in vulnerability modeling to illustrate dependencies among vulnerabilities. We present network attack path to reduce time complexity of attack graph construction and adapt single vulnerability exploit model based on Petri nets for automatic penetration testing. The verification method of vulnerability is achieved by combining attack graph with practical vulnerability exploit procedure. A prototype system named APTS is built to verify our approach. Experiment shows that our approach can realize automatic vulnerability modeling and verification efficiently for penetration testing and the evaluation on attack path and vulnerability severity can provide reference for network managers to harden the network.

Acknowledgements. This work is supported by Natural Science Foundation of Jiangsu Province (BK20150758), Foundation of Graduate Innovation Center in NUAA (kfjj20151609), Chinese Postdoctoral Science Foundation (No. 2014M561644), the Fundamental Research Funds for the Central Universities (No. NS2016096), Jiangsu Province Postdoctoral Science Foundation (No. 1402034C), and Open Project Foundation of Information Technology Research Base of Civil Aviation Administration of China (No. CAAC-ITRB-201405).

References

1. Guo, P., Wang, J., Li, B., Lee, S.: A variable threshold-value authentication architecture for wireless mesh networks. J. Internet Technol. **15**(6), 929–936 (2014)
2. Phillips, C., Swiler, L.P.: A graph-based system for network-vulnerability analysis. In: Proceedings of the Workshop on New Security Paradigms, pp. 71–79. ACM (1998)
3. Shen, J., Tan, H., Wang, J., Wang, J., Lee, S.: A novel routing protocol providing good transmission reliability in underwater sensor networks. J. Internet Technol. **16**(1), 171–178 (2015)
4. Tinghuai, M., Jinjuan, Z., Meili, T., Yuan, T., Abdullah, A.-D., Mznah, A.-R., Sungyoung, L.: Social network and tag sources based augmenting collaborative recommender system. IEICE Trans. Inf. Syst. **98**(4), 902–910 (2015)
5. McDermott, J.P.: Attack net penetration testing. In: Proceedings of the Workshop on New Security Paradigms, pp. 15–21. ACM (2001)

6. Sheyner, O., Haines, J., Jha, S., Lippmann, R., Wing, J.M.: Automated generation and analysis of attack graphs. In: Proceedings of the IEEE Symposium on Security and Privacy, pp. 273–284. IEEE (2002)
7. Ou, X., Boyer, W.F., McQueen, M.A.: A scalable approach to attack graph generation. In: Proceedings of the 13th ACM Conference on Computer and Communications Security, pp. 336–345. ACM (2006)
8. Bishop, M.: About penetration testing. IEEE Secur. Priv. 5(6), 84–87 (2007)
9. Yun, Y., Xishan, X., Zhichang, Q., Xueyang, W.: Attack graph generation algorithm for large-scale network system. J. Comput. Res. Dev. 10, 011 (2013)
10. Qiu, X., Wang, S., Jia, Q., Xia, C., Lv, L.: Automatic generation algorithm of penetration graph in penetration testing. In: Proceedings of the 2014 Ninth International Conference on P2P, Parallel, Grid, Cloud and Internet Computing, pp. 531–537. IEEE (2014)
11. Jha, S., Sheyner, O., Wing, J.: Two formal analyses of attack graphs. In: Proceedings of the 15th IEEE Workshop on Computer Security Foundations, pp. 49–63. IEEE (2002)
12. Ou, X., Govindavajhala, S., Appel, A.W.: MulVAL: a logic-based network security analyzer. In: Proceedings of the 14th Conference on USENIX Security Symposium, vol. 14, p. 8. USENIX Association (2005)
13. Jajodia, S., Noel, S., O'Berry, B.: Topological analysis of network attack vulnerability. In: Kumar, V., Srivastava, J., Lazarevic, A. (eds.) Managing Cyber Threats, pp. 247–266. Springer, Heidelberg (2005)
14. Kotenko, I., Stepashkin, M.: Attack Graph Based Evaluation of Network Security. In: Leitold, H., Markatos, E.P. (eds.) CMS 2006. LNCS, vol. 4237, pp. 216–227. Springer, Heidelberg (2006). doi:10.1007/11909033_20
15. Chen, F.: A Hierarchical Network Security Risk Evaluation Approach Based on Multi-goal Attack Graph. National university of defense technology, Chang sha (2009)
16. Noel, S., Jajodia, S., O'Berry, B., Jacobs, M.: Efficient minimum-cost network hardening via exploit dependency graphs. In: Proceedings of the 19th Annual Computer Security Applications Conference, pp. 86–95. IEEE (2003)
17. Wang, L., Noel, S., Jajodia, S.: Minimum-cost network hardening using attack graphs. Comput. Commun. 29(18), 3812–3824 (2006)
18. Wang, S., Zhang, Z., Kadobayashi, Y.: Exploring attack graph for cost-benefit security hardening: a probabilistic approach. Comput. Secur. 32, 158–169 (2013)
19. Wu, D., Lian, Y.-F., Chen, K., Liu, Y.-L.: A security threats identification and analysis method based on attack graph. Jisuanji Xuebao (Chin. J. Comput.), 35(9), 1938–1950 (2012)

Bandwidth Forecasting for Power Communication Using Adaptive Extreme Learning Machine

Zheng Zheng[1], Li Di[1], Song Wang[2], Min Xia[3(✉)], Kai Hu[3],
and Ruidong Zhang[3]

[1] State Grid Henan Economics Research Institute, Zheng Zhou 450052, China
[2] State Grid Henan Electric Power Company, Zheng Zhou 450052, China
[3] Jiangsu Collaborative Innovation Center on Atmospheric Environment
and Equipment Technology, Nanjing University of Information
Science and Technology, Nanjing 210044, China
xiamin@nuist.edu.cn

Abstract. Bandwidth demand forecasting is the basis and foundation of the power communication network planning. In view of the traditional neural network learning speed is slow, the number of iterations is large, and the local optimal problem, an adaptive extreme learning machine model based on the theory of extreme learning machine and K nearest neighbor theory is proposed to predict the bandwidth of electric power communication. The adaptive metrics of inputs can solve the problems of amplitude changing and trend determination, and reduce the effect of the overfitting of networks. The proposed algorithms are validated using real data of a province in China. The results show that this method is better than the traditional neural network, auto regressive model, self organization model, and single extreme learning machine model. It can be used in electric power communication bandwidth prediction.

Keywords: Electric power communication · Bandwidth prediction · Extreme learning machine · K nearest neighbor

1 Introduction

Information network is one of the important information infrastructure of power grid enterprises, which covers all units, substations, centralized control stations and power supply business [1]. And it is responsible for the connection with Internet, extranet. With the development of information technology, power communication network has more and more requirements on the processing capacity of the backbone network. In order to ensure the quality of service quality of network, it is necessary to make a reasonable forecast of bandwidth in the electric power communication planning stage, and to ensure the quality of service. The available network bandwidth requirement forecast algorithm is a technical problem which must be solved in the current planning system [2].

Using the model to analyze and study the problem of bandwidth prediction is one of the most important methods. Model selection plays a key role in forecasting

© Springer International Publishing AG 2016
X. Sun et al. (Eds.): ICCCS 2016, Part II, LNCS 10040, pp. 83–91, 2016.
DOI: 10.1007/978-3-319-48674-1_8

accuracy. If there is no reasonable modeling method, the prediction accuracy will be very low, given the wrong direction to the decision makers [3]. Bandwidth time series prediction has been a hot research topic in the field of forecasting [4–7]. For the time series, the domestic and foreign scholars have carried out a lot of research, forming a large number of forecasting methods [8–12], the main are: simple moving average, autoregressive moving average, linear regression, Kalman filtering and nonparametric regression model, etc. The traditional methods, such as regression analysis, exponential smoothing method and autoregressive integrated moving average model (ARIMA), are all based on linear models. All of these methods are assumed to be linear, and it is difficult to grasp the nonlinear phenomena in power communication system. In modern statistical learning theory, neural network is the most widely used in nonlinear time series model, the method has better forecasting performance and forecasting effect [13, 14], and can effectively achieve the short-term forecast of bandwidth data. Artificial neural network is characterized by its good nonlinear quality, flexible and effective self organization learning method and complete distribution of storage structure. Many documents prove that the effect of neural network method is better than other traditional methods in forecasting. Compared with other learning models, neural network has better robustness and fault tolerance, but the neural network has some disadvantages, such as slow learning speed, over fitting, iterative times and easy to fall into local minimum [15].

Extreme learning machine (ELM) is a new training method for neural network [15, 16]. In brief, it is a neural network algorithm model based on single layer feedforward neural network. As a new learning algorithm, ElM can improve the learning speed of the network, and avoid many problems, such as the local minimum, the number of iterations, the performance index and the determination of the learning rate [17]. However, due to the lack of analytical modeling for neural networks [18], it may suffer from under fitting or over fitting [19]. In order to solve this problem, this paper presents a novel neural network model based on the adaptive measurement of input data. The output data is evolved from a hybrid mechanism. The adaptive metric model can adapt to the trend and amplitude of local changes. The input of the network is historical data that most close to the sample to avoid the sharp increase in the prediction error due to the large difference between the training data and the input data. In the use of the proposed hybrid output mechanism, the relative error of the prediction results can be adjusted to make the prediction more accurate. Experimental results show that the model is superior to other traditional models.

2 Methodology

In this part, we introduce the proposed adaptive extreme learning machine (AD-ELM) algorithm for the electric power communication bandwidth prediction. In this work, the data are divided into training and testing sets. Based on the input and output weights obtained by training data, the electric power communication bandwidth can be predicted directly through the established AD-ELM.

2.1   Extreme Learning Machine

As a kind of single hidden-layer feed-forward network, ELM has fast learning speed with a higher generalization performance than traditional gradient-based learning algorithms [11]. Its network structure is shown in Fig. 1.

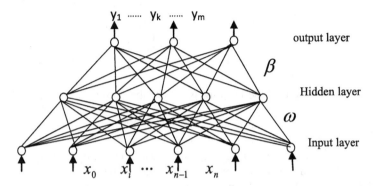

Fig. 1. The structure of the neural network

For N learning patterns (x_i, y_i), $x_i(x_i = [x_{i1}, x_{i2}, \ldots, x_{in}] \in R^n)$ is input pattern, $y_i(y_i = [y_{i1}, y_{i2}, \ldots, y_{im}] \in R^m))$ is the output pattern, where $i = 1, 2, \ldots, N$. If the number of the hidden nodes is $\tilde{N}$, the activation function $g(x)$ can be described as:

$$\sum_{i=1}^{\tilde{N}} \beta_i g_i(w_i x_j + b_i) = o_j, \ j = 1, 2, \ldots, N \tag{1}$$

where $w_i = [w_{i1}, w_{i2}, \ldots, w_{in}]^T$ is the input weight of the ith hidden node, o_j is the output of jth pattern, $g_i(w_i x_j + b_i)$ is the output of the ith hidden node for input x_i, $\beta_i = [\beta_{i1}, \beta_{i2}, \cdots \beta_{im}]^T$ is the connection weight between the ith hidden node and the output layer. In this work, the activation function $g(x)$ is set as Sigmoid function. Assuming that the network is able to approach the N learning sample without errors, that $\sum_{j=1}^{\tilde{N}} \left\| o_j - y_j \right\| = 0$.

$$\sum_{i=1}^{\tilde{N}} \beta_i g_i(w_i x_j + b_i) = y_j, \quad j = 1, 2, \ldots, N \tag{2}$$

Learning through N sample, the above equation can be expressed as:

$$H\beta = Y \tag{3}$$

$$
\begin{aligned}
&H(w_1, w_2, \ldots, w_{\tilde{N}}, b_1, b_2, \ldots, b_{\tilde{N}}, x_1, x_2, \ldots, x_N) \\
&= \begin{bmatrix}
g(w_1 x_1 + b_1) & \cdots & g(w_{\tilde{N}} x_1 + b_{\tilde{N}}) \\
\vdots & \ddots & \vdots \\
g(w_1 x_N + b_1) & \cdots & g(w_{\tilde{N}} x_N + b_{\tilde{N}})
\end{bmatrix}_{N \times \tilde{N}}
\end{aligned}
\tag{4}
$$

$$
\beta = \begin{bmatrix} \beta_1^T \\ \vdots \\ \beta_{\tilde{N}}^T \end{bmatrix}_{\tilde{N} \times m}, \quad
Y = \begin{bmatrix} y_1^T \\ \vdots \\ y_N^T \end{bmatrix}_{N \times m}
$$

The training objective of the network is to find the optimal weights:

$$
\min E(w) = \min \|H\beta - Y\|, \tag{5}
$$

Traditional neural networks usually use error back propagation to adjust weights. Different from the traditional learning mode, the hidden layer node bias value and the input weights of the ELM can be randomly given in the network training. Then the matrix H is a constant matrix, $H\beta = Y$ is the linear equations, Output weights can be obtained by the least square solution:

$$
\beta = H^+ Y \tag{6}
$$

H^+ is the generalized Moore-Penrose inverse of matrix H. Some characteristics of the network are obtained by the way of extreme learning: the minimum training error of the network can be obtained directly; it can obtain the minimum norm of the weight and get the optimal generalization performance; the weighted least squares solution is unique, and the network does not appear the local optimal solution. Because the weight of the extreme learning machine is obtained by Moore-Penrose generalized inverse, we often set $\tilde{N} \leq N$.

2.2 Adaptive Extreme Learning Machine

However, due to the lack of a systematic modeling of neural networks [11]. In order to reduce the impact of this shortcoming, this paper proposes a hybrid method based on K nearest neighbor and ELM for electric power communication bandwidth prediction. In this model, the test data may suffer from uncertainties, and the k nearest neighbor is used to pre process the input data to make the input data more close to the training sample, which makes the network output more reliable.

Firstly, initial test data $Q = [q^1, q^2, \ldots, q^n]$ $(q^j, j = 1, 2, \ldots, N)$. The test data $Q = [q^1, q^2, \ldots, q^n]$ is compared with the training data $X_i = [x_i^1, x_i^2, \ldots, x_i^n]$ using the k nearest neighbor method. In this paper, the Euclidean distance is used to define the difference between the test data and the training data:

$$D_i = \sqrt{(q^1 - x_i^1)^2 + (q^2 - x_i^2)^2 + \ldots + (q^n - x_i^n)^2} \qquad (7)$$

Based on this strategy, the $X_{d1}, X_{d2}, \ldots, X_{dk}$ is chosen as the K nearest neighbor. Based on K nearest neighbor preprocessing, the input vector of ELM network can be defined as:

$$Input_{ELM} = \left[\sum_{i=1}^{k} x_{di}^1/k, \sum_{i=1}^{k} x_{di}^2/k, \ldots, \sum_{i=1}^{k} x_{di}^n/k \right] \qquad (8)$$

For the neural network, even if there are the same learning samples, the network weights of each learning ELM are not the same, and the forecasting results are different. Therefore, this paper is to get the average value of s times, get higher accuracy and more reliable results. The steps of the proposed method are as follows:

Step 1: Train the neural network using training patterns. $x_i (x_i = [x_{i1}, x_{i2}, \ldots, x_{in}] \in R^n)$ is input training pattern, $y_i (y_i = [y_{i1}, y_{i2}, \ldots, y_{im}] \in R^m)$ is the output training pattern. Use ELM method to train the network.

Step 2: Comparison test data and training data based on Eq. (7) using Euclidean space distance.

Step 3: Based on Eq. (8), initialize the input data for neural network, choose the K nearest neighbor $X_{d1}, X_{d2}, \ldots, X_{dk}$ for test data.

Step 4: Preliminary forecast results are obtained by using neural network.

Step 5: Using the same data to repeat steps 1 and 4 for s times, and take the mean value of s times as the final prediction.

In order to compare with other methods, the normalized mean square error (NMSE) and the absolute mean percentage error (MAPE) are used as the standard. For a time series, the normalized mean square error is defined as follows:

$$NMES = \frac{\sum_{i=1}^{M}(y_i - \tilde{y}_i)^2}{\sum^{M}(y_i - \hat{y}_i)^2} = \frac{\sum_{i=1}^{M}(y_i - \tilde{y}_i)^2}{M\sigma^2}, \text{ where } \hat{y}_i = \frac{1}{M}\sum_{i=1}^{M} y_i$$

Where y_i is the real data, $\tilde{y}_i$ is the forecasting data, M is the number of the forecasting data. σ^2 is the variance of the estimates derived from the source data. Absolute average percentage error is considered as one of the standard statistical performance metrics, which is described as:

$$MAPE = \frac{1}{M} \sum_{i=1}^{M} \left| \frac{y_i - \tilde{y}_i}{y_i} \right| \cdot 100\%$$

3 Numerical Simulations Studies

In order to validate the proposed model, it is tested on a chaotic time series Duffing-equation chaotic time-series benchmarks. The Duffing-equation benchmarks [20] are well known for their evaluation of prediction methods. The time series is generated by the following nonlinear equation:

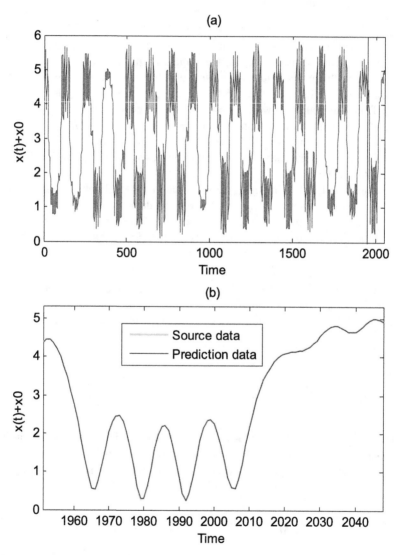

Fig. 2. (a) horizontal component of the time-series (vertical line showing the prediction start); (b) zoom of predicted values with different noise terms using AD-ELM model.

$$\begin{cases} \frac{dy}{dx} = -y + x - x^3 + \beta \cos(\alpha t) \\ \frac{dy}{dx} = y \end{cases}$$

The Duffing-equation chaotic time-series consists of 2050 observations, the first 1950 observations are used for training and the remaining observations for testing. The parameters k and m are set as 2 and 50 respectively. The prediction results are shown in Fig. 2. Figure 2 shows that the proposed model can give the accuracy forecasting results. The MAPE and NMSE are 0.323 and 6.76×10^{-6} respectively.

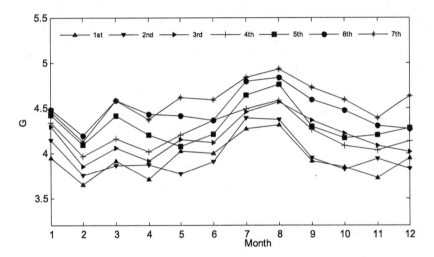

Fig. 3. 7 years real data of electric power communication bandwidth

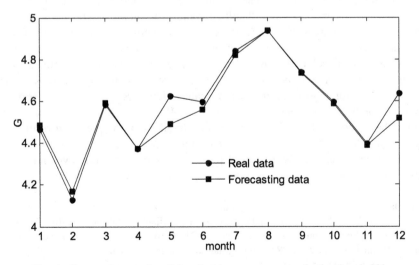

Fig. 4. Forecasting results of the electric power communication bandwidth

In this paper, the actual data of a province in China is tested to verify the usefulness of this method in electric power communication bandwidth prediction. And in this paper, the backbone node bandwidth of this province is forecasted. The Fig. 3 shows the 7 years real data of electric power communication bandwidth. In this paper, we use the previous 6 months real data as the input of the network to predict the next month's bandwidth. Therefore, the number of input nodes should be set to 6. And the number of hidden neurons is 8. The value of k is set as 3 for AD-ELM.

In this work, the proposed model is compared with the auto-regression (AR), artificial neural network (ANN), and extreme learning machine (ELM) model. For all methods $1 \sim 6$ years data is used for learning, and the 7th year data is used for testing. The Fig. 4 shows the forecasting results of electric power communication bandwidth. The simulation results are described in Table 1. The experimental results show that the proposed model outperforms the auto-regression (AR), artificial neural network (ANN), and extreme learning machine (ELM) model. The AD-ELM model is proved to benefit from the merits of the KNN and the ELM through its' novel structure with high robustness particularly for both chaotic and electric power communication bandwidth prediction.

Table 1. Forecasting results for different methods

	NMSE	MAPE
ANN	0.6424	23.23 %
AR	1.2632	31.21 %
ELM	0.6375	13.42 %
AD-ELM	0.0942	8.63 %

4 Conclusions

How to predict the future bandwidth is an important issue in the field of electric power communication. Achieving accurate bandwidth prediction has important support for decision making. The traditional bandwidth prediction model is based on the linear model, and the linear model is difficult to capture the nonlinear phenomena in the electric power communication process. The neural network is a kind of effective nonlinear method, but the traditional neural network method also has a variety of problems. In order to solve these problems, this paper proposes a new adaptive extreme learning model based on the theory of extreme learning machine and K nearest neighbor theory for power communication bandwidth forecasting. The experimental results generated with different metrics (MAPE, NMSE) show that this new method can improve the accuracy of time-series prediction. In addition, the predicted results generated by the AD-ELM are also compared with those by the ANN, ELM, and AR methods and indicate that the proposed model outperforms these conventional techniques, particularly in electric power communication bandwidth prediction.

Acknowledgments. This work is supported in part by, the National Natural Science Foundation of PR China (61105115), Six Talent Peaks Program of Jiangsu Province (2014-XXRJ-007), Natural Science Foundation of Jiangsu Province (BK20161533), Perspective Research Foundation of Production Study and Research Alliance of Jiangsu Province (BY2015007-01), and Laboratory open project of Nuist.

References

1. Jain, M., Dovrolis, C.: End-to-end estimation of the available bandwidth variation range. ACM Sigmetrics Perform. Eval. Rev. **33**(1), 265–276 (2005)
2. Dovrolis, C., Ramanathan, P., Moore, D.: Packet-dispersion techniques and a capacity-estimation methodology. IEEE/ACM Trans. Netw. **12**(6), 963–977 (2004)
3. Liu, X., Ravindran, K., Loguinov, D.: A stochastic foundation of available bandwidth estimation: multi-hop analysis. IEEE/ACM Trans. Netw. **16**(1), 130–143 (2008)
4. Nam, S.Y., Kim, S., Kim, J., et al.: Probing-based estimation of end-to-end available bandwidth. IEEE Commun. Lett. **8**(6), 400–402 (2004)
5. Park, K.J., Lim, H., Choi, C.H.: Stochastic analysis of packet-pair probing for network bandwidth estimation. Comput. Netw. Int. J. Comput. Telecommun. Netw. **50**(12), 1901–1915 (2006)
6. Zhang, M., Luo, C., Li, J.: Estimating available bandwidth using multiple overloading streams. Int. Conf. IEEE **2**, 495–502 (2006)
7. Liu, J., Zhang, D.: Toward accurate and efficient available bandwidth measurement. Telecommun. Syst. **41**(3), 211–227 (2009)
8. Li, M., Chang, C.R.: A two-way available bandwidth estimation scheme for multimedia streaming networks adopting scalable video coding. IEEE Sarnoff Symp. **1**, 1–6 (2009)
9. Guerrero, C.D., Labrador, M.A.: Traceband: "A fast, low overhead and accurate tool for available bandwidth estimation and monitoring". Comput. Netw. **54**(6), 977–990 (2010)
10. Guerrero, C.D., Labrador, M.A.: On the applicability of available bandwidth estimation techniques and tools. Comput. Commun. **33**(1), 11–22 (2010)
11. Dolama, M.V., Rahbar, A.G.: Modified smallest available report first: new dynamic bandwidth allocation schemes in QoS-capable EPONs. Opt. Fiber Technol. **17**(1), 7–16 (2011)
12. Huang, S.C.: Online option price forecasting by using unscented kalman filters and support vector machines. Expert Syst. Appl. **43**(4), 2819–2825 (2008)
13. Funahashi, K.I.: On the approximate realization of continuous mappings by neural networks. Neural Netw. **2**(3), 183–192 (1989)
14. Cybenko, G.: Approximation by superpositions of a sigmoidal function. Math. Control Sig. Syst. **2**(4), 303–314 (1989)
15. Huang, G.B.: Learning capability and storage capacity of two-hidden-layer feedforward networks. IEEE Trans. Neural Netw. **14**(2), 274–281 (2003)
16. Huang, G.B., Chen, L., Siew, C.K.: Universal approximation using incremental constructive feedforward networks with random hidden nodes. IEEE Trans. Neural Netw. **17**(4), 879–892 (2006)
17. Huang, G.B., Zhu, Q.Y., Siew, C.K.: Extreme learning machine: theory and applications. Neurocomputing **70**(1), 489–501 (2006)
18. Zhu, Q.Y., Qin, A.K., Suganthan, P.N., et al.: Evolutionary extreme learning machine. Pattern Recogn. **38**(10), 1759–1763 (2005)
19. Bartlett, P.L.: For valid generalization, the size of the weights is more important than the size. Adv. Neural Inf. Process. Syst. (NIPS) **9**, 134 (1997)
20. Wong, W.K., Xia, M., Chu, W.C.: Adaptive neural network model for time-series forecasting. Eur. J. Oper. Res. **207**(1), 807–816 (2010)

Narthil: Push the Limit of Cross Technology Coexistence for Interfered Preambles

Ping Li, Panlong Yang$^{(\boxtimes)}$, Yubo Yan, Lei Shi, Maotian Zhang, Wanru Xu, and Xunpeng Rao

PLA University of Science and Technology, Nanjing, China
pingli0112@gmail.com, panlongyang@gmail.com, yanyub@gmail.com,
shilei9018@gmail.com, maotianzhang@gmail.com, xwr88023@gmail.com,
raoxunpeng@gmail.com

Abstract. Recent studies show that cross technology interference is critically important for emergence of innovative applications in today's wireless networks. Existing approaches either suffer from the constraint of the need of clean preamble, or requiring technological similarities among cross technology systems.

This paper makes the first attempt for tackling this stalemate. We propose Narthil (Narthil is a sword in The Lord of the Rings and The Silmarillion. Narthil was broken in the overthrow of Sauron at the end of the Second Age and was later reforged.), an innovative coexistence system based on imperfect interference management, handling packet detection and symbol synchronization with interfered preambles. Moreover, it recovers the channel state information without the presents of clean preamble.

In Narthil, simple Butterworth bandstop filter is applied for an imperfect interference filtering. And the residual signals could be used for packet detection, symbol synchronization, and CSI estimation. The insight is, the inherent properties of preamble such as periodicity and modulation scheme, and the continuity in OFDM band could be effectively leveraged for some important operation such as signal detection, synchronization, and CSI estimation.

This inspiring design policy could be further leveraged for other cross technology signals. We implement Natrtil on our USRP/GNU radio platform, and evaluate its performance by using 15 USRP N210 devices. The experimental results demonstrates that Narthil could effectively perform the signal detection and synchronization, as well as CSI estimation without the presents of clean preamble.

Keywords: Cross-tech coexistence · Preamble · Interference · Recovery · Periodicity · Synchronization · CSI

1 Introduction

With the rapid development of wireless sensor network [1,2], cross technology coexistence is becoming vitally important, such as carbon dioxide monitoring

© Springer International Publishing AG 2016
X. Sun et al. (Eds.): ICCCS 2016, Part II, LNCS 10040, pp. 92–104, 2016.
DOI: 10.1007/978-3-319-48674-1_9

program "CitySee" deployed in Wuxi China, and "Smart Earth" project. In that, many densely deployed wireless networks are working in heterogeneous mode with the same ISM band, *e.g.*, WiFi, ZigBee, Bluetooth networks *etc.*. Most of the status quo solutions [7–10] focus on coordinating the heterogeneous signals with advanced interference management technology. For example, WizBee [9] exploits the energy diversity between WiFi and ZigBee, making efforts to decode WiFi and treating ZigBee signal as noise in temporary. ZigBee signal can be decoded after proper interference cancellation of WiFi. ZIMO [8] in the other hand leverages the assumption that not all preambles are interfered when signal collision occurs, and attempts to eliminate the signal with clean preamble. Then ZIMO decodes the remained interference free signal. Then, a customized interference cancellation is incorporated to cancel out the decoded signal to ensure the first signal is interference free.

Although these studies [6] have successfully settled down the heterogeneous interference coexistence problem fairly well, unresolvable limitations still exist [4]. Dependencies on bootstrapping procedure hinders the applicability and tolerability of status quo methods [3,5]. For example, WizBee needs a large energy diversity to guarantee its efficiency, and may not work without this premise. Moreover, ZIMO requires at least one clean preamble from both interfered signals to start the processing, while the clean preamble may not achieved in some scenarios. Actually, all these algorithms above are constrained by the need of clean preamble.

We propose Narthil, a novel method to break through this constraint. Narthil can perform packet detection, symbol synchronization, as well as CSI estimation, without the presents of clean preamble. To achieve these goals, two sample but efficient technologies are used to cope such challenges by leverage the inherent properties of preamble.

The first challenge is how to perform packet detection and symbol synchronization. When preamble is interfered, the periodicity of its training symbols is corrupted, thus makes the signal detection algorithm and synchronization algorithm fail, and cause a severe packet loss consequently. To cope such challenge, Narthil exploits the periodicity of preamble and proposes a filter based algorithm, which can recover the corrupted periodicity of preamble and ensure the performance of packet detection and symbol synchronization as well.

The second challenge caused by interfered preamble is how to obtain an accurate channel state information (CSI). Narthil leverages the diversity of bandwidth of both WiFi and ZigBee, and the frequency continuity of WiFi. Specifically, WiFi has a 10 times larger bandwidth than ZigBee, which means that not all subcarriers of WiFi are interfered by ZigBee, and Narthil can interpolate the CSI across all interfere-free subcarriers to estimate the CSI of interfered subcarriers.

We implement Narthil algorithm on our USRP/GUN radio platform and present a working system. Both WiFi and ZigBee transmissions are carefully scheduled to ensure both preambles are interfered. Experimental results show that, compare with other coexistence algorithms, Narthil can achieve an nearly

100 % accuracy in both packet detection and symbol synchronization. The channel estimation also has a very good performance.

In summary, this paper makes three major contributions:

- We propose Narthil, a method which break through the constraint of clean preamble. Narthil can performs packet detection and synchronization and CSI estimation without the presents of clean preamble. To the best of our knowledge, it is the first method to break through the constraint of clean preamble.
- Narthil provides an inspiring insight, that the inherent robustness in preamble (periodicity and module scheme) and the frequency continuity of WiFi signal could be effectively leveraged for signal detection, synchronization, and channel estimation. This design policy could be further applicable for other cross-tech coexistence scenes, especially when their preambles are interfered.
- We implement Narthil in our USRP platform, and test its performance of packet detection, symbol synchronization, and CSI estimation. The experimental results show that Narthil can achieve a favorable performance.

The rest of this paper is organized as follows. We investigate the property of preamble in Sect. 2, then we describe our algorithm in Sect. 3, and shows the experiment study in Sect. 4. After all, we give the conclusion in Sect. 5.

2   Investigation of Preamble

2.1   A Preamble Primer

Preamble is a sequence of known symbols sent before data transmission. It provides a period of time for several receiver functions such as signal detection, symbol synchronization and channel estimation.

A WiFi preamble sequence contains ten short symbols and two long symbols as depicted in Fig. 1, where t_0 to t_9 denote short training symbols (STS), T_1 and T_2 denote long training symbols (LTS), and GI is a 32-sample cyclic prefix that protects the long training symbols from intersymbol interference (ISI) caused by the short training symbols. The short training symbols are used to signal detection, auto gain control, coarse frequency offset estimation, while the long training symbols are used to fine synchronization, fine frequency offset estimation and channel estimation.

2.2   Periodicity of Training Symbols

Since WiFi and ZigBee is essentially a random access network, and the receiver does not know exactly when a packet starts, so the most important task of receiver is to detect the start of an incoming packet, and the receiver leverages the periodicity of preamble to perform packet detection.

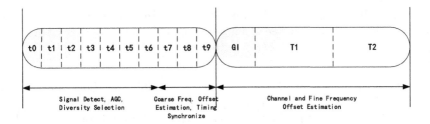

Fig. 1. Preamble format

Periodicity of Short Training Symbol. In wireless communication, receiver applies delay and correlate algorithm to detect the packet. This approach takes advantage of the periodicity of the short training symbols. The short training symbols contain ten identical duplicates and each are 16 symbols long. A short training symbol is modulated by the predefined sequence S,

$$
\begin{aligned}
S_{-26,26} = \sqrt{13/6} \times \{ & 0,0,1+j,0,0,0,-1-j,0,0,0, \\
& 1+j,0,0,0,-1-j,0,0,0,-1-j, \\
& 0,0,0,1+j,0,0,0,0,0,0,0,-1-j, \\
& 0,0,0,-1-j,0,0,0,1+j,0,0,0, \\
& 1+j,0,0,0,1+j,0,0,0,1+j,0,0 \}
\end{aligned}
\tag{1}
$$

and the waveform is generated according to the following equation:

$$
r_{SHORT}(t) = w_{TSHORT}(t) \sum_{k=-N_{ST/2}}^{N_{ST/2}} S_k exp(j2\pi k \Delta_F t)
\tag{2}
$$

where w_{TSHORT} is the time-windowing function, N_{ST} is the number of subcarriers, and Δ_F is the subcarrier frequency spacing, which is 312.5 kHz.

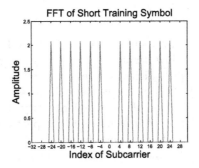

Fig. 2. FFT of STS

As Fig. 2 illustrated, a short training symbol utilizes 12 out of 52 subcarriers, and the frequency spacing between nonzero amplitude subcarriers is $4\Delta_F$, which results in a periodicity of $T_{FFT}/4$, $i.e.$ 16 symbols, where $T_{FFT} = 1/\Delta F$.

Corruption of Periodicity. The periodicity of training symbols can be easily corrupted when preamble is interfered. In this scene, the interference signal distorts some subcarriers of preamble and changes the amplitude of corresponding band. This amplitude changing also distorts the frequency spacing of training symbols, especially makes the Δ_F close to zero, thus makes the period approaches infinite, $i.e.$, corrupts its periodicity. On the other hand, the interference signal can also be regarded as an random additive noise, which makes short training symbols nonidentical, and corrupts the periodicity consequently. Figure 3 shows the corruption of periodicity of short training symbols in both frequency and time domain.

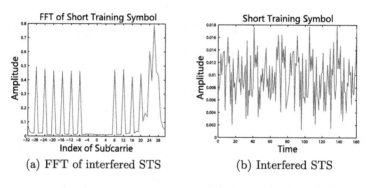

(a) FFT of interfered STS   (b) Interfered STS

Fig. 3. Periodicity of STS is corrupted by the interference.

As the periodicity of short training symbols is corrupted, the packet detection algorithm which based on such periodicity fails and the packet is lost consequently.

Periodicity Recovery. How can we recover the periodicity from corruption? To answer this question, we investigate the periodicity of training symbols. Equation 2 illustrates that the periodicity is determined by the subcarrier frequency spacing Δ_F, and the distortion of Δ_F is the main reason of periodicity corruption. But how this Δ_F distortion affects the periodicity of training symbols? We conduct a series of simulation to investigate the impact of Δ_F changing on the periodicity distortion. We first exam how the period of training symbols changes under different Δ_F. Table 1 shows the period changing among various subcarrier frequency spacings.

This simulation determines that, the bigger the frequency spacing is, the smaller the period is.

Table 1. With the increase of frequency spacing, the period of short training symbol is decrease.

Frequency spacing	Period
Δ_F	64 symbols
$4\Delta_F$	16 symbols
$8\Delta_F$	8 symbols
$16\Delta_F$	4 symbols

In the next simulation, we maintain the frequency spacing on one side, and change it on another side by filtering various number of successive subcarriers in Fig. 2. The results are shown in Table 2.

Table 2. Period is stable with various frequency spacing.

Filtered subcarrier index	Period
4	16 symbols
4,8	16 symbols
4,8,12	16 symbols
4,8,12,16	16 symbols
4,8,12,16,20	16 symbols
4,8,12,16,20,24	16 symbols

Surprisingly, the period of training symbols is stable with various frequency spacings. We analyze this phenomenon may comes from the unchanged band side, which has the constant frequency spacings during the simulation.

To validate this assumption, another two simulations are conducted. In the first simulation, we still maintain the subcarriers on one side, but filtering non-successive subcarriers instead of successive ones to obtain various frequency spacings. In the second simulation, we filtering some subcarriers in both sides but maintain some successive subcarriers in one side in Fig. 2. The results are shown in Table 3.

Table 3. Period is determined by the smallest frequency spacing.

Filtered subcarrier index	Period
8,16,24	16 symbols
8,12,20,24	16 symbols
−8,8,16,24	16 symbols
−12,−8,8,12,20,24	16 symbols

These simulations not only validate our assumption, but also show that the period of training symbols is determined by the smallest frequency spacing.

This is because the frequency spacing changing between nonzero amplitude subcarrier can only changes the period of its related subcarriers, while the period of the whole short training symbol is determined by the lowest common multiple (LCM) of all periods of their related subcarriers. This means that the period of short training symbols is only related to the smallest frequency spacing between nonzero amplitude subcarrier, *i.e.* 16 symbols in WiFi preamble.

Now we can easily recover the corrupted periodicity of training symbols by make the normal frequency spacing be the smallest ones. Briefly, filter those interfered subcarriers out. Figure 4 shows the effectiveness of this method.

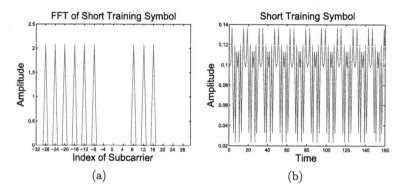

Fig. 4. After filtered interfered subcarriers out, the periodicity of short training symbols is recovered.

3   System Design

3.1   System Overview

Based on our deep investigation of preamble's periodicity, we propose an innovative coexistence scheme, Narthil, which can perform the packet detection, symbol synchronization without the presents of clean preamble, as well as channel estimation.

Four steps are involved in our system. Figure 5 provides the overview of Narthil. Since every WiFi band is overlapped with four ZigBee bands, so when the overlaped signals are received, Narthil needs to identify which band ZigBee signal occurs and applies a customized filter to filter ZigBee signal out. Then the receiver can perform a reliable WiFi packet detection and symbol synchronization sequently. After that, Narthil interpolates the CSI across all interfere-free subcarriers to estimate the CSI of interfered subcarriers, and obtain the whole CSI of WiFi packet consequently.

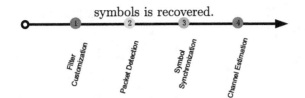

symbols is recovered.

Fig. 5. Algorithm diagram

3.2   Algorithm in Detail

Filter Customization. To filter ZigBee interference out, the receiver must know which channel ZigBee exists since every WiFi channel overlaps with four ZigBee channels. Narthil leverages the fact that, compare with WiFi packet, ZigBee packet has a much larger duration, so receiver can easily identify the band ZigBee occurs at the time slot when WiFi is not transmit, as the green box labeled in Fig. 6.

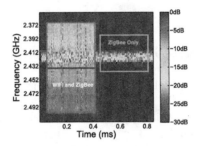

Fig. 6. The packet duration diversity between WiFi and ZigBee shows the opportunity to identify ZigBee's channel

Packet Detection. As we illustrated in Sect. 2, when ZigBee interference is filtered out, the periodicity of training symbols is recovered, and the packet detection algorithm can work as usual. Figure 7 shows that, after filtered the interference out, Narthil can correctly detect the incoming packet.

We note that in Fig. 7(b), besides the actual peak we desired at the beginning of WiFi packet, which labeled by the red circle, there is another peak around the end edge of WiFi frame ($Peak_{ending}$), which labeled by the green circle. This peak is caused by a high energy drop at the packet ending and is easy to identified.

Packet Synchronization. Packet detection only provides a coarse estimation of start edge of an incoming packet. To obtain a symbol level precision,

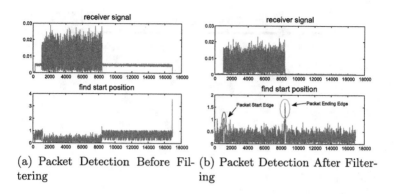

(a) Packet Detection Before Filtering   (b) Packet Detection After Filtering

Fig. 7. Interference filtering helps packet detection

receiver uses a simple cross-correlation based symbol timing algorithm. Specifically, receiver calculating the cross-correlation of the received signal r_n and a known reference t_k, *i.e.*, the long training symbols (LTS).

$$\hat{t}_s = argmax_n |\sum_{k=0}^{L-1} r_{n+k} t_k^*|^2 \tag{3}$$

The value of n that corresponds to maximum absolute value of the cross-correlation is the symbol timing estimate.

However, in our scenario, the original preamble is corrupted along with the interference filtering. Thus the above equation may not work well yet and make a synchronization error. Narthil cope this problem by rebuild a new LTS, which matches the filtered preamble.

Channel Estimation. When signal has been synchronized, channel coefficient can be estimated consequently. As Eq. 4 shows, Receiver estimates channel coefficient by comparing the received long training symbols (LTS) with the known after performs a DFT processing.

$$\hat{H}_k = \frac{1}{2}(R_{1,k} + R_{2,k})X_k^* \tag{4}$$

where H_k is the channel coefficient, X_k is one LTS, $R_{1,k}$ and $R_{2,k}$ are two received LTS respectively.

However, receiver can not calculate the right channel coefficient directly, since the received LTS is either interfered or partly filtered as Fig. 8(a) and (b) show respectively. Fortunately, two properties of WiFi signal can be leveraged to resolve this problem. The first property is that, compare with ZigBee, WiFi signal has a 10 times larger bandwidth, which means not all subcarriers of WiFi are interfered by ZigBee interference. The second property is the frequency continuity of WiFi. Narthil leverages both properties and interpolates the CSI across all interfere-free subcarriers to estimate the CSI of interfered ones. Figure 8(c) demonstrates the efficiency of our channel estimation, in which the red dash line is the estimated CSI of interfered subcarriers.

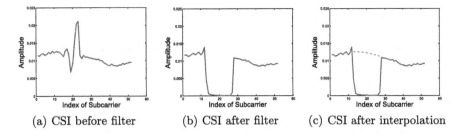

(a) CSI before filter   (b) CSI after filter   (c) CSI after interpolation

Fig. 8. Channel estimation

4   Performance Evaluation

4.1   Experiment Setup

To evaluate the performance of our algorithm, we implement Narthil on our GNURadio/USRP N210 software radio testbed. In our implement, two devices serve as senders to transmit WiFi and ZigBee packets respectively, and another two devices which connect with MIMO cable serve as a dual antenna receiver. The real-time trace is collected and then processed in Matlab.

The detailed parameters are shown in Table 4. We implement the OFDM PHY layer of WiFi and OQPSK PHY layer of ZigBee, the bandwidths of WiFi and ZigBee are 20 MHz and 2 MHz, respectively. The center frequency of WiFi and ZigBee are chosen in 2.342 GHz and 2.430 GHz, respectively. We select the WiFi and ZigBee payload length to be 256 Bytes and 20 Bytes respectively.

Table 4. Experiment parameter

Parameter	WiFi	ZigBee
Channel	2.432 GHz	2.430 GHz
Bandwidth	20 MHz	2 MHz
Payload length	256 Byte	20 Byte
Modulation	16 QAM	OQPSK
Trans-duration	0.358 ms	0.8325 ms

In order to evaluate the performance of our algorithm under the interfered preamble scene, we need to collect preamble collided packets. As a result, it is non-trivial to synchronize two USRPs, since the packet collision happens in signal-level. We exploit the time stamp mechanism provided by GNURadio community to deliberately create the WiFi/ZigBee collision. The period of both WiFi and ZigBee are adjusted to ensure both signal's preamble are collided.

To make a deep sense of our algorithm's performance, we set a series of Signal power ratio. In brief, we fix the ZigBee's signal strength at 8 dBm while adjust WiFi's signal strength in the range of 5 to 25 dBm. In each ratio, we transmit both packets in 5 times, and in each time, 100 WiFi packets and 100 ZigBee packets are transmitted.

4.2   Evaluation

We evaluate Narthil's performance in our GNURadio/USRP software radio testbed. Three main benchmarks are evaluated, which are packet detection, symbol synchronization, and CSI estimation.

Performance of Packet Detection. We first evaluate the performance of packet detection since packet detection is the first and most important task of receiver. As the failure of packet detection will causes packet loss, so it is easy to evaluate the performance of our packet detection algorithm. We count the packet number which receiver reported, and compare it with our original setting, *i.e.* 100 packets per times. All the reported packet number are collected and the statistic result are shown in Fig. 9(a).

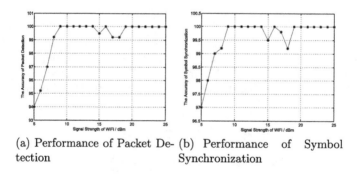

(a) Performance of Packet Detection

(b) Performance of Symbol Synchronization

Fig. 9. Performance of packet detection and symbol synchronization

As this figure shows, the accuracy of our packet detection always above 94 %, and achieves nearly 100 % when WiFi's signal strength is above 9 dBm.

Symbol Synchronization. The second benchmark we evaluated is the performance of symbol synchronization. Since one of the function of preamble is to delineate the signal field, which defines the code rate and modulation, as well as the length of payload, we can use signal field to determine whether our symbol synchronization performs well or poor. Since signal field is followed the preamble sequence, an error symbol synchronization would results in an error position of signal field, and make a error signal filed decoding. We check the decoded signal field information such as code rate and modulation, then compare them with our original setting. If the decoded signal field information is mismatched with our original setting, we determine the symbol synchronization performs poor and vice versa. The statistic results are shown in Fig. 9(b).

As the Fig. 9(b) illustrated, the accuracy of our symbol synchronization always above 97 %, and achieves nearly 100 % when WiFi's signal strength is above 9 dBm.

CSI Recovery. The last benchmark we study is the CSI estimation. CSI is an important information in packet decoding, without an accurate CSI, receiver can hardly decode the packet. To evaluate the performance of CSI estimation algorithm, we deliberately create a mutual interfered packets, where ZigBee's preamble is corrupted while WiFi's is clean. We first estimate the CSI by using the clean WiFi's preamble and serve this CSI value as the ground truth. Then we performs Narthil to estimates CSI independently and compare the resulted CSI with the ground truth in all three aspects, *i.e.* the real part of CSI value, the image part of CSI value, and the absolute CSI value. The performance of our CSI recovery algorithm is shown in Fig. 10.

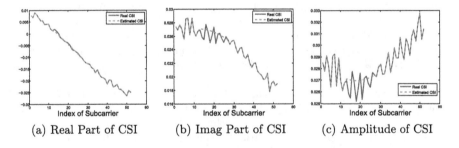

(a) Real Part of CSI   (b) Imag Part of CSI   (c) Amplitude of CSI

Fig. 10. CSI recovery performance

Where the blue solid line represents the real CSI which we estimated by using WiFi's clean preamble, and the red dash line represents the CSI Narthil estimated. As the Figure shows, both lines are very closely, thus demonstrate that our CSI recovery algorithm performs well.

5   Conclusion

In this paper, we propose an effective method, called Narthil, which can break through the constraint of the need of clean preamble. Narthil can detect the incoming packet without the present of clean preamble, and performs symbol synchronization by using the interfered preamble, as well as CSI estimation. All these information can used to resolve the cross-tech coexistence.

We implement Narthil on our USRP/GNU software radio platform and evaluate its performance in detail. The experimental result shows that Narthil can achieve an accuracy over 94 % and over 97 % in packet detection and symbol synchronization respectively, and can estimate the CSI pretty well. To the best of our knowledge, Narthil is the first attempt to break through the constraint of the need of clean preamble, and the first filter based algorithm to resolve such cross-tech coexistence problems. We claim that, this inspiring design policy could be further leveraged for other cross-tech signals.

Acknowledgement. This research is partially supported by NSF China under Grants No. 61272487, 61232018, Jiangsu Distinguished Young Scholar Awards under Grant No. BK 20150030, and Project PAPD and Project CICAEET.

References

1. Shen, J., Tan, H., Wang, J., Wang, J., Lee, S.: A novel routing protocol providing good transmission reliability in underwater sensor networks. J. Internet Technol. **16**(1), 171–178 (2015)

2. Guo, P., Wang, J., Li, B., Lee, S.: A variable threshold-value authentication architecture for wireless mesh networks. J. Internet Technol. **15**(6), 929–936 (2014)

3. Xie, S., Wang, Y.: Construction of tree network with limited delivery latency in homogeneous wirelsss sensor networks. Wirel. Pers. Commun. **78**(1), 231–246 (2014)

4. Fu, Z., Sun, X., Liu, Q., Zhou, L., Shu, J.: Achieving efficient cloud search services: multi-keyword ranked search over encrypted cloud data supporting paralled computing. In: IEICE Transactions on Communications, vol. E98-B, no. 1, pp. 190–200 (2015)

5. Ren, Y., Shen, J., Wang, J., Han, J., Lee, S.: Mutual verifiable provable data auditing in public cloud storage. J. Internet Technol. **16**(2), 317–323 (2015)

6. Zhangjie, F., Ren, K., Shu, J., Sun, X., Huang, F.: Enabling personalized search over encrypted outsourced data with efficiency improvement. In: IEEE Transactions on Parallel and Distributed Systems (2015). doi:10.1109/TPDS.2015.2506573

7. Tan, K., Liu, H., Fang, J.: SAM: enabling practical spatial multiple access in wireless LAN. In: Proceedings of The Annual International Conference on Mobile Computing and Networking (MobiCom), pp. 49–60. ACM (2009)

8. Yubo, Y., Panlong, Y., Xiangyang, L., Yue, T., Lan, Z., Lizhao, Y.: ZIMO: building cross-technology MIMO to harmonize zigbee smog with wifi flash without intervention. In: Proceedings of The Annual International Conference on Mobile Computing and Networking (MobiCom), pp. 465–476. ACM (2013)

9. Yubo, Y., Panlong, Y., Xiang-Yang, L., Yafei, Z., Jianjiang, L., Lizhao, Y., Jiliang, W., Jinsong, H., Yan, X.: WizBee: wise ZigBee coexisetence via interference cancellation with single antenna. IEEE Trans. Mob. Comput. **14**(12), 2590–2603 (2015)

10. Gollakota, S., Adib, F., Katabi, D., Seshan, S.: Clearing the RF smog: making 802.11 robust to cross-technology interference. ACM SIGCOMM Comput. Commun. Rev. **41**(4), 170–181 (2011)

VANET 2.0: Integrating Visible Light with Radio Frequency Communications for Safety Applications

Yao Ji[✉], Peng Yue, and Zongmin Cui

School of Telecommunications Engineering, Xidian University, Xi'an, China
{yji,zmcui}@stu.xidian.edu.cn, pengy@xidian.edu.cn

Abstract. Wireless communications and networking technologies are the foundations for road safety applications in Vehicular Ad hoc Networks (VANETs). Since VANET employing IEEE 802.11p only suffers from broadcast storm problems at a high vehicle density, many clustering schemes have been proposed and yet still can't effectively address the interference problems. Later, some scholars envisioned applying Visible Light Communications (VLC) as the wireless communication technology in VANET. However, VLC requires a strict line-of-sight transmission to maintain stable system performance. In this paper, we propose a hybrid architecture which integrates IEEE 802.11p based VANET with the VLC system. Then, we design a novel Multi-hop Clustering Scheme based on the weighed Virtual Distance Detection (MCSVDD) for the safety message delivery. Through network simulations, we demonstrate far superior performance of the IEEE 802.11p-VLC hybrid VANET architecture compared to that of NHop scheme through key metrics such as maximum delay and normalized goodput.

Keywords: Vehicular Ad Hoc Network (VANET) · Clustering · Visible Light Communication (VLC) · IEEE 802.11p · Safety applications

1 Introduction

In recent years, Vehicular Ad hoc Network (VANET) has attracted enormous attention throughout the whole world [1–3]. Many applications and services have been proposed in VANET, such as road safety improvement [1], autonomous driving [2], and content sharing [3]. Almost all of these applications require a both efficient and reliable data delivery, especially for safety-related information, such as Cooperative Awareness Message (CAM) and Basic Safety Message (BSM).

So far, researches on the safety data delivery in VANET are mainly based on IEEE 802.11p standard [4]. In IEEE 802.11p, a simplified version of carrier sense multiple access with collision avoidance (CSMA/CA) is chosen as the medium access control (MAC) layer protocol. Due to the characteristics of CSMA/CA, the channel access delay will be unbounded when the vehicle density is high, e.g., in multi-lane highway scenarios [5]. As a substitute of the IEEE 802.11p based VANET, cellular technologies such as the third generation mobile communication (3G) and Long Term Evolution (LTE) are proposed to be employed in VANET because of its wide communication range and high transmission rate. However, considering the high mobility of vehicles and the overload

© Springer International Publishing AG 2016
X. Sun et al. (Eds.): ICCCS 2016, Part II, LNCS 10040, pp. 105–116, 2016.
DOI: 10.1007/978-3-319-48674-1_10

of base station caused by broadcast problems at high traffic densities, a pure 3G/LTE technology is not practicable for vehicular communications [6].

Considering the benefits of the heterogeneous networks convergence, recently, a hybrid architecture merging IEEE 802.11p based VANET and 3G/LTE technology has been investigated [7]. Authors of [7] proposed a multi-hop cluster based IEEE 802.11p-LTE hybrid VANET architecture for the safety message dissemination in urban scenarios, which can provide a more reliable and scalable communication without changing existing network structures. However, the problem is that this hybrid architecture needs consume extra resources of 3G/LTE network, and system performance are probably constrained by the budget fluctuations of 3G/LTE system.

Compared to Radio Frequency (RF) based communication systems, several merits are offered by the Light Emitting Diode (LED) based Visible Light Communication (VLC) such as no need of frequency license, lower latency, lower channel interference, cost-efficient and no radiation on human bodies. Moreover, LEDs have been used for diverse light sources in vehicles, including daytime running lamps, headlights, taillights, brake lights, and front/rear frog lamps. Meanwhile, cameras deployed in vehicles for the driving image recording and automated parking are considered as data receiving candidates and shared with the original functions. For instance, the photonic receivers (PR) such as CMOS-based cameras which integrate with the photonic diode (PD) have a high receiving sensitivity of the visible light [8] and have achieved a considerable development in recent five years. Consequently, some scholars envisioned applying VLC based on LED as the wireless communication technology in VANET [8–10]. In [9], authors verified that the positioning error of a visible light related positioning technology, which is called as VLP, is on an order of tens of centimeters in comparison to an average positioning error more than 10 m in GPS.

Although the VLC-based VANET has many advantages, the transmission links of Visible Light (VL) is limited in a line-of-sight coverage and easily affected by the objective weather conditions such as rain, snow and heavy fog, which may lead to a severe attenuation of the transmitted beam, shorten the effective communication range and even provoke the communication outage. Furthermore, direct sunlight and ambient light can make the VLC receiver saturated, which also impacts the accuracy of the received messages.

Accordingly, merging the characteristics of the two communication systems, we propose a novel VANET architecture which integrates the IEEE 802.11p-based VANET with VLC system, and further present a Multi-hop Clustering Scheme based on the weighed Virtual Distance Detection (MCSVDD) for the safety message delivery. Since Vehicle to Vehicle (V2V) creates more complexity and scalability issues compared to the scenario with infrastructures, we only focus on the V2V scenario in this paper. To our knowledge, so far there is no relative literature investigating the IEEE 802.11p-VLC hybrid VANET architecture in detail.

The rest part is organized as follows. Section 2 describes IEEE 802.11p-VLC hybrid VANET architecture. Section 3 proposes a multi-hop clustering scheme named MCSVDD. The network simulation and performance analysis are showed in Sect. 4. Finally, Sect. 5 provides a summary of our contributions.

2   Network Architecture Model

The proposed IEEE 802.11p-VLC hybrid architecture is shown in Fig. 1. In this hybrid network, three kinds of node states form a muti-hop clustering topology. They are denoted as cluster head (CH), cluster member (CM) and non-cluster node (NC), respectively.

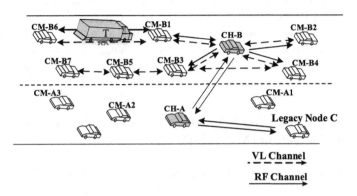

Fig. 1. IEEE 802.11p-VLC hybrid architecture for safety data delivery

CH can communicate with any states of nodes through both IEEE 802.11p and VL channels simultaneously and NC nodes communicate with CH only through IEEE 802.11p, whereas CM can correspond with any states except NC nodes and the transmission link of CM depends on the state that the node is in.

The state which a node will transfer to is determined by the information stored in the vehicle information table (VIT) of each node. VIT of a node owns the information of itself as well as its neighbors within the specified maximum hops.

The selection of a CH node is done by the clustering metrics. Once the CH is determined, vehicles which join the cluster managed by the CH are called CM. A CM node generally has two states. One is referred to as Cluster Member-Single Channel (CM-SC) state in which CM only can send messages via a VL channel, but receive data via both VL and RF channels. The other is named as Cluster Member-Dual Channel (CM-DC) state in which CM can send and receive messages via both VL and RF channel temporarily. CM nodes within the transmission range of the corresponding CH directly communicate with the CH via VL or RF channels according to the exact state. However, CM nodes out of both RF and VL coverage communicate with the corresponding CH via multi-hop relaying.

Those nodes which do not belong to any clusters are called NC. NC nodes include VLC-enabled nodes and Legacy nodes. VLC-enabled NC does not send and receive any safety data until it becomes CH or CM. A legacy node, which doesn't have the ability of VLC, have access to VANET only through RF channel and directly communicate with CH to maintain compatibility. It should be noted that legacy nodes probably suffer from the reliability degradation because legacy nodes are only permitted to communicate with CH. However, it could prompt users to update their vehicle into a VLC-enabled one.

In Fig. 1, there are seven CM nodes in the cluster managed by CH-B, which is denoted as CM-B1~B7 respectively. As is described previously, CH-B can send and receive data through RF and VL channels simultaneously, such as the communication link between CH-B and CM-B1. Communication links between CM-SC nodes experience VL channels only, such as CM-B3 and CM-B4 or CM-B5 and CM-B7. In addition, when the VL channel between two CM-SC nodes is blocked, CM-SC nodes will turn into state CM-DC and transmit packets through the RF channel. For instance, due to the blockage of the truck T, CM-B1 and CM-B6 transfer their states from CM-SC to CM-DC and transmit data through RF channels. As for legacy node C, it only has access to the VANET by communicating with CH-A via a RF channel, although there are some CM nodes around it.

3   Multi-hop Clustering Scheme Based on the Weighed Virtual Distance Detection (MCSVDD)

Clustering schemes in VANET is a good method which is used broadly for handling the broadcast storm problems. In the proposed scheme MCSVDD, the analyzing information in VIT is taken by a CMOS sensor.

Our proposed scheme has some characteristics. Firstly, whether a vehicle (CM) joins and leaves a cluster or not is determined by users themselves according to the information obtained by CMOS sensors periodically. Secondly, CH selection and maintenance is largely simplified because CH only updates one table which saves the information of itself and its cluster members periodically. Thirdly, when vehicles communicate with each other via VL channels, less interference among channels will be caused and broadcast storm problems will be constrained in comparison with a RF-based scheme. Finally, the function of the proposed scheme is independent from the GPS system because measurements of the metrics are achieved by the image sensor. Therefore, the proposed scheme can be suitable for much more diverse scenarios such as the highway tunnel where there is no GPS signal.

Next, we introduce MCSVDD through the following descriptions of some key points. They are vehicle states, vehicle information table (VIT) generation and update, metrics measurement and calculation, vehicle state transitions.

3.1   Vehicle States

INITIAL (IN) is the beginning of a vehicle.

IDENTITY CHOICE (IC) is the state of a vehicle where it decides the next state it will transfer to. In IC state, vehicle can exchange information with others via both VL and RF channels.

CH is the state of a vehicle in which the vehicle is selected as a cluster head.

CM-SC is the state of a vehicle in which the vehicle is affiliated with an existing cluster.

CM-DC is the state in which the vehicle is a member of an existing cluster. CM-DC nodes exist only when VL channels between CM-SC nodes are blocked.

3.2 VIT Generation and Update

In our proposed scheme, VIT is an important data structure and deployed at each node. VIT saves the information of itself and its neighbors within the maximum distance (MAX_DISTANCE) and maximum hops (MAX_HOP), which includes its relative distance and relative velocity between itself and its neighbors, its current vehicle state, the number of hops to the CH if it is a CM node, the ID of the vehicle, the ID of the corresponding CH, its clustering metric value and the sequence number of the currently generated packets.

VIT is updated when any change of its own information occurs or periodic HELLO_NEIGHBOR packets from its neighbors within the maximum distance and hops are received. It should be noted that MAX_DISTANCE changes with the different safety applications. Furthermore, if not updated within the preset time VIT_TIMER, the corresponding items of VIT are deleted.

HELLO_NEIGHBOR packets include the information of its current vehicle state, the ID of itself, the ID of the corresponding CH node, the latest value of metric, the current sequence number and its relative distance and velocity between itself and its neighbors within MAX_DISTANCE. To decrease the network payload, the transmission of HELLO_NEIGHBOR packets includes two ways, directional and non-directional VL transmission. For a directional VL transmission, when CM receives a HELLO_NEIGHBOR packet, forwarding procedure only occurs in the other direction apart from the orientation of the incoming packets. A self-generated packet will be sent to every direction covered by VLC, which means non-directional VL transmission.

3.3 Metrics Measurement and Calculation

In this paper, data is collected by CMOS-based image sensor presented in [8]. Without loss of generality, we adopt the layout of the transmitters and receivers as shown in Fig. 2.

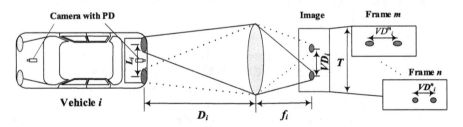

Fig. 2. Schematic for the measurement method of inter-vehicle distance and relative velocity

We use headlamps and taillights as the transmitters. A CMOS-based image sensor is placed on the front and back of each vehicle respectively. The spot of the corresponding vehicle light sources in the image taken by camera includes the information used to calculate the metrics.

The information in the data packets consists of an ID for identifying the left and right sides and the distances between the left and right light sources. Assuming the geometric center of a image is the location of the observer itself (vehicle i) whose reference coordinate is denoted as $(0,0)$, the geometric centers of two spots in the image corresponding to the left and right light sources are denoted as (x_i^L, y_i^L) and (x_i^R, y_i^R) respectively. Therefore, the virtual distance VD_i which describes the distance between left and right light sources in the image is denoted as

$$VD_i = \sqrt{(x_i^L - x_i^R)^2 + (y_i^L - y_i^R)^2} \tag{1}$$

A direct correspondence between the real inter-vehicle distance D_i and VD_i is given by

$$D_i = \frac{f_i \times L_i}{VD_i} = K_i \times \frac{1}{VD_i}, \ K_i = f_i \times L_i \tag{2}$$

where f_i is the focal length of vehicle i and L_i is the real distance between the left and right light sources. Usually, a typical CMOS-based camera can take 30~60 frames per second (fps). Therefore, the average relative velocity $AVRE\_V_i$ between itself and its neighbors can be obtained by selecting a appropriate frame interval. Assuming the frame interval between frame m and frame n is T seconds, then we have

$$AVRE\_V_i = \frac{|D_i^m - D_i^n|}{T} = \frac{K_i}{T} \left| \frac{VD_i^m - VD_i^n}{VD_i^m \cdot VD_i^n} \right| \tag{3}$$

According to (2) and (3), the clustering metric $AVRE\_VDD_i$ for vehicle i is calculated as

$$AVRE\_VDD_i = \begin{cases} \dfrac{1}{N(i)} \displaystyle\sum_{j=1}^{N(i)} \left(\dfrac{w_1 \cdot D_j}{MAX\{D_j\}} + \dfrac{w_2 \cdot AVRE\_V_j}{MAX\{AVRE\_V_j\}} \right), & N(i) \geq 1 \\ 1, & N(i) = 0 \end{cases} \tag{4}$$

where $N(i)$ is the number of the neighbors directly communicating with vehicle i via a VL channel within MAX_DISTANCE. $MAX\{D_j\}$ and $MAX\{AVRE\_V_j\}$ are the maximum value in all of the real distances D_j and the maximum value in all the $AVRE\_V_j$ detected by each directly connecting neighbor j of vehicle i. Affected by the real condition, w_1 and w_2 are the weighed factors which is used to adjust the proportion between VL and RF channels and obey the following relationship $w_1 + w_2 = 1$. The vehicle with the lowest $AVRE\_VDD$ is elected as CH.

3.4   Vehicle State Transitions

Figure 3 illustrates the possible five states of a node. The node begins at state IN. In state IN, vehicles construct their own VIT through exchanging HELLO_NEIGHBOR packets. When IN_TIMER is expired, the vehicle transfers to the state IC. According to its own VIT, a vehicle of IC state decides which state it will transfer to.

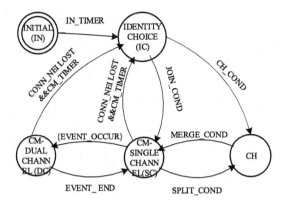

Fig. 3. MCSVDD state transition diagram

An IC node always attempts to join in an existing cluster rather than compete to be a CH. Therefore, an IC node transfers to state CM-SC if JOIN_COND is satisfied. Usually, JOIN_COND is related to the cluster scale, the number of hops, and the relative speed. It should be noted that in our proposed scheme, JOIN_COND can be customized according to the requirements of users. If several neighbors meet the preset JOIN_COND, the neighbor of the best condition is selected. If JOIN_COND is not met, an IC node transfers to CH state when CH_COND is satisfied, which means the node cannot connect to any neighbor CH or CM nodes, and has a minimum *AVRE_VDD* among all the neighbors in state IC.

A CH node makes its transition to state CM-SC when MERGE_COND is met. Generally, MERGE_COND refers to the conditions corresponding to the size of a cluster, driving direction, relative distance and speed. In this scheme, MERGE_COND is related to the scale of a cluster managed by CH i and the relative location between CH i and CM j which is the neighbor of CH i from a different cluster. We define the normalized virtual relative location NRE_VL_{ij} as

$$NRE\_VL_{ij} = \frac{\left| VD_{ij}^m - VD_{ij}^n \right|}{MAX(VD_{ij}^m, VD_{ij}^n)} \tag{5}$$

where VD_{ij}^m and VD_{ij}^n denote the distance between the left and right light sources of node j on the image m and n respectively. $MAX(a, b)$ is the maximum selection function.

MERGE_COND consists of two parts, the cluster scale SCALE_THRESHOLD and a preset value RE_LOCATION. RE_LOCATION is a preset value within the range of 0 to 1. If the scale of the cluster that node j stays in is not greater than SCALE_THRESHOLD and the normalized relative location NRE_VL_{ij} is not greater than the value RE_LOCATION as well, the corresponding CH i will try to join in the cluster in which node j stays through sending MERGE_REQ packet to node j. When node j receives MERGE_REQ packet from CH i, it updates its VIT and replies MERGE_CONF packet to CH i. Once receiving the MERGE_CONF packet, CH i changes its state into CM-SC, and sends a HELLO_NEIGHBOR packet including the updated information to its neighbors. And the CM nodes managed by CH i before quit the previous cluster and transfer their states into IC.

A CM-SC node will make different choices according to different conditions. If SPLIT_COND is satisfied, CM-SC transfers to state CH. Generally, SPLIT_COND is related to the received optical power. SPLIT_COND includes two essential parts, POWER_THRESHOLD and a Boolean quantity ON_PATH_CH. The value of POWER_THRESHOLD depends on the characteristics of PD integrated in CMOS and the demands for the quality of communication. ON_PATH_CH is used to indicate whether the received data is from a CH node or not. When the detected optical power cannot reach POWER_THRESHOLD and ON_PATH_CH is true, CM starts the procedure of a cluster splitting. It directly changes its state into CH and sends the updated information to its neighbors. The neighbors connecting to the original CH via that CM before become the CM of the new cluster.

If the event defined in the set of {EVENT_OCCUR} is triggered, a CM-SC node will change into CM-DC state. Besides the preset events like temporary blockage and direction changing, {EVENT_OCCUR} can be extended or pruned by users themselves to further enhance the communication performance and improve the user experience. If EVENT_END occurs, CM-DC transfers to state CM-SC. Whatever the exact state it is, a CM node will transfer to IC if it has lost connection to its neighbors and CM_TIMER is expired.

In order to avoid the possible conflicts caused by judging different conditions, a Round Robin (RR) scheme is used in our algorithm. That is to say, only one transition can be executed even if several conditions are met simultaneously.

4   Performance Evaluation

In this section, we implement NHOP [11], a typical relative speed based multi-hop clustering scheme in VANET, in comparison with the proposed scheme IEEE 802.11p-VLC hybrid VANET architecture. The simulations are performed in the network simulator OPNET [12]. We model the urban traffic environment at an isolated intersection.

As is shown in Fig. 4, the 4 km long road consists of two six-lane, two-direction and an intersection. The number of the vehicles on the road depends on vehicle densities. When a vehicle leaves from the road, the other one will be injected into the road to maintain the vehicle density. Once a vehicle is generated, the trail and speed of the vehicle will be configured randomly according to different lanes. For vehicles at the intersection on different lanes, we assume vehicles on the left, middle and right lane will turn left, go straight and turn right respectively. Moreover, we assume that VLC is limited in lanes. Several legacy vehicles are produced in random and used to block the VL channel between two vehicles. In the evaluation of the proposed scheme, we mainly focus on the maximum delay and normalized goodput. Tables 1 and 2 list out parameters of the VLC and IEEE 802.11p networks respectively.

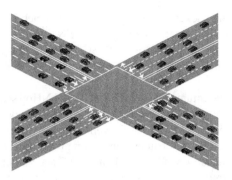

Fig. 4. Simulation scenario

Table 1. Main simulation parameters for VLC

Parameters	Description
Simulation Time	300 s
B	10 Mbps
Length of Vehicle	4 m
Distance between left and right lamp	1.5 m
Velocity on the lanes	10~20 m/s
HELLO_NEIGHBOR packet period	200 ms
HELLO_NEIGHBOR packet size	64 bytes
Safety Data Packet Period	100 ms
Safety Data Packet Size	218 bytes
MAX_ DISTANCE	500 m
EVENT_OCCUR	1. Blockage 2. Turn Left or Right
SCALE_THRESHOLD	2
RE_LOCATION	0.3
POWER_THRESHOLD	−30 dBm
IN_TIMER	1 s
CM_TIMER	5 s

Table 2. Main simulation parameters for IEEE 802.11p

Parameters	Description
Transmission range	300 m
MAC Layer	CSMA/CA
Data rate	6 Mbps
Pathloss Model	Friis Propagation Model

In Table 1, safety data packet size is set to 218 bytes which is the typical value of a generic CAM packet. In our simulations, the set of EVENT_OCCUR includes two events which are used to trigger the transition from CM-SC to CM-DC. According to the typical sensitivity of PIN with BER = 10^{-6} and B = 10 Mbps, we set POWER_THRESHOLD to −30 dBm.

Figure 5 shows the maximum delay of MCSVDD and NHop schemes versus vehicle density for 3 and 5 hops, respectively. From Fig. 5, the maximum delay of NHop schemes rise rapidly in comparison to MCSVDD as the vehicle density increases. This is because MAC access delay caused by the channel contention grows quickly for NHop with the increase of the vehicle density, while there is no MAC access delay for MCSVDD in the VLC mode. Furthermore, it is observed that the maximum delay of MCSVDD is less than 100 ms when the vehicle density is equal to 0.4/m, which means MCSVDD can satisfy the delay requirements for the safety applications whose allowable latency is limited by 100 ms.

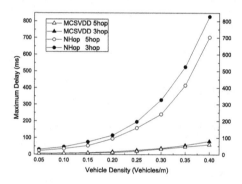

Fig. 5. Maximum delay of MCSVDD and NHop versus vehicle density

Next, we evaluate the performance of the goodput for MCSVDD and NHop schemes. The goodput is defined as the number of useful data bits delivered by the network to a certain destination per unit of time. Due to the lack of the re-transmission, the amount of data considered excludes protocol overhead, control packets, and redundant data packets. In our simulation, the normalized total goodput is expressed as shown below

$$NG_{total} = \frac{T_{receive} - T_{control} - T_{overhead} - T_{redundancy}}{T_{transmit}} \quad (6)$$

where NG_{total} denotes the normalized average goodput, $T_{transmit}$ denotes the total packets transmitted by all the vehicles within the simulation time, $T_{receive}$ denotes the total packets received by all the vehicles within the simulation time, $T_{control}$ denotes the total control packets for the VANET clustering within the simulation time, $T_{overhead}$ denotes the over-heads in data link layer, and $T_{redundancy}$ denotes the redundant packets received by vehicles within the simulation time.

Figure 6 shows NG_{total} of MCSVDD and NHop versus the vehicle density for 3 and 5 hops. NG_{total} of MCSVDD is observed far greater than that of NHOP. For instance,

NG_{total} of MCSVDD can maintain over 0.5 even if the vehicle density is high. However, for NHOP, NG_{total} is degraded by 0.2 below when the vehicle density is greater than 0.35. There are some reasons which lead to this result. First, according to the clustering mechanism of MCSVDD, most communications among vehicles occur upon the VL channel, leading to the lower channel contention compared to the IEEE 802.11p-based clustering scheme. Second, the clustering and protocol overhead of MCSVDD is far smaller than that of NHop, leading to the improvement of NG_{total}. Finally, due to the high directivity of VL, the number of the redundant packets decreases greatly in comparison to non-directional RF-based communication, which further improves the performance of NG_{total}.

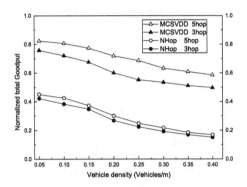

Fig. 6. Normalized goodput of MCSVDD and NHop versus vehicle density

5   Conclusion

In this paper, we present a novel IEEE 802.11p-VLC hybrid VANET architecture which integrates the VLC with IEEE 802.11p based VANET for the safety message dissemination. With this hybrid architecture, we profound a novel multi-hop clustering scheme called MCSVDD. Unlike many previous RF-based clustering schemes for VANETs in which GPS is necessary, MCSVDD collects data, used for metric measurements, by CMOS-based image sensors.

Based on the proposed scheme, we evaluate the performance and make an analysis of the IEEE 802.11p-VLC hybrid architecture. The simulation results show that the performance of the maximum latency and normalized goodput is far superior to that of NHop which is a typical relative speed based multi-hop clustering scheme for VANETs especially under the condition of a high vehicle density.

Acknowledgments. This work was supported by the National Nature Science Foundation of China grant No. 60902038, and the 111 project under Grant No. B08038. Moreover, the work was also supported by PAPD and CICAEET.

References

1. Lim, J.H., Kim, W., Naito, K., Yun, J.H., Cabric, D., Gerla, M.: Interplay between TVWS and DSRC: optimal strategy for safety message dissemination in VANET. IEEE J. Sel. Areas Commun. **32**(11), 2117–2133 (2014)
2. Gerla, M., Lee, E.K., Pau, G., Lee, U.: Internet of vehicles: from intelligent grid to autonomous cars and vehicular clouds. In: 2014 IEEE World Forum on Internet of Things (WF-IoT), Seoul, pp. 241–246 (2014)
3. Romoozi, M., Fathy, M., Babaei, H.: A content sharing and discovery framework based on semantic and geographic partitioning for vehicular networks. Wireless Pers. Commun. **85**(3), 1583–1616 (2015)
4. Han, C., Dianati, M., Tafazolli, R., Kernchen, R., Shen, X.: Analytical study of the IEEE 802.11p MAC sublayer in vehicular networks. IEEE Trans. Intell. Transp. Syst. **13**(2), 873–886 (2012)
5. Shi, L., Sung, K.W.: Spectrum requirement for vehicle-to-vehicle communication for traffic safety. In: 2014 IEEE 79th Vehicular Technology Conference (VTC Spring), Seoul, pp. 1–5 (2014)
6. Araniti, G., Campolo, C., Condoluci, M., Iera, A., Molinaro, A.: LTE for vehicular networking: a survey. IEEE Commun. Mag. **51**(5), 148–157 (2013)
7. Ucar, S., Ergen, S.C., Ozkasap, O.: Multihop-cluster-based IEEE 802.11p and LTE hybrid architecture for VANET safety message dissemination. IEEE Trans. Veh. Technol. **65**(4), 2621–2636 (2016)
8. Takai, I., Ito, S., Yasutomi, K., Kagawa, K., Andoh, M., Kawahito, S.: LED and CMOS image sensor based optical wireless communication system for automotive applications. IEEE Photonics J. **5**(5), 6801418 (2013)
9. Yu, S.H., Shih, O., Tsai, H.M., Wisitpongphan, N., Roberts, R.D.: Smart automotive lighting for vehicle safety. IEEE Commun. Mag. **51**(12), 50–59 (2013)
10. Takai, I., Harada, T., Andoh, M., Yasutomi, K., Kagawa, K., Kawahito, S.: Optical vehicle-to-vehicle communication system using LED transmitter and camera receiver. IEEE Photonics J. **6**(5), 1–14 (2014)
11. Zhang, Z., Boukerche, A., Pazzi, R.: A novel multi-hop clustering scheme for vehicular ad-hoc networks. In: Proceedings of the 9th ACM International Symposium on Mobility Management and Wireless Access, pp. 19–26. ACM (2011)
12. Optimized Network Technology. http://www.opnet.com.tw/

Temperature Error Correction Based on BP Neural Network in Meteorological Wireless Sensor Network

Baowei Wang[1,2,3(✉)], Xiaodu Gu[1,3], Li Ma[1,3,4], and Shuangshuang Yan[1,3]

[1] School of Computer and Software, Nanjing University of Information
Science and Technology, Nanjing 210044, China
wbw.first@163.com,1398499567@qq.com
[2] Jiangsu Collaborative Innovation Center on Atmospheric Environment
and Equipment Technology, Nanjing 210044, China
[3] Jiangsu Engineering Center of Network Monitoring,
Nanjing University of Information Science and Technology, Nanjing 210044, China
hotyss@hotmail.com
[4] Key Laboratory of Meteorological Disaster of Ministry of Education,
Nanjing University of Information Science and Technology, Nanjing 210044, China
mali1775088@163.com

Abstract. Using meteorological wireless sensor network to monitor the air temperature (AT) can greatly reduce the costs of monitoring. And it has the characteristics of easy deployment and high mobility. But low cost sensor is easily affected by external environment, often lead to inaccurate measurements. Previous research has shown that there is a close relationship between AT and solar radiation (SR). Therefore, We designed a back propagation (BP) neural network model using SR as the input parameter to establish the relationship between SR and AT error (ATE) with all the data in May. Then we used the trained BP model to correct the errors in other months. We evaluated the performance on the data sets in previous research and then compare the maximum absolute error, mean absolute Error and standard deviation respectively. The experimental results show that our method achieves competitive performance. It proves that BP neural network is very suitable for solving this problem due to its powerful functions of non-linear fitting.

Keywords: Wireless sensor network · Data correction · Artificial neural network · Solar radiation

1 Introduction

Meteorological parameter monitoring [27] is not only the base of weather forecast, climate prediction, scientific research, and the foundation of other kinds of meteorological services, but also the impetus of the development of Meteorological Science [16]. In the past many years, China affected by meteorological disasters seriously. In order to effectively reduce the meteorological disasters

© Springer International Publishing AG 2016
X. Sun et al. (Eds.): ICCCS 2016, Part II, LNCS 10040, pp. 117–132, 2016.
DOI: 10.1007/978-3-319-48674-1_11

caused economic losses, we urgently need a comprehensive, three-dimensional, continuous observation to the meteorological data to improve the monitoring accuracy.

At present, meteorological data monitoring in China mainly depends on the nationwide automatic weather station(AWS) [4,18]. Wide application of the automatic weather station has greatly improved the development of meteorological services. But there are still many deficiencies in the current observation mode: the site distribution of low density, location poor mobility, high cost and so on. Secondly, the deployment of automatic weather station is too single and the meteorological elements sensor deployment is too concentrated, it is difficult to ensure the best observation position. Finally, the current automatic weather station has the characteristic of poor mobility, high cost and long period. It is difficult to meet emergencies or natural disasters emergency encryption meteorological monitoring needs.

The application of wireless sensor network (WSN) [21,24,29] in meteorological observation and the formation of meteorological sensor network has many significant advantages. Firstly, the wireless communication technology makes the meteorological data no longer rely solely on the cable transmission, making deployment and data collection of meteorological sensors become more convenient, so as to enhance the emergency handling ability. Secondly, using a large number of sensor nodes and collect meteorological data, and results are obtained through the fusion processing [15] are more accurate than obtained by single sensor observation. It can also avoid the problem of deployed in a single location and easily affected by accidental factors. However, the professional meteorological sensor node is expensive and can not meet the large deployment requirements. Thus, many researchers are looking into the low price of the on-board sensors or non professional meteorological sensors, and use data fusion [12,20], data correction method to compensate the defect of low accuracy, in order to improve the measurement accuracy. This paper use the on-board temperature sensor for meteorological data collection, then the use of artificial intelligence algorithm [5,22,23] to correct the sampling data to improve the accuracy of meteorological sensor network data.

In this paper, we use the advantages of WSNs to collect the data of AT and other parameters. The sensor nodes were deployed in the university campus and automatic weather station nearby. In addition, our sensing node can be connected with specialized meteorological sensors. However, the cost still large if we apply specialized temperature sensor on every node. Thus, we use on-board temperature sensor. The sensor embedded in our nodes is SHT15 [1,2] which can collect humidity and temperature data and whose cost ranges from only 3 to 10 dollars. Comparing to the specialized meteorological sensor HMP45D [7,13], SHT15 is very cheap.

However, the accuracy of SHT15 is easily affected by external environment, often lead to inaccurate measurements. Many researchers are trying to improve the accuracy by using data fusion, data correction method to compensate the defect of low accuracy. So, this is also the work we want to do. Previous studies show that AT [14,28] is affected by SR [3,17] best. And our low cost sensor is affected by SR most seriously. So, it is reasonable for us to take SR into account in this work to correct the AT error (ATE).

Since there is a close relationship between ATE and SR, The most important thing is to find a method or formula to establish the relationship between them. But we can not find a precise formula to calculate the ATE of every SR. An existing work in [16] has given a approach using BP neural network to reduce the errors in sensing data. But they did not take the SR into account. This method needs to establish many BP models for each weather condition. And even in the same weather conditions, it also has to establish all kinds of BP models for different months. This method not only needs a lot of work, but also the effect of the correction is not very good. An other existing work on the improvement of the accuracy of AT collected by STH15 has given in [27]. It is a method which based on Statistics. They count the ATE corresponding to every possible SR which will be given a brief introduction in the related work. This is a method based on statistics analysis. But in practical application, it often lack the ability of generalization [26]. We draw the corresponding relationship between SR and ATE according to their statistical results as Fig. 1 shows.

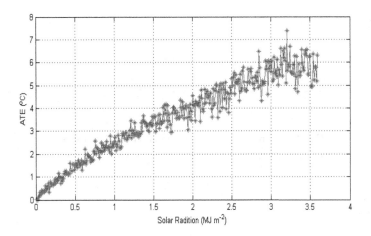

Fig. 1. ATE values corresponding to SR.

As is shown in Fig. 1, it illustrates the relationship between SR and ATE according to the results of [27], each SR corresponds to a unique ATE. Here, the ATE was collected by calculating the average ATE corresponding to every possible value of SR in May. Obviously we can see that, with the rise of SR intensity, ATE also showed an upward trend. But the problem is that, the fluctuation of ATE is too big. Although the difference between the values of the two SR is only 0.1, the statistics of the ATE will be a lot of difference. So, while in the process of correction, it may be cause a relatively large error. And Fig. 2 shows the performance in [27]. We can find that even if the original data curve of NodeAT is relatively smooth, the volatility of the results after the correction is still great. If we can find a function and a smooth curve to denote the trend of the change of ATE corresponding to SR, it will get a better result.

The BP neural network [10, 32] is one of the most widely used neural network models. It can learn and store a large amount of input-output models mapping relationship. Neural networks can be used to do classification [8], clustering [31], prediction [30], etc. In this paper, we use the same data sets in [27] and use BP neural network to build the relationship between ATE and SR due to its powerful ability of non-linear fitting [19]. Finally, we correct the ATE successfully and the experimental results show that our method can find a better relationship between ATE and SR than the method of statistics.

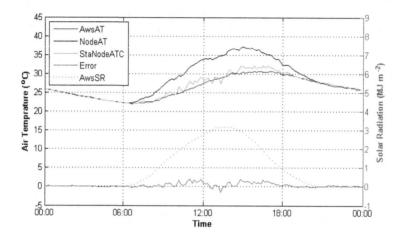

Fig. 2. Correction results using statistical analysis.

2   Proposed Approach

In this paper, we propose BATC, a BP neural network based Air Temperature Correction. The framework of is depicted in Fig. 3. There are four key steps in our framework: (1) Use interpolation method to add sample data. (2) The process of time translation is used to adjust the time coordinate to eliminate the sensing delay between specialized sensors and node sensors. (3) Set up BP neural network model and train it. (4) Use the trained model to calculate the ATE that should be corrected corresponding to SR and then correct the NodeAT.

2.1   Interpolation

First of all, we need to do interpolation with the original data because the sampling frequencies of NodeAT, AwsAT and AwsSR is different. The sampling

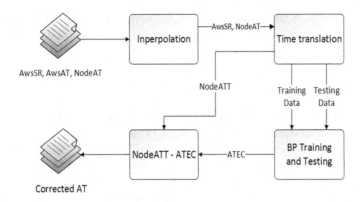

Fig. 3. The framework of data processing and correction.

frequencies of AwsAT, NodeAT and AwsSR is once per minute, once every three minutes and once per hour respectively. As we mentioned in the related work, we select cubic spline interpolation in this paper. We use the interpolation of NodeAT as an example.

Now, a set of raw data of NodeAT has been given as $(nodett_i, nodeAT_i)$, i = 0, 1, 2, ..., n, $nodett_0 < nodett_1 < nodett_2... < nodett_n$, interpolation involves the estimation of values of $nodeAT = f(nodett)$ at points $nodett$ in the interval $(nodett_0, nodett_n)$. Cubic spline interpolation can create a piecewise continuous curve passing through each value in the former data set. On each subinterval $(nodett_i, nodett_{i+1})$, we use spline function $S(x)$ to deal with the data to get an intermediate value that we want, where $nodett_i < x < nodett_{i+1}$. People interesting in the detailed information about the cubic spline interpolation algorithm are suggested to refer to paper [11]. In this paper, all the interpolation frequency of NodeAT, AwsAT and AwsSR are once every three minutes according to the sampling frequencies of AwsAT, NodeAT and AwsSR.

2.2 Time Translation

In our WSNs, we need to package for the low-cost sensor SHT15. In order to minimize the cost of our sensing node, the packaging materials we used is also cheap and unprofessional. The temperature of the packing shell can not be kept the same as the actual air temperature at the same time. We know that the temperature of an object which exposed in the air is the same as the temperature of air. When air temperature changes, the temperature of the object will change too with the change of temperature, but due to different specific heat capacity [25] of different materials, the change rate of the temperature will be different. And the thermal conductivity of our unprofessional packaging materials is not very good, it will cause a sensing delay between NodeAT and the actual AT. In addition, the earth and the packing shell will distribute long-wave radiation [6] to the air, these long-wave radiation will affect the sensor too, and these radiation will continue for some time. However, the sensors in AWS do not suffer from long-wave radiation. So, it is necessary to transform the time coordinate of NodeAT and AwsSR.

2.3   BP Neural Network Modeling

BP neural network is usually optimized through a learning method based on the type of mathematics and statistics. It is a kind of multilayer forward neural network based on error back propagation algorithm. It has the ability to learn and the training methods is supervised. It consists of an input layer, one or more hidden layers and one output layer. When the forward propagation, the direction of propagation is the input layer, the hidden layer, the output layer, the state of each layer of neurons only affects the neurons next layer of next layer. If the output layer can not get the desired output, then the reverse propagation process of the error signal is turned. Through the alternation of the two processes, in the right vector space execution error function gradient descent strategy, dynamic iterative search weight vector, the network error function achieves the minimum value, so as to complete the process of information extraction and the memory.

Hecht-Nielsen demonstrated a feed forward neural network which has three layer with one hidden layer can approximate any multivariate polynomial function [9]. Therefore, we use the three layer BP neural network to establish the model. The topological structure of BP neural network used in this paper is shown in Fig. 4.

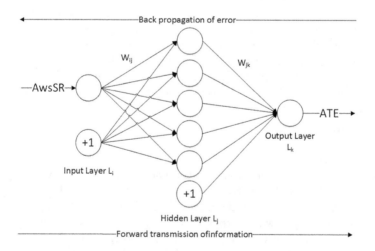

Fig. 4. The framework of data processing and correction.

Where we use $AwsSR$ ($AwsSR = [sr_0, sr_1, \cdots, sr_n]^T$) as the input value of BP neural network and ATE ($ATE = [ate_0, ate_1, \cdots, ate_n]^T$) as the predicted value of BP neural network. And w_{ij} and w_{jk} are the weights of BP neural network. The circle marked with '+1' is called a bias node. From Fig. 4 we can see that BP neural network can be regarded as a non-linear function. The input and output of BP neural network can seen as the independent variables and dependent variables of the function respectively. When the number of input nodes is n, the number of output nodes is m, the BP neural network is expressed the function mapping relationship from the n independent variables to the m dependent variables. The training steps of BP neural network include the following steps:

Step 1: Network initialization. Determines the network input layer node number n, hidden layer node number l, output layer node number m according to the input and output sequence $(AwsSR, ATE)$. Then randomly initialize the connection weights w_{ij} and w_{jk} between input layer, hidden layer and output layer. Then initialize the threshold b in hidden layer and the threshold a in output layer.

Step 2: Calculate the output H of the hidden layer nodes.

$$H_i = f\left(\sum_{i=1}^{n} w_{ij}x_i - a_j\right) \quad j = 1, 2, \cdots, l \tag{1}$$

where l is the node numbers in hidden layer. f is a kind of activation function and the function has many forms of expression. In order to map the data of AwsSR to a range of 0 to 1, we use sigmoid function as the activation function in this paper.

$$f(x) = \frac{1}{1 + e^{-x}} \tag{2}$$

Step 3: Calculate the output O of the output layer nodes according to H, w_{jk} and threshold b.

$$O_k = \sum_{j=1}^{l} H_j w_{jk} - b_k \quad k = 1, 2, \cdots, m \tag{3}$$

Step 4: Calculate the error e of the network according to predicted output O expected output ATE.

$$e = ATE_i - O_i \quad i = 1, 2, \cdots, m \tag{4}$$

Step 5: Update the weights w_{ij} and w_{jk} according to e.

$$w_{ij} = w_{ij} + \eta H_j (1 - H_j) x(i) \sum_{k=1}^{m} w_{jk} e_k \quad j = 1, 2, \cdots, n; k = 1, 2, \cdots, m \tag{5}$$

$$w_{jk} = w_{jk} + \eta H_j e_k \quad j = 1, 2, \cdots, l; k = 1, 2, \cdots, m \tag{6}$$

where η represent the learning rate of BP neural network.

Step 6: Update the threshold b and a according to e.

$$a_j = a_j + \eta H_j \left(1 - H_j\right) \sum_{k=1}^{m} w_{jk} e_k \quad j = 1, 2, \cdots, l \tag{7}$$

$$b_k = b_k + e_k \quad k = 1, 2, \cdots, m \tag{8}$$

Step 7: Determine whether the algorithm achieve the maximum number of iterations or meet the accuracy requirements. If not, turn back to step 2.

This is the whole training process of the BP neural network. After the training of the BP neural network, is means that we have established the relationship between AwsSR and ATE. While in the process of testing, we use AwsSR values corresponding to the NodeAT values as the input of the BP neural network to predict the errors that needed to be corrected. Then use the nodeAT values after the translation process to subtract the errors that needs to be corrected to obtain the corrected NodeAT.

3   Results and Discussion

3.1   Data Collection

The standard data of air temperature and solar radiation used in this research are collected from the AWS at Nanjing University of Information Science and Technology (NUIST). All the measured data also follow the World Meteorological Organization (WMO) requirements. Figure 5a shows a picture of pyranometer in AWS used to collected AwsSR. Figure 5b illustrates the temperature sensor in AWS used to collect AwsAT. Professional temperature sensor is placed in the thermometer screen to prevent the influence of direct radiation of sun and ground radiation, the thermometer screen is horizontally fixed on a special bracket and the height is about 125 cm.

(a)   (b)

Fig. 5. Pyranometer and temperature sensor in AWS at UNIST. (a) Temperature sensor (HMP45D) in thermometer screen; (b) The pyranometer in AWS.

Figure 6 shows the our own designed low-cost node that we used in meteorological WSNs. There are four interfaces in the bottom of the node. They are

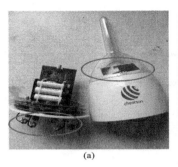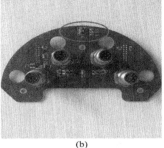

(a)   (b)

Fig. 6. Sensing node used in meteorological WSNs. (a) Interfaces on the bottom and solar cell panel in the shell. (b) On-board sensor SHT15 integrated on a circuit board.

used to connect with other meteorological sensors. So it is convenient for us to collect other meteorological factors.

The low-cost sensing node used in the experiment is placed in the vicinity of AWS as Fig. 7 shows. So it is close to the pyranometer which is used to monitor the SR. So we can treat solar radiation collected by AWS as the same as that from which the node suffered.

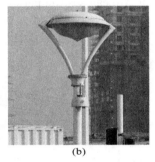

(a)   (b)

Fig. 7. Placement of sensor nodes. (a) A sensing node with several external meteorological sensors. (b) A sensing node without external sensor connections.

We focus on the same data set in [27] to evaluate the method for error correction in this paper. The data set consists of 8-month meteorological data from 1 May 2014 to 31 December 2014 including NodeAT, AwsAT, battery voltage of node and air humidity at Nanjing University of Information Science and Technology using WSNs and AWS with different kinds of sensors.

3.2 Performance of Time Translation

As is illustrated in Fig. 5, it shows the data of NodeAT, AwsSR and AwsAT before the process of time translation on 3 May 2014. These are the data we randomly selected used to illustrate the process of time translation.

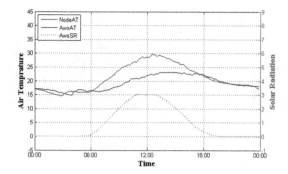

Fig. 8. NodeAT, AwsSR and AwsAT data before the process of time translation on 3 May 2014.

From Fig. 8 we can see that the value of AwsSR is zero in the evening. But theoretically, when the SR is zero, the NodeAT should be essentially consistent with the AwsAT. However, there is still a certain error between NodeAT and AwsAT even in the night. The reason for this phenomenon has been explained in some detail in Sect. 3. In order to eliminate the delay between the professional and the unprofessional sensors, we finally translate NodeAT and AwsSR to the future by 60 min. We can see the performance in Fig. 9.

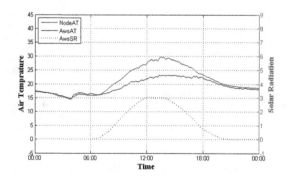

Fig. 9. NodeAT, AwsSR and AwsAT data after the process of time translation on 3 May 2014.

According to experimental result shows that when the translation time is 60 min, the performance gets to the best.

3.3   Performance Contrast of BP Neural Network and Statistical Analysis

In this experiment, we report the performance of the BP neural network model in Fig. 4 as this model achieve the best performance. This architecture is denoted as BP_{151}^s since the input parameter is only AwsSR (the superscript s) and the node numbers in each layer are 1, 5, 1 (the subscript 151). Here, the bias nodes not included. The number of nodes in the hidden layer is generally determined by the following formula:

$$q = \sqrt{n + m} + a \qquad (9)$$

where n is the input node number, m is the output node number, a is the constant between 1 to 10. According to the experimental results, we determine the optimal number of hidden layer nodes is 5 (bias node not included). We put the prediction results of BP_{151}^s and the results obtained by the statistical method in Fig. 9.

From Fig. 9 we can see that the blue curve is the prediction value of BP_{151}^s, it is a smooth curve. So there will not be much volatility when using this curve to correct the ATE values (Fig. 10).

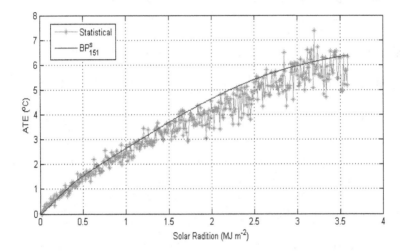

Fig. 10. ATE values corresponding to every possible value of SR.

3.4 Performance Evaluations

In order to show the superiority of our method numerically, we got the results in [27] and focus on the maximum absolute error, the mean absolute error and the standard deviation of the data to illustrate it. In addition, we use the formula (10) to calculate the correction efficiency in Tables 1, 2 and 3.

$$Efficiency = \frac{rawData - errorCorrected}{rawData} * 100\% \qquad (10)$$

In Table 1, we took two days of data per month from June to December to calculate their maximum absolute errors respectively. Raw data represents the

Table 1. Maximal absolute error in different correcting phases.

| Date | Maximal absolute error | | | |
	Raw data	Time translation	Error corrected	Efficiency
2014.06.04	7.55	5.96	1.87	75 %
2014.06.09	8.06	6.75	1.00	87 %
2014.07.04	2.76	2.26	0.56	80 %
2014.07.07	8.53	7.17	2.83	67 %
2014.08.08	2.03	1.35	0.57	72 %
2014.08.10	7.06	6.26	1.65	77 %
2014.09.03	6.10	4.80	1.65	73 %
2014.09.28	8.44	7.26	2.14	75 %
2014.10.02	5.84	4.56	1.10	81 %
2014.10.19	8.56	6.76	2.35	73 %
2014.11.11	7.10	4.66	2.46	65 %
2014.11.22	7.97	6.87	2.98	63 %
2014.12.07	6.21	5.23	1.16	81 %
2014.12.21	5.79	5.09	1.83	68 %
Average	**6.57**	**5.36**	**1.73**	**74 %**
Results in [27]	6.61	5.44	2.24	66 %

Table 2. Mean absolute error in different correcting phases.

| Date | Mean absolute error | | | |
	Raw data	Time translation	Error corrected	Efficiency
2014.06.04	2.78	2.22	0.48	83 %
2014.06.09	2.82	2.35	0.26	91 %
2014.07.04	0.73	0.65	0.16	78 %
2014.07.07	2.89	2.55	0.68	76 %
2014.08.08	0.68	0.63	0.28	59 %
2014.08.10	2.08	1.83	0.37	82 %
2014.09.03	1.62	1.54	0.33	80 %
2014.09.28	2.41	2.08	0.55	77 %
2014.10.02	1.87	1.45	0.31	83 %
2014.10.19	2.17	1.78	0.45	79 %
2014.11.11	1.83	1.50	0.61	67 %
2014.11.22	1.98	1.60	0.59	70 %
2014.12.07	1.96	1.39	0.44	78 %
2014.12.21	1.81	1.41	0.56	69 %
Average	**1.97**	**1.64**	**0.43**	**77 %**
Results in [27]	1.96	1.58	0.50	74 %

Table 3. Standard deviation in different correcting phases.

Date	Standard deviation			
	Raw data	Time translation	Error corrected	Efficiency
2014.06.04	3.06	2.31	0.57	81 %
2014.06.09	3.24	2.53	0.31	90 %
2014.07.04	0.91	0.66	0.19	79 %
2014.07.07	3.11	2.61	0.84	73 %
2014.08.08	0.49	0.32	0.22	55 %
2014.08.10	2.45	1.98	0.30	88 %
2014.09.03	1.93	1.52	0.45	77 %
2014.09.28	3.22	2.48	0.56	83 %
2014.10.02	2.09	1.51	0.34	84 %
2014.10.19	2.77	2.09	0.55	80 %
2014.11.11	2.25	1.57	0.67	70 %
2014.11.22	2.80	2.24	0.86	69 %
2014.12.07	2.65	1.94	0.65	75 %
2014.12.21	2.32	1.86	0.72	69 %
Average	**2.38**	**1.83**	**0.52**	**77 %**
Results in [27]	2.38	1.82	0.62	74 %

data without treatment and it can be seen that the error is the biggest. After the process of time translation, the error values were reduced by a small margin. The third column shows the maximum absolute error between the corrected data and the standard data with BP_{151}^s. This process greatly reduces the error. After the correction, our average maximal absolute error is 0.51 lower than that of them and the efficiency is improved by 8 % compared with the results in [27].

In Table 2, we calculated the mean absolute error of these days. Similarly, the errors gradually decreased with the process of time translation and correction. After the errors were corrected, our average maximal absolute error is 0.07 lower than that of them and the efficiency is improved by 3 % compared with the results in [27].

In Table 3, we calculated the error between the corrected data and the standard data. The greater the standard deviation, the greater the volatility. After the errors were corrected, our average maximal absolute error is 0.1 lower than that of them and the efficiency is improved by 3 % compared with the results in [27].

Comparing the average results and efficiency after error correction through these three indicators, we can find that our results are superior to the result in previous paper.

4   Conclusions

We use BP neural networks for error correction in this paper. We analyzed the data collected from the automatic weather station and wireless sensor network and did some pretreatments, and successfully fitted the function relationship between SR and ATE. We evaluated the performs of this model and finally corrected the errors. Experiment results show that the corrected data performs very well and the data of maximum absolute error, mean absolute error and standard deviation are all get reduced comparing with the performance of the method of statistical analysis, demonstrating its superior in ATE correction.

However, the cost of SR sensing is still very high. So in the future, we will study the relationship between the solar cell panel voltage and SR and then convert the voltage to the corresponding SR. If this method can be successful, we can use the voltage to replace the SR so that our correction will become more economical.

Acknowledgements. This work is supported by the National Science Foundation of China under Grant No. 61173136, U1536206, 61232016, U1405254, 61373133, 61502242, the CICAEET (Jiangsu Collaborative Innovation Center on Atmospheric Environment and Equipment Technology) fund and PAPD (Priority Academic Program Development of Jiangsu Higher Education Institutions) fund.

References

1. Arakawa, M., Okamoto, K., Yi, K., Terabayashi, M., Tsutsumi, Y.: Shrimp U-Pb dating of zircons related to the partial melting in a deep subduction zone: case study from the sanbagawa quartz-bearing eclogite. I. Arc **22**(1), 74–88 (2011)
2. Barroca, N., Borges, L.M., Velez, F.J., Monteiro, F., Grski, M., Castro-Gomes, J.: Wireless sensor networks for temperature and humidity monitoring within concrete structures. Constr. Build. Mater. **40**(3), 1156–1166 (2013)
3. Bojanowski, J.S., Vrieling, A., Skidmore, A.K.: A comparison of data sources for creating a long-term time series of daily gridded solar radiation for Europe. Sol. Energy **99**(1), 152–171 (2014)
4. Box, J.E., Rinke, A.: Evaluation of Greenland ice sheet surface climate in the HIRHAM regional climate model using automatic weather station data. J. Clim. **16**(9), 1302–1319 (2003)
5. Elfelly, N., Dieulot, J.Y., Benrejeb, M., Borne, P.: A multimodel approach of complex systems identification and control using neural and fuzzy clustering algorithms. In: International Conference on Machine Learning Applications, pp. 93–98 (2010)
6. Flerchinger, G.N., Xaio, W., Marks, D., Sauer, T.J., Yu, Q.: Comparison of algorithms for incoming atmospheric long-wave radiation. Water Resour. Res. **45**(3), 450–455 (2009)
7. Fu, X.: Test and analysis of temperature characteristics for HMP45D humidity sensors. Meteorol. Sci. Technol. (2009)
8. Gu, B., Sheng, V.S., Wang, Z., Ho, D., Osman, S., Li, S.: Incremental learning for v-support vector regression. Neural Net. Official J. Int. Neural Net. Soc. **67**(C), 140–150 (2015)

9. Hecht-Nielsen, R.: Theory of the backpropagation neural network. Neural Netw. **1**(1), 65–93 (1988)
10. Huang, G.B., Zhu, Q.Y., Siew, C.K.: Extreme learning machine: theory and applications. Neurocomputing **70**(13), 489–501 (2006)
11. Interpolation, C.S.: Cubic spline interpolation. Numer. Math. J. Chinese Univ. **64**(1), 44–56 (1999)
12. Izadi, D., Abawajy, J.H., Ghanavati, S., Herawan, T.: A data fusion method in wireless sensor networks. Sensors **15**(2), 2964–2979 (2015)
13. Jin, M.: Analysis and verification of HMP45D humidity sensor fault in dalian airport. Wireless Internet Technol. (2015)
14. Jing, Z., Jun, L.I., Schmit, T.J., Jinlong, L.I., Liu, Z.: The impact of airs atmospheric temperature and moisture profiles on hurricane forecasts: Ike (2008) and Irene (2011). Nat. Cell Biol. **32**(3), 966–972 (2015)
15. Kadar, I.: Perceptual reasoning in adaptive fusion processing. Proc. SPIE Int. Soc. Opt. Eng. **69**(1), 168–180 (2002)
16. Liu, H., Wang, B., Sun, X., Li, T., Liu, Q., Guo, Y.: DCSCS: a novel approach to improve data accuracy for low cost meteorological sensor networks. Inf. Technol. J. **13**(9), 1640–1647 (2014)
17. Liu, X., Cheng, X., Skidmore, A.K.: Potential solar radiation pattern in relation to the monthly distribution of giant pandas in foping nature reserve, China. Ecol. Model. **222**(3), 645–652 (2011). (online first)
18. Miller, F.P., Vandome, A.F., Mcbrewster, J.: Automatic weather station. Bioscience **196**(3366), 321–321 (2010)
19. Moroni, G., Syam, W.P., Petr, S.: Performance improvement for optimization of the non-linear geometric fitting problem in manufacturing metrology. Measur. Sci. Technol. **25**(8), 1409–1424 (2014)
20. Perez, P., Vermaak, J., Blake, A.: Data fusion for visual tracking with particles. Proc. IEEE **92**(3), 495–513 (2004)
21. Guo, P., Jin Wang, B.L., Lee, S.: A variable threshold-value authentication architecture for wireless mesh networks. J. Internet Technol. **15**(6), 929–935 (2014)
22. Prakash, D., Mageshwari, T.U., Prabakaran, K., Suguna, A.: Detection of heart diseases by mathematical artificial intelligence algorithm using phonocardiogram signals. Int. J. Innov. Appl. Stud. **3**(1), 145–150 (2013)
23. Roweis, S.T., Saul, L.K.: Nonlinear dimensionality reduction by locally linear embedding. Science **290**(5500), 2323–6 (2000)
24. Shen, J., Tan, H., Wang, J., Wang, J., Lee, S.: A novel routing protocol providing good transmission reliability in underwater sensor networks. J. Internet Technol. **16**(1), 171–178 (2015)
25. Sin, L.T., Rahman, W.A.W.A., Rahmat, A.R., Morad, N.A., Salleh, M.S.N.: A study of specific heat capacity functions of polyvinyl alcoholcassava starch blends. FEBS Lett. **31**(1–3), 3137 (2010)
26. Steiniger, S., Taillandier, P., Weibel, R.: Utilising urban context recognition and machine learning to improve the generalisation of buildings. Int. J. Geogr. Inf. Sci. **24**(24), 253–282 (2010)
27. Sun, X., Yan, S., Wang, B., Li, X., Liu, Q., Zhang, H.: Air temperature error correction based on solar radiation in an economical meteorological wireless sensor network. Sensors **15**(8), 18114–39 (2015)
28. Trontz, A., Cheng, B., Zeng, S., Xiao, H., Dong, J.: Development of metal-ceramic coaxial cable Fabry-Perot interferometric sensors for high temperature monitoring. Sensors **15**(10), 24914–24925 (2015)

29. Xie, S., Wang, Y.: Construction of tree network with limited delivery latency in homogeneous wireless sensor networks. Wireless Pers. Commun. **78**(78), 231–246 (2014)

30. Zhang, Y., Gao, X., Katayama, S.: Weld appearance prediction with BP neural network improved by genetic algorithm during disk laser welding. J. Manuf. Syst. **34**, 53–59 (2015)

31. Zheng, Y., Byeungwoo, J., Xu, D., Wu, Q.M.J., Zhang, H.: Image segmentation by generalized hierarchical fuzzy c-means algorithm. J. Intell. Fuzzy Syst. **28**(2), 4024–4028 (2015)

32. Zipser, D., Andersen, R.A.: A back-propagation programmed network that simulates response properties of a subset of posterior parietal neurons. Nature **331**(6158), 679–684 (1988)

An Energy-Efficient Data Gathering Based on Compressive Sensing

Ke-Ming Tang, Hao Yang[✉], Xin Qiu, and Lv-Qing Wu

School of Information Engineering, Yancheng Teachers University, Yancheng, China
tkmchina@126.com, classforyc@163.com, xinqiu.94@gmail.com,
wulvqing0523@sina.com

Abstract. To energy-efficient communication, Compressive Sensing (CS) has been employed gradually. This paper proposes a data gathering scheme based on CS. The network is divided into several blocks and each block sends data to the sink for reconstruction. Experiments demonstrate that our algorithm is feasible and outperforms other schemes.

Keywords: Compressive sensing · Data gathering · Wireless sensor network

1 Introduction

In WSN, to energy-efficient communication, Compressed Sensing (CS) [1, 2] has been gradually utilized to prolong the lifetime of networks in this field [3, 4].

As CS has been paid more and more attention in WSN, however, a doubt that whether this technique always outperforms traditional methods in practice has been proposed [5, 6]. In practice, plain CS may be not better than no-CS scheme. Compared to no-CS, edge nodes in the network cost more energy in CS when the scale of the network is not large.

To avoid unnecessary energy waste in practice, a hybrid approach is proposed in the paper, which decreases cost of edge nodes. Subsequently, Caione *et al.* [7] further elucidate this conclusion and verify in Zigbee network [8].

However, the problem of center region is still inevitable and the cost of sensors in this region is the overwhelming majority of energy consumption in the whole network. That is, the performance of the mix algorithm is greatly impacted in actual environments.

In this paper, we propose an effective data gathering scheme based on regionalization compressive sensing. Its basic idea is that the procedure of sampling via CS is carried out by regionalization via partitioning the topology of the network. In detail, the network is firstly divided into several blocks randomly. Subsequently, samplings are sent straight to the sink. Experiments reveal that it outperforms direct transmission, DCS by contrasting.

© Springer International Publishing AG 2016
X. Sun et al. (Eds.): ICCCS 2016, Part II, LNCS 10040, pp. 133–137, 2016.
DOI: 10.1007/978-3-319-48674-1_12

2   Preliminary

Compressed sensing [9, 10, 11] is an effective signal acquisition and compression technology, which is used to sample and compress data simultaneously. Suppose X is a N-dimensional signal, Φ is a $M \times N$ matrix $(M < N)$ and $Y = \Phi \times X$. Based on CS theory, it is probable that X could be recovery from Y and Φ as the signal X can be represented as a linear combination with K basis vectors.

Suppose C is a N-dimensional signal and ϕ is a M × N matrix (M < N). if $Y = \phi \times C$, then Y could be regarded as M measurements from C through the measurement matrix ϕ. Based on the theory of CS, it is probable that C could be reconstructed from Y if C can be represented as a linear combination of only K basis vectors.

To recover stably, ϕ must satisfy *Restricted Isometry Property* (RIP), which is expressed as: let $\theta \in (0, 1)$, for any $m \in [1, \min(N, M)]$, the restricted isometry constant of C is equal to the smallest quantity $\theta_m = \theta_m(\phi)$ such that

$$(1 - \theta_m)||C||^2 \le ||\phi_I C||^2 \le (1 + \theta_m)||C||^2 \tag{1}$$

CS provides a promising solution for extending the lifetime of sensor networks. According to CS theory, the procedures of both sampling and compression are combined together. That is, an asymmetric mode between the sampling end and the reconstruction end is constructed instead of a symmetric mode in WSN. Hence, energy costs are reduced in the process of sampling and the network's lifetime will be enlarged.

With CS theory, the sink could accurately recovery the original data via the required measurement. That is, the reconstruction accuracy is independent with data transmission schemes. In practice, however, inappropriate data gathering way will increase unnecessary energy cost of nodes tremendously and reduce the lifetime of the network greatly.

For adopting CS effectively, a proper data gathering scheme should be considered to prolong the lifetime of the network.

3   Design of Data Gathering Scheme

An obvious advantage of CS technique is that sensors closed to the sink cost the same energy as bottom ones in the network. Nevertheless, this theoretical superiority is probably not embodied in practice, even worse. Compared to no-CS methods, bottom sensors in the network cost more energy for CS in practical applications, that is, CS may result in unnecessary energy waste considerably.

To address this problem, we propose an effective data gathering scheme based on regionalization CS. An example is demonstrated. Suppose a sensor network with one sink is divided into two regions $\{r_i | i = 1, 2\}$, each of which includes several nodes. The sink obtains nodes' readings from two regions. In each region, a node is elected as center node in charge of compressing and relaying data. The strategy of election could be randomly assigning.

In the process of data gathering, regular nodes n_j forward its reading x_j to the center one c_i directly. Subsequently, the center node c_i implement regionalized CS. When all center nodes send its combination values, the sink will get a complete measurement.

4   Experiments

To evaluate the performance of our scheme, we have simulated evaluations considering Zigbee network, and the scale of the network varies from 20 to 1000 nodes.

The experiments adopt the temperature data set collected in the Pacific Sea at (7.0 N, 180 W) [12, 13], which contains 1000 readings obtained at different depth of sea, which are assigned to each node. The structure of the data package is the same with the definition in Sect. 3.

In this section, we compare our scheme to two typical data gathering approaches in previous literatures [6, 7], which are the direct transmission (DT), distributed compressed sensing (DCS). The size of Id of the data package is 2, 3, 4 bytes and the size of data is 1, 2, 3 bytes.

Figure 1 evaluate four schemes with fixed D_{id} and D_{data}. The network dimension is from [100, 1000]. For DT, it is nearly positive correlation with the network dimension, since it depends on the number of nodes in charge of relaying data. For DCS, it are more than the network dimension when the number of nodes is small.

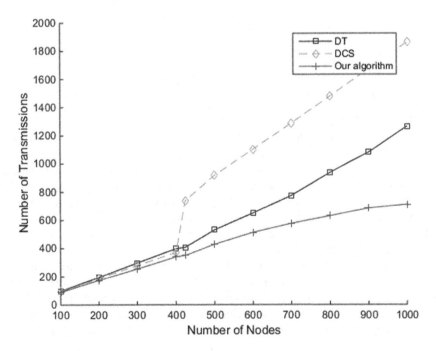

Fig. 1. Comparison the number of transmission among DT, DCS and Our Scheme.

As nodes are greater, it becomes less. However, each node may have to use two packages for loading the measurement value instead of one when the size of Id is large. When the scale of network enlarges, the merit of our scheme becomes obvious. As n is very large, the curve of transmission number turns to smooth. That is, its trend will not change rapidly as the number of nodes increasing.

In Fig. 2, simulations illustrates energy costs of three schemes. Here, we suppose that energy consumption is proportional to both the size and the number of data packets.

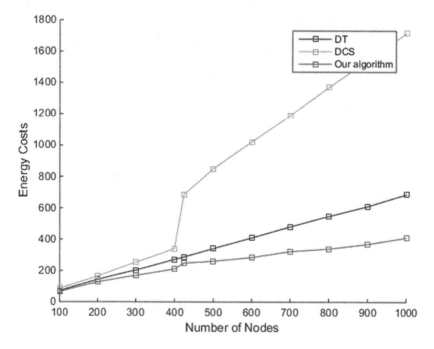

Fig. 2. Comparison the number of transmission among four schemes with 4, 6, 8 bytes Data

As Fig. 2 shown, the cost of DT is largest, since each node has to contain the size of data package in its data packet. The reason is that the transmission sequence number for each sensor could not be contained in its data packet by CS, since the sink is capable to identify it via measurement coefficients. For MA, it becomes smaller due to the increasing of the size of id of the data package, which leads that the center region enlarges In this case, energy cost augments slightly.

Our scheme outperforms them. When the size of id of the data package is small, it becomes large and the number of regionalization is few. In this case, there are few center nodes in the network and thus their consumption is less. As the size of the size of id of the data package growing up, regions increase and the corresponding cost for transmitting data enlarges. This relationship between the size of id of the data package and energy cost is not stable.

5   Conclusion

In this paper, we propose an effective data gathering scheme based on regionalization compressed sensing. This algorithm outperforms the previous schemes, including plain CS, straight forward. Experiments demonstrate that the proposed scheme outperforms the previous ones.

Acknowledgements. This work is supported by the National High Technology Research and Development Program (863 Program) of China (2015AA01A201), National Science Foundation of China under Grant No. 61402394, 61379064, 61273106, National Science Foundation of Jiangsu Province of China under Grant No. BK20140462, Natural Science Foundation of the Higher Education Institutions of Jiangsu Province of China under Grant No. 14KJB520040, 15KJB520035, China Postdoctoral Science Foundation funded project under Grant No. 2016M591922, Jiangsu Planned Projects for Postdoctoral Research Funds under Grant No. 1601162B, JLCBE14008, and sponsored by Qing Lan Project.

References

1. Donoho, D.L.: Compressed sensing. IEEE Trans. Inform. Theory **52**(4), 1289–1306 (2006)
2. Candès, E.J., Romberg, J., Tao, T.: An introduction to compressive sampling. IEEE Signal Proc. Mag. **25**(2), 21–30 (2008)
3. Jin, W., Tang, S.J., Yin, B.C., Li, X.Y.: Data gathering in wireless sensor networks through intelligent compressive sensing. In: IEEE INFOCOM (2012)
4. Caione, C., Brunelli, D., Benini, L.: Compressive sensing optimization for signal ensembles in WSNs. IEEE Trans. Ind. Inform. **10**(1), 382–392 (2014)
5. Luo, C., Wu, F., Sun, J., Chen, C.W.: Efficient measurement generation and pervasive sparsity for compressive data gathering. IEEE Trans. Wirel. Commun. **9**(12), 3728–3738 (2010)
6. Jun, L., Liu, X., Rosenberg, C.: Does compressed sensing improve the throughput of wireless sensor networks. In: IEEE ICC (2010)
7. Caione, C., Brunelli, D., Benini, L.: Distributed compressive sampling for lifetime optimization in dense wireless sensor networks. IEEE Trans. Ind. Inform. **8**(1), 30–40 (2012)
8. Baron, D., Duarte, M.F., Wakin, M.B., Duarte, M.F., Sarvotham, S., Baraniuk, R.G.: Distributed compressed sensing, arXiv.org, http://arxiv.org/abs/0901.3403
9. Candès, E., Tao, T.: Near optimal signal recovery from random projections and universal encoding strategies. IEEE Trans. Inform. Theor. **52**(12), 5406–5425 (2006)
10. Baraniuk, R., Davenport, M., DeVore, R., Wakin, M.: A simple proof of the restricted isometry property for random matrices. Constr. Approx. **28**(3), 253–263 (2008)
11. Maliootov, D.M., Sanghavi, S.R., Willsky, A.S.: Sequential compressed sensing. IEEE J-STSP **4**(2), 435–444 (2010)
12. NBDC CTD data. http://tao.noaa.gov/refreshed/ctd_delivery.php
13. Luo, C., Wu, F., Sun, J., Chen, C.W.: Compressive data gathering for large-scale wireless sensor networks. In: MOBICOM. ACM (2009)

Improving Data Credibility for Mobile Crowdsensing with Clustering and Logical Reasoning

Tongqing Zhou$^{(\boxtimes)}$, Zhiping Cai, Yueyue Chen, and Ming Xu

College of Computer, National University of Defense Technology, Changsha, China
{zhoutongqing,zpcai,yueyuechen,xuming}@nudt.edu.cn

Abstract. Mobile crowdsensing is a new paradigm that tries to collect a vast amount of data with the rich set of sensors on pervasive mobile devices. However, the unpredictable intention and various capabilities of device owners expose the application to potential dishonest and malicious contributions, bringing forth the important issues of data credibility assurance. Existed works generally attempt to increase data confidence level with the guide of reputation, which is very likely to be unavailable in reality. In this work, we propose CLOR, a general scheme to ensure data credibility for typical mobile crowdsensing application without requiring reputation knowledge. By integrating data clustering with logical reasoning, CLOR is able to formally separate false and normal data, make credibility assessment, and filter out the false ingredient. Simulation results show that improved data credibility can be achieved effectively with our scheme.

Keywords: Mobile crowdsensing · Data credibility · Clustering algorithm · Logical reasoning

1 Introduction

The past few years have witnessed the massive prevalence of human-carried computing devices equipped with a rich set of powerful embedded sensors. Such advancements have given rise to a new sensing paradigm, known as mobile crowdsensing (MCS) [1], where individuals use their own mobile devices to perform sensing task, and collect interested physical data for further analysis [2] in cloud-based platform. So far, a broad spectrum of MCS applications have been developed, including environment monitoring, city management, network measurement [3], etc.

A major challenge for the adoption of MCS is how to assure the credibility of collected sensory data [4]. Unlike the specialized sensors used in traditional wireless sensor networks (WSNs), MCS relies on individuals with unknown trustworthiness and varied capabilities. Generally, other than unintentionally false data, normal anonymous participants may tend to submit random measurements to get reward with minimal effort [5]. Further, potential malicious participants

© Springer International Publishing AG 2016
X. Sun et al. (Eds.): ICCCS 2016, Part II, LNCS 10040, pp. 138–150, 2016.
DOI: 10.1007/978-3-319-48674-1_13

intend to mislead the data analysis process for their own profit by injecting fabricated data. For instance, leasing agents may submit false low noise readings regarding a specific region to promote the rental for their houses. An Internet Service Provider may generate fictitious measurements to degrade its competitor's performance evaluation while increasing its own profit. Therefore, it is critical to design an effective scheme to verify the data in order to derive reliable conclusion from them.

Typically, previous works have investigated credibility assurance for sensory data from unreliable sources by either building reputation systems [6,7] or utilizing false detection [8–10] techniques. The former category attempts to evaluate the trustworthiness of the collected data based on participants' reputation information and related provenance, such as location proximity and real-time performance [6,7]. In [8] and [9], spatial-temporal compressive sensing technique and overall reputation of clusters are applied to detect false ingredient and improve data credibility. However, these approaches all rely on the prior knowledge of participants' reputation information, which may in fact be unavailable due to anonymity [11]. To address the problem of "trust without reputation", some works attempt to increase data credibility by identifying contributions that fail to pass location verification as false [12]. Unfortunately, it implicitly ignore a common unreliable form containing false sensory data with a valid location. Alternatively, in [13], the concept of provenance logic is introduced to evaluate data trust based on extended Event Calculus and Markov Logic Network. However, [13] only focus on several special application scenarios that collect data with finite domain of state (e.g. event happens or not), making it unable to handle the more common scenarios where numerical sensory data are collected [3].

In this work, we attempt to solve the problem of "trust without reputation" for general MCS applications. A Clustering and LOgical Reasoning based scheme (CLOR) is proposed to ascertain the credibility of multi-dimension numerical sensory data without requiring any prior knowledge from the participants. Specifically, two characteristics of MCS are exploited to achieve this goal. First, as crowd-contributed data for one MCS task are spatial correlated, clustering algorithm is performed to formally distinguish false ingredient from the normal part. Second, co-located events observed within a short period of time are very likely to share logical relations with the current MCS task, so logical reasoning is introduced to assess the credibility of sensory data through identifying potential logical supports.

The main contributions of our work are three-fold:

1. A novel clustering-and-merging based translation mechanism is presented to map the numerical sensory measurements to countable discrete levels and further represent them with First-Order Logic (FOL) predicates;
2. Given pre-defined logical relations between related events and MCS task, a logical reasoning based module is proposed to assess the credibility of quantization levels corresponding to sensory data clusters of that task;

3. A general data credibility assurance algorithm is developed by jointly applying clustering algorithm and logical reasoning to filter out false ingredient
   in the crowd-contributed sensory data, while no reputation information is
   required in this process.

The rest of this paper is organized as follows. Section 2 describes system
model, problem formulation and introduce logical reasoning knowledge. Then
we outline the key components of scheme CLOR, and introduce how CLOR
facilitates better data credibility in Sect. 3. In Sect. 4, simulation results that
indicate the effectiveness of the scheme are provided. Finally, conclusions are
drawn in Sect. 5.

2   Preliminaries

2.1   System Model

We consider a typical MCS architecture as shown in Fig. 1. It consists of a
cloud-based platform and a set of participants $U = \{u_1, ..., u_N\}$ that perform
sensing task T at location L. Among the three stages of a MCS application,
data credibility is considered as an crucial part of the utilization stage, and data
falsification threats arise as the crowd participants have various capabilities and
purposes. A sensing task normally specifies multiple modalities of sensory data
to be collected, so we consider that the collected data in MCS application are
multi-dimensional numerical sensor readings (e.g. temperature, noise level).

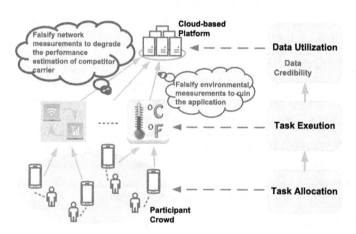

Fig. 1. Architecture of typical MCS applications. Network measurement and temperature monitoring are depicted as two illustrative example applications. Two potential
credibility threats are also listed.

During the execution of task T, u_i collects a series of measurements with K
different sensor types, where each can be denoted by $s_i(k)$, where $i \in [1, N]$, and

$k \in [1, K]$. Sensory data are submitted together with location l_i to the platform before time deadline. The contribution from u_i forms a tuple in key-value syntax, denoted as $d_i = <l_i, s_i>$. By the end of T, the centralized platform will obtain a data set $D = \{d_1, ..., d_N\}$, based on which some aggregation function f will be performed to derive statistical conclusion.

Finally, we assume that L refers to an area of interest within certain distance of L instead of a specific spot as physical measurements are usually spatial correlated, and all sensory data are aligned on measurement features. No additional information of the participants is required.

2.2   Problem Formulation

Data collected from individuals with unknown trustworthiness are unreliable. The potential erroneous or fabricated ingredient measurements injected in the collected data would deviate the analysis result from the expected true value. Here we consider data d_i as trust if its location component l_i and sensory measurement component s_i are both valid. We classify the state space of credibility of data d_i into four categories as shown in Table 1, where symbol T (F) means the value is true (false). Note that location attestation-based schemes like [12] try to assure data credibility by picking out data with invalid location in category B and category C, ignoring possibly false data in category A, which is more common in a MCS application especially when malicious intention is considered. Unlike these schemes, we propose to improve overall credibility through identifying the group of data with invalid measurement (Category A and C) in this work, we consider data fall in category B to be normal as its value is valid.

Table 1. Space state for validity of typical MCS data

s_i / l_i	T	F
T	Normal data	Category A
F	Category B	Category C

In view of the above-described false data forms, two types of adversary model are considered:

1. *Random Falsification.* Participants submit measurements with random value to minimize their efforts, or tamper the measurement to facilitate a misleading effect. For the latter intention, dishonest participants would try to deviate the aggregation result as much as possible.
2. *Falsification with Conspiracy Cooperation.* A group of adversaries collude with each other to intentionally induce the final aggregation result to a wrong

value. Moreover, in order to avoid being identified by statistical analysis-based abnormal detection method, the dishonest group is able to fabricate and submit data obeying normal distribution.

Collusion among participants would result in a more significant deviation, and the injected artificial data cannot be easily picked out. Taking average function f_{avg} as an example of the aggregation function, if we have a crowd contributed data set $D_{eg} = \{d_n^1, ..., d_n^N, d_f^1, ..., d_f^N\}$, where $d_n^i = <L, M>$ denotes a normal measurement, and $d_f^i = <L, 2M>$ denotes a false measurement, then we will have $f_{avg}(D_{eg}) = 1.5M$ which is 1.5 times larger than the actual value M. Additionally, we do not make any assumption or set any limitation on the number of dishonest participants in U, in which situation vote-based false detection approaches are not effective any more.

2.3   Logical Reasoning

Logical reasoning is the formal manipulation of the symbols representing a collection of something known to produce representations of new ones. It generally involves ontology, basic predicates, and knowledge base (KB). The underlying ontology can be time points, events (e.g. accident), and fluents (e.g. high temperature), while a predicate represents a property of or relation between ontology that can be true or false. A KB contains general axioms describing the relations between predicates. Resolution is one of the most widely used calculi for theorem proving in logical reasoning. It proves a theorem by negating the statement to be proved and adding this negated goal to the sets of axioms that are known to be true to tell whether it leads to a contradiction.

In this work, we consider to map and translate the sensory data collected during current MCS task into FOL predicates, and use resolution rules to tell whether the predicates are satisfiable by jointly considering the co-located events and basic KB. We assume the basic KB has been pre-established given a specific application scenario, and real time computation only involves translating related events into predicates and add them to the reasoning KB.

3   Design of CLOR

3.1   Overview

CLOR scheme tries to improve the overall credibility of crowd data in MCS through identifying and discarding the corrupted part with invalid sensory measurements (i.e. the data belonging to category A and C in Table 1). Theoretically, only normal part of the collected data remains after the processing.

Framework of CLOR is illustrated in Fig. 2, which basically consists of three modules. The quantization and representation module formally translates the input numerical sensory data into predicates, wherein clustering-and-merging mechanism, projection and translation operation are carried out sequentially. The KB construction module provides reasoning KB based on co-located events

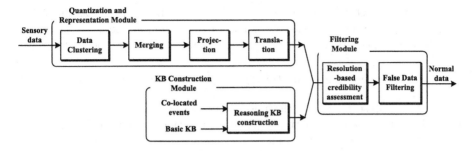

Fig. 2. Framework of CLOR

and pre-established casual logical relations in regard of the MCS tasks. The filtering module adopts logical resolution to find logical supports for each cluster and assess overall credibility for them. Finally, clusters with low assessment score are filtered out and aggregation function is performed on the filtering results.

CLOR improves data credibility, and provides space for privacy preserving. Essentially, CLOR improves the quality of service provided by a MCS application to the sensory information requesters.

3.2   Data Quantization and Representation

In this module, we aim to obtain several quantization levels from the sensory data and translate them into FOL predicates for further logical reasoning. The number of levels is application specific and dynamically determined by the distribution of the sensory measurements, and denoted as m. Each level represents the property of corresponding data cluster. The detail stages are introduced as follows.

(1) Data Clustering: Normally, physical measurements act as signatures that characterize a place of interest, which implies that measurements for the same location are correlated with each other, while on the other hand, false data behave abnormal in the feature space. Meanwhile, the collected data are mainly exploited at a community scale which provides sufficient participant density support for clustering the data around a specific location target. Hence, a fixed width clustering algorithm is first performed on D to group similar data instances into clusters with similar property. The first data is assigned to be the centroid of the first cluster. Then for every subsequent data d_i in D, distance between centroid of each cluster and data d_i is calculated as,

$$dis(s_i, s_c) = \sqrt{\sum_{k=1}^{K} (s_i(k) - s_c(k))^2} \tag{1}$$

where s_i is the sensory measurements in d_i, and s_c is the sensory values of cluster centroid. If the distance to one cluster is less than the cluster width ω, it is added to that cluster and the centroid of that cluster is adaptively adjusted to the mean of the inner data. Otherwise a new cluster is formed with that data as the initial centroid. Here, we novelly define ω as half of the minimum expected deviation from the true aggregation result for a potential falsify behavior among the crowd data, i.e.,

$$\omega = 1/2 \cdot \min_i\left(\left|f(D(i)) - f(\tilde{D})\right|\right) = 1/2 \cdot \sigma_{dev} \tag{2}$$

where $D(i)$ represents one of the possible collected data sets containing corrupted ingredient, f denotes the aggregation function during data analysis, $\tilde{D}$ denotes the set of normal data, and σ_{dev} denotes the minimum expected misleading degree. The value of parameter σ_{dev} is updated adaptively according to the application context, e.g., a dishonest participant may prefer to consider a deviation of at least $4\,°C$ as effective for a task that measures city temperature, while $10\,dB$ may be a meaningful value in an application of received signal strength measurement. The clustering operation generates a set of fixed width clusters $C = \{C_1, .., C_n\}$ in the feature space.

(2) Clusters Merging: In order to map the sensory data into several discrete levels, we introduce a merging stage to combine similar clusters together. The similarity between clusters can be measured by their inter-cluster distance. Hence, distance $dis(s_c^i, s_c^j)$ between each cluster C_i and C_j is calculated, and a merging operation is performed between the two clusters with the minimum inter-cluster distance to generate a new cluster. The new cluster combines the data points in the two neighbor clusters and is added into C to join the next round of comparison and merging. This iterative procedure is continued until the inter-cluster distances of remaining clusters are all bigger than width ω, making these distances the m largest ones.

Note that clusters with a bigger size do not inherently indicate higher credibility as the number of malicious participants may be more than the honest one, so vote-base approach can not help here.

(3) Projection: The above process provides us with m separated areas (i.e. clusters) in the K-dimension feature space. However, what we need are discrete levels, say, some points distributed in the space, so a mapping function is required to map one cluster into one single point. Generally, the centroid of a cluster can describe its property well, so we propose to use the centroid of clusters to represent them. Hence, the extracted m levels are defined as $Lev = \{s_c^1, ..., s_c^m\}$, and s_c^i equals to $f_c(i)$, which denotes the calculation of the centroid of cluster C_i.

(4) Translation: Each quantization level is a K-dimension feature vector, we propose to translate them independently. Specifically, each sensory measurement in s_c^i is first converted into linguistic variables $M(s_c^i(k))$ with function $M(x)$. There has already been many works on linguistic representation such as fuzzier in fuzzy logic, so we propose to rely on the state-of-art methods. For example, the value is replaced with "WA" or "CO" (Warm or Cold) according to its scale in a temperature monitoring application. Then we introduce a FOL predicate, denoted as $HoldsAt(F, T, L)$, which means Fluent F holds at time interval T at location L, to describe the statements corresponding to the linguistic variables.

Finally, the translation result regarding level i is defined as

$$T(i) = HoldsAt(M(s_c^i(1)), T, L) \wedge ... \wedge HoldsAt(M(s_c^i(K)), T, L) \qquad (3)$$

3.3 Knowledge Base Construction

The reasoning KB is constructed by incorporating related events into the basic KB. Physical phenomena sensed in the same region during a time period are often related, we define these phenomena as related events. Basically, the collection of related events can be obtained from two main sources: (i) the reports of other MCS applications from the same MCS platform, and (ii) the geo-tagged observations and information collected from social networks. For example, the degree of crowdedness in different regions of an urban area could influence the corresponding noise level, and practically, it can not only be identified through mobility-based sensing application [14], but also be detected from human observations with social sensing [15]. On the other hand, the basic KB contains a set of logical formulas representing the causal relations between events and the sensory phenomena of MCS applications, and it is application specific. The method of event collection and relation formulation are out the scope of this paper, we assume related events and basic KB are known prior, and denoted as E and KB_{basic}. Finally, the reasoning KB can be represented as $KB = E \cup KB_{basic}$.

3.4 Data Filtering

The quantization module formally map sensory data indicating different phenomenal property into discrete levels. We employ logical resolution to find evidence for each level of announced sensory phenomenon, and estimate its credibility.

The proposed algorithm is described in Algorithm 1, which will be repeated sequentially for each dimension in the K-dimensional of the m quantization levels. Initially, we introduce a variable A_c to denotes the credibility assessment score of levels in Lev. Then we adopt logical resolution to estimate A_c^i for each level i. Specifically, we first pick out the logical reasoning for one level's k-th sensory measurement and negate it to obtain a statement. We then use inference rules of resolution to iteratively perform resolution on the statement, axiom set E, and every formula in KB_{basic} to show whether this leads to a contradiction (logically, an empty clause). A contradiction means that this measurement of level i is logically supported by E, in which situation we propose to addictively increase A_c^i with a factor r_a. The rationale of the 3rd iteration (Line 5) is that with more events logically supporting the current level, it should be more reliable, while the 2nd iteration (Line 3) indicates that with more dimension of sensory measurements being supported, the current level should be more reliable. For each cluster, an estimation score would be generated with this iteration reasoning procedure. We normalize these estimation values and obtain an assessment for the credibility of each level (Line 13).

Algorithm 1. Cluster credibility assessment

Input:
   $M(s_c^i(k))$, KB_{basic}, E, additive increase factor r_a
Output:
   A_c^i: credibility assessment score of the i-th cluster
1: Set $A_c^i \leftarrow 0$ for $i = 1...m$
2: **for** $i = 1 \rightarrow m$ **do**
3:   **for** $k = 1 \rightarrow K$ **do**
4:     $statement = \neg HoldsAt(M(s_c^i(k)), T, L)$
5:     **for** $\forall f \in KB_{basic}$ **do**
6:       **if** $resolution(E, statement, f) \Rightarrow NIL$ **then**
7:         $A_c^i + = r_a$
8:       **end if**
9:     **end for**
10:    **end for**
11:   $A_c^i = \frac{A_c^i - \min(A_c^i)}{\max(A_c^i) - \min(A_c^i)}$ //Normalization
12: **end for**

Finally, the level with the highest credibility assessment is determined to be reliable, and the corresponding data cluster regarded as the container of normal data, i.e., $C^* = \arg\max_{C_i}\{A_c^i\}$. Other contributions in the data set are regarded as false and filtered out.

4   Evaluation

4.1   Settings

In this section, we aim to test the effectiveness of CLOR with a typical MCS-based environmental monitoring application. In such applications, portable sensors are equipped with mobile participants to collect physical information. Specifically, we choose an open source temperature measurement traces obtained from the CRAWDAD data set [16], which contains 5030 measurement items from 289 active taxicabs collected around the GPS location $(41.9, 12.5)$ in Rome. In order to simulate the potential dishonest behaviors that falsifies sensory data, some items of the data set are modified. Here, we consider the adversary model of falsification with conspiracy cooperation as it is harder to detect. Measurements of these items are replaced with random values generated from a normal distribution with mean parameter μ equalling to the value of misleading target S_{err} and standard deviation parameter $\sigma = 1$. Note that the false data are fabricated to obey normal distribution to imitate smart collusion among a dishonest group. Further, the synthetic data set is divided into two sets according to the submission time of the contribution to conduct two experiments independently. Finally, as mentioned above, we assume the KB has been pre-established given our application scenario.

We consider the minimum possible deviation caused by data falsification to be 4°, so the cluster width is set to be 2°. Meanwhile, the falsification target S_{err} for time period 1 and time period 2 are set to 14° and 8° to effectively mislead the aggregation results. Two sets of fabricated measurements are then generated and used to replace sensory measurements of the selected data items in the original data set. We assume that all the simulations are under a closed-world assumption, i.e., all relevant events are defined in the KB. For each time period, an complete KB is defined as presented in Table 2. Here we provide 3 levels (e.g. Cold, Warm, Hot) to quantize the collected temperature measurements, and we emphasize that other situations can be easily generalized.

We evaluate the effectiveness of CLOR using credibility metric $\Re_D$, given by

$$\Re_D = 1 - (\frac{\left| f(D) - f(\tilde{D}) \right|}{\min(f(D), f(\tilde{D}))}) \tag{4}$$

where $\tilde{D} = D - D_f$, and D_f is the set of false data. $\Re_D$ is a posterior value calculated by comparing the filtering results of CaPa with the ground truth. Obviously, the less false data in D, the more similar $f(D)$ and $f(\tilde{D})$ will be, and the higher credibility D could achieve. Without loss of generality, we adopt average function as the aggregation function f during data analysis.

Table 2. A complete knowledge base for logical reasoning

Period	(# of events, # of logical relations)		
	Cold ($< 10\,°C$)	Warm ($10 \sim 20\,°C$)	Hot ($> 20\,°C$)
Morning	(8,10)	(4,10)	(1,10)
Noon	(3,10)	(9,10)	(4,10)

4.2 Results

According to the scheme, collected data are first processed with the quantization and representation module to generate discrete levels for further reasoning. We evaluate the effectiveness of this procedure based on data of the two time periods. The results of each processing stage are shown in Fig. 3 (from left to right), separately. For time period 1, the data are first clustered into 15 groups, which are then merged by comparing their inter-cluster distance with 2, the cluster width, generating 3 new clusters with values distributed in the feature space. Centroid of the 3 clusters are extracted to project data cluster into discrete data point, and finally mapped to linguistic state "Cold", "Warm", "Cold", respectively. Similarly, 22 clusters are generated in time period 2, which are represented with state "Hot", "Cold", and "Warm" by merging, projection, and mapping. The number of output levels (3 for both periods) are mainly determined by cluster width (2 in our simulation). With application specific knowledge, proper width can be carefully chose to roughly separate normal and false ingredient into different groups. During the clustering phase, one data point is added to all the clusters within certain distance, so some clusters depicted in Fig. 3 are similar with each other. Note that the similarity (or redundancy) is significantly reduced with the merging phase.

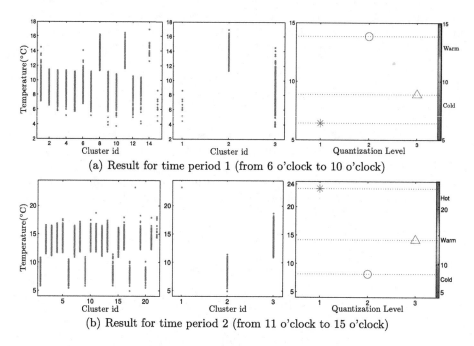

(a) Result for time period 1 (from 6 o'clock to 10 o'clock)

(b) Result for time period 2 (from 11 o'clock to 15 o'clock)

Fig. 3. Data quantization and representation results for two time periods. The result of data clustering, clusters merging, and projection are given, separately

Given the pre-established KB in Table 2, credibility of the discrete levels are assessed using logical reasoning. The normalized assessment scores are presented in Fig. 4. As expected, level with more supported events achieves higher score. Further, clusters are classified as normal or false based on their assessment score. Obviously, level 1 and 3 present the highest score (around 0.8) for time period 1, while the highest score of period 2 is level 3. Thus, cluster 1 and 3 generated from data of period 1 are labelled as normal, and cluster 3 is determined to be the normal container for time period 2. The remaining data points in the set are labelled as false.

Finally, we evaluate the performance of CLOR in Table 3. Since we assume all the unmodified measurements are reliable, the average temperature measurements are regarded as the ground truth value here. The falsification target is

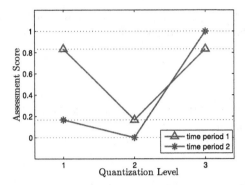

Fig. 4. Credibility assessment results of the quantization levels for the two periods

where the collusive group likes to mislead the aggregation result, and the falsification result is the real value it turns out to deviate to. Then the posterior credibility for both falsification result and CLOR output are evaluated. As illustrated in Table 3, CLOR improves the overall credibility from 0.84 and 0.83 to 0.99 for the two selected time periods.

Table 3. Performance evaluation of CLOR

Metric	Ground truth	Falsification			CLOR	
		Target	Result	Credibility	Result	Credibility
Period 1	8.85	14	10.27	0.84	8.81	0.99
Period 2	14.05	8	12.05	0.83	14.16	0.99

(**Comparison**) We consider CLOR as the first attempt to assess data credibility considering possible false forms without reputation information for typical MCS applications. Hence, we emphasize that the credibility advantage CLOR achieves is also relative to the location attestation-based scheme in [12], reputation-based scheme in [7] and provenance logic-based scheme in [13].

5   Conclusion

We have presented a Clustering and LOgical Reasoning based scheme CLOR to improve data credibility for typical MCS applications. In view of the potential data falsification threat, CLOR proposes to assess overall credibility of sensory data without the aid of reputation system. Clustering and logical reasoning techniques are introduced to exploit spatial correlation of data and logical relation of co-located events. We describe the corresponding processing and filtering module in detail. The simulation results show that CLOR can adequately improve the overall credibility under the cases considered.

Acknowledgment. This work is supported by National Key Basic Research Program of China (No.2012CB933504), National Natural Science Foundation of China under Grant Nos. 61379144, 61379145, 61402513.

References

1. Ganti, R.K., Ye, F., Lei, H.: Mobile crowdsensing: current state and future challenges. IEEE Commun. Mag. **49**(11), 32–39 (2011)
2. Gu, B., Sheng, V.S., Tay, K.T., Romano, W., Li, S.: Incremental support vector learning for ordinal regression. IEEE Trans. Neural Netw. Learn. Syst. **26**(7), 1403–1416 (2015)
3. Khan, W.Z., Xiang, Y., Aalsalem, M.Y., Arshad, Q.: Mobile phone sensing systems: a survey. IEEE Commun. Surv. Tutorials **15**(1), 402–427 (2013)
4. Reddy, S., Samanta, V., Burke, J., Estrin, D., Hansen, M., Srivastava, M.: Mobisense - mobile network services for coordinated participatory sensing. In: Proceedings of International Symposium on Autonomous Decentralized Systems (ISADS), pp. 1–6. IEEE (2009)
5. Downs, J.S., Holbrook, M.B., Sheng, S., Cranor, L.F.: Are your participants gaming the system? Screening mechanical turk workers. In: Proceedings of the SIGCHI Conference on Human Factors in Computing Systems, pp. 2399–2402. ACM (2010)
6. Wang, X., Cheng, W., Mohapatra, P., Abdelzaher, T.: Artsense: anonymous reputation and trust in participatory sensing. In: Proceedings of INFOCOM, pp. 2517–2525. IEEE (2013)
7. Amintoosi, H., Kanhere, S.S.: A reputation framework for social participatory sensing systems. Mob. Netw. Appl. **19**(1), 88–100 (2014)
8. Cheng, L., Kong, L., Luo, C., Niu, J., Gu, Y., He, W., Das, S.K.: False data detection and correction framework for participatory sensing. In: Proceedings of IEEE/ACM International Symposium on Quality of Service (IWQoS). IEEE/ACM (2015)
9. Zhou, T., Cai, Z., Xu, M., Chen, Y.: Leveraging crowd to improve data credibility for mobile crowdsensing. In: Proceedings of the 21th IEEE Symposium on Computers and Communications (ISCC). IEEE (2016)
10. Li, J., Li, X., Yang, B., Sun, X.: Segmentation-based image copy-move forgery detection scheme. IEEE Trans. Inf. Forensics Secur. **10**(3), 507–518 (2015)
11. Fu, Z., Ren, K., Shu, J., Sun, X., Huang, F.: Enabling personalized search over encrypted outsourced data with efficiency improvement. IEEE Trans. Parallel Distrib. Syst. (2015). doi:10.1109/TPDS.2015.2506573
12. Talasila, M., Curtmola, R., Borcea, C.: Improving location reliability in crowd sensed data with minimal efforts. In: Proceedings of the 6th Joint IFIP Wireless and Mobile Networking Conference (WMNC), pp. 1–8. IEEE (2013)
13. Wang, X., Fu, H., Xu, C., Mohapatra, P.: Provenance logic: enabling multi-event based trust in mobile sensing. In: Proceedings of IEEE International Performance Computing and Communications Conference (IPCCC), pp. 1–8. IEEE (2014)
14. Liu, S., Liu, Y., Ni, L., Li, M., Fan, J.: Detecting crowdedness spot in city transportation. IEEE Trans. Veh. Technol. **62**(4), 1527–1539 (2013)
15. Srivastava, M., Abdelzaher, T., Szymanski, B.: Human-centric sensing. Philos. Trans. R. Soc. Lond., Ser. A Math. Phys. Eng. Sci. **370**(1958), 176–197 (2012)
16. Alswailim, M.A., Hassanein, H.S., Zulkernine, M.: CRAWDAD dataset queensu/crowd temperature (v. 2015-11-20) (2015). http://crawdad.org/queensu/crowd_temperature/20151120

PTOM: Profit Concerning and Truthful Online Spectrum Double Auction Mechanism

Bing Chen[1], Tianqi Zhou[1]([⊠]), Ping Fu[2], and Xiangping Zhai[1]

[1] Nanjing University of Aeronautics and Astronautics, Nanjing, China
{cb_china,zhou_fly,blueicezhaixp}@nuaa.edu.cn
[2] Central Washington University, Ellensburg, USA
pingfu@cwu.edu

Abstract. In recent years, the auction has been widely applied in wireless communications for spectrum allocation. In this paper, we investigate the online spectrum double auction problem and propose a Profit concerning and Truthful Online spectrum double auction Mechanism (PTOM). Different from most previous works, we consider the dynamic arrival of primary users (PUs) and secondary users (SUs) and allow SUs to request distinct time slots for using the spectrum. By introducing the priority bid, we capture the online and location associated feature to improve the spectrum utility. Based on the priority bid, we design an efficient admission and pricing rule to improve the auctioneer's profit. Theoretical analyses are provided to prove that our mechanism has nice economic properties including individual rationality, budget-balance and resistance of time-based and value-based cheating.

Keywords: Wireless networks · Online auction · Truthful · Spectrum allocation

1 Introduction

With the rapidly increasing demand of spectrum from modern wireless equipments [1,2], the spectrum resource scarcity is becoming more and more urgent. However, spectrum utilization remains inefficient. Cognitive Radio (CR) [3] has been proposed to address this problem with the advantage of allocating spectrum flexibly and efficiently. One main feature of the CR technology is dynamic access which enables secondary users access the unused licensed spectrum at any time [4]. In the last few years, a variety of research has focused on the auction-based spectrum management. Moreover, the FCC (Federal Communications Commission) already used single-sided static auction to assign spectrum resources to wireless service providers.

Most of the previous works focused on static auction only, such as [5–9]. Zhou et al. [5] proposed the first truthful double auction mechanism TRUST. In [6], the authors presented a truthful double auction for heterogeneous spectrum units. It not only supported PUs' and SUs' diverse demands in quantity but also

© Springer International Publishing AG 2016
X. Sun et al. (Eds.): ICCCS 2016, Part II, LNCS 10040, pp. 151–162, 2016.
DOI: 10.1007/978-3-319-48674-1_14

considered the spectrum heterogeneity among SUs. However, the static auction is not fit for the condition that secondary users come in a stochastic way and an on-line [10] fashion, which is more realistic. Online auction is naturally suitable for the dynamic settings and has been concerned recently. A general model to design truthful online double auctions was presented in [11]. Wang et al. proposed the first truthful online double auction for spectrum allocation in [12]. But it modeled the conflict relationships of secondary users as a complete graph resulting in failing to capture the spatial reusability of spectrums. A location-aware online double auction mechanism was proposed in [13] to solve the spatial reusability problem. Both the two works assume that the PUs' information is static and all PUs arrive at the beginning time. To be more practical, online spectrum auction problem in which the auctioneer had no prior knowledge of primary users' activities was investigated in [14, 15]. However, they assumed each SU only demanded one time slot and paid little attention to the profit of the auctioneer.

To address the above issues, we design a profit concerning and truthful online spectrum double auction mechanism which allows buyers to request multiple time slots of one channel and take into consideration of the uncertain activities of PUs and the profit of the auctioneer. The main contributions are as follows:

1. To our best knowledge, we are the first to design an online auction mechanism which considers dynamic arrival of primary users and secondary users and allows secondary users to request multiple time slots. Meanwhile, We improve the profit of the auctioneer.
2. We propose the Priority Bid technique to recompute the secondary users' bid with the consideration of the online and location associated feature.
3. We prove our mechanism has nice economic properties including individual rationality, budget-balance and resistance of time-based and value-based cheating.

The rest of the paper is organized as follows. Section 2 introduces the system model and desired properties. Detailed mechanism design is described in Sect. 3. We provide our theoretical analysis in Sect. 4 and the simulation results are presented in Sect. 5. Finally, we conclude the paper in Sect. 6.

2   Preliminaries

2.1   System Model

Consider a Cognitive Radio Network with one primary base station (PBS) and m primary users (PUs). The primary users utilize their channels periodically and wish to lease their idle channels to secondary users (SUs) temporarily to gain profit. Meanwhile, there are some SUs in this network who are willing to purchase the usage of idle channels. Both activities of PUs and SUs are uncertain, which means that the supply of channels from PUs and the requests from SUs may come at any time. Thus, an online auction is held by the PBS to meet their demands and allocate the channels efficiently.

In our online auction model, we consider the time interval $[0, T]$ and the whole time is divided into time slots $\{0, 1, 2..., T\}$. The primary users and secondary users, all considered bidders, are the sellers and buyers in the auction. Their requests are characterized by a tuple $\theta_i = (r_i, a_i, d_i, t_i, v_i)$ where $r_i \in \{s, b\}$ indicates whether the request comes from a seller or a buyer, $a_i \in [0, T]$ is the arrival time of the request and $d_i \in [a_i, T]$ is the departure time. For a seller, the t_i is 0 and for a buyer, the t_i denotes the desired time slots. The v_i is the value of a request, which represents ask of a seller or bid of a buyer for one time slot.

One main character of spectrum auction is the temporal and spatial reusability of channels. The temporal reusability means that one channel can be leased to multiple SUs at different time slots. The spatial reusability reflects in that when SUs are located in distant areas, several SUs who don't interfere with each other can use one channel simultaneously. The online auction enables spatial reusability naturally and we capture the spatial reusability by modeling the SU network as a conflict graph $H = (N, E)$, which is adopted in most previous works [13,14]. The vertex set N of the graph is the requests from secondary users and the edge set E represents the conflict relationships. If two nodes n_i and n_j have a edge $(n_i, n_j) \in E$, they are conflicting with each other.

To make the problem more meaningful, we make the following assumptions:

1. Bidders can't misreport their desired time slot.
2. Preemption is not allowed, which means an allocated channel will not be allocated to other SUs until it is free.
3. There is no collusion among buyers and sellers.

2.2 Desired Properties

We consider the following economic properties:

1. *Truthfulness:* an online auction is truthful if for all bidders, the dominant strategy is to submit their true request. In other words, no one can improve his utility by misreporting his request $\theta_i' \neq \theta_i$.
2. *Individual rationality:* an auction is individual rationality if no winning seller is paid less than its ask and no winning buyer pays more than its bid.
3. *Budget balance:* an auction is budget balanced if the auctioneer's profit, which equals the total price paid by buyers minus the total payment to sellers, is non-negative.

3 Mechanism Design

In this section, we first introduce the **Priority Bid**, which reflects the impact of buyer's location and future opportunity on the current bid. Then we describe the admission and pricing rule.

3.1   Priority Bid

3.1.1   Expected Profit

In the online auction, a lost buyer in the current time slot can have multiple winning opportunities in the future time slots. This online feature should be considered when processing the current bid of that buyer. We assume the market clearing price in all time slots follows a stationary Gaussian process which is obtained from analysis of recent auctions. The probability density function of clearing price in time slot τ_i can be formulated as:

$$f_X(x, \tau_i) = \frac{1}{\sqrt{2\pi}\sigma(\tau_i)} exp[-\frac{(x - \mu(\tau_i))^2)}{2\sigma^2(\tau_i)}].$$
(1)

With a buyer's request $\theta_j = (r_j, a_j, d_j, t_j, v_j)$ and the average bid in the current time slot $\bar{v}$, we compute the winning possibility $\wp$ as:

$$\wp = \frac{v_j}{\bar{v} + v_j},$$
(2)

then the expected profit $\phi(\theta_j, \tau_i)$ is represented as:

$$\phi(\theta_j, \tau_i) = \sum_{k=\tau_i-a_j}^{d_j-t_j-\tau_i} \wp(1 - \wp)^k (v_j - E[X(\tau_i + k)]).$$
(3)

Because $X(t)$ is a stationary Gaussian process as assumed above, its expected value remains μ all the time and the Eq. (3) can be simplified as:

$$\phi(\theta_j, \tau_i) = \sum_{k=\tau_i-a_j}^{d_j-t_j-\tau_i} \wp(1 - \wp)^k (v_j - \mu).$$
(4)

3.1.2   Location Discount

Next, we introduce the location discount. As mentioned in [13], the recomputation of buyer's bid in an online auction should take the buyer's location into consideration. If a buyer (secondary user) locates in a critical place resulting in that many other buyers conflict with him, then the admission of such a buyer may cause a loss of spectrum utility and profit. Thus, for a buyer's request, given his interfering neighbours set δ, the location discount η is computed as:

$$\eta = \frac{v_i}{\sum v_j'/|\delta|},$$
(5)

where v_i is the buyer's bid, v_j' is his interfering neighbours' bid and $|\delta|$ denotes the size of his interfering neighbours set. This means if a user interferes with other users and his bid is not high enough (lower than the average bid of his interfering neighbours), there will be a discount on his bid. It also has a positive effect on improving the profit of the auction.

3.1.3   Bid Recomputation

With the expected profit and location discount, for a request θ_k, the priority bid in time slot τ_i can be computed as follow:

$$Pri(\tau_i, \theta_k) = (v_k - \phi(\theta_k, \tau_i))\eta. \tag{6}$$

The priority bid means that if a buyer has opportunities to win in the future or he interferes with many other buyers, his bid in current time slot will be reduced to improve the spectrum utility and profit.

3.2   Admission and Pricing

With the priority bid calculated, we are ready for making admission and pricing rules. The admission and pricing can be divided into three steps as follows:

Step1: Washing Out

In the online auction model, each time slot τ_i will generate a clearing price, which denotes the final price the buyers need to pay. The current admission price should take the historical information into consideration. The buyers who bid too low will be washed out for enhancing the efficiency of the auction and improving the profit of the auctioneer.

Here, we use the historical average clearing price as the metric. Consider the current time slot τ_i, the clearing prices of historical time slots are denoted as $p_1, p_2, \ldots, p_{i-1}$, then the average clearing price is calculated as:

$$\overline{p}_i = (\sum_{t=1}^{i-1} p_t)/(i-1). \tag{7}$$

For a buyer's request θ_k, we first check if $Pri(\tau_i, \theta_k)$ is higher than its original bid (true value). If this happens, we reset the $Pri(\tau_i, \theta_k)$ to its original bid to ensure the individual rationality. Then if the priority bid $Pri(\tau_i, \theta_k)$ is lower than $\overline{p}_i$, the request will be washed out. After the washing out process, the rest requests enter the next step.

Step2: Grouping

Two SUs who are not conflict with each other can use one channel at the same time slot. Therefore, different from traditional auction mechanisms, buyers in spectrum auction should be grouped according to their conflict relationships to reuse the channels spatially. With the conflict graph H, such process equals to finding the independent set of a graph. There are already many algorithms about this and we choose the Maximum Independent Set Algorithm [16].

We denote the buyer groups as $\psi_1, \psi_2, ..., \psi_m$ and each group is regarded as a super buyer in this auction. In the static auction, the group bid can be simply computed as $\beta_i = min\{v_{i1}, v_{i2}, ..., v_{in}\} \cdot |\psi_i|$ to make the auction truthful [5], where v_{ij} denotes the jth buyer's bid in group ψ_i, $|\psi_i|$ denotes the size of group ψ_i. However, in our online auction model, the buyers' requiring time slots are different and the interference condition and future state affect the current bid, which complicate the computation. Taking the above cases into consideration, we compute the group bid as follow:

$$\beta_i = \frac{Pri(\tau_i, \theta_{ik})t_{min}}{t_{max}}(|\psi_i| - 1) \qquad (8)$$

where $Pri(\tau_i, \theta_{ik})$ is the minimum per time slot priority bid of buyers in group ψ_i, t_{min} is the minimum requiring time slots in group ψ_i and t_{max} is the maximum requiring time slots in group ψ_i. Note that the buyer whose priority bid is the lowest in the group will lose the current auction. This is for ensuring truthfulness and the detail will be discussed in Sect. 4.

Step3: Competitive Pricing

Definition 1. *Let b be the bid vector of buyers sorted by descending order and s be the bid vector of sellers sorted by ascending order. $opt(b, s)$ denotes the optimal profit we can get from the pairs of buyers and sellers, i.e.,*

$$opt(b, s) = \underset{i}{argmax}\, i(b_i - s_i). \qquad (9)$$

Definition 2 *($ProfitExtract_R(b, s)$). The $ProfitExtract_R$ extracts the target profit R from the auction, which is defined as follows:*

(1) Sort the bid vector b in ascending order and sort the ask vector s in descending order.

(2) Find the largest k such that $k(b_k - s_k)$ is larger than R.

(3) If $k > 1$, the first k-1 sellers win the auction with payment s_k and the first k-1 buyers win the auction with price b_k.

For simplicity, We now refer to the buyer groups as buyers. The buyers' bid vector is denoted as β, the seller's bid vector is denoted as **v**. Here we can simply apply the traditional double auction mechanisms such as McAfee. However, this mechanism generates low profit for the auctioneer. Inspired by the idea of competitive auction [17], we design a mechanism that is suitable for spectrum double auction as well as generating high profit.

First, we randomly separate the buyers and sellers into two sets Ω_1 and Ω_2, and each set has the same amount of buyers and sellers. The sellers' bid vector in set one is denoted as ξ' and sellers' bid vector in set two is denoted as ξ''. Similarly, the buyers' bid vectors are denoted as ω' and ω''. Then we compute the optimal profit of each set. Let $op1 = opt(\xi', \omega')$ and $op2 = opt(\xi'', \omega'')$. By running $ProfitExtract_{op1}(\xi'', \omega'')$ on Ω_2 and $ProfitExtract_{op2}(\xi', \omega')$ on Ω_1, the winners of the auction and the price are determined.

The process including all steps in a time slot are presented in Algorithm 1.

4 Theoretical Analysis

In this section, we show that our mechanism satisfies all the desired economic properties. This is important because selfish bidders may misreport their requests

---

Algorithm 1. Auction Process

1: **for** every request θ_i in arrival requests in τ **do**
2:    **if** $Pri(\tau, \theta_i) > v_i$ and $v_i < \bar{p}$ **then**
3:       the request is washed out
4:    **else**
5:       **if** $Pri(\tau, \theta_i) < \bar{p}$ **then**
6:          the request is washed out
7:       **end if**
8:    **end if**
9: **end for**
10: group the remaining requests using maximum independent set algorithm
11: compute the group bid vector β using Equation (8)
12: randomly separate the group buyers and sellers two sets Ω_1 and Ω_2
13: divide sellers' bid vector into ξ', ξ''
14: divide buyers' bid vector into ω', ω''
15: compute optimal profit $op1 = opt(\xi', \omega')$ and $op2 = opt(\xi'', \omega'')$
16: **if** $op1 \leq op2$ **then**
17:    running $ProfitExtract_{op1}(\xi'', \omega'')$ on Ω_2
18: **else**
19:    running $ProfitExtract_{op2}(\xi', \omega')$ on Ω_1
20: **end if**
21: determine the final winners and price

---

to manipulate auction outcomes and gain unfair advantages, which is discussed in detail in [18]. The analysis includes two parts. The first part discusses the resistance of value-based cheating, which indicates that the buyers will report their values for spectrums truthfully and the second part discusses the resistance of time-based cheating, which motivates the buyers to report their arrival time and leaving time truthfully.

Lemma 1. *PTOM is individually rational.*

Proof. For a buyer's request θ_g, in the wash out step, the priority bid $Pri(\tau_i, \theta_g)$ is ensured to be less than or equal to v_g. Then in the group bid computing step, it is allocated into the group ψ_i and the group bid is computed as $\beta_i = \frac{Pri(\tau_i, \theta_{ik})t_{min}}{t_{max}}(|\psi_i| - 1)$, where $Pri(\tau_i, \theta_{ik})$ is the minimum per time slot priority bid of buyers in this group. Because the $ProfitExtract_R$ [17] is individually rational, if the group wins the auction, the payment of the group is no more than β_i. Then we have that the buyer's final per time slot payment $p' \leq \frac{\beta_i t_{max}}{(|\psi_i| - 1)t_g} \leq Pri(\tau_i, \theta_g) \leq v_g$. Thus, it is individually rational.

Lemma 2. *PTOM is budget-balanced.*

Proof. The winner determination and pricing step uses the $ProfitExtract_R$, which is proved to be budget-balanced in [17]. Thus, our mechanism is budget-balanced.

4.1   Resistance of Value-Based Cheating

Theorem 1 *([17]). The $ProfitExtract_R$ is truthful.*

Theorem 2 *([19]). A double auction is truthful if and only if it is bid-independent.*

Lemma 3. *Our online double auction is bid-independent.*

Proof. Our grouping process is based on the maximum independent set algorithm, thus it is independent of buyers' bids. When computing the group bid, we use the uniform bid strategy and the group bid is only based on the lowest bid in the group. Note that the buyer who bids lowest in the group will lose the auction and thus the group bid is still independent of all the possible winners' bids. Finally, together with Theorems 1 and 2, the pricing process is also bid-independent.

With Theorem 2 and Lemma 3, we prove that in our mechanism bidding truthfully is buyers' dominant strategy.

Lemma 4. *If a buyer wins by bidding truthfully as v_i, he will also win by bidding $\hat{v}_i > v_i$.*

Proof. Since the buyer is a winner in group g_k, v_i is not the minimum per time slot bid in group g_k. Therefore, the group bid will not be affected by a bid $\hat{v}_i > v_i$ and the buyer will still win if he bids higher.

4.2   Resistance of Time-Based Cheating

Lemma 5. *The priority bid of a request increases with the decreasing of its living time, i.e., $Pri(a_i, \theta_i) < Pri(a_i + 1, \theta_i) < ... < Pri(d_i, \theta_i)$.*

Proof. In the computation of priority bid, the winning possibility $\wp$ and the location discount δ remains unchanged over time slots. So we have $Pri(\tau_i, \theta_j) - Pri(\tau_i + 1, \theta_j) = \phi(\theta_j, \tau_i) - \phi(\theta_j, \tau_i + 1) = \sum_{k=\tau_i-a_j}^{d_j-t_j-\tau_i} \wp(1-\wp)^k(v_j - \mu) - \sum_{k=\tau_i+1-a_j}^{d_j-t_j-\tau_i} \wp(1-\wp)^k(v_j - \mu) = \wp(1-\wp)^{\tau_i-a_j}(v_j - \mu) > 0.$

We denote the untruthful request as $\hat{\theta}_i = (r_i, \hat{a}_i, \hat{d}_i, t_i, v_i)$ and prove this property by considering the following four cases:

1. $\hat{d}_i > d_i$: If the buyer wins at $\hat{d}_i > \tau > d_i$, it can't use the spectrum actually because it leaves at time slot d_i. However it still has to pay which results in a negative utility. If the buyer wins at $\tau < d_i$, according to Lemma 6, we have $Pri(\tau, \theta_i) > Pri(\tau, \hat{\theta}_i)$. Thus, according to Lemma 4, it will also win when it reports the leaving time truthfully.
2. $\hat{d}_i < d_i$: In this case, we assume the buyer wins at τ. If $\hat{d}_i - \tau < t_i$, its request won't be satisfied. If $\hat{d}_i - \tau > t_i$, we have $Pri(\tau, \theta_i) < Pri(\tau, \hat{\theta}_i)$. This is equivalent to bidding higher than its truthful value, which is discussed in the first part.

3. $\hat{a}_i > a_i$: In our mechanism, the priority bid of a request θ_i is only related to the d_i, v_i and its interference condition. So the cheating of arrival time will not influence its priority bid and only result in missing the winning opportunity, i.e., it could have won the auction at time slot $\tau < \hat{a}_i$.

4. $\hat{a}_i < a_i$: This case is similar to case 3 and has no positive effect on its auction result.

5   Simulation Results

5.1   Simulation Setup

In this section, we evaluate the performance of our mechanism using simulations. Since no prior work considers the absolutely same settings as in our work, we compare the auctioneer's (the PBS) profit with a most similar work in [14] by specifying that all primary users request a single time slot. Then, we explore the following performance metrics:

1. Buyer's satisfaction ratio: the ratio between winning buyers and total buyers.
2. Spectrum utilization rate: the spectrums sold in the auction divided by the total available spectrums.

We consider a wireless cognitive network where primary users and secondary users will arrive dynamically. The area size of the network is 800×800 and we assume two SUs are conflicting with each other if the distance between them is smaller than 300. The bids of PUs are uniformly distributed over $[10, 35]$ and the bids of SUs are uniformly distributed over $[10, 20]$. The time slot requirements of SUs are uniformly distributed over $[1, 30]$. The patient time of SU (patient time means the time between arrival time and departure time) is uniformly distributed between its desired time slots and 60 and the patient time of PU is uniformly distributed between $[50, 200]$. The arrival of PUs and SUs follow Poisson distribution with arrival rate λ_1, λ_2 and λ_1 is smaller than λ_2 so that there are more requests than demands. Also, we vary λ_1 and λ_2 to test the performance under different system load. The online auction's total time is 1000 time slots and the simulation results are averaged over 5 runs.

5.2   Results

We first compare the auctioneer's profit with VIOLET [14]. We set λ_1 to be 5 and λ_2 varies from 15 to 55 and the result is shown in Fig. 1. The profit is divided by 1000 and it will not affect the result. We can see that the profit of PTOM is much higher than the VIOLET. This is because we use priority bid to improve the utility of spectrums and use competitive pricing to collect the purchasing power of buyers.

Next we use different λ_1 to test the buyers' satisfaction ratio and spectrum utilization rate. Figure 2 shows the result of buyers' satisfaction ratio. We can see that for the same arrival rate of PUs, the buyers' satisfaction ratio decreases

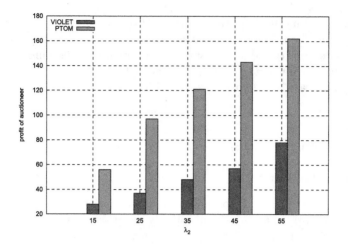

Fig. 1. Comparison of profit between PTOM and VIOLET

with the increment of buyers' arrival rate. This happens naturally because with a fixed λ_1, the competition among buyers becomes more intense with the increment of buyers. Then, for a fixed λ_2, we can see that the satisfaction ratio increases with λ_1 and this is because the competition among buyers will decrease when the supply increases.

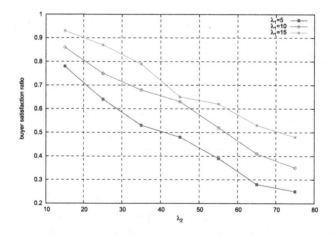

Fig. 2. Performance of buyers' satisfaction ratio

Figure 3 shows the result of the spectrum utilization rate. Here we make λ_1 larger to present the result more precisely. With a fixed λ_1, the spectrum utilization increases with the increment of buyers' arrival rate. This is because with more buyers, the buyer groups will become larger and thus the group bid

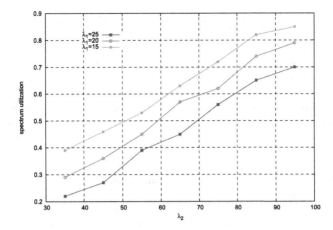

Fig. 3. Performance of spectrum utilization rate

increases. Then the successful transactions increase. Also, for a fixed λ_2, the spectrum utilization decreases with increment of λ_1 and this is quite reasonable.

6   Conclusion

In this paper, we proposed PTOM, a profit concerning and truthful online spectrum double auction. Different from previous works, we consider the dynamic arrival of primary users and secondary users. We use the novel priority bid and competitive pricing rule to improve the spectrum utilization and profit. Finally, we prove the mechanism is truthful and use simulation to show our mechanism works efficiently.

Acknowledgment. The work in this paper was partially supported by the Natural Science Foundation of Jiangsu Province (No. BK20140835), and the Postdoctoral Foundation of Jiangsu Province (No. 1401018B).

References

1. Guo, P., Wang, J., Li, B., Lee, S.: A variable threshold-value authentication architecture for wireless mesh networks. J. Internet Technol. **15**(6), 929–936 (2014)
2. Shen, J., Tan, H., Wang, J., Wang, J., Lee, S.: A novel routing protocol providing good transmission reliability in underwater sensor networks. J. Internet Technol. **16**(1), 171–178 (2015)
3. Haykin, S.: Cognitive radio: brain-empowered wireless communications. IEEE J. Sel. Areas Commun. **23**(2), 201–220 (2006)
4. Buddhikot, M.M.: Understanding dynamic spectrum access: models, taxonomy and challenges. In: Proceedings of DySPAN, pp. 649–663 (2007)
5. Zhou, X., Zheng, H.: TRUST: a general framework for truthful double spectrum auctions. In: Proceedings of IEEE INFOCOM, pp. 999–1007 (2009)

6. Zhan, S.C., Chang, S.C.: Design of truthful double auction for dynamic spectrum sharing. In: Proceedings of DySPAN, pp. 439–448 (2014)
7. Jing, T., Zhou, W.: Combinatorial auction based spectrum allocation under heterogeneous supply and demand. Comput. Commun. **60**, 109–118 (2015)
8. Yao, E., Lu, L., Jiang, W.: An efficient truthful double spectrum auction design for dynamic spectrum access. In: Proceedings of CROWNCOM, pp. 181–185 (2011)
9. Xiang, L., Sun, G., Liu, J., Wang, X., Li, L.: A discriminatory pricing double auction for spectrum allocation. In: Proceedings of WCNC, pp. 1473–1477 (2012)
10. Gu, B., Sheng, V.S., Tay, K.Y., Romano, W., Li, S.: Incremental support vector learning for ordinal regression. IEEE Trans. Neural Netw. Learn. Syst. **26**(7), 1403–1416 (2015)
11. Bredin, J., Parkes, D.C.: Models for truthful online double auctions. In: Proceedings of UAI (2005)
12. Wang, S., Xu, P., Xu, X.: TODA: truthful online double auction for spectrum allocation in wireless networks. In: Proceedings of DySPAN, pp. 1–10 (2010)
13. Chen, Y., Lin, P., Zhang, Q.: LOTUS: location-aware online truthful double auction for dynamic spectrum access. In: Proceedings of DySPAN, pp. 510–518 (2014)
14. Yi, C., Cai, J., Zhang, G.: Online spectrum auction in cognitive radio networks with uncertain activities of primary users. In: Proceedings of ICC, pp. 7576–7581 (2015)
15. Hyder, C.S., Jeitschko, T.D., Xiao, L.: Towards a truthful online spectrum auction with dynamic demand and supply. In: Proceedings of MILCOM, pp. 413–418 (2015)
16. Subramanian, A.P., Gupta, H., Das, S.R., Buddhikot, M.M.: Fast spectrum allocation in coordinated dynamic spectrum access based cellular networks. In: Proceedings of DySPAN, pp. 320–330 (2007)
17. Hartline, J.D., Goldberg, A.V.: Competitive auctions. Games Econ. Behav. **55**(2), 242–269 (2006)
18. Deek, L., Zhou, X., Almeroth, K., Zheng, H.: To preempt or not: tackling bid and time-based cheating in online spectrum auctions. In: Proceedings of INFOCOM, pp. 2219–2227 (2011)
19. Deshmukh, K., Goldberg, A.V., Hartline, J.D., Karlin, A.R.: Truthful and competitive double auctions. In: Proceedings of Algorithms-ESA, pp. 361–373 (2002)

Non-Technical Loss Fraud in Advanced Metering Infrastructure in Smart Grid

Wenlin Han and Yang Xiao$^{(\boxtimes)}$

Department of Computer Science, The University of Alabama,
342 H.M. Comer, Box 870290, Tuscaloosa, AL 35487-0290, USA
whan2@crimson.ua.edu, yangxiao@ieee.org

Abstract. Smart Grid employs Advanced Metering Infrastructure (AMI) to automatically manage metering and billing processes supporting various advanced features. Electricity theft is not limited to the traditional methods, such as bypassing power lines. In Smart Grid, adversaries could gain illegal benefit from the utility via various new ways, and we call this class of behavior as Non-Technical Loss (NTL) fraud. In this paper, we study various security issues in AMI and figure out which issues could be utilized by NTL fraud. We analyze various attacks in AMI and generalize attack tree of NTL fraud. We propose countermeasures for security issues to prevent NTL frauds.

Keywords: Smart grid security · Smart meter · Non-Technical Loss fraud · AMI

1 Introduction

Advanced Metering Infrastructure (AMI) is employed by Smart Grid to manage the metering and billing processes automatically [1–3]. Adversaries could utilize the two-way communication to gain illegal benefit. It causes economic loss to the utility, and the loss is not due to technical loss, such as electricity loss in transmission and distribution processes. We call this kind of loss as non-technical loss (NTL). This kind behavior is a fraud to the utility, and we call it NTL fraud.

According to a recent study, the utility in the U.S. lost six billion dollars per year because of NTL frauds [4]. In emerging market countries, such as China, economic loss due to NTL frauds is also huge. A recent report says that the top 50 emerging market countries lose 58.7 billion dollars each year [4].

In Smart Grid, not only the customers can steal electricity, the outside adversaries could steal electricity as well. They can control smart meters remotely to gain illegal benefit. At the same time, the traditional methods such as bypassing and slowing down meters are still applied to smart meters.

Intrusion Detection Systems (IDS) [5] are employed to secure Smart Grid, among which SCADA [6] and AMIDS [7] are popular applications. Many detection schemes have been proposed [4,8–11]. They either aim at addressing general security issues in Smart Grid or propose detection schemes to detect NTL

© Springer International Publishing AG 2016
X. Sun et al. (Eds.): ICCCS 2016, Part II, LNCS 10040, pp. 163–172, 2016.
DOI: 10.1007/978-3-319-48674-1_15

frauds. However, none of them analyze NTL fraud itself and how various attacks are related to an NTL fraud.

In this paper, we study various security issues in AMI and how they are related to NTL frauds. We generalize an attack tree for NTL frauds which describes how various attacks collaborate to commit NTL frauds. We propose countermeasures for these security issues to prevent NTL frauds.

The main contributions of this paper include:

– We analyze how various security issues relate to NTL frauds.
– We generalize an attack tree for NTL frauds.
– We propose countermeasures to prevent NTL frauds.

The rest of the paper is organized as follows: In Sect. 2, we introduce the framework of AMI. In Sect. 3, we introduce NTL frauds and the attack tree in details. We introduce security issues and propose countermeasures in Sect. 4. We conclude the paper in Sect. 5.

2   AMI Overview

AMI is an automatic pricing, metering, and billing infrastructure in Smart Grid which integrates with current state-of-the-art electronic hardware devices and software systems.

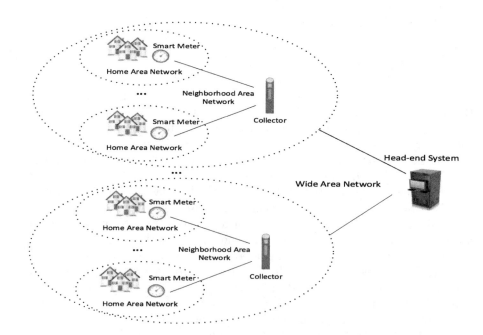

Fig. 1. The conceptual communication framework of AMI.

As shown in Fig. 1, a Home Area Network (HAN) [12] forms when home appliances and smart meters in a household join the AMI. In a community, a collector in installed to gather local information, thus forming a Neighbourhood Area Network (NAN) [1,2]. When several HANs are connected and report to the head-end systems, it is a Wide Area Network (WAN). In the U.S., the utility employs ANSI C12 serials as the communication protocol for AMI, including ANSI C12.18, 19, 21 and 22 [13].

3 NTL Fraud

In the traditional power grid, adversaries are limited to the customers of the utility. The forms of NTL fraud are limited to interrupting measurement physically. In Smart Grid, outside attackers could control smart meters remotely. The comparison between NTL fraud in the traditional power grid and Smart Grid is shown in Table 1.

Table 1. Comparison between NTL fraud in the traditional power grid and smart grid

	Adversary	Method
The traditional power grid	Inside customers	Interrupt measurement
Smart grid	Inside customers Outside attackers	Interrupt measurement Tamper meter Intrude network

We studied various security issues, vulnerabilities, threats, and attacks in AMI and generalized an attack tree for NTL fraud, shown in Fig. 2. There are three general ways to commit an NTL fraud including interrupt measurement, tamper meter, and intrude network.

4 NTL Related Security Issues and Countermeasures

After further analyzing on various security issues in Smart Grid, we identify some issues that could cause an NTL fraud, and we propose related countermeasures to deal with these issues.

4.1 Firmware Rewrite

A smart meter has firmware installed in its micro-controller. The firmware is the operating software to control the meter's operations, such as metrology and communication. If an adversary has the ability to modify or rewrite the firmware, (s)he can get full control of the meter.

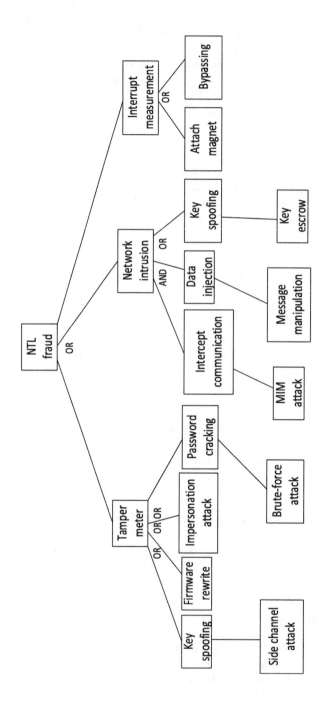

Fig. 2. The attack tree of NTL fraud showing how various attacks related to NTL fraud. "AND" means that the attacks on the left subtree are the prerequisite a NTL fraud. "OR" means that the attacks on either the left or the right subtree should occur to commit a NTL fraud.

Meter vendors often use foil seal, lockable micro-controller, and other tamper detection mechanisms to prevent smart meters from case opening, hardware probing and firmware reading. However, an adversary can sacrifice many devices to learn about the protection mechanisms. To prevent firmware manipulation, consistency checking of meter readings and sending 'heart beat' signals are often employed [14]. However, a skilled adversary with inside knowledge can still reprogram the firmware. The purpose of firmware rewrite is far beyond an NTL fraud, and usually committed by organized crime to sell meter hacking kit for profit. But, from a customer's point of view, stealing electricity without being detected might be the main concern.

To prevent firmware rewrite, the whole image of the firmware should be encrypted to ensure confidentiality. Moreover, all new firmware should be validated, authenticated, and checked for integrity upon installation. Here, we propose installing a tamper-resistant chip for each smart meter, which is a micro-controller responsible for keeping the meter secure. A RSA key pair is burned into each chip during manufacture process. The private key is used to generate symmetric session keys and never leaves the chip. Any change to the meter's firmware must be authenticated before committed. The public key pair is used to authenticate firmware update. The key size of RSA could be 2048 bits, since RSA claims that 2048-bit keys are uncrackable until 2030. Symmetric session keys are used to exchange messages in AMI since AMI protocols recommend symmetric cryptography, such as ANSI C12.21 that uses DES.

Traditionally, we talk more about how to develop security-focused software. However, the development cycle of firmware should be security-focused as well. The design vulnerabilities of firmware could be utilized by an adversary. The adversary may not be able to reprogram the whole firmware, but at least (s)he can inject code into the firmware. If the injected code is to manipulate billing time information of the meter, it is an NTL fraud. Buffer overflow might be the most commonly used vulnerability for code injection. Common methods to prevent buffer overflow in software design include: canary and non-executable (NX) bit. A canary is a random value placed between local variables and return address to alert the modification of the return address. However, smart meters have limited physical address space, so that canaries are practically guessable or cannot resist continuous probing. NX bit is to prevent a program segment from being executed. But, it is not supported by smart meter memory management. McLaughlin et al. [15] propose firmware diversity to solve buffer overflow problem, which encrypts the return address with three different keys before it is written to the stack. After further analysis, we find that the computational overhead is very large which may affect the performance of the meter. We propose encrypting the return address only once. With the support of tamper-resistant chip, we believe encrypting the return address once is enough.

4.2   Impersonation Attack

In Smart Grid, a customer may replace a legitimate meter with a fake one. A crime organization may steal firmware to clone meters and sell them for profit. A customer with inside knowledge may use a computer and special software to emulate a smart meter. If an adversary impersonates a smart meter and sends billing messages with manipulated time information, it is an NTL fraud.

Different from firmware rewrite that manipulates meters directly, impersonation attack does not affect the originality of meters. Therefore, the tamper-resistant chip cannot detect it. You may think about using the RSA key of the chip to authenticate communication each time, so that an adversary cannot impersonate a legitimate smart meter without this key. However, Public Key Infrastructure (PKI) does not fit in Smart Grid AMI. It needs support technicians to maintain the CA servers, to address various problems and to develop related documents. As reported, the ratio of support staff to certificate is 1:1000 [16]. Currently, the number of smart meters installed by utilities in the U.S. varies from 0 to 5 million, and the number keeps increasing [17]. Thus, if a utility installs 5 million smart meters with 5 million certificates, 500 support staffs will be needed to maintain normal operations. Therefore, we propose employing public keys without the need of certificates.

4.3   Password Cracking

Password cracking is where password is extracted by an adversary for a malicious purpose. In AMI, special table structures are defined in ANSI C12.19 to convey information exchanged within the networks of AMI. Passwords are bound to different roles to access these tables, which are defined by the access control policy. Passwords are stored in smart meters and they can even been transferred via messages. If an adversary obtained the passwords of these tables, (s)he could peak into the tables or even change the values of table items.

We summarize tables that could be used for NTL frauds and list them in Table 2. Table IDs 40 to 45 are security related tables. They define various security limits such as the minimum lengths of passwords and keys. They convey security information such as password, keys, and access control. Password spoofing on these tables does not directly lead to NTL frauds, but it may provide crucial information for adversaries to penetrate defense systems. Table IDs 50 to 55 are time related tables. They convey information of time, clock and TOU, which are used for timestamping, pricing, billing, and payment in AMI. If the passwords of these tables are spoofed, it could directly lead to NTL frauds. For example, if an adversary spoofs the password of the clock table, (s)he can increase or decrease the value of local clock, and thus drags a peak time billing to a non-peak time billing [13].

The minimum password length required in ANSI C12.19 is 20 bytes and they are randomly generated. Thus, for now, the password strength is fine, and it is not easy to crack the passwords by brute-force attacks on smart meters. However, ANSI C12.18 and ANSI C12.20 allow sending clear text passwords [18], and therefore, it is easy to hijack passwords in communication networks. As a countermeasure, the first thing is to band sending passwords in clear text.

Table 2. Security and time related tables in ANSI C12.19 and Password Cracking Consequences

Category	Table ID	Table Name	Description	Password cracking consequence
Security tables	40	Security Dimension Limits Table	Various security limits, such as password length limit and key length limit	Expose security strength
	41	Actual Security Limiting Table	Actually applied security limits	Exposes security strength
	42	Security Table	Stores passwords	Exposes real values of passwords
	43	Default Access Control Table	Access privileges of roles on tables by default	Exposes the bonds between tables and passwords
	44	Access Control Table	Access privileges of roles on tables	Exposes the bonds between tables and passwords
	45	Key Table	Stores encryption keys	Exposes encryption keys
Time and Time-of-use (TOU) tables	50	Time and Time-of-use (TOU) Dimension Limits Table	Various time and TOU limits, such as clock precision	Exposes timing information
	51	Actual Time and Time-of-use (TOU) Limiting Table	Actually applied time and TOU limits	Exposes timing information
	52	Clock Table	Stores local clock value	Changes this value could directly lead to NTL frauds
	53	Time Offset Table	Time offset between local time and global time	Changes this value could directly lead to NTL frauds
	54	Calendar Table	Year, month, date, daylight saving, etc.	Changes this value could directly lead to NTL frauds
	55	Clock State Table	States of local clock	Exposes local clock status

4.4 Key Spoofing

Key spoofing is where an adversary extracts encryption keys to decrypt messages or harass authentication processes. There are two general ways to spoof keys. The first way is to extract keys from smart meters, and this relies on various side channel attacks, such as side channel timing attack, cold boot attack and DMA attack. A tamper-resistant chip should be installed in each smart meter, and sensitive information, such as passwords and keys should be secured by hardware-level encryption.

The second way is to extract keys in communication networks. AMI networks employ symmetric key encryption and authentication, among which ANSI C12.21 employs DES of random token and ANSI C12.22 employs AES-EAX' with a key length of 128 bits [19]. It is well-known that DES is not secure. AES-EAX' is a choice for authentication on resource-constrained devices, but its security lacks of formal proofs for a long time. Minematsu et al. publish a formal security analysis on AES-EAX' in [20], which proves the security of AES-EAX' against a few attacks, such as chosen-message forgeries, chosen-ciphertext attack, chosen-plaintext attack, etc. However, they also prove that AES-EAX' is not secure when the cleartexts are shorter than one block. Moreover, the security of EAX' is built on AES 128 bits. If AES 128 bits is not secure, EAX' is not secure as well.

Beside security strength, another problem of symmetric keys in AMI is key management. We believe that Certificateless Public Key Cryptosystem (CL-PKC) is a good choice for AMI in Smart Grid. The concept of CL-PKC [21] was proposed by Al-Riyami in 2003. Similar to Identity-base cryptosystem, CL-PKC also needs a key generation center. However the key generation center does not have full control of the private keys. Instead, it generates partial private keys and distribute to users. The users choose secret values of their own, and combine with the partial private keys to generate their full private and public key pairs. CL-PKC does not need to maintain certificates and it does not suffer from key escrow. CL-PKC has low communication and storage cost, and thus, it is suitable for resource-constrained devices.

4.5   Man-in-the-middle Attack

Man-in-the-middle (MIM) attack in AMI is where an adversary intrudes the communication between two smart meters, or between a smart meter and the head end to make them believe they are communicating directly. MIM has no direct relationship with NTL frauds. However, MIM is a typical attack to eavesdrop sensitive information, such as passwords and keys in the networks. Thus, it often occurs with NTL frauds. As shown in Fig. 2, an adversary has to intercept communication before (s)he injects data, extracts keys or attacks time synchronization. MIM attack is one of the most typical attacks to intercept communication. Thus, to resist MIM attack, we need to build a reliable authentication mechanism. It is the same as to protect keys.

4.6   Message Manipulation Attack

Message manipulation attack in AMI is where an adversary alters the messages sent between two smart meters or between a smart meter and the head end. If the adversary alters the time related information of the billing messages, it could result in NTL frauds. For example, the adversary could alter the billing time at application layer to move it a few seconds earlier or a few seconds later, and both of the behaviors may drag the billing from a peak-time billing to a non-peak-time billing. As a countermeasure, we should compare the timestamps of the application layer and the mac layer to verify the billing time. Moreover, we should not discard the packets with obsolete timestamps directly as many existing systems do. It could result in NTL frauds. We should build up an efficient message authentication mechanism.

5 Conclusion

In this paper, we studied NTL fraud in AMI in Smart Grid. We analyzed various security issues, vulnerabilities, threats, and attacks in AMI. We eliminate unrelated attacks and generalized an attack tree for NTL fraud. We further studied each attack in the attack tree and proposed countermeasures. As a future work, we will refine the design of the proposed tamper-resistant chip for smart meters and key management in AMI.

Acknowledgement. This work was supported in part by the National Nature Science Foundation of China under the Grant 61374200, and the National Science Foundation (NSF) under Grant CNS-1059265.

References

1. Xiao, Z., Xiao, Y., Du, D.: Building accountable smart grids in neighborhood area networks. In: Proceedings of the IEEE Global Telecommunications Conference (GLOBECOM 2011), pp. 1–5, December 2011
2. Xiao, Z., Xiao, Y., Du, D.: Non-repudiation in neighborhood area networks for smart grid. IEEE Commun. Mag. **51**(1), 18–26 (2013)
3. Han, W., Xiao, Y.: IP^{2}DM for V2G networks in smart grid. In: Proceedings of the 2015 International Conference on Communications (ICC 2015), pp. 782–787, June 2015
4. Han, W., Xiao, Y.: FNFD: a fast scheme to detect and verify non-technical loss fraud in smart grid. In: International Workshop on Traffic Measurements for Cybersecurity (WTMC 2016), Xi'an, China, pp. 24–34, 30 May 2016. doi:10.1145/2903185.2903188
5. Han, W., Xiong, W., Xiao, Y., Ellabidy, M., Vasilakos, A.V., Xiong, N.: A class of non-statistical traffic anomaly detection in complex network systems. In: Proceedings of the 32nd International Conference on Distributed Computing Systems Workshops (ICDCSW 2012), pp. 640–646, June 2012
6. Gao, J., Liu, J., Rajan, B., Nori, R., Fu, B., Xiao, Y., Liang, W., Chen, C.L.P.: Scada communication and security issues. J. Secur. Commun. Netw. **7**(1), 175–194 (2014)
7. McLaughlin, S., Holbert, B., Zonouz, S., Berthier, R.: AMIDS: a multi-sensor energy theft detection framework for advanced metering infrastructures. In: Proceedings of the 2012 IEEE Third International Conference on Smart Grid Communications (SmartGridComm 2012), pp. 354–359, November 2012
8. Han, W., Xiao, Y.: NFD: a practical scheme to detect non-technical loss fraud in smart grid. In: Proceedings of the 2014 International Conference on Communications (ICC 2014), pp. 605–609, June 2014
9. Xia, X., Liang, W., Xiao, Y., Zheng, M.: BCGI: a fast approach to detect malicious meters in neighborhood area smart grid. In: Proceedings of the 2015 International Conference on Communications (ICC 2015), pp. 7228–7233, June 2015

10. Xia, X., Liang, W., Xiao, Y., Zheng, M., Xiao, Z.: Difference-comparison-based approach for malicious meter inspection in neighborhood area smart grids. In: Proceedings of the 2015 International Conference on Communications (ICC 2015), pp. 802–807, June 2015

11. Han, W., Xiao, Y.: CNFD: A Novel Scheme to Detect Colluded Non-technical Loss Fraud in Smart Grid. In: Yang, Q., Yu, W., Challal, Y. (eds.) WASA 2016. LNCS, vol. 9798, pp. 47–55. Springer, Heidelberg (2016). doi:10.1007/978-3-319-42836-9_5

12. Liu, J., Xiao, Y., Gao, J.: Achieving accountability in smart grids. IEEE Syst. J. **8**(2), 493–508 (2014)

13. Han, W., Xiao, Y.: Non-technical loss fraud in advanced metering infrastructure in smart grid. In: The 2nd International Conference on Cloud Computing and Security (ICCCS 2016), Part II. LNCS, vol. 10040, Nanjing, China (2016). doi:10.1007/978-3-319-48674-1_15

14. Skopik, F., Ma, Z., Bleier, T., Grneis, H.: A survey on threats and vulnerabilities in smart metering infrastructures. Int. J. Smart Grid Clean Energ. **1**(1), 22–28 (2012)

15. McLaughlin, S., Podkuiko, D., Delozier, A., Miadzvezhanka, S., McDaniel, P.: Embedded firmware diversity for smart electric meters. In: Proceedings of the 5th USENIX Conference on Hot Topics in Security (HotSec 2010), pp. 1–6, August 2010

16. Khurana, H., Hadley, M., Lu, N., Frincke, D.A.: Smart grid security issues. IEEE Secur. Priv. **1**(8), 71–85 (2010)

17. Utility-scale smart meter deployments: building block of the evolving power grid (2014). http://www.edisonfoundation.net/iei/Documents/IEI_SmartMeterUpdate_0914.pdf. Accessed 7 Jan 2016

18. Smartgrid, aeic ami interoperability standard guidelines for ansi c12.19, ieee 1377, mc12.19 end device communications, supporting enterprise devices, networks, related accessories (2013). http://aeic.org/wp-content/uploads/2013/07/AEIC-Guidelines-v2.1-2012-07-26clean.pdf

19. Moise, A., Beroset, E., Phinney, T., Burns, M.: EAX' cipher mode (2011). http://csrc.nist.gov/groups/ST/toolkit/BCM/documents/proposedmodes/eax-prime/eax-prime-spec.pdf. Accessed May 2011

20. Minematsu, K., Lucks, S., Morita, H., Iwata, T.: Attacks and security proofs of eax-prime. In: Proceedings of the 20th International Workshop on Fast Software Encryption, pp. 327–347, March 2013

21. Al-Riyami, S.S., Paterson, K.G.: Certificateless public key cryptography. In: Proceedings of the 9th International Conference on the Theory and Application of Cryptology and Information Security (ASIACRYPT 2003), pp. 452–473, December 2003

Compressive Sensing Based on Energy-Efficient Communication

Ke-Ming Tang[1], Hao Yang[1(✉)], Qin Liu[2], Chang-Ke Wang[2], and Xin Qiu[1]

[1] School of Information Engineering, Yancheng Teachers University, Yancheng, China
tkmchina@126.com, classforyc@163.com, xinqiu.94@gmail.com
[2] School of Foreign Language, Yancheng Teachers University, Yancheng, China
hobbyc@163.com, 77424610@qq.com

Abstract. In order to improve energy efficiency, Compressive Sensing has been employed gradually in the process of gathering data and transmitting information of sensors. In this paper, a mixed idea has been proposed based on classification for actual environments. At its heart lies a simple yet effective thought that the number of transmission of bottom sensors by no-CS schemes is less than ones by CS. In experiments, our scheme has been proved valuable and feasible.

Keywords: Compressive sensing · Energy efficiency · Wireless sensor networks

1 Introduction

To prolong the lifetime of sensor networks, Compressive Sensing (CS) [1–3], as a novel and effective signal transforming technology, has been proposed in the process of gathering data and transmitting information in WSNs [4–9]. Based on this technology, the transmitter only needs to send the sampled signals, which are obtained through a simple method of measurement with different coefficients, to the termination instead of encoding and compressing the original signals. After receiving the sampled signals, the termination can recover the original signals accurately through an effective recovery algorithm. The primary advantageous of the technique is that energy cost of top sensors which are closer to the sink is the same as ones of bottom sensors, which is valuable for the load balancing of the network.

However, this theoretical superiority is probably not embodied in actual environments, even worse. Consider N sensors are deployed in a localized region with one sink. That is, there are N sensors in the network and one of them is the sink sensor. If the number of measurement is M, then N−1 sensors must transmit their data packages M times according to CS theory.

On the contrary, the number of necessary transmission without CS only depends on the number of their hops to the sink. In practice, the number of hops is probably much less than M since the region is localized. That is, the required amount of transmission using CS is obvious more than the one without CS in practice.

As Fig. 1 shows, there are 13 sensors in the network and one sink sensor. Suppose the number of measurement is 4. The digits in parentheses denote the necessary number

© Springer International Publishing AG 2016
X. Sun et al. (Eds.): ICCCS 2016, Part II, LNCS 10040, pp. 173–179, 2016.
DOI: 10.1007/978-3-319-48674-1_16

of transmitting based on conventional methods (called no-CS). Obviously, the required amount of transmitting using CS is more than one using no-CS.

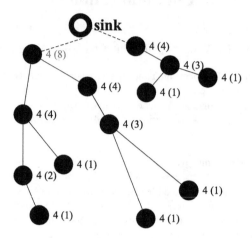

Fig. 1. The number of transmission through CS and No-CS

To address this problem, a simple yet effective mixed idea is considered, which is illustrated in Fig. 2. An essential difference is that each sensor which is close to the bottom only transmits its data to its upstream sensor using traditional methods until a certain sensor's children reaches to 3. In this case, these branch sensors only need to transmit the same number with one in parentheses. Afterwards, CS is applied in remaining sensors, the number of whose children is equal to or greater than 3.

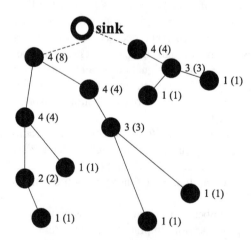

Fig. 2. The number of transmission through Mix-CS and CS

It is clearly that the number of transmitting decreases and energy cost reduces for the whole network. That is, this mixed communication framework is efficient for saving energy of sensors.

Furthermore, the accuracy of recovering the singles should be guaranteed when the number of measurement reduces. In other words, we need to know whether the received data by each measurement is effective for reconstruction based on CS.

Hence, this paper consists of two parts: mixed communication for reducing transmission and recovery guarantee for ensuring the effect of measurement. In the first part, we employ the mixed scheme to transmit data. Sensors in a certain class apply traditional schemes to send their gathering data to their head. Each head of classes accumulate all received values with measurement coefficients including its own value and send the sum to the sink using CS technique. In the second part, a sampling principle is proved to provide the stopping rule of measurement by the sink. According to this principle, the accuracy of reconstruction is guaranteed while the number of measurement reduces.

Our contributions in the paper are summarized as follows:

(a) A simple yet effective thought that both CS and no-CS are employed skillfully to mixed transmit signals, which effectively reduces energy cost of sensors.
(b) An optimization method has been given to further reduce energy in the process of communication.
(c) In experiments, our method has been proved valuable and feasible in realistic applications.

2 Compressive Sensing and Distributed Compressive Sensing

2.1 Compressive Sensing

Compressive sensing is the reconstruction of sparse signals from very few samples, which allows one to simultaneously sample and compress signals which are known to have a sparse representation in a known basis or dictionary along with the subsequent recovery by linear programming of the original signals with low or no error.

Consider C is an N-dimensional signal and Φ is M * N matrix, M < N, and set $Y = \Phi * C$, then Y is an M-dimensional vector and could be considered as M samples from C through the measurement matrix Φ. According to CS theory, it is probably that C could be reconstructed from Y if this signal can be represented as a linear combination of only K basis vectors (K < M).

For any subset I of ϕ, C could be recovered accurately with high probability by solving

$$\min \|c\|_1, \text{ such that } y = \Phi * c \tag{1}$$

Obviously, there are two aspects that need to be considered in the theory of CS. First, a special sparse transform is needed, which is used to transform the original signal C to a sparse signal. Second, a measurement matrix $\Phi(\Phi \in R^{M \times N}, M \ll N)$ should be irrelevant to the sparse transform. It is important to design an optimizing measurement matrix to increase the accuracy of CS reconstruction, which is the key point of this paper.

2.2 Distributed Compressive Sensing [10]

In practice, CS is particularly apt for distributed sensor network, where multiple singles are gathered. Distributed Compressed Sensing (DCS) is proposed to exploit both intra- and inter-signal correlation structures. This theory rests on a concept, which is called *Joint Sparsity Model* (JSM). Similar with the description of CS theory, consider signals $X\{x_1, x_2, \ldots x_j\}$, and $x_j \in R^N$ and there exists a sparse basis Ψ, in which x_j can be sparsely represented.

Based on JMS, the signal can be divided into two components, which are called sparse common component and innovations. In this case, all signals share a common sparse component while each individual signal contains a sparse innovation component. That is,

$$x_j = z + z_j, j \in \{1, 2, \ldots, J\} \tag{2}$$

With $z = \Psi\theta z$, $||\theta z||_0 = K$ and $Z_j = \Psi\theta j$, $||\theta_j z||_0 = K_j$ the sparsity of signal z is K, while the sparsity of signal z_j is K_j. Thus, the entire signals X have the same common component z and different individual components z_j.

3   Mixed Transmission Method

In WSNs, a practical application scene is that sensors are classed by the predefined rules. In inter-classes, each sensor sends its gathered data to its head h by traditional transmitting modes. After receiving data packages, h produce a new data h_{new} according to the requirements of CS technique.

It is clear for the whole network that the number of transmitting would decrease and energy cost of sensors would reduce, since (1) In general, the hops from the edge to the head in a class is probably less than the number of measurement owning to environment influences; (2) further features and characters, such as spatial-temporal correlation [4, 8], could be exploited and applied for CS technique after the head of each class receive all signals of the rest sensors in this class. As for in intra-classes, the head just need to transport its new value to the sink by CS.

It is noticed that the accuracy of reconstruction in this method is required for a higher standard than the one in traditional CS methods. Because the sink receives the processed values which is produced by the heads of classes, but not original signals or the required signals based on conventional CS.

In other words, these new values are just "intermediate data". To recover original signals accurately, intermediate data must be reconstruct very precisely to prevent error diffusion.

4   Optimization

Intuitively, the number of measurement should be large enough to recover signals high accurately according to CS theory [5]. Unfortunately, it is obvious that unnecessary transmissions would arise.

In this paper, a "good" measurement matrix and a sampling principle are presented for energy-efficient communication. It is used to guarantee incoherence between measurement matrices and transform matrices.

The set $\{-1, 0, 1\}$ is used to produce measurement matrices by probability selecting. The selection probabilities are 1/4, 1/2, 1/4 respectively. Therefore, the occurrence probability of zero in a measurement matrix is equal to one of non-zero in theory. In this case, our measurement matrix will be effective as well as random matrices [11], which are excellent candidates for incoherence between measurement matrices and transform matrices [1]. Hence, our measurement matrix is good for CS.

5   Experiments

In our simulations, after receiving all data gathered by sensors using no-CS methods, their heads transmit weighted values to the sink sensor using CS.

To display the stability of the performance in the real applications, sensors are divided into four groups, whose numbers are 100, 150, 200 and 300 respectively. To guarantee the accurate of the results, average values of the algorithms are calculated through 20 times.

We compare the mixed transmission scheme to the transmission method based on CS or no-CS. According to the Fig. 3, our method cost less energy than others. Both our scheme and no-CS are better than CS method, since the number of sensors in classes is less than the number of measurement. As the number of sensors increase, the advantages of CS are exploited and more energy is saved by our scheme.

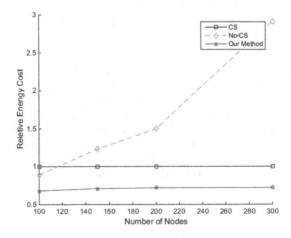

Fig. 3. Number of nodes and relative energy cost in three methods

Furthermore, we validate the state of balancing load using these three methods in Fig. 4. It is undoubted that the load of the network using CS is the optimal equilibrium; however, its energy cost is the most according to the analysis of Introduction. In practice, our mixed scheme cost the least energy as well as preserving load balancing. Meanwhile, the load of the network is stable as its scale enlarges, compared with more and more imbalanced situation using no-CS.

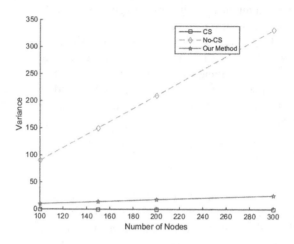

Fig. 4. Number of nodes and variance in three methods

6   Conclusion

An effective transmission scheme has been proposed to reduce energy cost of sensors and a principle of measurement has been proved to guarantee the accuracy of recovery. Sensors in each class transport their data to the head of the class, then the head process these values and convey to the sink. After the sink receives data, an optimization method is present. Experiment shows that our method outperforms natural CS in both energy cost and load balancing.

Acknowledgments. This work is supported by the National High Technology Research and Development Program (863 Program) of China (2015AA01A201), National Science Foundation of China under Grant No. 61402394, 61379064, 61273106, National Science Foundation of Jiangsu Province of China under Grant No. BK20140462, Natural Science Foundation of the Higher Education Institutions of Jiangsu Province of China under Grant No. 14KJB520040, 15KJB520035, China Postdoctoral Science Foundation funded project under Grant No. 2016M591922, Jiangsu Planned Projects for Postdoctoral Research Funds under Grant No. 1601162B, JLCBE14008, and sponsored by Qing Lan Project.

References

1. Donoho, D.L.: Compressed sensing. IEEE Trans. Inf. Theory **52**(4), 1289–1306 (2006)
2. Candes, E.: The restricted isometry property and its implications for compressed sensing. Compte Rendus de l'Academie des Sciences, Paris, vol. Series I,346, pp. 589–592 (2008)
3. Candes, E.J., Romberg, J., Tao, T.: Robust uncertainty principles: exact signal reconstruction from highly incomplete frequency information. IEEE Trans. Inf. Theory **52**(2), 489–509 (2006)
4. Roughan, M., Zhang, Y., Willinger, W., Qiu, L.: Spatio-temporal compressive sensing and internet traffic matrices. IEEE/ACM Trans. Netw. **20**(2), 662–676 (2015)
5. Charbiwala, Z., Chakraborty, S., Zahedi, S., Kim, Y., Srivastava, M.B., He, T., Bisdikian, C.: Compressive oversampling for robust data transmission in sensor networks. In: INFOCOM (2015)
6. Feng, C., Au, W.S.A., Valaee, S., Tan, Z.: Compressive sensing based positioning using RSS of WLAN access points. In: INFOCOM, pp. 1–9 (2014)
7. Wani, A., Rahnavard, N.: Compressive sampling for energy efficient and loss resilient camera sensor networks. In: INFOCOM (2014)
8. Yang, H., Huang, L.S., Xu, H., Yang, W.: Compressive sensing based on local regional data in wireless sensor networks. In: WCNC (2015)
9. Wang, J., Tang, S., Yin, B., Li, X.Y.: Data gathering in wireless sensor networks through intelligent compressive sensing. In: INFOCOM (2015)
10. Duarte, M.F., Sarvotham, S., Baron, D., Wakin, M.B., Baraniuk, R.G.: Distributed compressed sensing of jointly sparse signals. Asilomar Conf. Signals. Sys. Comput. 1537–1541 (2005)
11. Gilbert, A., Indyk, P.: Sparse recovery using sparse matrices. Proc. IEEE **98**(6), 937–947 (2010)

Energy-Efficient Data Collection Algorithms Based on Clustering for Mobility-Enabled Wireless Sensor Networks

Jian Zhang[1(✉)], Jian Tang[2], and Fei Chen[3]

[1] School of Computer and Software, Nanjing University of Information Science and Technology (NUIST), Nanjing 210044, China
jianzhang_neu@163.com
[2] Research Institute of Computing Technology, Beifang Jiaotong University, Beijing 100025, China
tjan001@126.com
[3] School of Digital Media, Jiangnan University, Wuxi 214122, China
chenf@jiangnan.edu.cn

Abstract. Energy consumption has always been a challenging issue in wireless sensor networks (WSNs). In this paper, we consider the collaboration optimization problem for load balancing with mobility-assisted features. In particular, we present a cluster-based network structure, in which sensor nodes are partitioned into layers according to transmission radius. Based on a distributed scheme for clustering and cluster heads, rendezvous points (RPs) are introduced and searched through greedy algorithm with geometrical relationship between a specific cluster head and its members. After that, mobile sinks are then introduced to replace the cluster heads in the place where RP has been found. Furthermore, mean squared error of energy in a cluster is used to reduce transmitted packets. Considering another factor, i.e. the data packet, of energy consumption model, we propose an energy optimal algorithm through the quantization approach to balance network load and allocate node's transmitted traffic. Finally, we analyze the cluster lifetimes in different scenarios and achieve balance to save significant energy.

Keywords: Wireless sensor network · Rendezvous points · Quantization · Mobile sinks

1 Introduction

Benefitting from the advantage of low cost, rapid deployment, self-organization capability and cooperative data processing, WSNs have been proposed as a practical solution for a wide range of applications [1]. One of the most important issues is how to prolong the network lifetime [2].

Basically, there exist two types of architectures. One is named as clustered architecture, such as LEACH [3], and their variants [4]. This architecture cannot guarantee that a cluster head is physically closer to the sink. Consequently, it may consume more energy to transmit data to the sink. The other one is called multi-hop layered

© Springer International Publishing AG 2016
X. Sun et al. (Eds.): ICCCS 2016, Part II, LNCS 10040, pp. 180–191, 2016.
DOI: 10.1007/978-3-319-48674-1_17

architecture [5]. Following the layered structure, PMRC structure is proposed in [6]. Clearly, due to the energy constraint on each sensor, it is very challenging to prolong the network lifetime, particularly in static WSNs. Sensors that are one hop away from the sink often become the bottleneck of the WSNs because they consume more energy forwarding the data from other sensors, and competing for the same radio resource. Experimental data in [7] show that the residual energy of sensor nodes far away from the sink has also up to 93 % of the initial energy, when sensor nodes near the sink runs out of energy.

In this paper, we discuss the problem of optimal collaboration for load balancing with mobility-assisted elements. In particular, we improve the PMRC structure where sensor nodes are partitioned into layers according to their distances. RPs are solved through greedy algorithm with geometrical relationship between cluster head and its members. In order to realize optimal/suboptimal energy consumption at every round, mobile sinks are then introduced to replace the role of cluster heads in the place where RPs has been found. In a cluster, active nodes are selected with mean squared error of energy to reduce energy consumption and balance the energy of cluster.

The rest of the paper is organized as follows. In Sect. 2, we will describe the Relation works. In Sect. 3, the problems and algorithms of network construction are discussed. In Sect. 4, loading analysis is presented and simulation results are discussed in Sect. 5. Section 6 concludes the paper.

2 Relation Works

Many energy efficient routing algorithms have been proposed to prolong network lifetime for WSNs [8, 9]. Because of the inevitable hot spot phenomenon [10] for the fact of fixed sinks, mobility strategies for WSNs are introduced in [11–14].

Due to difficulty for sensor devices powered by irreplaceable batteries to recharge, energy efficient network layer algorithms are designed to prolong the home network lifetime [15]. Generally sensor nodes close to sink node will have more traffic load to transmit than others, which will cause degraded network performance. By introducing mobility into WSNs, network performance such as energy efficiency, lifetime can be distinctly improved [16]. In [17], to optimize the trajectory of the mobile anchor node, a path planning scheme is presented to ensure that the trajectory of the mobile anchor node could improve network performance. [18] allows multiple mobile base stations to be deployed along the periphery of the sensor network field and develops some algorithms to dynamically choose the locations of base stations in order to improve network lifetime. In addition, energy efficient low-complexity algorithms are presented to determine the locations of the base stations. [19] utilizes mobile elements capable of carrying data mechanically to achieve significant energy saving by selecting a subset of nodes as the RPs. Using MIMO and Multi-hop, a controllable mobile sink that reduces the energy consumed in sensor transmission is also adopted for data collection in [20].

3 Network Construction

3.1 PMRC Structure

In [6], a rotational scheme for clustering is composed of nodes located in the same layer and within the transmission range of the cluster head located in one layer up, shown in Fig. 1.

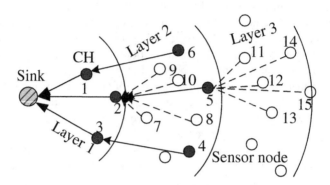

Fig. 1. PMRC structure

3.2 Distributed Clustering Based on Mobile Sinks

Although PMRC structure utilizes rotational schemes, that is, cluster heads in the same cluster rotating to receive and forward data and clusters at the same layer rotating to sense data, the problem of energy hole is still presence. Base on clustering and layering of PMRC, mobile sinks are introduced to restructure the network topology. According to the number of clusters in the same layer, corresponding mobile sinks whose trajectories are constrained on a series of concentric circles with radius $nR(n = 1, 2, \cdots, \max(layers))$ are needed. More specifically, sensor nodes in the first layer keep communication with the original fixed sink. Generally, as far as clusters in layer i, cluster heads for layer $i + 1$ are changed into source sensor nodes, and one mobile sink will be appointed as the cluster head. The metric is presented in Fig. 2.

In order to realize optimal energy consumption and load balancing, optimal RPs is necessary. However, how to look for so many suitable RPs? The following example illustrates this process of looking for RPs. Given one cluster of PMRC in Fig. 2, node 1 belongs to layer i as cluster head, and nodes 2, 3 and 4 in layer $i + 1$ as the members in the cluster. Connections between two nodes and cluster head are made to obtain arc $\overset{\frown}{AB}$ such that all intersections that connections between other nodes and cluster head with the circle belong to arc $\overset{\frown}{AB}$. Now, point O as shown in Fig. 3 is the optimal point as RP for a mobile sink taking minimum energy consumption and load balancing into account.

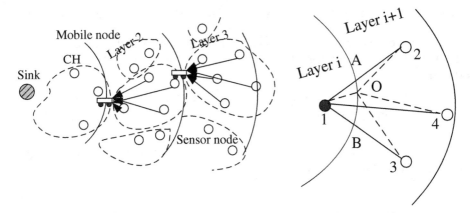

Fig. 2. Network structure based on PMRC   **Fig. 3.** RP in cluster based on PMRC

However, to find such a point O is not easy. A discrete search algorithm is used here. We divide arc $\overset{\frown}{AB}$ into N equally spaced sub-arcs, $\left\{ \overset{\frown}{AE_1}, \overset{\frown}{E_2E_3}, \cdots, \overset{\frown}{E_{N-1}B} \right\}$, and then, one point set $\{A, E_1, \cdots, E_{N-1}, B\}$ is produced. Finally, greedy algorithm is utilized to search RP in $\{A, E_1, \cdots, E_{N-1}, B\}$ under the condition with following the equation:

$$\min \sum_{i=1}^{N} (d_i^{\alpha} + c)$$

$$s.t. \frac{1}{N} \sqrt{(E_1 - \overline{E})^2 + (E_2 - \overline{E})^2 + \cdots + (E_N - \overline{E})^2} \leq \Phi \tag{1}$$

where N is the amount of the cluster, E_i is the residual energy of node i, $\overline{E}$ denotes average energy of the member of the cluster.

Note that the algorithm searches the suboptimal value associating with acceptable energy consumption. With the energy consumption of sensor nodes and the mobility of mobile sinks, clusters are restructured at every round according to the distance between mobile sinks and sensor nodes in the sense of the above equation.

4   Energy Consumption Analysis

4.1   Cluster Member Selection

In order to balance energy distribution, mobile nodes transmit selection information to each sensor node in their cluster. When the members receive the information from cluster head, the node determine whether to participate in data collection. So we can obtain C_M^K subsets in a cluster including M members, where $K = 1, 2, \cdots, M$.

$$S_K = \{S_{i1}, S_{i2}, \cdots, S_{iK} \mid S_{i1}, S_{i2}, \cdots, S_{iK} \in C, K = 1, 2, \cdots, M, i = 1, 2, \cdots, K\} \quad (2)$$

where C denotes sensor nodes in a cluster, S_{iK} is a sensor node in the cluster. In these subsets, we can use greedy algorithm again to select a subset to satisfy the following expression:

$$\min\left(\frac{1}{K}\sqrt{(E_1 - \overline{E})^2 + (E_2 - \overline{E})^2 + \cdots + (E_k - \overline{E})^2}\right) \quad (3)$$

In this way, only a part of members in a cluster transmit packets at every round. This is meaningful for dense deployment.

4.2   Energy Consumption

In this paper, we analyze the characteristic of the load distribution without considering the energy consumption of idle listening. The energy consumption in network construction phase is mainly consume to receive control packets, including *CP*, *HP*, *BP* and *CCP*. And then energy consumption E_{ci} in layer i is calculated as follows

$$E_{ci} = (cs \times cn + bs \times bn + hs \times hn + ccs \times ccn)E_{elec} \quad (4)$$

Assuming static sensor nodes evenly distribute within the circular area with density ρ, and each source node generates and sends λ bits every unit time. We also define the distance between two layers is equal to the transmission range r. So we could use the expression $\rho\pi(d^2 - (d - r)^2)$ to calculate the number of sensor nodes N_i in layer i. As a consequence, the energy consumption of each cluster in layer i at unit time is computed by

$$E_{tik} = \varepsilon\lambda \sum_{l=1}^{N_i} \left((x_l - x_{RPi})^2 + (y_l - y_{RPi})^2\right)^{\alpha/2} + N_i E_{elec} \quad (5)$$

Therefore, the total energy consumption of layer i is expressed by

$$\begin{aligned}
E_{ti} &= \sum_{k=1}^{n} E_{tik} + \frac{E_{ci}}{T_r} \\
&= \varepsilon\lambda \sum_{k=1}^{n} \sum_{l=1}^{N_i} \left((x_l - x_{RPi})^2 + (y_l - y_{RPi})^2\right)^{\alpha/2} + N_i n E_{elec} \\
&\quad + \frac{(cs \times cn + bs \times bn + hs \times hn + ccs \times ccn)E_{elec}E_{elec}}{T_r}
\end{aligned} \quad (6)$$

Where $1/T_r$ is the number of network construction at unit time. Meanwhile, sensor nodes in the layer one have to only transmit packets to the sink. In this sense, the energy consumption of nodes in layer one is calculated by

$$E_{t1} = \varepsilon\lambda \sum_{p=1}^{\rho\pi r^2} \left((x_p - x_{Sink})^2 + (y_p - y_{Sink})^2\right)^{\alpha/2} \tag{7}$$

4.3   Quantization

In order to further reduce the consumption of network energy under some constraints (e.g. accuracy), quantization technologies [21] are usually exploited.

We consider the reading of each node as follows

$$z_{i,t} = a_{i,t} + n_{i,t} \tag{8}$$

Where $a_{i,t}$ is the received signal, and $n_{i,t}$ stands for the measurement noise samples followed Gaussian distribution with parameters $N(0, \sigma^2)$. The quantized measurement $z_{i,t}$ of sensor is presented as

$$D_{i,t} = \begin{cases} 0 & -\infty < z_{i,t} < \eta_1 \\ 1 & \eta_1 < z_{i,t} < \eta_2 \\ \vdots & \vdots \\ L-1 & \eta_{(L-1)} < z_{i,t} < \infty \end{cases} \tag{9}$$

Where η_i in the Eq. (9) indicates the quantization thresholds, $L = 2^m$ is the number of quantization levels. The probability that $D_{i,t}$ takes value l is given by

$$p(D_{i,t} = l) = Q\left(\frac{\eta_l - a_{i,t}}{\sigma}\right) - Q\left(\frac{\eta_{l+1} - a_{i,t}}{\sigma}\right) \tag{10}$$

Where $Q(\cdot)$ is the complementary distribution of the standard normal distribution. In this sense, we design an optimal algorithm (i.e. Eq. (11)) to realize the goal of cluster-based minimum energy consumption under the condition of load balancing and packet allocation.

$$\min \sum_{i=1}^{N} (d_i^\alpha + c_i) \cdot l_i$$

$$s.t. \frac{1}{N}\sqrt{(E_1 - \overline{E})^2 + (E_2 - \overline{E})^2 + \cdots + (E_N - \overline{E})^2} \le \Phi \tag{11}$$

$$p(D_{i,t} = l) = Q\left(\frac{\eta_l - a_{i,t}}{\sigma}\right) - Q\left(\frac{\eta_{l+1} - a_{i,t}}{\sigma}\right)$$

5 Simulations

In this section, we evaluate the performance of schemes implemented with MATLAB. To evaluate the performance of the proposed mobile sinks based on the PMRC structure, extensive simulations have been conducted. As expressed in Sect. 4, main parameters used in the simulation are listed in Table 1.

Table 1. Simulation parameters

Parameters	Value	Parameters	Value
α	2 or 4	ε	10 J/bit /m^2
r	20 m	λ	400 bps
ρ	0.0088 /m^2	Number of nodes	100
T_r	200	Fixed sink	(0,0)
E_0	0.5 J	E_{elec}	50 nJ/bit
E_{amp}	0.0013PJ/bit.m^4	E_{DA}	5 nJ/(bit · signal)

In addition, we make use of parameters in [22]: cs(145 bits), hs(169 bits), bs(205 bits) and cs(259 bits) hn = 3.4, bn = 6.79, ccn = 3.4. For convenience, we name our algorithm mobile sinks based RP with quantization, short for MS-RP-Q.

We compare three metrics, No rotation, MS-RP-Q and PMRC. Seen from Fig. 4, because of no rotation and transmission and reception function of cluster head, especially for the nodes in layer one, the death for first node occurs at the earliest. Although PMRC uses rotation strategy for cluster or cluster head, the number of sensor nodes are elected as cluster head is limited after all. We introduce mobile sinks based on PMRC on the boundary of layers to replace the cluster head, so sensor nodes only transmit packets to the mobile sinks. Therefore, the lifetime of MS-RP-Q is longer.

Residual energy of every node is presented between PMRC and MS-RP-Q in Figs. 5 and 6, when the first node is dead. Seen from Fig. 6, the first node's death of PMRC appears and its ID is 71. Moreover, some nodes' residual energy will be exhausted, such as ID19, ID 49, ID50, ID60, ID72, and so on. The reason is that they are all in the first layer and transmit more packets. In addition, the distribution of residual energy of PMRC is nonuniform, and the node of the most residual energy existing in layer 4 is more than 0.45 J. At this point, residual energy of MS-RP-Q in Fig. 6 manifests that the numerical value is 0.42 around. From Fig. 7, as far as different layers, the tendency of residual energy is linear growth for PMRC, nodes of inlayer consume more energy, resulting in energy exhausting, when nodes in layer 4 sense is source node whose function is only sense and transmit data to the cluster head in the upper layer. None of them is responsible of relaying packets. Due to the introduction of mobile sink, the roles of cluster head in PMRC are changed into normal nodes. The energy consumption of every node is impacted by the distance between the node and its cluster head, i.e., mobile sink. Amplitude of variation of the line of MS-RP-Q is less. Therefore the residual energy in every layer is equivalent in general.

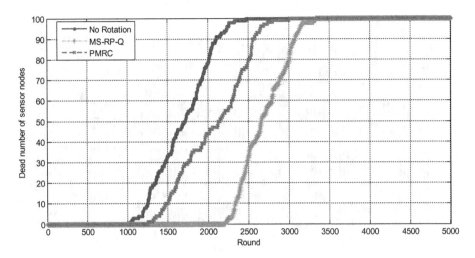

Fig. 4. Sensor nodes' death in network lifetime

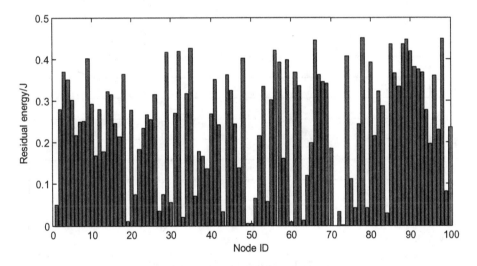

Fig. 5. Residual energy of layered structure

As shown in Fig. 8, we simulate the average energy consumption per packet. The average energy consumption per packet of MS-RP-Q decreases gradually. Because of greedy algorithm for optimal energy and choice of collection nodes in a cluster, the total packets with different density are not very different, and the total energy con-

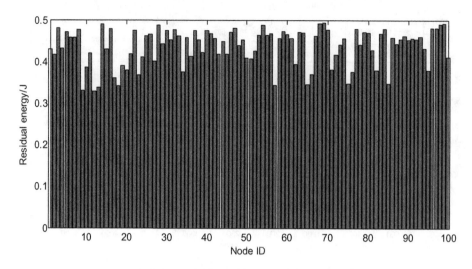

Fig. 6. Residual energy of MS-RP-Q

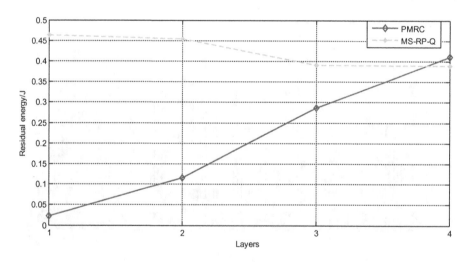

Fig. 7. Residual energy of every layer

sumption in different density is also almost equal. In order to demonstrate the selection scheme proposed in Sect. 4, Fig. 9 shows the results of PMRC and MS-RP-Q. It is evident that difference of average number of cluster members grows as the density increases.

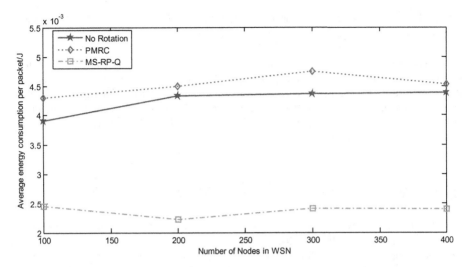

Fig. 8. Energy consumption per packet with different density

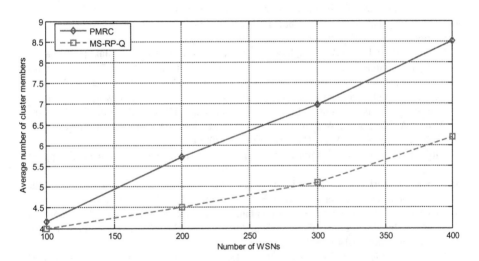

Fig. 9. Average number of cluster members

6 Conclusions

We improve the mobile sink-based structure where sensor nodes are partitioned into layers according to their distances. Firstly, RPs are searched through greedy algorithm with geometrical relationship between cluster head and its members to efficiently deal with the boundary problem. Secondly, to realize the goal of optimal/suboptimal energy consumption, optimize mechanism is proposed based on the mobile sink for a cluster. Thirdly, cluster member selection scheme is presented using greedy algorithm from a series of appointed subsets. In the end, the goal of optimal/suboptimal energy consumption in WSNs is realized.

Acknowledgement. This work was supported by Foundation of Nanjing University of Information Science and Technology (N1885014194, 2241101201101, 2201101401063), and A Project Funded by the Priority Academic Program Development of Jiangsu Higher Education Institutions(PAPD) and Jiangsu Collaborative Innovation Center on Atmospheric Environment and Equipment Technology (CICAEET) fund. In addition, the authors thank the anonymous reviewers for their constructive comments.

References

1. Akyildiz, I.F., Su, W., Sankarasubramaniam, Y., Cayirci, E.: A survey on sensor networks. IEEE Commun. Mag. **40**(8), 102–114 (2002)
2. Tashtarian, F., Hossein, Y.M.M., Sohraby, K., Effati, S.: On maximizing the lifetime of wireless sensor networks in event-driven applications with mobile sinks. IEEE Trans. Veh. Technol. **64**(7), 1 (2014)
3. Heinzelman, W.R., Sinha, A., Wang, A., Chandrakasan, A.P.: Energy-scalable algorithms and protocols for wireless microsensor networks, vol. 6, pp. 3722–3725 (2000)
4. Younis, O., Fahmy, S.: Distributed clustering in ad-hoc sensor networks: a hybrid, energy-efficient approach, vol. 1(3), pp. 629–640 (2004)
5. Salarian, H., Chin, K.W., Naghdy, F.: An energy-efficient mobile-sink path selection strategy for wireless sensor networks. IEEE Trans. Veh. Technol. **63**(5), 2407–2419 (2014)
6. Yang, M., Wang, S., Abdelal, A., Jiang, Y., Kim, Y.: An improved multi-layered architecture and its rotational scheme for large-scale wireless sensor networks. In: 4th IEEE Consumer Communications and Networking Conference, CCNC 2007, pp. 855–859 (2007)
7. Wadaa, A., Olariu, S., Wilson, L., Eltoweissy, M., Jones, K.: Training a wireless sensor network. Mob. Netw. Appl. **10**(1–2), 151–168 (2005)
8. Patil, M., Biradar, R.C.: A survey on routing protocols in wireless sensor networks, pp. 86–91 (2012)
9. Kumar, D.: Performance analysis of energy efficient clustering protocols for maximising lifetime of wireless sensor networks. IET Wirel. Sens. Syst. **4**(1), 9–16 (2014)
10. Heinzelman, W.: Energy-efficient communication protocols for wireless microsensor networks. In: Proceedings of the Hawaii International Conference on Systems Sciences, Hawaii, pp. 3005–3014 (2000)
11. Kim, H.S., Abdelzaher, T.F., Kwon, W.H.: Minimum-energy asynchronous dissemination to mobile sinks in wireless sensor networks. In: Proceedings of the International Conference on Embedded Networked Sensor Systems, vol. 13(9), pp. 193–204 (2010)
12. Gandham, S.R., Dawande, M., Prakash, R., Venkatesan, S.: Energy efficient schemes for wireless sensor networks with multiple mobile base stations. In: Global Telecommunications Conference, GLOBECOM 2003, vol. 1, pp. 377–381. IEEE (2004)
13. Marta, M., Cardei, M.: Improved sensor network lifetime with multiple mobile sinks. Pervasive Mob. Comput. **5**(5), 542–555 (2009)
14. Kim, J.W., In, J.S., Hur, K., Kim, J.W.: An intelligent agent-based routing structure for mobile sinks in WSNS. IEEE Trans. Consum. Electron. **56**(4), 2310–2316 (2010)

15. Wang, J., Yin, Y., Zhang, J., Lee, S., Sherratt, R.S.: Mobility based energy efficient and multi-sink algorithms for consumer home networks. IEEE Trans. Consum. Electron. **59**(1), 77–84 (2013)
16. Liu, W., Lu, K., Wang, J., Xing, G., Huang, L.: Performance analysis of wireless sensor networks with mobile sinks. IEEE Trans. Veh. Technol. **61**(6), 2777–2788 (2012)
17. Ou, C.H., He, W.L.: Path planning algorithm for mobile anchor-based localization in wireless sensor networks. IEEE Sens. J. **13**(2), 466–475 (2013)
18. Azad, A.P., Chockalingam, A.: Mobile base stations placement and energy aware routing in wireless sensor networks. In: IEEE Wireless Communications and Networking Conference, WCNC 2006, vol. 1, pp. 264–269 (2006)
19. Xing, G., Wang, T., Xie, Z., Jia, W.: Rendezvous planning in wireless sensor networks with mobile elements. IEEE Trans. Mob. Comput. **7**(12), 1430–1443 (2008)
20. Danpu, Z., Kailin, D.: Energy-efficient transmission scheme for mobile data gathering in wireless sensor networks. Wirel. Commun. Zigbee Automot. Inclination Meas. Chin. Commun. **10**(3), 114–123 (2013)
21. Cao, N., Brahma, S., Varshney, P.K.: Target tracking via crowdsourcing: a mechanism design approach. IEEE Trans. Signal Process. **63**(6), 1464–1476 (2014)
22. Qiao-Qin, L.I., Liu, M., Yang, M., Chen, G.H.: Load-similar node distribution for solving energy hole problem in wireless sensor networks. J. Softw. **22**(3), 451–465 (2011)

The Optimal Trajectory Planning for UAV in UAV-aided Networks

Quan Wang$^{(\boxtimes)}$ and Xiangmao Chang

College of Computer Science and Technology,
Nanjing University of Aeronautics and Astronautics, Nanjing, China
{quanwang,xiangmaoch}@nuaa.edu.cn

Abstract. Wireless Sensor Networks (WSNs) have been increasingly deployed in harsh environments for special applications such as ecological monitoring and Volcano monitoring. Harsh environments can easily cause the network to be unconnected, which lead to unable to collect data by multi-hops. The development of the Unmanned Aerial Vehicles (UAVs) makes it possible to collect data from ground sensor nodes by UAVs, and the UAV trajectory planning is necessary for energy conservation and data collection efficiency. The challenge of the trajectory planning is keeping the trajectory as short as possible while ensures the communication constraints to be satisfied. In this paper, we formulate the optimal UAV trajectory planning problem to a mixed integer programming (MIP) problem, and develop a heuristic algorithm to find a feasible solution to this problem. There are four steps of our scheme: initialization, rotation, optimization and smooth. The simulation results show that our trajectory planning scheme can shorten the length of the UAV's trajectory while satisfy communication constraints for every sensor nodes.

Keywords: UAV-aided networks · Trajectory planning · Communication constraints

1 Introduction

Recently, wireless Sensor Networks (WSNs) have been increasingly deployed in harsh environments for special applications such as ecological monitoring, Volcano monitoring, etc. In these cases, it's inconvenient to change batteries for key nodes, environmental corrosion and inclement weather can damage the nodes easily. These factors can cause the network to be unconnected with high probability, which lead to unable to collect data by multi-hops. The development of the Unmanned Aerial Vehicles (UAVs) opens a new window for collecting data from ground sensor nodes by UAVs [1]. UAV-aided networks, composed by some sensor nodes and one or several UAVs, are seemed to be an effective approach for data collecting in harsh environments. In the UAV-aided network, the UAV acts as a mobile collector and collect data by gliding around the sensing field. Since the UAV is powered by batteries or limited fuel, a well planed trajectory is

© Springer International Publishing AG 2016
X. Sun et al. (Eds.): ICCCS 2016, Part II, LNCS 10040, pp. 192–204, 2016.
DOI: 10.1007/978-3-319-48674-1_18

critical for saving UAV's energy. Moreover, a well planed trajectory can reduce the data collection cycle, so that to reduce the data collection delay.

Many UAV trajectory planing schemes have proposed in recent years. [2] proposed a scheme to improve the data collection efficiency by using the cooperation between UAV and WSN. [3] proposed an algorithm that chose some sensor nodes as waypoints to reduce the trajectory length and energy consumption. [4] planed a trajectory with the kinematic and dynamic constraints based on the solution of the Traveling Salesperson Problem (TSP). [5] planed a shortest trajectory for the UAV to pass all collection zone by using genetic algorithm and optimal rapidly-exploring random trees. [6] proposed a algorithm based on grid division to increase the efficiency of the path planning. [7] planned a trajectory that can maximum the amount of collected data by using knowledge of machine learning [8,9] and Particle Swarm Optimization algorithm. In these works, only part of sensor nodes (the cluster heads) which are separated far away from each other can communicate with the UAV, while other sensor nodes need to transmit their data to the cluster heads. This will bring heavy load to the cluster heads. Moreover, there are situations that the density of sensor nodes are too sparse to form clusters. In this situation, the UAV needs to collect data from each sensor node. This brings new challenges for planing the trajectory of the UAV.

A sensor node only can transmit its data to the UAV when the UAV flies over the communication range of the sensor node. When the trajectory is fixed, the transmission period that each sensor node can transmit data to the UAV is fixed too. Thus, the data volume that can be transmitted is limited. In order to transmit all data in the memory of each sensor node to the UAV, the trajectory should be well planed to assure enough transmission period for each sensor nodes. This issue is ignored by existing works ([2–6]) due to they assume the UAV only collect data from cluster heads which are separated far away.

In this paper, we investigate the problem that how to plan a shortest UAV's trajectory as well as satisfy the communication constraints. Firstly, we formulate the *Optimal Trajectory Planning for UAV (OTP)* problem as an optimal problem with graph constraints and communication constraints. We indicate that this problem is NP-hard as it is a mixed integer programming (MIP) problem, thus it is unpractical to get an exact solution. So, we propose a heuristic algorithm to solve this problem. we have taken the position of sensor nodes and the data size into the consideration of the trajectory planning. The trajectory is consisted by some edges that join some waypoints in wayponits set. Our algorithm contains four major steps to get the waypoints set: Initialization, Rotation, Optimization, Smooth. The former three steps are based on the position information and data size of the sensor nodes, we smooth the shape turn in the trajectory in fourth step. The simulation results show that our trajectory planning scheme not only reduces the length of the UAV's trajectory but also satisfies communication constraints for every sensor nodes.

The rest of the paper is organized as follows: In Sect. 2, we introduce the network model. In Sect. 3, we give the definition of the problem, and formulate the problem as an optimal problem. We propose our optimal trajectory planning scheme in Sect. 4. In Sect. 5, we conduct simulation experiments and discuss the results. We conclude our work in Sect. 6.

2   Network Model

Figure 1 shows the topology of the UAV-aided network, which is composed by a set of sensor nodes and a UAV, which the sensor nodes are homogeneous like the assumption in [10]. All sensor nodes are randomly deployed in a 2D sensing field. They probably can not form a connected network, due to reasons such as some key nodes burn out their energy or environmental factors. So it is unlikely to collect data by multi-hops. The UAV acts as a mobile data collector by gliding around the sensing field with a pre-planed trajectory. The average speed of the UAV is labeled as v and the flying hight is fixed to be h. Each sensor node can communicate with the UAV when their distance is less than R. As an example, field test results from [11] show that, the average delivery ratio and the throughput between a sensor node and the UAV are about 85 % and 13 Kbps respectively when their distance is less than 400 m. When there are more than one sensor nodes can communicate with the UAV simultaneously, in order to avoid the interference, they need to communicate with the UAV one by one.

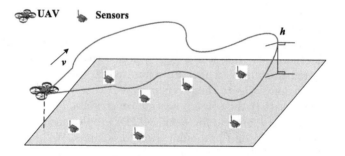

Fig. 1. The UAV-aided network topology

The UAV-aided network is delay-tolerant, each sensor node generates data periodically and stores the data in its memory. The UAV glide around the sensing field and collects data from each sensor node in cycle.

3   Problem Description and Analysis

3.1   Problem Definition

We now define the *Optimal Trajectory Planning for UAV (OTP)* problem in UAV-aided networks as follows.

Definition 1. *In a UAV-aided networks, given coordinates of all sensor nodes, the speed of the UAV and the sample rate of each sensor node, the OTP problem is to find the shortest trajectory of the UAV, such that all data in the memory of each sensor node can be collected by the UAV when the UAV flies over the sensor node.*

3.2 Problem Analysis

we assume that there is an UAV-aided network with N homogenous sensor nodes which denoted by set $\mathcal{N}$, randomly deployed in a rectangular sensing field. The UAV glides in the plane $\mathcal{Q}$ with the altitude of h meters, the UAV starts from the starting point $\mathcal{O}$, and returns to $\mathcal{O}$ after finishing data collection. The communication range of each sensor node in the plane $\mathcal{Q}$ is a circle with the radius R_{com}. Because the trajectory is planning in the plane $\mathcal{Q}$, we project the rectangular sensing field and the position of sensor nodes into $\mathcal{Q}$.

In order to describe the trajectory of the UAV, the projected sensing field is partitioned into small grids of size $a \times a$. Let graph $G = (V, E)$ represents the partitioned sensing field, where V is the set of all grids' vertex, and represents the alternative waypoints set of the UAV. The alternative edges set E is the set of edges between each waypoint i with its neighbor waypoints, which are the waypoints that are only a or $\sqrt{2}a$ away from i in V. The edges which are joined to a waypoint i are the available trajectories to next waypoint when the UAV locates at the position of i, and the UAV's trajectory is consisted by the edges in E.

The purpose of this paper is designing a shortest trajectory for the UAV, such that all sensor nodes' data can be collected after the UAV finishes a sorties. So, we give the formulation as follow:

$$minimize \sum_{e \in E} w_e \chi_e \tag{1}$$

subject to

$$\chi_e \begin{cases} = 1 & if\ e\ in\ the\ trajectory \\ = 0 & otherwise \end{cases} \quad \forall e \in E \tag{2}$$

Constraints: $\mathcal{G}$ constraints; $\mathcal{C}$ constraints

Equation (1) is our objective which is minimizing the length of UAV's trajectory, where w_e is the weight of the edge e and equals to a or $\sqrt{2}a$, χ_e is the indicator of whether a edge e in the trajectory. The set of the edges which $\chi_e = 1$ is denoted by E', and V' is endpoints set of the edges in E'. There are two constraints in this optimal problem, the first one is the graph constraints $\mathcal{G}$, the other one is the communication constraints $\mathcal{C}$. We give $\mathcal{G}$ as follow:

$\mathcal{G}$ constraints:

$$V' \bigcap \mathcal{O} \neq \emptyset \tag{3}$$

$$\lambda(\delta(i)) = 2 \quad \forall i \in V' \tag{4}$$

$$\lambda(\delta(S)) \geq 2 \quad \forall S \subset V' : 2 \leq |S| \leq |V'| - 2 \tag{5}$$

$$\lambda(F) = \sum_{e \in F} \chi_e \tag{6}$$

where Eq. (3) ensures the UAV's starting point $\mathcal{O}$ must in the planned trajectory. $\lambda(F)$ is the sum of χ_e where $e \in F$, and $\delta(S)$ is the set of edges with exactly one endpoint in S. Eq. (4) ensures that only two edges are joined with a waypoint i, one edge is the incoming edge and the other is the outgoing edge. Equation (5) is sometimes called the cycle elimination constraint and ensures that no cycle is found in the trajectory, S is the subset of V' with between 2 and $|V'| - 2$ members [4]. The graph constraints ensures the planned trajectory is available for the UAV, but maybe not all data can be collected. The trajectory also need satisfies the communication constraints, they are given as follow:

$\mathcal{C}$ constraints

$$\theta_j(e) \in R^+ \qquad \forall e \in E, j \in \mathcal{N} \tag{7}$$

$$0 \le \theta_j(e) \le \begin{cases} 1 & \text{if } \chi_e > 0 \text{ and } \sigma_j(e) = 2 \\ 1/2 & \text{if } \chi_e > 0 \text{ and } \sigma_j(e) = 1 \\ 0 & \text{otherwise} \end{cases} \tag{8}$$

$$\forall e \in E, j \in \mathcal{N}$$

$$\sum_{j=1}^{N} \theta_j(e) \le 1 \qquad \forall e \in E \tag{9}$$

$$\sum_{e \in E} w_e \theta_j(e) \ge \frac{M_j}{R_u} \times v \qquad \forall j \in \mathcal{N} \tag{10}$$

where $\theta_j(e)$ is the variable that represents the ratio of the e's length that allocated to the sensor node j, and it is a positive real number. Equation (8) is the value range of the $\theta_j(e)$, where the $\sigma_j(e)$ is the number of e's the endpoints that in the communication range of sensor node j. When e in the trajectory and $\sigma_j(e) = 2$, the upper bound of the $\theta_j(e)$ is 1, it means the whole edge can be allocated to the j to communicate with the UAV. Equation (9) ensures that the sum of the ratios which are allocated to all sensor nodes must less than 1 for each edge e. Equation (10) ensures that all sensor nodes' data can be collected, the left expression is the total length of all the section of edges that are allocated to j, and the right expression is the lower limit of contact length that the UAV can collect all data of j. M_j is the amount of data of sensor node j, R_u and v are the data receiving rate and UAV's velocity, respectively.

Note that, because we assume that M_j, R_u and v are constants, the right expression of Eq. (10) can be replaced by a constant RL which means the required length of the UAV in each sensor node's communication range. We replace the Eq. (10) by follow equation:

$$\sum_{e \in E} w_e \theta_j(e) \ge RL \qquad \forall j \in \mathcal{N} \tag{11}$$

Overview Eqs. (1) to (11), we have formulated the OTP problem to a mixed integer programming (MIP) problem. When grids' side length a is small, the cardinality of the alternative edges set E is very large. Due to the computational complexity of running the optimization problem, it is less practical to give the exact solution to OTP when the network has a large number of alternative edges. So, we have proposed a heuristic algorithm that efficiently finds a near-optimal solution of OTP problem.

4 Proposed Solution

In order to solve the OTP problem, we have considered the position and data size of the sensor nodes in the trajectory planning for the UAV. Our algorithm contains four major steps, and can be outlined as follow:

1. Initialization: determine the collection sequence and the initial waypoints pair for each sensor node by using the position information and data size of the sensor nodes.
2. Rotation: rotate the waypoints pairs between each two neighbor sensor nodes in the collection sequence.
3. Optimization: get inflected waypoint for each sensor node, remove some unreasonable waypoints in the trajectory, and update the waypoints.
4. Smooth: make the trajectory available for the UAV by smoothing the shape turn.

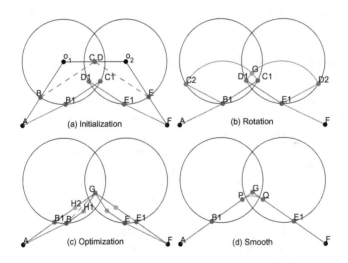

Fig. 2. The operation of waypoints

Then, we give the details of each step in our algorithm.

Step One: Initialization

The UAV starts from the starting point $\mathcal{O}$ and collects sensor nodes' data based on the collection sequence, and finally returns to $\mathcal{O}$, so we firstly need to determine the collection sequence. This is a Traveling Salesperson Problem (TSP) which consisted by the position of all sensor nodes and $\mathcal{O}$, and we solve it by the existing TSP solution [12]. After getting the collection sequence, we can get the initial trajectory for the UAV by joining $\mathcal{O}$ and the position of sensor nodes based on the sequence.

Let i represents the i_{th} sensor node in the collection sequence. The i's waypoints pair includes the waypoints WP_i^s and WP_i^o which are the position of start and over communication between the UAV and i. There are two cross points between the initial trajectory and sensor node i's transmission circle TC_i, if TC_i has no intersection with TC_{i-1} and TC_{i+1}, the cross points are temporary waypoints pair (WP_i^s, WP_i^o). But if the TC_i has intersection with TC_{i+1}, we let the central point of the intersection area be the WP_i^o or WP_{i+1}^s. As shown in the Fig. 2(a), the broken line $A \to o_1 \to o_2 \to F$ is a part of the initial trajectory, and the left circle is the sensor node o_1's communication range, the right circle is o_2's. So, the temporary waypoints pair of o_1 and o_2 are (B, C) and (D, E), and the waypoints C, D coincide.

As shown in Fig. 2(a), after getting the temporary waypoints pair (B, C) for sensor node o_1, the distance between B and C $DIS(B, C)$ maybe different with the required length RL that in Eq. (11). When $DIS(B, C) \le RL$, we let the temporary waypoints pair be the initial waypoints pair, but if $DIS(B, C) > RL$, we translate the line $\overline{BC}$ to the $\overline{B1C1}$, where the $DIS(B1, C1)$ equals RL, and $B1, C1$ on the circumference of o_1's transmission circle, then let the translated waypoints pair be the initial waypoints pair. We assume the initial waypoints pair don't change when $DIS(B, C) \le RL$, it will leads the sensor node's contact length less than the RL, we will deal with it in the successor step.

Step Two: Rotation

After the translation in step one, we find that the WP_i^o and WP_{i+1}^s maybe not coincide. There are a distance between them, we need to reduce the distance for the purpose of minimum the length of the trajectory. As shown in Fig. 2(b), the $(B1, C1)$ and $(D1, E1)$ are the waypoints pairs of sensor nodes o_1 and o_2, $C1$ and $D1$ are not coincide. Then, we let $B1$ and $E1$ be the center to form two circles, and the part which in the communication range of o_1 and o_2 are two arcs $\overparen{C1C2}$ and $\overparen{D1D2}$. The points on the arc $\overparen{C1C2}$ and $\overparen{D1D2}$ are the points set that can be used to replace $C1$ and $D1$. Then, we need to find the points pair in two arcs that minimum distance between two arcs. This process can be formulated to a optimal problem with two constraints. For the consideration of the computational complexity, we do not use the exact solution. We get a alternative points AP set for each arc, and find the pair that minimum the distance between two AP sets.

Assume that there are two arcs arc_1 and arc_2, the alternative points set for each arc has seven members, and AP_{arc}^i means the i_{th} member of arc's AP set, we get the AP set for two arcs as follow:

1. the cross points of circles that two arcs belonged, the cross points denoted by $AP^1_{arc_1,arc_2}$ and $AP^2_{arc_1,arc_2}$. If there are no cross points, we set them to infinite.
2. the cross points of the arcs and the line which joined the center of two arcs, $AP^3_{arc_1}$ and $AP^3_{arc_2}$
3. the cross points of the arcs and the line which joined the center of one arc and two endpoints of the other one arc, $AP^{4,5}_{arc_1}$ and $AP^{4,5}_{arc_2}$
4. the endpoints of arcs, $AP^{6,7}_{arc_1}$ and $AP^{6,7}_{arc_2}$

Note that, if anyone of the above alternative points isn't on the arc, we set it to infinite. After getting the AP set for each arc, we find the pair that minimum the distance between two arcs in two AP sets. Then,we use the points pair replace the original waypoints. As shown in Fig. 2(b), we let G replace $C1$ and $D1$.

Step Three: Optimization
As mentioned in step two, the distance between sensor node i's waypoints pair may be less than RL, so, we find a waypoint WP^z_i in the mid-perpendicular of the waypoints pair, and let the sum of $DIS(WP^s_i, WP^z_i)$ and $DIS(WP^z_i, WP^o_i)$ equals RL for sensor node i. We can understand it in Fig. 2(c), the waypoints pair (B, G) is the waypoints pair after rotation, we assume that the distance of it less than RL, so we let $H1$ as the inflected point to satisfy the communication constraints, the waypoints in transmission circle change from (B, G) to $(B, H1, G)$. If $DIS(WP^s_i, WP^o_i) \geq RL$, we chose the midpoint of the initial waypoints pair as the WP^z_i.

After the former process, we can get a waypoints set WPS which is consisted by the waypoints in all sensor nodes. The trajectory is formed by join the starting points $\mathcal{O}$ and the waypoints in WPS, the trajectory satisfies the communication constraints, but there are still some unreasonable waypoints in the trajectory. As shown in the Fig. 2(c), we will find the broken line $A \rightarrow B \rightarrow H1 \rightarrow G$ is unreasonable, because if we join A and G directly, it will not only reduces the length trajectory but also ensures all data can be collected. So, we remove some unreasonable waypoints by joining the waypoints to the successor waypoints.

The process as follow: for the i_{th} waypoint WPS_i in waypoints set, join the WPS_i with the final waypoint (WPS_f) in the WPS, if the length of intersection of line and all transmission circles is greater than RL, then directly join the two waypoints, and using the cross points of the line and circles update the waypoints from WPS_i to WPS_f. If the line don't satisfy the communication constraints, then try to the former waypoint of WPS_f until to the WPS_{i+1}. This process is done by all waypoints in WPS.

Step Four: Smooth
The trajectory in Fig. 2(c) is piecewise linear and not available for a UAV, the UAV can't take a shape turn because of the kinematic and dynamic constraints. So we adopt the C^1 continuous Bézier Curve [13] to smoothing the trajectory, and three control points are needed to make a quadratic Bézier curve. As shown in Fig. 2(d), there is a shape turn in G, we choose points P and Q in line $\overline{AG}$ and $\overline{GF}$, and let P, G, Q as the control points to smooth the turn. The distance

between the neighbor control points denoted by DC. The smoothed trajectory is different with the original trajectory, in order to reduce the difference of them, DC should be relatively small. We get the DC as follow:

$$DC = min\{D_{min}/2, DC_{upper}\} \qquad (12)$$

where D_{min} is minimum distance between two neighbor waypoints in WPS, DC_{upper} is the upper bound of the DC and it is a constant.

Algorithm 1 shows the pseudo-code of our optimal trajectory planning algorithm.

Algorithm 1. Optimal Trajectory Planning for the UAV

---

input: the position information of the network and data size

1: get the collection sequence by solving TSP
2: get the temporary waypoints pair for each sensor node
3: **for** each sensor node i **do**
4:     **if** $DIS(WP_i^s, WP_i^o) > RL$ **then**
5:         translate the waypoints pair
6:     **end if**
7: **end for**
8: **for** each sensor node i and its successor node j **do**
9:     **if** WP_i^o and WP_{i+1}^s not coincide **then**
10:        rotate the WP_i^o and WP_{i+1}^s
11:    **end if**
12: **end for**
13: **for** each sensor node i **do**
14:    **if** $DIS(WP_i^s, WP_i^o) < RL$ **then**
15:        get the WP_i^z
16:    **end if**
17: **end for**
18: **for** each waypoint WPS_i in WPS **do**
19:    **for** from waypoint WPS_f to the WPS_{i+1} **do**
20:        **if** can join WPS_i and WPS_j **then**
21:            update the waypoints between WPS_i and WPS_j
22:            break loop
23:        **end if**
24:    **end for**
25: **end for**
26: **for** each shape turn in trajectory **do**
27:    smooth the shape turn
28: **end for**

output: Trajectory of the UAV

---

5   Simulation

We evaluate the performance of the proposed OTP algorithm for different data size and density of sensor nodes. We compared our OTP strategies against the initial trajectory which get from the TSP solution in the trajectory length and the ratio of the sensor nodes which all data can be collected.

We simulated a 500 m × 500 m sensing field with sensor nodes, and sensor nodes randomly deployed in the sensing field. We assume that all sensor nodes have the same amount of data need to be collected, in the other word, the required length of all sensor node are same. The parameters used in our simulation are listed in Table 1. Note that, the transmission radius R_{com} of the senor node in the plane Q adopted from [2], which has shown the PRR in this range is higher than 98 % by real experiments. Each simulation result is averaged over 50 random deployments of sensor nodes.

Table 1. Simulation Parameters Value

Parameter	Description	Value
SF	Sensing field size	500 m × 500 m
R_{com}	Transmission radius	40 m
N_s	Number of all sensors	$\{5, 10, \ldots, 50\}$
M	Data size	$\{0, 2, \ldots, 20\}$ KB
v	UAV's speed	10 m/s
R_u	Data receiving rate	20 Kbps
DC_{upper}	Upper bound of DC	5 m

Figure 3 has shown the generation of the UAV's trajectory step by step in condition of 10 sensor nodes and data size equals 10 KB, the red circles are the communication ranges of sensor nodes. The blue triangles, green diamonds and black circles in sensor node i's communication range are WP_i^s, WP_i^z, WP_i^o, respectively. The red pentagram and blue curve are the UAV's initial position and trajectory. The number in the communication range is the order of the sensor nodes in the collection sequence, and the black curve is the solution of the TSP. After initialization, rotation, optimization and smooth, the terminal trajectory of the UAV is shown in Fig. 3(d).

Figure 4(a) shows the trajectory length comparison of OTP and TSP with different value of data size. The trajectory length of the OTP increases as the data size increases because the data size take apart in the trajectory planning of the OTP, but the trajectory length of the TSP is unrelated with the data size. We can see that the trajectory length of the OTP is less than the TSP when data size less than a critical value for both condition that the number of sensor nodes equals 10 and 30, and the difference of the trajectory length decreases as the data size increases from 0 to the critical value, when the data size larger than the critical value the trajectory length of the OTP is larger than the TSP, and the difference of the trajectory length increases as the required length increases. The reason of this phenomenon is that the OTP sacrifices the trajectory length for collecting data. We can understand it by Fig. 4(b).

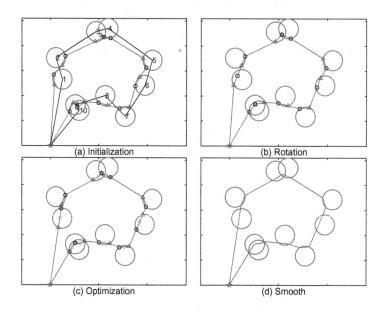

(a) Initialization   (b) Rotation

(c) Optimization   (d) Smooth

Fig. 3. The generation of the UAV's trajectory ($N_s = 10, M = 10\,\text{KB}$). (Color figure online)

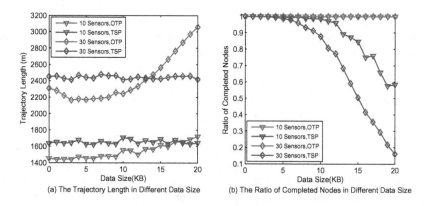

(a) The Trajectory Length in Different Data Size   (b) The Ratio of Completed Nodes in Different Data Size

Fig. 4. The performance of OTP and TSP in different data size: (a) the UAV's trajectory length; (b) the ratio of the sensor nodes that all data can be collected

Figure 4(b) shows the ratio of the sensor nodes that all data can be collected. We can see that the ratio of completed node decreases as the data size increases for the TSP. Because the neighbor two communication ranges have intersection, the contact length between the UAV and the sensor node will less than the 2 times radius, and it will divide equally to two sensor nodes. It directly causes the length in the sensor nodes' communication range too short to collect all data when data size is large. But all sensor nodes can satisfy the communication constraints in the OTP algorithm.

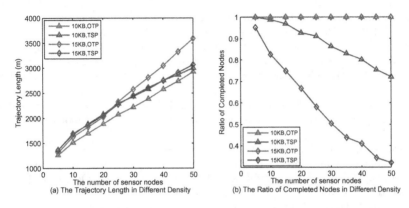

Fig. 5. The performance of OTP and TSP in different density of the sensor nodes: (a) the UAV's trajectory length; (b) the ratio of the sensor nodes that all data can be collected

Figure 5 show the trajectory length and ratio of completed nodes in different density of the sensor nodes. We can see that both the trajectory length of OTP and TSP increase as the the number of sensor nodes increases, because more sensor nodes means the UAV needs visit more position. We can find that the ratio of the completed nodes decreases as the density of the sensor nodes increases for the TSP. Because the sensing field is a bounded area, more sensor nodes will cause the distance between two neighbor sensor nodes decrease, and finally cause the contact length decreases. But the ratio of completed nodes of OTP always equals 1, and the trajectory length of the OTP always less than TSP when data size equals 10 KB.

Overview Figs. 4 and 5, the OTP scheme not only reduces the trajectory length of the UAV but also ensures all sensor nodes' data can be collected.

6   Conclusion

In this paper, we investigate the optimal trajectory planning for the UAV, and has formulated the *Optimal Trajectory Planning for the UAV (OTP)* problem to a mixed integer programming (MIP) problem. Because of the computational complexity to solve the MIP problem, we propose a heuristic algorithm to solve this problem. We have considered the information of position and sensor nodes data size in the process of trajectory planning. The proposed algorithm contains four major step of our scheme: Initialization, Rotation, Optimization, Smooth. And the simulation results show that the trajectory planned by our scheme not only can keep shortest but also ensures all data of sensor nodes can be collected.

References

1. Abdulla, A.E., Fadlullah, Z.M., Nishiyama, H., Kato, N., Ono, F., Miura, R., et al.: An optimal data collection technique for improved utility in uas-aided networks. In: 2014 IEEE Proceedings on INFOCOM, 736–744. IEEE (2014)
2. Martinez-de, J.R., Dios, J.R., Lferd, K., de San Bernabé, A., Núnez, G., Torres-González, A., Ollero, A.: Cooperation between uas and wireless sensor networks for efficient data collection in large environments. J. Intell. Robot. Syst. **70**(1–4), 491–508 (2013)
3. Ho, D.-T., Grøtli, E.I., Sujit, P., Johansen, T.A., Sousa, J.B.: Optimization of wireless sensor network and uav data acquisition. J. Intell. Robot. Syst. **78**(1), 159–179 (2015)
4. Wichmann, A., Korkmaz, T.: Smooth path construction and adjustment for multiple mobile sinks in wireless sensor networks. Comput. Commun. **72**, 93–106 (2015)
5. Alejo, D., Cobano, J.A., Heredia, G., Martínez-de Dios, J.R., Ollero, A.: Efficient trajectory planning for WSN data collection with multiple UAVs. In: Koubâa, A., Martínez-de Dios, J.R. (eds.) Cooperative Robots and Sensor Networks 2015. SCI, vol. 604, pp. 53–75. Springer, Heidelberg (2015). doi:10.1007/978-3-319-18299-5_3
6. Wang, C., Ma, F., Yan, J., De, D., Das, S.K.: Efficient aerial data collection with uav in large-scale wireless sensor networks. Int. J. Distrib. Sens. Netw. **2015**, 19 (2015)
7. Sujit, P., Lucani, D.E., Sousa, J.B.: Bridging cooperative sensing and route planning of autonomous vehicles. IEEE J. Sel. Areas Commun. **30**(5), 912–922 (2012)
8. Gu, B., Sheng, V.S., Tay, K.Y., Romano, W., Li, S.: Incremental support vector learning for ordinal regression. IEEE Trans. Neural Netw. Learn. Syst. **26**(7), 1403–1416 (2015)
9. Gu, B., Sun, X., Sheng, V.S.: Structural minimax probability machine. IEEE Trans. Neural Netw. Learn. Syst. (2016)
10. Xie, S., Wang, Y.: Construction of tree network with limited delivery latency in homogeneous wireless sensor networks. Wireless Pers. Commun. **78**(1), 231–246 (2014)
11. Teh, S.K., Mejias, L., Corke, P., Hu, W.: Experiments in integrating autonomous uninhabited aerial vehicles (uavs) and wireless sensor networks (2008)
12. Kaur, D., Murugappan, M.: Performance enhancement in solving traveling salesman problem using hybrid genetic algorithm. In: Fuzzy Information Processing Society: NAFIPS 2008. Annual Meeting of the North American, pp. 1–6. IEEE (2008)
13. Yang, K., Sukkarieh, S.: 3d smooth path planning for a uav in cluttered natural environments. In: IEEE/RSJ International Conference on Intelligent Robots and Systems, IROS 2008, pp. 794–800. IEEE (2008)

Wi-Play: Robust Human Activity Recognition for Somatosensory Game Using Wi-Fi Signals

Xiaoxiao Cao[1,2(✉)], Bing Chen[1,2], and Yanchao Zhao[1,2]

[1] College of Computer Science and Technology,
Nanjing University of Aeronautics and Astronautics, Nanjing, China
{xiaoxiao556655,cb_china,yczhao}@nuaa.edu.cn
[2] Collaborative Innovation Center of Novel Software Technology
and Industrialization, Nanjing, China

Abstract. Existing somatosensory games mainly use vision-based methods, which are affected easily by Line-of-Sight (LOS), occlusions, complex background, wearable devices, and so on. To address these limitations, we propose Wi-Play, a robust human activity recognition system using Wi-Fi signals. Based on the intuition that a specified activity introduces a unique pattern in the time-series of waveform for Channel State Information (CSI-waveform), Wi-Play leverages the unique pattern in the CSI-waveform values as the indicator of human activities. Wi-Play consists of two commercial Off-The-Shelf (COTS) WiFi devices, a TP-LINK TL-WR842N router as the transmitter and an Intel NUC D54250WYKH laptop as the receiver. As our major contributions, we propose a human activity detection algorithm for the extraction of CSI-waveform, build multi-classifiers to recognize human activities, and implement a real-time human activity recognition system using a series of novel technologies. Wi-Play achieves more than 88.3 % average recognition accuracy for recognizing human activities.

Keywords: Channel state information · Human activity · WiFi signals

1 Introduction

Recently human activity recognition has been a hot topic in academia and industry, which greatly promotes Human-Computer Interface (HCI), especially the development of somatosensory game. Existing human activity recognition technologies are mainly categorized into four classes: vision-based systems [1,2], hardware-based systems [3], sensor-based systems [4], and WiFi-based systems. Existing somatosensory games mainly use vision-based methods to recognize human activities, such as Leap Motion [1], Kinect [2]. However, vision-based systems have the fundamental limitations of LOS and brightness, and violate human privacy potentially. Sensor-based systems can get high-accuracy recognition but require human to wear sensors, and it is very inconvenient for the reason that users have to wear. There are also many other device-free localization works using sensor nodes in the literature [5,6]. Existing hardware-based

© Springer International Publishing AG 2016
X. Sun et al. (Eds.): ICCCS 2016, Part II, LNCS 10040, pp. 205–216, 2016.
DOI: 10.1007/978-3-319-48674-1_19

systems mainly utilize dedicated hardware to recognize human activities and they are costly and impractical to deploy. Recently, WiFi-based systems, such as Wi-Vi [7], CARM [8], are proposed leveraging wireless signals for recognizing human activities. WiFi-based systems are complementary to existing vision-based systems, hardware-based systems and sensor-based systems. They break the limitations of LOS, provide better coverage, ensure the security of privacy [9], and do not require human to wear any sensors.

In this paper, we propose Wi-Play, a robust human activity recognition for somatosensory game using Wi-Fi signals. Wi-Play is based on the intuition that human activities introduce multi-path distortions and each human activity generates a unique pattern in the time-series of CSI-waveform values. As is shown in Fig. 1, Wi-Play consists of two commercial COTS WiFi devices, namely, a router as transmitter, and a laptop as receiver. The transmitter continuously sends signals and the receiver continuously receives signals. When human activities happen, on the receiver end, Wi-Play detects human activity based on how CSI-waveform changes and achieves the recognition by matching extracted features to the best-fit profile. CSI-waveform contains the information of wireless phenomenon, including Doppler shift, fading and multi-paths in the given scenario. When human activities are performed, the Wi-Fi signal propagation path would be changed due to the effect of wireless phenomena. Based on the phenomena, we quantitatively build the correlation between CSI-waveform variance and a specific human activity. Wi-Play uses the correlation to recognize human activity. These testing activities are listed in Table 1.

To implement human activity recognition using Wi-Fi signals, we need to solve the following three challenges. The first challenge is how to denoise effectively. The original CSI-waveform is too noisy to be used for human activity recognition. Even in an absolutely static room without any human activity, CSI-waveform still suffers from air pressure temperature and surrounding electromagnetic noises. Moreover, the inherent state changes in Wi-Fi devices, such as transmission rates, transmit power levels and CSI reference levels, which result in burst and impulse noises in CSI-waveform. Traditional filters based denoising methods, such as low-pass filters or median filters cannot denoise effectively. Based on the observation that all CSI streams generated by human activity in all subcarriers of each TX-RX antenna pair are correlated, we leverage Principal Component Analysis (PCA) to extract useful variance in CSI-waveform.

The second technical challenge is how to automatically detect the start and end of human activity. As we know, in the absence of human activity, the CSI-waveform contains random noises and consequently extracted CSI streams using PCA are smooth. During human activities, collected CSI values in all subcarriers are correlated, and the mean absolute deviation (MAD) of CSI-waveform achieved by PCA becomes higher than those of no-activity. Based on the intuition mentioned above, we propose a human activity detection algorithm that utilizes the CSI-waveform of all transmit-receive (Tx-Rx) antenna pairs to detect the approximate start and end of human activity by continuously comparing MAD to threshold.

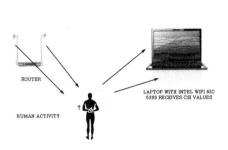

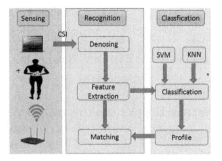

Fig. 1. Wi-Play system   **Fig. 2.** Framework of Wi-Play

The last technical challenge is how to build classification models for human activities. To address the challenge, we propose a multi-classifiers model method. Wi-Play utilizes Support Vector Machine(SVM) based on conventional features extracted from CSI-waveform and k-nearest neighbor classification(KNN) using CSI-waveform as the feature to build classifiers for multiple Tx-Rx antenna pairs. Then Wi-Play calculates the final result by voting on the decisions of all classifiers.

The main contributions of this paper can be summarized as follows:

- We propose a human activity detection algorithm to automatically identify the start and end of human activities using a sliding window approach.
- We propose multi-classifiers model to recognize human activities using SVM and KNN methods. Wi-Play recognizes human activities by voting on the decisions of all classifiers from training samples for all Tx-Rx antenna pairs.
- We implement a real-time human activity recognition system for somatosensory game using a series of novel technologies. We conduct experiments in two different-sized rooms to demonstrate that Wi-Play accurately achieve more than 88.3 % average recognition accuracy for recognizing human activities.

The rest of this paper is organized as follows. In Section 2, we introduce the related work. Section 3 gives an overview of wireless technology and system framework relevant to our work. The detailed system design and methodology are in Sect. 4. Section 5 describes the implementation and experimental results of Wi-Play. Finally, the conclusions and future work are given in Sect. 6.

2   Related Work

In this section, we introduce some prior works on human activity recognition related to our work, including Dedicated Radio Frequency(RF) Hardware-based, Received Signal Strength(RSS) based and CSI-based.

Dedicated RF Hardware-Based: Dedicated RF Hardware-based systems mainly utilize special dedicated hardware to transmit and receive custom modulated signals for human activity recognition [3,7,10]. WiSee [3] applies USRPs

Table 1. Human activities

AC1	AC2	AC3	AC4	AC5	AC6	AC7
Hand forward	Hand left	Hand right	Hand up	Hand down	Sit down	Stand up

to extract Doppler effect to recognize human gestures. WiTrack [10] uses a specific frequency modulated carrier wave radio frontend to track human activities behind a wall. Wi-Vi [7] uses ISAR technology to detect human activities. Although these systems break the limitations of LOS, they all require a dedicated WiFi monitor for extracting CSI values.

RSS-Based: RSS-based systems leverage the intuition that human activities cause the signal strength changes. Sigg et al. propose an activity recognition framework to recognize four human activities, including lying down, crawling, standing up, and walking [11,12]. To improve the granularity of RSSI values and the accuracy of activity recognition, they apply USRPs which provide RSS values. However, RSS-based systems get low accuracy of human activity recognition for the reason that RSS values contain coarse-grained information about channel state changes and cannot provide fine-grained information about multi-path effects and small scale fading.

CSI-Based: CSI values are available in COTS WiFI network interface cards (NICs) including Intel 5300 and Atheros 9390. Recently, CSI has been used for indoor localization [13,14], large scale activity [8,15,16] and small scale motion [17,18]. Han et al. proposed Wi-Fall that uses CSI variances to detect a single human falling activity [15]. Zou et al. proposed Electronic Frog Eye that uses CSI values to count the number of people in a room [16]. Wang et al. proposed CARM based on the underpinnings of CSI-speed model and CSI-speed model [8]. Wang et al. proposed WiHear that leverages MIMO beamforming focusing on the targets mouth to "hear" words [17]. Ali et al. proposed Wi-Key that uses the CSI-waveform as the feature to recognize keystroke [18]. Compared to RSS, CSI values provide fine-grained information to get higher recognition accuracy.

3   Preliminaries

In this section, we briefly introduce the background of Wi-Play, including channel state information and the overview of Wi-Play.

3.1   Channel State Information

Existing Wi-Fi devices almost all support IEEE 802.11a/g/n standards which are based on Orthogonal Frequency Division Multiplexing(OFDM). In an OFDM system, These WiFi devices continuously quantify Channel State Information to effectively perform transmit rate adaptations and power allocations from all (TX-RX) antenna pairs such that the available capacity of each OFDM channel can be maximally utilized. Each MIMO channel between each Tx-Rx antenna pair consists of Sc selected subcarriers, and each CSI measurement contains Sc matrices with dimensions $N_{tx} \times N_{rx}$ which represent the number of transmitting and receiving antennas respectively.

In frequency domain, the MIMO system can be modeled by the following equation:

$$Y = HX + N \tag{1}$$

where Y and X are the received and transmitted vectors respectively, H represents Channel State Information and N are the noise matrix. Also, we can estimate H as:

$$\widehat{H} = \frac{Y}{X} \tag{2}$$

From the above equation, we observe that CSI is the estimation of H. We can depict the amplitudes and phases in each subcarrier using the following equation:

$$H(k) = \| H(k) \| e^{j \angle H(k)} \tag{3}$$

$H(k)$ represents the CSI of the k_{th} sub-carriers, $\| H(k) \|$ and $\angle H(k)$ represent the amplitude and phase of k_{th} sub-carriers respectively. From the equation, we observe that CSI provides a finer-grained information about multi-path effects and small scale fading. Next, we will give the system overview.

3.2 System Overview

Wi-Play is a wireless system working on COTS WiFi devices, which leverages CSI to indicate the human activities for somatosensory game. Figure 2 gives an overview of Wi-Play, and we observe that Wi-Play mainly consists of four modules: data collection, noise removal, feature extraction, classification.

Wi-Play consists of two COTS Wi-Fi devices: a Laptop with Intel 5300 NIC, and a router at 5 GHz. First, Wi-Play samples CSI values from PHY layer at a rate of up to 2500 samples/second. Second, we use Butterworth and PCA filters to remove noises. Third, we detect the start and end of CSI-wavefrom caused by human activity using a human activity detection algorithm. Last, we use machine learning methods to build multi-classifiers for the recognition of human activity.

4 Methodology

In this section, we will give details of Wi-Play based on the four technologies: data collection, noise removal, feature extraction and classification.

4.1   CSI Data Collection

CSI values are collected from Intel 5300 NICs and a modified driver using an open CSI Tool at a rate of 2500 samples/s. In order to get fine-grained information about CSI, we leverage MIMO technology to multiply the capacity of a radio link with two antennas in transmitter and three antennas in receiver. As a result, we form a 3×2 MIMO system to exploit multipath propagation. Thus we can divide the CSI into 6 streams and every stream has 30 subcarriers. We use the following matrix to represent the time-series of CSI data:

$$
\begin{pmatrix}
H_{1,1} & H_{1,2} & \cdots & H_{1,29} & H_{1,30} \\
H_{2,1} & H_{2,2} & \cdots & H_{2,29} & H_{2,30} \\
\vdots & \vdots & \ddots & \vdots & \vdots \\
H_{5,1} & H_{5,2} & \cdots & H_{5,29} & H_{5,30} \\
H_{6,1} & H_{6,2} & \cdots & H_{6,29} & H_{6,30}
\end{pmatrix}
\tag{4}
$$

where $H_{i,j}$ represents the j_{th} subcarrier in the i_{th} stream.

4.2   Noise Removal

Original CSIs values are inherently noisy due to internal and environmental factors [19]. To recognize human activities using CSI values provided by COTS WiFi NICs, we must remove these noises effectively. Some recent related works use conventional denoising techniques including Birge-Massart Filter, Weighted Moving Average Filter and Butterworth Filter. Unfortunately, a simple conventional filter cannot denoise the CSI-waveform values very efficiently. To address this, Wi-Play leverages our observation that the variations in the series of CSI-waveform for all subcarriers caused by human activity are correlated. Thus, we utilize PCA for further denoising.

Butterworth. Wi-Play first passes the original CSI values from the Butterworth filter to remove high frequency noises. Butterworth filter is referred to as a maximally flat magnitude filter and does not distort CSI-Waveform caused by human activity much. The frequency response (gain) of Butterworth is:

$$
G(w)^2 = \mid H(jw) \mid^2 = \frac{G_0{}^2}{1 + (\frac{w}{w_c})^{2n}}
\tag{5}
$$

where w is the angular frequency; G_0 is the DC gain; w_c is the cutoff frequency; n represents the order of filter; $G(w)$ is the gain of filter.

Our experiments show that the frequencies of the variations in CSI time series caused by human activities are no more than 280 Hz in the CFR power. As the sample rate of CSI data is 2500 samples/s, we set w_c at 0.7 rad/s ($w_c = \frac{2\pi * f}{F} = \frac{2\pi * 280}{2500} \approx 0.7$ rad/s).

Principal Component Analysis. After removing noises using Butterworth filter, our observation that the variations in the series of CSI-waveform for all subcarriers caused by human activity are correlated. Despite the correlated change is not identical, we can use PCA to calculate the principal components from all CSI-waveform, and then select these principal components representing most common correlated changes. There are four steps in the process of PCA:

- *Data Preprocessing:* Wi-Play first collect N CSI packets, and remove noises using Butterworth filter. Then we can get an $N \times S_n$ dimensional matrix $H_{t,r}$ by the following equation:

$$H_{t,r} = [H_{t,r}(1) \mid H_{t,r}(2) \mid .. \mid H_{t,r}(N)]^T \tag{6}$$

  where $H_{t,r}(j)$ represent a $S_n \times 1$ dimensional vector containing CSI values of all s_n subcarriers at the (t, r) antenna pair for the j_{th} collected CSI packet.
- *Covariance Matrix:* In this step, we normalize the $H_{t,r}$, and get the normalized version $Z_{t,r}$ of $H_{t,r}$ with zero mean and unit variance. After that, Wi-Play calculates the correlation matrix.
- *Eigen Decomposition:* Wi-Play gets the eigenvectors ϱ through eigen decomposition of the covariance matrix.
- *Principal Components:* By the step, Wi-Play achieves top p principal components by the following equation:

$$Z_{t,r}^{\{1:p\}} = Z_{t,r} \times \varrho^{\{1:p\}} \tag{7}$$

Due to the high correlation, noises are mainly captured in the first component $Z_{t,r}^1$ along with human activities. Based on the observation, Wi-Play removes the first component and retains the next $p - 1$ principal components. Since the first principal component only contains one orthogonal component and the others are retained in the rest PCA components, they are uncorrelated. Thus we can remove the first principal component without distorting much information.

4.3   Activity Detection

In recent systems, there are many techniques to extract the CSI-waveform caused by human activity. WiFall leverages Local Outlier Factor (LOF), it can detect the activity but cannot work in real time. Wikey proposes a keystroke detection algorithm based on the observation that the waveforms of different keys show a similar rising and falling trends in the changing rate of CSI values. The detection algorithm cannot be directly adapted for our system for the randomness of the trends in the changing rate of CSI-waveforms caused by human activity. To address the challenge, we propose a writing detection algorithm based on the intuition that the mean absolute deviation(MAD) of CSI-Waveform caused by human activity is much higher [20].

Our algorithm uses a moving window approach to calculate the MAD and detect the starting and ending point. As described in Algorithm 1. The input W_n is the collection of windows for a particular TX-RX antenna pair. The output

---

Algorithm 1. Activity Detection

Input: W_n.
Output: The starting and ending point, (s_m, e_m).

1 $S_u = 0$, $S_v = 0$, $(s_m, e_m) = (null, null)$;
2 **for** *each window W_j in W_n* **do**
3   Calculate the MAD of W_j for each principal component,$\triangle m_j$;
4   Get the summation MAD for all principal components,$\triangle M_j$;
5   **if** $\triangle M_j > T_v$ **then**
6   //When $\triangle M_j > T_v$, it means that the window contains significant information;
7   **if** *s_m is null* **then**
8   set the current window as the s_m;
9   increment the S_u and S_v by 1;
10   **else**
11   increment the S_u and S_v by 1;
12   **else**
13   **if** *s_m is not null* **then**
14   increment the S_u by 1;
15   **if** $S_u - S_v > T_s$ **then**
16   //When S_u is in the range of the length for each activity, S_u is valid;
17   **if** *s_m is not null and S_u is valid* **then**
18   set the current window as the e_m;
19   return (s_m, e_m);
20   **else**
21             $S_u = 0$, $S_v = 0$, $(s_m, e_m) = (null, null)$;

(s_m, e_m) represents the starting and ending point. For each window, we first calculate the MAD for CSI-waveforms as the following equations:

$$\triangle m_j[k] = \frac{\Sigma_{i=j}^{j+L} \mid Z_{t,r}^{\{k\}}(i) - \overline{Z_{t,r}^{\{k\}}}(j:j+L) \mid}{L}; \tag{8}$$

$$\triangle M_j = \Sigma_{k=2}^{p} \triangle m_j[k]; \tag{9}$$

where L is the size of window, $\overline{Z_{t,r}^{\{k\}}}(j:j+L)$ represents the mean of the k_{th} projected CSI stream, $\triangle m_j[k]$ is the MAD of the k_{th} principal component and $\triangle M_j$ is the summation MAD for all principal components. The above step is shown in line 3 to line 4. From line 5 to line 11, if $\triangle M_j$ is larger than T_v, it means the window may contain significant variance, thus we can set the starting point and record S_u representing the number of all traversed windows and S_v representing traversed windows on condition that $\triangle M_j > T_v$. From line 15 to line 19, if $S_u - S_v > T_s$, the algorithm records the ending point e_m and returns (s_m, e_m) on condition that the starting point is found and S_u is valid. Both T_v and T_s are the threshold we get experimentally.

4.4   Classification

After the above steps, we obtain the CSI-waveforms, which are caused by different human activity. To achieve recognition result, we build multi-classifiers based on Support Vector Machine(SVM) and K Nearest Neighbor (KNN).

Support Vector Machine. Based on the extracted CSI-waveform, we choose the following features to characterize different activities: (1) the MAD, (2) the mean value(MEAN), (3) signal entropy, (4) Amplitude Amount, (5) the max value(MAX). Then we use non-linear SVM which can map the input samples to high dimensional space and seek a maximum classification hyper plane for classification. The model can be described as:

$$\min_{\omega,\varepsilon,\rho} \frac{1}{2}\|\omega^2\| + C\sum_i \varepsilon_i - \rho \tag{10}$$

subject to

$$(\omega \cdot \varphi(X_i)) \geq \rho - \varepsilon_i, \varepsilon_i \geq 0 \tag{11}$$

The discriminant function $F(x)$ is described as:

$$F(x) = sign(\omega \cdot \varphi(x) - \rho) \tag{12}$$

Then we choose a quadratic polynomial kernel as the kernel function:

$$K(x,y) = (< x,y > +1)^2 \tag{13}$$

K Nearest Neighbor. Since some CSI-waveforms caused by different human activities have similar characteristics, conventional features used in SVM cannot discriminate activities exactly. To solve this problem, we leverage the CSI-waveform as the feature based on the intuition that CSI-waveform contains all the information about human activity. To enhance the computing efficiency, we first use Discrete Wavelet Transform(DWT) to reduce the number of CSI values without distorting the information. Then we build separate classifiers for sampled CSI-Waveforms from each Tx-Rx antenna pair. After that, Dynamic Time Warping(DTW) is used to match the testing CSI-waveform to the best profile.

By now, we have built multi-classifiers including both SVM and KNN for $p-1$ principal components from each extracted sample, then we make a decision to choose the human activity by voting on the results of each classifier.

5   Implementation and Evaluation

In this section, we first introduce the implementation and experimental settings of Wi-Play. Then we evaluate the human activity recognition result.

5.1   Implementation

Wi-Play consists of two COTS hardware devices: an Intel NUC D54250WYKH laptop with an Intel Link 5300 WiFi NIC as a receiver and a TP-LINK TL-WR842N router as transmitter. The NUC laptop has 2.0 GHZ Intel Core i5 4250U processor with 8 GB of RAM, and we operate Wi-Play with Matlab in Ubuntu 12.04. The router has 2 antennas and the laptop has 3 antennas, and they all run in 802.11n AP mode at 5 GHz. Thus we can sample 6 CSI streams from Intel 5300 NIC in 2×3 MIMO system using CSITool developed by Halperin *et al.* Also we need an extra laptop continuously send packets to the receiver via router using iperf tool, and the receiver collects CSI values at the rate of about 2500 packets/s. The higher sampling rate makes sure that the collected CSI-Waveform contains enough information about human activity.

5.2 Experimental Setting

We collect training samples of 7 human activities for somatosensory game in our lab, and these samples are from 8 volunteers, including 4 male and 4 female students. We evaluate the performance of Wi-Play through two sets of experiments. One experiment is to evaluate the extraction accuracy in the trained and untrained environments, and the other is to evaluate accuracy by increasing the number of trained samples. We let volunteers perform within a certain area faced to the receiver and wait for 2 s before the next activity. Wi-Play detects the activity features caused by arm $(AC1 - AC5)$ and body $(AC6 - AC7)$. The distance between users and receiver is about 2 m, and each activity is at a size of 60 cm–80 cm.

5.3 Evaluation

We evaluate human activity recognition accuracy through two sets of experiments. In the first set of experiments, we perform experiments in the trained and untrained environments. In the second set of experiments, we build classifiers by increasing the number of training samples to observe the impact of increment in the number of samples on recognition accuracy.

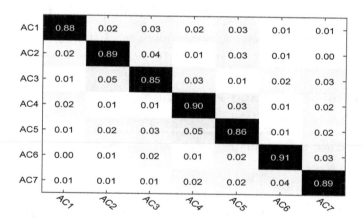

Fig. 3. Color map of confusion matrix

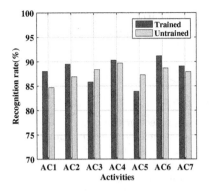 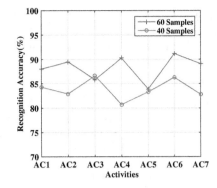

Fig. 4. Accuracy with trained and untrained environments

Fig. 5. Accuracy with 24 and 48 samples

Accuracy with Trained and Untrained Environments. We investigate the performance of Wi-Play in trained and untrained environment, and present the average accuracy of 10-fold cross validation for each human activity. In addition, every classifier has 60 samples for each human activity. In Fig. 4, we observe that Wi-Play achieves 88.3 % recognition accuracy in trained environment and 87.7 % recognition accuracy in untrained environment. The result indicates that all our predefined activities can be recognized with high accuracy in the trained and untrained environment, and it proves that our system is robust.

Impact of Number of Samples. To determine the effect of the number of training samples on the accuracy of Wi-Play for each human activity, we perform experiments by increasing the number of training samples from 40 to 60 in each classifier for all volunteers. From Fig. 5, we observe that the recognition accuracy for the number of samples in each classifier varying from 40 to 60, and the average accuracy for all written letters increases from 83.8 % to 88.3 %. Thus we can improve recognition accuracy by increasing the number of training samples.

The confusion matrix achieved by 10-fold cross validation on 60 training samples over all users is shown in the Fig. 3. The darker areas represent higher rate of correct recognition, and the average recognition accuracy is about 88.3 %.

6   Conclusions and Future

In this paper, we propose a robust human activity recognition for somatosensory system using WiFi signals: Wi-Play. Wi-Play collects CSI values from COTS WiFi devices, and remove noises leveraging Butterworth and PCA filters. Then Wi-Play uses a human activity detection algorithm that automatically extracts the CSI-Waveform for each of human activity. Last, Wi-Play build a multi-classifier model using SVM and KNN to make a decision by voting on the results.

Our system achieves more than 88.3 % average recognition accuracy for recognizing human activities. As future work, we plan to use multiple receivers to ensure the long-distance performance.

References

1. Leap motion. https://www.leapmotion.com
2. Microsoft kinect. http://www.microsoft.com/en-us/kinectforwindows
3. Qifan, P., Gupta, S., Gollakota, S., Patel, S.: Whole-home gesture recognition using wireless signals. In: Proceedings of ACM MobiCom, pp. 27–38. ACM (2013)
4. Park, T., Lee, J., Hwang, I., Yoo, C., Nachman, L., Song, J.: E-gesture: a collaborative architecture for energy-efficient gesture recognition with hand-worn sensor and mobile devices. In: Proceedings of the ACM SenSys, pp. 260–273. ACM (2011)
5. Pan, W., Xiaobing, W., Chen, G., Shan, M., Zhu, X.: A few bits are enough: energy efficient device-free localization. Comput. Commun. **83**, 72–80 (2016)
6. Pan, W., Chen, G., Zhu, X., Wu, X.: Minimizing receivers under link coverage model for device-free surveillance. Comput. Commun. **63**, 72–80 (2015)
7. Adib, F., Katabi, D.: See through walls with WiFi! In: Proceedings of the ACM SIGCOMM, pp. 75–86. ACM (2013)
8. Wang, W., Liu, A.X., Shahzad, M., Ling, K., Sanglu, L.: Understanding and modeling of WiFi signal based human activity recognition. In: Proceedings of ACM MobiCom, pp. 65–76. ACM (2015)
9. Xia, Z., Wang, X., Sun, X., Wang, Q.: A secure and dynamic multi-keyword ranked search scheme over encrypted cloud data. IEEE Trans. Parallel Distrib. Syst. **27**(2), 340–352 (2015)
10. Adib, F., Kabelac, Z., Katabi, D., Miller, R.C.: 3D tracking via body radio reflections. In: Proceedings of USENIX NSDI, pp. 317–329. USENIX Association (2014)
11. Sigg, S., Shi, S., Buesching, F., Ji, Y., Wolf, L.: Leveraging RF-channel fluctuation for activity recognition: active and passive systems, continuous and RSSI-based signal features. In: Proceedings of ACM MobiCom, pp. 43:43–43:52. ACM (2013)
12. Sigg, S., Scholz, M., Shi, S., Ji, Y., Beigl, M.: RF-sensing of activities from non-cooperative subjects in device-free recognition systems using ambient and local signals. IEEE Trans. Mob. Comput. **13**(4), 907–920 (2014)
13. Kotaru, M., Joshi, K.R., Bharadia, D., Katti, S.: SpotFi: decimeter level localization using WiFi. In: Proceedings of ACM SigCom, pp. 269–282 (2015)
14. Yang, Z., Zhou, Z., Liu, Y.: From RSSI to CSI: indoor localization via channel response. ACM Comput. Surv. **46**(2), 25:1–25:32 (2013)
15. Han, C., Wu, K., Wang, Y., Ni, L.M.: WiFall: device-free fall detection by wireless networks. In: Proceedings of IEEE INFOCOM, pp. 271–279 (2014)
16. Xi, W., Zhao, J., Li, X.Y., Zhao, K., Tang, S., Liu, X., Jiang, Z.: Electronic frog eye: counting crowd using WiFi. In: IEEE INFOCOM 2014 - IEEE Conference on Computer Communications, pp. 361–369 (2014)
17. Wang, G., Zou, Y., Zhou, Z., Wu, K., Ni, L.M.: We can hear you with Wi-Fi! In: Proceedings of ACM MobiCom, pp. 593–604. ACM (2014)
18. Ali, K., Liu, A.X., Wang, W., Shahzad, M.: Keystroke recognition using WiFi signals. In: Proceedings of ACM MobiCom, pp. 90–102. ACM (2015)
19. Ren, Y., Shen, J., Wang, J., Han, J., Lee, S.: Mutual verifiable provable data auditing in public cloud storage. J. Internet Technol. **16**(2), 317–323 (2015)
20. Zhangjie, F., Ren, K., Shu, J., Sun, X., Huang, F.: Enabling personalized search over encrypted outsourced data with efficiency improvement. IEEE Trans. Parallel Distrib. Syst., p. 1 (2015)

A Glance of Child's Play Privacy in Smart Toys

Patrick C.K. Hung[1,3(✉)], Farkhund Iqbal[1,2], Shih-Chia Huang[1,3],
Mohammed Melaisi[1], and Kevin Pang[1]

[1] Faculty of Business and Information Technology,
University of Ontario Institute of Technology, Oshawa, Canada
patrick.hung@uoit.ca,
{mohammed.melaisi,kevin.pang}@uoit.net
[2] College of Technological Innovation, Zayed University, Dubai, UAE
farkhund.iqbal@zu.ac.ae
[3] Department of Electronic Engineering,
National Taipei University of Technology, Taipei, Taiwan
schuang@ntut.edu.tw

Abstract. A smart toy is defined as a device consisting of a physical toy component that connects to one or more toy computing services to facilitate gameplay in the Cloud through networking and sensory technologies to enhance the functionality of a traditional toy. A smart toy in this context can be effectively considered an Internet of Things (IoT) with Artificial Intelligence (AI) which can provide Augmented Reality (AR) experiences to users. Referring to the direction of the United States Federal Trade Commission Children's Online Privacy Protection Act (COPPA) and the European Union Data Protection Directive (EUDPD), this study adopts the definition of a child to be an individual under the age of 13 years old. In this study, the first assumption is that children do not understand the concept of privacy. The second assumption is that children will disclose as much information to smart toys as they can trust. Breaches of privacy can result in physical safety of child user, e.g., child predators. While the parents/legal guardians of a child strive to ensure their child's physical and online safety and privacy, there is no common approach for these parents/guardians to study the information flow between their child and the smart toys they interact with. This paper discusses related privacy requirements for smart toys in a toy computing environment with a case study on a commercial smart toy called Hello Barbie from Mattel.

Keywords: Smart toys · Toy computing · Cloud computing · Children protection · Privacy

1 Introduction

A toy is an item or product intended for learning or play, which can have various benefits to childhood development. The modern toy industry is comprised of establishments primarily engaged in manufacturing dolls, toys and games. As such a substantial part of human development, toys have continued to maintain a presence in the daily lives of billions of individuals of all ages. A smart toy is defined as a device

© Springer International Publishing AG 2016
X. Sun et al. (Eds.): ICCCS 2016, Part II, LNCS 10040, pp. 217–231, 2016.
DOI: 10.1007/978-3-319-48674-1_20

consisting of a physical toy component that connects to one or more toy computing services to facilitate gameplay in the Cloud through networking and sensory technologies to enhance the functionality of a traditional toy (Ren et al. 2015). A smart toy in this context can be effectively considered an Internet of Thing (IoT) with Artificial Intelligence (AI) which can provide Augmented Reality (AR) experiences to users. Examples of these are Mattel's Hello Barbie and Cognitoys' Dino. Toy computing is a recently developing concept which transcends the traditional toy into a new area of computer research using services computing technologies (Hung 2015). In this context, a toy is a physical embodiment artefact that acts as a child user interface for toy computing services in a cloud computing environment. A smart toy can also capture child user's physical activity state (e.g., voice, walking, standing, running, etc.) and store personalized information (e.g., location, activity pattern, etc.) through camera, microphone, Global Positioning System (GPS), and various sensors such as facial recognition or sound detection. Referring to Fig. 1, a new invention called the "Google Toy" like a humanoid toy has caused many criticisms from the media as people express concern about privacy breaching and safety issues by Google.

Fig. 1. What the public is worrying on Google Toy?

More specifically, the toy makers are confronted with the challenge of better understanding the consumer needs, concerns and exploring the possibility of adopting such data-collected smart toys to rich information interface in this emerging market. For example, many toy designers have been researching the balance between the level of private information a toy collected from a child and the level of personalized features the toy provided to the child. Referring to the direction of the United States Federal Trade Commission Children's Online Privacy Protection Act (COPPA) and the European Union Data Protection Directive (EUDPD), this study adopts the definition of a child to be an individual under the age of 13 years old. In this study, the first assumption is that children do not understand the concept of privacy. The second assumption is that children will disclose as much information to smart toys as they can trust. Some research studies found out that children have emotional interactions with dolls and stuffed toys in anthropomorphic design (Tanaka and Kimura 2009). Some children even prefer to take the toy to the dinner table or make a bed for it next to the child's own (Plowman and Luckin 2004). For example, many studies found that anthropomorphic toys such as teddy bears or bunny rabbits serve a specific purpose, as children trusted such designs and felt at ease disclosing private information.

Breaches of privacy can result in physical safety of child user, e.g., child predators (Schell et al. 2007). While the parents/legal guardians of a child strive to ensure their child's physical and online safety and privacy, there is no common approach for these parents/guardians to study the information flow between their child and the smart toys they interact with (Xia et al. 2015). As smart toys are able to collect variety of data such as text, picture, video, sound, location, and sensing data, this makes the context far more complicated than many other smart devices in particular given that the subjects are mainly children in a physical and social environment. Parental control is a feature in a smart toy for the parents to restrict the content the children can provide to the toy. Though the toy industry has also issued regulations for toy safety, these regulations have no mention of privacy issues in this toy computing paradigm. This paper discusses related privacy requirements for smart toys with a case study on a commercial smart toy called Hello Barbie from Mattel. This paper is organized as follows. Section 2 provides a literature review. Section 3 will discuss the privacy requirements for smart toys with a case study of Hello Barbie, and Sect. 4 will conclude the paper with future works.

2 Literature Review

Recently the topic of smart toy technologies is gaining more and more public interest. For example, Yahoo Canada published a report called "Electronic toy maker VTech's zero accountability clause puts onus for hacks on parents" on Feb 12, 2016, which said: *"the collection of data through toys and apps geared towards children presents a growing challenge. In Canada we have a very restrictive and well defined privacy act for the healthcare domain. In the toy industry, they see all those safeguards and guidelines and they only talk about the safety of a toy. Those guidelines haven't caught up to the information collecting aspect."* This report is one of the examples that shows the public concerns on the toy safety and privacy issues in our society. However, there is limited research on this specific cross-disciplinary research topic in toy computing. For example, AlHarthy and Shawkat (2013) discuss a security solution to protect the network data from unauthorized access from controlling unmanaged smart devices, but they do not provide a generic privacy-preserving data model for this paradigm. Next, Armando et al. (2014) describe a technical approach to secure the smart device paradigm based on a given organization's security policy, but without discussing the privacy policy from the perspective of users. Then, Peng et al. (2013) present threat detection and mitigation mechanisms on mobile devices in a prioritized defense deployment, but they do not cover a technical architecture to tackle the requirements of accessing mobile services. Referring to the research works in IoT, Alqassem and Svetinovic (2014) describe the challenges to tackling IoT privacy and security requirements as follows: (1) It is difficult to determine what information should be protected, when to protect it, and to whom access should be granted/restricted; (2) The IoT consists of diverse technologies and the integration of these technologies may lead to unknown risks; and (3) The changing nature of the environment plays an important role when dealing with the privacy and security vulnerabilities of the IoT. Though there is a lot of related research in security and privacy of IoT, there is no standardized framework which focuses on smart toys in this paradigm. For example, Sun et al. (2014) proposes a personal privacy protection policy model based on homomorphism encryption in IoT, but there is no specific design which is compliant with the privacy laws. Since smart toys are still an emerging research topic, there have not been many related research works done in privacy. Smart TVs have a lot of common attributes as smart toys. In a Smart TV, personalized services are provided to the user based on context data collected and inferred through sensors and other environment data (Schmidt 2005). While allowing context data to be collected for services can prove to be of great benefit to users, there is an ongoing trade-off between utility and privacy (Chakraborty et al. 2013). Their research states that a large amount of users do not even know that such information is being stored, and in some cases, still happens even if the user has explicitly restricted such data to be collected. This goes against the privacy principle of having the users consent before collecting this information. The amount of information collected often results in a trade-off required between disclosing sensitive data and receiving context-aware services in Smart TV. However, the related research on Smart TVs does not only focus on a specific user group, e.g., children. On the other hand, privacy technologies have also been investigated for a period of time. For example, the Platform for Privacy Preferences (P3P) working group at W3C develops the P3P specification for enabling Web sites to express their privacy practices (W3C 2002). The P3P framework is not designed for tackling toy computing privacy issues. In summary, smart toys which embrace sensory and networking capabilities open up new threats to privacy (Heurix et al. 2015), stimulate new user requirements, and establish a unique case for privacy requirements in toy computing.

3 Privacy Requirements in Smart Toys

Information privacy is defined by Hung and Cheng (2009) as "an individual's right to determine how, when, and to what extent information about the self will be released to another person or to an organization." Privacy rules can be achieved through privacy preserving mechanisms such as access control. In order to provide the most relevant content, the smart toy will need to collect certain context data such as the child's location, and also potential profile information such as age and gender to help determine what their interests may be based on demographic. To gain even more context of the child, the smart toy may collect and retain historical data on the child such as previous movement patterns via GPS, camera and various sensors, to determine where the child is likely to be at certain times, if the child is travelling, or previous interactions with the smart toy such as which content they had previously been interested in. It is clear that the more information is collected on the child, the more relevant services can be provided to the child. However, the user may not be comfortable with the level of data that is collected and inferred on them (Shen et al. 2015). There are countless types of data that can be collected from smart toys that must be considered when evaluating the scope of privacy. This is true of collected sensory data, and also from within other applications, sensitive data can be collected such as a user's profile information, contact list, or calendar. All of this information can be collected and analyzed to determine context data about the children and then the smart toy may provide personalized functions (Tath 2006).

Referring to Fig. 2, the children (users) may interact with different smart toys from different toy makers in a physical and social environment such as Mattel's Hello Barbie and Cognitoys' Dino. Mattel introduced Barbie in early 1959, the doll has then gone through many phases, allowing it to sell over 800 million units around the world. Thus Barbie has become a fashion doll icon. Hello Barbie is introduced as *"the first fashion doll that can have a two-way conversation with girls"* with speech recognition and cloud computing technologies. The smart toys may be equipped with camera, microphone, GPS, and various sensors for face and sound detection. These smart toys may send the collected information such as text, picture, video, sound (voice), location and sensing data to the toy computing services, which are published and managed by different toy computing providers and even bind with other third party services, in the Cloud. Each smart toy should have its own privacy policy which outlines information including how it will collect, manage, share, and retain the user's personal data (Fu et al. 2015). This paper assumes that although the information disclosure practices are outlined in the privacy policy on smart toys, and the parents/guardians have provided their consent for their children, the parents/guardians are not actually aware due to the fact that they did not read or understand the policy. For example, ToyTalk.com, which is the Cloud service provider of Mattel, outlines the Hello Barbie privacy statement (Taylor and Michael 2016): *"[...] use, store, process, convert, transcribe, analyze or review Recordings in order to provide, maintain, analyze and improve the functioning of the Services, to develop, test or improve speech recognition technology and artificial intelligence algorithms, or for other research and development and data analysis purposes."* Content unawareness occurs when the user is unaware of the information that is collected on them, e.g., their location via GPS on the toy. While parents strive to ensure their child's physical and online safety and privacy, they may wish to be in control of how their personal data is shared through the devices they are using (Salomon 2010). Based on the privacy requirements for toy computing, Table 1 shows the analysis of Hello Barbie privacy policy on ToyTalk.com. The third column shows the related statements on the ToyTalk's Hello Barbie privacy policy (https://toytalk.com/hellobarbie/privacy/) which is related to each privacy requirements for toy computing (Hung 2015).

On the other side, the parents/guardian (authorized user) should have a data visualization model with related activities on their children in the form of dashboard on their smart device (Tracy and Westeyn 2012), e.g., smart phone or tablet. This dashboard should have two major functions: (1) *Privacy Preferences*: define the preferences for how and which of their data will be collected, shared, retained, etc. associated with the privacy policy of each smart toy. These preferences will be used to generate a set of privacy rules at the smart toy. The privacy rule states what subject is allowed to perform which operation on which object for what purposes, to which recipients, and under what obligations and retention; and (2) *Alert Mechanism*: inform the user if there

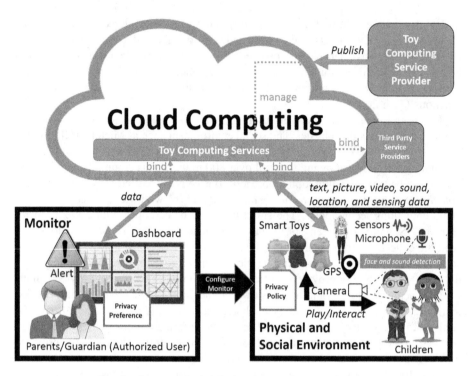

Fig. 2. Conceptual model of toy computing environment

Table 1. Analysis of Hello Barbie privacy policy on ToyTalk.com

	Privacy requirement for toy computing (Hung 2015)	Hello Barbie privacy policy last revised: January 5, 2016 (https://toytalk.com/hellobarbie/privacy/)
1	The right for a parent/guardian to request restrictions on the use or disclosure of private information of their child. This allows parents/guardians to provide restrictions to purpose, recipients, obligations, and retention regarding their child's information	*We use Recordings only for limited purposes as described in this Policy. We use Recordings in order to provide and maintain the Services. We may also use, store, process, convert, transcribe, analyze or review Recordings in order to provide, maintain, analyze and improve the functioning of the Services, to develop, test or improve speech recognition technology and artificial intelligence algorithms, or for other research and development and data analysis purposes. We do not use Recordings or their content, including any personal information that may be captured therein, to contact children or to advertise to them*

(*continued*)

Table 1. (*continued*)

	Privacy requirement for toy computing (Hung 2015)	Hello Barbie privacy policy last revised: January 5, 2016 (https://toytalk.com/hellobarbie/privacy/)
2	The right for a parent/guardian to access, copy, and inspect collected records on their child. This allows a parent/guardian to access their child's records to see that data that is collected on them	*ToyTalk uses parental email in order to obtain parental consent for your children's use of the Services and to create a parent account, which allows you to access the Parental Settings section of the ToyTalk website. For your convenience, ToyTalk offers a unified parent account so if your children also use or want to use other ToyTalk children's products or services, you may use the same account to manage your children's use of all such products or services*
3	The right for a parent/guardian to request deletion of their child's private data records, or correction if records are inaccurate. This allows parents/guardians to request that their child's location records be deleted, or to request a correction if their child's records are in-complete or incorrect	*We cannot prevent children from providing personal information when they talk with Hello Barbie, and such information may be captured in the Recordings. However, it is our policy to delete such personal information where we become aware of it and we contractually require our service providers to do the same*
4	The right for a parent/guardian to request acknowledgements through a communication channel when private information of their child is collected. This allows parents to set up a communication channel such as phone number or email address to receive acknowledgements there is an update pertaining to the collection of their child's records. This allows parents/guardians to keep track of how their child's information	*We may change this Policy from time to time. If we make changes, we will notify you by revising the date at the top of the Policy and, in some cases, we will provide you with additional notice (such as adding a statement to our web site's homepage or sending you a notification) and/or obtain your prior verifiable consent*
5	The right to file complaints to toy company. If a parent/guardian believes that their child's data has been mishandled in any way by the toy company or service provider, or if they believe that they have not acted in compliance with their policies, they are able to file complaints	*If you have any questions about this Policy or any concerns about your privacy, please email us at privacy@toytalk.com or contact us at: ToyTalk, Inc. Attn: Chief Privacy Office 77 Maiden Lane, San Francisco, CA 94108 Tel. 415-890-4446*
6	The right to find out where the child's private data has been shared for purposes other than a game. This allows a parent/guardian to be notified if their child's records have been shared with another party for any purpose other than for a game	*We will not share the personal information we collect through the Services with third parties, except as described in this Policy*

is any privacy violation or suspicious events in the physical and social environment. Parental control is a feature in a smart toy for the parents to restrict the content the children can provide to the toy (Noor et al. 2012). For example, ToyTalk's privacy policy claims *"All references to the term "you" or "parent" in this privacy policy shall include legal guardians, and all references to "children" or "child" shall mean children under 13 years of age. The use of Hello Barbie™ requires parental consent, and by providing consent, you are certifying that you are the parent for the children who use the Services."*

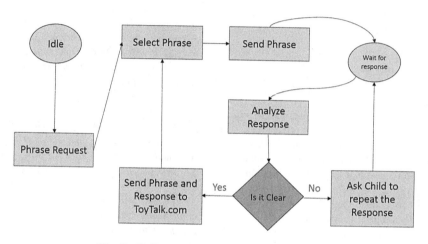

Fig. 3. Hello Barbie conversation flow diagram

Child users exhibit a varying level of awareness when it comes to their online activities and understanding of privacy risks. Children must be protected from risks which they can be vulnerable to online including violence, harassment, stalking, grooming, sexual abuse or exploitation, or personal data misuse. Furthermore, children also take up a large segment of the consumer population and are of particular interest to market researchers who may attempt to collect their personal data and usage patterns for targeted advertising (Salomon 2010). Third party advertisers can infer a great amount of information about a child based on their location via GPS, collecting detailed behavioral profiles that may be used for unknown or unwanted purposes. Referring to Hello Barbie, Mattel's privacy policy explicitly claims *"There is no advertising content within Hello Barbie"* and *"Your children's conversations are not used to advertise to your child."* Further, ToyTalk's privacy policy has explicitly described three types of data they will collect from the users: (1) *Active Collection*: Collect a parental email and password, their child's birthday, what holidays to remember, and other conversation options that are used to improve the conversational experience; (2) *Recordings*: Capture the conversation between children and Hello Barbie (see the Hello Barbie's conversation flow diagram in Fig. 3); and (3) *Passive Collection*: Automatically collect certain information about the configuration of hardware and software.

Context is defined succinctly by Dey and Abowd (1999) as "any information that can be used to characterize the situation of an entity." Schilit et al. (1994) defined context as location, identities of nearby people and objects, and changes to those objects. Heurix et al. (2015) further categorized the elements for describing context information into five categories: individuality, activity, location, time, and relations. Individuality is personal information about a user, activity is data regarding physical activity, location is the GPS location, time is discrete time, and relations are inferences between two or more pieces of context data. In smart toys, the fusion of data from cameras and sensors allow for a more comprehensive and non-obtrusive observation of people for user behaviour analysis (Salah et al. 2013). The context data model is built up in terms of the children human factors (User, Social Environment, and Tasks) and their physical environment (Conditions, Infrastructure, and Location). In general, a context data model is classified into three types (World Economic Forum 2011) as follows: (a) Volunteered Data: data that is explicitly provided by the children. This can include personal profile information or preference settings, e.g., *Active Collection* and *Recordings*; (b) Observed Data: data not directly given by the children, but is detected by the smart toys often through a sensor, e.g., *Passive Collection*; and (c) Inferred Data: data deduced based on analysis of a combination of volunteered and/or observed data. A lot can be evaluated about a child and their environment through inferences based on context data by third party influencing, e.g., integrate with the information from social networking sites and Google Map. Referring to the context data model of Hello Barbie as of November 17, 2015, she can speak 56,367 total words and 3,935 unique word forms in 8,000 phrases. Figure 4 shows the analysis of the 8,000 phrases by Voyant and it does not show any evidence that Hello Barbie will explicitly ask any private information from the child. Most frequent words in the phrases are: like (599); oh (591); know (365); love (353); think (329). While Hello Barbie does not ask for the private information directly, we conducted an analysis on the 8,000 phrases, that it is possible for a child to reveal such information indirectly. Table 2 shows some phrases and the privacy concerns and some illustrative examples of potential children responses.

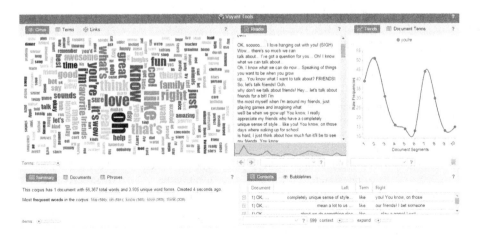

Fig. 4. Hello Barbie's phrases analysis by Voyant (http://voyant-tools.org/)

Table 2. Analysis of the 8,000 phrases in Hello Barbie

Keyword (Times)	Hello Barbie phrases	Appeared on page number	Potential privacy concerns	Example of a child's answers
Name (48)	"What's your middle name?"	18	Revealing the child middle name or the parents name	My middle name is Jean, My full name is Alice Jean Mark
	My mom's name is Margaret, and my dad's name is George	66	Revealing the parents name.	My mom name is Mary and my father name is George
	I'll be a visitor and you'll show me around! So… what's the name of your family's town?	94	Revealing the child current town	My family town is Toronto
	This is so cool. But so tell me, bestie, about one of your other friends. What's your friend's name?	154	Revealing the child's friend name	My best friend name is Bill
Old (9)	(GIDDY) I've been waiting all year to sing that! And remind me… how old are you today? Oh that's right… So? How does it feel being five?	58	The system identifies the child age	I am six years old
	Oh that's right… So? How does it feel being six?	58	This phrase repeated the ages from six to ten	I am happy to be six years old
Born (1)	Oh, well, I was born in Wisconsin, but I live in Malibu now	64	This phrase could lead the child to say their place of birth	Oh nice, I was born in Calgary, but I live in Toronto now
School (67)	How different do you think high school will be from Kindergarten?	151	The system can identify the child's grade	I am still in junior high school

(*continued*)

Table 2. (*continued*)

Keyword (Times)	Hello Barbie phrases	Appeared on page number	Potential privacy concerns	Example of a child's answers
	How different do you think high school will be from 1st Grade?	151	This phrase repeated the grades from 1st to 5th grade	I am still in junior high school
Teacher (26)	A teacher? That's a great idea! What made you want to be a teacher?	116	This could lead the child to say their teacher's name	My science teacher Mrs. Marui, she is smart and funny
	Oh, ok. Well, what class have you had fun in? Or is there a class where you really like the teacher?	116	This could lead the child to provide more information about their school	Mathematics class as it is the best in York High School
Bank (19)	Oh, a bank! You have to be responsible to work there. Who in your family runs the bank?	107	If a family member is actually working in a bank the child may reveals that information	My father works at TD Bank in Markham
	I have a piggy bank that I put money into all the time. I'm saving it all up for something special - I just don't know what yet!	107	If the child has a piggy bank, he could reveal his financial status	I have a lot of money in my piggy bank
Money (5)	My dad has always taught my sisters and me why it's important to save the money we make for doing chores or allowance or whatever. And it's fun to save up to buy really special things!	108	The child could reveal their parents' saving plans	My parents are saving a lot of money to buy a house

(*continued*)

Table 2. (*continued*)

Keyword (Times)	Hello Barbie phrases	Appeared on page number	Potential privacy concerns	Example of a child's answers
Jewelry (22)	(CUTE GASP) A jewelry store! So sparkly and pretty! Who in your family runs the jewelry store?	103	Similar to the bank situation	Similar to the bank situation
	My mom has lots of jewelry, but what she loves most is the macaroni necklace Chelsea made her in school!	103	The child could reveal their mother's jewelry information	My mother love jewelry as well. She keeps them in her bedroom
Necklace (3)	Honestly, my favorite necklace doesn't have a jewel in it. It's the first necklace my parents got me, and it says my name. It's more precious to me than any diamond!	103	The child could reveal information about their necklace. If the child wear it all the time, she may reveals her appearance	I have a golden necklace with a heart shape and I wear it all the time even when I go to school
Job (28)	(LAUGHS) There you go! Ok, so what job might you like…	145	Information about a family member's occupation	I would like to be a computer expert like my father who work at TD Bank
Home (28)	(EXCITED) Oh I just know your home will look so amazing!! Tell me more!	30	The child may miss understand the phrase and may start describing his actual house	I live in a house with a big front yard and we have a fish tank in the front
	Is your home decorated in red, black, and green?	35	More details about the child house	My house is red color
	Home IS where the heart is! Why do you like drawing your house?	188	More details about the child house	I like to draw flowers on the front door

(*continued*)

Table 2. (*continued*)

Keyword (Times)	Hello Barbie phrases	Appeared on page number	Potential privacy concerns	Example of a child's answers
House (20)	My dream house is in Malibu, California!	67	The location of the house	My dream house is in Florida
	My parents helped my sisters and me build a treehouse! That was such a fun day!	102	More details about the appearance of the house	We have big backyard so my father built a tree house
	You have a vacation house? Do you go there every year?	203	Details about a vacation house such as location and time of being there could be reveals	We go to our vacation house near the beach every year in December
Town (9)	I'll be a visitor and you'll show me around! So… what's the name of your family's town?	94	A direct question of the family's town	It is Toronto!
Driver's license (10)	Oh, totally! I'm pretty sure my sister Stacy already has her license, 'cause, let me tell you, she can Drive	152	The child might reveal his parents' car information	My father has a black car and my mother has a blue car

4 Conclusions and Future Works

Children's data is widely considered to be particularly sensitive and should be treated with extreme care by law and legislation in a toy computing environment (Hinske and Langheinrich 2009). Privacy can result in physical safety of child user. A children protection framework is required for smart toys which can achieve privacy goals by minimizing the collection and retention of potentially sensitive user data, as well as involving the user (or parent) in the control of their child's data (Livingstone et al. 2011). In summary, end user requirements need to consider that the main user base is children, who have unique requirements as they are especially vulnerable and in order to protect their sensitive data, parents/guardians require a framework to implement privacy controls on their child's data. This paper gives an overview of the related privacy challenges and issues with a case study of Mattel's Hello Barbie. In particular, we can assume that smart toys will have more advanced software (e.g., face and sound detection algorithms) and hardware (e.g., various sensors) in the coming future. Thus there is a need for a privacy quantification that enables the parents/guardians to decide whether to share its children's private data to smart toys (Hadzovic et al. 2015).

Acknowledgement. This work was supported by the Ministry of Science and Technology (MOST), Taiwan, under MOST Grants: *105-2923-E-027 -001 -MY3, 105-2221-E-027 -113, 105-2811-E-027 -001, 104-2221-E-027 -020, 103-2221-E-027 -031 -MY2, 103-2923-E-002 -011 -MY3, & 103-2221-E-027 -030 -MY2*; the Research Office - Zayed University, Abu Dhabi, United Arab Emirates, under Research Projects: *R15048 & R15046*; and the Natural Sciences and Engineering Research Council of Canada (NSERC), under NSERC Discovery Grants Program: *RGPIN-2016-05023*.

References

AlHarthy, K., Shawkat, W.: Implement network security control solutions in BYOD environment. In: The 2013 IEEE International Conference on Control System, Computing and Engineering (ICCSCE), pp. 7–11 (2013)

Alqassem, I., Svetinovic, D.: A taxonomy of security and privacy requirements for the Internet of Things (IoT). In: The 2014 IEEE International Conference on Industrial Engineering and Engineering Management (IEEM), pp. 1244–1248 (2014)

Armando, A., Costa, G., Verderame, L., Merlo, A.: Securing the bring your own device paradigm. Computer **47**(6), 48–56 (2014)

Chakraborty, S., Raghavan, K.R., Johnson, M.P., Srivastava, M.B.: A framework for context-aware privacy of sensor data on mobile systems. In: The Fourteenth Workshop on Mobile Computing Systems and Applications (HotMobile2013) (2013)

Dey, A.K., Abowd, G.D.: Towards a Better Understanding of Context and Context-Awareness, Georgia Institute of Technology, College of Computing (1999)

Fu, Z., Ren, K., Shu, J., Sun, X., Huang, F.: Enabling personalized search over encrypted outsourced data with efficiency improvement. IEEE Trans. Parallel Distrib. Syst. (2015)

Hadzovic, S., Serval, D., Kovacevic, S.: Regulatory aspects of child online protection. In: The 38th International Convention on Information and Communication Technology, Electronics and Microelectronics (MIPRO), pp. 409–412 (2015)

Heurix, J., Zimmermann, P., Neubauer, T., Fenz, S.: A taxonomy for privacy enhancing technologies. Comput. Secur. **53**, 1–17 (2015)

Hinske, S., Langheinrich, M.: An infrastructure for interactive and playful learning in augmented toy environments. In: The IEEE International Conference on Pervasive Computing and Communications (PerCom 2009), pp. 1–6 (2009)

Hung, P.C.K.: Mobile Services for Toy Computing. Applications and Trends in Computer Science. Springer International Publishing, Switzerland (2015)

Hung, P.C.K., Cheng, V.S.Y.: Privacy, Encyclopedia of Database Systems, pp. 2136–2137. Springer, New York (2009)

Livingstone, S., Haddon, L., Gorzig, A., Olafsson, K.: Risks and Safety on the Internet: The Perspective of Europan Children, Full findings and policy implications from the EU Kids Online survey of 9–16 year olds and their parents in 25 countries, London School of Economics and Political Science, London (2011)

Noor, R., Sahila, S., Jamal, S., Zakaria K.H.: Parental module control system for children's internet use. In: The 2012 International Conference on Information Society (i-society), pp. 511–513 (2012)

Peng, W., Li, F., Han, K.J., Zou, X.K., Wu, J.: T-dominance: prioritized defense deployment for BYOD security. In: The 2013 IEEE Conference on Communications and Network Security (CNS), pp. 37–45 (2013)

Plowman, L., Luckin, R.: Interactivity, interfaces, and smart toys. Computer **37**(2), 98–100 (2004)

Ren, Y., Shen, J., Wang, J., Han, J., Lee, S.: Mutual verifiable provable data auditing in public cloud storage. J. Internet Technol. **16**(2), 317–323 (2015)

Salah, A.A., Lepri, B., Pentland, A., Canny, J.: Understanding and changing behavior. Pervasive Comput. **12**(3), 18–20 (2013)

Salomon, D.: Privacy and Trust, Elements of Computer Security, pp. 273–290 (2010)

Schmidt, A.: "Interactive Context-Aware Systems Interacting with Ambient Intelligence," Ambient Intelligence. IOS Press, pp. 159–178 (2005)

Schell, B.H., Martin, M.V., Hung, P.C.K., Rueda, L.: Cyber child pornography: a review paper of the social and legal issues and remedies, aggression and violent behavior. Elsevier **12**(1), 45–63 (2007)

Schilit, B., Adams, N., Want, R.: Context-aware computing applications. In: The First Workshop on Mobile Computing Systems and Applications, pp. 85–90 (1994)

Shen, J., Moh, S., Chung, I.: Enhanced secure sensor association and key management in wireless body area networks. J. Commun. Netw. **17**(5), 453–462 (2015)

Sun, G., Huang, S., Bao, W., Yang, Y., Wang, Z.: A privacy protection policy combined with privacy homomorphism in the internet of things. In: The 23rd International Conference on Computer Communication and Networks (ICCCN), pp. 1–6 (2014)

Tanaka, F., Kimura, T.: The use of robots in early education: a scenario based on ethical consideration. In: The 18th IEEE International Symposium on Robot and Human Interactive Communication, pp. 558–560 (2009)

Tath, E.I.: Context data model for privacy. In: PRIME Standardization Workshop, IBM Zurich, 6 pages (2006)

Taylor, E., Michael, K.: Smart toys that are the stuff of nightmares. IEEE Technol. Soc. Mag. **35**(1), 8–10 (2016)

Tracy, L., Westeyn, G.D.: Monitoring children's developmental progress using augmented toys and activity recognition. Pers. Ubiquit. Comput. **16**(2), 169–191 (2012)

World Economic Forum. Personal Data: The Emergence of a New Asset Class, World Economic Forum (2011)

W3C. The Platform for Privacy Preferences 1.0 (P3P1.0) Specification, World Wide Web Consortium (W3C) Recommendation (2002)

Xia, Z., Wang, X., Sun, X., Wang, Q.: A secure and dynamic multi-keyword ranked search scheme over encrypted cloud data. IEEE Trans. Parallel Distrib. Syst. **27**(2), 340–352 (2015)

Grid Routing: An Energy-Efficient Routing Protocol for WSNs with Single Mobile Sink

Qi Liu[1,2(✉)], Kai Zhang[2,3], Xiaodong Liu[4], and Nigel Linge[5]

[1] Jiangsu Collaborative Innovation Center of Atmospheric Environment and Equipment Technology (CICAEET), Nanjing University of Information Science and Technology, Nanjing, China
qi.liu@nuist.edu.cn

[2] School of Computer and Software, Nanjing University of Information Science and Technology, Nanjing, China
zh_zhangkai@163.com

[3] Jiangsu Engineering Centre of Network Monitoring, Nanjing University of Information Science and Technology, Nanjing, China

[4] School of Computing, Edinburgh Napier University, 10 Colinton Road Edinburgh EH10 5DT, UK

[5] The University of Salford, Salford Greater Manchester M5 4WT, UK

Abstract. In a traditional wireless sensor network with static sinks, sensor nodes close to the sink run out of their batteries quicker than other nodes due to the increased data traffic towards the sink. These nodes with huge data traffic are easy to become hotspots. Therefore, such networks may prematurely collapse since the sink is unreachable for other remote nodes. To mitigate this problem, sink mobility is proposed, which provides load-balanced data delivery and uniform energy dissipation by shifting the hotspots. However, the latest location update of the mobile sink within the network introduces a high communication overhead. In this paper, we propose Grid Routing, an energy-efficient mobile sink routing protocol, which aims to decrease the advertisement overhead of the sink's position and balance local energy dissipation in a non-uniform network. Simulation results indicate that Grid Routing shows better performance in network lifetime when compared with existing work.

Keywords: Hotspots · Hierarchical structure · Sink mobility · Non-uniform network

1 Introduction

Wireless sensor networks are composed of lots of low-cost, dime-size, multifunctional sensor nodes in a self-organized manner [1]. Due to advantages of cheapness, easy implementation, reliability and small footprint, WSNs have been widely applied into different kinds of applications, such as environmental monitoring and protection, medical care, mine safety, home automation and forest fire detection [2–4]. However, the battery capacity of sensor devices is limited and batteries cannot be

© Springer International Publishing AG 2016
X. Sun et al. (Eds.): ICCCS 2016, Part II, LNCS 10040, pp. 232–243, 2016.
DOI: 10.1007/978-3-319-48674-1_21

replaced in most typical deployment scenarios. Therefore, energy efficiency is always a challenge for WSNs [5].

In a static sink scenario, sensor nodes in the vicinity of the sink suffer from a large number of data forwarding tasks towards the sink, which makes these nodes consume more battery power than other nodes. These nodes are easy to become hotspots [5]. For this purpose, sink mobility is proposed to alleviate hotspot problem, which helps achieving uniform energy consumption to extend the network lifetime by shifting the hotspots. Mobile sinks also implicitly provide load-balancing by distributing extra workload over other nodes. During the WSN operation, isolated sensor islands may be formed due to non-uniform node distribution or hotspot effect. Mobile sinks can link the isolated sensor islands to improve the network connectivity by accessing the portions of the network one by one to receive data, which might not be realized in a static sink case.

Mobile sinks although bring lots of advantages to WSNs, a series of new problems also comes with them. Exploring mobile sinks, how to maintain the fresh routes towards mobile sinks is a core problem [6]. Unlike static sink scenarios, the network topology becomes dynamic as the sink moves. Frequent location updates will cause frequent unpredictable topology changes. Flooding the location update packets of mobile sinks within the network is the simplest approach, whereas this method will introduce a high communication head.

The usage of the hierarchical architecture significantly decreases the advertisement overhead of the sink's position [7]. Only a limited set of nodes which is high-tier nodes in the hierarchical architecture need to keep track of the latest location of mobile sinks. Other regular nodes complete data delivery by retrieve high-tier nodes to get the sink's position. It is obvious that high-tier nodes cause a higher communication overhead than low-tier nodes, which makes the hierarchical structure collapse early. So in order to keep the network running smoothly, a high-tier structure maintenance mechanism is necessary to distribute extra communication overhead over a set of regular nodes [8].

For these problems, in this paper, we propose Grid Routing, an energy-efficient mobile sink routing protocol, suitable for time-sensitive applications. We highlight some key features and the contributions of Grid Routing as follows:

- Grid Routing is a hierarchical mobile sink routing protocol targeted for periodic data reporting in a large-scale networks.
- Grid Routing uses a routes dynamic adjustment scheme to maintain the fresh routes towards the mobile sink with minimal communication cost. Sensory data from source nodes can be easily forwarded to destination nodes.
- A simple high-tier structure maintenance mechanism is adopted to prevent the high-tier nodes from dying quickly. Grid Routing enables the high-tier nodes to switch roles with regular nodes when their energy level is below a certain energy threshold.

The rest of this paper is organized as follows: Section 2 gives a brief introduction of routing protocols employing different hierarchical structures. Section 3 gives the system model, including network characteristics and energy model. In Sect. 4, the methodology of Grid Routing is described in detail. We shows how to construct a grid structure and how data is delivered among sources and sinks. Section 5 shows simulation environment and further analyzes simulation results. Finally, we conclude this paper in Sect. 6.

2   Related Work

2.1   Virtual Infrastructure-Based Routing Protocols

There have been many hierarchical approaches to the problem of routing in WSNs with mobile sinks [9]. Overlaying a virtual infrastructure over the physical network significantly decreases the advertisement overhead of the sink's position. The high-tier nodes keep track of the latest location of mobile sinks, which means that only a limited set of nodes are employed to communicate with the sink. Low-tier nodes get the sink's position by querying the high-tier nodes. A successful hierarchy can enable the latest location of mobile sinks to be easily forwarded to the hierarchical structure and regular nodes to acquire the sink's position from the virtual high-tier infrastructure. In the remainder of this section, we explore several hierarchical mobile sink routing protocols and analyze their respective relative merits.

A distributed load balanced clustering and dual data uploading (LBC-DDU) is a cluster-based hierarchical routing protocol [10], which is proposed for sensors to self-organize themselves into clusters and realize dual data uploading by imposing multi-user multi-input and multi-output (MU-MIMO) technique. The network is partitioned into separate clusters with two cluster-heads of each cluster. LBC-DDU employs a mobile car to access each polling points selected in each cluster to collect data within a tolerable delay. It is clear that LBC-DDU is not suitable for time-sensitive applications. If the mobile car does not reach each polling points on time, data packets will be dropped after a certain period of time.

Cluster-based structure is the most popular hierarchical structure but not the only one. Two-Tier Data Dissemination (TTDD) is a virtual grid-based hierarchical routing protocol [11]. Every source node establishes a virtual grid-based network structure when existing sensory data and itself becomes a crossing point of this grid. Mobile sinks flood a query within a local grid. The request packet will be forwarded to the source node and generated sensory data will be sent to the mobile sink along the opposite direction of the originating path. Although TTDD limits flooding overhead within a local grid, grid construction cost for every source node is immense.

Obviously, TTDD is not suitable for the network where events occur frequently. In order to overcome TTDD's shortcoming of grid construction, a Grid-Based Energy-Efficient Routing (GBEER) from multiple sources to multiple mobile sinks is presented [12], which constructs only one grid structure for all the source nodes using global location information. Data request packets are sent from the sink along the horizontal direction while the source node sends data announcement packets along the vertical direction, ensuring that there must be a header to receive both two data packets. Data request packets will be forwarded to the source node along the reverse of the path taken by data announcement packets. Although GBEER significantly decreases grid construction cost and enables high overhead to be limited in a separate cell, headers which process data request and announcement are easy to become hotspots and deplete their energy quicker than other nodes.

Similar to GBEER and TTDD, a virtual Grid-Based Dynamic Routes Adjustment (VGDRA) scheme is put forward [6], aiming to reduce the routes reconstruction cost to extend the network lifetime. VGDRA adopts four communication rules to dynamically readjusting routes, facilitating the sink's location update within the virtual high-tier infrastructure. Moreover, high-tier nodes can easily spread extra load to other nodes of every cell via a cell-header rotation mechanism. Even though dynamic routes adjustment scheme is a good solution for the problem of the sink's position update, VGDRA has no good performance in a non-uniform network.

Area-based approaches are also adopted to the problem of the sink's position advertisement in a hierarchical mobile sink routing protocol. LBDD [13] and Railroad [14] are typical area-based routing protocols.

Line-Based Data Dissemination (LBDD) protocol defines a vertical virtual line, where in-line nodes belong to high-tier nodes. Source nodes forward the data to the nearest in-line nodes while generating some new data. The sink sends a query to the line and in-line nodes share this query until the destination node is reached. The data is then directly forwarded to the sink. However, LBDD suffers from the hotspot problem. Especially for large-scale networks, the line has to be wide enough to alleviate the hotspot problem since sharing queries on the line will introduce a high communication overhead.

Railroad constructs a virtual rail structure, which is a closed loop of a strip of nodes. When a source node generates data, it sends an event notification message to the nearest rail node. This rail node constructs a new station and floods this notification message in the station. The sink sends a query to the nearest rail node and share this query in two directions until this query reaches the station. The station node receiving the query informs the source node of the sink's position. The source node forwards sensory data directly to the sink. However, Railroad may introduce a high data delivery delay due to a much longer structure travelled by the query and a long distance between the rail node and the source node.

Grid Routing establishes a virtual grid structure that imposes dynamic routes adjustment scheme to easily deliver the latest location of mobile sinks to cell-headers (high-tier nodes) with minimal communication overhead. On the other hand, Grid Routing improves the grid maintenance mechanism to enable the cell-headers to distribute more reasonably, which helps decreasing the overall energy consumption of every cell.

2.2   Energy-Aware Transmission Range Adjusting

As we know, a node with a large communication range will have amounts of neighbors. This means this node will suffer from a large number of data forwarding tasks. If a sensor node keeps the same transmission range of a "healthy" node all the time during the WSN operation, it will run out of its battery resource quickly.

Wang proposed an energy-aware transmission range adjusting scheme to adjust the communication range of sensor nodes based on their current residual energy [15]. Assuming that the total battery capacity of a "healthy" sensor node is B and its transmission range is r, the battery capacity of sensor nodes can be divided into three types.

As shown in Fig. 1, a sensor node will adjust its communication range according to the current residual energy.

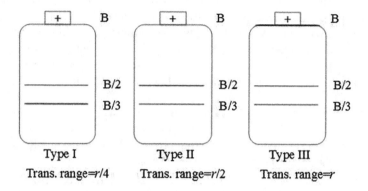

Fig. 1. The energy-aware transmission range adjusting mechanism

3   System Model

Grid Routing establishes a virtual grid-based network structure which divides the network into the optional number of cells of the same size. The optional number of cells is calculated based on the total number of sensor nodes in the sensor field. The mobile sink moves around the clockwise\counterclockwise around the sensor field to collect data from the network.

3.1   Network Characteristics

We make some assumptions about network characteristics before introducing our Grid Routing protocol.

- Sensor nodes shows non-uniform distribution.
- All sensor nodes have the same limited initial energy level, whereas the battery of the mobile sink is rechargeable, where it has no resource constraints.
- Each sensor node can adjust its communication range referring to the energy-aware transmission range adjusting mechanism described in Related Work.
- There is no communication obstacle between any two nodes.

3.2   Energy Model

Grid Routing adopts the first order radio energy model as energy consumption model [13]. When a sensor node transmits l-bit length data packet at distance d, energy consumed by the sender node can be got by the following Eq. 1.

$$E_{Tx}(l, d) = \begin{cases} lE_{elec} + l\varepsilon_{fs}d^2, \ d < d_0 \\ lE_{elec} + l\varepsilon_{mp}d^4, \ d \geq d_0 \end{cases} \tag{1}$$

where l is the length of data packets, E_{elec} is energy consumption to transmit or receive one-bit length data, ε_{fs} and ε_{mp} are energy required for the transmitter amplifier according to different transmission ranges. d_0 is a constant, which can be calculated by $\sqrt{\varepsilon_{fs}/\varepsilon_{mp}}$.

When a sensor node receives l-bit length data, energy consumption can be easily calculated:

$$E_{Rx}(l, d) = lE_{elec} \tag{2}$$

4 Grid Routing

In this section, the methodology of Grid Routing is described in detail, which divides the network into cells of equal size on the basic of the total number of sensor nodes in the sensor field. Utilizing this grid construction approach, only a limited set of nodes need to keep track of the latest location of mobile sinks, thereby decreasing the communication cost of this process. The hierarchy can be kept during the WSN operation by reelecting cell-headers in every cell. Adjacent cell-headers communicate with each other via gateway nodes.

4.1 Grid Construction

Initially, the network is partitioned into several uniform-size cells. The number of cells is determined by the total number of sensor nodes. If a large number of nodes are divided into a small amount of cells, cell-headers will run out of their batteries quickly and cell-header reelection process will be performed frequently. If a small number of sensor nodes are divided into excessive cells, too many high-tier nodes will lead to a high communication overhead while updating the sink's position.

To determine the optional number of high-tier nodes, we refer to the heuristics used in LEACH [16], which considers 5 % of the total number of sensor nodes. Considering load-balancing and uniform energy dissipation, Eq. 3 is adopted to divide the sensor field with N sensor nodes into K cells of equal size, where K is a square number.

$$K = \begin{cases} 4 & N \times 0.05 \leq 6; \\ 9 & 6 < N \times 0.05 \leq 12; \\ 16 & 12 < N \times 0.05 \leq 20; \\ \vdots & \vdots \end{cases} \tag{3}$$

The virtual grid structure will not change once constructed successfully. Sensor nodes put themselves into their respective cells based on network partitioning results from the mobile sink. Initially, nodes closest to the mod-point of their respective cell will be determined as the cell-header. Only those nodes whose distance to the mid-point of cells is below a certain distance threshold will be qualified to be a cell-header candidate. Elected cell-headers informed their member nodes and adjacent cell-headers of their roles.

As shown in Fig. 2, the mobile sink is first placed at *Cell* 1 while the network is initially partitioned into 16 cells. The mobile sink moves counterclockwise around the sensor field to collect data.

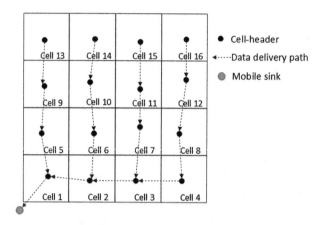

Fig. 2. The backbone of virtual grid structure

4.2 The Sink's Position Update Mechanism

As the mobile sink changes its position, the topology becomes dynamic and routes towards the mobile sink should be reset. Flooding the update packets of mobile sinks within the network is the most efficient way, however, the significant communication overhead will cause a short network lifetime.

In this paper, Grid Routing adopts a dynamic routes adjustment scheme to facilitate the sink's location update, which maintains the fresh routes towards the mobile sink. A propagation rule is performed while updating routes towards the mobile sink. The specific process is as follows:

- Rule 1: The mobile sink sends a location update packet to its immediate cell. Then nodes upon receiving this packet will forward it to their cell-header. If the current cell-header (CH) is the originating cell-header (OCH), which communicates directly with the mobile sink, the current CH informs the mobile sink to transmit data directly. Otherwise, rule 2 will be executed.
- Rule 2: The current CH becomes OCH, and forwards this location update packet to its immediate downstream cell-header. The next downstream cell-header upon receiving the update packet checks whether its next-hop is the sender node. If not, this cell-header set its next-hop as the sender node, and continues to relay this update packet to its downstream cell-header. If the downstream cell-header is NULL, the update packet is discarded.

- Rule 3: The current OCH also shares the sink's position update to the previous OCH. The previous OCH upon receiving the update packet adjusts its route by setting the current OCH as its next-hop towards the mobile sink.

As illustrated in Fig. 3(a), a mobile sink starting from *Cell* 2 moves a small distance and still sojourns at *Cell* 2, routes towards the mobile sink remain the same according to rule 1. However, if the mobile sink moves out to the current cell, routes towards the mobile sink will change. In Fig. 3(b), the mobile sink moves from *Cell* 2 to *Cell* 3, blue arrows represent adjusted data delivery routes.

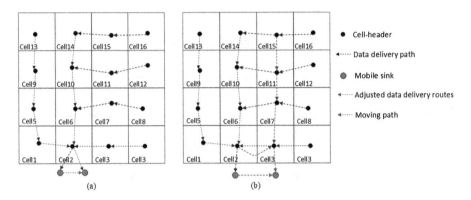

Fig. 3. Dynamic routes adjustment scheme

4.3 Grid Maintenance

To ensure a long network lifetime, the grid structure should be kept during the WSN operation. Hence, a grid maintenance mechanism is necessary in Grid Routing. Reelecting cell-headers to replace current cell-headers in every cell is a good way to extend the hierarchy lifetime.

We define a certain energy threshold to trigger cell-header reelection process. When the current residual battery energy of a cell-header is below this threshold, a cell-header reelection process occurs among nodes whose distance to the mid-point of cells is below a distance threshold. Since sensor nodes remain non-uniform distribution, the node density in local regions is different, leading to non-uniform energy consumption in every cell. We adopt the number of neighbor nodes to represent the node density and take it into consideration when reelecting a new cell-header. It is clear that the overall energy consumption in a cell will be decreased if the node with more neighbor nodes becomes the cell-header, since more nodes have less hops towards the cell-header.

In the reelection process, the node with a higher residual energy level and more neighbor nodes are more likely to be a new cell-header compared to other candidates. If no node meets the requirement in the search zone, the searching scope will be slightly expanded or the energy level is decreased progressively. In order to protect the grid structure, cell-headers will share information of new cell-headers with their respective member nodes and adjacent cell-headers in their neighborhood.

5   Performance Evaluation

5.1   Simulation Environment

We use Matlab R2012b to evaluate the performance of our proposed Grid Routing protocol. 300 sensor nodes are randomly deployed in a rectangular region of 200×200 m^2. As shown in Fig. 2, the mobile sink is placed at *Cell* 1 and then moves counterclockwise around the sensor field to collect data at a constant speed. According to Eq. 3, the sensor field is divided into 16 cells. Specific simulation parameters are listed in Table 1.

Table 1.   Simulation parameters

Parameter	Definition	Unit
E_0	Initial battery capacity of sensor nodes	2 J
E_{elec}	Energy dissipation to run the radio unit	50 nJ/bit
ε_{fs}	Free space radio propagation model of transmitter amplifier	10 pJ/bit/m^2
ε_{mp}	Multi-path radio propagation model of transmitter amplifier	0.0013 pJ/bit/m^4
l	Packet length	2000 bits

5.2   Results Analysis

Compared with VGDRA [6], we adopt energy-aware transmission range adjusting scheme to adaptively change the communication range of a sensor node to avoid a long distance communication in our proposed Grid Routing protocol. Furthermore, we improve the cell-header reelection process to achieve uniform energy dissipation in every cell. Therefore, in a given period of time, Grid Routing can save more energy theoretically. We define one time of data reporting as one round. It is clear that Grid Routing, which can achieve uniform energy dissipation in the local region, has a longer network lifetime and also has higher residual energy level in the same rounds than VGDRA.

In our experiments, we estimated the network lifetime in terms of the number of rounds of the mobile sink around the sensor field till all nodes die due to energy depletion. Figure 4 presents the network lifetime of Grid Routing and VGDRA with different rounds. In VGDRA, sensor nodes suffer from more energy dissipation due to non-uniform node distribution. On the basic of the cell-header role rotation process, more nodes experience a long distance data delivery to forward data to the cell-header if the cell-header locates at a place with low node density. However, in our Grid Routing, we put local node density into consideration when reelecting cell-headers, which enables cell-header to distribute more reasonably. As described in Fig. 5, Grid Routing consumes less energy than VGDRA in the same rounds.

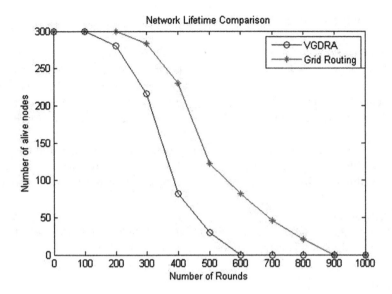

Fig. 4. Network lifetime comparison

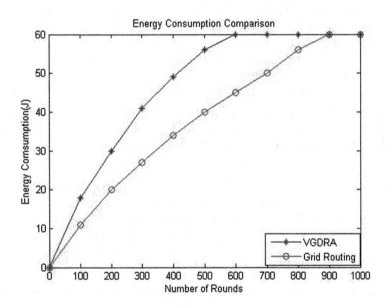

Fig. 5. Energy consumption comparison

6 Conclusions and Future Work

In this paper, we proposed an energy-efficient hierarchical mobile sink routing protocol, called Grid Routing, which enable a mobile sink to move counterclockwise around the sensor field to collect data. Grid Routing maintains the fresh routes towards the mobile sink with minimal communication cost and imposes the cell-header reelection process to get uniform energy consumption in local region. Simulation results of Grid Routing show good performance compared to existing work.

In the future, we hope to analyze the performance of Grid Routing at different sink's speeds and different moving paths. And we will work on constructing a grid structure with cells in different sizes to get uniform energy consumption in the whole sensor field.

Acknowledgements. This work is supported by the NSFC (61300238, 61300237, 61232016, 1405254, 61373133), Marie Curie Fellowship (701697-CAR-MSCA-IFEF-ST), Basic Research Programs (Natural Science Foundation) of Jiangsu Province (BK20131004) and the PAPD fund.

References

1. Akyildiz, I.F., Su, W., Sankarasubramaniam, Y., Cayirci, E.: Wireless sensor network: a survey. Comput. Netw. **40**(8), 393–422 (2002)
2. Chen, M., Gonzalez, S., Vasilakos, A., Cao, H., Leung, C.M.: Body area networks: a survey. Mob. Netw. Appl. **16**(2), 171–193 (2011)
3. Yick, J., Mukherjee, B., Ghosal, D.: Wireless sensor network survey. Comput. Netw. **52**(12), 2292–2330 (2008)
4. Shen, J., Tan, H., Wang, J., Wang, J., Lee, S.: A novel routing protocol providing good transmission reliability in underwater sensor networks. J. Internet Technol. **16**(1), 171–178 (2015)
5. Tunca, C., Isik, S., Donmez, M.Y., Ersoy, C.: Distributed mobile sink routing for wireless sensor networks: a survey. IEEE Commun. Surv. Tutorials **16**(2), 877–897 (2014)
6. Khan, A.W., Abdullah, A.H., Razzaque, M.A., Bangash, J.I.: VGDRA: a virtual grid-based dynamic routes adjustment scheme for mobile sink-based wireless sensor networks. IEEE Sens. J. **15**(1), 526–534 (2015)
7. Xie, S., Wang, Y.: Construction of tree network with limited delivery latency in homogeneous wireless sensor networks. Wirel. Pers. Commun. **78**(1), 231–246 (2014)
8. Guo, P., Wang, J., Li, B., Lee, S.: A variable threshold-value authentication architecture for wireless mesh networks. J. Internet Technol. **15**(6), 929–936 (2014)
9. Tunca, C., Isik, S., Donmez, M.Y., Ersoy, C.: Ring routing: an energy-efficient routing protocol for wireless sensor networks with a mobile sink. IEEE Trans. Mob. Comput. **14**(9), 1947–1960 (2015)
10. Zhao, M., Yang, Y., Wang, C.: Mobile data gathering with load balanced clustering and dual data uploading in wireless sensor networks. IEEE Trans. Mob. Comput. **14**(4), 770–785 (2015)
11. Luo, H., Ye, F., Cheng, J., Lu, S., Zhang, L.: TTDD: two-tier data dissemination in large-scale wireless sensor networks. Wirel. Netw. **11**(1–2), 161–175 (2005)
12. Kweon, K., Ghim, H., Hong, J., Yoon, H.: Grid-based energy-efficient routing from multiple sources to multiple mobile sinks in wireless sensor networks. In: Proceedings of 4th IEEE International Symposium on Wireless Pervasive Computing, pp. 1–5 (2009)

13. Hamida, E.B., Chelius, G.: A line-based data dissemination protocol for wireless sensor networks with mobile sink. In: Proceedings of 2008 IEEE International Conference on Communications, pp. 2201–2205 (2008)
14. Shin, J.-H., Kim, J., Park, K., Park, D.: Railroad: virtual infrastructure for data dissemination in wireless sensor networks. In: Proceedings of the 2nd ACM International Workshop on Performance Evaluation of Wireless Ad Hoc, Sensor, and Ubiquitous Networks, pp. 168–173 (2005)
15. Wang, C.-F., Shih, J.-D., Pan, B.-H., Wu, T.-Y.: A network lifetime enhancement method for sink relocation and its analysis in wireless sensor networks. IEEE Sens. J. **14**(6), 1932–1943 (2014)
16. Heinzelman, W.B., Chandrakasan, A.P., Balakrishnan, H.: An application-specific protocol architecture for wireless microsensor networks. IEEE Trans. Wirel. Commun. **1**(4), 660–670 (2002)

A Method for Electric Load Data Verification and Repair in Home Environment

Qi Liu[1,2(✉)], Shengjun Li[2,3], Xiaodong Liu[4], and Nigel Linge[5]

[1] Jiangsu Collaborative Innovation Center of Atmospheric Environment
and Equipment Technology (CICAEET), Nanjing University of Information
Science and Technology, Nanjing 210044, China
qi.liu@nuist.edu.cn
[2] School of Computer and Software,
Nanjing University of Information Science and Technology, Nanjing, China
846579040@qq.com
[3] Jiangsu Engineering Centre of Network Monitoring,
Nanjing University of Information Science and Technology, Nanjing, China
[4] School of Computing, Edinburgh Napier University, 10 Colinton Road,
Edinburgh EH10 5DT, UK
[5] The University of Salford, Salford, Greater Manchester M5 4WT, UK

Abstract. Most people do not have a consciousness of energy saving. For this phenomenon, the governments are building smart grids to take measures for the energy crisis. Electric load data records the electric consumption and plays an important role in operation and planning of the power system. However, in home, electric load data usually has the abnormal, noisy and missing data due to various factors. With wrong data, we can not analysis the data correctly, then can not take the right actions to avoid the energy wastes. In this paper, we propose a new solution for the electric load data verification and repair in home environment. As the result shows, proposed method have a better performance than the up to date methods.

Keywords: Data repair · Power data quality · Power system · Home energy management

1 Introduction

Recent years, the smart grid develops rapidly, the load data has been a essential role for electric utilities [1, 2]. To get the load data, we must complete the smart grid, so smart meters are necessary to be built in various environment. In this way, we can get the load data, and gather the information about how appliances consume electric energy, and even the consuming patterns. For electric industry, the analysis of electric load data is important for the day-to-day operation, system analysis, energy saving and energy planning. For energy consumer, they can use the feedback information to help them save the cost.

In home environment, gathering load data accurately is a challenging task. There is often missing and wrong data in the process of collecting and transferring. It is caused

© Springer International Publishing AG 2016
X. Sun et al. (Eds.): ICCCS 2016, Part II, LNCS 10040, pp. 244–253, 2016.
DOI: 10.1007/978-3-319-48674-1_22

by many factors, such as smart meters malfunction, communication failures, equipment outages and other factors. These cause a significant deviation in load, and can not represent the correct energy consuming pattern. If we work on these wrong data sets, the results would be useless, even misleading. So it is important to identify and correct the wrong data and fill the missing data.

Currently, many approaches are presented to detect and repair wrong load data, but few researchers focus on the load data repair in home environment. In this paper, we propose a novel method to verify and repair the load data. Missing data is treated as a special case of wrong data. There are three challenges in solving the problems. First, traditional statistical methods can not be used if a relatively large portion of data is wrong or missing. Second, it is difficult to judge whether a relatively large deviation represents wrong data or an underlying change in data patterns. Third, due to in home environment, it is hard to deal with its real randomness and uncertainty in electricity consumption.

The contributions of this work are as follows. First, we propose a "1 + N" method to validate if the data is correct, repair the wrong data. Second, we focus on the random electric consumption in home environment, the method can avoid the influence of the load data's aperiodicity in home. Also, the solution can be robust to a relatively large portion of missing data, and it can identify whether the deviation represents wrong data or an underlying change in patterns. The results demonstrated the effectiveness and high performance of the proposed solution.

2 Related Work

A closely related area to the load repair is outlier detection, which has been broadly studied in lots of fields, such as data mining and statistics. For outlier detection, researchers identify the outliers first, then find a proper way to correct them.

As these methods develop, outliers detection in time series has become a general mathematical concept in statistic field to be studied [3]. In statistic domain, the mean and median method suggested in [4] considers a given periodicity and replaces missing and corrupted data using the average or medians of the corresponding observations at different periods. This method does not fully take data distribution into consideration. A lot of methods assume that the data follow an underlying known probability distribution. Tang et al. split the data into some portrait data sets from a brand new perspective, they assume that the data sets follow some distributions, and find the outliers according to the distribution, replace the outliers with the estimated values finally [5]. Assuming data follow a certain distribution can convert the detection problem to finding the abnormal areas in time series. However, the distribution can not be precisely known to us all the time. What's more, traditional statistical methods can not handle the data which a relatively large portion of it are missing.

Some other methods [6−10] are regression-based. They assume that the load data have some certain pattern, but to home environment, the randomicity is a important feature which need to be considered. People's lives are not set carved in stone, incidents occur everyday, resulting in the strong stochastic load data. So these methods inevitably have large error and over-fitting problems. Other methods employ smoothing techniques.

Chen et al. [11] proposed a non-parametric regression method based on B-spline and kernel smoothing to fit the load curve data, then set a confidence interval to judge whether a point is an outlier or not. In general, the regression-based methods are based on their parameters. Smoothing techniques are sensitive to their training data, if missing data are out of the training data's range or training data can not represent the original data, the outcome will be bad. As a result, the consequence will be subject to these factors.

In the domain of data mining, a lot of methods based on similarity were proposed to detect outliers. Such as k-nearest neighbor [12], k-means clustering [13], and the neural network methods such as RNNs [14] are used. According the same features, they classify the observations, and find the observations which are far from the clusters. However, most of these methods are designed for structured relational data, and they are also time consuming for training process.

3 Problem Definition

A load curve data is a time series where the load values are collected at a certain time frequency such as every 1 s or hourly. The load data record status of domestic appliances, such as their current, voltage, power. The data is also influenced by various factors such as meter failures, communication interruptions or errors, and dynamism of customers. So, a load curve data consists of not only white noises but also some corrupted data.

Nowadays, the technology for smart meters is mature, the precision of smart meters is very high, and the fault rate is low. In home environment, smart meters are used to collected the data. The meters usually use zigbee to deliver domestic appliances' status data, due to the short transmission distance of zigbee, there will be communication interruptions sometimes, and it brings missing data. So the corrupted data is usually caused by the communication interruptions. As a result, the corrupted data in this paper is referred to the missing data. Under these circumstances, the data repair process is mainly to replacing the missing data.

In addition, traditional data cleansing methods check that if the observation is follow a certain pattern to identify whether the observation is corrupted or not. But the observation which does not follow the pattern may not be really corrupted. And in home environment, modern people's irregular lifestyle may not follow a so-called pattern. So defining a corrupted data in that way is not precise, and we need to find the corrupted data more precisely.

Definition 1: A load curve data is a time series $S = \{(y_i, t_i)\}_{i=1}^n$ that is an n-values sequence ordered by time where t_i is the timestamp and y_i is the observation at the time t_i.

In this paper, we focus on two tasks: First, validate if an observation is corrupted precisely. Second, fill the missing data caused by the communication interruptions.

4 Proposed Methods

As mentioned earlier, modern domestic consumers will not use appliances regularly, that is to say, the habits of people's using appliances do not follow a certain pattern. So we proposed a new solution to get rid of the influence of domestic consumers' irregular lifestyles.

4.1 System Construction

To collect data, we proposed a new way to get the data. Assume that the family has N appliances that needed to be measured, then we install N smart meters to get their data respectively. In addition, we install a smart meter at the power bus for the house. At last, put the server for receiving signals just besides the power bus to ensure the server can receive the signal from the power bus. Figure 1 shows the system layout. In this way, we have constituted our 'N + 1' model to get the data we want. In this paper, the data we collect is power.

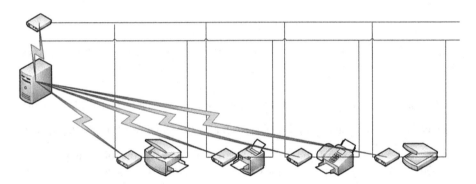

Fig. 1. System layout

4.2 Validate Data Quality

As we know, household electrical circuit is a parallel circuit, so that we can use the following formula to describe the relationship between the power bus and various domestic appliances:

$$P_{All} = \sum_{i=0}^{n} P_i + \varepsilon \qquad (1)$$

where the P_{All} is the value of the power bus, P_i is the value of ith domestic appliance and there are n of the appliances, ε is the error, it mainly refers to the line loss and white noise. Figure 2 shows that some value of ε when all the appliances work stably.

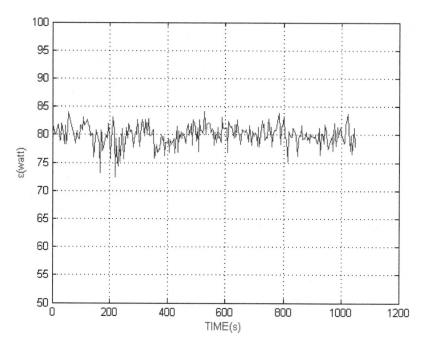

Fig. 2. The difference between the values of power bus and sum of appliances when appliances work stably and well

While all domestic appliances and smart meters work stably and well, then the difference between P_{All} and $\sum_{i=0}^{n} P_i$, i.e. ε is less than a threshold, we consider the data is correct and true in this situation. Even there are some observations obviously deviate from their so-called regular patterns, the data is real and true. Because we get the values of power bus and various domestic appliances, according to (1), they can verify each other. Also, this could identify the outliers more precisely.

4.3   Fill Missing Data

As mentioned earlier, corrupted data refers to missing data and it is caused by the communication interruptions in home environment. And we consider that the data from the power bus is real and correct because of the system layout, it overcome the problem that the short communication distance of zigbee brings.

If only one appliance miss its data, we can easily use (1) to fill the data.

$$P_k = P_{All} - \left(\sum_{i=1}^{k-1} P_i + \sum_{i=k+1}^{N} P_i + \varepsilon \right) \tag{2}$$

However, there are more than one appliances lose their data sometimes, interpolation techniques are used to help fill it. Interpolation techniques utilize the existing observed points to generate a new interpolation function, and this function will be carried out to get the interpolation to fill the missing data.

4.3.1   Lagrange Interpolation

$x_0, x_1, \ldots, x_n$ are the $n + 1$ nodes of the time series, utilize them to construct the interpolation polynomial $L_n(x)$. Assume that they meet the following condition:

$$L_n(x_j) = y_j(j = 0, 1, \ldots, n) \tag{3}$$

Where y_j is the real value. To construct $L_n(x)$, define the interpolation basis function as following:

Definition 2: Given a polynomial of degree n, $L_j(x)(j = 0, 1, .., n)$, it satisfy the following conditions on $n + 1$ observations $x_0 < x_1 < \ldots < x_n$:

$$L_n(x_j) = \begin{cases} 1, & k = j; \\ 0, & k \neq j. \end{cases} (j, k = 0, 1, \ldots, n) \tag{4}$$

call these $n + 1$ $L_0(x), L_1(x), \ldots, L_n(x)$ polynomials of degree n are the interpolation basis functions of the nodes $x_0, x_1, \ldots, x_n$. The n degree interpolation basis function is:

$$L_k(x) = \frac{(x - x_0)\ldots(x - x_{k-1})(x - x_{k+1})\ldots(x - x_n)}{(x_k - x_0)\ldots(x_k - x_{k-1})(x_k - x_{k+1})\ldots(x_k - x_n)} (k = 0, 1, \ldots, n) \tag{5}$$

it obviously satisfies (4). Then the interpolation polynomial $L_n(x)$ which meets the condition (3) could be expressed as following:

$$L_n(x) = \sum_{k=0}^{n} y_k l_k(x) \tag{6}$$

the polynomial like $L_n(x)$ called Lagrange interpolation.

4.3.2   b-spline Interpolation

Given the control nodes $P_0, P_1, \ldots, P_n$, so that the b-spline curve of degree $k((k-1)$-th power) can be expressed as:

$$P(t) = \sum_{i=0}^{n} P_i N_{i,k}(t) \tag{6}$$

where $N_{i,k}(t)$ are the basic functions of the b-spline curve of degree k, every one of them is called a b-spline.

The b-spline basic function $N_{i,k}(t)$ is k order, it can be expressed as following:

$$N_{i,k}(t) = \frac{1}{k!} \sum_{j=0}^{k-i} (-1)^k \cdot C_{k+1}^j \cdot (t+k-i-j)^k (0 \leq t \leq 1, i = 0, 1, 2, \ldots k) \quad (8)$$

de Boor Cox's recursive definition:

$$N_{i,0}(t) = \begin{cases} 1, t_i \leq t < t_{i+1}; \\ 0, t < t_i \, or \, t \geq t_{i+1} \end{cases},$$

$$N_{i,k}(t) = \frac{t - t_i}{t_{i+k} - t_i} N_{i,k-1}(t) + \frac{t_{i+k+1} - t}{t_{i+k+1} - t_{i+1}} N_{i+1,k-1}(t), k > 0$$

$$\text{assume that:} \frac{0}{0} = 0 \quad (9)$$

The recurrence formula shows that: the i-th b-spline $N_{i,k}(t)$ of degree k is obtained depend on $t_i, t_{i+1}, \ldots, t_{i+k+1}$ k + 2 nodes.

4.3.3   Interpolation Fusion Method

Here we proposed a new interpolation fusion method to fill the missing data, in the case of more than one appliance lose their information. It based on the system layout, Lagrange interpolation and the b-spline interpolation. As the interpolation technique just simulate the data's trend roughly, it can not restore the data precisely. For simplicity, so there will be two situations: first, two interpolation methods' outcome are all larger or smaller than the real value, and one of them is closer. Second, one of them is larger than the real value, and the other is lower than the real value.

As mentioned above, we proposed a new interpolation fusion method to fill the missing data when there are more than one appliance lose data, the pseudo code of the algorithm is shown in Table 1.

Table 1. Interpolation fusion method

Algorithm interpolation fusion($D_0, D_1, \ldots, D_n; E_0, E_1, \ldots, E_n$)
1. $P_{l1}s$=Lagrange interpolation($D_0, D_1, \ldots, D_n$);
2. $P_{l2}s$=Lagrange interpolation($E_0, E_1, \ldots, E_n$);
3. $P_{b1}s$=b-spline interpolation($D_0, D_1, \ldots, D_n$);
4. $P_{b2}s$=b-spline interpolation($E_0, E_1, \ldots, E_n$);
5. compare $P_{l1}s + P_{l2}s$ with $P_{all} - P_{known} - \varepsilon$;
6. compare $P_{b1}s + P_{b2}s$ with $P_{all} - P_{known} - \varepsilon$;
7. compare $\frac{(P_{l1}s+P_{b1}s)}{2} + \frac{(P_{l2}s+P_{b2}s)}{2}$ with $P_{all} - P_{known} - \varepsilon$;
8. take the value which is more closer to $P_{all} - P_{known} - \varepsilon$;

$D_0, D_1, \ldots, D_n$ and $E_0, E_1, \ldots, E_n$ are the observations of the appliances which have missing data, $P_{l1}s$ and $P_{l2}s$ are the outcomes of the Lagrange interpolation, and $P_{b1}s$ and $P_{b2}s$ are the outcomes of the b-spline interpolation, P_{known} is the sum of the power that appliances which have no missing data.

5 Implementation and Performance

In this section, we implement our electric load data verification and repair method in home environment.

5.1 Data Verification

In this paper, we use the REDD data sets [16], and assume that the appliances work stably, i.e. working appliances' number will not change, so that the ε mentioned before will be steady, as Fig. 2 shows. In other words, we consider one situation of the working appliances' combination, the others are the same. When another kind of combination, the ε will also be steady.

As domestic appliances work stably, the error ε is steady, and we can use the average value of training data to represent the error ε. And we use the most deviate observation as the bound value, if an observation deviate the average value more than the bound one, this will be thought as an outlier. After training, here we take 100 test observations randomly. These observations are observed real and correct in advance. Table 2 shows the consequence.

Table 2. Data verification and outlier detect

Mostly deviate from ε	Number of test observations	Observations that $\geq \varepsilon$	Observations that $\leq \varepsilon$	Accuracy
9.32 %	100	0	100	100 %

As the Table 2 shows, our methods could certificate the data's quality.

5.2 Fill Missing Data When Only One Appliance Miss Data

When only one appliance loses its data, we can use (1) to fix the data and get the following formula:

$$P_{loss} = P_{all} - \sum P_{unloss} - \varepsilon$$

where P_{all} is the value of the power bus, P_{unloss} is the value of every value of the appliance which has no missing data, ε is the error, here we used the existing data's average value.

The performance of the b-spline and our proposed method, as Table 3 shows.

Table 3. Performances when one appliance miss data

Number of missing data appliance	Loss percent of the data	b-spline	Proposed method
1	50 %	96.37 %	98.42 %
1	20 %	88.79 %	96.32 %

As seen in Table 3, proposed method's performance is better than the b-spline which is the up-to-date method in outlier repair, and it is robust to the loss rate of data. Because the data is randomly corrupted, and the number of the working appliance is stationary, data is relatively stable. Also, we did not take some actual accidents into the experiment, so the b-spline have a relatively high repair accuracy. If we take some simulation situations of accidents, our method will be even better theoretically and the b-spline's performance will be bad for some special situations.

Proposed method can handle the condition that one appliance totally loses its data. As the data's loss rate raises, b-spline and other traditional methods will not work.

5.3   Fill Missing Data When More Than One Appliance Miss Data

When more than one appliance loses data, the method for one appliance losing data is not worked. So here we need two interpolation methods and our proposed system to construct the interpolation fusion method to repair the missing data. As the Table 1 shows how the proposed algorithm works. It can handle more than one appliance miss its data (Table 4).

Table 4. Performances when more than one appliance miss data

Number of missing data appliance	Loss percent of the data	b-spline	Proposed method
2	50 %	93.94 %	95.92 %
2	80 %	90.32 %	93.86 %

Proposed method fuses two interpolation methods, it seems just make a relatively little improvement as to b-spline method. But the method provide a good way to verify which outcome is better.

6   Conclusion and Future Work

This paper proposed a new data verification and repair method in home environment. The method considered the real condition that happens in home, and it collected the information of all appliances and the power bus, to make them verify each other. It also can handle the randomicity problem which has a big affect on the repair accuracy. As a result, it could verify the data quality precisely, and it can repair the missing data better than the up-to-date method. Its advantage is to solve the traditional method's inherent drawback that they assumed the data follows certain pattern or period.

But the proposed method did not consider the change of the working appliances, it assumed that the number of working appliances is stationary. In the future work, we must consider the data fluctuation caused by the domestic users. So far, we just focus on the missing data, next we will also fix the corrupted data which caused by the mistake of the smart meters or the communication process.

Acknowledgements. This work is supported by the NSFC (61300238, 61300237, 61232016, 1405254, 61373133), Marie Curie Fellowship (701697-CAR-MSCA-IFEF-ST), Basic Research Programs (Natural Science Foundation) of Jiangsu Province (BK20131004) and the PAPD fund.

References

1. Chen, J., Li, W., Lau, A., Cao, J., Wang, K.: Automated load curve data cleansing in power systems. IEEE Trans. Smart Grid **1**(2), 213–221 (2010)
2. Chen, S.-Y., Song, S.-F., Li, L., Shen, J.: Survey on smart grid technology. Power Syst. Technol. **33**(8), 1–7 (2009)
3. Hodge, V.J., Austin, J.: A survey of outlier detection methodologies. Artif. Intell. Rev. **22**, 5–126 (2004)
4. Weron, R.: Modeling and Forecasting Electricity Loads and Prices—A Statistical Approach. Wiley, New York (2006)
5. Tang, G., Kui, W., Lei, J., Bi, Z., Tang, J.: From landscape to portrait: a new approach for outlier detection in load curve data. IEEE Trans. Smart Grid **5**, 1764–1773 (2014)
6. Fox, A.J.: Outliers in time series. J. Roy. Stat. Soc. Ser. B Stat. Methodol. **34**, 350–363 (1972)
7. Ljung, G.M.: On outlier detection in time series. J. Roy. Stat. Soc. Ser. B Stat. Methodol. **55**, 559–567 (1993)
8. Abraham, B., Yatawara, N.: A score test for detection of time series outliers. J. Time Ser. Anal. **9**, 109–119 (1988)
9. Abraham, B., Chuang, A.: Outlier detection and time series modeling. Technometrics **31**, 241–248 (1989)
10. Schmid, W.: The multiple outlier problems in time series analysis. Aust. J. Stat. **28**, 400–413 (1986)
11. Chen, J., Li, W., Lau, A., Cao, J., Wang, K.: Automated load curve data cleansing in power systems. IEEE Trans. Smart Grid **1**, 213–221 (2010)
12. Ramaswamy, S., Rastogi, R., Shim, K.: Efficient algorithms for mining outliers from large data sets. ACM Sigmod Rec. **29**, 427–438 (2000)
13. Nairac, A., Townsend, N., Carr, R., King, S., Cowley, P., Tarassenko, L.: A system for the analysis of jet engine vibration data. Integr. Comput. Aided Eng. **6**, 53–66 (1999)
14. Hawkins, S., He, H., Williams, G., Baxter, R.: Outlier detection using replicator neural networks. In: Proceedings of the 4th International Conference on Data Warehousing Knowledge Discovery, pp. 170–180 (2002)
15. Kolter, J.Z., Johnson, M.J.: REDD: a public data set for energy disaggregation research. In: Proceedings of the SustKDD Workshop on Data Mining Applications in Sustainability (2011)

An Introduction of Non-intrusive Load Monitoring and Its Challenges in System Framework

Qi Liu[1,2(✉)], Min Lu[2,3], Xiaodong Liu[4], and Nigel Linge[5]

[1] Jiangsu Collaborative Innovation Center of Atmospheric Environment and Equipment Technology (CICAEET), Nanjing University of Information Science and Technology, Nanjing 210044, China
qi.liu@nuist.edu.cn
[2] School of Computer and Software, Nanjing University of Information Science and Technology, Nanjing, China
bmbboy@163.com
[3] Jiangsu Engineering Centre of Network Monitoring, Nanjing University of Information Science and Technology, Nanjing, China
[4] School of Computing, Edinburgh Napier University, 10 Colinton Road Edinburgh EH10 5DT, UK
[5] The University of Salford, Salford Greater Manchester M5 4WT, UK

Abstract. With the increasing of energy demand and electricity price, researchers gain more and more interest among the residential load monitoring. In order to feed back the individual appliance's energy consumption instead of the whole-house energy consumption, Non-Intrusive Load Monitoring (NILM) is a good choice for residents to respond the time-of-use price and achieve electricity saving. In this paper, we discuss the system framework of NILM and analyze the challenges in every module. Besides, we study and compare the public data sets and recent approaches to non-intrusive load monitoring techniques.

Keywords: NILM · System framework · Challenge · Public data set

1 Introduction

Nowadays, with the rapid urbanization and greenhouse effect, people put more attention on energy saving and environment protection. Related statistics show that residential energy account for almost 30 % of the total carbon dioxide in the UK and the figure can achieve 10 % reduction by taking some simple energy efficiency measures [1]. Domestic energy consumption makes up over one fifth of the total energy use in the United States and over 40 % of this power is wasted [2]. Statistics show direct feedback methods (i.e., real-time energy consumption information of appliance-specific) can achieve maximum energy saving instead of indirect feedback methods (i.e., monthly bills and irregular energy usage suggestions) [3]. Motivated by this, Appliance Load Monitoring (ALM) has been put forward to reach the goal of energy conservation and emission reduction. ALM not only can provide useful feedback to the residents, but also be qualified in fault detection for industry. This can be achieved by two major approaches:

© Springer International Publishing AG 2016
X. Sun et al. (Eds.): ICCCS 2016, Part II, LNCS 10040, pp. 254–263, 2016.
DOI: 10.1007/978-3-319-48674-1_23

- Intrusive Load Monitoring – ILM requires individual device and appliance to be installed a sensor with digital communication function to acquire energy usage, then the local area network take charge of gathering and sending electricity consumption information [4].
- Non-Intrusive Load Monitoring – NILM was first proposed by George Hart in the 1980 s [5], which only needs to set one sensor to gather aggregated energy information of the total load at the house entry point. Then the raw current and voltage data will be analyzed to estimate the appliances that are turned on.

Although ILM have potential high accuracy, the hardware cost and difficulty of implementation will relevantly increase [6]. Due to the existence of multi-sensors, some reliability problems may occur if any sensor does not work, which could lead to a system failure [7]. In addition, ILM is not scalable and has poor user acceptance. On the other hand, NILM approaches need no more additional devices and can be easily accepted by consumers because of its convenience and economic efficiency.

In this paper, we explain the resources and algorithms of non-intrusive load monitoring. In Sect. 2, we introduce some basic concepts of NILM methods. In Sect. 3, we describe the system framework of NILM approaches. In Sect. 4, the public data sets are listed and compared. Challenges and conclusions are finally presented.

2   Concepts and Definitions in Non-intrusive Load Monitoring Methods

2.1   Load Signature

Load signature means reliable and unique load feature, which represents the significant electrical behavior when individual appliance is working. Load signature is the amount that can distinguish the operating state and temporal behavior of appliances. Since every appliance has its own internal structure, working pattern and working environment, load signature is highly contributing to the identification of different appliances, and it is one of the most fundamental elements of the energy disaggregation problems.

2.2   Categories of Load Signature

In [8], the authors have divided two forms of load signature. The first one is called snapshot form. In this form, the signature is shown by transient snapshot of appliances' electric behavior at any fixed time intervals. This form usually contains more than one appliance's operating behavior simultaneously, which refers to the composite load. The second one is named delta form. This form tells the difference between two sequential snapshot form load signatures. If the time interval is small enough, we can regard the delta form signature as a single appliance's load behavior more likely than composite load.

2.3   Categories of Consumer Appliances

The goal of NILM methods is to identify individual working appliance and determine their operating states and corresponding energy consumption. The types of appliances which NILM approaches are intended to disaggregate can be classified as follows [9]:

- Type-I: On-off appliances. These are appliances that only have two states of operation (ON/OFF), such as table lamp, electric kettle, etc.
- Type-II: Finite state machines (FSM). These refer to the appliances with limited number of operating states, including washing machine, electric fan, etc.
- Type-III: Continuously variable devices (CAD). This type of appliances has no fixed power draw and no obvious switching signs when it changes the states. Thus it becomes an obstacle to load disaggregation algorithm.
- Type-IV: Permanent consumer devices. In [10], the authors present the type of appliances which remains active and has approximately constant power draw in a time period. The devices that belong to this type are hardwired smoke detector and cable TV receivers (Fig. 1).

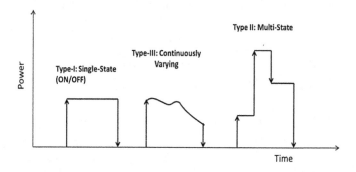

Fig. 1. Power curves of three types of loads.

3   System Framework of NILM and Technical Challenges

The general framework of NILM methods can be broadly separated into six modules, including data acquisition module, data processing module, event detection module, feature extraction module, load disaggregation module and application module. Figure 2 shows the logic block diagram of NILM. The following section introduces the structure and function of every steps of the framework in detail.

3.1   Data Acquisition Module

Data acquisition module is used to get measurement of aggregated load for follow-up work. Now, there are various available commercial power meters on the market. In general, the sampling rate of power meters can be classified as low-frequency meters

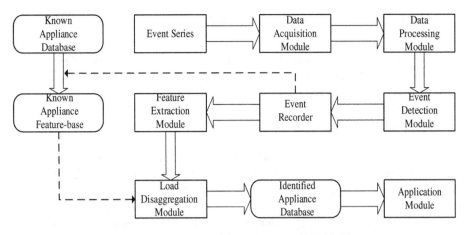

Fig. 2. General logic block diagram of NILM [8].

and high-frequency meters, which decides the features that can be extracted from the acquired data. Usually, the power meters measure three values: voltage, current and power factor.

Low-frequency meters: Its aim to capture steady-state features. According to the Nyquist-Shannon sampling theorem, if sampling rate is two times more than the highest frequency of the electrical signal, the digital signal can remain the information of original signal completely.

High-frequency meters: Its aim to capture transient state and collect fine-grained data to get more unique load features. Since the sampling rate needs to reach a range of 10 to 100 MHz to record waveforms, high resolution power meters usually need to be custom-made and high cost.

Challenge: (1) For the same device, different kinds of power meters could gather different data, which leads to the mismatching of whole-house data and the sum of circuit-level data. (2) The color noise that generated by variable speed devices and white noise that generated by permanent consumer devices will reduce the accuracy of raw data. (3) Data compression in the power meters will cause the loss of raw data as well.

3.2 Data Processing Module

Data processing module is used to adjust and process the gathered data, it usually contains three steps:

- Resampling, it requires aligning the current signal with the voltage signal to compute their proper phase relationship.
- Quantizing, with the initial data standardized, we can calculate useful features, such as reactive power, spectral envelop, higher harmonics and so on.
- Extracting features, we can get specific features using filter bank and down-samples. The task of filtering is to get a good approximate of original waveform and minimize

the loss of information. Down-sampling can help us get the appropriate resolution data for further use.

Challenge: Since the information we need is not computed from raw data but from the down-sampled data, the loss of raw data is unavoidable and the amount depends on the resolution that we choose.

3.3 Event Detection Module

Event detection module is used to decide whether an actual appliance's state switching event occurs by analyzing the total power-level changes. The methods to detect events are major divided into two kinds: using edge detection on the aggregated power curve and probability–based approaches.

Event-based methods usually calculate the difference of continuous values in a sample and compare it to the predefined threshold. Some methods compare two windows of samples using a probabilistic way to judge whether an event occurs. In recent year, non-event-based methods have been proposed which do not depend on the edge detection. The examples can refer to Hidden Markov Model, which take every sample of total power into account for classification and inference.

Challenges: Between the event-based methods and non-event-based methods, the former is more computationally efficient because not the whole data need to be calculated and estimated. But due to the threshold of edge, if the value is too small, the rate of false detection may increase; if the value is too big, the rate of miss detection may raise up.

3.4 Feature Extraction Module

Feature extraction module is used to capture features around the event points. The features can be divided into two types according to the sampling frequency: steady-state features and transient-state features. We discuss the advantages and disadvantages of each kind of features below.

A. Steady-State Features

- Power change. Choosing the variation of real power and reactive power as features can easily identify the high-power electrical appliances, but it only works well with on-off devices. Because of the overlapping features in P-Q plane, the performance in identifying type-II,type-III and type-IV appliances is poor.
- Time-frequency analysis of V-I waveform. It needs higher sampling rate to get steady-state harmonics. According to the harmonics, we can easily tell the difference between resistive, inductive and electronic loads. But the accuracy for type-III appliances is low and it is difficult to identify the events that happen at the same time.
- V-I trajectory. It mainly analyzes the shape features of V-I trajectory such as looping direction, area enclosed, number of self-intersections and so on. It enables the appliances can be distinguished in a detailed way. But it needs complex computational work and the devices with small power consumption have no unique trajectory features.

- Steady-State voltage noise. Due to the EMI features, motor-based appliances and devices with SMPS (Switching Mode Power Supply) can be recognized. It is also able to detect the simultaneous activation events. The shortcomings of this feature are not every appliance has SMPS and it is sensitive to signal noise.

B. Transient-State Features
- Transient power. The advantages to use spectral envelopes are feasibility to recognize type-I, type-II and type-III appliances, even including the devices with same power characteristics. But it requires continuous monitoring at high sampling frequency.
- Start-up current. The current spikes, size and duration can help us distinguish the appliances with multi-states and the accuracy is acceptable. But in the situation of simultaneous activation, the accuracy can be poor. It also does not support type-III and type-IV appliances.
- Transient-State voltage noise. According to the noise FFT (Fast Fourier Transform), multi-states appliances and devices with SMPS can be easily distinguished. But it needs complexity and large calculating quantity.

3.5   Load Disaggregation Module

Load disaggregation module is used to do the classification by using the extracted features. Current NILM algorithms can broadly be divided into the supervised learning and unsupervised learning based on whether the approaches using the labeled data sets for training the classifier. We discuss the supervised learning and unsupervised learning approaches below.

Supervised Learning
- Optimization Methods. Optimization methods try to treat the problem of load disaggregation as an optimization problem. Once an appliance's event has been detected, this approach extracts feature vector of target event and compare it with the feature vector of known appliance' event stored in the signature database to find the closest possible match. The idea of optimization is quite simple, but it becomes more and more complicated when taking the combination of appliances into account. Besides, if an unknown appliance without training occurs, the accuracy can be poor. The algorithms belonging to the optimization methods are integer programming, genetic algorithms and so on.
- Pattern Recognition Methods. Pattern recognition is one of the most common used approaches by researches to deal with the problem of load monitoring. This approach classifies the captured features by using machine learning techniques. These algorithms including artificial neural networks (ANN) [11], naïve Bayes classifier, support vector machines (SVM) [12], k-nearest neighbor (kNN) and so on. The shortcomings of these algorithms is the lack of test samples and the overlapping signatures of low power-consuming appliances.

Unsupervised Learning. Since the supervised learning approaches need labeled data set to train classifier and manual labeling is fallible and time-consuming, the unsupervised learning approaches become a hot research content. These approaches base on the mathematical probability models, which including blind source separation, genetic k-means, motif mining, FHMM (Factorial Hidden Markov Model) and its variety. Although these algorithms can reduce human's work, but it is computationally expensive because it takes every part of samples into account and the load disaggregated accuracy is not so satisfactory. Besides, it also needs to assume that the number of devices is already known.

3.6 Application Module

Since the changes of devices' states have been recognized, application module is used to track the operation pattern and power consumption of individual appliance. Based on this, some personalized and useful suggestions will be provided. Besides, some prediction can also be made to help electric power company know more about the energy demand side.

4   Public Data Set

Nowadays, more and more approaches from data mining and machine learning have been used to solve the problem of energy. Although these advanced techniques are presented, it is still hard to put into use and test without the public data sets. The reasons why it is not practical to build their own data sets by every researcher are including:

- Time-consuming, building a data set needs to take a duration of time to capture and collate data, at least takes a week or much more longer.
- High-costing, not only need to measure the aggregate load at one point, we also require distributed sensors to get the individual appliance load as ground truth to train and test load disaggregation algorithms. If the features are transient state, high-frequency sampling will greatly increase the cost.
- Hard to compare, just assume that every researcher develops different algorithms on their own data sets, it is actually unable to evaluate the results and judge which method is better.
- Privacy, recording appliance usage and geographical location information may reveal what appliances do occupants have and their usage pattern.

Since the Reference Energy Disaggregation Data Set (REDD) was publically released by MIT in 2011, which has been widely used in the disaggregation community, the number of data sets from different countries is increasing greatly. We list the public data set so far in Table 1. It should be noted that the abbreviations of features: current (I), voltage (V), power factor (PF), frequency (f), active power (P), reactive power (Q), apparent power (S), energy (E) and phase angle (Φ).

Table 1. The existing public data set for energy disaggregation research

Data set	Country	Houses	Sensors (per house)	Features	Granularity	Duration
AMPds [13]	Greater Vancouver	1	19	I, V, PF, f, Q, S	1 min	1 year
BLUED [14]	Pittsburg	1	Aggregated	I, V, switch events	12 kHz	8 days
GREEND [15]	Austria, Italy	8	9	P	1 Hz	1 year
iAWE [16]	India	1	33	V, I, f, P, S, E, Φ	1 Hz	73 days
REDD [17]	Boston	6	9–24	Aggregated: V, P; Sub-metered: P	15 kHz (aggregated), 3 s (sub-metered)	3–19 days
Smart* [18]	Western Massachusetts	3	25 circuits, 29 appliance monitors	Circuits: P, S; Sub-metered: P	1 Hz	3 months
Tracebase [19]	Germany	15	158 appliances in total (43 types)	P	1–10 s	N/A
UK-DALE [20]	UK	5	House 1:54; house 2–4:5–26	Aggregated: P; Sub-metered: P, switch-states	16 kHz (aggregated), 6 s (sub-metered)	655 days

5 Challenges and Conclusions

In this paper, we introduce the system framework and its challenges in individual module. Besides, the public data sets are also studied and compared. Although the non-intrusive load monitoring gains a lot of attentions in recent year because of the economic efficiency and convenience, it is still difficult to put the NILM into commercial due to the following reasons:

1. The compatibility of load signatures. Since the factors of different kinds, manufacturers and sizes of appliances will affect the performance of load disaggregation algorithms. Moreover, there are no widely applicable load signatures can model the operations of the four types of appliances well.
2. The comparison of load disaggregation algorithms. As mentioned in Sect. 4, without the standard and unified public reference dataset, it is quite difficult to fairly compare and test different load disaggregation algorithms.
3. The overlap of load features. Low-power appliances have similar power consumption characteristics and it is difficult to discern them at low-frequency sampling, due to the ambiguous overlapping of steady-state features in the P-Q plane.
4. Manual labeling. For supervised learning approaches, it is quite boring and fallible to turn on/off every appliance in proper order to build a signature database and train the algorithms for classification.

5. The update of signature database. The supervised learning approaches need signature database to do off-line training. Since any unknown appliances which are not in the appliance signature database appear, the precision of load disaggregation will be poor.

6. Imperfect appliance models. For unsupervised learning approaches, the appliance model generated by the HMM and house power consumption established by the FHMM suffer from non-Gaussian. And since the imperfect manufacturing process and the influence of environment, the precision will decline.

7. Different types of appliances. The precision of load disaggregation for on/off appliances is quite high (more than 90 %) so far. But to multi-state appliances, continuously variable devices and rarely used devices, the result is not so satisfactory. And the simultaneous switch events of appliances (like PC and printer etc.) make the disaggregation of load more complex.

8. The security of data transmission. Because most of the data transmission approaches are wireless, thief may analyze the presence of house owner by counting the number of packets. So it is necessary to reinforce the security of the wireless communications [21].

9. The robustness of algorithms. The NILM approach should be scalable in the sense because the number of used appliance of a typical family can up to 20–30 [22].

Acknowledgements. This work is supported by the NSFC (61300238, 61300237, 61232016, 1405254, 61373133), Marie Curie Fellowship (701697-CAR-MSCA-IFEF-ST), Basic Research Programs (Natural Science Foundation) of Jiangsu Province (BK20131004) and the PAPD fund.

References

1. Sundramoorthy, V., Cooper, G., Linge, N., Liu, Q.: Domesticating energy-monitoring systems: challenges and design concerns. IEEE Pervasive Comput. **10**(1), 20–27 (2011)

2. Alahmad, M.A., Wheeler, P.G., Schwer, A., Eiden, J., Brumbaugh, A.: A comparative study of three feedback devices for residential real-time energy monitoring. IEEE Trans. Ind. Electron. **59**(4), 2002–2013 (2012)

3. Ehrhardt-Martinez, K., Donnelly, K.A., Laitner, S.: Advanced Metering Initiatives and Residential Feedback Programs: A Meta-review for Household Electricity-Saving Opportunities. American Council for an Energy-Efficient Economy, Washington, DC (2010)

4. Ridi, A., Gisler, C., Hennebert, J.: A survey on intrusive load monitoring for appliance recognition. Biochem. Biophys. Res. Commun. **94**(4), 3702–3707 (2014)

5. Hart, G.W.: Nonintrusive appliance load monitoring. Proc. IEEE **80**(12), 1870–1891 (1992)

6. Froehlich, J., Larson, E., Gupta, S., Cohn, G., Reynolds, M.S., Patel, S.N.: Disaggregated end-use energy sensing for the smart grid. IEEE Pervasive Comput. **10**(1), 28–39 (2011)

7. Laughman, C., Lee, D., Cox, R., Shaw, S., Leeb, S., Norford, L., Armstrong, P.: Power signature analysis. IEEE Power Energ. Mag. **1**(2), 56–63 (2003)

8. Liang, J., Ng, S.K.K., Kendall, G., Cheng, J.W.M.: Load signature study—Part I: basic concept, structure, and methodology. IEEE Trans. Power Delivery **25**(2), 551–560 (2010)

9. Zoha, A., Gluhak, A., Imran, M.A., Rajasegarar, S.: Nonintrusive load monitoring approaches for disaggregated energy sensing: a survey. Sensors **12**(12), 16838–16866 (2012)

10. Zeifman, M., Roth, K.: Nonintrusive appliance load monitoring: review and outlook. IEEE Trans. Consum. Electron. **57**(1), 76–84 (2011)

11. Xuezhi, W., Ling, S., Yu, X., Wei, F.: A rapid learning algorithm for vehicle classification. Inf. Sci. **295**(1), 395–406 (2015)

12. Bin, G., Victor, S.S., Keng, Y.T., Walter, R., Shuo, L.: Incremental support vector learning for ordinal regression. IEEE Trans. Neural Netw. Learn. Syst. **26**(7), 1403–1416 (2015)

13. Makonin, S., Popowich, F., Bartram, L., Gill, B., Bajic, I.V.: AMPds: a public dataset for load disaggregation and eco-feedback research. In: Proceeding of 2013 IEEE Conference on Electrical Power and Energy (EPEC), pp. 1–6 (2013)

14. Anderson, K., Ocneanu, A., Benitez, D., Carlson, D., Rowe, A., Berges, M.: BLUED: a fully labeled public dataset for event-based non-intrusive load monitoring research. In: Proceedings of the 2nd KDD Workshop on Data Mining Applications in Sustainability (SustKDD), pp. 1–5 (2012)

15. Monacchi, A., Egarter, D., Elmenreich, W., D'Alessandro, S., Tonello, A.M.: GREEND: an energy consumption dataset of households in Italy and Austria. In: Proceedings of 2014 IEEE International Conference on Smart Grid Communications (SmartGridComm), pp. 511–516 (2014)

16. Batra, N., Gulati, M., Singh, A., Srivastava, M.B.: It's different: insights into home energy consumption in India. In: Proceedings of the 5th ACM Workshop on Embedded Systems for Energy-Efficient Buildings, pp. 1–8 (2013)

17. Kolter, J.Z., Johnson, M.J.: REDD: a public data set for energy disaggregation research. In: Proceedings of the SustKDD Workshop on Data Mining Applications in Sustainability (SustKDD), San Diego, CA, USA, August 2011

18. Barker, S., Mishra, A., Irwin, D., Cecchet, E., Shenoy, P., Albrecht, J.: Smart*: an open data set and tools for enabling research in sustainable homes. In: Proceedings of the 1st KDD Workshop on Data Mining Applications in Sustainability (SustKDD), San Diego, California, USA, August 2012

19. Reinhardt, A., Baumann, P., Burgstahler, D., Hollick, M., Chonov, H., Werner, M., Steinmetz, R.: On the accuracy of appliance identification based on distributed load metering data. In: Proceedings of the 2nd IFIP Conference on Sustainable Internet and ICT for Sustainability (SustainIT), October 2012

20. Kelly, J., Knottenbelt, W.: UK-DALE: a dataset recording UK domestic appliance-level electricity demand and whole-house demand. arXiv, April 2014

21. Jian, S., Haowen, T., Jin, W., Jinwei, W., Sungyoung, L.: A novel routing protocol providing good transmission reliability in underwater sensor networks. J. Internet Technol. **16**(1), 171–178 (2015)

22. Zeifman, M.: Disaggregation of home energy display data using probabilistic approach. IEEE Trans. Consum. Electron. **58**(1), 23–31 (2012)

A Survey on the Research of Indoor RFID Positioning System

Jian Shen[1,2,3,4(✉)], Chen Jin[1,4], and Dengzhi Liu[1,4]

[1] Jiangsu Engineering Center of Network Monitoring,
Nanjing University of Information Science and Technology, Nanjing, China
s_shenjian@126.com
[2] Jiangsu Collaborative Innovation Center on Atmospheric
Environment and Equipment Technology, Nanjing University of Information
Science and Technology, Nanjing, China
[3] Jiangsu Technology and Engineering Center of Meteorological
Sensor Network, Nanjing University of Information Science
and Technology, Nanjing, China
[4] School of Computer and Software, Nanjing University of Information
Science and Technology, Nanjing, China

Abstract. The success of the Global Positioning System (GPS) makes the demand for location-based services increase rapidly. However, in the indoor environment, since the reception of the satellite signal is disrupted severely, the accuracy of GPS positioning can not meet the requirements. Radio Frequency Identification (RFID) technology with the advantages of non-contact, non-visibility, low cost and high positioning accuracy, begins to get more and more attention and becomes the most suitable indoor positioning technology. RFID location is a technique which is based on signal strength positioning, using the received signal strength indication (Received Signal Strength Indicator, RSSI) to determine the position of the object. In recent years, the indoor positioning technology has made great progress, especially on the verity of the localization algorithm. In this paper, we will briefly describe the basic principles of RFID, then we introduce the algorithms of existing indoor RFID positioning system. Finally, we analyze their strengths and weaknesses.

Keywords: RFID · Positioning algorithm · Security · RSSI · Indoor positioning

1 Introduction

Radio Frequency Identification (RFID) technology can be traced back to the World War II, but due to technical and cost reasons, was not widely used at that time [15]. In recent years, with the development of large scale integrated circuits, network communications and information security technology, RFID technology has been coming into the stage of commercial application. Location services have an important application not only in military service, general science service, and commercial activity, but also in emergency rescue and disaster relief effort. Mobile positioning technology has become an important research direction in present life. Since the RFID has many

© Springer International Publishing AG 2016
X. Sun et al. (Eds.): ICCCS 2016, Part II, LNCS 10040, pp. 264–274, 2016.
DOI: 10.1007/978-3-319-48674-1_24

characteristics, such as the high-speed moving object recognition, multi-target recognition and identification of non-contact, it has shown the great potential for development and the huge space of application. The RFID is considered to be one of the most promising information technologies in the 21st century [10].

2 Key Issues in RFID Positioning

2.1 The Basic Concept of RFID

Radio frequency identification (RFID) is a technology that uses radio waves to transfer data from an electronic tag, called RFID tag or label, attached to an object, through a reader for the purpose of identifying and tracking the object. It is a non-contact automatic identification technique, whose basic principle is using the transmission characteristics of radio frequency signal and spatial coupling (electromagnetic coupling or electromagnetic propagation) to automatically identify the target object [2, 11].

2.2 Composition

There are usually two major components of a simplest RFID system—a tag and a reader. The tag and the reader communicate through radio waves [12,14]. A RFID tag usually has two key parts: an integrated circuit for executing commands and storing data; and an antenna coil for receiving and transmitting RF signals [13]. All RFID tags use radio frequency energy to communicate with the readers [16].

A RFID reader is a device which used to modulate and demodulate RF signals to communicate with supported RFID tags through one or several antennas. RFID readers have two interfaces. The first one is a RF interface which communicates with the tags in their read range in order to retrieve tags' identities. The second one is a communication interface, for communicating with the servers. Finally, one or several servers configured the third part of an RFID system. They collect tags' identities sent by the reader and perform calculation such as applying a localization method. They also embed the major part of the middleware system and can be interconnected between each other's (Fig. 1).

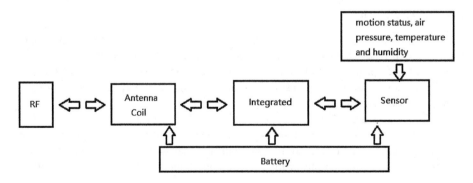

Fig. 1. RFID tag structure

2.3   Distance Estimation and Position Calculation

Knowing the electromagnetic waves attenuation law, the emission power of the signal and its attenuation, the distance between the tag and the reader can be estimated. Since the results obtained are only estimations, we will attempt to enhance them with empirical rules which aid in finding the most accurate result [5].

Using the obtained distances at the first step, mathematical algorithms are applied for obtaining the node's global coordinates. There are two methods suitable for distance related measurements: Trilateration and Multi-point positioning.

After knowing the distance of the tag from the readers, we can use trilateration to calculate the coordinate of the tag with respect to the readers. It is a range-based algorithm as it needs to know the position of the reader with minimum three anchor nodes, to localize a target node in 2D plane.

Trilateration uses circle geometry to calculate a node's position from another three known locations. Preferably, three points are enough to find the exact coordinates of a node, but considering that distances measured are not extremely accurate, we can use more points in order to obtain low error rates in the calculated position. Ideally, the intersection of the three circles will be a point, but because of errors, the intersection will be a zone (Figs. 2 and 3).

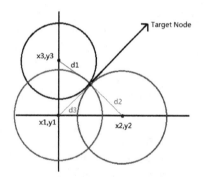

Fig. 2. Get the location by trilateration

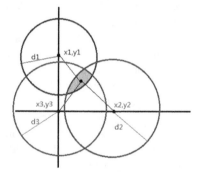

Fig. 3. Trilateration with errors

2.4   RFID Security

Universally deploying RFID tags offers many potential security benefits, yet may expose new privacy threats. Embedding RFID tags as seals of authenticity in documents, designer products, and currency may discourage forgery. While RFID tags improve certain security properties in these applications, they may exacerbate privacy threats or pose new security risks [3].

RFID systems are different from other means of identification because RF communication is non-contact and non-line-of-sight, where as other means of identification are either contact-based or require line-of-sight. In other words, it is more difficult for the owner of the RF tag to physically impede communication with the tag [17,19].

Accepting short-term limitations on low-cost tag resources, we discuss a simple RFID security scheme based on a one-way hash function. In practice, a hardware optimized cryptographic hash function would suffice, assuming it may be implemented with significantly fewer resources than symmetric encryption. In this design, each hash-enabled tag contains a portion of memory reserved for a "meta-ID" and operates in either an unlocked or locked state. While unlocked, the full functionality and memory of the tag are available to anyone in the interrogation zone [3].

3 Key Technologies in RFID Positioning

Several mature indoor positioning scheme based on RFID will be mentioned next, including LANDMARC scheme, VIRE scheme and SpotON scheme [2].

3.1 Two-Dimensional Localization Scheme

3.1.1 LANDMARC Scheme

LANDMARC is an effective system using RFID positioning technology [1]. In the LANDMRC method, it uses cheaper active tags to assist RFID readers for position location. LANDMARC system uses active sensor notes with a larger read range and higher response ability to be the hardware specifications of tags in actual process [2]. K-nearest neighbor's algorithm is used and the distance between tags is represented by the size of the signal intensity differences. The positioning accuracy is heavily dependent on the number of reference tags and the obstacles. First, some reference tags are arranged as a foundation for positioning according to certain way in substantial environment. Second, readers measure the RSSI values of target tags and reference tags respectively; finally, the database is established for processing [6].

In addition, using LANDMARC algorithm can fix some blind spots of the traditional positioning methods. Because of doing the studies for the various positioning systems in different actual environments, the reliability of the positioning data calculated by LANDMARC method is greatly enhanced.

3.2 VIRE Scheme

In order to overcome some limitations in Landmark system, we propose a new algorithm called VIRE based on Landmark scheme. There are two main ideas: (1) Using the virtual grid label. Without increasing the number of reference tags, we apply a large number of virtual tags. The RSSI value is obtained by its known signal strength value of the reference tags, so it increases a lot of reference points for the tested labels. Therefore, it can greatly improve the density of labels. (2) Establish a fuzzy map by calculating the difference of RSSI numerical between virtual tags and test tags. Remove grid positions that the targets impossibly appear. Then add two weighted calculation, further improve the positioning accuracy.

3.3   Three-Dimensional Localization Scheme

3.3.1   SpotON Scheme

The first system to use RFID technology for indoor positioning is SpotON. In this positioning system, SpotON uses an aggregation algorithm for three dimensional location sensing based on radio signal strength analysis to calculate the collected signal strength.

In SpotON method, the positioning of the unknown object is not intensively managed by the central system, but in a manner of distributed calculating by other perception points that have the same hardware specifications. These perception points dispersed in the environment will collect the received signal strength and feedback, and finally, calculate the predicted position of the unknown object by using positioning algorithm. Positioning methods in the SpotON system is using a number of tags and the RFID sensor reader to construct an indoor wireless sensor network environment of a certain range. SpotON tags use received radio signal strength information as a sensor measurement for estimating inter-tag distance. Meanwhile, in the process of collecting the signal strength, the SpotON approach also introduces a regression model to estimate the signal strength, so the data collected can be expected more accurate. However, a complete system has not yet been made available [8].

4   Algorithms Classification

In a real indoor environment, fading, absorbing, reflection, and interference are major issues affecting the RF waves' strength, direction, and distribution. This make the variation of the RF signal propagation not easily modeled. Since the theoretical model is not applicable, numerous positioning algorithms have been developed [7]. Several major types are summarized and introduced as follows, while many varieties exist. The two largest groups are determined by whether the algorithm ranges the RF signal to an estimated distance or not.

4.1   Range-Based Localization

4.1.1   Based on Signal Strength

Received Signal Strength Indicator (RSSI). RSSI, which is a standard feature in most wireless radios, has attracted a lot of attention in recent literature. It is considered that the simplest approach for ranging since almost no additional cost is needed to collect the RSSI data which is provided by most systems. RSSI is defined as the voltage measured by a receiver's received signal strength indicator (RSSI) circuit. It eliminates the need for additional hardware in small wireless devices and exhibits favorable properties with respect to power consumption, size and cost [4,18].

Using RSSI in localization also has some disadvantages. RSSI depends on the type of antennae used in the receiver and the transmitter and on the orientation of the antennae. RSSI values change if either of the nodes move away from the line of sight. Equations are presented below:

$$(x_1 - x)^2 + (y_1 - y)^2 = d_1^2 \qquad (1)$$

$$(x_2 - x)^2 + (y_2 - y)^2 = d_2^2 \qquad (2)$$

$$(x_n - x)^2 + (y_n - y)^2 = d_n^2 \qquad (3)$$

The readers' coordinates are from x_1 to x_n, and d_1 to d_n are the distances measured from the first step. The coordinates to be calculated is (x, y).

In matrix form:

$$S = \begin{bmatrix} 2(x_1 - x_n) & 2(y_1 - y_n) \\ 2(x_2 - x_n) & 2(y_2 - y_n) \\ \cdots\cdots & \cdots\cdots \\ 2(x_{n-1} - x_n) & 2(y_{n-1} - y_n) \end{bmatrix} \qquad (4)$$

$$H = \begin{bmatrix} \left(x_1^2 - x_n^2\right) + \left(y_1^2 - y_n^2\right) + \left(d_1^2 - d_n^2\right) \\ \left(x_2^2 - x_n^2\right) + \left(y_2^2 - y_n^2\right) + \left(d_2^2 - d_n^2\right) \\ \cdots\cdots \\ \left(x_{n-1}^2 - x_n^2\right) + \left(y_{n-1}^2 - y_n^2\right) + \left(d_{n-1}^2 - d_n^2\right) \end{bmatrix} \qquad (5)$$

At last, we can get the result: $X = (S'S) - 1 (S')H \cdot (x, y)$ is the predicted position where the probability of the presence of the target node is maximum.

Adaptive Power Multilateration (APM). Another approach is called Adaptive Power Multilateration (APM), which measures the estimated distance from the reader to the tag by reducing or increasing the reader transmission power until the tag disappears or appears. The corresponding power level is then translated into distance based on a pre-calibrated chart. At last, the tag's position is determined using the multilateration method on distances estimated from all readers. The accuracy of APM heavily relays on two things.

One is the edge tolerance of the power circle. A perfect clear cut at the edge may not exist. The other one is the environmental impacts. The pre-calibrated chart may not be valid under complex circumstance.

4.1.2 Based on Distance

Time Difference of Arrival(TOA). The Time of Arrival (TOA) is a method using the signal propagation time and it's based on a theoretical propagation model of an RF signal. If we measure the travel time of the signal between two points, then we can determine the distance between them. When we get the distance between the two points, we should finally use the mathematical algorithms to give an estimate of the location. Therefore, the TOA method requires all readers and tags to be strictly precisely synchronized, and all signals to be time-stamped (Fig. 4).

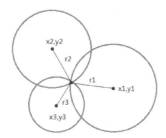

Fig. 4. Cycle intersection for TOA

Time Difference of Arrival (TDOA). Similar to TOA, the Time Difference of Arrival (TDOA) approach also relies on precisely synchronized readers and tags. By measuring the arrival time to readers, we can determine the distance between two points. If we know the distance between the tag and each reader, the position of the tag can be determined. However, the absolute time is generally more difficult to measure, by comparing the time differences of the signal to various readers, we are able to get a hyperbola with readers being the focus and distance difference being the major axis. Then, the intersection of those hyperbola is ought to be the position of the tag (Fig. 5).

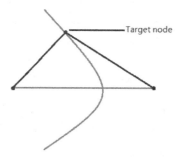

Fig. 5. First step of multilateration for TDOA

4.1.3   Based on Angle

Angle of Arrival (AOA). AOA is a typical localization algorithm based on the distance, sensing the arrival direction of signal transmitting nodes by some hardware device. AOA is a common wireless sensor network algorithm, with the feature of low spending and high positioning accuracy.

The basic idea of Angle of Arrival (AOA) is simple. Consider a triangle for example. Given the coordinates of any two points are known, the third one can be located if and only if the angles from these two known points to the unknown point are provided [9] (Fig. 6).

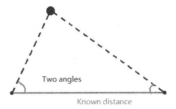

Fig. 6. Triangulation for AOA

4.2   Range-Free Localization

4.2.1   k Nearest-Neighbor (kNN)

The fingerprinting technique applied in the improved RSSI approach is also used in the k Nearest-Neighbor (kNN) method but without ranging. Similarly, the reference anchors are deployed in cells. The Eucledian distances between the RSSI values from the unknown tag and all anchors are calculated. Subsequently, the k anchors with lowest distances to this tag are selected as its k-nearest neighbors. The coordinates of

Table 1. Summary *of localization algorithms in RFID*

Algorithms		Pros	Cons	Accuracy
Range-based	RSSI	1. Supported by most systems 2. Low cost	Depends on the type of antennae	Low accuracy level
	APM	1. Low cost 2. No reference tags needed	Not suitable in complex environments	Low accuracy level
	TOA	High accuracy level	High requirements for the hardware	High accuracy level
	TDOA	High accuracy level	High cost for synchronized devices	High accuracy level
	AOA	1. High accuracy level 2. Provide orientation information	1. High cost for customized hardware 2. Pre-calibration need	High accuracy level
Range-free	kNN	1. Low cost 2. Suitable for varying environments	Relies on dense deployment of reference tags	Low accuracy level
	Proximity	1. Low cost 2. Easily deployed	1. Relies on dense deployment of readers or antennas 2. Not suitable in complex environments	Low accuracy level

this tag can be estimated using the centroid of these anchors. An enhanced method call weighted kNN further applies the Eucledian distances from the unknown tag to its k-nearest neighbors as weights to improve the approximation.

Overall, the kNN approach is suitable for complex non-isotropic and varying environments.

4.2.2   Proximity

In the proximity approach, each antenna has a predefined coverage area, which may be an approximation or calibrated result. If the unknown tag is detected by more than one antenna, the location of this tag can be estimated by the intersection of the coverage areas of these antennas. The density of antenna deployment heavily affects the system resolution. Furthermore, the coverage area may be difficult to be clearly defined since the RF signals fade away gradually at the edge and the theoretical propagation model may not be an appropriate simulation for real indoor environments.

5   Comparison

The following table summarizes the pros and cons of different localization algorithms in RFID. Nowadays, the RSSI approach is mostly cost effective and reliable for indoor environments with the advantages of low cost and wide range of applications. And other algorithms also have their own features (Tables 1 and 2).

Table 2. Comparison among typical location system

Location System	Data source	Range-based	Range-free	Beacon	Used algorithm	Signal coverage	Accuracy
LANDMARC	RF, acitve RFID	N	Y	Y	Top-KNN	<45 m	<2 m 50th:1 m
SpotON	RF, acitve RFID	Y	N	N	Triangulation	N/A	N/A
VIRE	RF, Acitve RFID	N	Y	Y	VIRE	<300 m	0.47 m

Y denotes satisfication
N denotes dis-satisfication

6   Conclusion

At present, the radio frequency identification (RFID) is the most widely used positioning technology in the indoor environment. RFID uses radio frequency through electromagnetic field to realize no-contact two-way communication to identify and achieve non-contact automated data exchange. In the near future, the RFID technology will be embedded into our lives like other identification technologies. In this paper, we list some common algorithms in detail, the advantages and disadvantages of each algorithm have been discussed with comparison results as well. Although many studies related to RFID were done so far, there are still many challenges to be solved. For example, we can optimize current algorithms to get a new method getting a more accurate result or there may be a more efficient way to solve the security problem of RFID.

Acknowledgement. This work is supported by the National Science Foundation of China under Grant No. 61300237, No. U1536206, No. U1405254, No. 61232016 and No. 61402234, the National Basic Research Program 973 under Grant No. 2011CB311808, the Natural Science Foundation of Jiangsu province under Grant No. BK2012461, the research fund from Jiangsu Technology & Engineering Center of Meteorological Sensor Network in NUIST under Grant No. KDXG1301, the research fund from Jiangsu Engineering Center of Network Monitoring in NUIST under Grant No. KJR1302, the research fund from Nanjing University of Information Science and Technology under Grant No. S8113003001, the 2013 Nanjing Project of Science and Technology Activities for Returning from Overseas, the 2015 Project of six personnel in Jiangsu Province under Grant No. R2015L06, the CICAEET fund, and the PAPD fund.

References

1. Bolic, M., Simplot-Ryl, D.: RFID Systems Research Trends and Challenges. Wiley, Hoboken (2011)
2. Du, H.: Research on Indoor Positioning Technology Based on RFID. China. School of Information Engineering, Communication University of China, Beijing (2013)
3. Sanjay, E., Stephen, A., Daniel, W.: RFID Systems and Security and Privacy Implications. In: Sarma, S.E., Weis, A., Engels. D.W. (eds.) Cryptographic Hardware and Embedded Systems. 4th International Workshop Redwood Shores, CA, USA. LNCS, Vol. 2523, pp. 454–469. Springer, Heidelberg (2002). doi:10.1007/3-540-36400-5_33
4. Shetty, A.: Weighted K-nearest neighbor algorithm as an object localization technique using passive RFID tags. M.S. thesis, Rutgers University, New Brunswick, NJ (2010)
5. Sorin, D., Dan, S.: RSSI-Based Localization in Low-cost 2.4 GHz Wireless Networks. Polytechnic University of Bucharest, Bucharest, Romania (2012)
6. Xue, J., Wang, W., Zhang, T.: An active RFID indoor positioning system mechanism based on sleep modeL. In: Zhong, Z. (ed.) Proceedings of the International Conference on Information Engineering and Applications (IEA) 2012. Lecture Notes in Electrical Engineering, vol. 218, pp. 733–740. Springer, London (2013)
7. Shen, J., Tan, H., Sangman, M., Chung, I., Wang, J.: An efficient RFID authentication protocol providing strong privacy and security. J. Internet Technol., 17(3) (2016). SCI
8. Wu, J.: Three-Dimensional Indoor RFID Localization System. The Graduate College at the University of Nebraska, Lincoln, Nebraska (2012)
9. Zhou, J., Zhang, H., Mo, L.: Two-dimension localization of passive RFID tags using AOA estimation. In: Instrumentation and Measurement Technology Conference, Hangzhou, China, 10–12 May 2011, pp. 1–5. IEEE (2011)
10. Shahzad, M., Liu, X.: Fast and accurate estimation of RFID tags. IEEE/ACM Trans. Netw. **23**, 241–254 (2015)
11. Yang, L., Cao, J., Zhu, W., Tang, S.: Accurate and efficient object tracking based on passive RFID. IEEE Trans. Mob. Comput. **14**, 2188–2200 (2015)
12. Brandl, M.: Accuracy of RFID position estimation using SAW compressive receivers. Procedia Eng. **120**, 320–323 (2015)
13. Huang, W., Ding, C., Wang, S.: A comprehensive method to combine RFID indoor targets positioning with real geographic environment. Comput. Sci. Inf. Syst. **12**, 1149–1169 (2015)

14. Yang, Z., Zhang, P., Chen, L.: RFID-enabled indoor positioning method for a real-time manufacturing execution system using OS-ELM. Neurocomputing **174**, 121–133 (2016)

15. Attaran, M.: The coming age of RFID revolution. J. Int. Technol. Inf. Manag. **15**(4), 77–88 (2016)

16. Oliveira, B., Lisboa, C., Fonseca, A., Silva, J., Adriano, R.: Low-cost antenna design for RFID readers using multiobjective optimization. Microw. Opt. Technol. Lett. **58**, 905–908 (2016)

17. Wang, S., Liu, S., Chen, D.: Security analysis and improvement on two RFID authentication protocols. Wirel. Pers. Commun. **82**, 21–33 (2015)

18. Zhou, Z., Chen, B., Yu, H.: Understanding RFID counting protocols. IEEE/ACM Trans. Netw. **24**(1), 291–302 (2013)

19. Dass, P., Om, H.: A secure authentication scheme for RFID systems. Procedia Comput. Sci. **78**, 100–106 (2016)

A RFID Based Localization Algorithm for Wireless Sensor Networks

Jian Shen[1,2,3,4(✉)], Anxi Wang[4], Chen Wang[4], Yongjun Ren[4], and Xingming Sun[4]

[1] Jiangsu Engineering Center of Network Monitoring,
Nanjing University of Information Science and Technology, Nanjing, China
[2] Jiangsu Technology and Engineering Center of Meteorological Sensor Network,
Nanjing University of Information Science and Technology, Nanjing, China
[3] Jiangsu Collaborative Innovation Center on Atmospheric Environment and Equipment
Technology, Nanjing University of Information Science and Technology, Nanjing, China
[4] School of Computer and Software, Nanjing University of Information Science and Technology,
Nanjing, China
s_shenjian@126.com

Abstract. The localization technology takes an important role in real-time alarm and rapid response. In this paper, we propose a novel localization method for wireless sensor network which is based on Radio Frequency Identification technology (RBLOCA). This method combines above both techniques and achieves the localization in WSN. The method not only has the advantages of real-time monitoring and low cost of WSN, but also has the characteristics of fast and repeatable use of RFID technology. Experimental results show that the proposed method can achieve a higher positioning accuracy. At the same time, the energy consumption of nodes is also very low. Therefore, we can get the method has a wide range of applications in a number of scenarios such as the forest fire alarm system, underwater sensor network.

Keywords: Localization technology · Wireless sensor network · RFID technology · Real-time

1 Introduction

A Hierarchical Wireless Sensor network (HWSN) comprises thousands of sensor nodes, which can be classified as Cluster Head (CH) nodes and Normal nodes. The CH nodes were selected from Normal nodes. What's more, the CH will be changed in the overwhelming majority of cases. In some networks, clustering algorithms are implemented locally [1–5]. The locations of the both nodes are unknown, but in some cases the location information of the nodes is very important. WSNs have application in various areas such as target tracking, intrusion detection, fire alarm system, underground monitoring [6], underwater detection, outer space explorations, etc. In WSN, sensor node acquires some physical data about the environment around the deployed region, such as temperature, humidity, pressure, wind speed, etc. The collected information, aggregated and transferred by the CHs, enables us to develop real-time intelligent monitoring systems.

© Springer International Publishing AG 2016
X. Sun et al. (Eds.): ICCCS 2016, Part II, LNCS 10040, pp. 275–285, 2016.
DOI: 10.1007/978-3-319-48674-1_25

Enhanced quality and efficiency were provided by such unattended monitoring systems, because each node for monitoring environmental change is fast and accurate. The cellular networks were originally taken the advantage of wireless localization, since it is required to provide location services to is's consumers by many innovative applications [7]. Currently, the need of location information has become a crucial component for a serious of applications such as Navigation, taxi-hailing apps and so on.

Since the features of such network, the energy resource of nodes is limited. The so-called good steel should be used in the blade. The constrained energy should be used to gather and transfer data from local region to the base station. What's more, the data received at the BS is always transferred by multi-hop routings, making the localization of node be a hard task in HWSNs. A lot of solutions have been used to realize the localization of nodes in WSNs over the past decade. To accurately localize each CH or normal node, these algorithms require the information of the distance between the nodes to be positioned and at least three location-aware nodes. Since it is the same to the HWSN that normal nodes have no chance to communicate directly with the BS, the distance between each nodes pair is usually measured by the shortest path. The latter is obtained by counting the number of nodes which are located on the shortest path between the two nodes. Taking the process used to estimate distance into consideration, localization algorithms may be divided into parts: measurement, exploration, and analytical.

In this paper, we only take our attention on the range-based measurements. For the reason that it can provide higher accuracy in most cases. In the range-based measurements, the core part is to get the distance between two nodes. However, in our algorithm the position-aware nodes are replaced by the RFID Tags which are arranged in advance. And the sender nodes which report to the BS are treated as the RFID readers. To achieve the interested information, it is necessary to enable node communication, which can be cooperative or non-cooperative. Only in this way the tags can get the energy resource to decide the senders. The RFID Tags can calculate the distance to the source by the received signal strength. The detail description of RFID technology is given in the following section. The range-based measurement can be realized in distributed or centralized mode. But the first mode is sensitive to the error and may need long time recalculation. For the reason above, we focus on the centralized mode. To achieve the fast and correct calculation of the source nodes, the position of RFID Tags and readers is known to the BS priorly.

The remainder of this paper is organized as follows. In Sect. 2, the related work and current research are introduced briefly. In Sect. 3, we introduces the main part of RBLOCA. The simulation is summarized in Sect. 4. Finally, in Sect. 5, we summarize the main conclusions.

2   Related Work

2.1   RFID Technology

In a RFID system [8], the main component is consisted of three parts: RFID readers, the BPS, the Tags. And in this system there is no need of line-of-sight contact when the Tags should communicate with RFID readers. The relational between the readers and tags is one-to-multi, that means the readers can communicate with multiple tags and get the related information from them. Therefore, the information from one or more RFID tags is gathered simultaneously. The interested information is generated after several communication. We cannot but mention that the RFID tag just can indirectly communicate with the BPS. Instead, the readers act as the link to connect the tags and the BPS. Accordingly, the readers are assumed to have enough energy to calculate and enough space to storage messages. In the traditional RFID positioning system, the RFID tag exposures radio signals to the readers through the wireless channel. Thus the position of the tag can be computed by at least three readers from a mathematical point of view only with small energy consumption. However, signal may be crosstalk and the correct rate of positioning will drop.

RFID readers [9] use the antenna to communicate with RFID tags through wireless tunnel. They also can be achieved on the tag identification code and memory data read or write operation. RFID technology can identify high-speed moving objects and can identify multiple tags at the same time by distributing RFID readers into it's region. The rate of data transmission between readers and tags is fast and convenient. Last but not least, the RFID reader takes the role of power center, is deemed to be the core part of RFID system. We allow the source node to act as the reader.

According to the working state the RFID tags can be divided into three categories: active tag, passive tag and semi-active tag, are the cheapest RFID device that is vulnerable to security risks. Thanks to the recent technology development, the cost of RFID tags has been dropped to a relatively low level. Nevertheless, these low-cost tags can provide real-time and accurate monitoring. Due to the resource limitation in terms of computation, communication and memory, the RFID tag cannot keep location information in it for a long period. Note here that the RFID tag referred in this paper is low-cost passive tag which gets power from the interaction with the source nodes.

2.2   Current Research

There are a lot of measurements designed to calculate the distance between nodes depending on the radio signal transmitted, such as received signal strength (RSS) [10–11], time-difference-of-arrival (TDOA) [12], time-of arrival (TOA) [13], round trip-time (RTT) [14], or angle-of-arrival (AOA) [15] measurements. The balance between the localization accuracy and the implementation complexity are the vital role we should considered in choosing which one to be in use.

In the conventional RSS measurement, the distance was calculated by switching the power loss which is consumed during the data transmission on the routing protocol. Unluckily, the calculated distance is not accurate owing to the noise between the nodes. That's will lead to the unliable localization. In [16], different weighting schemes for the multidimensional scaling (MDS) formulation were presented and compared. It was shown that the solution of the MDS can be used as the initial value for iterative algorithms, which then converge faster and attain higher accuracy when compared with random initial values. Angle of AOA location algorithm is based on the arrival angle. Unknown nodes through ZR36504TQCG antenna array and multiple ultrasonic receiver perceived beacon node sends signals to the direction. Between unknown nodes and beacon nodes azimuth the calculation is accomplished through the measurement of angle calculation the location of the unknown node. Because the additional hardware support is necessary to the AOA algorithm, the distance measurement process is easy to be affected by the external environment, so the algorithm is not suitable for large-scale network.

From the name of TOA, we can confirm that what we need to calculate the distance is the time. That's means we require high resolution clock and accurate synchronization between the sender and receiver. This requirement will increase the size of nodes. The another drawback of TOA is the energy consumption. Sum up, the demands of TOA measurement are not suitable to the development of WSN. However, we can study the main of them to design enhanced localization algorithm to improve the performance of it.

As far as former localization algorithms [10–16] are discussed briefly, they also have a common drawback. In most of these traditional algorithms, the main aim of achieving localization is realized by the anchor nodes. However, the anchor nodes are the main part of multi-hop WSNs. That means the limited energy resource of anchor nodes is wasted in localization. This causes an undesired prohibitive overhead and power consumption, thereby increasing the overall energy consumption of the network. In this paper, we focus on providing a good localization accuracy by using RFID technology.

3   Localization Algorithm

In this section, the details of RBLOCA is going to be discussed. We assume that micro sensor nodes are distributed randomly in the network area. Each sensor node has a limited built-in battery, and the battery cannot be replaced after the node has been deployed. Once the deployment of the network is totally completed, the location of the sensor node will not be changed. In addition, The location information of the node is unknown to the node itself. We also assume each node does know the position of the BS. But its remaining energy can be achieved at any time. The shape of the whole tested area nodes distributed in is a rectangle. We set the lower left corner of the whole region to be the origin point. In RBLOCA, CH nodes have multi-hop path communication with the BS. We set the number of RFID tags at the percentage of 20 % at the beginning of the simulation. According to the time period, the running process of the whole RBLOCA is divided into three stages: Setup phase, Compute phase and Localization phase.

3.1   Setup Phase

The nodes is first distributed into the network randomly. After that, the RFID tags are deployed into this region too. The node distribution graph is shown in Fig. 1. The blue color indicates that this is a location-unaware node. The red field shows that it is a RFID tag.

The main task of the setup phase is to deploy nodes and RFID tags in the WSN region. At first, the nodes are unknown to the environment factors. In our model, we make the communication more simplify. Nodes do not communicate with others. We just take the localization into consideration. Messages between the BS and the sensor nodes is ignored too. The messages in the network mainly contain the location and the

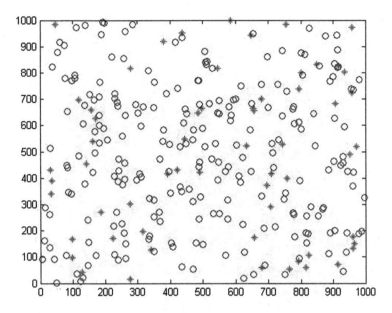

Fig. 1. The node distribution graph (Color figure online)

distance between the nodes with the tags. The energy dissipation of the whole network is measured by the transmission distance of RFID. The RFID tags are chosen by the source node in the first round and the greatest transmission distance. After the implementation of the whole phase, the exchange information will be stored in the RFID tags and sensor nodes. In addition, the information of the routing table is just kept by the source node.

3.2 Compute Phase

After the setup phase is finished, the source node broadcast the radio signal to find out the nearest three tags whose distance is most equal to the radio range. Specially, the first round of tags selection is random because the tags are unknown to sensor nodes. The tag is ready to sense the signal around it. The selection criteria include the most suitable three tags and the whole network area which should be monitored being covered by RFID tags. In fact, in the first tag selection phase, each tag in the network is all ready to work.

Compute phase is mainly to compute the distance between the source node and the tags. After this phase, the topology of network is shown as Fig. 2. The tags complete the identification of the broadcast information of the source node. When the three tags are all compute out the distance by the signal strength, this phase is finished. Note here that when the node is deployed far away from the tags, this phase will take a good while. In RBLOCA when a node's position has been confirmed, the node will turn into a "tag" to help other nodes. In other words, the node itself will change it's role and opens the receiving antenna to prepare for helping other sensor nodes after the node's position has been confirmed. When all the nodes' distance to their neighbours are computed, the node closes the transmitting antenna to save energy and the tags send the distance and their own position information to the BS to prepare for next phase.

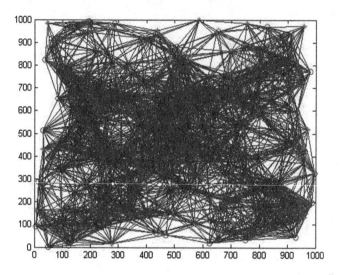

Fig. 2. Neighbor relation graph

3.3 Localization Phase

After the compute phase, the localization phase start. In RBLOCA, the trilateration localization algorithm [17] is united completely. The principle of trilateration localization algorithm is shown in Fig. 3.

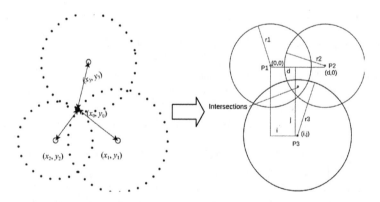

Fig. 3. The principle of trilateration localization algorithm

Position of the unknown node is pointed at (x, y), make the first spherical P1 center coordinates $(0, 0)$, P2 in the same vertical coordinates, center coordinates of $(d, 0)$, P3 of center coordinates (i, j), three spherical radius respectively, and r1, r2, r3, and z is three spherical intersection point and level surface height [18]. We can use Eqs. (1), (2) and (3) to calculate the acquired factors to decide the x of unknown node.

$$r_1^2 = x^2 + y^2 + z^2 \tag{1}$$

$$r_2^2 = (x - d)^2 + y^2 + z^2 \tag{2}$$

$$r_3^2 = (x - i)^2 + (y - j)^2 + z^2 \tag{3}$$

In other model, the value of z is 0. So the x of node is shown in Eq. (4).

$$x = \frac{(r_1^2 - r_2^2 + d^2)}{2d} \tag{4}$$

Next, we deform the Eq. (2) and take the z^2 in Eq. (1) into Eq. (2). After that, the value of y can be figured out and is shown in Eq. (5).

$$y = \frac{[r_1^2 - r_3^2 - x^2 + (x - i)^2 + j^2]}{2j} \tag{5}$$

4 Performance Evaluation

In this section, the simulation and analysis of RBLOCA are implemented by using MATLAB. We consider a wireless sensor network with N = 300 nodes [19] randomly

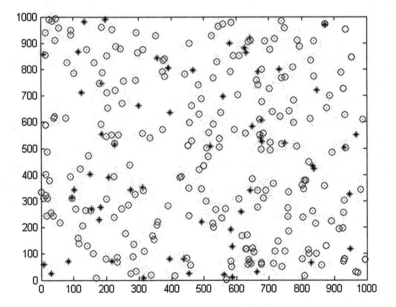

Fig. 4. The positional error of RBLOCA (Color figure online)

distributed in a 1000 m * 1000 m field. 60 RFID tags are deployed in the region too. The communication ranges of nodes and tags are all set at 200 m [20]. The radio model is Regular Model. After compute phase, the average connectivity of the network is calculated and is shown as follows: 33.3333. What's more, the average number of RFID tags in the network is 6.1867.

The typical Centroid Localization algorithm, DV-HOP algorithm and RBLOCA algorithm are simulated in this part and each of them are analyzed from positioning error, aspects, which are named as number of sensors have the wrong position [21]. The detailed comparisons are shown as follows.

In Figs. 4, 5 and 6, blue short term used to indicate the positioning error of the unknown nodes. From Fig. 4, we can draw the conclusion that the most of unknown nodes are located correctly. Even than the most of nodes in Figs. 5 and 6 are located, the correct rate is not satisfactory [22].

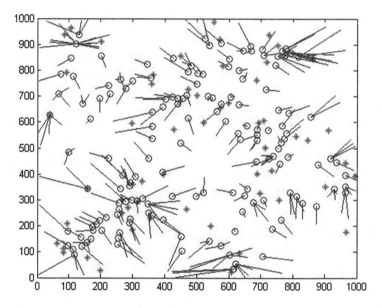

Fig. 5. The positional error of Centroid Localization algorithm (Color figure online)

The detail analysis of three algorithms is shown in Table 1. Performance of the main analysis of the following indicators for the following three: the positioning error, the average connectivity of the network and the average number of RFID tags. From the performance analysis, the RBLOCA has a lower positioning error even when the average connectivity of the network is low [23].

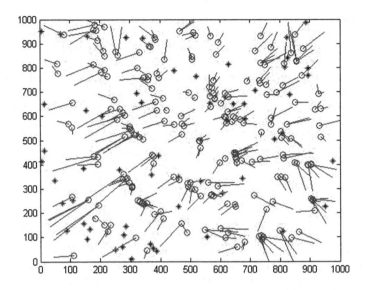

Fig. 6. The positional error of DV-HOP algorithm (Color figure online)

Table 1. The detail analysis of three algorithms

	The positioning error	The average connectivity of the network	The average number of RFID tags
RBLOCA	1.9835e−15	31.4667	6.21
Centroid	0.33895	31.8933	6.5533
DV-HOP	0.31305	32.3067	6.4267

So the algorithm we designed has better performance than the two traditional algorithms.

5   Conclusion and Future Work

In this paper, we propose a RFID based localization algorithm for wireless sensor networks in order to improve the correct rate of the localization algorithm by combining the RFID technology into WSN, which is popular in the field of positioning technology. We also make use of the trilateration localization algorithm to compute the position information of nodes. From the simulation results, when the average connectivity of the network and the average number of RFID tags are lower, the EBLOCA could achieve a higher correct rate. In the further work, we want to improve the algorithm by finding the most suitable average number of RFID tags in the network. What's more, we want to improve the performance of trilateration localization algorithm by making the full use of the radio signal. We hope that our future algorithm can perform better when the network is more complex.

Acknowledgment. This work is supported by the National Science Foundation of China under Grant No. 61300237, No. U1536206, No. U1405254, No. 61232016 and No. 61402234, the National Basic Research Program 973 under Grant No. 2011CB311808, the Natural Science Foundation of Jiangsu province under Grant No. BK2012461, the research fund from Jiangsu Technology & Engineering Center of Meteorological Sensor Network in NUIST under Grant No. KDXG1301, the research fund from Jiangsu Engineering Center of Network Monitoring in NUIST under Grant No. KJR1302, the research fund from Nanjing University of Information Science and Technology under Grant No. S8113003001, the 2013 Nanjing Project of Science and Technology Activities for Returning from Overseas, the 2015 Project of six personnel in Jiangsu Province under Grant No. R2015L06, the CICAEET fund, and the PAPD fund.

References

1. Heinzelman, W.R., Chandrakasan, A., Balakrishnan, H.: Energy-efficient communication protocol for wireless microsensor networks. In: Proceedings of the 33rd Annual Hawaii International Conference on System Sciences, vol. 2. IEEE (2000). 10 pp.
2. Yektaparast, A., Nabavi, F.-H., Sarmast, A.: An improvement on leach protocol (cell-leach). In: 2012 14th International Conference on Advanced Communication Technology (ICACT), pp. 992–996. IEEE (2012)
3. Heinzelman, W.B.: Application-specific protocol architectures for wireless networks. Ph.D. dissertation, Massachusetts Institute of Technology (2000)
4. Manjeshwar, A., Agrawal, D.P.: Teen: a routing protocol for enhanced efficiency in wireless sensor networks. In: Null, p. 30189a. IEEE (2001)
5. Manjeshwar, A., Agrawal, D.P.: APTEEN: a hybrid protocol for efficient routing and comprehensive information retrieval in wireless sensor networks. In: IPDPS, p. 0195b. IEEE (2002)
6. Shen, J., Tan, H., Wang, J., Wang, J., Lee, S.: A novel routing protocol providing good transmission reliability in underwater sensor networks. J. Internet Technol. **16**(1), 171–178 (2015)
7. Lee, J., Kim, Y., Lee, J., Kim, S.: An efficient three-dimensional localization scheme using trilateration in wireless sensor networks. IEEE Commun. Lett. **18**(9), 1591–1594 (2014)
8. Shen, J., Tan, H., Moh, S., Chung, I., Wang, J.: An efficient RFID authentication protocol providing strong privacy and security. J. Internet Technol. **17**(3) (2016). doi:10.6138/JIT.2016.17.3.20141219
9. Shen, J., Tan, H., Wang, Y., Ji, S., Wang, J.: An enhanced grouping proof for multiple RFID readers and tag groups. Int. J. Control Autom. **7**(12), 239–246 (2014)
10. Ren, H., Meng, M.Q.-H.: Power adaptive localization algorithm for wireless sensor networks using particle filter. IEEE Trans. Veh. Technol. **58**(5), 2498–2508 (2009)
11. Rezazadeh, J., Moradi, M., Ismail, A.S., Dutkiewicz, E.: Superior path planning mechanism for mobile Beacon-assisted localization in wireless sensor networks. IEEE Sens. J. **14**(9), 3052–3064 (2014)
12. Cong, L., Zhuang, W.: Hybrid TDOA/AOA mobile user location for wideband CDMA cellular systems. IEEE Trans. Wirel. Commun. **1**(3), 439–447 (2002)
13. Hong, S., Zhi, D., Dasgupta, S., Chunming, Z.: Multiple source localization in wireless sensor networks based on time of arrival measurement. IEEE Trans. Sign. Process. **62**(8), 1938–1949 (2014)
14. Niculescu, D., Nath, B.: Ad hoc positioning system (APS). In: Proceedings of IEEE Global Telecommunication Conference, San Antonio, TX, USA, 25–29 November 2001

15. Niculescu, D., Nath, B.: Ad hoc positioning system (APS) using AOA. In: Twenty-Second Annual Joint Conference of the IEEE Computer and Communications, INFOCOM 2003, IEEE Societies, vol. 3, pp. 1734–1743. IEEE (2003)
16. Li, X.: Collaborative localization with received-signal strength in wireless sensor networks. IEEE Trans. Veh. Technol. **56**(6), 3807–3817 (2007)
17. Boukerche, A., Oliveira, H.A.B.F., Nakamura, E.F., et al.: Localization systems for wireless sensor networks. IEEE Wirel. Commun. **14**(6), 6–12 (2007)
18. Guo, P., Wang, J., Li, B., et al.: A variable threshold-value authentication architecture for wireless mesh networks. J. Internet Technol. **15**(6), 929–936 (2014)
19. Wen, X., Shao, L., Fang, W., et al.: Efficient feature selection and classification for vehicle detection. IEEE Trans. Circ. Syst. Video Technol. **25**(3), 508–517 (2015)
20. Li, J., Li, X., Yang, B., et al.: Segmentation-based image copy-move forgery detection scheme. IEEE Trans. Inf. Forensics Secur. **10**(3), 507–518 (2015)
21. Zhangjie, F., Xingming, S., Qi, L., et al.: Achieving efficient cloud search services: multi-keyword ranked search over encrypted cloud data supporting parallel computing. IEICE Trans. Commun. **98**(1), 190–200 (2015)
22. Buschmann, C., et al.: Radio propagation-A ware distance estimation based on neighborhood comparison. In: Proceedings of 4th European. Conference Wireless Sensor Networks, The Netherlands, 29–31 January 2007
23. Huang, B., Yu, C., Anderson, B.D.O., Mao, G.: Estimating distances via connectivity in wireless sensor networks. Wirel. Commun. Mob. Comput. **14**(5), 541–556 (2014)

Multimedia Applications

SA-Based Multimedia Conversion System for Multi-users Environment

Hsin-Hung Cho[1]([⊠]), Fan-Hsun Tseng[1], Timothy K. Shih[1], Li-Der Chou[1], and Han-Chieh Chao[2,3,4,5,6]

[1] Department of Computer Science and Information Engineering
at National Central University, Taoyuan, Taiwan, ROC
{hsin-hung,fanhsuntseng}@ieee.org
timothykshih@gmail.com, cld@csie.ncu.edu.tw
[2] College of Computer and Software,
Nanjing University of Information Science and Technology, Nanjing, China
[3] College of Mathematics and Computer Science,
Wuhan Polytechnic University, Wuhan, China
[4] Department of Electrical Engineering,
National Dong Hwa University, Hualien, Taiwan, ROC
[5] Department of Computer Science and Information Engineering,
National Ilan University, Yilan, Taiwan, ROC
hcc@niu.edu.tw
[6] School of Information Science and Engineering,
Fujian University of Technology, Fujian, China

Abstract. Nowadays multimedia applications surround our life. The relevant technologies of multimedia have been widely used anywhere, e.g. education, medicine, research, transportation and recreation, as long as people who has a mobile device. The computing ability of mobile device is growing rapidly, but it still has its limitations. One of significant influence on most mobile devices is the active time of them depend on the capacity of battery. Multimedia may make battery runs out quickly because it usually carries a large amount of information and data so that it leads to a great quantity of calculation and bandwidth requirement. In order to alleviate the computation amount of mobile devices, we propose an adaptive cloud-based multimedia conversion system to eliminate energy consumption and unnecessary occupancy on bandwidth in accordance with the capability and network state of users' mobile devices. Then we propose a Simulated Annealing-based algorithm to solve the optimization problem of scheduling for a multi-user environment.

Keywords: Multimedia · Cloud computing · Metaheuristics · Simulated annealing

1 Introduction

Visualization is not an innovative concept but is a basic demand of human [1]. For a most representative example, the medium is evolved from radio to television

© Springer International Publishing AG 2016
X. Sun et al. (Eds.): ICCCS 2016, Part II, LNCS 10040, pp. 289–300, 2016.
DOI: 10.1007/978-3-319-48674-1_26

when people wants to receive news. Another example is that traditional mobile phone is gradually replaced by smartphone. These instances represent human quite able to accept seeing is believing. Media technologies play a very important role in such kind of instances. However, technological development is progressing rapidly so that early media technologies have been unable to meet the demands of modern people, because people want higher quality, less time and more types of services. Therefore, multimedia technology has been proposed to bear these heavy responsibility [2]. Multimedia is able to store more information than the traditional media, even let those informations have relationship so that they can be effectively machined that includes storage, transmission, compression and so on. It means that multimedia can achieve more diversified and quality services for people.

Generally, multimedia is composed of a large number of digital data so that it will occupies a lot bandwidth and spends more downloading time. To solve this problem, multimedia usually be compressed into a smaller format, but it must be through a more complex computation. Fortunately, the current computers have powerful computing ability to deal such complex process even cloud computing technique has matured [3,4]. They are able to easily decode and encode a high quality video even if this video is encapsulated very many information [5]. However, most smartphone have not enough computing power to do that. Even if they have, their battery will run out soon, because energy consumption and computational complexity are in a direct proportion. As well as smartphone usually use mobile communication network that the throughput is obviously inadequate than the optical network [6]. It means that smartphone has a bottleneck for use of multimedia.

Human always like to watch high definition videos and prefer to watch them on smartphone. But we know that screen of most smartphone is far less than the personal computer's screen. It means that high definition video is watched by smartphone seems overkill. According to this observation, we know that original smartphone may only need the video which has lower resolution. Therefore, used of bandwidth and computing power will be decreased if the lower resolution video is downloading for smartphone. In an existed research [7], authors use Hadoop [8] and ffmpeg to implement a conversion system. However, it only consider to how to quickly convert video from large to small but not taking network states and detail smartphone capabilities into account. In this paper, we propose an adaptive cloud-based multimedia conversion architecture so that we can find out a really suitable resolution for conversion process via cloud computing then users can downloaded the appropriate version. Due to scenario of real world exist very many users to watch video in the same time. Their network environment, ability of smartphone and video want to watch are different so that the interaction may very huge. It means that this problem can be formulated into an optimization problem. Therefore, we will use simulated annealing-based (SA) algorithm [9] to find an optimal tasks scheduling policy for proposed cloud-based multimedia conversion architecture.

The simulation results show that the proposed method can reduce more unnecessarily delay. It represents that this method also provides a stable network environment. The rest of the paper is organized as follows. Section 2 introduces background and related works. Section 3 will give the problem definition then we will introduce our proposed cloud-based multimedia conversion architecture and SA-based algorithm. The simulation results present in Sect. 4. Finally, we will summarize research contributions and discussing the future works in last section.

2   Background and Related Works

2.1   Distributed Media Conversion System (DMCS)

Distributed Media Conversion System (DMCS) has been proposed at 2010 by Hsu [7]. Authors found smartphone can not quickly decode high quality video so that users must wait some times before watching video. They think that media should be converted into the easier format for decoding of smartphone. In order to decrease the decodeding time, they use Hadoop as a computing platform then use of MapReduce algorithm decodes the original coding and then encodes it to a compressed format. First step is "Map" process that media can be parted into several blocks then assign to work nodes by head end node. Second step is to run the ffmpeg so that any blocks can be covert into specified format. Third, these blocks will put into the "Reduce" process after they have completed the conversion. Finally, user can download a simple format version.

However, they did not consider to more metrics which may impact user experience. Therefore this method may produces unfair situation in real scenario. Any users may use different network type so that data rate of them are not same, therefore even the smartphone has high computing power that it is still not fit to download the high quality video. Moreover, there are many people watch video in the same time so that the interaction between multi-user will become frequent. It means that only dealing video of single user is not enough. This is a scheduling problem, so we must consider to the features of any tasks, such as task reach time, task work time and so on. When considerations become more, general algorithms may cause the results fall into local optimal. Therefore, a fast metaheuristic-based algorithm is worth considered.

3   Adaptive SA-Based Multimedia Conversion (ASAMC) Architecture

3.1   System Model

In order to overcome some drawbacks of DMCS, we try to design a complete system model which takes network states, capability of smartphone and so on any possible arguments into account. This system composed of controller, cloud nodes, media server and at least one smartphone. Controller is responsible as a bridge between smartphone and server as well as it must monitor the network states. It can be a agent or SDN controller. In this paper, SDN controller is chosen for this system, because it has strong ability for monitor the network traffic as well as it is able to flexibly configure any needed functions. Firstly, user will finds a video want to watch, then smartphone 1 will sends a request $Req(Server1, Video1, P1)$ to controller that this request includes server 1's IP address, video 1 and own various information. The third step is that controller will helps smartphone 1 to download video 1 as well as ask server 1 for the related information of video 1. In this moment, controller has obtained the information from both of video 1, smartphone 1 and its network state then sent them to the master node of Hadoop platform that shown in step 4 of Fig. 1. Master node can calculated a policy which can suit with smartphone 1's capability and network state. Step 5 and 6 show that when a suitable version of video 1 has been converted completely, it will sent back to smartphone 1. The whole process are shown in Fig. 1. We called this method as Adaptive SA-based Multimedia Conversion(ASAMC) Architecture.

In multi-users environment, controller may need to deal many requests so that master node will received several commands from controller. These commands will continue to influx, but complex conversion process has some time for computing which includes conversion process time, scheduling time and MapReduce time. In order to avoid congestion, we set several standby node to deal some cases which are more urgent. This component can be regarded as a faster counter in the service industry. When standby nodes were not working, they will work with work nodes. They will interrupts the current job as long as an urgent job is reaching. The major mission of master node is find an optimal scheduling. We will introduce this scheduling optimization problem and its solution in the following two subsection.

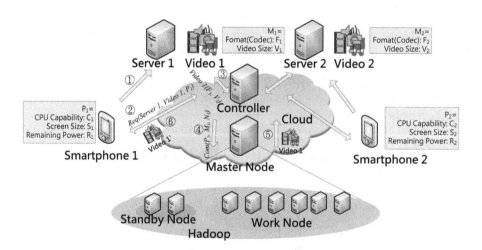

Fig. 1. Adaptive SA-based Multimedia Conversion (ASAMC) architecture

3.2   Problem Definition

In order to clearly depict multi-user video conversion problem, all symbols will be used are listed in the Table 1.

Table 1. Important symbol list

Values	Definition
n	Number of smartphone
M_i	Information of video i
F_i	Format of video i
V_i	Size of video i, $V \in \{1080, 702, 480, 360, 240, 144\}$
P_i	Information of smartphone i
C_i	CPU capability of smartphone i
S_i	Screen size of smartphone i, $S \in \{1080, 702, 480, 360, 240, 144\}$
R_i	Remaining power of smartphone i
$N_{i,j}$	Network speed from smartphone i to server j
D_i	Delay time of smartphone i
$T_{(arrival,i)}$	Arrival time that video i arrived to Hadoop platform.
$T_{(deadline,i)}$	Deadline of video i
$T_{(expected,i)}$	Expected end time that smartphone i received video i
$T_{(actual,i)}$	Actual end time that smartphone i received video i
$T_{(conversion,i)}$	Consumed conversion time of video i
$T_{(transmission,i)}$	Consumed transmission time of video i travelling between smartphone and server

Providing an efficient multimedia service is a basic requirement. In the problem definition, we will try to minimize the delay time for all users of whole network as well as ensure that size of video will not smaller than the size of smartphone screen. According to the standard scheduling problem, all of videos has own arrival time and deadline. In general, deadline must less than arrival time. The value of them are based on user behavior as well as some video may has limited lifetime. In this way, when all of videos arrived to Hadoop platform, they have been roughly arranged into orderly, so that we can easy to depict problem definition by linear programming model [10] that shown in Table 2. Because the time is an important metric which help us to schedule all of conversion tasks, we will detail to derive the needed time metric. The so call delay time can be calculated by Eqs. (1) to (3):

$$D_i = T_{(actual,i)} - T_{(expected,i)} \tag{1}$$

where expected end time can be obtained as follows:

$$T_{expected} = \frac{V_i(kb)}{N_{i,j}(kbs)} \tag{2}$$

Table 2. Linear programming model

Minimize $\sum_{i=1}^{n} D_i$

s.t.

$$V_i \geq S_i$$
$$T_{(deadline,i)} > T_{(arrival,i)}$$

---

and actual end time is a summation of conversion time and transmission time that shown in Eq. (3)

$$T_{actual} = T_{transmission} + T_{conversion} \tag{3}$$

The solution will be found in the range which restricted by our linear programming model. Next assignment is to design an efficient scheduling algorithm. We know that this problem is not easy, multi-user case especially. Because in multi-user environment, work nodes are the resource for users so that they all want to be able to compete to the chance for use. But computing resource is limited so that there are some tasks must to line up in the queue. In this moment, some urgent tasks cannot be completed on time. Although there are several standby nodes are set, the may still be in short supply. In simple terms, multi-users lead problem become difficult due to the intense competition. Therefore we have to use a metaheuristic-based algorithm to solve it, however most of this kind of algorithm may spend more computing time. Hence we choose simulated annealing (SA) algorithm [11] as a core of proposed method. The major reason is that SA is faster than the other metaheuristic-based algorithms [12]. Because SA is a single-threaded method and it not only has concept of greedy algorithm but also has ability to escape local optimal.

3.3 Adaptive SA-Based Multimedia Conversion Algorithm

Our main goal is to efficiently reduce delay time, hence we must ensure that any work nodes can not have too much idle time so that the number of completed tasks are largest within a specified time. Based on this view, we can further design the coding of solution that show in Fig. 2. X-axis represents a continuous time and Y-axis is number of work nodes that both two axis size can be specified by administrator. *Com* is the received command which includes information of smartphone, video and network states. Video size has six types can be chosen that are 1080, 720, 480, 360, 240, 144 respectively. We assume length of each video is same and each type of solution is exactly equal to an unit block. For instance, Com_1 occupied an unit block that represents its resloution is 144p, so the consumed time is also an unit time. In other words, the needed time of *Com* may be changed if V was changed according our algorithm. We can easy

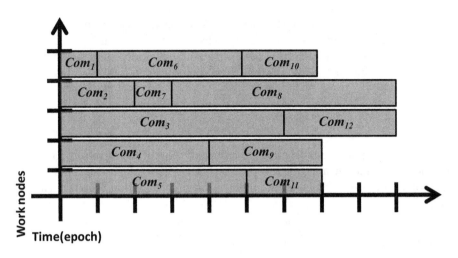

Fig. 2. Coding of solution

to find that our mission is to fill up this space completely. This diagram can be translated into a formal matrix Sol_i as follows:

$$
Sol_i = \begin{pmatrix}
Com_1 & Com_3 & Com_3 & Com_3 & Com_3 & Com_{10} & Com_{10} & \phi & \phi & \phi \\
Com_2 & Com_2 & Com_7 & Com_8 & Com_8 & Com_8 & Com_8 & Com_8 & Com_8 & \phi \\
Com_4 & Com_4 & Com_4 & Com_4 & Com_4 & Com_4 & Com_{12} & Com_{12} & Com_{12} & \phi \\
Com_5 & Com_5 & Com_5 & Com_5 & Com_9 & Com_9 & Com_9 & \phi & \phi & \phi \\
Com_6 & Com_6 & Com_6 & Com_6 & Com_6 & Com_{11} & Com_{11} & \phi & \phi & \phi
\end{pmatrix}
$$

Any solutions of original SA can compare with their neighbors in every iterations. In this problem, we will randomly change V from a stochastic Com. In general case, V usually is became small. When length of Com is changed, rear Com will filled ahead or putting any siutable Com to fill. So we may got an adjacent solutions such as:

$$
Sol_{i+1} = \begin{pmatrix}
Com_1 & Com_3 & Com_3 & Com_3 & Com_3 & Com_{10} & Com_{10} & \phi & \phi & \phi \\
Com_2 & Com_2 & Com_7 & Com_8 & Com_8 & Com_8 & Com_8 & Com_8 & Com_8 & \phi \\
Com_4 & Com_4 & Com_4 & Com_4 & Com_4 & Com_4 & Com_{12} & Com_{12} & \phi & \phi \\
Com_5 & Com_5 & Com_5 & Com_5 & Com_9 & Com_9 & Com_9 & \phi & \phi & \phi \\
Com_6 & Com_6 & Com_6 & Com_6 & Com_6 & Com_{11} & Com_{11} & \phi & \phi & \phi
\end{pmatrix}
$$

Any Com can be cutted to distribute to other work nodes, this operation will be executed after above mentioned step. Then we will get a new solution:

$$
Sol_{i+2} = \begin{pmatrix}
Com_1 & Com_3 & Com_3 & Com_3 & Com_3 & Com_{10} & Com_{10} & Com_8 & \phi & \phi \\
Com_2 & Com_2 & Com_7 & Com_8 & Com_8 & Com_8 & Com_8 & Com_8 & \phi & \phi \\
Com_4 & Com_4 & Com_4 & Com_4 & Com_4 & Com_4 & Com_{12} & Com_{12} & \phi & \phi \\
Com_5 & Com_5 & Com_5 & Com_5 & Com_9 & Com_9 & Com_9 & \phi & \phi & \phi \\
Com_6 & Com_6 & Com_6 & Com_6 & Com_6 & Com_{11} & Com_{11} & \phi & \phi & \phi
\end{pmatrix}
$$

In order to highlight the difference after resolution of video be changed. We assume that any resolutions exactly need twice as long as transmission time with next level. For example, 1080p is level 1 that it has double transmission time then the 720p which is level 2. Therefore, we can derived $T_{transmission}$ as Eq. (6):

$$T_{transmission} = \sum_{i=1}^{6} \frac{\frac{1}{i} \times V(kbs)}{N(kbs)} \tag{4}$$

Conversion time depends on the consumed time of an iteration so that it only be got by measuring. Since we want to know how much time to speed up after solution has been changed, we use a variation of iteration time to formulate $T_{conversion}$:

$$T_{conversion} = \Delta T_{iteration} \tag{5}$$

then we can find a better solution via fitness function f_i:

$$f_i = \sum_{i=1}^{n} D_i \tag{6}$$

The main body of proposed algorithm is shown in the following:

Algorithm 1. Adaptive SA-based Multimedia Conversion (ASAMC)

Input: $Com(P, M, N)$
Output: Sol_{best} Constant: T, Ψ
1: Specifying size of X-axis and Y-axis;
2: Randomly fill up the candidate space from $Com = \{Com_1, ..., Com_n\}$;
3: **repeat**
4:     Randomly generate a new Sol from Sol_{best};
5:     **If** Sol is better than Sol_{best} $|| T < \Psi$
6:         $Sol_{best} = Sol$;
7:     **End**
8:     $T = T \times 0.9$;
9: **until** Find out a Sol_{best} that f is minimum

---

where Ψ is used in deciding whether the solution is a probability of accepting nonimproving. The definition is shown in

$$\Psi = e^{\left(-\frac{f(Sol_{best} - Sol)}{T}\right)} \tag{7}$$

The algorithm will be terminated if solution has converged or the temperature T is already close to 0°c. T will be slightly decreased after an iteration has finished. Too quick reduction of T will leads solution can be prematurely convergented, hence we limit T dropped only 10 % in every times.

Table 3. Simulation parameters

Parameters	Values
Number of woek nodes	100
Number of users	10−800
Distribution of video size	Uniform distribution: $\{1080, 720, 480, 360, 240, 144\}$
Distribution of screen size	Uniform distribution: $\{1080, 720, 480, 360, 240, 144\}$
Distribution of network speed	Uniform distribution: $\{10, 50, 100, 150, 200, 250\}$(kbs)
Initial temperature T	1,000 °c

4 Simulation

4.1 Simulation Setting

The simulation is performed by utilizing MATLAB (Version 7.11, R2010b). In order to make a fair comparison, most of distribution models adopte uniform as their distribution. The reason is that although the real case is more complicated, the special cases always in the minority, hence we do not think they will have too much influence for our method. So we think use of uniform distribution is acceptable. The detail parameters setting are listed in Table 3.

4.2 Simulation Results

Figure 3 shows a comparison of delay time between ASAMC and DMCS. In the beginning, ASAMC has more delay time in the fewer user case, because it needs some times for operation of SA. Generally, when SA want to initially generated a solution, it must to collect several *Com* firstly. Otherwise, too few *Com* will causes SA easier to fall into local optimal. This situation will be continued until when number of users is equal to 250. DMCS began to significantly delay. Because DMCS always put *Com* to currently idle work nodes so that some work nodes may be occupied for a long time. Therefore, many users must to wait that leading the summation of their delay time will rapidly increased. Therefore in the more users case, although delay time of ASAMC also began to grow, the growth trend is relatively milder than DMCS.

Typically, metaheuristics need huge computing time. Most of time is used to ensure whether solution fall into local optimal. This point will be impacted by coding of solution. In order to evaluate the efficacy of ASAMC, we depict convergence curve of it that is shown in Fig. 4. We set scenario in the 800 user case. ASAMC need about 25 iteration to find the best solution. This is acceptable speed, because it is only equal to 200 (s) that can contrast with Fig. 3.

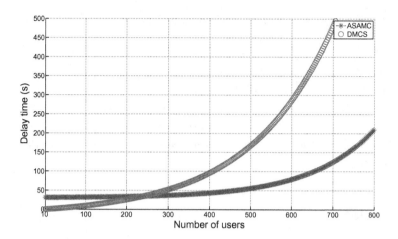

Fig. 3. Comparison of delay time between ASAMC and DMCS

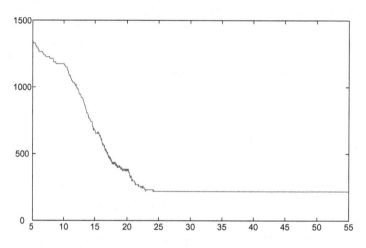

Fig. 4. Convergence curve of ASAMC

5   Conclusion

In this paper, we use SA to design the adaptive cloud-based multimedia conversion architecture and algorithm. Smartphone can watch a multimedia video with acceptable resolution so that the energy consumption will be decreased. Most important point is this method is able to reduce more delay time that users can obtain better experience. In the future works, we will consider to more metrics so that our method has ability to implement in a real environment, such as different length of video, movable users, security issues [13,14] and so on. In addition, we will enhance ASAMC so that it can deal the streaming process [15]. This is a very demanding challenge, because group of pictures (GOP) scheduling will generate a very large computation costs. Therefore, this problem needs a faster method.

Acknowledgments. This research was partly funded by the National Science Council of the R.O.C. under grants MOST 104-2221-E-197- 014 - and 105-2221- E-197 -010 - MY2.

References

1. Ten, D.W.H., Manickam, S., Ramadass, S., Bazar, H.A.A.: Study on advanced visualization tools in network monitoring platform. In: Third UKSim European Symposium on Computer Modeling and Simulation (EMS 2009), pp. 445–449. IEEE, 25–27 November 2009
2. Lee, C.D., Jeong, T.W.: Fuzzy filtering-based segment grouping for user-centered multimedia streaming service in P2P distribution mobile networks. J. Internet Technol. 11(5), 651–658 (2010)
3. Tseng, F.-H., Chou, L.-D., Chiang, H.-P., Yu, W.-J.: Implement efficient data integrity for cloud distributed file system using Merkle hash tree. J. Internet Technol. (JIT) 15(2), 307–316 (2014)
4. Fu, Z., Sun, X., Liu, Q., Zhou, L., Shu, J.: Achieving efficient cloud search services: multi-keyword ranked search over encrypted cloud data supporting parallel computing. IEICE Trans. Commun. **E98–B**(1), 190–200 (2015)
5. Pan, Z., Zhang, Y., Kwong, S.: Efficient motion and disparity estimation optimization for low complexity multiview video coding. IEEE Trans. Broadcast. **61**(2), 166–176 (2015)
6. Cho, H.-H., Lai, C.-F., Shih, T.K., Chao, H.-C.: Integration of SDR and SDN for 5G. IEEE Access **2**, 1196–1204 (2014)
7. Hsu, S.-W., Chen, C.-Y., Shih, W.-K., Chao, H.-C.: Distributed media conversion system over cloud environment. In: Personalized Service Over Cloud (PSoC 2012) (in Conjunction with HumanCom2012), Gwangju, Korea, 6–8 September 2012
8. Shvachko, K., Kuang, H., Radia, S., Chansler, R.: The Hadoop distributed file system. In: Proceedings of the 26th IEEE Symposium on Massive Storage Systems and Technologies, MSST 2010 (2010)
9. Tsai, C.-W., Rodrigues, J.J.P.C.: Metaheuristic scheduling for cloud: a survey. IEEE Syst. J. **8**(1), 279–291 (2014)
10. Dantzig, G.B.: Linear Programming and Extensions. Princeton University Press, Princeton (1963)
11. Aarts, E., Korst, J.: Simulated Annealing and Boltzmann Machines: A Stochastic Approach to Combinatorial Optimization and Neural Computing. Wiley, New York (1989)
12. Chien, W.-C., Cho, H.-H., Chen, C.-Y., Chao, H.-C., Shih, T.K.: An efficient charger planning mechanism of WRSN using simulated annealing algorithm. In: IEEE International Conference on Systems, Man, and Cybernetics (SMC 2015), Hong Kong, 9–12 October 2015
13. Tseng, F.-H., Chen, C.-Y., Chou, L.-D., Chao, H.-C.: Implement a reliable and secure cloud distributed file system. In: 2012 International Symposium on Intelligent Signal Processing and Communications Systems (ISPACS), pp. 227–232 (2012)

14. Xia, Z., Wang, X., Sun, X., Wang, Q.: A secure and dynamic multi-keyword ranked search scheme over encrypted cloud data. IEEE Trans. Parallel Distrib. Syst. **27**(2), 340–352 (2015)
15. Padmanabhan, V.N., Wang, H.J., Chou, P.A., Sripanidkulchai, K.: Distributing streaming media content using cooperative networking. In: Proceedings of the 12th International Workshop on Network and Operating Systems Support for Digital Audio and Video, ACM NOSSDAV 2002, pp. 177–186 (2002)

Color Image Quality Assessment with Quaternion Moments

Wei Zhang, Bo Hu$^{(\boxtimes)}$, Zhao Xu, and Leida Li

School of Information and Electrical Engineering,
China University of Mining and Technology, Xuzhou 221116, China
`15262004211@163.com`

Abstract. Color information is important to image quality assessment (IQA). However, most image quality assessment methods transform color image into gray scale, which fail to consider color information. In recent years, color image processing by using the algebra of quaternions has been attracting tremendous attention. Extensive moments based on quaternion have been introduced to deal with the red, green and blue channels of color images in a holistic manner, which have been proved more effective in color processing. With these inspirations, this paper presents a full-reference color image quality assessment metric based on Quaternion Tchebichef Moments (QTMs). QTMs are first employed to measure color and structure distortions simultaneously. Considering that moments are insensitive to weak distortions in high-quality images, gradient is incorporated as a complementary feature. Luminance is also considered as an auxiliary feature. Finally, a QTM-feature-based weighting map is proposed to conduct the pooling, producing an overall quality score. The experimental results on five public image quality databases demonstrate that the proposed method outperforms the state-of-the-arts.

Keywords: Image quality assessment · Full-reference · Quaternion moment · Image gradient

1 Introduction

Image quality assessment (IQA) aims to design reliable algorithms to predict the quality of images automatically. IQA is a fundamental issue in many image processing problems [1–3]. According to the availability of a reference image, the current IQA metrics can be classified into full-reference (FR), reduced-reference (RR) and no-reference (NR) approaches [4–6]. In this paper, we focus on FR-IQA model, which is important for benchmarking image processing algorithms.

Several FR-IQA metrics have been addressed in the literature. Mean squared error (MSE) and peak signal-to-noise ratio (PSNR) are the most commonly used FR-IQA metrics, which operate directly on the intensity of image. However, they do not correlate well with the subjective ratings [7]. In the past decade, several IQA methods have been proposed based on human visual system (HVS) and achieved remarkable results. In [7], Wang *et al.* introduced structural similarity

© Springer International Publishing AG 2016
X. Sun et al. (Eds.): ICCCS 2016, Part II, LNCS 10040, pp. 301–312, 2016.
DOI: 10.1007/978-3-319-48674-1_27

(SSIM), where image quality was measured by quantifying structure, luminance and contrast distortions. Then SSIM was extended to the multi-scale version with improved performance, i.e., MS-SSIM [8], which incorporated the influence of varying viewing conditions. Wang and Li [9] proposed the information-content-weighted SSIM (IW-SSIM), accounting for the fact that different regions of an image have different contributions on perceived quality. Sheikh and Bovik [10] proposed the visual information fidelity (VIF) metric based on natural scene statistics. They measured image quality using an information fidelity criterion, which was obtained by calculating the mutual information between the reference and distorted images. Larson and Chandler [11] proposed the most apparent distortion (MAD) metric. Two separate models were first used to evaluate the qualities of high-quality and low-quality images. Then they were combined to evaluate the overall quality of an image. Zhang *et al.* [12] adopted phase congruency (PC) to represent image structures and proposed the feature similarity (FSIM). In [13], Liu *et al.* claimed to measure structure and contrast distortions simultaneously using gradient similarity (GSM). Xue *et al.* [14] proposed the gradient magnitude similarity deviation (GMSD) model, where the standard deviation of gradient magnitude similarity map was computed as the quality score. Kolaman *et al.* [15] proposed quaternion structural similarity (QSSIM), which is a vectorial expansion of structure similarity using quaternion. Most of the current IQA metrics are achieved in gray scale domain, so they are limited in evaluating the quality of color images.

Color and structure are important to color IQA. Quaternion-based moments can capture both color and structure information simultaneously. On the one hand, the red, green and blue channels of an color image can be represented using a pure quaternion. Therefore, quaternion-based moments contain the color information and can be used to evaluate color distortions. On the other hand, it has been widely accepted that distortions give rise to structure changes in images [7]. In practice, we find that structure distortions change the shape of visual objects. Since orthogonal moments are effective shape descriptors, it is straightforward to employ moments to measure the structure changes caused by distortions. Inspired by these facts, we propose to use Quaternion Tchebichef Moments (QTMs) for image quality assessment, which are more effective on color images. In this paper, QTMs of image blocks are used to design features for measuring both color and structure distortions in an image. Image gradient is used as a complementary feature to capture weak distortions in high-quality images. Luminance information is also considered to make the proposed method more accurate. Experimental results on five public databases demonstrate the advantages of the proposed method.

2   Quaternion Tchebichef Moments

In this section, we briefly review some basic definitions of the quaternion and Tchebichef moments.

2.1 Quaternion

Quaternions, a generalization of the complex numbers, were introduced by the mathematician Hamilton in 1843 [16]. A quaternion with one real part and three imaginary parts can be written as follows:

$$q = a + bi + cj + dk, \tag{1}$$

where a, b, c and d are real numbers, and i, j, k are three imaginary units obeying the following rules:

$$i^2 + j^2 + k^2 = -1, \tag{2}$$

$$ij = -ji = k, jk = -kj = i, ki = -ik = j. \tag{3}$$

As shown in (3), the quaternion multiplication is not commutative. If a=0, then $q = bi + cj + dk$ is called a pure quaternion, and if q has unit norm ($\mid q \mid = 1$), then it is called unit pure quaternion.

For any two quaternions p and q, $\overline{pq} = \overline{q}.\overline{p}$ holds. Eulers formula holds for quaternions, namely $e^{q\varphi} = cos\varphi + q\sin\varphi$, with $\mid e^{q\varphi} \mid = 1$. In [17], Sangwine proposed to encode the three channel components of a RGB image using the three imaginary parts of a pure quaternion. In other words, a RGB format color image can be represented as

$$f(x, y) = f_R(x, y)i + f_G(x, y)j + f_B(x, y)k, \tag{4}$$

where $f_R(x, y)$, $f_G(x, y)$ and $f_B(x, y)$ represent the red, green and blue components, respectively. A more complete discussion on the properties of quaternion can be found in [18].

2.2 Tchebichef Moments

The computation of Tchebichef moments is based on a set of orthogonal Tchebichef kernels. The nth order, N-point Tchebichef kernel is defined as [19]:

$$t_n(x; N) = n! \sum_{k=0}^{n} (-1)^{n-k} \binom{N-1-k}{n-k} \binom{n+k}{n} \binom{x}{k}. \tag{5}$$

In order to avoid numerical instabilities, weighted Tchebichef kernel is usually used:

$$\tilde{t}_n(x; N) = \sqrt{\frac{w(x; N)}{\rho(n, N)}} t_n(x; N), \tag{6}$$

where $w(x; N) = \frac{1}{N+1}$, $\rho(n; N) = \frac{(2n)!}{N+1} \binom{N+n+1}{2n+1}$, are the weight and norm, respectively. With the weighted kernels, the $(m+n)th$ order Tchebichef moments of an $M \times N$ image $f(x, y)$ is defined as:

$$T_{mn} = \sum_{x=0}^{M-1} \sum_{y=0}^{N-1} \tilde{t}_m(x; M)\tilde{t}_n(y; N)f(x, y), \tag{7}$$

where $m \in \{0, 1, 2, ..., M - 1\}, n \in \{0, 1, 2, ..., N - 1\}$. T_{00} equals the average intensity value of an image, which denotes the DC component [19].

2.3   Quaternion Tchebichef Moments

QTMs generalize Tchebichef moments from complex domain to hypercomplex domain using quaternion algebras. Given an $N \times N$ color image $f(x, y)$, the right-side quaternion Tchebichef moment of an image is defined as [20]:

$$QTM_{mn}^{R}(f) = \sum_{x=0}^{N-1} \sum_{y=0}^{N-1} (f_R(x,y)i + f_G(x,y)j + f_B(x,y)k)\tilde{t}_m(x)\tilde{t}_n(y)\mu, \quad (8)$$

and the left-side QTM is defined similarly:

$$QTM_{mn}^{L}(f) = \sum_{x=0}^{N-1} \sum_{y=0}^{N-1} \mu(f_R(x,y)i + f_G(x,y)j + f_B(x,y)k)\tilde{t}_m(x)\tilde{t}_n(y), \quad (9)$$

where μ is a unit pure quaternion, which is set to $\mu = (i + j + k)/\sqrt{3}$ in this paper.

3   Proposed Method

The flowchart of the proposed metric is illustrated in Fig. 1. The proposed metric consists of three components, namely QTM-based feature similarity, complementary feature similarity and luminance correlation. QTM-based feature similarity is the main component of the proposed method, where features are extracted for measuring the color and structure distortions in an image. Complementary feature similarity is used to compensate for the insensitiveness of moments to weak distortions in high-quality images. Luminance information is also considered for the proposed method. In this section, we will first introduce the QTM-based feature similarity. Then complementary feature similarity and luminance correlation are discussed in detail. Finally, a QTM-based weighting function is proposed to conduct the pooling, producing the overall quality score.

3.1   QTM-Based Feature Similarity

Given a reference image and a distorted image, both of size $M \times N \times 3$, they are first converted into quaternion domain, which are denoted by $\mathbf{I}^r$ and $\mathbf{I}^d$, respectively. Then they are divided into non-overlapping blocks of size $R \times R$, which are denoted by $\{\mathbf{B}_{ij}^r\}$ and $\{\mathbf{B}_{ij}^d\}$, $i = 1, 2, ..., \lfloor M/R \rfloor$, $j = 1, 2, ..., \lfloor N/R \rfloor$, and $\lfloor . \rfloor$ is the floor operation. For each block-pair, the quaternion Tchebichef moments up to the $(m + n)th$ order are computed:

$$\mathbf{T}_{ij}^r = \begin{pmatrix} t_{00}^r & t_{01}^r & \cdots & t_{0n}^r \\ t_{10}^r & t_{11}^r & \cdots & t_{1n}^r \\ \vdots & \vdots & \ddots & \vdots \\ t_{m0}^r & t_{m1}^r & \cdots & t_{mn}^r \end{pmatrix}, \quad (10)$$

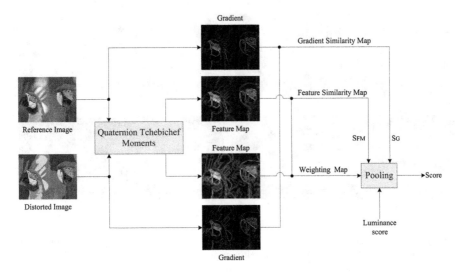

Fig. 1. Flowchart of the proposed method.

$$\mathbf{T}_{ij}^d = \begin{pmatrix} t_{00}^d & t_{01}^d & \cdots & t_{0n}^d \\ t_{10}^d & t_{11}^d & \cdots & t_{1n}^d \\ \vdots & \vdots & \ddots & \vdots \\ t_{m0}^d & t_{m1}^d & \cdots & t_{mn}^d \end{pmatrix}, \tag{11}$$

where $m, n \in \{0, 1, 2, ..., (R-1)\}$. Then the root of sum of squared non-DC moment values, namely root of AC energy, is computed as:

$$E_{ij}^r = \sqrt{\sum_{p=0}^m \sum_{q=0}^n (t_{pq}^r)^2 - (t_{00}^r)^2}, \tag{12}$$

$$E_{ij}^d = \sqrt{\sum_{p=0}^m \sum_{q=0}^n (t_{pq}^d)^2 - (t_{00}^d)^2}. \tag{13}$$

The root of AC energy of all blocks are arrayed according to the position of corresponding block to generate feature map. The two feature maps, i.e., $\mathbf{E}^r = \{E_{ij}^r\}$ and $\mathbf{E}^d = \{E_{ij}^d\}$, are used to capture color and structure distortions. Figure 2 shows an original image and several distorted versions, together with their feature maps. These distortion types include image color quantization with dither, quantization noise, and gaussian blur. It is observed that the feature maps are indicative of color and structure distortions. Based on this finding, we employ them to measure the distortions in images. The similarity between the feature maps is computed as:

$$\mathbf{S}_F(i,j) = \frac{2\mathbf{E}^r(i,j)\mathbf{E}^d(i,j) + c_1}{[\mathbf{E}^r(i,j)]^2 + [\mathbf{E}^d(i,j)]^2 + c_1}, \tag{14}$$

Fig. 2. Images and moment-induced feature maps. (a) Reference image; (b) Image color quantization with dither; (c) Quantization noise; (d) Gaussian blur; (e)–(h) Feature maps. (Color figure online)

where c_1 is a constant used to ensure numerical stability. The similarity of the feature maps is computed pixel-wisely, so $\mathbf{S}_F$ serves as a local quality map, which indicates local distortions in an image.

3.2 Gradient Similarity

When using moments for IQA, it should be noted that moments are robust to noise and contrast changes [19]. This indicates that moment-based features are mainly effective for low-quality images, where severe distortions are present. By contrast, they are not very effective in capturing the weak distortions in high-quality images. As a result, we incorporate image gradient as a complementary feature, which is more sensitive to weak distortions in high-quality images.

In this work, the gradients are computed using the Scharr operator [13]. Image gradients are denoted by $\mathbf{G}^r$ and $\mathbf{G}^d$ for reference and distorted images, respectively. Then the local gradient similarity is computed as:

$$\mathbf{S}_G(i,j) = \frac{2\mathbf{G}^r(i,j)\mathbf{G}^d(i,j) + c_2}{[\mathbf{G}^r(i,j)]^2 + [\mathbf{G}^d(i,j)]^2 + c_2}, \tag{15}$$

where c_2 is a constant used to ensure numerical stability.

3.3 Luminance

Luminance change is also considered, which makes this metric more accurate and applicable to a wider range of distortions. Specifically, luminance change is measured using the DC component of the moments, i.e., zeroth order moments $|t^r_{00}|$ and $|t^d_{00}|$. First, all zeroth order moment pairs are selected and denoted by

$m^{ref} = \{m_i^{ref}\}_{i=1}^L$ and $m^{dis} = \{m_i^{dis}\}_{i=1}^L$, where L is the number of moment pairs. Then the absolute errors of all the pairs are computed, i.e., $A = |m^{ref} - m^{dis}|$. Second, we select available pairs as follow:

$$(m^r, m^d) = \{(m_i^{ref}, m_i^{dis}) \mid A_i \geq T_m\}, \tag{16}$$

where $T_m = C_m \cdot median(A)$. In this paper, we set $C_m = 1.3$. Finally, the luminance similarity score is computed as:

$$Q_L = \frac{\sum_{i=1}^K (m_i^r - \mu(m^r)).(m_i^d - \mu(m^d)) + c_3}{\sqrt{\sum_{i=1}^K (m_i^r - \mu(m^r))^2 . \sum_{i=1}^K (m_i^d - \mu(m^d))^2} + c_3}, \tag{17}$$

where $\mu(.)$ is the mean operation, K is the number of available block pairs, and c_3 is a constant.

3.4 Weighting and Pooling

So far, we have obtained the QTM-based feature similarity map $\mathbf{S}_F$, gradient similarity map $\mathbf{S}_G$ and luminance similarity score Q_L. In order to generate an overall quality score, we propose a QTM-based weighting function to conduct the pooling. Having noted that the moment-induced feature map also indicates the relative importance of local contents on the perception of image quality, we construct the weighting function $\mathbf{W}$ as follows [12]:

$$\mathbf{W}(i, j) = max(\mathbf{E}^r(i, j), \mathbf{E}^d(i, j)). \tag{18}$$

With the weighting map $\mathbf{W}$, the feature similarity map $\mathbf{S}_F$ and gradient similarity map $\mathbf{S}_G$ are pooled, producing two overall quality scores:

$$Q_F = \frac{\sum_{i=1}^M \sum_{j=1}^N \mathbf{S}_F(i, j) \cdot \mathbf{W}(i, j)}{\sum_{i=1}^M \sum_{j=1}^N \mathbf{W}(i, j)}, \tag{19}$$

$$Q_G = \frac{\sum_{i=1}^M \sum_{j=1}^N \mathbf{S}_G(i, j) \cdot \mathbf{W}(i, j)}{\sum_{i=1}^M \sum_{j=1}^N \mathbf{W}(i, j)}. \tag{20}$$

It should be noted that both the similarity map and the weighting map are resized to the same size before pooling. With Q_F, Q_G and Q_L, the final image quality score is obtained as follows:

$$Q = (Q_F)^\alpha . (Q_G)^\beta . (Q_L)^\gamma, \tag{21}$$

where α, β, γ are used to adjust the relative importance of moment, gradient and luminance in the final quality measure, and $\alpha, \beta, \gamma \in (0, 1)$. In this paper, we set $\alpha = 0.4$, $\beta = 0.1$, $\gamma = 0.3$ by experiments. The quality score lies in the range $(0, 1]$, where higher score indicates better quality.

4   Experiments

4.1   Experimental Settings

We evaluate the performance of the proposed method on five popular image quality databases, i.e., IVC [21], LIVE [22], CSIQ [11], TID2008 [23], and TID2013 [24]. Three commonly used criteria are employed to evaluate the performances of these metrics, i.e., Pearson linear correlation coefficient (PLCC), Spearman rank order correlation coefficient (SRCC) and root mean squared error (RMSE). SRCC is calculated according to the rankings of the scores, and it is used to evaluate the prediction monotonicity. PLCC and RMSE are used to evaluate the prediction accuracy. To compute PLCC and RMSE, a logistic mapping is first conducted between the subjective and predicted scores. In this paper, the five-parameter logistic function is adopted [25]:

$$f(x) = \tau_1(\frac{1}{2} - \frac{1}{1 + e^{\tau_2(x-\tau_3)}}) + \tau_4 x + \tau_5, \qquad (22)$$

where τ_i, $i = 1,2,...,5$, are the parameters to be fitted.

In our experiments, the images are divided into 8×8 blocks ($R = 8$), and the order of the computed QTMs is 12 ($m = n = 6$). The proposed method is compared with ten FR-IQA metrics, including PSNR, SSIM [7], MS-SSIM [8], IW-SSIM [9], VIF [10], MAD [11], FSIM [12], GSM [13], GMSD [14], and QSSIM [15]. These metrics are implemented using the codes released by the authors with default parameters.

4.2   Performance Evaluation

In this section, the performances of the proposed method and ten compared metrics are evaluated in terms of PLCC, SRCC and RMSE values. The experimental

Table 1. Summary of experimental results of the proposed method and compared FR-IQA metrics.

Database	Criterion	PSNR	SSIM	MS-SSIM	VIF	IW-SSIM	MAD	FSIM	GSM	GMSD	QSSIM	Proposed
IVC	PLCC	0.7196	0.9119	0.9108	0.9028	0.9231	0.9210	**0.9378**	**0.9390**	0.8926	0.9033	**0.9483**
	SRCC	0.6884	0.9018	0.8980	0.8964	0.9125	0.9146	**0.9262**	**0.9291**	0.9146	0.8906	**0.9399**
	RMSE	0.8460	0.4999	0.5029	0.5239	0.4686	0.4746	**0.4228**	**0.4190**	0.5494	0.5227	**0.3865**
LIVE	PLCC	0.8682	0.9212	0.9489	**0.9604**	0.9522	**0.9675**	0.9597	0.9512	0.9595	0.9281	0.9576
	SRCC	0.8730	0.9226	0.9513	**0.9636**	0.9567	**0.9669**	0.9634	0.9561	0.9603	0.9306	**0.9634**
	RMSE	13.558	10.632	8.6184	**7.6137**	8.3472	6.9073	7.6742	8.4326	7.6937	10.171	7.8747
CSIQ	PLCC	0.8276	0.8579	0.8991	0.9277	0.9144	**0.9500**	0.9118	0.8964	**0.9541**	0.8591	**0.9467**
	SRCC	0.8389	0.8719	0.9133	0.9195	0.9213	**0.9466**	0.9240	0.9108	**0.9570**	0.8732	**0.9508**
	RMSE	0.1474	0.1349	0.1149	0.0980	0.1063	**0.0820**	0.1078	0.1164	**0.0786**	0.1344	**0.0846**
TID2008	PLCC	0.5309	0.6803	0.8451	0.8084	0.8579	0.8306	**0.8738**	0.8422	**0.8788**	0.6949	**0.8833**
	SRCC	0.5245	0.6779	0.8542	0.7491	0.8559	0.8340	**0.8804**	0.8504	**0.8907**	0.6979	**0.8886**
	RMSE	1.1372	0.9836	0.7173	0.7899	0.6895	0.7473	**0.6527**	0.7235	**0.6404**	0.9649	**0.6291**
TID2013	PLCC	0.6729	0.7895	0.8329	0.7720	0.8319	0.8267	**0.8589**	0.8463	**0.8553**	0.7457	**0.8651**
	SRCC	0.6873	0.7417	0.7859	0.6677	0.7779	**0.8083**	0.8022	0.7946	**0.8044**	0.7155	**0.8301**
	RMSE	0.9437	0.7608	0.6861	0.7880	0.6880	0.6976	**0.6349**	0.6603	**0.6423**	0.8259	**0.6218**

results on the five databases are summarized in Table 1. For each performance criterion and each database, the best three results are marked in boldface.

It can be seen from Table 1 that the proposed method performs consistently well on the five databases. On IVC and TID2013 databases, it outperforms all the other metrics in terms of both prediction accuracy and monotonicity. As we all known, TID2013 database contains three kinds of color distortions with five levels of distortions, namely change of color saturation, image color quantization with dither, and chromatic aberrations. It is shows that the proposed method effective in processing color distortions. On CSIQ and TID2008, the proposed method outperforms most of the state-of-the-art metrics. Specifically, on TID2008, it produces the best prediction accuracy while the prediction monotonicity is slightly worse than GMSD. On LIVE and CSIQ, although it is not the best, the proposed method performs only slightly worse than the best metrics.

Scatter plots of subjective ratings versus objective scores obtained on the largest TID2013 database are shown in Fig. 3, where each point represents one test image. It can be seen from the figure that the quality scores predicted by the proposed method are highly consistent with subjective evaluations.

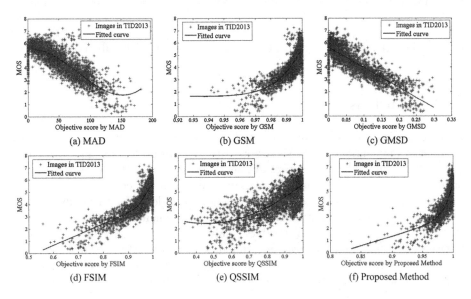

Fig. 3. Scatter plots of subjective scores against predicted scores by different metrics on the TID2013 database.

Figure 4 shows the performance of the proposed method on color distortions. It is observed from the figure that for all images, with the decrease of the mean opinion scores (MOS), the objective quality scores degrades accordingly. This indicates that the effectiveness of the proposed method to different color dis-

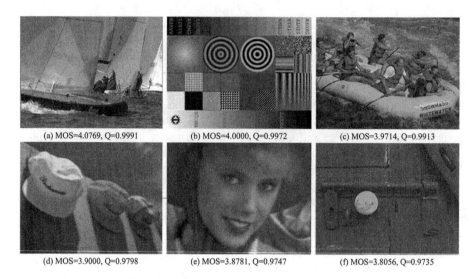

Fig. 4. Performance of the proposed method on color distortions. (a) and (b) are distorted by change of color saturation; (c) and (f) are distorted by image color quantization with dither; (d) and (e) are distorted by color saturation. (Color figure online)

tortions in a perceptual way and have high correlation with subjective quality evaluation.

5   Conclusions

In this paper, we have presented a FR-IQA metric based on quaternion Tchebichef moments. The QTMs are used to capture both color and structure information simultaneously. Image gradient is incorporated to capture complementary structure distortions in high-quality images, which cannot be effectively represented by moment features. Luminance is considered as an auxiliary feature for more efficient quality assessment. The experimental results have shown that the proposed method can produce quality scores consistent well with subjective evaluations and can evaluate different color distortions. We have also compared our method with ten popular image quality metrics, and the results have demonstrated that our method achieves state-of-the-art performance.

Acknowledgment. This work is supported by the National Natural Science Foundation of China (61379143) and the Fundamental Research Funds for the Central Universities (2015XKMS032, 2015QNA66).

References

1. Xia, Z.H., Wang, X.H., Sun, X.M., Wang, B.W.: Steganalysis of least significant bit matching using multi-order differences. Secur. Commun. Netw. **7**(8), 1283–1291 (2014)
2. Li, J., Li, X.L., Yang, B., Sun, X.M.: Segmentation-based image copy-move forgery detection scheme. IEEE Trans. Inf. Forensics Secur. **10**(3), 507–518 (2015)
3. Zheng, Y.H., Jeon, B., Xu, D.H., Wu, Q.J., Zhang, H.: Image segmentation by generalized hierarchical fuzzy C-means algorithm. J. Intell. Fuzzy Syst. **28**(2), 961–973 (2015)
4. Lin, W.S., JayKuo, C.-C.: Perceptual visual quality metrics: a survey. J. Vis. Commun. Image Represent. **22**(4), 297–312 (2011)
5. Cai, H., Li, L.D., Qian, J.S., Pan, J.S.: Image blur assessment with feature points. J. Inf. Hiding Multimedia Signal Proces. **6**(3), 482–490 (2015)
6. Zhang, W., Li, L.D., Zhu, H.C., Cheng, D.Q., Chu, S.C., Roddick, J.F.: No-reference quality metric of blocking artifacts based on orthogonal moments. J. Inf. Hiding Multimedia Signal Proces. **5**(4), 701–708 (2014)
7. Zhang, W., Bovik, A.C., Sheikh, H.R., Simoncelli, E.P.: Image quality assessment: from error visibility to structural similarity. IEEE Trans. Image Process. **13**(4), 600–612 (2004)
8. Wang, Z., Simoncelli, E.P., Bovik, A.C.: Multi-scale structural similarity for image quality assessment. In: Proceedings of IEEE Asilomar Conference on Signals, Systems and Computers, pp. 1398–1402 (2003)
9. Wang, Z., Li, Q.: Information content weighting for perceptual image quality assessment. IEEE Trans. Image Process. **20**(5), 1185–1198 (2011)
10. Sheikn, H.R., Bovik, A.C.: Image information and visual quality. IEEE Trans. Image Process. **15**(2), 430–444 (2006)
11. Larson, E.C., Chandler, D.M.: Most apparent distortion: full-reference image quality assessment and the role of strategy. J. Electr. Imaging **19**(1), 001006:1–001006:21 (2010)
12. Zhang, L., Zhang, L., Mou, X.Q., Zhang, D.: FSIM: a feature similarity index for image quality assessment. IEEE Trans. Image Process. **21**(4), 1500–1512 (2012)
13. Liu, A.M., Lin, W.S., Narwaria, M.: Image quality assessment based on gradient similarity. IEEE Trans. Image Process. **20**(8), 2378–2386 (2011)
14. Xue, W.F., Zhang, L., Mou, X.Q., Bovik, A.C.: Gradient magnitude similarity deviation: a highly efficient perceptual image quality index. IEEE Trans. Image Process. **22**(2), 684–695 (2014)
15. Kolaman, A., Pecht, O.Y.: Quaternion structural similarity: a new quality index for color images. IEEE Trans. Image Process. **21**(4), 1526–1536 (2012)
16. Hamilton, W.R.: Elements of Quaternions. Longmans Green, London (1866)
17. Sangwine, S.J.: Fourier transforms of color images using quaternion or hypercomplex numbers. Electr. Lett. **32**(21), 1979–1980 (1996)
18. Kantor, I.L., Solodovnikov, A.S.: Hypercomplex Number: An Elementary Introduction to Algebras. Springer, New York (1989)
19. Mukundan, R., Ong, S.H., Lee, P.A.: Image analysis by Tchebichef moments. IEEE Trans. Image Process. **10**(9), 1357–1364 (2001)
20. Zhu, H.Q., Li, Q., Liu, Q.: Quaternion discrete Tchebichef moments and their applications. Int. J. Signal Process. Image Process. Pattern Recogn. **7**(6), 149–162 (2014)

21. Le Callet, P., Autrusseau, F.: Subjective Quality Assessment IR-CCyN/IVC Database. http://www.irccyn.ecnantes.fr/ivcdb/
22. Sheikh, H.R., Sabir, M.F., Bovik, A.C.: A statistical evaluation of recent full reference image quality assessment algorithms. IEEE Trans. Image Process. **15**(11), 3440–3451 (2006)
23. Ponomarenko, N., Lukin, V., Zelensky, A., Egiazarian, K., Carli, M., Battisti, F.: TID2008 - a database for evaluation of full-reference visual quality assessment metrics. Adv. Mod. Radioelectron. **10**(4), 30–45 (2009)
24. Ponomarenko, N., Ieremeiev, O., Lukin, V., Egiazarian, K., Jin, L., Astola, J., Vozel, B., Chehdi, K., Carli, M., Battisti, F., Jay Kuo, C.-C.: Color image database TID2013: peculiarities and preliminary results. In: European Workshop on Visual Information Process, pp. 106–111 (2013)
25. Final Report from the Video Quality Experts Group on the Validation of Objective Models of Video Quality Assessment, Phase II. http://www.vqeg.org

Data Aggregation and Analysis:
A Fast Algorithm of ECG Recognition
Based on Pattern Matching

Miaomiao Zhang$^{(\boxtimes)}$ and Dechang Pi

College of Computer Science and Technology,
Nanjing University of Aeronautics and Astronautics,
29 Jiangjun Avenue, Nanjing 211106, Jiangsu, People's Republic of China
Snowmmy0123@yeah.net, dc.pi@nuaa.edu.cn

Abstract. This paper presents a fast algorithm for the aggregation and analysis of ECG data. The whole process of fusion and analysis can be divided into three stages. ECG signal de-noising is the first stage. A combined filter is used to cut out the noises from ECG signals. In the second stage, a simple method named SDTW (the Sample Dynamic Time Wrapping) is proposed to improve the time efficiency of DTW. Then SDTW and K-means algorithm are applied to attain templates as well as compress templates. The last stage is to train a BP neural network with the compressed templates and other ECG features. Experiments with the MIT-BIH arrhythmia database shows that our algorithm can efficiently improve the recognition accuracy and shorten the recognition time.

Keywords: ECG recognition · Dynamic Time Wrapping (DTW) · Sample Dynamic Time Wrapping (SDTW) · K-means · BP neural network

1 Introduction

ECG is a convenient and reliable way to monitor patients' health conditions. An electrocardiogram signal is able to contain much valuable heart information. ECG cycle has a variety of shapes. Normal beats usually have similar wave forms, while abnormal beats are consist of different shapes. Therefore, experienced doctors can diagnose different kinds of heart disease due to different ECG shapes.

The ECG data of the human body can be collected under different conditions. For example, ECG data can be collected using the hospital ECG instrument or using portable equipment outdoor. All of the collected data need to be pre processed before they can be used. Therefore, a lot of corresponding de-noising methods have been adopted. Sadhukhan and Mitra [1] proposed an ECG noise reduction technique based on suppression of the fourier coefficients corresponding to the noise frequency bands. Wei [2] uses matching pursuit (MP) algorithm to decompose the signal.MP algorithm's dictionary is composed of Gabor atoms, so it can reflect the properties of the signal. Samadi and Shamsollahi [3] presented an EMD-based approach which uses the time interval between two adjacent zero crossings within an Intrinsic Mode Function (IMF) to distinguish noise components from the main ECG signal. Mallick [4]

© Springer International Publishing AG 2016
X. Sun et al. (Eds.): ICCCS 2016, Part II, LNCS 10040, pp. 313–323, 2016.
DOI: 10.1007/978-3-319-48674-1_28

implemented several different filters to remove baseline drift. Cuomo et al. [5] proposed a novel O(n) numerical scheme which based on Infinite Impulse Response (IIR) noise reduction algorithms to remove ECG signal noise. Experiments show that it proves to be very fast on many devices.

In recent years, more and more scholars are interested in ECG signal classification by means of Data Mining. Shaharm and Nayebi [6] adopted an ECG beat classification method which is mainly based on clustering and a cross-distance analysis algorithm. Polat et al. [7] used a least square support vector machine (LSSVM) to classify arrhythmia from an ECG dataset and get good test results. Exarchos et al. [8] proposed fuzzy expert systems for ischemia and arrhythmic beat classification which combined a fuzzy model with a set of rules extracted from a decision tree. Saini et al. [9] developed a KNN algorithm to locate the waveform components' boundaries. The algorithm is tested on their ECG dataset and attain high accuracy rate. Shadmand and Mashoufi [10] combined block-based neural network (BBNN) with particle swarm optimization (PSO) algorithm to classify ECG heartbeats of a specific patient. Each block is a neural network. This method has a good classification result.

The rest of the paper consists of the following parts. Section 2 describes the procedure of ECG signal noise reduction. Section 3 concentrates on the data aggregation and analysis algorithm. And the algorithm is tested on the MIT-BIH arrhythmia database in Sect. 4. And the paper is concluded in Sect. 5.

2 ECG Signal De-noising

ECG signals are recorded by placing electrodes on the patients' body surface, so it easily contaminated by noise such as motion artifacts, power-line noise, and electrode contact noises, all of which declines the accuracy of ECG interpretation [1]. This paper adopt a series of filter to reduce the noises. The main types of noises and their reduction methods are as follows: (i) 60 Hz power-line interference. It's created by the power line of the ECG signal measurement systems which usually is with 60 Hz harmonics. The 60 Hz notch filter is suitable for rejecting the power-line interference (see Fig. 1). (ii) Motion artifacts. Motion artifact is a short baseline change caused by the relative movement of the electrode and the human body. It can produce larger amplitude signals in the ECG, and its duration time is about 100–500 ms. Wavelet transform is a powerful tool for signal analysis and signal de-noising. Hence, this paper adopts wavelet transform to remove motion artifacts (see Fig. 2). (iii) Baseline drifts. Many reasons can lead to baseline drift, such as patient breathing, bad electrodes, or improper electrode site, etc. Its frequency range is usually below 0.5 Hz. Therefore, this paper uses a high-pass filter with cut-off frequency 0.5 Hz to remove the interference by baseline drift. And the result shows that Chebyshev high-pass filter works better than Butterworth high-pass filter in dealing with ECG (see Fig. 3). (vi) Myopotential Interference. It comes from muscle electrical activity. In the ECG signal, EMG interference appears as rapid fluctuations which have about 50 ms duration and it vary faster than ECG waves. Low-pass filter can be used to eliminate the high frequency EMG (see Fig. 4).

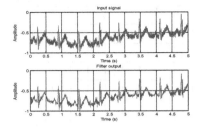

Fig. 1. 60 Hz notch filter

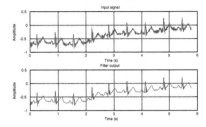

Fig. 2. Wavelet transform

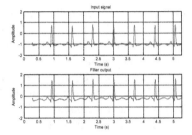

Fig. 3. Chebyshev high-pass filter

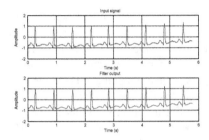

Fig. 4. Chebyshev low-pass filter

3 The Fast Data Aggregation Algorithm Based on Sample Dynamic Time Wrapping for ECG Signal

3.1 Sample Dynamic Time Wrapping (SDTW)

ECG signal as a kind of biological signals can be regarded as time series. Comparison of medically abnormal pattern of electrocardiogram can be transformed into comparison of time series. The dynamic time warping (DTW) is a classic similarity measure which can compute the similarity of time series is suitable to handle ECG signal matching issue. Besides, even the same person's normal heart beats in different times, may not have the same length of time. In these complex cases, it cannot effectively find the distance (or similarity) between two time series by using the traditional Euclidean distance. DTW based on dynamic programming can warp time series in order to get the similarity of the two series (see Figs. 5 and 6). The formula of computing path is shown as Eq. (1):

$$g(i,j) = \min \begin{cases} g(i-1,j) + d(i,j) \\ g(i-1,j-1) + d(i,j) \\ g(i,j-1) + d(i,j) \end{cases} \tag{1}$$

where $g(i,j)$ denotes the total minimum distance of the two templates which from the start component of the successive match to this step, $d(i,j)$ indicates the distance of the current step.

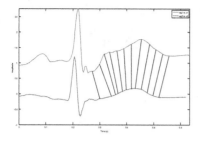

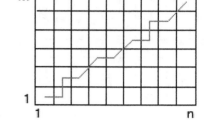

Fig. 5. Warping time series   **Fig. 6.** Distance matrix and computing path

Although DTW can compare the similarity between two series, it's will cost a lot of time to compute the time series that have many sample points. For a large number of data, the waiting time is even intolerable. So it is worth thinking about how to keep the recognition accuracy and enhance recognition efficiency at the same time. Sample dynamic time wrapping (SDTW) is a simple way to enhance the DTW's efficiency as well as ensures the accuracy. Firstly, SDTW sample the signals to compress the ECG cycle, For instance, sampling a ECG cycle with 200 points and the number of points will be reduced to 100 (see Fig. 7). Then SDTW adopts DTW algorithm to compute the distance of the sampled signals. By this way, the distance matrix can be greatly scaled down (see Fig. 8). m and n denote the length of segment1 and segment2. Segmnet1 and segment2 are ECG cycles. If the two signals are quite different in wave forms, the two sampled signals will have a comparatively large distance value.

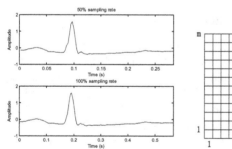

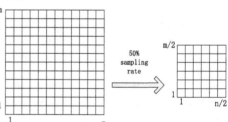

Fig. 7. 50 % sampling ECG   **Fig. 8.** 50 % sampling distance matrix

For example, to attain the distance between segment1 and segment2, we firstly sample them by 10 % and use DTW to calculate the distance. If the distance is bigger than 100, we consider these two segments are quite different and assign 150 to the distance. If the distance is less than 100, we sample segment1 and segmnet2 by 30 %. Then use DTW to calculate the distance again, and compare it with 50 repeat those steps until the distance no longer need to be compared. This paper regards the result as sdtw value or distance. Here is the SDTW algorithm flow chart (see Fig. 9):

Algorithm 1. Sample dynamic time wrapping

Input: segment1, segment2, the ratio of extracted samples $R[N]$, the threshold of extracted samples $Th[N]$, the constant sequence $A[N]$.

Output: the distance $Dist$ between segment1 and segment2

Begin

Step1: Let $i = 1$.

Step2: If $i \leq N$, sample segment1 and segment2 by $R[i]$ to generate uniform sample points $SR1$ and $SR2$, go to Step4.

Step3: Else use DTW to calculate the distance $Dist$ of segment1 and segment2 by $R[N+1]$, return $Dist$.

Step4: Use DTW to calculate the distance $Dist$ of $SR1$ and $SR2$.

Step5: If $Dist > Th[i]$, then $Dist = A[i]$, return Dist. Else back to Step2, $i = i+1$.

End

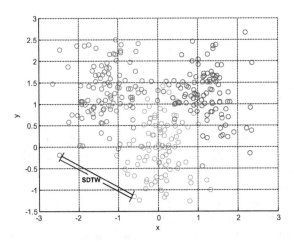

Fig. 9. K-means & SDTW

3.2   The Fast Template Compression Algorithm Based on Improved k-means

The extracted templates can be used to construct a feature template library. Based the above distance between two time series (sdtw value), this section presents an improved K-means for compress the ECG data. K-means usually attains clustering center by calculating the Euclidean distance between points and points, but the similarity between the ECG signals can not be calculated using Euclidean distance. Therefore, each ECG signal can be regarded as a point, and the distance between the points can be computed by the SDTW algorithm. It can be seen from Fig. 9. Here segments is termed as segs. Each circle represents a ECG segment.

Algorithm 2 Fast template **compression algorithm based on improved k-means**

Input: Segments without classification $Seg[len]$, the number of cluster centers K.

Output: Sequence of cluster centers U .

Begin

Step1. Randomly select K different Segs as the initial centers.

Step2. Assign each Seg to the least sdtw value centers, dataset become K clusters.

Step3. As for each cluster, calculate sdtw value between every Seg and the rest of Segs and find the least one. That Seg is the new center.

Step4. Compare the previous cluster centers with the new centers. If the sdtw value between previous centers and new centers are less than threshold, output the centers. Otherwise, back to Step 2.

End

3.3   The Data Aggregation with BP Neural Network

According to morphological features, there are many important general features in ECG signals, such as the height of the R wave crest, length of QRS wave group, P wave's width, etc. These features can be used as important criterions for doctors to diagnose heart rate disorders. Whereas, DTW can merely consider the similarity of the ECG waveform morphology while ignore these conventional features. Due to SDTW comes from DTW, the combination of the two should have the same performance. Therefore, this paper uses the BP neural network to integrate the medical knowledge and the morphological characteristics of extracted templates. And it is termed as Data Aggregation SDTW (DA-SDTW).

Theoretically, for a BP network with three layers or above, the network can approximate a nonlinear function with any precision, as long as the number of neurons in the hidden layer is large enough. Because it has powerful nonlinear processing ability, it can be better to carry out nonlinear classification. However, people have to set the number of input samples in advance before training a neural network. That is to say, neural network has a limit in dealing with time series of non fixed length or other variable length data. In order to avoid this weakness and take advantages of the strengths of neural network, it's naturally to think of combining neural network with SDTW which is good at handling variable length data. The basic steps and procedure of DA-SDTW is described as Algorithm 3.

Algorithm3 The Data Aggregation with Sample Dynamic Wrapping

Input: Segment without classification $S[lenS]$, General characteristics of electrocardiogram $C[lenC]$, the number of templates (N), Templates T .

Output: Classification results($R[lenR]$)

Begin:

Step1. Each S compares with all templates T in turn according to 1NN (1-Nearst Neighbor) algorithm. For each instance, if $S[i]$ has least sdtw value with $T[j]$, then $S[i].type = j$.

Step2. Compute the general characteristics value of each S and save as SC, SC:={SC[1,1], SC[1,2],...,SC[lenS, lenC]}.For example, the n-th general characteristics value of S[i] is SC[i,n].

Step3. Input the type of each type and C values to the neural network and get the classification results which save as R.

End

3.4   The Procedure of ECG Recognition with Data Aggregation

SDTW is a fast way to find out the waveform features of ECG signals. In order to classify different ECG waveforms, we extract some templates by K-means method. To judge whether the signal is abnormal or not can not only look at the morphological characteristics, but the other general features. And neural network is a good way to link all features together (Fig. 10).

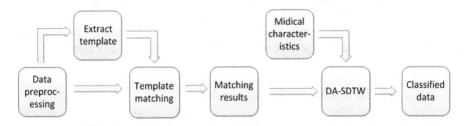

Fig. 10. The flow chart of ECG recognition with data aggregation

4   Experiments and Analysis

In the first experiments, we compared the performance of SDTW and DTW. By comparison, we chose SDTW to extract templates instead of DTW. The next experiments, we compared the SDTW template matching algorithm and the DA-SDTW algorithm. All experiments are carried out with the MATLAB version of the 2014Ra and run on a PC with Inter CPU i5 and 4.0 RAM.

Currently internationally recognized as the standard ECG database has three, respectively, MIT-BIH provided by the Massachusetts Institute of Technology in the study of arrhythmia database, the AHA database of the American Heart Association and the European AT-T ECG database. MIT-BIH database which is widely used in recent years is used to evaluate the proposed algorithm.

4.1   Effectiveness of SDTW

In order to verify the effectiveness of proposed algorithm, the ECG signals with different segments (100, 150, 200, 250, 300) are employed. Figure 11 shows the matching accuracy of 4 templates, and Fig. 12 describes the shapes of sampled ECG signals. As we can see from Fig. 11, the accuracy of the sample matching is getting close to the original data with the increase of the sampling ratio. From Fig. 12, the shape of sampled ECG signals is more similar to the original signals.

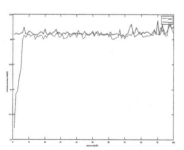
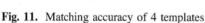
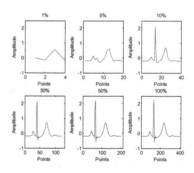

Fig. 11. Matching accuracy of 4 templates   **Fig. 12.** Sampled ECG

According the first experiment, we implement the SDTW algorithm at the ratio by 5 %, 10 %, 50 % and threshold by 3, 4. Table 1 lists the result of contrast of run time. From Table 1, it's obvious that SDTW algorithm is much faster than DTW algorithm, and SDTW's classification accuracy is very similar to the DTW algorithm.

4.2   Experimental Results of Data Aggregation

In this part, we choose some ECG records in MIT-BIH arrhythmia database, and each tape have thousands ECG cycles. Each record is divided into two parts, the test set and

Table 1. The contrast of run time

ECG segments	SDTW		DTW		Time saving ratio (%)
	time (s)	accuracy ratio (%)	time(s)	accuracy ratio (%)	
50	22.06	90.00	158.67	92.00	86.10
100	91.66	91.00	649.82	94.00	85.89
150	226.16	90.00	1486.37	90.67	84.78
200	413.48	92.50	2718.96	91.50	84.79
250	665.75	92.40	3391.21	92.80	80.37
300	937.05	92.00	4906.02	93.67	80.90

the training set. Both SDTW and DA-SDTW is tested on 10 templates which extracted by improved K-means. And we implement SDTW algorithm at the ratio by 5 %, 10 %, 30 % and threshold by 3, 4 in this test, so as the corresponding DA-SDTW.

In order to test performance of proposed algorithm, two different sizes of training set are selected, which are 30 % and 80 % of data set. Note that these training sets are uniformly selected from the record. Table 2 lists the computational results of 30 % and 80 % of data set. From Table 2, it can be found that the DA-SDTW algorithm can make the prediction results more accurate. Through the comparison of above two training set, it can be found that when the training set is less, the performance of the DA-SDTW is better. That is to say, DA-SDTW is more suitable for use in the absence of data. In general, most of the records show better accuracy when the training set is larger, but some cases have no obvious growth because of the change of cluster centers. The following experimental results are measured in percentage units.

Table 2. Comparitional results of 30 % and 80 % training set

Tape#	30 % training set			80 % training set		
	SDTW	DA- SDTW	Improved ratio	SDTW	DA- SDTW	Improved ratio
200	91.92	96.60	5.09	95.77	97.16	1.45
201	90.25	93.48	3.58	92.39	95.30	3.15
202	94.32	96.54	2.35	96.23	96.23	0
203	92.22	94.92	2.93	93.60	96.66	1.06
205	96.84	97.30	0.48	97.92	97.93	0.01
208	92.51	94.06	1.68	92.49	93.88	1.50
209	84.69	90.32	6.65	90.20	93.04	3.15
213	86.08	88.75	3.10	86.21	87.45	1.44
215	91.90	97.59	6.19	95.02	96.46	1.52
220	95.71	97.08	1.43	93.78	95.32	1.64
228	96.10	98.99	3.01	98.23	99.16	0.95
232	84.50	97.77	15.70	85.22	98.44	15.51
233	92.58	95.58	3.24	98.37	98.38	0.01

4.3   Discussion

This section discusses the results of comparison with other existing algorithms for ECG signal recognition.

(1) DTW is a good method to classify ECG signals. However, it is time consuming when the amount of data is large. Compared to the DTW, the Sample Dynamic Time Wrapping (SDTW) proposed in this paper is more suitable to handle large dataset. Tables 1 and 2 show that SDTW can not only maintain the accuracy of the data recognition, but also significantly reduce the time of recognition.

(2) By means of improved K-means algorithm compressing templates, a small amount of data can achieve a good recognition rate. A small amount of templates can achieve a high matching rate of the data which usually have thousands of segments.

(3) The DA-SDTW algorithm uses templates (extracted by improved K-means) and other general features as input, and its performance is better than SDTW algorithm. It can be concluded that using neural network for data aggregations could improve the recognition accuracy. However, as seen in Table 2, the approach proposed has less improved rate with high rate training set, which demonstrate that our method is more suitable for processing inadequate data.

5   Conclusions

ECG pattern recognition is of great significance for human health. In this paper, four kinds of noise and corresponding de-noising methods were presented. Then, a fast way to compute the similarity of ECG signals was proposed. Next, the K-means was also been improved to extract features from ECG signals. Finally, we introduced the BP neural network for data aggregation. Furthermore, in order to illustrate the validity and feasibility of the above methods, the MIT-BIH arrhythmia database was used to test the algorithm. Although experiments show that our algorithm is effective, there are many other aspects needed to be improved. For instance, find the best proportion of the training set in order to obtain better classification results; the comparison among different individuals and other feature extraction methods need to be test.

Acknowledgements. The research work was supported by National Natural Science Foundation of China (U1433116) and the Aviation Science Foundation of China (20145752033).

References

1. Sadhukhan, D., Mitra, M.: ECG noise reduction using fourier coefficient suppression. In: International Conference on Control, Instrumentation Energy and Communication, pp. 142–146 (2014)
2. Wei, A.Y.: ECG de-noising based on MP algorithm. Appl. Mech. Mater. **433–435**, 510–513 (2013)

3. Samadi, S., Shamsollahi, M.B.: ECG noise reduction using empirical mode decomposition based on combination of instantaneous half period and soft-thresholding. In: The Proceedings of Middle East Conference on Biomedical Engineering (MECBME), Doha, Qatar, pp. 244–248 (2014)
4. Mallick, P.K.: Baseline Drift Removal of ECG Signal: Comparative Analysis of Filtering Techniques. Information Resources Management Association (IRMA) (2016)
5. Cuomo, S., De Pietro, G., Farina, R., Galletti, A., Sannino, G.: A novel O(n) numerical scheme for ECG signal denoising. Procedia Comput. Sci. **51**(1), 775–784 (2015)
6. Shaharm, M., Nayebi, K.: Classification of multichannel ECG signals using a cross—distance analysis. In: IEEE 23rd Annual International Conference of Engineering in Medicine & Biology Society (EMBC), Istanbul, Turkey, pp. 2182–2185 (2001)
7. Polat, K., Akdemir, B., Gunes, S.: Computer aided diagnosis of ECG data on the least square support vector machine. Digit. Sig. Proc. **18**(1), 25–32 (2008)
8. Exarchos, T.P., Tsipouras, M.G., Exarchos, C.P., et al.: A methodology for the automated creation of fuzzy expert systems for ischaemic and arrhythmic beat classification based on a set of rules obtained by a decision tree. Artif. Intell. Med. **40**(3), 187–200 (2007). Elsevier
9. Saini, I., Singh, D., Khosla, A.: Delineation of ECG wave components using K-Nearest Neighbor (KNN) algorithm: ECG wave delineation using KNN. In: 2013 Tenth International Conference on Information Technology: New Generations (ITNG), vol. 25(1), pp. 712–717, 15–17 2013
10. Shadmand, S., Mashoufi, B.: Personalized ECG signal classification using block-based neural-network and particle swarm optimization. In: International Conference of the IEEE Engineering in Medicine & Biology Society, vol. 3(37), pp. 2182–2185 (2001)

Original Image Tracing with Image Relational Graph for Near-Duplicate Image Elimination

Fang Huang[1], Zhili Zhou[1(✉)], Tianliang Liu[2], and Xiya Liu[1]

[1] School of Computer and Software and Jiangsu Engineering Center of Network Monitoring,
Nanjing University of Information Science and Technology, No. 219, Ningliu Road
Nanjing 210044, China
zhou_zhili@163.com
[2] Department of Telecommunications and Information Engineering,
Nanjing University of Posts and Telecommunications, No. 66, The New Model Road
Nanjing 210003, China

Abstract. In this paper, we propose a novel method for near-duplicate image elimination by tracing the original image of each near-duplicate image cluster. To generate a similarity matrix of each cluster, both global feature and local feature are extracted to accurately evaluate the visual similarity of each image pair. According to the similarity matrix, an Image Relational Graph (IRG) is constructed. Then we adopt the graph model based link analysis algorithm PageRank to analyze the contextual relationship between images on this IRG. In this way, the original image will be correctly traced with the highest rank, while other redundant near-duplicate images in the cluster will be eliminated. To validate the performance of our proposed method, large amount of near-duplicate images mixing with distracting images are applied for experiments, and the experimental results indicate the effectiveness of our method.

Keywords: Near-duplicate detection · Global feature · Local feature · Contextual relationship · Image copy detection

1 Introduction

In day-to-day life, the increasing ability of digital images has brought great convenience to people for their working and learning. Once a hot and popular image is shared by a user, it cannot resist being republished by other users in different channels on the Internet, usually after some modifications or editing. Accordingly, a large amount of near-duplicate images with the same original image are spread on the Internet, especially in the searching results of the keyword-based image search engines. And near-duplicate image elimination is a challenging problem for network resource management. In this context, near-duplicate image refers to a pair of images in which one is generated from the other due to some digital editing [1]. Some typical editing operations include cropping, captioning, illumination changing and Gaussian convolution, etc. Figure 1 illustrates three examples of near-duplicate images.

© Springer International Publishing AG 2016
X. Sun et al. (Eds.): ICCCS 2016, Part II, LNCS 10040, pp. 324–336, 2016.
DOI: 10.1007/978-3-319-48674-1_29

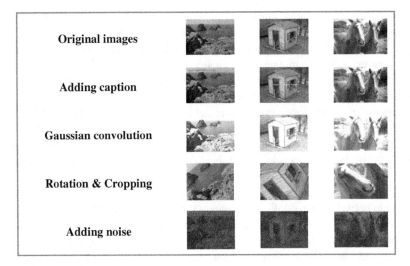

Fig. 1. Examples of near-duplicate images. Those near-duplicate versions of the original images are generated from some digital editing such as: adding caption, Gaussian convolution, rotation & cropping and adding noise.

Comparing with similar methods which are mainly devoted to image analysis [2] or copy detection [3], we apply some popular technologies of image processing to a more meaningful application. Given several sets of clustered near-duplicate images, our objective is to find the best representative image of each cluster and eliminate other redundant images. With the fact that most near-duplicate images on the Internet are derived from one original source, the best representative image of a near-duplicate image cluster is the original image. Thus, assuming that the original images exist in relevant near-duplicate image clusters, we aim to trace the original image of each cluster for redundancy elimination.

The basic method for representative image selection is to select the image that has the minimal sum of distance to other images in its cluster. However, this method is lack of robustness with the increase of complexity of digital images and their near-duplicate versions. Moreover, there are several methods devote to near-duplicate image elimination, and some techniques are proposed for representative image selection. For example, Liu J et al. [4] propose an approach of near-duplicate elimination for geo-tagged photo. In this method, photo fate simply depends on the visual distance between photos and their clustering centroid, and the image closest to the clustering centroid will be selected to be reserved. However, we think this centroid based method cannot accurately choose the original image. As another example, the representative image selection in [5] is based on the evaluation of image quality. However, the image of the highest quality may not be the original version of other near-duplicate images, and it is insufficient to represent the cluster.

It is obvious from Fig. 1 that most copy attacks will not destroy the semantic meaning of images and the generated near-duplicate images are contextually related with each other [6]. Since the existing methods for near-duplicate image elimination completely ignore the contextual relationship between near-duplicate images, we attempt to mine this relationship to better choose the representative image of a cluster. If the original image exists in a near-duplicate image cluster, it will be traced through contextual relationship analysis between images in the cluster. However, if the original image does not exist in the cluster, the most relevant image to other images of the cluster will be traced, *i.e.*, the image that closest to the original image.

In this paper, we propose a normal original image tracing method for near-duplicate image elimination. We focus on that near-duplicate images are contextual related to each other and this relationship can be utilized to trace the original image as the representative image. In the proposed work, global feature and local feature are combined to accurately evaluate the similarity of image pairs. Based on the corresponding similarity matrix, a structure named Image Relational Graph (IRG) is constructed to reflect the contextual relationship between near-duplicate images according to the relevant feature matching. Moreover, the IRGs according with different features will be fused for further link analysis. Then we adopt the PageRank algorithm to analyze the contextual relationship between images in each near-duplicate image cluster. Finally, each image will have a convergent rank value, and image with the highest rank value will be regarded as the original image of other near-duplicate images. Experiments demonstrate that our proposed method achieves considerable results in tracing the original image for near-duplicate elimination.

2   Overview of the Proposed System

In the proposed method, we present a system of original image tracing for near-duplicate image elimination. The framework of our method is illustrated in Fig. 2. As is shown in the figure, our system is composed of three stages: feature extraction, IRG generation and fusion, and contextual relationship analysis for original image tracing. In Sect. 2.1, we extract both global feature and local feature to evaluate the visual similarity of near-duplicate images. In Sect. 2.2, the IRGs based on global feature matching and local feature matching respectively are constructed. And these two IRGs are fused as a comprehensive IRG_{fusion} to reflect the contextual relationship between near-duplicate images. Finally in Sect. 2.3, we use the PageRank algorithm to analyze the contextual relationship between near-duplicate images based on the IRG_{fusion} above. As a result, the image with the highest rank value will be regarded as the original image of other near-duplicate images, and other redundant images will be eliminated to achieve de-duplication.

2.1   Feature Extraction

To our knowledge, any applications for near-duplicate images are based on the techniques of feature matching. For examples, near-duplicate image detection [7], image clustering [8], and personal photo collection [9], etc. These existing applications can be classified into two main categories according to the attributes of visual features they used for near-duplicate matching: global feature based methods and local feature based

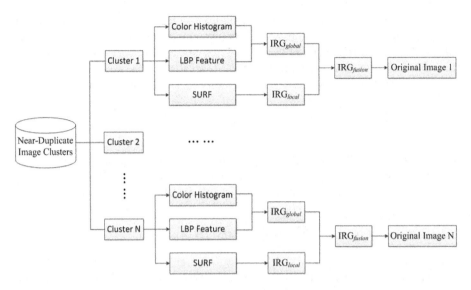

Fig. 2. Overview of the proposed framework: original image tracing for near-duplicate image elimination.

methods. However, it has been more and more noticed that a single type of feature is impossible preferable in all cases, and feature fusion is a reasonable option to leverage multiple advantages [10]. Therefore, to accurately obtain representative descriptions of an image, it is necessary for us to combine both global feature and local feature. In this section, feature extraction is elaborated in detail.

2.1.1   Global Feature Extraction

To provide a more accurate global feature based similarity evaluation, we consider both color property and texture property of an image. Thus color histogram [11] and local binary pattern feature (LBP) [12] are combined. Moreover, image partition is achieved in three ways to avoid negative effects of image segmentation and background changes on similarity evaluations. As is shown in Fig. 3, color histogram and LBP feature are extracted from these $\sum_{j=0}^{2} 2^j \times 2^j = 31$ grids, separately.

$2^0 \times 2^0 \ (j=0)$ $2^1 \times 2^1 = 4 \ (j=1)$ $2^2 \times 2^2 = 16 \ (j=2)$

Fig. 3. Gridded image for global feature extraction.

Color histogram is a typical global feature used to represent the image content on color space. In this paper, we adopt HSV color histogram as one of the image descriptor, and map the color histogram into 128 bins to represent the color distribution of an image. Then the computational equation for similarity evaluation between two images is proposed. Given two images u and v, their similarity $S_h(u,v)$ on color histogram matching can be defined as:

$$S_h(u, v) = e^{-M_h(u,v)/h_{max}} \tag{1}$$

where $M_h(u,v)$ is the average error between u and v on the matching of their color histogram on gridded images; h_{max} is the maximal M_h in the image cluster of u and v ($M_h(u,v)$ is normalized by the maximum M_h value). And $M_h(u,v)$ is defined as:

$$M_h(u, v) = \frac{1}{R} \sum_{j=0}^{R-1} \frac{1}{2^j \times 2^j} \sum_{i=1}^{2^j \times 2^j} MSE(H_i(u), H_i(v)) \tag{2}$$

where $MSE(H_i(u), H_i(v))$ is the Mean Squared Error (MSE) between image u and v on their color histogram at the i-th grid; $j = 0, 1, ..., R$ represent the corresponding j-th grid resolutions. The number of image partition ways in our paper is 3, so that $R = 2$ for j starts from 0.

Not limited to color property, we also describe texture property of an image with LBP feature. Then we extract LBP features of each gridded image. During this process, LBP feature of each grid contains 256 bins for histogram statistic. Thus, similar to the similarity definition on color histogram matching, the similarity $S_l(u,v)$ on LBP feature matching of image u and v is defined as:

$$S_l(u, v) = e^{-M_l(u,v)/l_{max}} \tag{3}$$

where $M_l(u,v)$ is the average error between u and v on the feature matching of their LBP features; l_{max} is the maximal M_l in the image cluster of u and v, and $M_l(u,v)$ is defined as:

$$M_l(u, v) = \frac{1}{R} \sum_{j=0}^{R-1} \frac{1}{2^j \times 2^j} \sum_{i=1}^{2^j \times 2^j} MSE(L_i(u), L_i(v)) \tag{4}$$

where $MSE(L_i(u), L_i(v))$ is the MSE between image u and v on their LBP feature matching at the i-th grid; $j = 0, 1, ..., R$ represent the corresponding j-th partition way.

Then these two kinds of global descriptors can be characterized more accurately by fusing the similarities based on them, and the fusion equation for the finally global feature based similarity S_{global} can be defined as:

$$S_{global}(u, v) = \frac{S_h(u, v) + S_l(u, v)}{2} \tag{5}$$

where the visual similarities on color histogram and LBP feature are assigned with their respective weightings. However, the proposed method is not restricted to the weighting allocation in this internal distribution of global features, so the relevant two weightings are all equal to 0.5. Finally, each near-duplicate image cluster will obtain a similarity matrix SM_{global} which records the global feature based similarity of every two images in the cluster.

2.1.2 Local Feature Extraction

Local feature based image matching aims to recognize more sophisticated near-duplicate images with rich descriptors, while global feature based image matching focuses on rapid identification at the sacrifice of accuracy. Thus, we also extract local features from images to make more accurate similarity evaluation and contextual relationship analysis between near-duplicate images. In this section, SURF [13] model is employed to describe local features of images. As a speed up version of SIFT feature [14], SURF reduces the computational cost for feature extraction. For each image, there might exist hundreds of feature points. Thus we can evaluate the similarity of two images according to the proportion of local features they shared.

Given two images u and v, their visual similarity $S_{local}(u,v)$ on SURF feature matching can be defined as:

$$S_{local} = \frac{m}{\min(m_u, m_v)} \tag{6}$$

where m is the number of SURF features they shared; m_u and m_v are the total number of feature points in u and v, respectively; $\min(m_u, m_v)$ is the smaller one between m_u and m_v. Thus the similarity matrix SM_{local} that stores cues of the contextual relationship between near-duplicate images in one cluster, will be constructed according to local feature based matchings.

2.2 IGR Construction and Fusion

Considering that further analysis of the contextual relationship between near-duplicate images is on the basis of an appropriate link analysis algorithm, we organize the images in each near-duplicate cluster with a graph model. In this section, a graph model IRG used to organize the contextual relationships between images is proposed. Moreover, the method for graph fusion on global feature based IRG and local feature based IRG is also provided.

To construct the IGR, we take each I_i in a near-duplicate image cluster C as a node and link it with its top-K nearest images. In more detail, if I_j is another image in C and I_i is the top-K nearest image of I_j, then there exists an edge from I_i to I_j. Accordingly, all image nodes make up a vertex set and the links between them make up an edge set. Thus, the IRG can be described as: IGR = $<I_c, E>$, where I_c represents the images in C; E represents the links between near-duplicate images. Furthermore, referring to the similarity matrix SM_{global} or SM_{local}, each edge in the IRG will be assigned with a weight according to the corresponding similarity matrix.

As mentioned above, the similarity matrix is calculated with the similarity of each image pair in C. Then we mark the similarity matrix as $SM_{m\times m}$, where m is the total number of images in C. If I_i and I_j are two images in the cluster C, $SM[i, j]$ is equal to the visual similarity of I_i and I_j. Therefore, the IRG marked with edge weights according to $SM_{m\times m}$ can effectively reflect the contextual relationship between near-duplicate images in cluster C. Moreover, the more relevant an image is to another image, the higher weight will be assigned to their link. In Sect. 2.1, we extract two kind of visual features to separately evaluate similarities between images. Thus in this section, we construct both the global feature based IRG_{global} and the local feature based IRG_{local} to combine the advantages of global features and local features. And the corresponding weights could be obtained from SM_{global} or SM_{local}, separately. For easier analysis in the next section, we fuse these two IRGs into a comprehensive IRG_{fusion}, and the IRG_{fusion} has incorporative edges of the same vertex set as two previous IRGs. The process of IRG fusion is illustrated in Fig. 4.

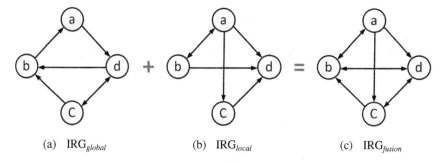

(a) IRG_{global} (b) IRG_{local} (c) IRG_{fusion}

Fig. 4. The process of IRG fusion.

In the comprehensive IRG_{fusion}, the corresponding link weight of each edge should be updated according to the weights of two previous IRGs. Since the link weights are indicated by the similarity matrix, the fused similarity matrix SM_{fusion} is defined as:

$$SM_{fusion} = (1-\alpha)SM_{global} + \alpha SM_{local} \qquad (7)$$

where SM_{global} is the similarity matrix based on global feature matching and SM_{local} is the similarity matrix of local feature based matching. And $1-\alpha$ and α are the importance factors of global feature and local feature, respectively. Accordingly, the link weights of the fused IRG_{fusion} are updated referring to this fused similarity matrix SM_{fusion}.

2.3   Contextual Relationship Analysis

Given an IRG_{fusion} fused by a global feature based IRG_{global} and a local feature based IRG_{local} that corresponding to one near-duplicate image cluster, the edges of the IRG_{fusion} can reflect the contextual relationship between images in the cluster. Benefiting from the fact that the more relevant an image is in the cluster, the more likely it will appear at the outgoing links of other images. Thus it motivates us to select an effective link analysis algorithm to find the best representative image of each image cluster. Moreover, the analysis for the contextual relationship between images is essential to find the best representative image on the visual content of a cluster. Therefore, the above observations prompt us to adopt the PageRank algorithm [15] to complete this step.

PageRank is a graph-based ranking algorithm which usually used to evaluate the importance of a webpage. So for the IRG_{fusion}, we can use this algorithm to evaluate the relevance and importance of each image in the cluster. In addition, the more relevant an image is, the more possible it will be visited, and it will achieve higher ranking value after the PageRank analysis. However, it is necessary to note that the weights of each column in the similarity matrix SM_{fusion} should be normalized to ensure that the sum weight of all outgoing links of each node is equal to 1.

In the process of contextual relationship analysis, the PageRank will iteratively update the authority of each image node until convergence. Considering of time consumption, we set the number of iterations for 5 times to achieve a balance between convergence and time consumption. This analysis process is formulated in Fig. 5. Finally, each image will be assigned with a ranking value which could represent its relevance and importance on visual content. Based on the truth that the original image will have the highest relevance to other images, we consider the image with the highest ranking value as the original image. After original image tracing, each original image in its cluster will be reserved as the representative image, to achieve accurately redundancy elimination.

Algorithm 1 Contextual Relationship Analysis

Input: An IRG, the similarity matrix SM_{fusion} corresponding to the IRG.
Output: the original image I_o.
  1: Update the similarity matrix SM_{fusion} according to the constraint
     of top-K nearest image;
  2: Normalize SM_{fusion} so that the weights of each column sum to 1;
  3: int num = the total number of images in the IRG.
  4: Initialize a $1 \times num$ node vector V whose initial element
     value is $1/num$;
  5: **while** $p<5$ **do**
  6:   Update V with the normalized SM_{fusion};
  7:   p++;
  8: **end while**
  9: Compute the maximum value of V;
10: Return the corresponding image of the maximum value.

Fig. 5. The algorithm for contextual relationship analysis between near-duplicate images, which returns the original image of the current image cluster.

3   Experimental Results and Discussions

The famous INRIA Copydays database is a set of images which are composed of personal holiday photos. Each image has suffered three kinds of digital attacks: JPEG, cropping and "strong". To further increase the number of near-duplicate images, we additionally conduct 16 kinds of common attacks or hybrid attacks on each image. Then we merge each original image with its near-duplicate images into an image cluster. Thus, we obtain a set of near-duplicate clusters corresponding to different original images, and these clusters constitute the validation dataset of parameter determination in our paper. Moreover, distracting images crawled from the Internet are randomly inserted into these clusters to form the final testing dataset of our experiment. In this section, we conduct several experiments with the above mentioned dataset to verify the effectiveness of our method. Evaluated by the MAP value, the experimental results achieve good performance in accordance with our expectation.

A. Evaluation Criteria. MAP is the abbreviation of Mean Average Precision, which can be applied to systems that refer to image ranking (the MAP metric here is not referred to geometrical area under the precision-recall curve). AP (Average precision) value emphasizes ranking relevant images higher, and the original image is expected to have the highest ranking, so we can use this evaluative criteria to evaluate the precision of our original image tracing system for near-duplicate elimination. The MAP is defined as:

$$MAP = \frac{\sum_{m=1}^{N} AP_m}{N} \tag{8}$$

where m is the current retrieved near-duplicate image cluster; N is the total number of near-duplicate image clusters; AP is the average precision which is computed at each image cluster in the ranked image sequence, and the AP value is defined as:

$$AP = \frac{\sum_{r=1}^{n} P(r) \times rel(r)}{\text{number of relevant images}} \tag{9}$$

where r is the rank; n is the number of retrieved images in the current cluster; and $rel(r)$ is a binary (0/1) function on the relevance of a given rank. $P(r)$ is the precision at a given cut-off rank, which is defined as:

$$P(r) = \frac{|\{\text{relevant retrieved images of rank } r \text{ or less}\}|}{r} \tag{10}$$

where $|*|$ is the number of $*$.

In our paper, the relevant image of each cluster is only the original image, and all the images in the cluster are considered to be successfully retrieved. Thus, the computation of the AP value is very simple. Moreover, for the above mentioned $rel(r)$, the given rank of the original image is equal to 1. That is to say, only the rel corresponding to the rank of the original image is equal to 1, rel values corresponding to the ranks of other near-duplicate images are equal to 0.

B. Parameter Determination. In this section, we configure the settings of the weighting parameter α (in the importance allocation for global feature and local feature) and the parameter K (in the top-K nearest image selection). The validation dataset is composed of 100 image clusters with pure near-duplicate images, where the original images are extracted from the Copydays dataset and each cluster has 20 near-duplicate images. Firstly, we set K as 20 (i.e., all near-duplicate images in the cluster are connected with each other), and report the MAP values of different settings of α. The weighting parameter α is set from 0 to 1, while $1-\alpha$ is from 1 to 0. Figure 6(a) illustrates the effects of α on the MAP value. From Fig. 6(a), we can conclude that the MAP value reaches the top at $\alpha = 0.3$. That is to say, when we set the importance weighting of global feature as 0.7 and local feature as 0.3, the performance of our method will achieve the best state. Thus, we adopt this setting of parameter α for further validation.

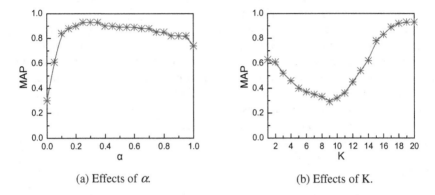

(a) Effects of α.   (b) Effects of K.

Fig. 6. The effects of different parameter settings on MAP value: (a) reflects the effects of α on MAP and (b) reflects the effects of K on MAP.

Based on the above parameter setting of α, we then test the influence of parameter K involved to the top-K nearest image selection. Figure 6(b) illustrates the effects of different settings of K on the MAP value. From this figure, we find that different settings of parameter K have an unsteadily impact on the MAP value. When K is set from 1 to 20, the MAP decrease first, then increase to the expected value until K is near to 20. This indicates that we should better set K as the ground-truth number of near-duplicate images when those near-duplicate images are accompanied with several distracting images. On the fact that the original images in our paper have suffered in total 19 kinds of different copy attacks and each image cluster in the validation dataset has 20 near-duplicate images, we set K as 18 to balance the performance and computation complexity at the following testing experiments.

C. Performance Analysis. To validate the general performance of our proposed method, we add several distracting images into each near-duplicate image cluster and each cluster has a random number of distracting images. Since the number of original images in the Copydays dataset is 157, there are 157 near-duplicate image clusters all together. To further expand the testing dataset, we also download other 143 original images of different scenes from the Internet and do the same copy attacks as above mentioned attacks. Then the testing dataset in this section is composed of 300 near-duplicate clusters. Moreover, distracting images crawled from the Internet are randomly inserted into these clusters.

Following the parameter settings in the above section, we conduct the proposed method of original image tracing to achieve near-duplicate elimination. Moreover, we compare our original image tracing method with other three methods: the basic method, the centroid based seed selection method [4] which is denoted as "Geo-Tag", and the fuzzy logic reasoning method [5] which is denoted as "FAIDA". The basic method for representative image selection is to select the image that has the minimal sum of distance to other images in the cluster; the "Geo-Tag" method considers the photo nearest to the centroid of its cluster should be the representative photo, where the centroid is the mean of all the photos; the "FAIDA" method takes image quality into consideration and uses fuzzy logic reasoning to select representative images.

With different size of distracting images, we firstly compare the impacts of distracting image of our method with the above mentioned three methods on the MAP value. Figure 7 shows the comparison results or the corresponding methods. From Fig. 7, it can be observed that our method outperform than other three methods in the MAP value with the increase of distracting images. Moreover, the rate of decrease of our method is the lowest, while the basic method for representative image selection is most sensitive to the increase of distracting images.

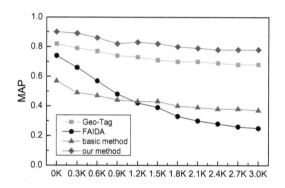

Fig. 7. The change of MAP value on different size of distracting images.

Next, we use time consumption to evaluate the efficiency of our method on the total response time. Figure 8 shows the comparative results. From the figure, we can conclude that the FAIDA has the lowest time consumption due to only global feature based image matching, which can achieve rapid identification with compact descriptors but sacrifice some accuracy. The efficiency of our method on representative image selection is higher than Geo-Tag because the processing of geographic information for feature matching and NIG identification will cost some time which cannot be neglected. Moreover, it is necessary to note that the total response time of our method and the basic method are almost the same because very little time consumption on the iteration of PageRank is negligible.

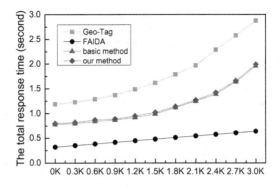

Fig. 8. The change of total response time on different size of distracting images.

4   Conclusion

In this paper, we introduce a framework of original image tracing to accurately eliminate near-duplicate images. To better evaluate the similarity of near-duplicate images, both global feature and local feature are extracted to describe different properties of each image. Moreover, a graph based model named IRG is constructed to reflect the contextual relationship between near-duplicate images with their visual similarities. And IRGs corresponding to different features are fused to develop a comprehensive IRG. Based on the PageRank algorithm, which is a superior link analysis algorithm to rank items with their relevance and importance, we trace the original image of each near-duplicate cluster by iteratively updating the authority of each image in the comprehensive IRG. Thus the image with the highest rank will be regarded as the representative image of the cluster and other near-duplicate versions will be eliminated. Experiments show that our method could accurately trace the original image as the representative image, which could withstand the test of large-scale distracting images.

Acknowledgments. This work was supported in part by the National Natural Science Foundation of China under Grant 61602253, Grant U1536206, Grant 61232016, Grant U1405254, Grant 61373133, Grant 61502242, and Grant 61572258, in part by the Jiangsu Basic Research Programs-Natural Science Foundation under Grant BK20150925, in part by the Priority Academic Program Development of Jiangsu Higher Education Institutions (PAPD) fund, in part by the Collaborative Innovation Center of Atmospheric Environment and Equipment Technology (CICAEET) fund, and in part by College Students Practice Innovation Training Program under Grant 201610300022, China.

References

1. Yao, J., Yang, B., Zhu, Q.: Near-duplicate image retrieval based on contextual descriptor. IEEE Sig. Proc. Lett. **22**(9), 1404–1408 (2015)
2. Chen, B., Shu, H., Coatrieux, G., et al.: Color image analysis by quaternion-type moments. J. Math. Imag. Vis. **51**(1), 124–144 (2014)

3. Li, J., Li, X., Yang, B., et al.: Segmentation-based image copy-move forgery detection scheme. IEEE Trans. Inf. Forensics Secur. **10**(3), 507–518 (2015)

4. Liu, J., Huang, Z., Cheng, H., et al.: Presenting diverse location views with real-time near-duplicate photo elimination. In: 2013 IEEE 29th International Conference on Data Engineering (ICDE), pp. 505–516. IEEE (2013)

5. Ming, C., Wang, S., Yun, X., et al.: FAIDA: a fast and accurate image deduplication approach. J. Comput. Res. Dev. **50**(1), 101–110 (2013)

6. Costa, F.D.O., Oikawa, M.A., Dias, Z., et al.: Image phylogeny forests reconstruction. IEEE Trans. Inf. Forensics Secur. **9**(10), 1533–1546 (2014)

7. Lei, Y., Qiu, G., Zheng, L., et al.: Fast near-duplicate image detection using uniform randomized trees. ACM Trans. Multimedia Comput. Commun. Appl. **10**(4), 181–184 (2014)

8. Wang, X.J., Zhang, L., Liu, C.: Duplicate discovery on 2 billion internet images. In: Proceedings of the 2013 IEEE Conference on Computer Vision and Pattern Recognition Workshops, pp. 882–889. IEEE Computer Society (2013)

9. Vonikakis, V., Jinda-Apiraksa, A., Winkler, S.: PhotoCluster: a multi-clustering technique for near-duplicate detection in personal photo collections. In: 2014 International Conference on Computer Vision Theory and Applications (VISAPP), pp. 153–161. IEEE (2014)

10. Luo, Q., Zhang, S., Huang, T., Gao, W., Tian, Q.: Hybrid-indexing multi-type features for large-scale image search. In: Cremers, D., Reid, I., Saito, H., Yang, M.-H. (eds.) ACCV 2014. LNCS, vol. 9003, pp. 446–460. Springer, Heidelberg (2015)

11. Liu, C., Lu, X., Ji, S., et al.: A fog level detection method based on image HSV color histogram. In: 2014 International Conference on Progress in Informatics and Computing (PIC), pp. 373–377. IEEE (2014)

12. Amit, S., Xudong, J., How-Lung, E.: LBP-based edge-texture features for object recognition. IEEE Trans. Image Process. Publ. IEEE Sig. Process. Soc. **23**(5), 1953–1964 (2014)

13. Bay, H., Tuytelaars, T., Gool, L.V.: SURF: speeded up robust features. Comput. Vis. Image Underst. **100**(3), 404–417 (2006)

14. Lowe, D.: Distinctive image features from scale–invariant keypoints. Int. J. Comput. Vis. **60**(2), 91–110 (2004)

15. Yushi, J., Shumeet, B.: VisualRank: applying pagerank to large-scale image search. IEEE Trans. Pattern Anal. Mach. Intell. **30**(11), 1877–1890 (2008)

Hierarchical Joint CNN-Based Models for Fine-Grained Cars Recognition

Maolin Liu, Chengyue Yu, Hefei Ling$^{(\boxtimes)}$, and Jie Lei

Huazhong University of Science and Technology,
Luoyu Road, Wuhan 430074, China
{liumaolin,lhefei,ycy}@hust.edu.cn, leijie@ncu.edu.cn

Abstract. For the purpose of public security, car detection and identification are urgently required in the real time traffic monitoring system. However, fine-grained recognition is a challenging task in the area of computer vision due to the subtle inter-class and huge intra-class differences. To tackle this task, this paper provided a novel approach focussed on two main aspects. On the one hand, the most discriminative local feature representations of regions of interests (ROIs) magnified many details. On the other hand, the hierarchical relations within the fine-grained categories can be simulated by probability formulas. Our proposed model consists of two modules: (i) a region proposal network to generate plenty of ROIs and (ii) a joint CNN-based model to learn the multi-grained feature representations simultaneously.

The proposed joint CNN-based model was implemented and tested on the Stanford Cars dataset and the CompCars dataset. Our experimental results are compared with those of other methods, and verify the superior performance of the proposed model.

Keywords: CNN-based models · Security models · Big data · Fine-grained recognition

1 Introduction

Recent years have witnessed great concern about public safety issues due to the social instability. Nowadays major cities in China are committed to building the *Safety City* system, in which the intelligent traffic monitoring system is an integral part. As an application, recognizing the brand and model of a specific car is a necessary task when fighting against vehicle crime or looking for the suspect in monitor videos [1]. For humans, even for avid car enthusiasts, it is fairly hard and time-consuming to identify the specific model of a car from thousands of categories accurately. So we are devoted to constructing classification model of cars from the perspective of computer vision.

Thanks to the rapid development of deep convolutional neural networks (CNNs) [2], a great many of achievements has been completed in the area of object recognition. Especially, visual recognition of fine-grained object is a popular topic among them due to the potential applications. In contrast to general

© Springer International Publishing AG 2016
X. Sun et al. (Eds.): ICCCS 2016, Part II, LNCS 10040, pp. 337–347, 2016.
DOI: 10.1007/978-3-319-48674-1_30

object recognition, fine-grained recognition is more challenging because of (i) the small differences between different subcategories, and (ii) the large visual variances within instances of the same subcategory caused by a variety of factors such as pose, viewpoint, illumination, and partially occlusion. Figure 1 illuminates that recognizing the specific model of cars is a challenging task.

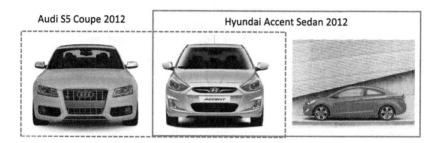

Fig. 1. Examples of small inter-class and large intra-class variances. Left cars in red dotted box with similar appearance belong to different subcategories. Right cars in blue solid box with different appearance belong to the same brand.

The significant features of images required by fine-grained tasks can be extracted by several well designed CNN models. Up to now, a number of researches have shown that the CNN-based approaches can achieve state-of-the-art accuracy in fine-grained object recognition tasks [3–8]. Many methods extracted the saliency local features based on the manually annotated part annotations [3,4,7,8]. Although the part-based approaches achieved good performances, they require a large number of expensive part annotations at training time. To solve this problem, we obtain our discriminative local features from ROIs generated by the region proposal methods. Inspired by the tree structure in the computer network [9–11], we propose a joint CNN-based model which takes advantages of the hierarchical relations of fine-grained and coarse-grained categories by adding a little extra hierarchical augmented information.

The rest of this paper is organized as follows. Section 2 discusses related work. Section 3 details our overall framework based on the proposed method. Experimental results are reported in Sect. 4 and we conclude in Sect. 5.

2   Related Work

Based on CNN variations and their joint models, many fine-grained recognition methods performed well. The CaffeNet model [12] is a variation of the most commonly used CNN model-AlexNet [2] and the GoogLeNet model [13] is designed to improve the performance of AlexNet by making network structure deeper. Lin et al. [5] proposed a bilinear CNN model, which is a novel recognition architecture consists of two networks. The feature extractors produced by the two networks are combined to obtain image descriptors. Sudowe et al. [6] treated fine-grained recognition as multiple binary attribute classification tasks. They proposed a multi-task CNN model, in which the visual knowledge is shared by attribute categories simultaneously.

In order to capture subtle difference among fine-grained categories, a lot of studies focused on learning parts of the objects and aligning the contours of objects within the same class. Based on the Region-based CNN [14], Zhang et al. [3] performed pose-normalized bird classification by learning whole-object with part detectors and enforcing geometric constraints between them. Lin et al. [7] showed that part localization, alignment, and classification can be incorporated into one recognition system. Krause et al. [4] combined co-segmentation and alignment to generate parts using only image-level labels. Simon et al. [8] learned part models in a completely unsupervised manner without given bounding boxes during training.

Usually, the fine-grained datasets are small-scale because the labeled fine-grained data is much harder to be collected and labeled than general data. There are several ways to tackle this problem such as fine-tuning, which should be treated as a manner of data augmentation to enable learning a large-scale CNN model with small-scale dataset. Some studies like [8] adopted a more straightforward way to data augmentation i.e. adding more related data from the Internet or other datasets. Chen et al. [15] proposed a double-path deep domain adaptation network to model the data from the domain of unconstrained images captured and online shopping stores mined jointly. It's worth mentioned that we haven't introduced additional data except for the ImageNet dataset.

3   Proposed Method

When recognizing a specific object, our eyes first find where the target is and then determine the object-level category. In the next moment, we recognize the coarse-grained and fine-grained category of the object step by step. Automatically fine-grained cars recognition performs in the same way as our eyes. For instance, finding an Audi S5 Coupe in an image entails the process of first estimating the location of the car, then recognizing its type (coupe) and brand (Audi) by its overall style, finally determining the specific model from the details. Similarly, we use two modules to describe our framework. First, the region proposal generation module is adopted to generate a great many of ROIs which expand local features in the original basis during training and roughly located the target object at test time. Secondly, the joint CNN-based model which makes use of the hierarchical relationship of coarse-grained and fine-grained categories is trained on the region proposals generated by the former module. In the sequel, the terms *ROIs* and *region proposals* are used interchangeably.

3.1   ROIs Generation

The combination of object location and classification is a promising approach to recognize fine-grained object. The details of objects can be well described by the local feature representations extracted from the randomly generated region proposals. For these reasons, we prefer training our models on ROI patches of the raw images rather than on the expanded datasets consist of simple image deformations. There are many ways to generate ROI patches, such as the most widely used selective search [16] method, which performed with high quality but poor efficiency in practice. For the trade-off between efficiency and accuracy, we utilize the region proposal networks, which is recently proposed in [17] to generate initial candidate ROIs for each raw image.

As is shown in Fig. 2(a), we pre-train an object-level detector on the original dataset. Our learned detector can effectively localize the site of cars. Compared with the bottom-up methods, region proposal networks share convolutional parameters with the detection networks, that is to say, they generate candidate region proposals and extract features simultaneously. The proposals produced by region proposal networks retain the objectness that is helpful for the recognition task. After that, we discard the proposals with abnormal aspect ratio and size and adopt non-maximum suppression (NMS) to limit the quantity of similar patches for high efficiency training.

3.2   Joint CNN-Based Model

As an example depicted in Fig. 3, the hierarchical structures inherent in many fine-grained datasets are able to be displayed clearly by manually annotated coarse-grained labels with minimal labor. Different from several literatures such as augmenting datasets by introducing hyper-class data [18] or constructing

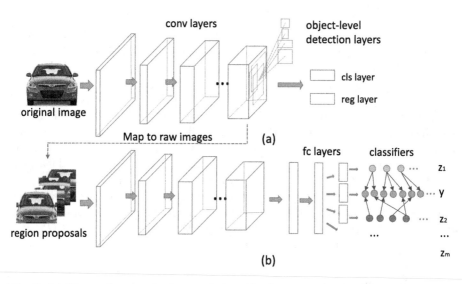

Fig. 2. (a) The region proposal network is utilized to generate initial candidate ROI patches for each image. (b) The joint CNN-based model is trained with the hierarchical relations among multi-grained categories.

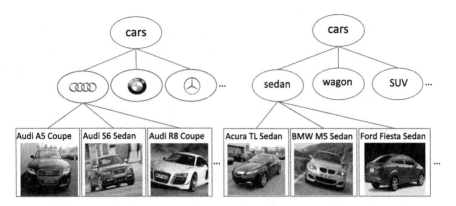

Fig. 3. The tree structures of car models. From the perspective of brand (left), each brand contains several models of cars but each fine-grained car model only belongs to only one coarse-grained brand. From the perspective of type (right), the relationship of type-model is similar to brand-model.

hierarchy by clustering with distributed graphs [19], we explore the hierarchical relations of multi-grained labels by deducing the formulas of probability distribution relationships.

In our method, models are trained by different grained labels respectively. However, based on our observations, features extracted from the last convolutional layer of the different models are quite similar. It's feasible to share parameters of the first layers among multi-grained labels. Unlike the commonly used CNN which only has one classifier, the last layers of our CNN structure are multi-grained classifiers described by different loss functions. The structure of our proposed method is illustrated in Fig. 3(b). It's worth noting that we add fully-connected layers before the corresponding classifiers in order to retain the variations among them.

There are N images labeled with F fine-grained subcategories and C_m coarse-grained categories. Notice that, there may be various relations between coarse and fine grained classes such as type-model and brand-model. Here suppose we have M coarse-grained classes and m is the index. We use $x_i, i \in 1, \ldots, N$ to denote the feature representations of the i-th image produced by the last fully-connected layer of the shared network structure. The corresponding fine-grained label is represented as $y_i, y_i \in 1, 2, \ldots, F$ and the coarse-grained label is $z_{mi}, z_{mi} \in 1, 2, \ldots, C_m$. y_i are able to be contained by a certain z_{mi}. Our ultimate goal is improving the accuracy of predicting the fine-grained label by constructing a probability distribution model of multi-grained categories. We let $\hat{p}_{y_i,m}$ denote the probabilities of the i-th image belonging to the fine-grained class y_i after introducing the coarse-grained class z_{mi} and $\hat{p}_{z_{mi}}$ is the probabilities of it belonging to the coarse-grained class z_{mi}. $\hat{p}_{y_i|z_{mi}}$ specifies the conditional probability when given the coarse-grained class z_{mi}. The probability relations among them are modeled by

$$\hat{p}_{z_{mi}} = \frac{e^{w_{z_{mi}}^T x_i}}{\sum\limits_{z_{mi}=1}^{C_m} e^{w_{z_{mi}}^T x_i}}, \tag{1}$$

and

$$\hat{p}_{y_i|z_{mi}} = \frac{1\{y_i \in z_{mi}\}e^{v_{y_i|z_{mi}}^T x_i}}{\sum\limits_{y_i=1}^{F} 1\{y_i \in z_{mi}\}e^{v_{y_i|z_{mi}}^T x_i}}. \tag{2}$$

So multiplying (1) and (2) together by conditional total probability formula, we obtain the following probability predicted for the specific fine-grained class y_i

$$\hat{p}_{y_i,m} = \sum_{z_{mi}=1}^{C_m} \hat{p}_{z_{mi}} \cdot \hat{p}_{y_i|z_{mi}} = \sum_{z_{mi}=1}^{C_m} \frac{e^{w_{z_{mi}}^T x_i}}{\sum\limits_{z_{mi}=1}^{C_m} e^{w_{z_{mi}}^T x_i}} \cdot \frac{1\{y_i \in z_{mi}\}e^{v_{y_i|z_{mi}}^T x_i}}{\sum\limits_{y_i=1}^{F} 1\{y_i \in z_{mi}\}e^{v_{y_i|z_{mi}}^T x_i}} \tag{3}$$

In Fig. 2(b), the fully-connected layers are followed by a group of vari-size grained loss layers which have certain relations among them. To make use of the hierarchical relations, we sum all grained loss with well-chosen weights together. The joint loss function is summarized as follows

$$Loss = -\frac{1}{N} \sum_{i=1}^{N} \sum_{m=1}^{M} \left(\sum_{j=1}^{F} 1\{y_i = j\} \log \hat{p}_{y_i,m} + \beta_m \sum_{k=1}^{C_m} 1\{z_{mi} = k\} \log \hat{p}_{z_{mi}} \right) \tag{4}$$

where β_m is the weight of the m-th coarse-grained loss and it is selected by the validation method. In our experiment, we set β_m to 0.2. Here we ignore the penalty term for the convenience of expression, but it is crucial to whole design in practice. In the next section, we will minimize the improved joint loss function by iteratively training.

4   Experiments

4.1   Datasets

The proposed method is assessed on two public fine-grained recognition datasets-Stanford Cars [20] and CompCars [21]. Each image in the datasets have a single bounding box annotation. The Stanford Cars dataset contains 196 car classes with model annotated for each of the 16,185 images, split into 8,144 training set and 8,041 test set. We manually divided them into 9 types of passenger cars, including convertible, SUV, sedan, hatchback, coupe, wagon, cab, van and minivan. Another coarse-grained hierarchical structure is the car brands, including 49 classes such as Audi, BMW, Benz, etc. Since the whole CompCars dataset is too huge, we follow [21] to select a subset from the CompCars dataset which contains 431 car models with a total of 30,955 images capturing the entire car. Similar coarse-to-fine multi-label hierarchical structures as Stanford Cars are apply equally to this dataset.

4.2   Implement Details

During the training phase, the provided training set is adopted to train an object-level detection network. We create our training and validation sets by dividing the original training set into two subsets with a ratio of 9:1 and implement the produced detector on the training and validation data to generate a variety of region proposals. After ignoring the unreasonable size and aspect ratios, we use the remaining patches as the augmented dataset. To utilize the limited data and avoid over-fitting, we select the strategy of fine-tuning. We fine-tune our joint CNNs on the models pre-learned from the ImageNet dataset. For the convenience to implement, we complete the experiments with the deep learning framework-Caffe [12].

The CNN structure adopted by our object-level region proposals generation is consistent with the joint CNN learned for multi-grained recognition. Learning from [17], we assign a positive label to the proposals that have an Intersection-over-Union (IoU) overlap higher than 0.7 with the ground-truth box and abandon bad samples resulting in about 2k patches per image left. Since the training results of multi-grained categories are affected by the quality of proposals, we have to set a strict filter criteria for them. Fortunately, we don't need to worry too much about the region proposals generated by the region proposal net, because the proposal scoring is effective enough that we use the highest scored 50 proposals which have at least 0.5 IoU with the ground-truth. In order to illuminate the role of region proposals, we use the model fine-tuned on data augmentation [12] with flipped and cropped patches as a baseline without region proposals.

During the test phase, we first put the test set into the detection network to roughly locate the cars and generate the highest scored proposals. Then the NMS is adopted to roughly determine the position coordinates of the cars. The detected cars is further recognized by our joint CNN-based model.

4.3   Result of Hierarchical Joint Models

Our final accuracy and the results of other recently reported state-of-the-art methods are presented in Table 1. Method [4] generates parts by image segmentation and method [5] trained with two parallel CNNs. Method [18] is closely related to our method in the way of introducing hyper-class data. The difference is that [18] utilizes large amounts of images from the Internet. These augmented images are too messy, so they do not have our accurate results. For comparison purpose, the results are all trained from the variant of CaffeNet [12] architecture which contains 5 convolutional and 3 fully connected layers with fine-tune strategy. The GoogLeNet [13] model is designed to improve the performance of AlexNet by making network structure deeper. The performance of model trained by GoogLeNet is also showed in Table 1, where we just compare it with that of our CaffeNet models and unsurprisingly GoogLeNet-based model achieves better performance. As far as we know, there are few literatures reporting results on Compcars dataset, so we use the test result in [21] as our benchmark. Similarly, the results of our models implemented on Compcars dataset is showed in Table 2 which indicates that we have achieved promising results on this dataset as well. In Tables 1 and 2, we use S to represent the small networks (CaffeNet) and L to represent the large networks (GoogLeNet).

4.4   Performance and Error Analysis

When predicting a given image, we put it into the detector and further recognize it by the joint CNN-based model. In practice, the model learned on the actual data performs well on the surveillance video datasets. With two GTX Titan X, it approximately spends 200 ms on detecting the location of car, 100 ms on extracting high-level features and further recognition.

However, we found that most of the wrong predictions belong to the same brands or the same types as the test images. In order to examine the cross-category noise, we draw the confusion matrix of provided labels versus predicted labels for 100 categories on Stanford Cars test set and 100 categories on Compcars test set in Fig. 4. Since the adjacent rows or columns belong to the same cars brands, we confirm that the errors mainly come from the same coarse-grained categories due to the similar appearance. This is the main drawback of our method, although plentiful region proposals can solve this at a certain extent. We will try to solve this problem in future researches.

Table 1. Accuracy on Stanford Cars dataset

Method	Acc(S)	Acc(L)
Baseline	79.4%	86.7%
PD+DCoP [4]	81.8%	N/A
HAR-CNN [18]	86.3%	N/A
B-CNN [5]	86.5%	N/A
Ours (proposals)	85.2%	90.9%
Ours (jointCNN)	81.7%	87.6%
Ours (proposals+jointCNN)	**86.8%**	**92.1%**

Table 2. Accuracy on Compcars dataset

Method	Acc(S)	Acc(L)
Baseline	76.9%	87.2%
Ours (proposals)	86.7%	93.4%
Ours (jointCNN)	78.0%	89.9%
Ours (proposals+jointCNN)	**87.9%**	**95.0%**

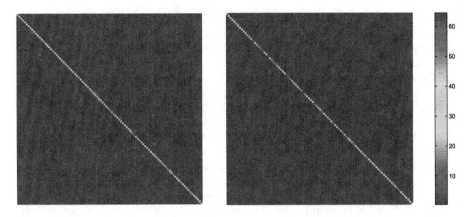

Fig. 4. Confusion matrices of the predicted and provided label for 100 categories on Stanford Cars test set (left) and 100 categories on Compcars test set (right). Most of the wrong predictions come from the same car brands or the same types as the test images.

5   Conclusions

In this paper, we proposed a joint CNN-based model to tackle the fine-grained cars recognition task. Our researches are significant to the content security issues because the trained model can be used to identify cars models in video monitoring system. First, we extract a plurality of discriminative local features from the region proposals generated by the region proposal networks. Then we trained the joint CNN models by taking advantages of the hierarchical relations between fine-grained subcategories and coarse-grained categories. Our method only require almost negligible additional coarse-grained labels instead of part annotations. Experimental results on two challenging datasets demonstrate that our method achieves state-of-the-art predictions.

In future work, we intend to solve the problem of wrong predictions within coarse-grained categories and apply our framework to more datasets.

Acknowledgments. This work was supported in part by the Natural Science Foundation of China under Grant U1536203 and 61272409, in part by the Major Scientific and Technological Innovation Project of Hubei Province under Grant 2015AAA013.

References

1. Wen, X., Shao, L., Xue, Y., Fang, W.: A rapid learning algorithm for vehicle classification. Inf. Sci. **295**(1), 395–406 (2015)
2. Krizhevsky, A., Sutskever, I., Hinton, G.E.: Imagenet classification with deep convolutional neural networks. In: Advances in Neural Information Processing Systems (NIPS), vol. 1, pp. 1097–1105. Curran Associates, Inc. (2012)

3. Zhang, N., Donahue, J., Girshick, R., Darrell, T.: Part-based R-CNNs for fine-grained category detection. In: Fleet, D., Pajdla, T., Schiele, B., Tuytelaars, T. (eds.) ECCV 2014. LNCS, vol. 8689, pp. 834–849. Springer, Heidelberg (2014). doi:10.1007/978-3-319-10590-1_54

4. Krause, J., Jin, H., Yang, J., Fei-Fei, L.: Fine-grained recognition without part annotations. In: Proceedings of the IEEE Conference on Computer Vision and Pattern Recognition (CVPR), vol. 1, pp. 5546–5555. IEEE (2015)

5. Lin, T.-Y., RoyChowdhury, A., Maji, S.: Bilinear CNN models for fine-grained visual recognition. In: Proceedings of the IEEE International Conference on Computer Vision (ICCV), vol. 1, pp. 1449–1457. IEEE (2015)

6. Sudowe, P., Spitzer, H., Leibe, B.: Person attribute recognition with a jointly-trained holistic CNN model. In: Proceedings of the IEEE International Conference on Computer Vision Workshops (ICCVW), vol. 1, pp. 87–95. IEEE (2015)

7. Lin, D., Shen, X., Cewu, L., Jia, J.: Deep LAC: deep localization, alignment and classification for fine-grained recognition. In: Proceedings of the IEEE Conference on Computer Vision and Pattern Recognition (CVPR), vol. 1, pp. 1666–1674. IEEE (2015)

8. Simon, M., Rodner, E.: Neural activation constellations: unsupervised part model discovery with convolutional networks. In: Proceedings of the IEEE International Conference on Computer Vision (ICCV), vol. 1, pp. 1143–1151. IEEE (2015)

9. Xie, S., Wang, Y.: Construction of tree network with limited delivery latency in homogeneous wireless sensor networks. Wireless Pers. Commun. **78**(1), 231–246 (2014)

10. Shen, J., Tan, H., Wang, J., Wang, J., Lee, S.: A novel routing protocol providing good transmission reliability in underwater sensor networks. J. Internet Technol. **16**(1), 171–178 (2015)

11. Guo, P., Wang, J., Li, B., Lee, S.: A variable threshold-value authentication architecture for wireless mesh networks. J. Internet Technol. **15**(6), 929–936 (2014)

12. Jia, Y., Shelhamer, E., Donahue, J., Karayev, S., Long, J., Girshick, R., Guadarrama, S., Darrell, T.: Caffe: convolutional architecture for fast feature embedding. In: Proceedings of the ACM International Conference on Multimedia (ACM MM), vol. 1, pp. 675–678. ACM (2014)

13. Szegedy, C., Liu, W., Jia, Y., Sermanet, P., Reed, S., Anguelov, D., Erhan, D., Vanhoucke, V., Rabinovich, A.: Going deeper with convolutions. In: Proceedings of the IEEE Conference on Computer Vision and Pattern Recognition (CVPR), vol. 1, pp. 1–9. IEEE (2015)

14. Girshick, R., Donahue, J., Darrell, T., Malik, J.: Rich feature hierarchies for accurate object detection and semantic segmentation. In: Proceedings of the IEEE Conference on Computer Vision and Pattern Recognition (CVPR), vol. 1, pp. 580–587. IEEE (2014)

15. Chen, Q., Huang, J., Feris, R., Brown, L.M., Dong, J., Yan, S.: Deep domain adaptation for describing people based on fine-grained clothing attributes. In: Proceedings of the IEEE Conference on Computer Vision and Pattern Recognition (CVPR), vol. 1, pp. 5315–5324. IEEE (2015)

16. Uijlings, J.R.R., van de Sande, K.E.A., Gevers, T., Smeulders, A.W.M.: Selective search for object recognition. Int. J. Comput. Vis. (IJCV) **104**(2), 154–171 (2013)

17. Ren, S., He, K., Girshick, R., Sun, J.: Faster R-CNN: towards real-time object detection with region proposal networks. In: Advances in Neural Information Processing Systems (NIPS), vol. 1, pp. 91–99. Curran Associates, Inc. (2015)

18. Xie, S., Yang, T., Wang, X., Lin, Y.: Hyper-class augmented and regularized deep learning for fine-grained image classification. In: Proceedings of the IEEE Conference on Computer Vision and Pattern Recognition (CVPR), vol. 1, pp. 2645–2654. IEEE (2015)
19. Zhang, L., Yang, Y., Wang, M., Hong, R., Nie, L., Li, X.: Detecting densely distributed graph patterns for fine-grained image categorization. IEEE Trans. Image Process. **25**(2), 553–565 (2016)
20. Krause, J., Stark, M., Deng, J., Fei-Fei, L.: 3d object representations for fine-grained categorization. In: Proceedings of the IEEE International Conference on Computer Vision Workshops (ICCVW), vol. 1, pp. 554–561. IEEE (2013)
21. Yang, L., Luo, P., Loy, C.C., Tang, X.: A large-scale car dataset for fine-grained categorization and verification. In: Proceedings of the IEEE Conference on Computer Vision and Pattern Recognition (CVPR), vol. 1, pp. 3973–3981. IEEE (2015)

Towards Interest-Based Group Recommendation for Cultural Resource Sharing

Jing Zhou[1]([✉]), Weifeng Xie[2], and Chen Zhang[1]

[1] Communication University of China, Beijing 100024, China
zhoujing@cuc.edu.cn
[2] PLA Logistics Academy, Beijing 100858, China
http://cs.cuc.edu.cn/zhoujing/index.htm

Abstract. We presented in this paper a usage scenario in which cultural resources in a public context, items on display in a historical museum for instance, should be recommended to groups of visitors in response to their interest (or preferences), thus conserving computational resources and reducing network traffic. Motivated by the scenario, we set out to design and implement a group recommender system, Museum Guides for Groups (MGG), that provides visitors to a museum with a sequence of items of interest by efficiently clustering visitors of similar user profiles into groups and computing recommendations for each group. Our work in progress was reported, focusing on the system design and the selection of an appropriate clustering algorithm for dividing visitors. We evaluated the efficiency of three candidate clustering techniques, including the bisecting K-Means, DBSCAN, and improved CURE, using the MovieLens dataset with 1M ratings.

Keywords: Clustering algorithm · Group recommendation · User profile

1 Introduction

Inevitably, we came across to situations in which recommender systems were anticipated to provide items to a group of users instead of an individual, for instance, a movie for friends to watch together or a restaurant for co-workers to spend some time for fun. For such cases, items should be recommended to groups of users in response to their interest (or preferences) rather than individual users. Group recommendation techniques [10] deal with this issue by aggregating information from individual user profiles, modeling the affective state for groups consisting of similar users, and producing recommendations to each group.

Similar to traditional recommender systems that serve single users, group recommenders rely on acquiring user profiles to gain an insight into user interest or preferences. However, there exist additional challenges that group recommender systems have to overcome:

– *How to form groups that consist of users share similar interest or preferences?*
In a public context as the historical museum mentioned in Sect. 2, clustering

X. Sun et al. (Eds.): ICCCS 2016, Part II, LNCS 10040, pp. 348–357, 2016.
DOI: 10.1007/978-3-319-48674-1_31

visitors of similar interest into smaller (virtual) groups and providing recommendations to each of such groups are mostly attributed to the concern of conserving computational resources and reducing network traffic, given the potential number of visitors within any timeframe. Various clustering algorithms have been proposed and investigated in a number of areas of data mining and information retrieval, and we will embark on the clustering problem of museum visitors by drawing on well-established techniques from related communities. In particular, we employed the following algorithms: bisecting K-means [12], DBSCAN [4], and an improved variant of the standard CURE [7].

– *How to adapt recommendations to a group of users as a whole based on the information in user profiles?* To this end, two approaches are typically available for use: recommendation aggregation and profile aggregation [3]. In the first case, recommendations for individual members of a group are generated and then consolidated to produce a group recommendation. In contrast, the profiles of all members from a group are aggregated into a group model in the second case and a group recommendation is then generated according to the model. In MGG, after clustering users into smaller groups, each group will then be treated as a *virtual user* and a profile will be created for this user. Group recommendations can then be generated to the member of the virtual user.

– *How to produce recommendations to users in an adaptive (but not intrusive) way when more knowledge about individual interest is discovered over time?* Intuitively, a user is not supposed to belong to a single group all the time while she visits a museum. This is particularly true if MGG knows nothing or little about her interest the first time she uses the service since MGG may be able to update her profile as more information about user interest can be accumulated along her visiting path within the museum. However, as the user profile keeps being updated, carrying out user clustering and delivering recommendations to a user constantly may not seem to be a good idea. We call this "adaptive group recommendations" since it is distinct from recommending a movie for a bunch of friends (only if they all like it), neither is it similar to recommending a sequence of songs to shoppers in a bookstore (as long as they do not dislike them). Adaptive group recommendations indicate performing clustering of users and generating recommendations at proper intervals, unless users explicitly seek for new recommendations, rather than only once.

The remainder of the paper is organized as follows. Section 2 presents a usage scenario that inspired our work on interest-based group recommendation for cultural resource sharing. We describe the system design of a group recommender, MGG, and report our findings on how three well-established clustering techniques are used to divide the users of MGG into smaller groups in Sect. 3. This is followed by an experimental evaluation of the efficiency of all the clustering algorithms in Sect. 4. Related work on group recommendation techniques is given in Sect. 5. Finally, we conclude the paper by identifying the future work in Sect. 6.

2   A Usage Scenario for Cultural Resource Sharing

A tour group comprising a few hundred people is going to visit the Palace Museum. In view of the fact that the members of the group vary in age, occupation, goals, and even in understanding of the nature of the items on display, the Palace Museum supplies each visitor with a downloadable application called Museum Guides for Groups (MGG) for their smartphones free of charge. MGG is able to recommend a sequence of items of interest to individual visitors by capturing user interest or preferences from certain sources (for instance, the browsing history captured by smartphones) if permissions are granted from the visitors. Furthermore, MGG is able to gradually enrich the content of user profiles by observing user visiting behaviors over time and identifying their preferences. Therefore, not only the extensive workload of the tour guide will be reduced considerably, but more importantly, tour members are more likely to obtain a personalized guide service, which typically leads to a satisfactory visiting experience.

Most recommender systems cannot avoid the cold–start problem and MGG is no exception to this. In a public context as the Palace Museum mentioned in the scenario, most visitors might have never used MGG before. Even if they had, information about their interest or past activities in the museum might not have been recorded by MGG because people are unlikely to register for a service they would probably use only once in a while. Hence, user ratings of items on display as typically used by collaborative filtering or content-based recommendations may be unavailable for MGG to use in creating user profiles. In the community of electronic commerce, the effectiveness of a Web page can be evaluated by measuring the time spent on viewing the page by visitors. MGG adopts a similar approach to getting to know more about a new visitor: It may announce new findings on user interest if the visitor is observed to spend a long time on viewing a certain item on display.

3   System Design

In this section, we describe the design of a recommender system, MGG, that is intended to provide group recommendations to the members sharing interest in common. Moreover, we will report our findings on how three well-established clustering techniques are used to allocate the users of MGG to distinct groups.

3.1   Architecture

The architecture of MGG is based on the client/server paradigm, see Fig. 1.

The client side consists of the following components: the user interface, the user behavior collector, and the user profile generator. With the user interface, a user of MGG is able to: (1) express her wish to make use of the recommendation service provided by MGG; (2) grant permissions to MGG for accessing her browsing history recorded by her smartphone, thus building up her user profile

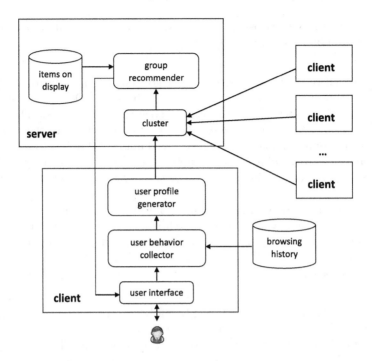

Fig. 1. The software architecture of MGG

in the first place; (3) and indicate her location within a public place, for example a museum, and allow the user behavior collector to capture the viewing time she spends on each item on display. The user profile generator can establish a model that characterizes the interest of a user by coupling the observations on the user visiting behavior within the museum with her browsing history if possible.

The cluster, the group recommender, and a database for storing information on items on display in a museum, are housed at the server side of MGG. After obtaining user profiles from all the users of MGG, the cluster is going to form a certain number of groups, each of which incorporating users sharing similar interest in common, using one of the clustering techniques introduced in Sect. 3.2. The group recommender will create a *group profile* for each group and generate recommendations based on the profile to each member of a group.

3.2 Clustering Techniques

Bisecting K-Means. Bisecting K-means is a simple variant of K-means, an iterative centroid-based divisive algorithm, and was introduced in [12] as an effective document clustering technique. It starts with a cluster that contains all the documents. Then, the basic K-means is used to split the cluster into two sub-clusters (referred to as the bisecting step). Repeat the bisecting step for ITER (a tunable parameter) times and select the split that produces the clustering with the highest overall similarity. The above steps are repeated until the desired number of clusters is found.

DBSCAN. DBSCAN is a density-based algorithm for discovering clusters of arbitrary shape in large spatial databases with noise [4]. Density in DBSCAN is defined as the number of points within a specified radius (*Eps*). The density of points within a cluster is considerably higher than outside of the cluster. A point is a core point if it has more than specified number of points *MinPts* within Eps, whereas a border point has fewer points than MinPts within Eps but is in neighborhood of a core point. The rest of the points are referred to as noise points.

The algorithm starts with an arbitrary point p from the dataset and retrieve all the points density-reachable from p with respect to Eps and MinPts. If p is a core point, a cluster is formed. If p is a border point, no points are density-reachable from p. Then, DBSCAN picks up another unvisited point from the dataset and processes it as described above so as to discover another cluster.

Improved CURE. CURE (Clustering Using Representatives) is an agglomerative algorithm from hierarchical clustering. The algorithm starts with each point as a separate cluster. It then selects a constant number c of well scattered points in a cluster. The chosen scattered points are then shrunk towards the centroid of the cluster by a fraction α. After shrinking, the scattered points will be used as representatives of the cluster. CURE will merge the clusters that have the closest pairs of representative points at each step of the algorithm until target k clusters are found.

In view of the fact that the worst-case time complexity of CURE is $O(n^2 \log n)$, we therefore consider reducing the scale of the points in the original dataset by preprocessing it with K-means, thus leading to k_1 ($k_1 > k$) clusters each of which consists of a smaller scale of points. CURE is then employed to perform further clustering on the k_1 clusters.

4   Evaluation

We present in this section an experimental evaluation of the cluster quality of bisecting K-means, DBSCAN, and improved CURE using the MovieLens dataset. To begin with, we explain why the dataset was selected and how it was adapted for evaluation. We then describe the experimental settings and metrics that facilitate a fair comparison among these clustering techniques. Finally, we provide the result accompanied by a brief analysis.

4.1   Original Dataset: MovieLens

We used the MovieLens 1M ratings dataset [6] for evaluation purposes, the statistics of which is shown in Table 1.

Table 1. Statistics of MovieLens 1M ratings dataset

# users	# movies	# ratings
6,040	3,706	1,000,209

The MovieLens datasets describe user's expressed preferences for movies by collecting information about user interactions with the MovieLens online recommender system over the course of years [9]. The preferences take the form of tuples as in <user_id, movie_id, rating, timestamp, gender, age, occupation, zip, title, genres>.

4.2 Dataset Processing

In order to better model the situation in our scenario, we preprocessed the dataset by reducing each tuple to contain only five elements: user_id, movie_id, rating, timestamp, and genres. In the processed dataset, ratings that users give to movies of different genres can be simulated as user interest in items on display in our scenario while information on the genre of a movie can be used to model the characteristics of each item.

For the MovieLens 1M ratings dataset, we computed the user interest vector of all distinct 6,040 users (see Table 1). The value for each component in the user interest vector was then normalized to a range from 0.0 to 1.0. An example user interest vector is presented in Fig. 2.

Drama	Animation	Romance		Horror	Documentary
(0.135,	0.040,	0.081,	... ,	0.021	0.002)

Fig. 2. An example user interest vector of 18 dimensions

We shuffled the user interest vectors of the 6,040 users and picked up the first 5 % vectors, thus forming a set of 302 user interest vectors to generate a user dataset D. This step was repeated for 30 times and we obtained 30 datasets for use in evaluation.

4.3 Experimental Settings and Metrics

All experiments were conducted on a notebook with Intel Core i3-2310M CPU @2.1 GHz, 4 GB physical memory, running Windows 7 64 bit. The three clustering algorithms were implemented and run using Python 2.7.10. All result data was averaged over 30 runs.

We define a metric called the clustering quality S to evaluate the efficiency of all three clustering algorithms as follows.

1. For each user i involved in the dataset D, compute her user interest vector $\mathbf{V}_i = (V_i^1, V_i^2, \cdots, V_i^n)$, where the extent to which the user i likes a movie of genre j ($j \in [1, n]$) is referred to as the interest intensity V_i^j, and n is equal to 18 since it represents the total number of genres of movies (see Sect. 4.2). We give the following definition:

$$V_i^j = \sum r_k$$

   where r_k is a rating that the user i gives to the movie k that is of genre j.
2. Apply a clustering algorithm to all $\mathbf{V}_i$ derived from D and compute a weighted interest vector $\mathbf{Q}^c$ for each cluster C. We define $\mathbf{Q}^c = (q_1^c, q_2^c, \cdots, q_n^c)$, where q_j^c represents the interest weight all the users from cluster C assign to the movies of genre j and is defined as:

$$q_j^c = \frac{\alpha_{inter}^c}{\alpha_{intra}^c} * \frac{\sum V_l^j}{|C|}$$

   where l is any user from cluster C and $|C|$ denotes the total number of users in cluster C. If β is used to represent the set of all clusters, then $|\beta|$ denotes the number of all clusters. So,

$$\overline{\mathbf{V}_c} = \frac{1}{|C|} \sum_{l=1}^{|C|} \mathbf{V}_l$$

$$\alpha_{intra}^c = \frac{\sum_{l=1}^{|C|} \|\mathbf{V}_l - \overline{\mathbf{V}_c}\|}{|C|}$$

$$\alpha_{inter}^c = \frac{\sum_{m=1}^{|\beta|} \|\overline{\mathbf{V}_m} - \overline{\mathbf{V}_c}\|}{|\beta|}$$

   It is clearly that α_{inter}^c is used to measure the Euclidean distance between $\overline{\mathbf{V}_m}$ and $\overline{\mathbf{V}_c}$, indicating how far the mean of the interest intensity all users from all clusters is spread out from the mean of the interest intensity of all users from a particular cluster C. In the meantime, α_{intra}^c is adopted to evaluate the Euclidean distance between $\mathbf{V}_l$ and $\overline{\mathbf{V}_c}$, revealing how far the interest intensity of any single user l from cluster C is spread out from the mean of the interest intensity of all users from the same cluster. Ideally, the greater α_{inter}^c (or the less α_{intra}^c) is, the greater the interest weight q_j^c is. This is in correspondence with the primary objective of user clustering: grouping users with similar interest as close as possible while keeping those of distinct nature apart.
3. For a given algorithm, its clustering quality S to evaluate the efficiency of clustering is then defined as follows:

$$S = \sum_{c \in \beta} (\mathbf{Q}^c \cdot \sum \mathbf{V}_l)$$

where l still denotes any user from cluster C and β is the set of all clusters. According to the properties of the dot product, we can tell that the more precisely the weighted interest vector $\mathbf{Q}^c$ can describe the interest intensity of users from cluster C to all genres of movies (that is, the better clustering quality is), the greater S is.

4.4 Results and Analysis

We collected experimental data and listed them in Table 2.

Table 2. Experimental results of S for different clustering algorithms

Bisecting K-means (k = 10)	DBSCAN	Improved CURE (k = 10)
7.712	0.931	4.910

With the experimental settings as described in Sect. 4.3, the bisecting K-means (k = 10) has achieved the greatest S, indicating the best clustering quality. Moreover, it is the most straightforward clustering algorithm. While the bisecting K-means algorithm only requires the number of the desirable clusters K as an input, DBSCAN needs to determine both Eps and MinPts and the improved CURE takes into account three parameters including the number of desirable clusters K, shrink factor α, and the number of representative points.

DBSCAN delivered the worst clustering quality and other disadvantages of DBSCAN include that it is difficult to determine an appropriate value for both Eps and MinPts. We therefore had to carry out extensive experiments for this purpose. The experimental results shown in Table 2 reveal the fact that DBSCAN does not work well for high-dimensional data in terms of clustering quality. However, compared with other two algorithms, DBSCAN does not need the desirable number of clusters K. Besides, it has proved to be able to exclude the undesirable impact from noise.

The improved CURE algorithm delivered a performance in terms of clustering quality inferior to that of bisecting K-means and it spent the longest time to accomplish the clustering task compared with the other two algorithms in the evaluation.

5   Related Work

As discussed in Sect. 1, two widely used approaches to producing group recommendations include recommendation aggregation and profile aggregation. Interested readers can refer to [10] for a detailed summary of both strategies and the group recommenders in which these strategies were used.

Other group recommendation techniques tackle the problem from different perspectives. For example, Gorla et al. proposed a probabilistic relevance framework, based on the information matching model, for group recommendation [5].

To define the group relevance, this model takes into account both an item's relevance to each user as an individual and as a member of the group. It was shown that recommendations of higher quality can be generated by shifting the focus toward better modeling of group members other than simply merging individual's ranked recommendations as in [2].

Amer-Yahia et al. formalized the problem of group recommendation and defined its semantics as a consensus function that is targeted at minimizing the disagreement among group members while maximizing item relevance [1]. Their work demonstrated that taking disagreements among group members into consideration is critical to both quality and efficiency of group recommendation. In this regard, MGG used clustering techniques to form groups of users sharing similar interest, which roughly corresponds to minimizing the disagreement of group members.

6   Conclusions

Group recommendation techniques that facilitate users to share cultural resources in a public context, a historical museum for instance, are confronted with the issues that traditional recommender systems would rarely have to address. As we analyzed in Sect. 1, a group recommender systems like MGG will need to perform clustering of visitors into smaller groups in the first place. Moreover, MGG has to take into account whether a group recommendation should be generated by combining user profiles or consolidating recommendations for individual users. As time goes by, more knowledge about user interest can be accumulated by MGG and the contents of group recommendations should also be updated and delivered to better serve MGG users in an adaptive and non-intrusive manner.

We have yet to provide an all-inclusive approach to the above problems but only reported our work in progress. After designing the overall system architecture, we tentatively selected three well-established clustering algorithms and performed a series of experiments to evaluate their effectiveness and efficiency. Among others, the bisecting K-means has proved to be a straightforward yet efficient clustering technique for dividing users into groups with most similar interest according to the clustering quality rating S that we defined for the evaluation.

We plan to investigate the issue of aggregating user profiles from the member of a group to establish a group profile based on which a group recommendation will then be generated. Ideally, if the clustering quality is good enough, MGG may select the user profile of any user within a group and directly use it as the group profile. Otherwise, a *representative* user profile, which may be derived from consolidating all user profiles within a group or directly chosen according to certain criteria, will be used to serve as a group profile. Our future work also includes determining a proper time interval at which MGG can take the initiative to deliver new recommendations [8, 11, 13].

Acknowledgments. This work was funded by the Open Project Program of Jiangsu Engineering Center of Network Monitoring and Nanjing University of Information Science and Technology Project (PAPD and CICAEET). The authors would also like to acknowledge the input of the National Key Technology R & D Program (No. 2015BAK25B03).

References

1. Amer-Yahia, S., Roy, S.B., Chawlat, A., Das, G., Yu, C.: Group recommendation: semantics and efficiency. Proc. VLDB Endow. **2**(1), 754–765 (2009)
2. Baltrunas, L., Makcinskas, T., Ricci, F.: Group recommendations with rank aggregation and collaborative filtering. In: Proceedings of the 4th ACM Conference on Recommender Systems (RecSys 2010), ACM, pp. 119–126 (2010)
3. de Campos, L.M., Fernández-Luna, J.M., Huete, J.F., Rueda-Morales, M.A.: Managing uncertainty in group recommending processes. User Model. User Adap. Interact. **19**(3), 207–242 (2009)
4. Ester, M., Kriegel, H.-P., Sander, J., Xiaowei, X.: A density-based algorithm for discovering clusters in large spatial databases with noise. In: Proceedings of the 2nd International Conference on Knowledge Discovery and Data Mining, pp. 226–231. AAAI Press (1996)
5. Gorla, J., Lathia, N., Robertson, S., Wang, J.: Probabilistic group recommendation via iinformation matching. In: Proceedings of the 22nd International Conference on World Wide Web (WWW 2013), pp. 495–504. ACM (2013)
6. GroupLens: MovieLens. http://grouplens.org/datasets/movielens/. Accessed Apr 2016
7. Guha, S., Rastogi, R., Shim, K.: CURE: an efficient clustering algorithm for large databases. In: Proceedings of the 1998 ACM SIGMOD International Conference on Management of Data (SIGMOD 1998), pp. 73–84. ACM (1998)
8. Guo, P., Wang, J., Li, B., Lee, S.: A variable threshold-value authentication architecture for wireless mesh networks. J. Internet Technol. **15**(6), 929–936 (2014)
9. Harper, F.M., Konstan, J.A.: The MovieLens datasets: history and context. ACM Trans. Interact. Intell. Syst. **5**(4), 19:1–19:19 (2015)
10. Masthoff, J.: Group recommender systems: combining individual models. In: Ricci, F., Rokach, L., Shapira, B., Kantor, P.B. (eds.) Recommender Systems Handbook, pp. 677–702. Springer, Boston (2011)
11. Shen, J., Tan, H., Wang, J., Wang, J., Lee, S.: A novel routing protocol providing good transmission reliability in underwater sensor networks. J. Internet Technol. **16**(1), 171–178 (2015)
12. Steinbach, M., Karypis, G., Kumar, V.: A comparison of document clustering techniques. In: Proceedings of the KDD Workshop on Text Mining (2000)
13. Xie, S., Wang, Y.: Construction of tree network with limited delivery latency in homogeneous wireless sensor networks. Wireless Pers. Commun. **78**(1), 231–246 (2014)

Human Facial Expression Recognition Based on 3D Cuboids and Improved K-means Clustering Algorithm

Yun Yang[1], Borui Yang[1], Wei Wei[2], and Baochang Zhang[1(✉)]

[1] Beihang University, Beijing 100191, China
{yangyun,yangborui,bczhang}@buaa.edu.cn
[2] Logistics Engineering University, Chongqing, China

Abstract. This paper focuses on human facial expression recognition in video sequences. Different from the methods of two-dimensional image recognition and three-dimensional spatial-temporal interest point detection, our approach highlights human facial expression recognition in complex spatial-temporal video datasets. The major challenge in facial expression recognition is how to obtain a feature dictionary from extracted cube pixel windows based on clustering algorithm. In this paper, our contributions are mainly concentrated on two aspects. Firstly, we combine discrete linear filter with key parameters selection procedure to extract 3D cuboids. Secondly, we propose a novel seed spot selection method to optimize K-means clustering algorithm. The proposed algorithms are evaluated on open databases. The results show that our approach can achieve outstanding results and the proposed approach is significantly effective.

Keywords: Facial expression recognition · Interest point detection · Clustering algorithm

1 Introduction

Human behavior recognition from video sequence is a challenging and dramatic task in the field of computer vision [1]. With the development of computer intelligence, accurate behavior recognition has attracted much attention in recent years [2–6]. Based on an understanding of high-level visual information, computer vision is applied to analyzing abnormal action expressions in video surveillance, providing convenience to disabled person with special needs and human-computer interaction. Nowadays, many researchers have achieved human behavior recognition based on spatial-temporal interest point detection method [7–9]. Specifically, interest point detection method is adopted as the following steps.

1. Interest point detection.
2. Describe pixel windows centered on interest point under specifically definition.
3. Quantify spatial-temporal features of above mentioned pixel windows.

This paper focuses on detection method of interest points, extraction and quantification algorithm of spatial-temporal features [10]. Sequentially, human behaviors

© Springer International Publishing AG 2016
X. Sun et al. (Eds.): ICCCS 2016, Part II, LNCS 10040, pp. 358–367, 2016.
DOI: 10.1007/978-3-319-48674-1_32

including different kinds of movements and expressions are recognized with high recognition rates utilizing simple classifiers.

Currently, it is a mainstream trend to utilize sparse feature points with necessary information to detect and recognize target objects [11]. Sparse feature descriptor is also conducive to increase robustness of feature with noise and decrease disturbance due to the change of posture. In this paper, we extend and improve spatial-temporal feature extraction method. Explicitly, it is not enough to detect two-dimensional (2D) interest points by common approaches in three-dimensional (3D) space-time video sequences. Instead, our proposed algorithm is based on spatial-temporal composited pixel window, which is feasible for various datasets including behaviors of human and rodents. As shown in Fig. 1, noisy maps, different backgrounds of action sequences, and free styles in performing actions may cause large intra-class variations in the dataset.

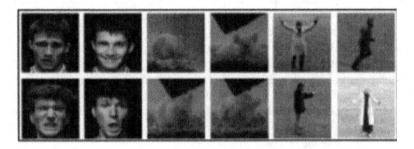

Fig. 1. Applied examples of human behavior recognition

The challenge for facial expression recognition is that posture, morphology and size of the target may change with complicated external condition. The dynamic change of background also adds more difficulty to recognition. In addition, the representations of the same kind facial expression are often different. To address this problem, our proposed approach aims to extract typical sparse features of target. These features describe various human facial expressions sufficiently and decrease the disturbance from change of posture and background [12, 13].

In the following sections we describe our algorithm in detail. In Sect. 2.1, we talk about detection of spatial interest points and introduce our method to extract 3D cuboids in the spatio-temporal domain. We describe improved K-means clustering algorithm in more detail in Sect. 2.2. In Sect. 3, we utilize extracted 3D cuboids and improved k-means algorithm in all of our experiments. Some concluding remarks are drawn in Sect. 4.

2 Algorithm

Our idea is inspired by the work of Dollár et al. [14]. Based on manifold structure of video data, we calculate pre-processed video data by convolution to extract cube pixel windows. Sequentially, the feature dictionary is acquired through K-means clustering and then passed to a classifier model. Support vector machine (SVM) and Random Forest classifiers are utilized in our experiments.

2.1 3D Cuboid Interest Point Extraction

Currently the most popular algorithm for interest point detection is corner detection in 2D space [15]. The corner is defined as the point near a region where gradient vectors are orthogonal. To obtain the gradient vector, we smooth the first order derivate image. Sequentially, the corner is extracted based on response intensity of each point. Then the pixel window near the corner and relative position of corner would be effective features for object detection and recognition. On account of various selected features, algorithms differ slightly from each other.

The interest point detection in 3D spatial-temporal space is similar to that in 2D space-time. However, in some fields such as human facial expression and facial expression recognition, the corner detection in 3D space is not employed frequently. Because corners are rare in 3D space-time, even totally vanish sometimes. Although the corner is detected, it is not what we need. In 3D space where time dimension is considered, corners may come from the background. Thus pixel windows around the corner and relative location of the corner would be useless in object detection or recognition. Therefore, an extended algorithm is adopted in this paper. Different from other interest point detectors, the response function we proposed is calculated with discrete linear filters [16]. We define the response function as

$$R = (I * g * h_{ev})^2 + (I * g * h_{od})^2, \tag{1}$$

where $g(x, y; \sigma)$ is a 2D Gaussian smoothing kernel utilized in space dimension. h_{ev} and h_{od} are 1D orthogonal Gabor filters which are applied to time dimension. Specifically, $g(x, y; \sigma)$ is defined as:

$$G(x, y; \sigma) = \frac{1}{2\pi\sigma^2} e^{\frac{x^2 + y^2}{2\sigma^2}}, \tag{2}$$

where h_{ev} is defined as:

$$h_{ev}(t; \tau, \omega) = -\cos(2\pi t\omega)e^{-t^2/\tau^2}, \tag{3}$$

and h_{od} is defined as:

$$h_{od}(t; \tau, \omega) = -\sin(2\pi t\omega)e^{-t^2/\tau^2}, \tag{4}$$

where σ, τ and ω are control parameters.

Subsequently, we propose some original methods to select parameters mentioned above. For odd Gabor filter function in the form of sin ($\cdot$), the integral of the function equals to 0 referring to the interval which is symmetrical to zero. However, for even Gabor function in the form of cos ($\cdot$), the integral is not identically zero in interval symmetrical to zero. Thus static background also generates large response value refer to even Gabor filter, especially in area with high-brightness. To address this problem, appropriate parameters of τ and ω are selected to make the integral value of $-\cos(2\pi t\omega)e^{-t^2/\tau^2}$ be zero. In practice, τ is discrete and the equation can be expressed as:

$$h_{ev}(t; \tau, \omega) = -\cos(2\pi t\omega)e^{-t^2/\tau^2}. \tag{5}$$

Because the size of the selected convolution window in time dimension is limited, any one parameter of τ and ω can be computed with both the other one and the size parameter of convolution window. Take the calculation of τ for example, when the size of convolution window is in the range of [−5, 5] and $\omega = 0.9$, we get $\tau = 7.93$, but if $\omega = 0.1$ with size parameter keeps unchanged, corresponding τ doesn't exist anymore. Therefore, we choose several groups of parameters to explore the best one in advance.

Generally, parameter σ can be initialized as any arbitrary value. However, the size of convolution window in space dimension needs to be coordinated with σ as much as possible to guarantee that the weights of convolution window's edge region reach negligible small number.

2.2 Improved K-means Algorithm

The simple description of cube pixel window is to arrange it into one-dimension (1D) vector directly, but this direct pattern could make the dimensionalities of vector very large. Moreover, as the numbers of cube pixel windows extracted from each frame differ, the dimensions of corresponding arranged vector are also different. Thus we propose to utilize feature dictionary to describe cube pixel windows. Generally, the feature dictionary is acquired based on K-means clustering algorithm. Its basic idea is to cluster space points centering on k points. After k centers are randomly chosen, space points are clustered to the nearest one from k centers, and then all space points could be clustered through iteration. Specifically, the clustering centers are updated successively until the best clustering result is acquired [17–20].

The proposed algorithm expects to divide all cube pixel windows into different typical features, such as eye-open, eye-closing mouth-uptrending, knee-bending and handshakes. In order to acquire these typical features, it is very important to select reasonable initial centers and reserve the manifold structure of video data. One simple method is to choose the first few cube windows as initial clustering centers. However, K-means algorithm results in poor outcomes if the initial centers are not properly arranged.

As shown in Fig. 2, the clustering centers for the simulated data (1) are chosen as (1, 1), (1, 2) and (2, 2), then the classification results are shown in Fig. 3.

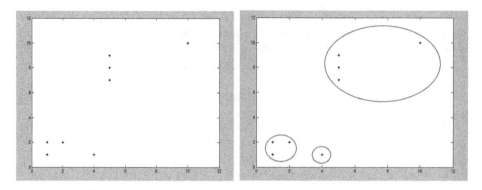

Fig. 2. Distribution of simulated data (1)   **Fig. 3.** Results after clustering (1)

Obviously, the variance of one cluster is too much bigger than the others in Fig. 3. The clustering result is so unsatisfactory that affects the final recognition results seriously. Another typical example is discussed as follows, and the distribution of simulated data (2) is shown in Fig. 4.

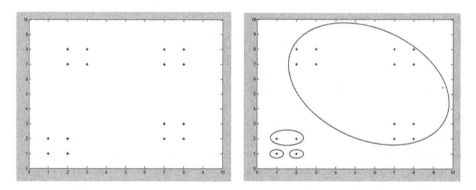

Fig. 4. Distribution of simulated data (2)   **Fig. 5.** Results after clustering (2)

As shown in Fig. 4, the clustering centers for the simulated data (2) are chosen as (1, 1), (1, 2), (2, 1) and (2, 2), and corresponding classifications are shown in Fig. 5.

Compared with Fig. 3, results after clustering in Fig. 5 are worse. Therefore a reasonable principle is required to select original clustering centers for obtaining better clustering results. The drawback of K-means algorithm is that selecting original clustering centers are quite intensive, but it is expected that the original clustering centers are far away from each other. In other words, those original centers should be loose, thus the adopted steps are as follows.

1. Choose two points with the biggest distance as two original clustering centers;
2. Find the point with the biggest distance sum to selected centers, and define the point as the original clustering center too;
3. Repeat (2) until all clustering centers are selected.

The improved K-means algorithm is deployed in the aforementioned two simulated dataset. The result is shown in Figs. 6 and 7. As we can see, our proposed algorithm achieves the result which is most near to the real. The feature dictionary is obtained after clustering all of cube pixel windows by K-means algorithm. In such method, a video data sample is compressed to one vector with the same numbers of dimensions and clustering centers, and each dimension represents the corresponding feature number in the sample feature dictionary. It has been proved that this description is simple and practical.

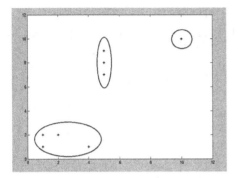   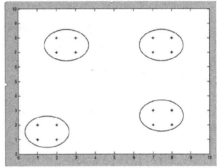

Fig. 6. Improved results after clustering (1)   **Fig. 7.** Improved results after clustering (2)

3   Experiment Results

We experiment on the dataset which is collected by Piotr Doll'ar's team (http:// vision.ucsd.edu). As shown in Fig. 8, there is a group of facial expressions from one person. The emotional expressions are anger, disgust, fearful, happy, sad and surprised. Some expressions are distinct, such as sad and happy, but some expressions are similar, such as fearful and surprised. In the experiments, each conduct is requested to repeat each expression 8 times. To simplify the segmentation process of human facial expression video sequence, every subject begins with the natural expression and ends with the natural one too.

Fig. 8. Six different facial expressions in dataset

3.1   Results with SVM Classifier

In the experiment, the size of convolution window is $5 \times 5 \times 5$, $\sigma = 6$, $\tau = 7.93$, $\omega = 0.9$. The confusion matrix results of human facial expression recognition are shown in

Table 1. Some parameters are collected to analyze their influence for results, including the size of feature dictionary and Gaussian parameters of convolution detector. With a set of experiments, a group of optimal parameters are calculated as follows: the size of convolution window is $5 \times 5 \times 5$, the size of cube pixel window is $10 \times 10 \times 5$, $\sigma = 6$, $\tau = 7.93$, $\omega = 0.9$, the size of feature dictionary is 70, the thresh value for extracting is $T = 0.25$, and complete Euclidean distance is employed for the distance formula of K-means clustering algorithm. As shown in Figs. 9 and 10, we fine-tune a few parameters to estimate optimal parameters.

Table 1. Confusion matrix of human facial expression recognition performances

	Anger	Disgust	Fearful	Happy	Sad	Surprised
Anger	0.625	0	0.125	0.125	0	0.125
Disgust	0	0.875	0.125	0	0	0
Fearful	0	0	1.0	0	0	0
Happy	0	0	0	1.0	0	0
Sad	0.125	0	0.5	0	0.375	0
Surprised	0	0	0	0	0	1.0

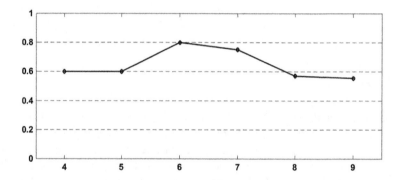

Fig. 9. The accuracy with the size of feature dictionary by SVM classifier

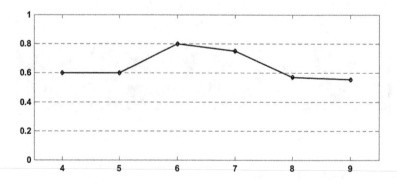

Fig. 10. The accuracy with σ in Gaussian detector

3.2   Results with Random Forest Classifier

In Table 2, we compare results of different classifiers utilizing 3D cuboids feature and improved K-means clustering method. It is shown that recognition results with Random Forest classifier are better than those with SVM [21], SRC [22, 23] and K Nearest Neighbor (KNN). The highest recognition rate is reached with the following parameters as follows: the size of cube pixel window is $20 \times 20 \times 10$, the size of convolution window for Gaussian function and Gabor function is $5 \times 5 \times 5$, $\sigma = 6$, $\tau = 7.93$, $\omega = 0.9$, the size of feature dictionary fd is 15, then the accuracy rate is 89.6 %.

Table 2. Recognition accuracy compared with other methods

	KNN	SVM	Random Forest
$\sigma = 6$ $fd = 10$	0.330	0.675	0.850
$\sigma = 6$ $fd = 15$	0.360	0.796	0.896
$\sigma = 6$ $fd = 25$	0.310	0.690	0.810
$\sigma = 6$ $fd = 30$	0.220	0.500	0.750

4   Conclusion

In this paper, we have proposed an improved K-means clustering algorithm and demonstrated the feasibility of applying a novel spatial-temporal interested point detection method to human facial expression recognition. We also introduce an extended corner detection algorithm in 3D space to extract cube pixel windows. The experimental results demonstrate that our method is practicable and effective. In the future, we would focus on fusing spatial-temporal layouts of cube pixel windows, for example the relative position information. We would discuss how to choose dimension of feature dictionary based on the results of feature extraction in our follow-on work.

Acknowledgements. This work was supported in part by the Natural Science Foundation of China under Contract 61272052, 61473086, 61672079 and 61601466, in part by PAPD, in part by CICAEET, and in part by the National Basic Research Program of China under Grant 2015CB352501. The work of B. Zhang was supported by the Program for New Century Excellent Talents University within the Ministry of Education, China, and Beijing Municipal Science & Technology Commission Z161100001616005.

References

1. Ali, S., Shah, M.: Human action recognition in videos using kinematic features and multiple instance learning. IEEE Trans. Pattern Anal. Mach. Intell. **32**(2), 288–303 (2010)
2. Wu, B., Yuan, C., Hu, W.: Human action recognition based on context-dependent graph kernels. In: Proceedings of the IEEE Conference on Computer Vision and Pattern Recognition (CVPR), pp. 2609–2616. IEEE (2014)
3. Lin, Y., Hua, J., Tang, N., Chen, M., Liao, H.: Depth and skeleton associated action recognition without online accessible rgb-d cameras. In: Proceedings of the IEEE Conference on Computer Vision and Pattern Recognition (CVPR), pp. 2617–2624. IEEE (2014)
4. Kantorov, V., Laptev, I.: Efficient feature extraction, encoding and classification for action recognition. In: Proceedings of the IEEE Conference on Computer Vision and Pattern Recognition (CVPR), pp. 2593–2600. IEEE (2014)
5. Zhang, B., Perina, A., Li, Z., Murino, V., Liu, J., Ji, R.: Bounding multiple gaussians uncertainty with application to object tracking. Int. J. Comput. Vision **118**(3), 364–379 (2016)
6. Du, Y., Wang, W., Wang, L.: Hierarchical recurrent neural network for skeleton based action recognition. In: Proceedings of the IEEE Conference on Computer Vision and Pattern Recognition (CVPR), pp. 1110–1118. IEEE (2015)
7. Zhang, H., Zhou, W., Reardon, C., Parker, L.: Simplex-based 3D spatio-temporal feature description for action recognition. In: Proceedings of the IEEE Conference on Computer Vision and Pattern Recognition (CVPR), pp. 2059–2066. IEEE (2014)
8. Zhang, B., Li, Z., Perina, A., Del Bue, A., Murino, V.: Adaptive Local Movement Modelling (ALMM) for object tracking. IEEE Trans. Circuits Syst. Video Technol. **99**(1051–8215), 1 (2016)
9. Wang, J., Wu, Y.: Learning maximum margin temporal warping for action recognition. In: Proceedings of the IEEE Conference on Computer Vision and Pattern Recognition (CVPR), pp. 2688–2695. IEEE (2013
10. Ballas, N., Yang, Y., Lan, Z., Delezoide, B., Preteux, F., Hauptmann, A.: Space-time robust representation for action recognition. In: Proceedings of the IEEE International Conference on Computer Vision (ICCV), pp. 2704–2711. IEEE (2013)
11. Zheng, J., Jiang, Z.: Learning view-invariant sparse representations for cross-view action recognition. In: Proceedings of the IEEE International Conference on Computer Vision (ICCV), pp. 3176–3183. IEEE (2013)
12. Tulsiani, S., Malik, J.: Viewpoints and keypoints. In: Proceedings of the IEEE Conference on Computer Vision and Pattern Recognition (CVPR), pp. 1510–1519. IEEE (2015)
13. Laptev, I.: On space-time interest points. Int. J. Comput. Vision **64**(2), 107–123 (2005)
14. Dollár, P., Rabaud, V., Cottrell, G., Belongie, S.: Behavior recognition via sparse spatio-temporal features. In: Proceedings of the IEEE International Workshop on Visual Surveillance and Performance Evaluation of Tracking and Surveillance (PETS), pp. 65–72. IEEE (2005)
15. Lowe, D.: Distinctive image features from scale-invariant key points. Int. J. Comput. Vision **60**(2), 91–110 (2004)
16. Yang, M., Zhang, L.: Gabor feature based sparse representation for face recognition with gabor occlusion dictionary. In: Daniilidis, K., Maragos, P., Paragios, N. (eds.) ECCV 2010. LNCS, vol. 6316, pp. 448–461. Springer, Heidelberg (2010). doi:10.1007/978-3-642-15567-3_33
17. Celebi, M., Kingravi, H., Vela, P.: A comparative study of efficient initialization methods for the k-means clustering algorithm. Int. J. Expert Syst. Appl. **40**(1), 200–210 (2013)
18. Ghosh, S., Dubey, S.: Comparative analysis of K-means and fuzzy C-means algorithms. Int. J. Adv. Comput. Sci. Appl. **4**(4), 34–39 (2013)

19. Wen, X., Shao, L., Xue, Y., Fang, W.: A rapid learning algorithm for vehicle classification. Inf. Sci. **295**(1), 395–406 (2015)
20. Zheng, Y., Jeon, B., Xu, D., Wu, Q., Zhang, H.: Image segmentation by generalized hierarchical fuzzy C-means algorithm. J. Intell. Fuzzy Syst. **28**(2), 961–973 (2015)
21. Gu, B., Sheng, V., Tay, K., Romano, W., Li, S.: Incremental support vector learning for ordinal regression. IEEE Trans. Neural Netw. Learn. Syst. **26**(7), 1403–1416 (2015)
22. Zhang, B., Perina, A., Murino, V., Del Bue, A.: Sparse representation classification with manifold constraints transfer. In: Proceedings of the IEEE Conference on Computer Vision and Pattern Recognition (CVPR), pp. 4557–4565 (2015)
23. Li, J., Li, X., Yang, B., Sun, X.: Segmentation-based image copy-move forgery detection scheme. IEEE Trans. Inf. Forensics Secur. **10**(3), 507–518 (2015)

Multimedia Security and Forensics

Palmprint Matching by Minutiae and Ridge Distance

Jiali Chen and Zhenhua Guo[✉]

Graduate School at Shenzhen, Tsinghua University, Shenzhen 518055, China
chenjiali_cjl@foxmail.com,
zhenhua.guo@sz.tsinghua.edu.in

Abstract. Palmprint is an essential biometrics for personal identification, especially in forensic security. Due to the large valid region of palmprint, palmprint recognition is very time-consuming. Fast and accurate palmprint recognition is an urge problem. To speed up matching, some methods based on classification and indexing are proposed, in which accuracy may be dropped. Ridge distance is often used as an auxiliary feature in palmprint recognition. In this paper, a novel minutiae matching algorithm incorporating ridge distance is proposed. Firstly, we incorporate ridge distance to conventional minutiae. Then, with the restriction of ridge distance, palmprint alignment could be greatly sped up. Experimental results show that our method could not only reduce time cost for matching, but also improve matching accuracy.

Keywords: Minutiae · Ridge distance · Palmprint identification

1 Introduction

Nowadays biometric recognition systems are playing more and more important role in security applications. Among them, palmprint recognition is one of the most widely used in both forensic and civil applications, for its high level of reliability and convenience [1]. Palmprint has a much larger valid area and contains much more features than fingerprint, indicating palmprint is more discriminative than fingerprint [2].

Although lots of palmprint matching systems have achieved good matching accuracy, palmprint matching is still not fast enough for large databases. It is mainly because palmprint matching is more complex than fingerprint matching. For example, a typical fingerprint (500 * 500 pixels, 500 ppi) contains about 100 minutiae, while the average number of minutiae in a typical palmprint (2040 * 2040 pixels, 500 ppi) is 800. Assuming the complexity of the algorithm is $O(n^2)$, where n denotes the number of minutiae in the fingerprint or palmprint, palmprint matching is 64 times slower than fingerprint. Thus, complexity improvement is a critical problem in palmprint matching.

There are mainly three approaches to solve the above mentioned problem, palmprint classification (classifying palmprints into disjoint categories), indexing (continuous classification) [1, 3] and other methods. Unlike fingerprint, there is no widely accepted classification criterion for palmprint classification. Existing works are mainly based on principal lines [4, 5]. However in high-resolution palmprint the middle part of the print is often missing due to metacarpal bones and touch-based capture method, so

© Springer International Publishing AG 2016
X. Sun et al. (Eds.): ICCCS 2016, Part II, LNCS 10040, pp. 371–382, 2016.
DOI: 10.1007/978-3-319-48674-1_33

few palmprints contain all the principal lines. Thus this approach is only used in low-resolution and touchless palmprint recognition. Indexing is another more popular way [6–8]. Some of these techniques are based on line feature [9], minutiae [8, 10–12], texture feature [13–15] and so on. Most of these methods need additional retrieving process to maintain the accuracy. Besides the above mentioned methods, there are some other research work, such as hierarchical way [16], coarse matching [6], and region-based matching [17]. Yet most of them are based on some specific conditions, for example, calibration.

Like fingerprint, palmprint friction ridge features are generally described at three different levels: level-1 features such as principle line, level-2 features such as minutiae, and level-3 features such as pores and ridge contours. Among them, minutiae are considered as the uppermost feature. Alignment as an essential process in palmprint matching is mostly done through Generalized Hough Transformation (GHT) using minutiae [17–19]. Density map and other features are aligned by the transformation parameters. However it's very time-consuming. Besides, spurious and missing minutiae also make the problem difficult.

In order to speed up the palmprint matching, we propose a novel minutiae matching algorithm incorporating ridge distance. The main advantage of our proposal is that, unlike other methods, there is no need of retrieving and the accuracy is improved. Firstly, we add ridge distance to every single conventional minutia. With this extra information minutiae are proved to be more discriminative. Then the difference of ridge distances near the minutiae is calculated, and only the pairs with similar ridge distance are considered during GHT voting. Thus the number of minutiae comparison is greatly reduced. Our method can not only reduce time cost, but also improve the accuracy considerably. Since ridge distance is simultaneously extracted with orientation field [18], it costs tiny computation.

The rest of the paper is organized as follows. In Sect. 2, we introduce some previous knowledge. In Sect. 3, we describe our new method. In Sect. 4, experimental results are represented. Finally, in Sect. 5, some conclusions are drawn.

2   Previous Work

In this section we mainly discussed the two important features, minutiae and ridge distance. To align two sets of minutiae, GHT is also introduced. After transforming one set of minutiae, score of two palmprints can be calculated.

2.1   Ridge Distance Estimation

Palmprint and fingerprint ridge distance is defined as the length of the segment connecting the centers of two adjacent and parallel ridges along the line perpendicular to the ridges, as showed in Fig. 1 [20]. Strictly speaking, the ridge distance we used here is local average ridge distance in the blocksize of 16 * 16 pixels, which forms density map. In this case, we firstly draw the density map, and then define the ridge distance of the blocksize where the minutia locates as minutiae ridge distance. There are mainly

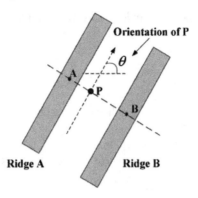

Fig. 1. Illustration of ridge distance. The distance between point A and B is the ridge distance at point P.

two ways to compute ridge distance. One is geometric method, and the other is spectral method [21]. Formally speaking, ridge period in the spectral method is not the same as ridge distance despite the frequent interchangeability of these two terms in the literature.

In this paper, we used the method proposed in paper [18], in which density map is simultaneously obtained with orientation field. The orientation field is extracted by the composed algorithm consisting of discrete Fourier transformation (DFT) [19] and Radon transformation [18], then a region growing algorithm [19] is used for post-smoothing.

After the orientation field estimation and binarization of the enhanced image, ridge distance is extracted following the geometric way proposed in paper [20]. To get the coarse density map, we draw a line passing the given point perpendicular to the ridges, and then detect the nearest two central points of two neighboring ridges on the line. The distance between the two center points is defined as the ridge distance on that point. Then a weighted polynomial approximation is added for improvement and smoothness. The polynomial is written as:

$$p(x,y) = \sum_{i=0}^{n} \sum_{j=0}^{n} a_{ij} x^i y^j \qquad (1)$$

where n is the order of the polynomial, p denotes the modified ridge distance, x and y represent the x-coordinate and y-coordinate respectively. The coefficients of the polynomial can be obtained through Weighted Least Square (WLS) algorithm by minimizing the weighted square error between the polynomial and the coarse density map, the minimizing function is as follows,

$$J = \sum_{k=1}^{K} w_k [z_k(x_k, y_k) - p(x_k, y_k)]^2 \qquad (2)$$

where K denotes the number of samples, $z_k(x_k, y_k)$ is the density value at (x_k, y_k), and w_k is a weight factor on the point (x_k, y_k). w_k is calculated as follows:

$$w_k = \exp\left(-\frac{\sigma^2}{8}\right) \tag{3}$$

where σ^2 denotes the variance of ridge distance computed in the neighborhood of the given point.

In order to solve the Eq. (2), a singular value decomposition method (SVD) is used [22]. And the polynomial order is set to 4 ($n = 4$) for the tradeoff between complexity and accuracy.

2.2   Minutiae Extraction

Minutiae are extracted as the ending and bifurcation points of ridge lines. After image preprocessing, orientation field extraction, ridge enhancement, binarization and thinning, minutiae extraction is performed. The minutiae set of a palmprint is denoted by $M_q = \{m_1, m_2, ..., m_l\}$, where $m_i = \{x_i, y_i, \theta_i\}$, x_i, y_i and θ_i represent the i th minutiae's x-coordinate, y-coordinate and direction, respectively. And l is the number of minutiae.

2.3   Minutiae Alignment

Alignment of two minutiae sets M_q and M_t is a key process of matching. In order to calculate the matching minutiae pairs, the two minutiae sets should be registered with certain translation and rotation. It is essentially a point pattern matching problem and is usually solved by GHT voting [23] with the time-complexity of $O(vw)$, where v denote the number of minutiae in set M_q and w in M_t. Table 1 summarizes the main procedure.

3   Proposed Method

In this section, we introduce our new minutiae representation, and its applications in both alignment and matching score.

3.1   New Minutiae Representation

As minutiae ridge distance does not change along the rigid transformation, and it has good discrimination in palmprint images. So based on the traditional minutiae $m_i(x_i, y_i, \theta_i)$, we add the ridge distance d_i in the neighborhood of the given minutiae point [18]. Thus we get a more powerful minutia representation $p_i(x_i, y_i, \theta_i, d_i)$. In this situation, two minutiae are considered as matched with an additional condition:

Table 1. Pseudocode of the GHT voting algorithm.

Function Alignment(M_q, M_t)

Input: the minutiae set, M_q and M_t

Output: the transformation parameters, (Δx, Δy, $\Delta \theta$)

set V, the voting space;

for each m_i in M_q **do**

  for each m_j in M_t **do**

    Compute translation parameters

$$\theta^+ = \min(|\theta_i - \theta_j|, 360 - |\theta_i - \theta_j|)$$

$$\Delta \theta_k^+ = \arg \min_{\theta_t \in V} |\theta^+ - \theta_t|$$

$$\begin{bmatrix} \Delta x^+ \\ \Delta y^+ \end{bmatrix} = \begin{bmatrix} x_j \\ y_j \end{bmatrix} - \begin{bmatrix} \cos \theta_k^+ & -\sin \theta_k^+ \\ \sin \theta_k^+ & \cos \theta_k^+ \end{bmatrix} \begin{bmatrix} x_i \\ y_i \end{bmatrix}$$

$$\Delta x_k^+ = \arg \min_{\Delta x_t \in V} |\Delta x^+ - \Delta x_t|$$

$$\Delta y_k^+ = \arg \min_{\Delta y_t \in V} |\Delta y^+ - \Delta y_t|$$

$$V|\Delta x_k^+, \Delta y_k^+, \Delta \theta_k^+ \models V|\Delta x_k^+, \Delta y_k^+, \Delta \theta_k^+| + 1$$

  end

end

$$(\Delta x, \Delta y, \Delta \theta) = \arg \max_{\Delta x_t^+, \Delta y_t^+, \theta_t^+} V[\Delta x_t^+, \Delta y_t^+, \Delta \theta_t^+]$$

$$|d_i - d_j| < Thresh_d, \tag{4}$$

where $Thresh_d$ is set for tolerance of distortion error.

3.2 Minutiae Alignment

In the proposed alignment method we make use of the ridge distance in a quite different way. Figure 2 shows the minutiae ridge distance is universally distributed between 7–14 pixels in palmprint. This also shows discriminative ability of ridge distance. We index the minutiae according to their ridge distance. In the GHT-based alignment stage, only the minutiae with similar ridge distance are considered. This physical indexing decreases the spurious minutiae during Hough transformation voting greatly, as shows in Fig. 3. Although there is a general decrease in similarity score, the drop between impressions from different palms is rapid, which can distinguish the true pairs. And the

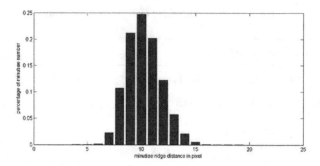

Fig. 2. The average distribution of minutiae ridge distance in a full palmprint.

general decrease is mainly because of the stricter criterions during scoring stage. Our method also makes a speedup with less computation. Table 2 summarizes the main procedure.

3.3 Matching Score Computation

From the above generalized Hough transformation, we get the translation and rotation parameters. With these parameters, the query minutiae set P_q is transformed. Then greedy match is performed between each minutiae pair, only the pair that satisfies Eq. (4), spatial and angle criterions is counted as a matched minutiae pair. With the additional strict condition, spurious minutiae pairs will be reduced obviously. The minutiae score is calculated as follows,

$$S = \sqrt{\frac{N^2_{matched}}{N_q N_t}}, \tag{5}$$

where N_q and N_t denote the number of minutiae in set P_q and P_t. $N_{matched}$ is the number of matched minutiae pairs.

During the matching score stage, minutiae pairs also follow the strict new criterion (4) as well as the conventional conditions. There is a tendency that minutiae share high consistency in the neighborhood. This makes trouble in matching minutiae pairs, since a given minutia is probably have several corresponding minutiae. With the more strict condition, spurious minutiae pairs will be reduced obviously. Thus this problem will ease. In our matching score process, if a minutiae in the query minutiae set find its minutiae pair in the template set, then it is counted as a matched pair and skip to the next minutiae in the query minutiae set. Thus, each minutia in the query set is counted at most once.

Table 2. Pseudocode of the proposed alignment algorithm.

Function Alignment(P_q , P_t)

Input: the minutiae set, P_q and P_t

Output: the transformation parameters, (Δx , Δy , $\Delta \theta$)

set V, the voting space;;

for each p_i in P_q **do**

  for each p_j in P_t **do**

    ridgeDist $= | d_i - d_j |$

    if ridgeDist < $Thresh_d$

$$\theta^+ = \min(|\theta_i - \theta_j|, 360 - |\theta_i - \theta_j|)$$

$$\Delta\theta_k^+ = \arg \min_{\theta_t \in V} |\theta^+ - \theta_t|$$

$$\begin{bmatrix} \Delta x^+ \\ \Delta y^+ \end{bmatrix} = \begin{bmatrix} x_j \\ y_j \end{bmatrix} - \begin{bmatrix} \cos\theta_k^+ & -\sin\theta_k^+ \\ \sin\theta_k^+ & \cos\theta_k^+ \end{bmatrix} \begin{bmatrix} x_i \\ y_i \end{bmatrix}$$

$$\Delta x_k^+ = \arg \min_{\Delta x_t \in V} |\Delta x^+ - \Delta x_t|$$

$$\Delta y_k^+ = \arg \min_{\Delta y_t \in V} |\Delta y^+ - \Delta y_t|$$

$$V|\Delta x_k^+, \Delta y_k^+, \Delta\theta_k^+ |= V|\Delta x_k^+, \Delta y_k^+, \Delta\theta_k^+ |+1$$

  end

  end Δy_k^+

end

(Δx , Δy , $\Delta \theta$) = $\arg \max_{\Delta x_t^+, \Delta y_t^+, \theta_t^+} V[\Delta x_t^{+}, \Delta y_t^{+}, \Delta\theta_t^{+}]$

---

4   Experimental Results

This section mainly describes the experiments carried out for performance comparison between previous work and our proposed method.

4.1   Database and Evaluation Protocol

Experiments are conducted on the public available high-resolution palmprint database, the Tsinghua Palmprint Database (THUPALMLAB) [24]. It contains 1280 palmprint images from 80 subjects, two palms per person (one left palm, and one right palm) and

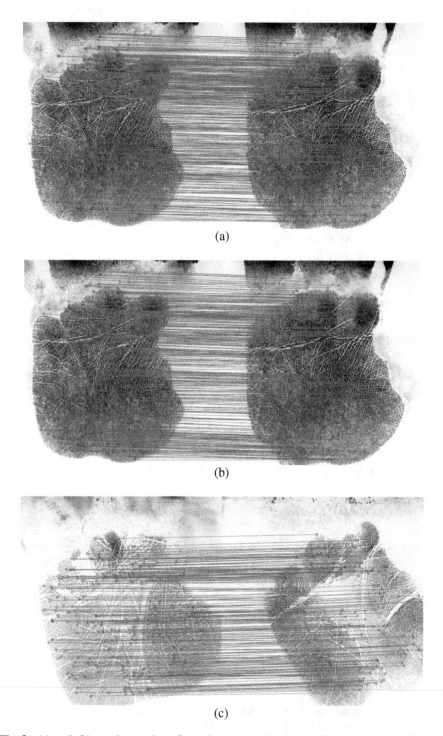

Fig. 3. (a) and (b) are impressions from the same palm, (a) similarity score is 0.2986 in conventional method. (b) similarity score is 0.2579 in our proposed method. (c) and (d) are impressions from different palms. (c) similarity score is 0.2121. (d) similarity score is 0.06922.

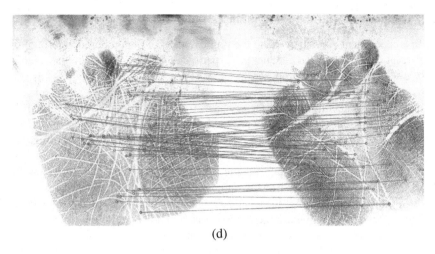

(d)

Fig. 3. (continued)

eight impressions per palm. The image is 2040 * 2040 pixels. The resolution is 500 PPI with 256 gray levels. They were all collected by a Hisign palm scanner [24]. In our experiments, we separate the THUPALMLAB database into two sets: (1) training set and (2) test set. The former contains 320 palmprints (from 40 different palms). The latter contains the rest 960 palmprints (from 120 different palms). Training set is used to empirically select parameters and test set is used evaluate performance.

The protocol used to evaluate the proposed method is as the following:

- Genuine match: each impression is compared against other impressions of the same palm to calculate the false rejection rate (FRR). The total number of genuine match is: (8 * 7/2) * 120 = 3360. FalseRejectionNumber is the number of different impressions from the same palm with lower similarity.

$$FRR = \frac{FalseRejectionNumber}{GenuineMatchNumber} * 100\%$$

- Imposter match: each impression is compared against each impression of other palms to compute the false acceptance rate (FAR). The total number of imposter match number is ((8 * 120) * (8 * 119)/2) = 456960. FalseAcceptionNumber is the number of impressions from different palms with higher similarity.

$$FAR = \frac{FalseAcceptionNumber}{ImposterMatchNumber} * 100\%$$

- Equal Error Rate (EER) is the value when FRR is equal to FAR.
- Area Under Curve (AUC) represents the area below the Receiver Operating Characteristic (ROC). The AUC value is equivalent to the probability that a randomly chosen positive example is ranked higher than a randomly chosen negative example.

4.2   Comparison with the Conventional Minutiae-Based Algorithm

The first experiment aims to evaluate the improvement of the proposed algorithm over the conventional method. To conduct the experiment, we obtain the minutiae and ridge distance with the algorithm proposed in paper [17].

As the ROC curves show in Fig. 4, our proposed method shows great superiority than the conventional one in almost every aspect. As show in Table 3, the EER values of the conventional method and proposed method are 0.65 % and 0.29 %, respectively. This drop of EER mainly benefit from more accurate alignment and scoring, since spurious minutiae pairs decrease, as shown in Fig. 3. As for the speed, our proposed method also shows satisfying performance. The matching time falls to 89 ms from 195 ms. This improvement is because indexing based on the ridge distance cut the greedy minutiae comparisons during the GHT-based alignment. The computational costs of different algorithms are measured on a PC with Intel(R) core (TM) i7 CPU 2.8 GHz and Windows 8 × 64 operating system. The algorithm is written in C++ language. As for the additional extraction time for ridge distance, since density map is extracted simultaneously with the orientation field, the execution time of the ridge distance from density map is limited.

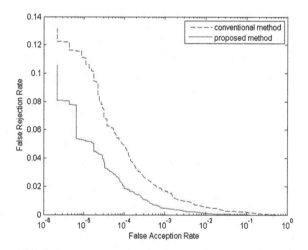

Fig. 4. The ROC curves of the conventional GHT-based minutiae matching algorithm and the proposed method on THUPALMLAB.

Table 3. Performance comparison of conventional method and the proposed method.

	EER	AUC	Time
Conventional method	0.65 %	0.9992	195 ms
The proposed method	**0.29 %**	**0.9999**	**89 ms**

4.3   Comparisons with Other Methods

We compare our proposed method with two state-of-art algorithms. One is the hierarchical matching approach in paper [16], the other is procedure proposed in paper [17]. As show in Table 4 our method is faster and with a much lower EER than approach in [16]. The hierarchical method is rather unstable due to the limitation of threshold (the max value in voting space), since the voting space is considerably sparse, which means a change of threshold will bring great change of result. Compared with approach in [17], our method also perform satisfyingly.

Table 4. Comparisons of the proposed method with approaches in [16, 17], H means the number of decomposed steps [16].

		EER	AUC	Time
Chen et al. [16]	H = 1	0.65 %	0.9992	195 ms
	H = 2	1.31 %	0.9911	152 ms
	H = 3	1.86 %	0.9855	130 ms
	H = 4	2.14 %	0.9815	135 ms
	H = 5	1.12 %	0.9940	110 ms
Dai and Zhou [17]		2.69 %	0.9854	2150 ms (calibration) + 17.2 ms (matching)
The Proposed method		**0.29 %**	**0.9999**	**89 ms**

5   Conclusion

In this paper, a novel algorithm for palmprint minutiae identification is proposed, which not only saves the matching time, but also improves the accuracy. Through the simple comparison of the ridge distance, spurious minutiae comparisons are greatly reduced. At the same time, the accuracy improves. Experimental results show that the proposed algorithm cost less time and reduce EER greatly. It can also be integrated to other identification or verification systems conveniently. In our future work, we will study this method to local matching for palmprint.

References

1. Kong, A., Zhang, D., Kamel, M.: A survey of palmprint recognition. Pattern Recogn. **42**(7), 1408–1418 (2009)
2. Jain, A.K., Ross, A., Prabhakar, S.: An introduction to biometric recognition. IEEE Trans. Circuits Syst. Video Technol. **14**(1), 4–20 (2004)
3. Maltoni, D., et al.: Handbook of fingerprint recognition. Springer, London (2009)
4. Wu, X., et al.: Palmprint classification using principal lines. Pattern Recogn. **37**(10), 1987–1998 (2004)
5. Fang, L., et al.: Palmprint classification. In: IEEE International Conference on Systems, Man and Cybernetics, SMC 2006. IEEE (2006)

6. Yang, X., Feng, J., Zhou, J.: Palmprint indexing based on ridge features. In: 2011 International Joint Conference on Biometrics (IJCB). IEEE (2011)

7. Paulino, A.A., et al.: Latent fingerprint indexing: fusion of level 1 and level 2 features. In: 2013 IEEE Sixth International Conference on Biometrics: Theory, Applications and Systems (BTAS). IEEE (2013)

8. Muñoz-Briseño, A., Hernández-Palancar, J., Gago-Alonso, A.: Minutiae based palmprint indexing. In: Garain, U., Shafait, F. (eds.) IWCF 2012 and 2014. LNCS, vol. 8915, pp. 10–19. Springer, Heidelberg (2015)

9. Li, F., Leung, M.K.: Hierarchical identification of palmprint using line-based hough transform. In: 18th International Conference on Pattern Recognition, ICPR 2006. IEEE (2006)

10. Cappelli, R., Ferrara, M., Maltoni, D.: Minutia cylinder-code: a new representation and matching technique for fingerprint recognition. IEEE Trans. Pattern Anal. Mach. Intell. **32** (12), 2128–2141 (2010)

11. Cappelli, R., Ferrara, M., Maltoni, D.: Fingerprint indexing based on minutia cylinder-code. IEEE Trans. Pattern Anal. Mach. Intell. **33**(5), 1051–1057 (2011)

12. Cappelli, R., Ferrara, M., Maio, D.: A fast and accurate palmprint recognition system based on minutiae. IEEE Trans. Syst. Man Cybern. Part B Cybern. **42**(3), 956–962 (2012)

13. Paliwal, A., Jayaraman, U., Gupta, P.: A score based indexing scheme for palmprint databases. In: 2010 17th IEEE International Conference on Image Processing (ICIP). IEEE (2010)

14. Li, W., You, J., Zhang, D.: Texture-based palmprint retrieval using a layered search scheme for personal identification. IEEE Trans. Multimedia **7**(5), 891–898 (2005)

15. Yue, F., et al.: Hashing based fast palmprint identification for large-scale databases. IEEE Trans. Inf. Forensics Secur. **8**(5), 769–778 (2013)

16. Chen, F., Huang, X.: Zhou, J: Hierarchical minutiae matching for fingerprint and palmprint identification. IEEE Trans. Image Process. **22**(12), 4964–4971 (2013)

17. Dai, J., Feng, J., Zhou, J.: Robust and efficient ridge-based palmprint matching. IEEE Trans. Pattern Anal. Mach. Intell. **34**(8), 1618–1632 (2012)

18. Dai, J., Zhou, J.: Multifeature-based high-resolution palmprint recognition. IEEE Trans. Pattern Anal. Mach. Intell. **33**(5), 945–957 (2011)

19. Jain, A.K., Feng, J.: Latent palmprint matching. IEEE Trans. Pattern Anal. Mach. Intell. **31** (6), 1032–1047 (2009)

20. Wan, D., Zhou, J.: Fingerprint recognition using model-based density map. IEEE Trans. Image Process. **15**(6), 1690–1696 (2006)

21. Choi, H., Choi, K., Kim, J.: Fingerprint matching incorporating ridge features with minutiae. IEEE Trans. Inf. Forensics Secur. **6**(2), 338–345 (2011)

22. Press, W.H.: Numerical Recipes. The Art of Scientific Computing, 3rd edn. Cambridge University Press, Cambridge (2007)

23. Ratha, N.K., et al.: A real-time matching system for large fingerprint databases. IEEE Trans. Pattern Anal. Mach. Intell. **18**(8), 799–813 (1996)

24. Tsinghua Univ. Dept. Autom., i-Vision Group Web Site. http://ivg.au.tsinghua.edu.cn

Anomaly Detection Algorithm for Helicopter Rotor Based on STFT and SVDD

Yun He[✉] and Dechang Pi

College of Computer Science and Technology,
Nanjing University of Aeronautics and Astronautics,
29 Jiangjun Avenue, Nanjing 210016, Jiangsu, People's Republic of China
1561850387@qq.com, dc.pi@nuaa.edu.cn

Abstract. Anomaly detection for helicopter rotor provides fault early warning and failure detection to avoid catastrophic accidents and major downtime. It is difficult to extract effective fault features from non-stationary and non-linear vibration data of rotor. A novel time-frequency feature is presented based on short-time Fourier transform in the paper. Due to lack of abundant fault data in practice, support vector data description is also exploited to detect damages by building a model only with normal data. We experimentally evaluate the performance of the proposed anomaly detection on realistic vibration data of helicopter rotor. The results demonstrate that the time-frequency features are closely related to the states of rotor, and the anomaly detection algorithm can clearly detect damages.

Keywords: Anomaly detection · Helicopter rotor · Time-frequency features · Short-time fourier transform · Support vector data description

1 Introduction

Helicopter rotor as a lifting and controlling surface is vital to flight safety [1]. Once it breaks down, it would lead to catastrophic accidents and major downtime [2]. To ensure helicopter rotor safety and reliability, maintenance inspections, parts replacement and overhauls must be performed regularly. But maintenance is a kind of expensive and time-consuming task. Fortunately, anomaly detection can solve such problems for helicopter rotor system.

Anomaly detection refers to the process of finding the unexpected patterns in data whose behavior is abnormal [3]. These unexpected patterns are often called anomalies or outliers, which imply critical actionable information [4]. There are three main steps for helicopter rotor system's anomaly detection: the first step is feature extraction from rotor vibration data, the second is to build a model based on normal features, and the third one is anomaly detection.

There are many studies about fault classification for helicopter rotor, mostly focused on imbalance fault, but seldom on anomaly detection. Some conventional damage diagnoses utilize classification algorithms, especially, artificial neural networks and support vector machines which have achieved remarkable results in classification [5]. However, these classification algorithms require plenty of fault data, which makes

© Springer International Publishing AG 2016
X. Sun et al. (Eds.): ICCCS 2016, Part II, LNCS 10040, pp. 383–393, 2016.
DOI: 10.1007/978-3-319-48674-1_34

it difficult to detect diagnosis for helicopter rotor with its limited fault data. According to the situation above, only normal data is available, based on which whether the rotor appears abnormal is need to be detected. The problem of anomaly detection is more common in real-world applications, and also harder than conventional damage diagnosis [6]. Thus support vector data description (SVDD) [7] is introduced to detect damages. One of the great advantages to use SVDD is that there is no need for any prior knowledge of the detected object [8]. SVDD can build a flexible description boundary to construct a hyper-sphere in feature space. The hyper-sphere tends to enclose most of normal samples and minimize the chance of accepting anomalies simultaneously. The sample within the hyper-sphere is regarded as the normal, otherwise, an anomaly.

How to extract features from vibration data is another key problem in anomaly detection of helicopter rotor system. Due to the complicated structure and working condition, the vibration data of rotor is non-stationary and nonlinear. It is difficult to detect anomaly in an effective way only in time domain or frequency domain. The time-frequency method displays the time and the frequency information together in two-dimension. Typical time-frequency methods include short-time Fourier transform (STFT), wavelet analysis, Wigner-Ville distribution, Choi-Williams distribution and Hilbert-Huang transform [9].

This research aims to propose an anomaly detection method for helicopter rotor. As a result of extensive attempts, an effective feature extraction method is presented to obtain rotor fault features. And SVDD is used to detect anomalies by building a model with normal data [10]. Besides, the vibration data is collected on the real helicopter rotor. We experimentally find the appropriate dimension of fault features, and then compare them with common statistical features.

The rest of the paper is organized as follows. Section 2 describes the experimental data sets. In Sect. 3, time-frequency is presented and the anomaly detection method is introduced in Sect. 4. Section 5 experimentally demonstrates the effectiveness of the proposed method. Finally the conclusion summarizes the paper in Sect. 6.

2   Experimental Data

The experimental data sets are provided by China Helicopter Research and Development Institute. The rotor rotating speed is 212 rpm, and these five vibration data sets are sampled at 4096 Hz during 1500 s. Figure 1 shows five original vibration signals denoted by *data1*, *data2*, *data3*, *data4*, and *data5*.

Five data sets are measured from three accelerometers denoted by *ac1*, *ac2* and *ac3*, which are attached to different locations of a real helicopter. The detailed locations are shown with the blue arrow in Fig. 2.

data1 and *data2* are collected by *ac1* in two different directions. Similarly, *data4* and *data5* are from *ac3*. And *data3* comes from *ac2*.

According to experts' description, the rotor performed normally within the first 500 s. After that, a minor failure occurred at 1075 s.

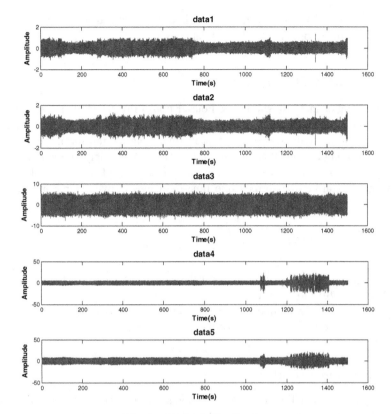

Fig. 1. Original vibration data

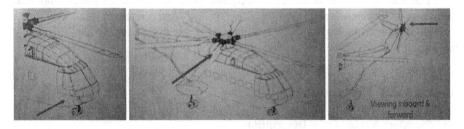

Fig. 2. Installation positions of *ac1*, (left), *ac2* (median) and *ac3* (right) (Color figure online)

3 Feature Extraction

Vibration signals of helicopter rotor are complicated and contain a great deal of information. With the rotor state changing, the vibration signals will change simultaneously. Selecting appropriate analysis tools can make anomaly detection much easier and more reliable. The feature extraction method is based on short time Fourier transform (STFT). STFT is chosen to obtain both the time and frequency information because of its simple principle and good capacity [9].

3.1 Short Time Fourier Transform

Proposed by Gabor in 1946, short time Fourier transform (STFT) is a typical method for time-frequency analysis, and it has been widely used in signal processing field [11]. STFT is a significant improvement of proverbial Fourier transform. Time window which moves along the signal is introduced to STFT. By multiplying the time window and signals, the non-stationary signal are approximately considered as a local stationary process, then it can be transformed into time-frequency domain. Time indexed spectrum is captured as formula (1).

$$STFT(t, \omega) = \int x(\tau)g(\tau - t)\exp(-j\omega\tau)d\tau \tag{1}$$

where $x(t)$ is the signal to be considered, t is the time, and the ω is the frequency. $g(t)$ is a sliding window function, and Hanning window is the most popular one. In our study, we just consider the amplitude spectrum of $STFT(t, \omega)$ which contains rotor fault information that we need, regardless of the phase spectrum.

3.2 Fault Feature Extraction

Assume that the rotational frequency of helicopter rotor is f. The amplitude spectrum of f and its multiple-frequencies always contain rich information about rotor state, which can be exploited to detect rotor anomalies. For signal $x(t)$, STFT is applied to obtain the joint distribution of time domain and frequency domain. Then we select amplitude spectrums of harmonic frequencies, i.e. f, $2f$, $3f \ldots nf$. And n refers to multiplier. These n amplitude spectrums construct the fault feature matrix of helicopter rotor. The data of the feature matrix will be normalized into $[-1, 1]$.

4 Anomaly Detection Algorithm

4.1 Support Vector Data Description

Support vector data description (SVDD) is one-class classification method. The goal of SVDD is to minimize the volume of the hyper-sphere which encloses most normal data. Capturing the minimum feature space can reduce the probability of accepting outlier samples. Assume that the target dataset $X = \{x_1, x_2, \ldots, x_n\}$, and the optimization function is constructed as formula (2).

$$\min_{R,a,\xi} \quad R^2 + C\sum_{i=1}^{l} \xi_i \qquad s.t. \quad ||\phi(xi) - a|| \leq R^2 + \xi_i, \qquad \xi_i \geq 0, \quad i = 1, \ldots, n \tag{2}$$

Where R and a are the radius and center of the hyper-sphere respectively. ξ_i represents the error term, and function $\phi(\cdot)$ can map x_i into a higher dimensional feature space. To avoid over-fitting, penalty parameter C is introduced when data point x_i locates outside the hyper-sphere. Formula (3) is the Lagrange dual problem.

$$\min_{\alpha} \sum_{i=1}^{n}\sum_{j=1}^{n}\alpha_i\alpha_j(\phi(x_i)\cdot\phi(x_j)) - \sum_{i=1}^{n}\alpha_i(\phi(x_i)\cdot\phi(x_i)) \quad s.t. \quad \sum_{i=1}^{n}\alpha_i=1, \; 0\leq\alpha_i\leq C, i=1,2,\ldots,n$$

(3)

where α_i is a Lagrange multiplier. Generally, $(\phi(x_i)\cdot\phi(x_j))$ is replaced by Gaussian radial basis function $K(x_i, x_j)$. Assume that the number of support vectors is N_{sv}, and x_m is a support vector, then

$$a = \sum_{i=1}^{n}\alpha_i K(x_i, x_i)$$

(4)

$$R^2 = K(x_m, x_m) - 2\sum_{i}^{N_{sv}}\alpha_i K(x_i, x_m) + \sum_{i=1}^{N_{sv}}\sum_{j=1}^{N_{sv}}\alpha_i\alpha_j K(x_i, x_j)$$

(5)

For a new sample x, the distance from the center a is calculate as formula (6),

$$d = ||x - a||^2 = K(x,x) - 2\sum_{i}^{N_{sv}}\alpha_i K(x_i, x) + \sum_{i=1}^{N_{sv}}\sum_{j=1}^{N_{sv}}\alpha_i\alpha_j K(x_i, x_j)$$

(6)

To test a new sample x, the decision function is defined as formula (7)

$$f(x) = ||x - a||^2 - R^2 = d - R^2$$

(7)

Generally $f(x) \leq 0$, x is regarded as the normal data. If the decision values of multiple sequential samples are larger than zero, it will be determined as failures.

4.2 Anomaly Detection Scheme Based on STFT and SVDD

The flow chart of the whole strategy is presented in Fig. 3. The implementation steps are briefly described as follows.

- In the stage of fault feature extraction, STFT is chosen to realize the time-frequency analysis, then the amplitude spectrums of specific frequencies are obtained to form feature matrix, and finally the matrix is normalized.
- The data is divided into two sets: training set and testing set. When training, SVDD is selected to construct the hype-sphere on the feature of training set. Then the center a and radius R are obtained.
- In testing stage, the testing set is detected by the exiting SVDD model, calculating the decision values to achieve anomaly detection.

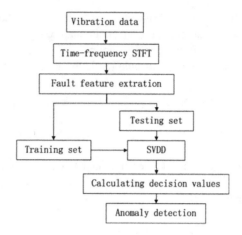

Fig. 3. Flow chart of the anomaly detection system

5 Experiments and Analysis

The SVDD method are trained and tested with the extracted fault features. The five data sets of 1500 s are used to analyze, where data from the first 500 s is used for training to construct the hyper-sphere and the rest for testing. For parameters in SVDD, we set σ to be 0.7, and C to be 0.3.

5.1 Helicopter Rotor Fault Feature Extraction

According to the information mentioned above, the rotational frequency f of rotor is 3.5 Hz. Applying STFT on data2 and data4 for example, time-varying signal components of different frequencies are obtained first. Then we select amplitude spectrums of harmonic frequencies, f, $2f$, $3f$, ..., nf. n denotes the dimension of feature, and it obviously has direct effect on anomaly detection performance.

n is set as different values for analysis in order to find the optimal one. In the experiments, we set n as 2, 4, 6, and 8 respectively. The anomaly detection results for data2 in different amplitude spectrums are displayed in Fig. 4. When n takes 2 in Fig. 4, there is an obvious jump at about 1075 s, which is indicated with a red dashed line. Before 1075 s, nearly all decision values are smaller than zero, it implies the extracted features behave normally. After that, decision values seriously deviate from the previous values. When n takes 4, the effects of anomaly detection are similar to those when n is 2. While the value of n is 6 and 8, a few of abnormal states occur before 1075 s. It also illustrates that some features irrelevant to rotor faults are extracted when n is 6 and 8. If n is too small, the extracted fault features may be insufficient, whereas if n is too big, the extracted fault features may contain some irrelevant information which would interfere anomaly detection results. We can get the same analysis conclusion from Fig. 5. In conclusion, $n = 4$ is the optimal value in our study.

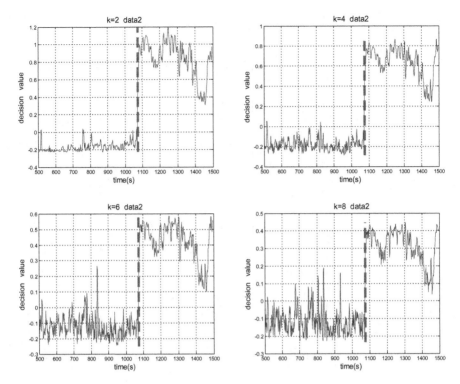

Fig. 4. The analysis results on *data2* with different *n* values

5.2 Anomaly Detection Experiments

In order to demonstrate the effectiveness of the extracted features, some common statistical features are also employed to detect abnormal conditions of helicopter rotor, like root mean square (RMS), kurtosis, skewness, peak-peak(P-P), crest factor, impulse factor, margin factor [12]. These statistical features are defined as follows:

$$RMS = \left(\frac{1}{N}\sum_{i=0}^{N} x_i^2\right)^{1/2} \qquad Kurtosis = \frac{1}{N}\sum_{i=0}^{N-1}\left(x_i - \bar{x}\right)^3/\sigma^4$$

$$Skewness = \frac{1}{N}\sum_{i=0}^{N-1}\left(x_i - \bar{x}\right)^3/\sigma^3 \qquad P - P = x_{\max} - x_{\min}$$

$$crest\ factor = \frac{\max|x_i|}{RMS} \qquad impulse\ factor = \max|x_i|/\frac{1}{N}\sum_{i=0}^{N-1}|x_i|$$

$$m\ \arg\ in\ factor = \max|x_i|/\left(\frac{1}{N}\sum_{i=0}^{N-1}|x_i|^{1/2}\right)^2$$

$$(8)$$

where $\bar{x}$ and σ refer to the mean and variance of $x(t)$ respectively.

Each data set is divided into 1500 groups in chronological order, and the sampling time for each group is 1 s. These seven statistical features are calculated within each group. We still use the features of the first 500 s as training data, and the last 1000 s as testing data. The comparative results are displayed in Fig. 6. Time-frequency features refer to the extracted features with the method proposed in this paper.

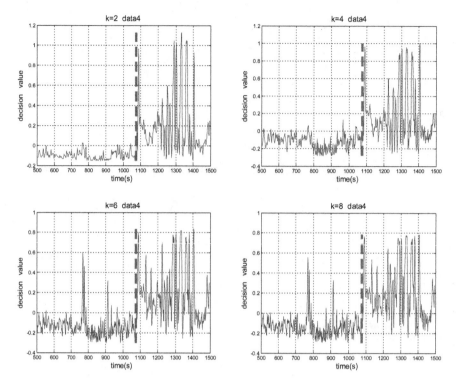

Fig. 5. The analysis results on *data4* with different *n* values

As Fig. 6 shows, the extracted statistical features on *data1*, *data2*, and *data3* can hardly detect the anomaly accurately. Although the decision values based on statistical features show a jump at 1075 s for *data4* and *data5*, the decision values during 1100 s to 1200 s seem to be normal. However, the detection effects on time-frequency features are pretty well for every data set, it consistently detects anomalous behavior with a visible jump when damage occurs. The vibration data of helicopter rotor is non-stationary and nonlinear, it is difficult to detect anomaly by statistical features only in time domain analysis. The time-frequency features we proposed are closely related to the states of rotor.

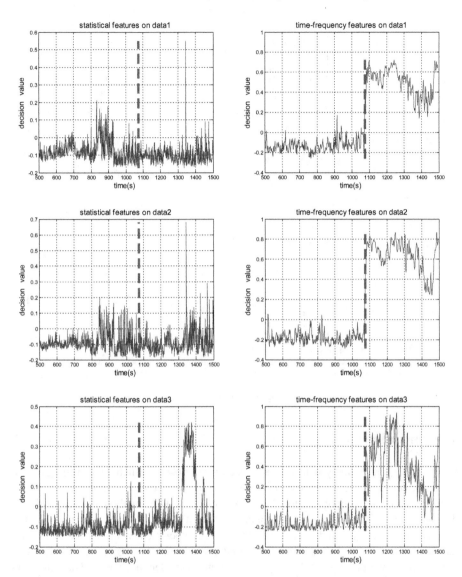

Fig. 6. The anomaly detection results based on statistical features (left) and time-frequency features (right)

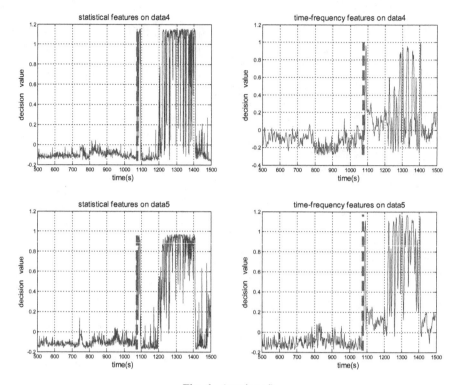

Fig. 6. (continued)

6   Conclusions

In this paper, an anomaly detection approach is proposed for helicopter rotor system. And a novel time-frequency features are extracted based on short time Fourier transform (STFT). The support vector data description (SVDD) method is used to detect damages by constructing a hyper-sphere only with normal data. To evaluate the effectiveness of the anomaly detection method, we experiment with vibration data of a real helicopter. First, we experimentally find the optimal dimension of features. The dimension of feature affects the veracity of detection. Second, we evaluate the performance of time-frequency features proposed in this paper by comparing with some common statistical features. The results demonstrate that the time-frequency features are closely related to the states of rotor, and the anomaly detection method can clearly detect the damages.

Acknowledgments. This paper is supported by National Natural Science Foundation of China (U1433116), Foundation of Graduate Innovation Center in NUAA (kfjj20151602).

References

1. Ganguli, R.: Health monitoring of a helicopter rotor in forward flight using fuzzy logic. AIAA J. **40**(12), 2373–2381 (2002)
2. Samuel, P.D., Pines, D.J.: A review of vibration-based techniques for helicopter transmission diagnostics. J. Sound Vib. **282**(1–2), 475–508 (2005)
3. Agrawal, S., Agrawal, J.: Survey on anomaly detection using data mining techniques. Procedia Comput. Sci. **60**, 708–713 (2015)
4. Akoglu, L., Tong, H., Koutra, D.: Graph based anomaly detection and description: a survey. Data Mining Knowl. Discovery **29**(3), 626–688 (2015)
5. Li, W., Zhu, Z., Jiang, F., et al.: Fault diagnosis of rotating machinery with a novel statistical feature extraction and evaluation method. Mech. Syst. Signal Process. **50–51**, 414–426 (2015)
6. Tax, D.M.J., Duin, R.P.W.: Outliers and data descriptions. In: Proceedings of the 7th Annual Conference of the Advanced School for Computing and Imaging, pp. 234–241 (2001)
7. Lv, F., Li, H., Sun, H., et al.: Method of fault diagnosis based on SVDD-SVM classifier. In: Jia, Y., Du, J., Li, H., Zhang, W. (eds.) Proceedings of the 2015 Chinese Intelligent Systems Conference, LNEE, pp. 63–68. Springer, Heidelberg (2016)
8. Chen, G., Zhang, X., Wang, Z.J., et al.: Robust support vector data description for outlier detection with noise or uncertain data. Knowl.-Based Syst. **90**(C), 129–137 (2015)
9. Gao, H., Lin, L., Chen, X., et al.: Feature extraction and recognition for rolling element bearing fault utilizing short-time fourier transform and non-negative matrix factorization. Chin. J. Mech. Eng. **28**(01), 96–105 (2015)
10. Zhang, Y., Shi, H., Zhou, X., et al.: Vibration analysis approach for corrosion pitting detection based on SVDD and PCA. In: 2015 IEEE International Conference on Cyber Technology in Automation, Control, and Intelligent Systems (CYBER), pp. 1534–1538. IEEE (2015)
11. Greitāns, M.: Advanced processing of nonuniformly sampled non-stationary signals. Elektronika ir elektrotechnika **59**(3) (2015)
12. Yu, J.B.: Bearing performance degradation assessment using locality preserving projections. Expert Syst. Appl. **38**(6), 7440–7450 (2011)

A Novel Self-adaptive Quantum Steganography Based on Quantum Image and Quantum Watermark

Zhiguo Qu[1]([✉]), Huangxing He[2], and Songya Ma[3]

[1] Jiangsu Engineering Center of Network Monitoring,
Nanjing University of Information Science and Technology,
Nanjing 210044, People's Republic of China
qzghhh@126.com
[2] School of Electronic and Information Engineering,
Nanjing University of Information Science and Technology,
Nanjing 210044, People's Republic of China
740061231@qq.com
[3] School of Mathematics and Statics, Henan University,
Kaifeng 475004, People's Republic of China
masongya0829@126.com

Abstract. Quantum steganography is an important branch of quantum information hiding. It integrates quantum secure communication technology and classical steganography, which embeds the secret information into public channel for covert communication. In this paper, based on the novel enhanced quantum representation (NEQR), a new quantum steganography algorithm is proposed to embed the secret information into the quantum carrier image and the quantum watermark image. The second least significant qubit (LSQb) of quantum carrier image is replaced with the secret information by implementing quantum circuit for good imperceptibility. Compared with the previous quantum steganography algorithms, the key shared by communicating parties can recover the secret information even if it was tampered while the tampers can be located effectively as well. In the experiment result, the Peak Signal-to-Noise Ratio (PSNR) is calculated with different quantum carrier images and quantum watermark images, which demonstrates the imperceptibility is good.

Keywords: Quantum steganography · Quantum least significant bit · Quantum carrier image · Quantum watermark

1 Introduction

Steganography [1] is an important research direction in the field of information security. To achieve covert communication, it embeds the secret information into the network medium [2, 3], such as the text, voice, image, video and so on. In recent years, with the development of quantum computer and quantum network, the quantum steganography has become a new research field, which attracted the attention of a large number of researchers on domestic and abroad. The essential parameters of quantum steganography mainly include three aspects: imperceptibility, security and capacity.

© Springer International Publishing AG 2016
X. Sun et al. (Eds.): ICCCS 2016, Part II, LNCS 10040, pp. 394–403, 2016.
DOI: 10.1007/978-3-319-48674-1_35

According to different hidden strategies, quantum steganography can be classified into two categories, QDH (Quantum data hiding) and QS (Quantum steganography). In 2001, Terhal [4] et al. proposed the first quantum data hiding protocol based on the Bell state. Which builds up hidden channel within normal quantum channel to transmit secret messages. In 2005, Hayden [5] proposed a quantum data hiding protocol with the laid of threshold access structures, and their work provided the foundation for hiding the large capacity data. These protocols are the classical protocols of QDH.

The second category is the narrow quantum steganography (QS). In 2002, J. Gea-Banacloche [6] adopted QECC (Quantum Error Correcting Code) to hide secret messages as errors in arbitrary quantum data files. In 2011, Shaw et al. [7] proposed a novel quantum steganography protocol for quantum noisy channels, which make the protocol have a good secrecy. G. Mogos et al. [8], using three-dimensional qubits to represent RGB (Red, Green and Blue) pixels, proposed a novel algorithm for transmitting the quantum secret messages in digital color images. In 2007, K. Martin et al. [9] presented a novel quantum steganographic communication protocol. It analyzed imperceptibility and security in detail, and accurately calculated capacity of this type of hidden channel. In 2010, Z.G. Qu et al. [10] proposed a quantum steganography algorithm by using χ state entanglement swapping and super dense coding. In 2013, Y. Zhang et al. [11] proposed a NEQR image representation based on Flexible Representation of Quantum Images (FROI) [12]. In 2015, Wang et al. [13] proposed a least significant qubit (LSQb) information hiding algorithm for quantum image based on NEQR.

In this paper, on the basis of the NEQR image representation, we proposed a novel quantum steganography algorithm based on quantum carrier image and quantum watermark, which owns an unique self-adaptive mechanism to recover the tamped secret information. The simple quantum circuit we designed has the merits of easy to operate, which makes the process of embedding the quantum watermark image into the quantum carrier image to be safe and practical.

2 Preliminaries

In 2015, a novel enhanced quantum representation (NEQR) for digital images was proposed by Zhang et al. [14]. The new representation model of a quantum image for a $2^n \times 2^n$ image is described as follows:

$$|I\rangle = \frac{1}{2^n} \sum_{i=0}^{2^{2n}-1} |f(i)\rangle |i\rangle = \frac{1}{2^n} \sum_{i=0}^{2^{2n}-1} \left| M_{q-1}^i M_{q-2}^i \cdots M_0^i \right\rangle |i\rangle \tag{1}$$

Wang et al. [13] proposed a quantum comparator to judge whether two qubits are same or not. In new algorithm, by virtue of the quantum bit comparator, we can judge whether the least significant bit of the original carrier image are equal to quantum secret information or not for embedding secret information.

For convenience, the embedded secret information is composed of two parts, which are embedded into the quantum carrier image and quantum watermark image, respectively. In order to avoid possible overlap of two part of embedded secret information, the method of ZigZag conversion operation and key location are adopted to avoid this issue.

According to [13], the quantum circuit is designed to replace a bit of gray value in the quantum carrier image to achieve the embedding of watermark image in the new algorithm.

3 The Proposed Quantum Steganography Algorithm

3.1 Embedding of LSQb Secret Information in Quantum Carrier Image

Firstly, the sender prepares a $2^n \times 2^n$ quantum carrier image, which can be denoted as follows:

$$|Q\rangle = \frac{1}{2^n} \sum_{i=0}^{2^{2n}-1} |f(i)\rangle |i\rangle = \frac{1}{2^n} \sum_{i=0}^{2^{2n}-1} \left| C_{q-1}^i C_{q-2}^i \cdots C_0^i \right\rangle |i\rangle \tag{2}$$

Among them, $|Q\rangle$ represents the quantum carrier image, and C_m^i ($m \in [0, q-1]$) denotes the gray value of i-th pixel in the quantum carrier image. Here, $|i\rangle$ is used to show the position information of pixels, which includes the vertical coordinate and the horizontal coordinate values.

The secret information needed to be embedded in the quantum carrier image is denoted as S_N, N represents its bit length. The sender embeds the secret information into the corresponding positions of the quantum carrier image according to the key k_{s1}. Before the secret information is embedded, the sender compares the secret information $|S_0^n\rangle$ embedded (the superscript n represents the $n-th$ secret information embedded in S_N, subscript 0 indicates that the embedded position is the least significant bit) with the least significant bit $|C_0^i\rangle$ (the superscript i represents the i-th pixel of the quantum carrier image. Then, according to the output of the quantum comparator circuit, we can decide which unitary transform need to be performed on the quantum state.

(1) If $|S_0^n\rangle = |C_0^i\rangle$, the unitary transformation is given as follow.

$$U_j = I^{\otimes q} \otimes \left(\sum_{j=0}^{2^{2n}-1} |j\rangle\langle j| \right) \tag{3}$$

(2) Otherwise $|S_0^n\rangle \neq |C_0^i\rangle$, the unitary transformation is defined as follow.

$$U_i = I^{\otimes q-1} \otimes U \otimes |i\rangle\langle i| + I^{\otimes q} \otimes \left(\sum_{j=0, j\neq i}^{2^{2n}-1} |j\rangle\langle j| \right) \tag{4}$$

Here, $U = \begin{pmatrix} 0 & 1 \\ 1 & 0 \end{pmatrix}$.

Next, the following two steps are performed to embed the secret information.

(1) If the output two values from quantum comparator are same, which means $|S_0^n\rangle = |C_0^i\rangle$. That is, the secret information $|S_0^n\rangle$ embedded are equal to the least significant bit C_0^i, so nothing will be done.

(2) If the output two values from quantum comparator are different, $|S_0^n\rangle \neq |C_0^i\rangle$. That is, the embedded secret information $|S_0^n\rangle$ are not equal to the least significant bit C_0^i. As a result, the following unitary transformation will be performed on the quantum carrier image.

$$
\begin{aligned}
U_i(|Q\rangle) &= \left(I^{\otimes q-1} \otimes U \otimes |i\rangle\langle i| + I^{\otimes q} \otimes \left(\sum_{j=0, j \neq i}^{2^{2n}-1} |j\rangle\langle j| \right) \right) \left(\frac{1}{2^n} \sum_{i=0}^{2^{2n}-1} \left| C_{q-1}^i C_{q-2}^i \cdots C_0^i \right\rangle |i\rangle \right) \\
&= \frac{1}{2^n} \left| C_{q-1}^i C_{q-2}^i \cdots C_1^i \right\rangle U \left| C_0^i \right\rangle |i\rangle + \frac{1}{2^n} \sum_{j=0, j \neq i}^{2^{2n}-1} \left| C_{q-1}^j C_{q-2}^j \cdots C_0^j \right\rangle |j\rangle \qquad (5) \\
&= \frac{1}{2^n} \left| C_{q-1}^i C_{q-2}^i \cdots C_1^i \right\rangle |S_0^n\rangle |i\rangle + \frac{1}{2^n} \sum_{j=0, j \neq i}^{2^{2n}-1} \left| C_{q-1}^j C_{q-2}^j \cdots C_0^j \right\rangle |j\rangle
\end{aligned}
$$

Where $|S_0^n\rangle = \begin{cases} |1\rangle, |C_0^i\rangle = |0\rangle \\ |0\rangle, |C_0^i\rangle = |1\rangle \end{cases}$.

Assuming the length of the secret information sequence is $N = 2^4 \times 2^4$, then the sender apply the operation $\prod_{i=0}^{2^8-1} U_i$ to the quantum carrier image $|Q\rangle$. It can realize the aim of hiding the secret information to the quantum carrier image and get the following embedded carrier image.

$$
|Q'\rangle = \frac{1}{2^n} \sum_{i=0}^{2^8-1} \left| C_{q-1}^i C_{q-2}^i \cdots C_1^i \right\rangle |S_0^n\rangle |i\rangle \qquad (6)
$$

3.2 Embedding of LSQb Secret Information in Quantum Carrier Image

The sender also prepares a quantum watermark image, and the size is $2^m \times 2^m$. The quantum watermark image is smaller than the size of the quantum carrier image ($m < n$). So the quantum watermark image can be denoted as follow:

$$
|R\rangle = \frac{1}{2^m} \sum_{h=0}^{2^{2m}-1} |f(h)\rangle |h\rangle = \frac{1}{2^m} \sum_{h=0}^{2^{2m}-1} \left| W_{q-1}^h W_{q-2}^h \cdots W_0^h \right\rangle |h\rangle \qquad (7)
$$

Where $|R\rangle$ is the whole quantum state storage of quantum carrier image, W_m^i $m \in [0, q-1]$, represents the gray value bit of the quantum watermark image $|h\rangle$ is the position information, which includes the vertical information and the horizontal information.

The secret information sequence needed to be embedded in the quantum watermark image is described as T_M. M represents the length of the sequence. Next, the sender embeds the secret information into the position of the quantum watermark image with the k_{s2}. The same as the previous embedding method, the sender compares the secret information $|T_0^m\rangle$ embedded (the superscript m represents the m-th secret information embedded in the information sequence T_M, subscript 0 indicates that the embedded position is the least significant bit) with the least significant bit $|W_0^h\rangle$ (the superscript h represents the h-th pixel of the quantum watermark image) of the quantum watermark image. Then according to the output of the quantum comparator circuit, we can judge which unitary transform shall be performed on the quantum state.

(1) When $|T_0^m\rangle = |W_0^h\rangle$, we define the following unitary transformation.

$$U_l = I^{\otimes q} \otimes \left(\sum_{l=0}^{2^{2m}-1} |l\rangle\langle l| \right) \tag{8}$$

(2) When $|T_0^m\rangle \neq |W_0^h\rangle$, we define the following unitary transformation.

$$U_h = I^{\otimes q-1} \otimes U \otimes |h\rangle\langle h| + I^{\otimes q} \otimes \left(\sum_{l=0,l\neq h}^{2^{2m}-1} |l\rangle\langle l| \right) \tag{9}$$

Here, $U = \begin{pmatrix} 0 & 1 \\ 1 & 0 \end{pmatrix}$.

Then, the secret information is embedded through the following two steps operation. The first step is consistent with the operation described in the embedding of LSQb secret information in quantum carrier image. Here we only discuss the second step, the different values returned from the quantum comparator, which is $|T_0^m\rangle \neq |W_0^h\rangle$.

$$\begin{aligned} U_h(|R\rangle) &= \left(I^{\otimes q-1} \otimes U \otimes |h\rangle\langle h| + I^{\otimes q} \otimes \left(\sum_{l=0,l\neq h}^{2^{2m}-1} |l\rangle\langle l| \right) \right) \left(\frac{1}{2^m} \sum_{h=0}^{2^{2m}-1} \left| W_{q-1}^h W_{q-2}^h \cdots W_0^h \right\rangle |h\rangle \right) \\ &= \frac{1}{2^m} \left| W_{q-1}^h W_{q-2}^h \cdots W_1^h \right\rangle U |W_0^h\rangle |h\rangle + \frac{1}{2^n} \sum_{l=0,l\neq h}^{2^{2m}-1} \left| W_{q-1}^l W_{q-2}^l \cdots W_0^l \right\rangle |l\rangle \\ &= \frac{1}{2^m} \left| W_{q-1}^h W_{q-2}^h \cdots W_1^h \right\rangle |T_0^m\rangle |h\rangle + \frac{1}{2^m} \sum_{l=0,l\neq h}^{2^{2m}-1} \left| W_{q-1}^l W_{q-2}^l \cdots W_0^l \right\rangle |l\rangle \end{aligned} \tag{10}$$

Where $|T_0^m\rangle = \begin{cases} |1\rangle, |W_0^h\rangle = |0\rangle \\ |0\rangle, |W_0^h\rangle = |1\rangle \end{cases}$.

Assuming the length of the secret information sequence is M, that $M = 2^4 \times 2^4$. Then the sender apply the operation $\prod_{h=0}^{2^8-1} U_h$ to the quantum watermark image $|R\rangle$,

Which can realize the aim of hiding the secret message M into the quantum watermark image and get the following embedded watermark image.

$$|R'\rangle = \frac{1}{2^m} \sum_{h=0}^{2^8-1} \left| W_{q-1}^h \, W_{q-2}^h \cdots W_1^h \right\rangle \left| T_0^m \right\rangle |h\rangle \tag{11}$$

3.3 Secret Information Extraction of LSQb from Quantum Carrier Image and Watermark Image

For the process of extracting secret information, only need to extract the last qubit of color encoding of the stego image (embedded quantum carrier image and quantum watermark image). Owing to LSQb stego carrier image is a complex vector in Hilbert space which the size is 2^{q+2n}, So we decompose the vector into the direct product of color and correspondingly position. Take $2^2 \times 2^2$ as an example, the LSQb stego carrier image vector is X. Then we ought to disintegration X as the following form:

$$X = C_1 \otimes \begin{pmatrix} 1 \\ 0 \\ 0 \\ \vdots \\ 0 \\ 0 \end{pmatrix} + C_2 \otimes \begin{pmatrix} 0 \\ 1 \\ 0 \\ \vdots \\ 0 \\ 0 \end{pmatrix} + \cdots\cdots + C_{15} \otimes \begin{pmatrix} 0 \\ 0 \\ 0 \\ \vdots \\ 1 \\ 0 \end{pmatrix} + C_{16} \otimes \begin{pmatrix} 0 \\ 0 \\ 0 \\ \vdots \\ 0 \\ 1 \end{pmatrix} \tag{12}$$

According to the secret key K_{s1}, the receiver converts every first part of the direct product (color information) to binary data. The number of binary bit is equivalent to the number of bits of quantum carrier image's color encoding. In the above example, it means converting C_2, C_7, C_{12} to the appropriate binary data C_{2b}, C_{7b}, C_{12b}. Then, the last bit of each binary data is extracted. These bits from a binary code stream which is the secret information. That is to extract the last bit of C_{2b}, C_{7b}, C_{12b}. and choose these bits as the secret information.

The LSQb stego watermark image is a complex vector in Hilbert space with the size of 2^{q+2m}, So we also decompose the vector into the direct product of color and correspondingly position. Taking 2×2 as an example, the LSQb stego watermark image vector is Y. Then we ought to disintegration Y as the following form:

$$Y = W_1 \otimes \begin{pmatrix} 1 \\ 0 \\ 0 \\ 0 \end{pmatrix} + W_2 \otimes \begin{pmatrix} 0 \\ 1 \\ 0 \\ 0 \end{pmatrix} + W_3 \otimes \begin{pmatrix} 0 \\ 0 \\ 1 \\ 0 \end{pmatrix} + W_4 \otimes \begin{pmatrix} 0 \\ 0 \\ 0 \\ 1 \end{pmatrix} \tag{13}$$

The receiver converts every first part of the direct product (color information) to binary data by using the secret key K_{s2}. In the formula (13), it means converting W_1, W_3, W_4 to the appropriate binary data W_{1b}, W_{3b}, W_{4b}. These bits from a binary code stream which is the secret information. That is to extract the last bit of W_{1b}, W_{3b}, W_{4b}. and arrange these bits as the secret information.

3.4　Recovery of Secret Information and Localization of Tampered Position

Although the secret information is difficult to be detected by the unauthorized third party in the process of quantum image transmission. However, the image is easy to be tampered with or damaged by the unauthorized third party when the image is delivered, which leads to the loss of the secret information embedded in the least significant bit of the image. Therefore, in order to make the secret information embedded in the quantum carrier image or quantum watermark image can be recovered after being destroyed. The sender and the receiver use the key K_t hared in advance, shown as $K_t = \{X, I, X, I, I, I, X, X \cdots I, X\}$. Here, $X = \begin{pmatrix} 0 & 1 \\ 1 & 0 \end{pmatrix}$, $I = \begin{pmatrix} 1 & 0 \\ 0 & 1 \end{pmatrix}$. Then the relationship of recovering secret information is built as follows:

$$K_t \cdot WS = CS \tag{14}$$

The secret information sequence extracted from the quantum watermark image is called WS, meanwhile, the secret information sequence extracted from the quantum carrier image is called CS. Suppose $WS = \{|0\rangle, |1\rangle, |1\rangle, |0\rangle, |1\rangle, |0\rangle, |0\rangle, |1\rangle\}$, $CS = \{|1\rangle, |1\rangle, |0\rangle, |0\rangle, |1\rangle, |0\rangle, |1\rangle, |0\rangle\}$.

As can be seen from Table 1, as long as any one side in the process of quantum image transmission was tampered with, the receiver can recover the tampered party by using the key K_t. For the sender, also can know which secret information of the position in the quantum image is destroyed or tampered with.

Table 1. Recovery of secret information

WS	$|0\rangle$	$|1\rangle$	$|1\rangle$	$|0\rangle$	$|1\rangle$	$|0\rangle$	$|0\rangle$	$|0\rangle$
K_t	X	I	X	I	I	I	X	X
CS	$|1\rangle$	$|1\rangle$	$|0\rangle$	$|0\rangle$	$|1\rangle$	$|0\rangle$	$|1\rangle$	$|0\rangle$

4　The Experiment Result and Performance Analysis

In classical LSB algorithm, PSNR is used to evaluate its hidden effect. In this paper, PSNR is also introduced to evaluate the imperceptibility of quantum stego image.

First of all, the new quantum steganography algorithm is simulated on the MATLAB R2014a. And then, the PSNR is introduced and calculated for proving the imperceptibility of the new algorithm. It is most easily defined via the mean squared error (MSE), which can be defined as Eq. (16). Assuming there are two $2^n \times 2^n$ images I and J. (I is the original carrier image, J is the embedded carrier image), $I(i,j)$ and $K(i,j)$ representing the pixel values of pixel (i, j).

$$MSE = \frac{1}{mn} \sum_{i=0}^{2^m-1} \sum_{j=0}^{2^n-1} \left[(I(i,j) - K(i,j))^2 \right] \quad (15)$$

$$PSNR = 20 \times \log_{10} \left(\frac{MAX_I}{\sqrt{MSE}} \right) \quad (16)$$

Here, MAX_I is the maximum possible pixel value of the image. Figure 1 shows the experimental results of the proposed steganography algorithm. In which the carrier image is selected the size of 512×512 of the gray-scale image, the watermark image is the size of 256×256 of the gray-scale image. and their corresponding PSNR values with different watermark images are presented in Table 2.

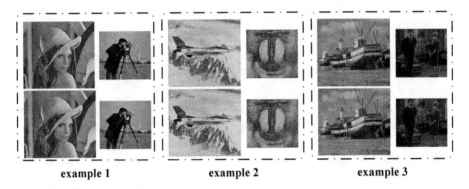

example 1   example 2   example 3

Fig. 1. In three groups of pictures, the left upper are the stegano carrier images, the right upper are the stegano watermark images, the left down are the embedded stegano carrier images, the right down are the extracted watermark images.

Table 2. PSNR values of three examples in our simulation

stegano carrier image	stegano watermark image	PSNR/db
Lena	Camera	44.6946
airplane	Baboon	45.0959
fishingboat	Couple	45.1287

From the left down image in Fig. 1, we can see that it's impossible for users of the stegano carrier image to become aware of the existing of stegano watermark images and the secret information embedded in the carrier image. So the security of the secret information is proved to be greatly improved. From Table 2, we can see that the PSNR values of the embedded stegano carrier image are high enough for different carrier images and watermark images. Through three PSNR values in our simulation, we can conclude that the quantum steganography algorithm based on quantum carrier image and quantum watermark image proposed has very good imperceptibility and high level security.

5 Conclusion

In this paper, based on the NEQR, a new quantum steganography algorithm is proposed to embed the secret information into the quantum carrier image and the quantum watermark image. In order to covertly communicate, the sender substitutes the least significant bit of the quantum carrier image and quantum watermark image with the secret information by using QLSb image information hiding algorithm. Compared with the previous quantum steganography algorithms, the new algorithm proposed can not only improve the imperceptibility of the secret information by virtue of the quantum watermark, but also, the security of the information embedded has been greatly improved by virtue of its self-adaptive mechanism.

Acknowledgements. This work was supported by the National Natural Science Foundation of China (No. 61373131, 61303039, 61232016, 61501247), PAPD and CICAEET funds.

References

1. Xia, Z., Wang, X., Sun, X., Wang, B.: Steganalysis of least significant bit matching using multi-order differences. Secur. Commun. Netw. 7(8), 1283–1291 (2014)
2. Zheng, Y., Jeon, B., Danhua, X., Jonathan Wu, Q.M., Zhang, H.: Image segmentation by generalized hierarchical fuzzy C-means algorithm. J. Intell. Fuzzy Syst. 28(2), 961–973 (2015)
3. Chen, B., Shu, H., Coatrieux, G., Chen, G., Sun, X., Coatrieux, J.-L.: Color image analysis by quaternion-type moments. J. Math. Imaging Vis. 51(1), 124–144 (2015)
4. Terhal, B.M., DiVincenzo, D.P., Leung, D.W.: Hiding bits in Bell states. Phys. Rev. Lett. 86, 5807–5813 (2001)
5. Hayden, P., Leung, D., Smith, G.: Multiparty data hiding of quantum information. Phys. Rev. A 71, 062339 (2005)
6. Gea-Banacloche, J.: Hiding messages in quantum data. J. Math. Phys. 43, 4531–4536 (2002)
7. Shaw, B.A., Brun, T.A.: Quantum steganography with noisy quantum channels. Phys. Rev. A 83, 022310 (2011)
8. Mogos, G.: A quantum way to data hiding. Int. J. Multimedia Ubiquit. Eng. 4, 13–20 (2009)
9. Martin, K.: Steganographic communication with quantum information. In: Furon, T., Cayre, F., Doërr, G., Bas, P. (eds.) IH 2007. LNCS, vol. 4567, pp. 32–49. Springer, Heidelberg (2008)

10. Qu, Z.G., Chen, X.B., Luo, M.X., Niu, X.X., Yang, Y.X.: Quantum steganography with large payload based on entanglement swapping of -type entangled states. Opt. Commun. **284**, 2075–2082 (2011)
11. Zhang, Y., Lu, K., Gao, Y.H., Wang, M.: NEQR: a novel enhanced quantum representation of digital images. Quantum Inf. Process. **12**(8), 2833–2860 (2013)
12. Le, P.Q., Dong, F., Hirota, K.: A flexible representation of quantum images for polynomial preparation, image compression and processing operations. Quantum Inf. Process. **10**(1), 63–84 (2010)
13. Wang, S., Sang, J., Song, X., Niu, X.M.: Least significant qubit (LSQb) information hiding algorithm for quantum image. Measurement **73**, 352–359 (2015)
14. Wang, N., Lin, S.: Watermarking scheme for quantum images based on least significant bit. Chin. J. Quantum Electron. (量子电子学报) **32**(3), 263–269 (2015). (in chinese)

Rotation Invariant Local Binary Pattern for Blind Detection of Copy-Move Forgery with Affine Transform

Pei Yang, Gaobo Yang$^{(\boxtimes)}$, and Dengyong Zhang

School of Information Science and Engineering,
Hunan University, Changsha 410082, China
yanggaobo@hnu.edu.cn

Abstract. For copy-move forgery, the copied region may be rotated or flipped to fit the scene better. A blind image forensics approach is proposed for copy-move forgery detection using rotation invariant uniform local binary patterns ($LBP_{P,R}^{riu2}$). The image is first filtered and divided into overlapped blocks with fixed size. The features are extracted from each block using $LBP_{P,R}^{riu2}$. Then, the feature vectors are sorted and block pairs are identified by estimating the Euclidean distances of these feature vectors. Specifically, a shift-vector counter C is exploited to detect and locate tampering region. Experimental results show that the proposed approach can deal with multiple copy-move forgeries, and is robust to JPEG compression, noise, blurring region rotation and flipping.

Keywords: Passive image forensics · Copy-move forgery · Local binary pattern (LBP) · Rotation · Flipping

1 Introduction

With the prevalence of advanced image editing tools such as PhotoShop, it becomes much easier to create forgery images which are difficult to be distinguished by naked eyes. The abusive use of tampered images is a serious problem to maintain public confidence. Digital image forensics, which aims at verifying the trustworthiness of images, has emerged as a hot research topics in the field of image security. Especially, passive forgery detection does not require any prior knowledge of original images or any auxiliary data such as watermarks or signatures. Instead, passive image forensics only utilizes the available forged image itself to detect the tampering traces [1,2]. Copy-move forgery is most common, in which a part of an image is replicated from one area to another area of the same picture to hide an object or create more objects. An intuitive idea of copy-move detection is to divide the image into blocks and find similar block pairs within an image [3,4]. However, the copied region may be rotated and/or scaled so as to fit the scene better. That is, copied regions might suffer from further affine transform before pasting. Moreover, tampered images can be post-processed with

© Springer International Publishing AG 2016
X. Sun et al. (Eds.): ICCCS 2016, Part II, LNCS 10040, pp. 404–416, 2016.
DOI: 10.1007/978-3-319-48674-1_36

blur, noise and JPEG compression. Thus, it is challenging to detect copy-move forgery with affine transform [5].

To address this issue, a straightforward idea is to seek more robust features which are invariant to image scaling, translation, and rotation. In this paper, a simple yet effective forensics approach is proposed to detect and localize copy-paste forgery with affine transform. Local binary pattern (LBP) is an excellent texture descriptor widely-used in computer vision and image forensics for its simplicity and robustness to illumination change. However, LBP is sensitive to scaling, rotation and non-rigid deformation. There are lots of variants such as pyramid LBP (PLBP), dominant LBP (DLBP), center-symmetric LBP (CS-LBP) and completed LBP (CLBP). Among them, a generalized gray-scale and rotation invariant operator $(LBP_{P,R}^{riu2})$ is claimed to have desirable discriminability, which is a combination of $LBP_{P,R}^{ri}$ and $LBP_{P,R}^{u2}$. We are motivated to extract the $LBP_{P,R}^{riu2}$ features to resist rotation in copy-move forgery detection. Moreover, the uniform pattern $(LBP_{P,R}^{u2})$ is used for dimension reduction. The matching is achieved by estimating the Euclidean distances of features. A shift vector counter C is used to detect and locate tampered regions.

The remainder of the paper is organized as follows. Section 2 briefly introduces the related works. Section 3 briefly introduces LBP and $LBP_{P,R}^{riu2}$. Section 4 presents the proposed detection approach. Section 5 reports experimental results. Conclusion is made in Sect. 6.

2   Related Work

There are many copy-move forgery detection approaches, which can divided into two categories: block-based methods and keypoint-based methods. Block-based methods always divide image into rectangular or circle regions. For each region, feature vectors are computed, and similar feature vectors are subsequently matched. To reduce the computational complexity of searching duplicate blocks, lexicographic sorting is used to identify similar feature vectors since the performance of block-based copy-move forgery detection depends on block matching. To reduce the probability of false matches, these features should accurately represent block content. Some approaches exploit frequency-based features such as discrete cosine transform (DCT) [3,4], Fourier-Mellin Transform (FMT) [5] and Polar Harmonic Transform (PHT) [6]. In addition, moment-based features such as Zernike moments and blur-invariant moments are used for block-based feature extraction [7,8]. There are also some texture features such as Local Binary Patterns (LBP) [9] and Multi-resolution LBP (MLBP) [10].

Recently, an alternate approach is to exploit interest points including scale-invariant feature transform (SIFT) [11] and speed up robust feature (SURF) [12]. Keypoint-based methods start from interest point extraction. By identifying correspondences between SIFT points within an image, duplicate image regions are exposed. In general, most keypoint-based methods are robust to geometrical transformations and occlusions [13]. However, some small and smooth forged areas do not have strong SIFT key points. Thus, some duplicate regions or copied regions with little structure may cannot be identified, which considerably decreases the performance of keypoint-based approaches.

3 Local Binary Patterns (LBP)

In the original LBP operator, each central pixel is compared with its neighboring pixels in a 3×3 block. This binary pattern is multiplied by a weighted matrix with powers of two, and the LBP value of central pixel is obtained by summation of these weighted elements. Later, the basic LBP was extended to include circular neighborhoods with radius R, as shown in Fig. 1. That is,

$$LBP_{P,R} = \sum_{p=0}^{P-1} s(g_p - g_c)2^P, s(x) = \begin{cases} 1, & x \geq 0 \\ 0, & x < 0 \end{cases} \tag{1}$$

where g_c is the gray values of the central pixel, g_p is the value of its neighbors. P is the total number of neighboring pixels, and R is the radius of circularly neighboring set. Let the coordinate of g_c be $(0, 0)$. The coordinate of each neighboring pixel g_p is then determined in terms of its index p and parameter (P, R) as $(Rcos(2\pi p/P), Rsin(2\pi p/P))$. The gray values of the neighbors, which do not locate at the image grids, can be estimated by an interpolation operation.

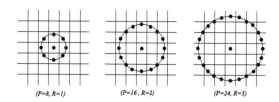

(P=8, R=1)   (P=16, R=2)   (P=24, R=3)

Fig. 1. Circularly symmetric neighboring sets with three different values.

LBP operator is invariant to monotonic gray-scale transformations, which preserves the pixel intensity order in local neighborhoods. But if an image is rotated in a plane, the surrounding neighbors around the central pixel will move along the perimeter of the circle, resulting in a different LBP value. To remove rotation effect, a rotation-invariant LBP is proposed in [14], which labels the its minimum value after the original LBP code is circularly rotated.

$$LBP_{P,R}^{ri} = min\{ROR(LBP_{P,R}, i)|i = 0, 1, 2, ... P - 1\} \tag{2}$$

where $ROR(x, i)$ means a circular bitwise right shift to the P-bit binary number x for i times ($|i| < P$), and the superscript ri stands for "*rotation invariance*".

It is possible to use only a subset of 2^p binary patterns to describe the texture of images. These patterns are denoted as $LBP_{P,R}^{u2}$ which contain at most two bitwise transitions from 0 to 1 or vice verse when the binary string is considered circularly. To extract the most fundamental structure and rotation invariance patterns from LBP, the uniform and rotation invariant operator $LBP_{P,R}^{riu2}$ is given as:

$$LBP_{P,R}^{riu2} = \begin{cases} \sum_{p=0}^{P-1} s(g_p - g_c), \, if \quad U(LBP_{P,R}) \leq 2 \\ P+1, \qquad \qquad \quad otherwise \end{cases} \tag{3}$$

where the U value of an LBP pattern is defined as the number of spatial transitions (bitwise 0/1 changes) in that uniform pattern. That is,

$$U(LBP_{P,R}) = |s(g_{p-1} - g_c) - s(g_0 - g_c)| + \sum_{p=1}^{P-1} |s(g_p - g_c) - s(g_{p-1} - g_c)|. \tag{4}$$

When the LBP pattern of each pixel has been identified, a LBP histogram can be calculated to represent the texture as follows:

$$H(k) = \sum_{i=1}^{W} \sum_{j=1}^{H} f(LBP_{P,R}^{riu2}(i,j),k), k \in [0, K-1].$$

$$f(x,y) = \begin{cases} 1, \, x = y \\ 0, \, otherwise \end{cases} \tag{5}$$

where K is the number of patterns, which is equal to $P + 2$. W and H are the height and width of this image, respectively. The proportion of the pixels in the non-uniform patterns usually takes a small part in a texture image when accumulated into a histogram. Based on the statistical properties of different patterns, the uniform and rotation invariant operator feature has a strong capability to discriminate textures. Therefor, the $LBP_{P,R}^{riu2}$ histogram features are extracted to represent image blocks in this paper.

4   Proposed Detection Scheme

Figure 2 is the proposed copy-move forgery detection scheme, which includes three steps: feature extraction, block matching, and post-processing.

4.1   Feature Extraction

Color images are firstly converted to grayscale images I using color space conversion. Considering that high frequency components are not stable when the image is subject to signal processing operations, low frequency features are used in feature matching. Thus, a Gaussian low pass filter with size of 3×3 and standard deviation of 3.0 is adopted to reduce high frequency disturbances.

To identify forged regions, the input image is firstly divided into overlapping blocks of $L \times L$ pixels. That is, adjacent blocks only have one different row or column. Moreover, we assume that the sizes are smaller than the size of duplicated regions to be detected. A square with $L \times L$ pixels slides once the input image from the upper left corner right down to the lower right corner, so the total number T of overlapping blocks for an image of $M \times N$ pixels will be $(M - L + 1) \times (N - L + 1)$. Then, $LBP_{P,R}^{riu2}$ is employed to extract the feature from each block. Typically, a feature vector is extracted from a block, thus $(M-L+1) \times (N-L+1)$ LBP features are obtained. In the following, we consider eight neighbors for calculating the local histogram. Following Eqs. (3)–(5), the local histogram has 10 bins. The resulting histogram is used as a descriptor vector to represent each block. The dimensions of this feature vector are lower than those used in other block-based detection method [3, 4]. For an image with the size of $M \times N$, all features are arranged into a matrix A with the size of $(M - L + 1)(N - L + 1) \times 10$.

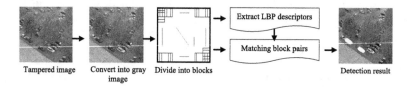

Tampered image   Convert into gray   Divide into blocks   Detection result
                  image

Fig. 2. Diagram of detection algorithm.

4.2   Block Matching

In the matching step, the feature matrix A is lexicographically sorted. The lexicographically sorted matrix is denoted as β. Block matching is exploited to match block pairs and identify regions that are likely to have been forged. Block pairs are identified by estimating the Euclidean distances of feature vectors. In the proposed scheme, the Euclidean distance D between adjacent pairs of β is calculated. If the distance is smaller than a present threshold $D_{similar}$, then we initialize a black map with the size of $M \times N$ and consider the inquires blocks as a pair of candidate for forgery detection. Meanwhile, Since the duplicated regions are assumed to be not overlapping and the divided blocks may be overlapping, another parameter the distance threshold Td is also imported in this step. That is, only the two corresponding blocks whose distance d is larger than Td are counted. To accurately identify the forged region, the distance threshold Td and the threshold of similarity $D_{similar}$ should be predetermined. In this manner, the distance threshold Td is defined in terms of the length of block L. Let V_i and V_j denote the ith row and jth row of β, and corresponding block coordinate is defined as the top-left corner's coordinate of block noted as (x_i, x_j) and (y_i, y_j), then the Euclidean distance between V_i and V_j and the two corresponding blocks distance are computed as follows:

$$D(V_i, V_j) = \sqrt{\sum_{k=1}^{10} [\beta_i(k) - \beta_j(k)]^2} \tag{6}$$

$$d = \sqrt{(x_i - x_j)^2 + (y_i - y_j)^2} \tag{7}$$

The matching of the blocks begins in the first row of matrix β. For a feature located in the ith row of β, distances in the vicinity of ith rows are computed, and the Euclidean distance between the ith row and nearby j rows is obtained as follows:

$$D(V_i, V_{i+j}) = \sqrt{\sum_{p=0}^{10} [V_i(k) - V_{i+j}(k)]^2} \leq D_{similar} \tag{8}$$

In this paper, we set $j = 10$. That is, there are 10 adjacent feature vectors distances which are compared.

From the above, each pair of consecutive vector V_i, V_j is tested whether they are similar, and the distance between two corresponding blocks is test whether it is greater than Td. If they are, the shift vector s between the two corresponding blocks is calculated and normalized as:

$$s = (s_1, s_2) = (x_i - x_j, y_i - y_j).$$

Because the shift vectors $-s$ and s correspond to the same shift, the shift vectors s are normalized, if necessary, by multiplying by -1 so that $s_1 \geq 0$. For each matching pair of blocks, we increment the normalized shift vector counter C by one: $C(s_1, s_2) = C(s_1, s_2) + 1$. The shift vectors are calculated and the counter C incremented for each pair of consecutive matching rows in the sorted matrix β. The shift vector C is initialized to zero before the algorithm starts. At the end of the matching process, the counter C indicates the frequencies with which different normalized shift vectors occur.

4.3   Post-processing

Then the algorithm finds all normalized shift vectors $s(1), s(2), ..., s(K)$, whose occurrence exceeds a user-specified threshold $T : C(s(r)) > T$ for all $r = 1, ..., K$. For all normalized shift vectors, the matching blocks that contributed to that specific shift vector are stored and thus identified as segments that might have been copied and moved. This algorithm outputs a black map image, regions which are considered to be duplicated are marked with a special color than black. Morphologic operations are applied to the map image to fill the holes in the marked regions and remove the isolated regions, then output the final result. With the map image and human visual judgment, it can be quickly determined whether the input image is original or tampered.

5   Experimental Results and Analysis

5.1   Experimental Setup

For our experiments, there are two databases adopted to evaluate the proposed methodology. The first is obtained from the CoMoFoD database [15]. All the images were 512 × 512 pixels RGB image saved in png format. The second dataset of high resolution images are obtained from the Image Manipulation Dataset [13] with the resolution varying from 1280 × 854 to 3888 × 2592 pixels. Figure 3 presents the forged images used in the experiments. All experiments were performed on a personal computer with 2.1 GHz CPU and 2 GB memory running Matlab R2010b. In our experiments, without specific specification, all the parameter in the experiment were set as: $L = 32, D_{similar} = 0.0625, T_d = 32$ by default.

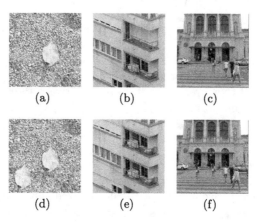

(a)   (b)   (c)

(d)   (e)   (f)

Fig. 3. Examples of copy-move forgery: (a)–(c) original image, (d)–(f) tampered image.

5.2   Evaluation Metrics

To illustrate the performance of the proposed algorithm, we referenced two evaluation criteria, the correct detection ratio F_c and the false detection ratio F_f, defined as follows:

$$F_c = \frac{|\mu \cap \mu^c| + |\omega \cap \omega^c|}{|\mu| + |\omega|} \qquad (9)$$

$$F_f = \frac{|\mu^c - \mu| + |\omega^c - \omega|}{|\mu^c| + |\omega^c|} \qquad (10)$$

where μ and ω respectively denote pixels of original region and forgery region in original image, and μ^c and ω^c respectively denote pixels of original region and forgery region in the image displaying detected results. Obviously, the more F_c was close to 1 and F_f was close to 0, the more precise the method would be. In the following experiment, to evaluate the degree to which the size of the duplicated regions influences detection, sub-blocks of three sizes (16 × 16 pixels, 32 × 32 pixels and 48 × 48 pixels) were used in the tests.

5.3   Experiments

(I) Simple Copy-Move Forgery Images. The detection result of this copy-move forgery is presented in Fig. 4. The statistical detection rates for different size of

sub-blocks are presented in Table 1, in which F_c is generally greater than 0.9 and F_f is nearly 0. Experiments results demonstrated the ability of the algorithm to identify images forged using translation. Moreover, the correct detection ratio is affected by the size of sub-blocks. That is due to the fact that portions of the forged regions are so small that they cannot be detected when using a larger block size. Thus, as long as the tampered regions are larger than the blocks employed, the proposed algorithm is able to locate forgery with a high degree of precision.

Table 1. Detection results of copy-move forgery with different sub-blocks

Block size	16×16	32×32	48×48
F_c	0.986	0.967	0.836
F_f	0.019	0.041	0.208

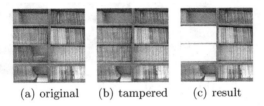

(a) original   (b) tampered   (c) result

Fig. 4. Detection results using images manipulated through translation.

Table 2. Detection results of images distorted by rotation

Rotated angle (F_c/F_f)	16×16	32×32	48×48
90°	100.00/0.14	100/0.26	99.87/1.87
180°	100.00/0.09	100.00/0.32	99.86/1.54
270°	100.00/0.23	100.00/0.45	99.88/2.03
Flipping horizontally	100.00/0.15	100.00/0.23	99.93/1.96
Flipping vertically	100.00/0.21	100.00/0.34	99.82/2.31

(II) Rotation and Flipping Duplication Forgery. The proposed scheme has an advantage of resisting region rotation and flipping. The visual result of these tampered image is shown in Fig. 5, when the copied region is rotated by 90°, 180°, 270° degrees or flipping, both horizontally and vertically. The simulation results and comparisons with PHT [6] are shown in Fig. 6. It can be easily seen that a lot of false matches are obtained based on the PHT method. It is not difficult to understand, because when the image is rotated by 90°, 180°, or 270° degrees, there is no interpolation error. Consequently, block matching is very accurate. The statistical detection rates F_c/F_f are shown in Table 2.

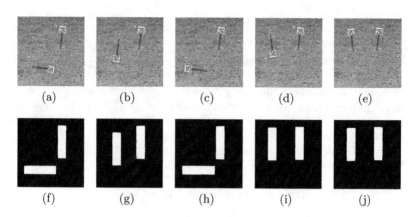

(a)   (b)   (c)   (d)   (e)

(f)   (g)   (h)   (i)   (j)

Fig. 5. Detection results on rotation regions: (a)–(e) forgery image: 90°, 180°, 270°, vertically and horizontally flipping. (f)–(j) detection result.

(a) original   (b) tampered   (c) PHT[6]   (d) proposed

Fig. 6. Detection results on region rotation: 180°.

Table 3. Detection results of tampered images distorted by blurring

Filter size (F_c/F_f)	16 × 16	32 × 32	48 × 48
3 × 3	99.35/0.75	98.25/1.76	88.36/9.96
5 × 5	98.05/1.85	96.78/2.94	86.94/11.87
7 × 7	95.84/5.45	94.03/5.97	80.75/12.30

(III) Robust to Blurring, Brightness and Color Reduction Attack. Post-processing operation are often used to conceal the forged region. Figure 7 shows the detection results of a forged image that underwent blurring, brightness and Color reduction attack. The statistical detection rates of duplication regions using different blurring averaging filters, different conditions of brightness, and distorted by color reduction are present in Tables 3, 4 and 5, respectively. Experiment results show that the method works better when dealing with these attack.

(IV) Multiple Copied Regions and Combined Transformations. The copy regions are often encountered several perturbations concurrently and pasted to several different regions of the image. Figures 8 and 9 show the examples of multiple copy-move and combined Transformations detection. In Fig. 8. F_c/F_f are 89.52 %/4.06 %, 93.54 %/5.70 % and 95.45 %/13.6 % of each row. In Fig. 9, the

Table 4. Detection results of images distorted by adjustment of brightness

Ranges (F_c/F_f)	16×16	32×32	48×48
$[0.01, 0.95]$	99.36/0.77	97.87/2.03	87.35/10.96
$[0.01, 0.9]$	98.04/1.97	96.45/2.36	85.96/11.25
$[0.01, 0.8]$	97.55/3.35	94.76/3.82	79.79/12.46

Table 5. Detection results using images distorted by color reduction

Levels (F_c/F_f)	16×16	32×32	48×48
32	98.56/3.84	97.36/4.03	81.09/7.13
64	98.89/3.05	97.72/3.95	83.45/6.73
128	99.07/1.95	98.34/2.57	88.57/3.21

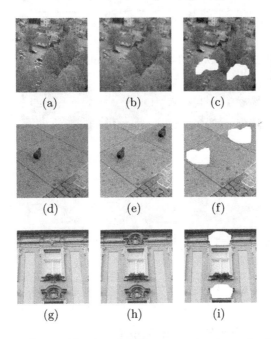

Fig. 7. Detection results on blurring, brightness, and color reduction attack (Color figure online)

top left image is forged by $180°$ rotation and an additional noise of 23.38 db. The bottom left image is under the transformations of horizontally flipping and Gaussian blurring. These are well proved that the method has a good robustness to multiple copied regions and combined transformations forgery.

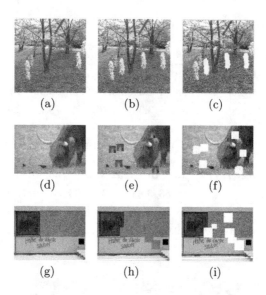

Fig. 8. Detection results of multiple forgery.

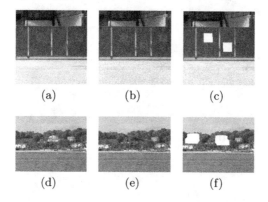

Fig. 9. Detection results of combined forgery.

5.4   Comparison with Existing Approaches

In this section, the detection performance of the proposed method is compared to other existing methods based on DCT [3], PCA [4] and SIFT [11]. Overall performance comparisons of F_c/F_f are presented in Fig. 10. From Fig. 10, we notice that the proposed method has better discriminating features in cases where the regions were modified by blurring, color reduced, brightness, with $F_c \geq 90\%$ and providing the lowest F_f.

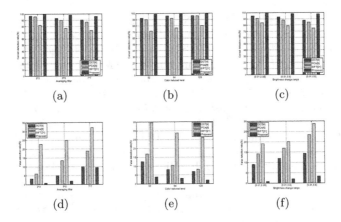

Fig. 10. F_c/F_f for DCT, PCA, SIFT, and the proposed method using various averaging filters, color reduction levels, brightness adjustment and rotated angle with a block size of 16×16. (Color figure online)

6 Conclusions

In this paper, a copy-move image forgery detection is proposed, which puts emphasis on detecting duplicated regions with rotation or flipping. The proposed approach employs rotation invariant uniform local binary patterns to extract block-based features. Experimental results show the advantages of the proposed approach. However, similar to existing block-based detection approaches, the proposed approach still does not work well if the duplicated region is largely scaled or rotated. In future work, we will investigate multi-scale invariant block features [16] and introduce machine learning to further improve detection accuracy [17,18].

Acknowledgements. This work is supported in part by the National Natural Science Foundation of China (61379143, 61232016, U1405254), the Specialized Research Fund for the Doctoral Program of Higher Education (SRFDP) under grant 20120161110014 and the PAPD fund.

References

1. Al-Qershi, O.M., Khoo, B.E.: Passive detection of copy-move forgery in digital images: state-of-the-art. Forensic Sci. Int. **231**(1), 284–295 (2013)
2. Li, J., Li, X., Yang, B., et al.: Segmentation-based image copy-move forgery detection scheme. IEEE Trans. Inf. Forensics Secur. **10**(3), 507–518 (2015)
3. Huang, Y., Lu, W., Sun, W., et al.: Improved DCT-based detection of copy-move forgery in images. Forensic Sci. Int. **206**(1), 178–184 (2011)
4. Farid, A.P., Popescu, A.C.: Exposing digital forgeries by detecting duplicated image regions. Technical report, TR2004-515, Department of Computer Science, Dartmouth College, Hanover, New Hampshire (2004)

5. Bayram, S., Sencar, H.T., Memon, N.: An efficient and robust method for detecting copy-move forgery. In: Proceedings of International Conference on Acoustics, Speech and Signal Processing (ICASSP), pp. 1053–1056. IEEE (2009)
6. Li, L., Li, S., Zhu, H., et al.: Detecting copy-move forgery under affine transforms for image forensics. Comput. Electr. Eng. **40**(6), 1951–1962 (2014)
7. Mahdian, B., Saic, S.: Detection of copy-move forgery using a method based on blur moment invariants. Forensic Sci. Int. **171**(2), 180–189 (2007)
8. Ryu, S.J., Lee, M.J., Lee, H.K.: Detection of copy-rotate-move forgery using zernike moments. In: Proceedings of Information Hiding (LH), pp. 51–65 (2010)
9. Li, L., Li, S., Zhu, H., et al.: An efficient scheme for detecting copy-move forged images by local binary patterns. J. Inf. Hiding Multimedia Sig. Process. **4**(1), 46–56 (2013)
10. Davarzani, R., Yaghmaie, K., Mozaffari, S., et al.: Copy-move forgery detection using multiresolution local binary patterns. Forensic Sci. Int. **231**(1), 61–72 (2013)
11. Amerini, I., Ballan, L., Caldelli, R., et al.: A sift-based forensic method for copy-move attack detection and transformation recovery. IEEE Trans. Inf. Forensics Secur. **6**(3), 1099–1110 (2011)
12. Shivakumar, B.L., Baboo, L.D.S.S.: Detection of region duplication forgery in digital images using SURF. IJCSI Int. J. Comput. Sci. Issues **8**(4), 223–229 (2011)
13. Christlein, V., Riess, C., Jordan, J., et al.: An evaluation of popular copy-move forgery detection approaches. IEEE Trans. Inf. Forensics Secur. **7**(6), 1841–1854 (2012)
14. Huang, D., Shan, C., Ardabilian, M., et al.: Local binary patterns and its application to facial image analysis: a survey. IEEE Trans. Syst. Man Cybern. Part C Appl. Rev. **41**(6), 765–781 (2011)
15. Tralic, D., Zupancic, I., Grgic, S., et al.: CoMoFoD-new database for copy-move forgerydetection. In: Proceedings of 2013 55th International Symposium on ELMAR, pp. 49–54. IEEE (2013)
16. Pan, Z., Zhang, Y., Kwong, S.: Efficient motion and disparity estimation optimization for low complexity multiview video coding. IEEE Trans. Broadcast. **61**(2), 166–176 (2015)
17. Gu, B., Sheng, V.S., Tay, K.Y., et al.: Incremental support vector learning for ordinal regression. IEEE Trans. Neural Netw. Learn. Syst. **26**(7), 1403–1416 (2015)
18. Gu, B., Sheng, V.S., Wang, Z., et al.: Incremental learning for v-support vector regression. Neural Netw. **67**, 140–150 (2015)

An Efficient Passive Authentication Scheme for Copy-Move Forgery Based on DCT

Huan Wang, Hongxia Wang$^{(\boxtimes)}$, and Canghong Shi

School of Information Science and Technology,
Southwest Jiaotong University,
Chengdu 610031, China
hxwang@home.swjtu.edu.cn

Abstract. Digital images can be easily manipulated due to availability of powerful image processing software. Passive authentication as a common challenge method of digital image authentication is extensively used to detect the copy-move forgery images. In this paper, a passive authentication scheme is proposed to authenticate copy-move forgery based on discrete cosine transform (DCT). At the feature extraction step, DCT is applied to image blocks and makes use of the means of DCT coefficients to represent image blocks. The size of feature vectors are optimized. At the matching step, a set number of packages is used to store the feature vectors. The similar blocks can be found by comparing the feature vectors that are contained in adjacent packages. The experimental results demonstrate that the proposed scheme can locate irregular and meaningful tampered regions and multiply duplicated regions. In addition, it can also locate the duplicated regions in digital images that are distorted by adding white Gaussian noise, Gaussian blurring and their mixed operations.

Keywords: Passive authentication · Copy-move forgery · Feature extraction · Packages

1 Introduction

Nowadays, digital media becomes more and more important in our life with the popular of low-cast and high-resolution digital cameras. Digital images as a kind of digital media can be tampered. It will pose a serious social problems that how much of their content can be trusted whether these digital images are authentic or tampered. Especially, these digital images are used to as the witnesses in courtrooms or insurance claims. Therefore, digital image forensics become more and more urgent [1]. Generally, there are two classes of image authentication techniques, i.e., active authentication and passive authentication [2]. The former is based on digital watermarking technologies [3,4] that conceal one or more watermarks into digital images. The receivers can extract the concealed watermarks to determine whether the images have been tampered. These methods are convenient and useful for authenticators. However, the watermarks

© Springer International Publishing AG 2016
X. Sun et al. (Eds.): ICCCS 2016, Part II, LNCS 10040, pp. 417–429, 2016.
DOI: 10.1007/978-3-319-48674-1_37

should be generated by some specially methods and inserted into the images in advance. In addition, the subsequent process for the original images may degrade the image visual quality. In the contrary, passive authentication is a process of detecting whether a digital image is tampered without any additional information except for itself [5]. Thus, passive authentication is widely used in more and more industries.

Copy-move forgery is the most common method in image tampering methods where some regions in an image are copied and pasted to other non-intersecting regions in the same image to conceal important elements or to emphasize particular objects. Since the duplicated regions come from a same image, their most important characteristics are compatible with the remainder of the image, such as the color palettes, noises and dynamic ranges. In a copy-move detection algorithm, lexicographic sorting methods are most popular for identifying similar features. Every feature vector extracted from each block becomes a row in a matrix. Therefore, a matrix will be formed. This matrix can be sorted with its row elements and the most similar features will appear in adjacent rows.

DCT technologies are generally used in image processing because they have a strong energy compaction property. By performing DCT in a digital image, the image energy usually focus on low frequency coefficients and noises are concentrated in high frequency parts. Therefore, the DCT coefficients of each block can be considered as a feature vector to replace the pixels of the block during the block matching processes. Fridrich et al. [8] analyzed the exhaustive search algorithms and proposed a block matching detection method based on discrete cosine transform (DCT), which is one of the landmark methods for copy-move forgery detection. Popscu and Farid [6] presented a PCA-based scheme to conduct copy-move forgery detection. Duplicated regions can be detected by lexicographically sorting all of image blocks. This method can locate multiply duplicated regions. However, the robustness of the presented method is weak. The authors of [7] proposed two similar algorithms based on DWT and PCA to reduce the computational time.

In the above mentioned methods, feature vector sizes are reduced. However, some of them do not consider the reasonable robustness for the suspicious images with post-processing. In real cases, digital images may suffer from different post-processing to conceal the forgery clues, such as additive noises, Gaussian blurring, JPEG compression, image rotation and their mixed operations. Therefore, the detection methods for copy-move forgery are required to improve the detection precise as well as locating the tampered regions of the post processed suspicious images.

Huang et al. [9] improved the method proposed in [8] by reducing the number of features to a quarter. These features are located in the low frequency parts. However, the detection accuracy is unsatisfactory since some useful DCT coefficients that are located in the intermediate frequency parts are truncated as well. Wang et al. [10] applied DWT and DCT on image blocks, respectively. The resulting coefficients are combined to form the feature vectors. This method is robust against JPEG compression and additive noises but it cannot resist other types of post-processing and the mixed operations. Kumar *et al.* proposed a DCT-PCA based method for copy-move forgery detection in [11]. In the proposed method, DCT and PCA are used to represent and compress the feature vector of overlapping blocks, respectively. This method can also robust against some post-processing. However, a high number of false positives can be produced which affect the detection results. Yu *et al.* [12] proposed an effective method to analyze the DCT coefficients of image blocks based on cluster analysis methods. This method can effectively detect copy-move forgery in digital images and resist the post-processing operations, such as Gaussian blurring, adding white Gaussian noise, and JPEG compression in digital images. However, it cannot work well if tampered images suffer from the mixed operations of some types of post-processing.

In this study, an image forgery detection method based on DCT is proposed. The means of DCT coefficients for each image block are calculated to represent the image block and the size of feature vectors is optimized to sixteen. In the matching step, the pixel mean of each image block is calculated and all image blocks are put into 64 packages to detect the copy-move regions instead of using lexicographic order methods to find the copy-move regions. The proposed method can detect the multiply duplicated regions in an image with the mixed operations of adding white Gaussian noises and Gaussian blurring rather than single post-processing.

The rest of this paper is organized as follows. In Sect. 2, the proposed method is presented. Section 3 introduces the experiment results. Finally, Sect. 4 concludes this paper.

2   The Proposed Detection Scheme

The key point of detecting copy-move forgery is to detect the similar regions in an image. However, the size and shape of the duplicated regions are indeterminate. In this paper, a passive authentication method for detecting copy-move forgery is proposed based on DCT. It can locate the multiply duplicated regions. In addition, the proposed scheme can also deal with some post-processing including some mixed operations.

2.1   Algorithm Framework

In existing algorithms, feature vectors matching contains two main steps. Firstly, lexicographically sorting is applied to all feature vectors. The next step is to compare the feature vectors based on the sorted results. In fact, the above mentioned two steps may generate a large number of false positives that will affect the detection results. In the proposed method, in order to improve the detection precision, the method of matching in the packages is adopting to avoid the lexicographically sorting processes and reduce the times of block comparing.

As we know, the pixel values are similar if two regions are duplicated and the means of them are basically identical. Therefore, all blocks and their feature vectors can be put into different packages according to the pixel means of blocks. The blocks that belong to the duplicated regions will be put into a same package. We only need to match the feature vectors of any two blocks that belong to a same package to find the similar blocks and then the duplicated regions are located. Figure 1 shows the processes of the proposed scheme.

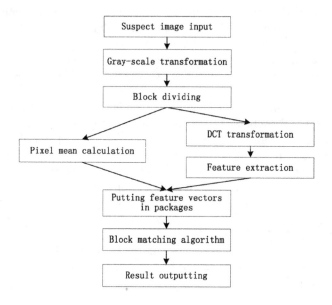

Fig. 1. The diagram of the proposed scheme.

2.2 Pre-processing the Image

If suspicious image A' is a color image, it should be converted into a gray scale image A by using the following formula.

$$I = 0.299R + 0.587G + 0.114B \tag{1}$$

where R, G and B represent the red, green and blue components of A', respectively.

2.3 Extracting the Features

In this section, three steps are used to describe the details of feature extraction in the proposed scheme.

Step 1: Dividing the converted grey-scale image into overlapping blocks with a fixed-size. At this step, the converted gray-scale image A with the size $M \times N$ is divided into $(M - b + 1) \times (N - b + 1)$ overlapping blocks by sliding the window of $b \times b$ pixels along with image A from the upper-left corner right down to the lower-right corner. The size of each image block is $b \times b$ pixels. The image blocks are represented by B_{ij}, where $1 \leq i \leq (M - b + 1)$ and $1 \leq j \leq (N - b + 1)$.

Step 2: Applying DCT to each image block to generate the coefficient matrix for each image block. At this step, DCT is applied to all blocks to obtain the DCT coefficient matrices. In the proposed method, we assume $b = 8$. The DCT coefficient matrices can be expressed as $(C_{ij})_{8\times8}$, where $1 \leq i \leq (M - b + 1)$ and $1 \leq j \leq (N - b + 1)$. Each DCT coefficient matrix contains 64 (8×8) elements.

Step 3: Extracting the features from their coefficient matrices for image blocks. One characteristic of DCT for an image is that the energy focuses on the low frequency parts and the high frequency coefficients play an insignificant role. In the proposed method, each block will be divided into sixteen sub-blocks denoted as $C_{ij}^1 - C_{ij}^{16}$, as shown in Fig. 2.

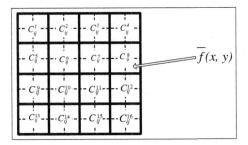

Fig. 2. The sixteen sub-blocks of a block.

Let $t_1 - t_{16}$ represent the DCT coefficient means of the sixteen sub-blocks. Then t_k can be calculated as follows.

$$t_k = \frac{\sum_{x=1}^{2}\sum_{y=1}^{2}\overline{f}_k(x,y)}{2^2} \qquad (2)$$

where $1 \leq k \leq 16$ and $\overline{f}_k(x,y)$ indicates the DCT coefficient values at xth row and yth column in kth sub-blocks. Therefore, we can use the average energy (DCT coefficient mean) to represent each sub-block. For each block, the combination of t_i, denoted as $T = (t_1, t_2, t_3, t_4, t_5, t_6, t_7, t_8, t_9, t_{10}, t_{11}, t_{12}, t_{13}, t_{14}, t_{15}, t_{16})$, can be considered as the feature vector to represent the image block. The size of block feature vectors is reduced from 1×64 (or 1×16) to 1×16 compared with the methods proposed in [8] (or [9]).

2.4 Matching Similar Regions

In this section, the matching method is described by five steps.

Step 1: Calculating the pixel mean for each image block. At this step, the pixel means of image blocks B_{ij}, denoted as P_{ij} ($1 \leq i \leq (M - b + 1)$ and $1 \leq j \leq (N - b + 1)$), are calculated as follows.

$$P_{ij} = \frac{\sum_{x=1}^{b}\sum_{y=1}^{b}f_{ij}(x,y)}{b^2} \tag{3}$$

where $f_{ij}(x,y)$ indicates the pixel values at xth row and yth column in ijth blocks.

Step 2: Putting the features and coordinates of image blocks into corresponding packages according to the pixel means of blocks. At this step, the packages are generated to store the feature vectors. Since the pixel range of a gray scale image is 0 to 255, we can assume that there are 64 package B_k, $k = 1, 2, ..., 64$, where the offset of each package is four. Let P_{ij} be the mean value of block B_{ij}. Then, block B_{ij} will be put into the $([P_{ij}/4] + 1)$th package, where [] represents the round-off to integer. For example, assume $P_{23} = 67$. Then, block B_{23} will be put into 17th package. This indicates that the pixel range of 6th package is 64, 65, 66, and 67. According to this method, all blocks and their feature vectors will be put into the 64 packages.

Step 3: For each package, the similar image block pairs are matched according to their features and a map is labeled according to the coordinates. Any two blocks that are belong to a same package will be compared to determine whether they are copy-move blocks. Let B_{ij} and B_{mn} be two blocks that belong to a same package, (x_1, y_1) and (x_2, y_2) be the coordinates of B_{ij} and B_{mn}, respectively.

To avoid some false matches, the algorithm needs to pay a close attention to the mutual positions of each block pair in a package and outputs a specific block pair only if there are many other matching pairs in the same mutual position, that is, they have the same shift vector. Towards this goal, the shift vector between any two block in a same package is calculated. The positions of each pair of blocks are stored in two separated lists and a shift vector counter C is increased. The shift vector S between B_{ij} and B_{mn} is calculated as follows.

$$S = (x_1 - x_2, y_1 - y_2) \tag{4}$$

Due to the shift vector $-S$ and S correspond to the same shift, the shift vectors are normalized, if necessary, by multiplying by -1 so that $S \geq 0$. For each pair of blocks in a same package, the normalized shift vector counter C is calculated as follows.

$$C = C + 1 \tag{5}$$

The shift vector counter C is initialized to zero. At the end of matching step, the counter C indicates the frequencies of different normalized shift vectors occur. Therefore, all normalized shift vectors $S_1, S_2, ..., S_k$ are generated. If $C(S_r) > T$, the pairs of blocks have the same shift vector S_r can form the candidate duplicated region, where $r = 1, 2, ..., K$. It is worth to mention that the value of the threshold T is related to the size of the smallest region that can be identified by the algorithm. Larger values may cause the algorithm to miss some not so closely matching blocks, while a too small value of T may result many false matches.

Furthermore, the feature vectors of two neighboring blocks may also be similar to each other. Therefore,the coordinate distance of the two blocks should be considered. The actual coordinate distance m between a pair of candidate blocks can be calculated as follows.

$$m = \sqrt{(x_1 - x_2)^2 + (y_1 - y_2)^2} \tag{6}$$

If $m > M$, the pair of blocks is considered as an actual forgery, where M is a preset threshold and $M = 20$ at the default state.

Step 4: Let B_1, B_2, $\cdots$, and B_{64} be the 64 packages. $\forall B \in B_i$ and $\forall B' \in B_{i+1}$, blocks B and B' should be matched with the similar methods of step 3. The purpose is to increase the precision of the proposed method because the adjacent blocks that belong to two contiguous packages may also be the similar image blocks.

Step 5: Outputting the map that includes the detecting results. A map is generated with the same pixel value (it is 0 in this algorithm). Morphologically open operation is applied to fill the holes in marked regions and remove the isolated blocks, then output the final detection.

3 Experimental Results

All experiments are carried out on the platform with Intel Core 3.30 GHZ and MATLAB 7.1. Photoshop 8.0 is used to modify the images and the tampered images are generated based on two data sets.The first data set contains 100 images that are randomly chosen from the miscellaneous volume of $USC-SIPI$ database with the size of 256×256 pixels and 512×512 pixels [13]. The second data set contains 100 uncompressed PNG true color (24 bits per pixel) images with the size of 768×512 pixels [14] which are released by the Eastman Kodak company for unrestricted usage.

3.1 Performance Evaluation

In the proposed scheme, DCT is used to reduce the computational complexity and enhance the performance of the proposed algorithm for some post-processing, such as adding white Gaussian noises and Gaussian blurring. A method can be used to evaluate the performance of a detection method in practical applications from pixel level. It is used to evaluate the accuracy of duplicated regions that have been detected.

From the pixel level, let ω_s and ω_t be the pixels of original regions and copy-move regions in a suspicious image, respectively, and $\widetilde{\omega}_s$ and $\widetilde{\omega}_t$ be the pixels of original regions and copy-move regions in detected result image, respectively.

Detection accuracy rate (DAR) and false positive rate (FPR) are calculated as follows.

$$DAR = \frac{|\omega_s \cap \widetilde{\omega}_s| + |\omega_t \cap \widetilde{\omega}_t|}{|\omega_s| + |\omega_t|} \tag{7}$$

$$FPR = \frac{|\widetilde{\omega}_s - \omega_s| + |\widetilde{\omega}_t - \omega_t|}{|\widetilde{\omega}_s| + |\widetilde{\omega}_t|} \tag{8}$$

where the DAR indicates the performance of correctly locating the pixels of duplicated regions in the tampered images, and the FPR reflects the percentage of pixels that are contained in the detected results but not included in duplicated regions. Then we can calculate the performance of the proposed method from image level and pixel level.

3.2   Accuracy and Effectiveness Test

To evaluate the accuracy and effectiveness of the proposed method, some color images with the size of 768×512 pixels are collected from the second data set to carry out the following experiments. These images are divided into three parts. In the first part, the sizes of duplicated regions are 32×32 pixels and 64×64 pixels, respectively. In the second part, the duplicated regions are irregular and meaningful objects. In the third part, there is more than one duplicated region in each image. In these experiments, all the tampered images are without any post-processing operation and the experiment results are shown in Figs. 3, 4 and 5. The DAR and FPR are calculated to show the performance of the proposed scheme.

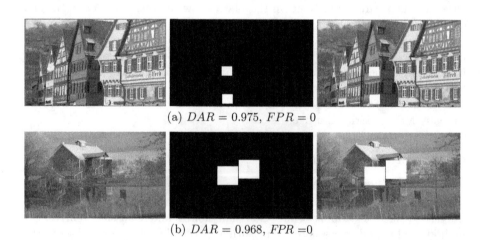

(a) $DAR = 0.975$, $FPR = 0$

(b) $DAR = 0.968$, $FPR = 0$

Fig. 3. Two tampered images with regular duplicated regions (the size of duplicated region in top row is 32×32 pixels, in bottom row is 64×64 pixels) and detection results.

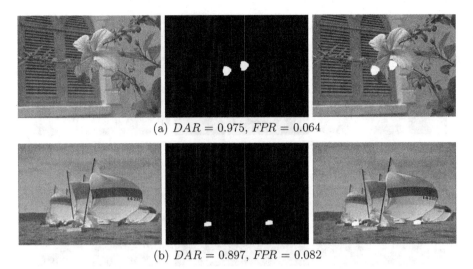

(a) $DAR = 0.975$, $FPR = 0.064$

(b) $DAR = 0.897$, $FPR = 0.082$

Fig. 4. Two tampered images with irregular duplicated regions and detection results.

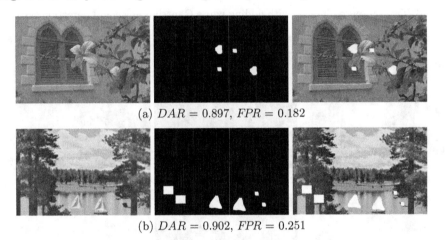

(a) $DAR = 0.897$, $FPR = 0.182$

(b) $DAR = 0.902$, $FPR = 0.251$

Fig. 5. Two tampered images with two irregular and meaningful duplicated regions and the detection results.

We can obtain from Fig. 3 that the three DAR are larger than 0.95 (it is close to 1), and the FPR are zero. This indicates that the duplicated regions can be detected by using the proposed method. Figure 4 shows that the proposed scheme can locate the irregular and meaningful duplicated regions with satisfactory FPR and DAR. Figure 5 demonstrates that the images with multiple duplicated regions can be detected by performance the proposed method. The DAR and FPR are satisfactory. However, the method proposed in [8] cannot detect these tampered images.

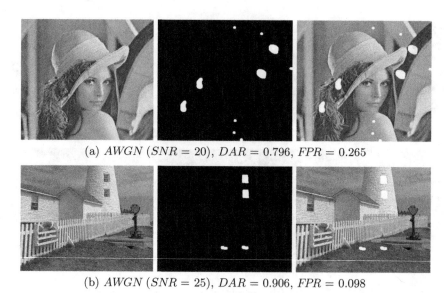

(a) *AWGN (SNR = 20), DAR = 0.796, FPR = 0.265*

(b) *AWGN (SNR = 25), DAR = 0.906, FPR = 0.098*

Fig. 6. Two tampered images with adding white Gaussian noise and detection results.

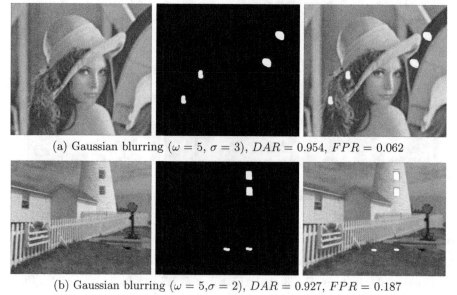

(a) Gaussian blurring ($\omega = 5$, $\sigma = 3$), *DAR = 0.954, FPR = 0.062*

(b) Gaussian blurring ($\omega = 5$, $\sigma = 2$), *DAR = 0.927, FPR = 0.187*

Fig. 7. Two tampered images with Gaussian blurring and detection results.

3.3   Robustness Test

The robustness tests will investigate the performance of the proposed method with adding white Gaussian noises, Gaussian blurring, and their mixed

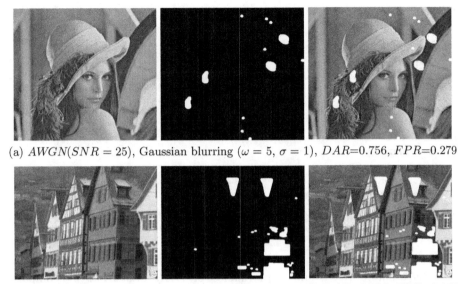

(a) $AWGN(SNR = 25)$, Gaussian blurring ($\omega = 5$, $\sigma = 1$), DAR=0.756, FPR=0.279

(b) $AWGN(SNR = 30)$, Gaussian blurring ($\omega = 6$, $\sigma = 2$), DAR=0.784, FPR=0.245

Fig. 8. Two tampered images with adding white Gaussian noise and Gaussian blurring and detection results.

operations, respectively. In these experiments, 200 images are doctored from the two data sets, there are two irregular and meaningful duplicated regions in each doctored image. The tampered images are added white Gaussian noises, Gaussian blurring, and their mixed operations, respectively. These duplicated regions can be located with a high DAR. A few of detecting results are shown in Figs. 6, 7 and 8. Figure 6 indicates that the proposed method can locate the irregular and meaningful duplicated regions in tampered images that are adding white Gaussian noises with different SNR. Moreover, the proposed method can also resist Gaussian blurring, as is shown in Fig. 7. For the mixed operation of adding white Gaussian noises and Gaussian blurring, the proposed algorithm works well, Fig. 8 shows the results of detecting the tampered images that suffer from the operations above-mentioned. However, the DCT-based [8] and the improved DCT [9] fail to consider such cases.

3.4 Comparison of the Performances with Other Methods

In the last experiment, the performance of the proposed method is compared with the existing classic methods of DCT-based [8] and improved DCT [9]. There are 200 tampered images that are created by using photoshop 8.0 from the two data sets. We randomly copy a region with the size of 32×32 pixels and past it into another non-overlapping region in a same image and applying post-processing on this image. Now, we comparing the proposed method with other two classic methods as follows.

Table 1. DAR and FPR for [8,9], and the proposed scheme (denoted as [P]) with white Gaussian noises

	$SNR = 10$			$SNR = 20$			$SNR = 30$			$SNR = 40$			$SNR = 50$		
	[8]	[9]	[P]	[8]	[9]	[P]	[8]	[9]	[P]	[8]	[9]	[P]	[8]	[9]	[P]
DNR	0	0.75	0.86	0.35	0.94	0.96	0.77	0.98	1.00	0.96	0.98	1.00	0.99	0.99	1.00
FPR	0	0.14	0.06	0.34	0.05	0.04	0.32	0.05	0.03	0.21	0.04	0.02	0.07	0.04	0.02

Table 2. DAR and FPR for [8,9], and the proposed scheme (denoted as [P]) with Gaussian blurring

	$\omega = 3, \sigma = 0.5$			$\omega = 3, \sigma = 1.0$			$\omega = 3, \sigma = 1.5$			$\omega = 3, \sigma = 2.0$			$\omega = 3, \sigma = 2.5$		
	[8]	[9]	[P]	[8]	[9]	[P]	[8]	[9]	[P]	[8]	[9]	[P]	[8]	[9]	[P]
DNR	0.85	0.92	0.98	0.81	0.91	0.97	0.80	0.90	0.95	0.75	0.88	0.92	0.71	0.82	0.91
FPR	0.10	0.09	0.07	0.11	0.09	0.06	0.12	0.10	0.08	0.13	0.11	0.09	0.16	0.13	0.10

Table 1 shows the overall performance of DAR and FPR by comparing over 200 tampered images. In Table 1, white Gaussian noises ($SNR = 10, 20, 30, 40, 50$) are adding to each tampered image. With the increasing of SNR, the DAR and FPR change as well. We can obtain from the table that the method of [8] has the lowest DAR in the three methods especially SNR is smaller than 40. The method of [9] has better results than [8] but its DAR is lower than the proposed method. It is clear that the method of [8] has a unsatisfactory FPR compared with other two methods especially SNR is greater than 20. It is sensitive for noise adding. However, the proposed method has lower FPR.

In the cases of Gaussian blurring, Table 2 shows the overall performance of DAR and FPR of the three methods. It indicates that the proposed method gains higher performance than other two methods with the increasing of blurring radius. The DAR and FPR of [8] methods become discontent and the identical parameters of [9] are better than them. Nevertheless, the proposed method has better performance in the three methods.

4   Conclusions

A passive authentication scheme is proposed to detect the copy-move forgery in the absence of digital watermarks. The method adopts DCT and makes use of the means of DCT coefficients in sub-blocks to represent an image block. It can reduce the size of feature vectors for each image block. Furthermore, the proposed method optimizes the time complexity by using the package method to replace the lexicographic order methods. The accuracy of locating is optimized comparing the existing methods of DCT-based and improved DCT. The experiment results indicate that the proposed method not only can locate the multiple copy-move duplicated regions but also can resist adding white Gaussian noises, Gaussian blurring, and their mixed operations.

Acknowledgments. This research is supported by the National Natural Science Foundation of China (NSFC) under the grant No. U1536110.

References

1. Chang, S.-F., Sebe, N., Liu, Y., Zhuang, Y., Huang, T., Chang, S.F.: Blind passive media forensics: motivation and opportunity. In: Sebe, N., Liu, Y., Zhuang, Y., Huang, T.S. (eds.) MCAM 2007. LNCS, vol. 4577, pp. 57–59. Springer, Heidelberg (2007). doi:10.1007/978-3-540-73417-8_11
2. Lian, S., Kanellopoulos, D.: Recent advances in multimedia information system security. Informatica **33**, 3–24 (2009)
3. Mishra, A., Goel, A., Singh, R., Chelty, G., Singh, L.: Anovel image watermarking scheme using extreme learning machine. In: The 2012 International Joint Conference on Neural Networks (IJCNN), pp. 1–6 (2012)
4. Tong, X., Liu, Y., Zhang, M., Chen, Y.: A novel chaos-based fragile watermarking for image tampering detection and self-recovery signal process. Image Commun. **28**, 301–308 (2013)
5. Zhou, L., Wang, D., Guo, Y., Zhang, J.: Blur detection of digital forgery using mathematical morphology. In: Nguyen, N.T., Grzech, A., Howlett, R.J., Jain, L.C. (eds.) KES-AMSTA 2007. LNCS (LNAI), vol. 4496, pp. 990–998. Springer, Heidelberg (2007). doi:10.1007/978-3-540-72830-6_105
6. Popscu, A.C., Farid, H.: Exposing digital forgeries by detecting duplicated image regions. Technical report TR2003-515, Dartmouth College (2004)
7. Zimba, M., Xingming, S.: DWT-PCA (EVD) based copy-move image forgery detection. Int. J. Digital ContentTechnol. Appl. **5**(1), 251–258 (2011)
8. Fridrich, J., Soukalm, D., Lukas, J.: Detection of copy-move forgery in digital images. In: Digital Forensic Research workshop, Cleveland, pp. 19–23 (2003)
9. Huang, Y.P., Lu, W., Sun, W., Long, D.Y.: Improved DCT-based detection of copy-move forgery in images. Forensic Sci. Int. **206**(1–3), 178–184 (2011)
10. Wang, X., Zhang, X., Li, S., Wang, S.: A DWT-DCT based passive forencis method for copy-move attacks. In: 2011 Third International Conference on Multimedia Information Networking and Security, pp. 304–308 (2011)
11. Kumar, S., Desai, J., Mukherjee, S.: DCT-PCA based method for copy-move forgery detection. In: Satapathy, S.C., Avadhani, P.S., Udgata, S.K., Lakshminarayana, S. (eds.) ICT and Critical Infrastructure: Proceedings of the 48th Annual Convention of Computer Society of India - Volume II. Advances in Intelligent systems and computing, vol. 249, pp. 577–583. Springer, Cham (2014)
12. Yu, J., Han, Q.L.: Detection of copy-move forgery in digital images using discrete cosine transform and cluster analysis. In: International Conference on Computer Networks and Information Security (CNIS), pp. 73–76 (2015)
13. The USC-SIPI Image Database. http://sipi.usc.edu/database/
14. Kodak Lossless True Color Image. http://r0k.us/graphics/kodak/

Audio Tampering Detection
Based on Quantization Artifacts

Biaoli Tao, Rangding Wang[✉], Diqun Yan, Chao Jin, Yanan Chen,
and Li Zhang

College of Information Science and Engineering,
Ningbo University, Ningbo 315211, China
wangrangding@nbu.edu.cn

Abstract. MP3 is one of the common formats in the recording equipments. The authenticity and integrity of MP3 audio is widely concerned. We analyzed quantization characteristic of MP3 encoding, and studied the effect of quantified in frame offset and non offset frame. Then we combined statistical characteristics of zero spectral coefficients before and after quantization. Finally, a tampering detection method based on quantitative characteristics is proposed. According to the disadvantage of existing frame offset method that cannot detect high rate compression, this paper in the quantization artifacts description according to the characteristics of the line frequency distribution used in front of the 16 band. We can further effectively solve tamper detection problem of high bit rate compression by studying 16 band quantization. The experimental results show that the accuracy rate of proposed detection method can reach up to 99 %, the compression rate of detection can reach 256 Kbps, and the complexity of compared with the existing methods is significantly reduced.

Keywords: MP3 audio · Tampering detection · Frame offset · Quantitative artifact

1 Introduction

Digital audio forensic technology is an important part of digital multimedia forensics. Its aim is to verify the integrity and authenticity of the digital audio. Deletion, insertion and splicing are the most typical tampering operations. Deletion is to discard one or more segments of the original audio. Insertion is to insert homologous or heterologous segments into the original audio. Splicing often combines with deletion and insertion.

Till now, a few digital audio forensic methods have reported in the open literatures. Ikram and Malik [1] proposed a method to determine the audio's integrity based on correlation similarity measure. Background noise is considered in this method. In [2], the MFCC and log MFCC have been taken as the detection features to identify the recording environment. As for MP3 audio forensic [3, 4], it has been found that the frame structure of MP3 audio will be destroyed once the tampering operation happens. More works have been done based on electric network frequency (ENF) to identify the audio's integrity [5–7]. Chen et al. [8] utilized singularity analysis based on wavelet packet transform to detect and locate the forgeries in time domain. In [9], by exploiting

© Springer International Publishing AG 2016
X. Sun et al. (Eds.): ICCCS 2016, Part II, LNCS 10040, pp. 430–439, 2016.
DOI: 10.1007/978-3-319-48674-1_38

the traces left by double compression in the statistics of quantized modified discrete cosine transform coefficients, a single measure has been derived that allows to decide whether an MP3 file is singly or doubly compressed.

As mentioned above, digital audio tampering detection has got lots of concern and achievements [10–13]. However, there are still some challengeable issues needed to be solved. For example, when the suspicious audio is compressed with a high compression ratio (i.e. 256 kbps), it becomes very difficult to detect the forgery trace. On the other hand, for the lack of an accurate model for the recording device, it is still a hard problem to identify the source of the testing audio.

In this work, the MP3 encoding technique was introduced in Sect. 2. The detection algorithm was proposed based on quantization artifacts in Sect. 3. Then, in Sect. 4 the proposed scheme was evaluated and compared with the related work [4]. Finally, in Sect. 5, some conclusions about our research are drawn.

2 Review of MP3 Encoding

MP3 is a lossy compression of digital audio coding format. The procedure of MP3 encoding is as follows (Fig. 1):

(1) Through a polyphase filterbank analysis, each sequence of consecutive 1152 PCM samples are filtered into 32 subbands with equal bandwidth according to the Nyquist frequency of the PCM signal.

(2) Each sub-band signal is further divided into 18 finer subbands by applying a modified discrete cosine transform (MDCT), and 576 subbands form a granule. MDCT coefficients can be given by vector xr: $xr = [xr_0 \cdots xr_i \cdots xr_{575}]$.

(3) Meanwhile, the same input PCM signal is also transformed to the frequency domain through a fast Fourier transform (FFT) in order to obtain a higher frequency resolution and information about the spectral changes over time.

(4) The frequency information from the FFT output is provided to the psychoacoustic model to identify audible parts of the audio signals. The current FFT spectra and the previous spectra are compared. If considerable differences are found, a request to adopt short windows will be sent to the MDCT block. As soon as the difference fades away, the MDCT block will be informed to change back to long windows. At the same time, the psychoacoustic model detects the dominant tonal components and masking thresholds are calculated for each critical band. Frequency components below the thresholds are masked out.

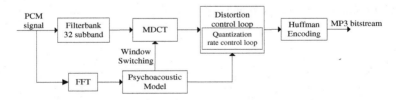

Fig. 1. Block diagram of MP3 encoding

(5) Scaling and quantization are applied to 576 spectral values at a time, and carried iteratively in two nested loops: a distortion control loop (an outer loop which aims to keep the quantization noise below the masking threshold) and a rate control loop (an inner loop which determines the quantization step size).

(6) The Huffman encoding, which inner loop is completed. The frequency domain coefficients of quantitative are encoded without distortion of Huffman. All parameters generated by the encoder reside in the side information part of the frame. The frame header, side information, CRC, Huffman coded frequency lines, etc., are put together to form frames.

It should be noted that quantized MDCT coefficients in Step (5) are calculated by Eq. (1),

$$xr_Q(i) = \text{nint}\left(\left[\frac{|xr(i)|}{2^{\frac{stepsize}{4}}}\right]^{\frac{3}{4}} - 0.0946\right) \tag{1}$$

where $xr_Q(i)$ represents the ith quantized MDCT coefficient, and $xr(i)$ is the ith MDCT coefficient. nint() denotes the nearest integer function and *stepsize* is the quantization step size determined in the inner loop.

3 Proposed Detection Algorithm

3.1 Quantization Artifacts Caused by Tampering

From Eq. (1), it can be seen that MDCT coefficients with similar values will be quantized to a same integer. This phenomenon can be called as quantitative artifacts. We find that when quantized coefficients is 0, the corresponding the value of the MDCT coefficients was 0 or $\pm 10^{-6}$ in most cases, from Fig. 2. Here, Ac denotes the number of MDCT coefficients which values are 0 and $\pm 10^{-6}$. Qc denotes the number of the quantized coefficients with value 0. In Fig. 3a, the difference between Ac and Qc denoted as Δ_{AQ} is close to 0 when no tampering is applied to the original audio (offset = 0). Figure 3b shows the case that the first sample of the original audio is deleted (offset = −1). It can be seen that the range of Δ_{AQ} fluctuates from $-100 \sim -50$. Similarly, when an extra sample is inserted at the beginning of the original audio (offset = +1), the range is also from $-100 \sim -50$ (See Fig. 3c). It means that once the tampering operation happens, the value of Δ_{AQ} will diverge from zero obviously. For example, the segment of 0.5 s long in a 10 s audio is deleted, which is located at 7 to 7.5 s. Figure 4 shows the value of Δ_{AQ}. It can be seen that the range of Δ_{AQ} before tampering position is around zero and goes into the range of $-100 \sim -50$.

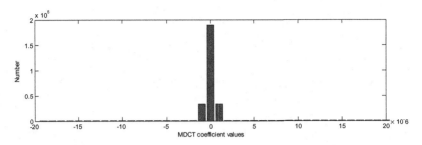

Fig. 2. The distribution of the number of the corresponding MDCT coefficient when the coefficient of quantification is 0 in 10 s audio

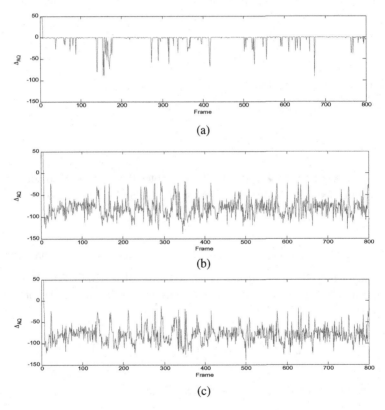

Fig. 3. Δ_{AQ} in different offsets (a) offset = 0 (b) offset = -1 (c) offset = $+1$

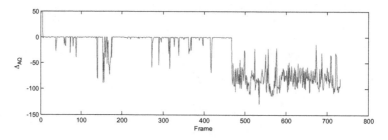

Fig. 4. Tempering detection of deletion

3.2   Detection Algorithm

The proposed detection procedures are described as follows,

(1) For a given audio signal X with L samples, divide it into 1152 samples for each frame by Eq. (2), and each frame has 50 % overlap. The total number of frames is $N = L/576 - 1$

$$[x_0, x_1, x_2, \ldots, x_{N-1}] = FX \tag{2}$$

where F is the window function.

(2) Each frame is applied filter banks and MDCT,

$$S_i = M(x_i) \quad i = 0, 1, \ldots, N - 1 \tag{3}$$

M denotes the filter bank and MDCT. S_i denotes the ith MDCT coefficient. Then count the number of the coefficients which value is 0 and $\pm 10^{-6}$. That is,

$$Ac_i = T(S_i) \quad i = 0, 1, 2, \ldots, N - 1 \tag{4}$$

where T is a count function. And the number of spectral coefficients expressed as Ac_i.

(3) The quantized MDCT coefficient $xr_Q(i, j)$ can be calculated by Eq. (1). Qc, which is the number of the quantized coefficients with value 0, can be obtained by Eq. (5),

$$Qc_i = T(xr_Q(i)), \quad i = 0, 1, 2, \ldots, N - 1 \tag{5}$$

(4) Once Qc is obtained, Δ_{AQ} can be expressed as,

$$\Delta_{AQ}(i) = Ac_i - Qc_i \tag{6}$$

(5) Final calculate

$$result = \begin{cases} i, & if \; length(find(\Delta_{AQ}(i) : \Delta_{AQ}(i+5)) = 0) \leq \theta \& i < N-1 \\ N, & else \end{cases} \tag{7}$$

Where the 'find' function indicates that the position was returned when the value is not equal to 0. θ represents the threshold. It indicates that index was returned when haven't 4 times 0 value. The detecting precision is the 6/3 frame when the sliding frame number 6.

4   Experimental Results

4.1   Experimental Settings

A dataset with 600 audio clips has been constructed. The format of all clips is WAV, 3 s long, 44.1 kHz sampling rate, 16-bit quantization and mono. All the clips are coded by LAME3.99.5 with 6 compression ratios: 32, 64, 96, 128, 192 and 256 kbps. The dataset is randomly divided into 300 positive clips and 300 negative clips. For negative clips, three typical tempering operations including deletion, insertion and splicing are applied respectively. The tampering positions are randomly determined. The threshold in Step (5) of the algorithm sets to 4.

4.2   Detection Accuracy

The detection accuracy AR can be calculated by Eq. (8),

$$AR = (1 - \frac{f_p + f_n}{2}) \times 100 \% \tag{8}$$

where f_p is false positive rate that non-tampered audio is classified as tampered one and f_n is false negative rate that tampered audio is classified as non-tampered one.

From the results shown in Table 1, it can be seen that when the compression ratio is from 32 kbps to 96 kbps, the detection accuracy is more than 99 % and higher than the method in [4].

In [4], the number of non-zero coefficients is used to detect the tampering. However, the method in [4] is not suitable for the case that the compression ratio is larger than 128 kbps. More details in frequency domain will be reserved at high compression ratio and then the numbers of non-zero coefficients are greatly increased. In this case, the number of non-zero coefficients will not reflect the quantitative artifacts.

In the proposed method, only the coefficients in the 16 lowest Frequency-bands are considered for the compression ratio 128, 192 and 256 kbps. As shown in Fig. 5(d), the Δ_{AQ} values of first part of the deleted location still fluctuate around zero, while the corresponding values of the tampering position have large deviation. So the Δ_{AQ} values

Table 1. Detection accuracy at compression ratios 32, 64 and 96 kbps ([5]/proposed)

Compression ratio	Tampering	f_p (%)	f_n (%)	AR (%)
32	Deletion	0.33/1.00	3.67/0.33	98.00/99.34
	Insertion	0.33/1.00	5.67/0.00	94.00/99.50
	Splicing	0.33/1.00	5.33/0.00	97.17/99.50
64	Deletion	0.67/0.67	0.67/1.00	99.33/99.17
	Insertion	0.67/0.67	4.33/0.00	95.00/99.68
	Splicing	0.67/0.67	5.67/0.00	93.57/99.68
96	Deletion	3.67/0.00	2.33/0.33	94.00/99.84
	Insertion	3.67/0.00	6.67/0.17	89.64/99.92
	Splicing	3.67/0.00	4.33/0.00	92.00/100.00

can be used for detecting the tampering position for 128 kbp audios. Similarly, the values also able to identify tampering with location at 192 kbps, as shown in Fig. 5(e). However, Fig. 5(f) reveals that it is very difficult to find the tampering location when the compression bit rate is 256 kbps. Generally, more spectrum detail will be retained and the number of Ac will be increased with the increasing of compression ratio. Therefore, the Δ_{AQ} values are close to zero for high bit rate audios, and these values will fail to reflect the quantitative artifacts caused by tampering.

Table 2 shows the detection results at higher compression ratios. It can be seen that the proposed method can still keep a good accuracy at 128 and 192 kbps. However, the accuracy declines about 20 % when the compression ratio up to 256 kbps.

4.3 Algorithm Complexity

The algorithm complexities of Yang's and the proposed methods are compared. The algorithm can be divided into several modules as shown in Fig. 6.

The complexity of Yang's algorithm can be expressed as,

$$576t_1 + 576t_2 + 2 \times 576t_3 + t_4 \tag{9}$$

where $576t_1$ denote the running time of applying frame offset, $576t_2$ denote the running time of extracting the MDCT coefficients, $576t_3$ denote the running tine of counting the number of non-zero coefficients and calculating frame offset. t_4 denote the running time of detecting the location with frame offset.

The complexity of the proposed algorithm is,

$$t_2' + 2t_3 + t_4 \tag{10}$$

Where denote the running time of extracting the quantitative MDCT coefficients.

From Eqs. (9) and (10), it can be seen that the complexity of [4] is about 576 times higher than the proposed algorithm. The testing experiment for complexity is evaluated

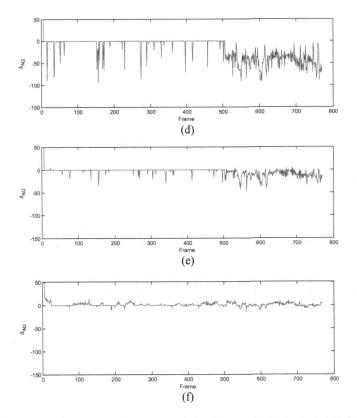

Fig. 5. Tampering detections of compression ratio in different. (d) The ratio is 128 kbps, (e) the ratio is 192 kbps, (f) the ratio is 256 kbps.

Table 2. Detection accuracy at high compression ratios

Compression ratio	Tampering	f_p (%)	f_n (%)	**AR** (%)
128	Deletion	0.00	0.13	99.95
	Insertion	0.00	0.33	99.84
	Splicing	0.00	0.00	100.00
192	Deletion	0.33	2.33	98.68
	Insertion	0.33	0.00	99.84
	Splicing	0.33	0.00	99.84
256	Deletion	23.00	23.00	77.00
	Insertion	23.00	18.40	79.30
	Splicing	23.00	18.00	79.50

on a HpZ820 computer. Its CPU is Xeon(R) 2.50 GHz and the memory is 64G. The program code runs on MATLAB2012. The experimental result shows that the running time of proposed algorithm is 1.314 s. It is obvious lower than that of [4] which is 628.917 s.

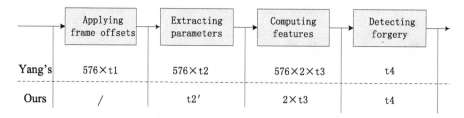

Fig. 6. Algorithm flowchart

5   Conclusions

Audio tampering detection is becoming more and more challenging due to the unre-lenting advances in audio processing. A tampering detection method based on quan-tization artifact is proposed in this paper. We used quantization characteristics to reflect the frame offset. Then we combined statistical characteristics of zero spectral coeffi-cients before and after quantization. The experimental results show that the detection accuracy is nearly to perfect. Meanwhile, the proposed method can also effectively detect the tampering position for high bit rate audio.

There are some interesting issues that can be considered for further research. For example, our method can detect tampering with the start position, but can't detect the end position. And the proposed method only detects the first location if the audio was tampered at multiple positions. So we will aim to solve these problems in the future work.

Acknowledgments. This work was supported by the National Natural Science Foundation of China (Grant No. 61300055, 61672302), Zhejiang Natural Science Foundation (Grant No. LZ15F020002), Ningbo University Fund (Grant No. XKXL1405, XKXL1503) and K.C. Wong Magna Fund in Ningbo University.

References

1. Ikram, S., Malik, H.: Digital audio forensics using background noise. In: IEEE International Conference on Multimedia and Expo, vol. 41, no. 3, pp. 106–110 (2010)
2. Malik, H., Hong, Z.: Recording environment identification using acoustic reverberation. In: International Conference on Acoustics, Speech, and Signal Processing, vol. 22, no. 10, pp. 1833–1836 (2012)
3. Rui, Y., Zhenhua, Q., Jiwu, H.: Detecting digital audio forgeries by checking frame offsets. In: International Multimedia Conference, Processing of the 10th ACM Workshop on Multimedia and Security, pp. 21–26 (2008)
4. Rui, Y., Zhenhua, Q., Jiwu, H.: Exposing MP3 audio forgeries using frame offsets. ACM Trans. Multimedia Comput. Commun. Appl. **8**(2), 1651–1654 (2012)
5. Lv, Z., Hu, Y., Li, C.T., et al.: Audio forensic authentication based on MOCC between ENF and reference signals. In: IEEE China Summit and International Conference, pp. 427–431 (2013)

6. Su, H., Garg, R., Hajj-Ahmad, A., et al.: ENF analysis on recaptured audio recordings. In: International Conference on Acoustics, Speech and Signal Processing (ICASSP), vol. 32, pp. 3018–3022 (2013)
7. Garg, R., Varna, A.L., Hajjahmad, A., et al.: Seeing ENF: power-signature-based timestamp for digital multimedia via optical sensing and signal processing. IEEE Trans. Inf. Forensics Secur. **8**(9), 1417–1432 (2013)
8. Chen, J., Xiang, S., Huang, H.: Detecting and locating digital audio forgeries based on singularity analysis with wavelet package. Multimedia Tools Appl. **75**, 2303–2325 (2016)
9. Bianchi, T., Rosa, A.D., Fontani, M.: Detection and localization of double compression in MP3 audio tracks. EURASIP J. Inf. Secur. **1**, 1–14 (2014)
10. Milani, S., Piazza, P.F., Bestagini, P.: Audio tampering detection using multimodal features. In: IEEE International Conference on Acoustics, Speech and Signal Processing (ICASSP). vol. 152a, pp. 4563–4567 (2014)
11. Korycki, R.: Time and spectral analysis methods with machine learning for the authentication of digital audio recordings. Forensic Sci. Int. **230**(1–3), 117–126 (2013)
12. Cuccovillo, L., Mann, S., Tagliasacchi, M.: Audio tampering detection via microphone classification. In: IEEE International Workshop on Multimedia Signal Processing, vol. 51, no. 7, pp. 177–182 (2013)
13. Zhaoqing, P., Yun, Z., Sam, K.: Efficient motion and disparity estimation optimization for low complexity multiview video coding. IEEE Trans. Broadcast. **61**(2), 166–176 (2015)

Improvement of Image Universal Blind Detection Based on Training Set Construction

Min Lei[1(✉)], Huaifeng Duan[2], Chunru Zhou[1], Huihua Wang[2],
and Yin Li[1]

[1] Information Security Center, Beijing University of Posts
and Telecommunications, Beijing, China
leimin@bupt.edu.cn
[2] School of Information Engineering, Beijing Institute of Graphic
Communication, Beijing, China

Abstract. The detection rates of existing universal blind detection reduced greatly in practical applications due to the generalization problem. According to the principle of orthogonal design, this paper builds three sample sets of embedding rates mismatch, embedding algorithms mismatch and image sources mismatch between the training sample and the testing sample. The three sets are used to test the detection error rates of Rich Model in the case of embedding rates mismatch, embedding algorithm mismatch and image source mismatch. This paper proposes several methods to improve the generalization ability of the universal blind detection, including training the sample by small embedding rates, learning various kinds of embedding algorithms, pre-classifying the testing sample and improving the IQM algorithm. The results show that the practicability of the universal blind detection will be improved.

Keywords: Universal blind detection · Generalization ability · Rich model

1 Introduction

With the rapid development of Internet and computer technology, the society today has become an information society. The damage, tampering and loss of information make people aware of the issue of the information security has become more and more serious. Information hiding technology is a research hotspot in information security. Steganography and steganalysis are two important branches of information hiding technology, they are opposites. The purpose of steganalysis is to detect the existence of secret information and destroy the information. Steganalysis is the key technology to solve the problem of illegal use of steganography.

Now steganalysis algorithms mainly use machine learning methods to detect the existence of secret information. With the improvement of the efficiency of feature extraction and the performance of classifier, the performance of the universal blind detection method has become better and better, and it can detect many kinds of algorithms [1]. The existing steganalysis algorithms mainly focus on the design of features, but rarely focus on practicality. In fact, steganalysis has the same generalization problem

© Springer International Publishing AG 2016
X. Sun et al. (Eds.): ICCCS 2016, Part II, LNCS 10040, pp. 440–449, 2016.
DOI: 10.1007/978-3-319-48674-1_39

with machine learning in practical applications. If the generalization problem can't be solved, it is difficult to put the steganalysis into practice.

This paper analyzes the generalization abilities of a representative steganalysis algorithms: Rich Model algorithm. This paper do the research from three aspects: embedding rates mismatch, embedding algorithm mismatch and image source mismatch. At the same time, this paper propose several methods to improve the generalization ability of the universal blind detection according to the test results.

2 Analysis of Steganalysis Algorithm

2.1 Analysis of Rich Model

Fridrich et al. [2] proposed a steganalysis algorithm by subtractive pixel adjacency matrix (SPAM) in 2009. SPAM models the differences between adjacent pixels using first-order and second-order Markov chain. The algorithm computes the differences from eight directions, and the statistical histogram of the mean of the differences in $\uparrow, \downarrow,$ $\leftarrow, \rightarrow, \searrow, \searrow, \nearrow, \swarrow$ directions are used as features for steganalysis.

In one direction as an example, the calculation formula of the difference array D is shown as follows:

$$D_{i,j}^{\rightarrow} = I_{i,j} - I_{i,j+1} \tag{1}$$

$i \in \{1,\ldots,m\}, j \in \{1,\ldots,n-1\}.$

The first-order SPAM features model the difference arrays D by a first-order Markov process:

$$M_{u,v}^{\rightarrow} = P(D_{i,j+1}^{\rightarrow} = u | D_{i,j}^{\rightarrow} = v) \tag{2}$$

where $u, v \in \{-T,\ldots,T\}.$

The second-order SPAM features model the difference arrays D by a second-order Markov process:

$$M_{u,v,w}^{\rightarrow} = P(D_{i,j+2}^{\rightarrow} = u | D_{i,j+1}^{\rightarrow} = v, D_{i,j}^{\rightarrow} = w) \tag{3}$$

where $u, v, w \in \{-T,\ldots,T\}.$

Finally, the transition probability matrix is converted to an one-dimensional vector, and calculate the average of the four results in horizontal and vertical direction. The result matrix is converted to an one-dimensional vector too.

$$\begin{aligned} F_{1,\ldots,k} &= \frac{1}{4}[M^{\rightarrow} + M^{\leftarrow} + M^{\uparrow} + M^{\downarrow}] \\ F_{k+1,\ldots,2k} &= \frac{1}{4}[M^{\searrow} + M^{\nwarrow} + M^{\swarrow} + M^{\nearrow}] \end{aligned} \tag{4}$$

where $k = (2T+1)^2$ for the first-order features and $k = (2T+1)^3$ for the second-order features.

Fridrich et al. [3] proposed the Rich Model steganalysis algorithm 2012. The algorithm extracts useful features from spatial domain, and it contains 106 submodels and 34671 dimensional effective features. It is an improved steganalysis algorithm based on the SPAM algorithm. The steps of Rich Model algorithm are as follows:

(1) Computing Residuals: Input an image X, and computing the residuals by the following form:

$$R_{ij} = \widehat{X}_{ij}(N_{ij}) - cX_{ij} \tag{5}$$

where c is the residual order, N_{ij} is a local neighborhood of pixel X_{ij}, and $\widehat{X}_{ij}$ is a predictor of cX_{ij}. The residual type includes "spam" type and "minmax" type, and the "spam" residual can be divided into five classes: 1st, 2nd, 3rd, EDGE and SQUARE [4]. In one direction as an example, the calculation formulas are shown as follows:

$$
\begin{aligned}
1st: \quad & R_{ij} = X_{i,j+1} - X_{ij} \\
2nd: \quad & R_{ij} = X_{i,j-1} + X_{i,j+1} - 2X_{ij} \\
3rd: \quad & R_{ij} = -X_{i,j+2} + 3X_{i,j+1} - 3X_{ij} + X_{i,j-1} \\
EDGE: \quad & Rij = -X_{i-1,j-1} + 2X_{i-1,j} + X_{i-1,j+1} + 2X_{i,j-1} - 4X_{ij} + 2X_{i,j+1} \\
SQUARE: \quad & Rij = -X_{i-1,j-1} + 2X_{i-1,j} + X_{i-1,j+1} + 2X_{i,j-1} - 4X_{ij} + 2X_{i,j+1} \\
& \quad -X_{i+1,j-1} + 2X_{i+1,j} - X_{i+1,j+1}
\end{aligned} \tag{6}
$$

The "minmax" residual can be divided into three classes: 1st, 2nd and EDGE, the calculation formulas are shown as follows:

$$
\begin{aligned}
1st: \quad & R_{ij} = \min \, or \, \max\{X_{i-1,j-1} - X_{ij}, X_{i-1,j} - X_{ij}, X_{i-1,j+1} - X_{ij}, X_{i,j+1} - X_{ij}\} \\
2nd: \quad & R_{ij} = \min \, or \, \max\{X_{i,j-1} + X_{i,j+1} - 2X_{ij}, X_{i-1,j} + X_{i+1,j} - 2X_{ij}\} \\
EDGE: \quad & R_{ij} = \min \, or \, \max\{-X_{i-1,j-1} + 2X_{i-1,j} - X_{i-1,j+1} + 2X_{i,j-1} - 4X_{ij} + 2X_{i,j+1}, \\
& \quad -X_{i-1,j+1} + 2X_{i-1,j} - X_{i+1,j+1} + 2X_{i,j+1} - 4X_{ij} + 2X_{i+1,j}, \\
& \quad -X_{i+1,j+1} + 2X_{i,j+1} - X_{i+1,j-1} + 2X_{i+1,j} - 4X_{ij} + 2X_{i,j-1}\}
\end{aligned} \tag{7}
$$

(2) Truncation and Quantization: Each submodel is formed from a quantized and truncated version of the residual

$$R_{ij} \leftarrow trunc_T\left(round\left(\frac{R_{ij}}{q}\right)\right) \tag{8}$$

where $q > 0$ is a quantization step. The quantization makes the residuals more sensitive to the changes caused by the embedded information. The purpose of truncation is to limit the residuals in an appropriate dynamic range.

(3) Co-Occurrence: The effect of the co-occurrence matrix of the main diagonal and the diagonal direction is very small. So Rich Model algorithm only use the horizontal co-occurrence $C_d^{(h)}$ and the vertical co-occurrence $C_d^{(v)}$

$$C_d^{(h)} = \frac{1}{Z} \left| \{ R_{ij}, R_{i,j+1}, R_{i,j+2}, R_{i,j+3} | R_{i,j+k-1} = dk, k = 1, \ldots, 4 \} \right|$$
$$C_d^{(v)} = \frac{1}{Z} \left| \{ R_{ij}, R_{i+1,j}, R_{i+2,j}, R_{i+3,j} | R_{i+k-1,j} = dk, k = 1, \ldots, 4 \} \right|$$

(9)

where Z is the normalization factor ensuring that $\sum_{d \in T4} C_d^{(h)} = 1$ and $\sum_{d \in T4} C_d^{(v)} = 1$.

(4) Due to truncation and quantization, as well as the symmetry of the co-occurrence matrix, the dimensions of each "spam" submodel are decreased from 2625 to 338, all "spam" residuals are symmetrized sequentially by applying the following two rules:

$$\bar{C}_d \leftarrow C_d + C_{-d}$$
$$\bar{\bar{C}}_d \leftarrow \bar{C}_d + \bar{C}_{\vec{d}}$$

(10)

where $d = (d_1, d_2, d_3, d_4) \in T_4$, $\vec{d} = (d_4, d_3, d_2, d_1)$ and $-d = (-d_1, -d_2, -d_3, -d_4)$.
    The dimensions of each "minmax" submodel are decreased from 625 to 325, all "minmax" residuals are symmetrized sequentially by applying the following two rules:

$$\bar{C}d \leftarrow C_d^{(\min)} + C_{-d}^{(\max)}$$
$$\bar{\bar{C}}d \leftarrow \bar{C}d + \bar{C}\vec{d}$$

(11)

where $C^{(\min)}$ and $C^{(\max)}$ are the "min" and "max" co-occurrence matrices computed from the same residual.

2.2 Ensemble Classifier

The idea of ensemble classifier [5, 6] is to combine the classifiers which have independent decision making abilities to form a strong classifier. In general, the predictive ability of ensemble classifier is much better than the predictive ability of the single classifier. Random forest [7] is an ensemble method in the machine learning, based on bagging and random feature selection, number of decision trees (base classifiers) is generated and majority voting is taken for classification. Random forest algorithm has a great advantage compared to other algorithms, it can deal with high dimensional data and has a faster speed of learning, and the random forest can detect the interaction between different features.

The ensemble classifier uses Fisher Linear Discriminants (FLDs) as base learners due to their simple and fast. The basic idea of Fisher linear discriminant is to find a projection direction and the high dimensional problem is reduced to one dimension to be solved. The one dimensional data need to have the following properties: the similar samples gather together as close as possible and different samples should far away from each other.

3   Algorithm Design

The image sources used for experiments are the BOSSBase ver. 1.01 database [8]. The BOSSBase database consists of 10000 grayscale images in PGM format and the sizes of the images are 512512. They are all original images without other additional processing, so the database can reflect the problems better. Six kinds of classical embedding algorithms are used to embed the secret information. The six classical algorithms are: LSB Matching algorithm (LSB $\pm$ 1) [9], edge-adaptive algorithm (EA) [10], HUGO algorithm [11], Syndrome-Trellis Codes algorithm (STC) [12, 13], SSTDM algorithm [14] and PATCHWORK algorithm. The above six kinds of embedding algorithms almost cover all the features of the spatial domain. The generalization abilities of Rich Model are tested in the experiments. Ensemble classifier is used in the experiments, and the experiments include the analysis of embedding rates mismatch, embedding algorithm mismatch and image source mismatch.

3.1   Analysis of Embedding Rates Mismatch

The distance between the features of cover images and stego images has an important relationship with the embedding rates [15], so this paper test the stego images with different embedding rates first. According to the principle of orthogonal design, the embedding rates which are selected are 10 %, 50 % and 80 %. And in order to improve the confidence coefficient of the experimental result, this paper divide the BOSSBase database into two groups. One group is the training sample contains 9000 cover images and 9000 stego images, and the other one is the testing sample contains 1000 cover images and 1000 stego images embedded by different embedding rate from the stego images in training sample. This paper take the test for ten times and then averaged. The detection error rates of Rich Model algorithm are shown in Table 1.

It can be seen from Table 1 that in terms of the specific embedding algorithm, the Rich Model algorithm performs well in the detection of LSB algorithm, MLSB algorithm and LSB Matching algorithm, and for other algorithms, the detection error rates are still low. When the embedding rate of the training sample is 10 % and the embedding rate of the testing sample is 50 % or 80 %, the detection error rates are low. But when he embedding rate of the training sample is 50 % or 80 % and the embedding rate of the testing sample is 10 %, the detection error rates are so high.

Table 1. The detection error rates of Rich Model algorithm in the test of embedding rates mismatch

	train 50% test 10%	train 10% test 50%	train 10% test 80%	train 80% test 10%	train 80% test 50%	train 50% test 80%
▩ EA	0.5	0.0778	0.0772	0.4635	0.1148	0
▩ STC	0.3227	0.0688	0.0602	0.4865	0.224	0.0195
▩ LSB±1	0.4818	0.0198	0.016	0.4965	0.0553	0.0055
▩ SSTDM	0.394	0.0515	0.0423	0.4768	0.0948	0.03

3.2 Analysis of Embedding Algorithms Mismatch

Because of the varied of embedding algorithms, it is difficult to enumerate all the algorithms in the training phase. In practical application, the detector will encounter algorithms which not appear in the training sample, and the gaps of embedding principles between different embedding algorithms are also different, so the detection accuracy may changes greatly. If the problem can't be solved, the practicality of the steganalysis algorithm will be badly affected. Aiming at this problem, this paper do a test with the Rich Model algorithm. In order to improve the confidence coefficient of the experimental result, this paper also divide the BOSSBase database into two groups. One group is the training sample contains 9000 cover images and 9000 stego images, and the other one is the testing sample contains 1000 cover images and 1000 stego images embedded by different embedding algorithms from the stego images in training sample. This paper take the test for ten times and then average these results. The detection error rates of Rich Model algorithm are shown in Table 2.

From Table 2 we can see that in the aspect of embedding algorithms mismatch, in terms of overall performance, Rich Model algorithm performs well. In terms of the specific embedding algorithm, when the training samples and test images using same embedding algorithms, the detection error rate is the lowest. When the training samples and test images using different embedding algorithms, the results are different. If the

Table 2. The detection error rates of Rich Model algorithm in the test of embedding algorithm mismatch

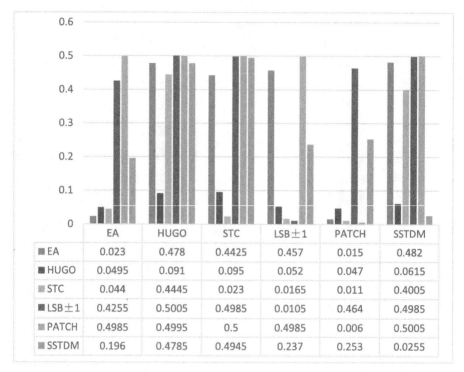

	EA	HUGO	STC	LSB±1	PATCH	SSTDM
■ EA	0.023	0.478	0.4425	0.457	0.015	0.482
■ HUGO	0.0495	0.091	0.095	0.052	0.047	0.0615
■ STC	0.044	0.4445	0.023	0.0165	0.011	0.4005
■ LSB±1	0.4255	0.5005	0.4985	0.0105	0.464	0.4985
■ PATCH	0.4985	0.4995	0.5	0.4985	0.006	0.5005
■ SSTDM	0.196	0.4785	0.4945	0.237	0.253	0.0255

embedding principles of different embedding algorithms are similar, the detection error rates of Rich Model algorithm are very low, such as LSB Matching algorithm and LSB algorithm, MLSB algorithm and LSB algorithm. Rich Model algorithm could detect plenty of embedding algorithms, and detection error rate is low.

3.3   Analysis of Image Source Mismatch

Image properties have a great influence on the accuracy of steganalysis, and the detection rates will make a big difference between different image sources. The performance of the detector may decrease greatly when the image source of the training sample and the image source of the testing sample are different [16]. This paper do tests in the case of image source match and image source mismatch. In the test of image source match, this paper divide the BOSSBase database into two groups. One group is the training sample contains 9000 cover images and 9000 stego images, and the other one is the testing sample contains 1000 cover images and 1000 stego images using same embedding algorithm with the stego images in training sample. In the test of image source mismatch, this paper use BOSSBase database as training sample, and the training sample contains 9000 cover images and 9000 stego images. This paper use

MAP database as the testing sample, the testing sample contains 1000 cover images and 1000 stego images embedded by same embedding algorithm with the stego images in training sample. The embedding rates of the stego images are all 50 %. The features of the MAP database are different from the features of BOSSBase database, so use the two databases can reflect the problem well. This paper take the test for ten times and then averaged. The detection error rates of Rich Model algorithm in the test of image source match and image source mismatch are shown in Table 3.

Table 3. The detection error rates of Rich Model algorithm in the test of image source match and image source mismatch

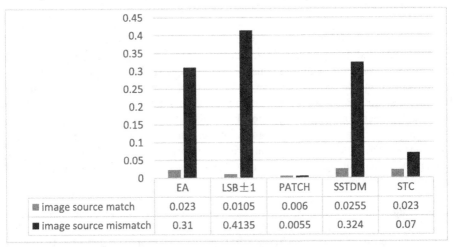

	EA	LSB±1	PATCH	SSTDM	STC
■ image source match	0.023	0.0105	0.006	0.0255	0.023
■ image source mismatch	0.31	0.4135	0.0055	0.324	0.07

It can be seen from Table 3 that in the aspect of image source mismatch, in terms of overall performance, the performances of Rich Model algorithm is decreased in different degrees. In terms of the specific embedding algorithm, Rich Model algorithm performs well in the detection of LSB algorithm, MLSB algorithm, PATCHWORK algorithm and STC algorithm, the detection error rates are low.

4   Improved Methods

This paper puts forward several methods to improve the generalization ability of the universal blind detection through the analysis of the experimental data.

For the problem of embedding rates mismatch, because when the embedding rate of the training sample is small and the embedding rate of the testing sample is big, the detection error rates are low, so we can put stego images whose embedding rates are small as the training sample to solve the problem of embedding rates Mismatch.

For the problem of embedding algorithms mismatch, it can be seen from the experiment that if the embedding principles of embedding algorithms of the training sample and testing sample are similar, the detection error rates are very low. So we can construct the training sample which consists of various kinds of embedding algorithms. By this method, the detection rate can be improved.

For the problem of image source mismatch, we could classify the images according to the features of the images first, and then detect the images by corresponding detector. We can also improve the IQM steganalysis algorithm to solve the problem. Firstly, the imagesare processed by filtering, and then compute the difference of the noise of the images before and after filtering. If the difference is too large, then the images are stego images.

5 Conclusion

The principles of Rich Model algorithm are introduced and the generalization ability of the universal blind detection is analyzed in this paper. This paper puts forward several methods based on the training set construction to improve the generalization ability of the universal blind detection. To solve the problem of embedding algorithms mismatch by putting stego images whose embedding rates are small as the training sample. To solve the problem of embedding algorithms mismatch by learning various kinds of embedding algorithms during the training phase. And we can pre-classify the images and improve the IQM steganalysis algorithm to solve the problem of image source Mismatch. In the future, we could improve the practicability of the universal blind detection in color images.

Acknowledgment. This work was supported by the National Key Technology Support Program (2015BAH08F02). Open Foundation of Jiangsu Engineering Center of Network Monitoring (Nanjing University of Information Science & Technology) (Grant No. KJR1509). The PAPD fund and CICAEET fund.

References

1. Wan, B.J., Zhang, T., Hou, X.D., Zhu, Z.H.: Image steganalysis method based on boosting algorithm fusion. Comput. Eng. **39**, December 2013. (in Chinese)
2. Pevny, T., Bas, P., Fridrich, J.: Steganalysis by subtractive pixel adjacency matrix. IEEE Trans. Inf. Secur. Forensics **5**(2), 215–224 (2010)
3. Fridrich, J., Kodovsky, J.: rich models for steganalysis of digital images. IEEE Trans. Inf. Forensics Secur. **7**(3), 868–882 (2012)
4. Li, C.X.: Reasearch of steganography and steganalysis of adaptive EA algorithm in spatial domain. Dalian University of Technology, Dalian (2013). (in Chinese)
5. Kodovský, J., Fridrich, J., Holub, V.: Ensemble classifiers for steganalysis of digital media. IEEE Trans. Inf. Forensics Secur. **7**(2), 432–444 (2012)
6. Kodovský, J., Pevný, T., Fridrich, J.: Modern steganalysis can detect YASS. In: Proceedings of SPIE, Electronic Imaging, Security Forensics of Multimedia XII, San Jose, CA, vol. 7541, pp. 02-01–02-11, 17–21 January 2010
7. Breiman, L.: Random forest. Mach. Learn. **45**(1), 5–32 (2001)

8. Filler, T., Pevný, T., Bas, P.: BOSS (Break Our Steganography System) (2014). http://agents.fel.cvut.cz/stegodata/BossBase-1.01-cover.tar.bz2

9. Sharp, T.: An implementation of key-based digital signal steganography. In: Proceedings of the 4th International Workshop on Information Hiding, London, UK, pp. 13–26 (2001)

10. Luo, W., Huang, F., Huang, J.: Edge adaptive image steganographybased on LSB matching revisited. IEEE Trans. Inf. Forensics Secur. 5(2), 201–214 (2010)

11. Pevný, T., Filler, T., Bas, P.: Using high-dimensional image models to perform highly undetectable steganography. In: Böhme, R., Fong, P.W., Safavi-Naini, R. (eds.) IH 2010. LNCS, vol. 6387, pp. 161–177. Springer, Heidelberg (2010). doi:10.1007/978-3-642-16435-4_13

12. Filler, T., Fridrich, J., Judas, J.: Minimizing embedding impact in steganography using Trellis-coded quantization. In: Proceedings of SPIE, EI, Media Forensics and Security XII, San Jose, CA, pp. 1–14, 18–20 January 2010

13. Filler, T., Judas, J., Fridrich, J.: Minimizing additive distortion in steganography using Syndrome-Trellis codes. IEEE Trans. Inf. Forensics Secur. 6(3), 920–935 (2011)

14. Chen, B., Wornell, G.: Quantization index modulation: a class of provably good methods for digital watermarking and information embedding. IEEE Trans. Inf. Theory. 47(4), 1423–1443 (2001)

15. Wu, A., Feng, G.: Payload mismatch detection of image steganalysis using ensemble linear discriminant clustering. IEEE Trans. Signal Process. 1–4 (2015)

16. Dong, Y., Zhang, T., Hou, X., Xu, C.: A new steganalysis paradigm based on image retrieval of similar image-inherent statistical properties and outlier detection. In: Wireless Communications and Signal Processing (WCSP), pp. 1–5 (2015)

An Efficient Forensic Method Based on High-speed Corner Detection Technique and SIFT Descriptor

Bin Yang[(✉)] and Honglei Guo

School of Design, Jiangnan University, Wuxi 214122, China
{Yewind2002,guohonglei200}@163.com

Abstract. Image manipulation has become commonplace with growing easy access to sophisticated photo editing softwares. One of the most common types of image forgeries is the copy–move forgery, wherein a region from an image is replaced with another region from the same image. Many existing forensic methods suffer from their inability to detect the cloned area, which is subjected to various transformations such as scaling, rotation, flipping and blurring. In this paper, we propose a novel forensic method based on high-speed corner detection (HSCD) technique and improved scale invariant features transform (SIFT) descriptor. Machine learning technique is used to detect feature points which greatly decreasing the processing time compare to other feather detectors. Experimental results show the efficacy of this technique in detecting copy-move forgeries and estimating the geometric transformation parameters. Compared with the state of the art, our approach obtains a higher true positive rate and a lower false positive rate.

Keywords: Image forensics · High-speed corner detection · Copy-move forgery detection · SIFT · Descriptor

1 Introduction

Different types of digital cameras and user-friendly image editing software people can create and manipulate digital images easily. A digitally changed photograph can be indistinguishable from an authentic photograph. As a result, photographs no longer hold the unique stature as recording of events. Copy-Move forgery is performed with the intention to make an object "clone" or "disappear" from the image by covering it with a small block copied from another part of the same image. Since the duplicated region come from the same image, noise components, Brightness, the color palette, and the other properties will be well- matched with the rest of the image, therefore it is very difficult for a human eye to detect such forgery. To better hide the tampering, additional postprocessed transformations are often used. These include scaling, rotation, lossy compression, noise addition, blurring, among others. Figure 1 shows two example of copy-move forgery. Since the duplicated region is selected from the image itself, the noise components, texture and color patterns are compatible with the rest of the image. The counterfeit parts are not easily to detect. Moreover, there might be post-processing operations that can even increase the difficulty of exposing such forgery. To detect such

© Springer International Publishing AG 2016
X. Sun et al. (Eds.): ICCCS 2016, Part II, LNCS 10040, pp. 450–463, 2016.
DOI: 10.1007/978-3-319-48674-1_40

forgeries reliably and be robust to some of post-processing operations, a number of approaches have been recently carried out.

(a)   (b)

Fig. 1. Examples of copy-move forgery: (a) the original image (b) the forged image

CMFD techniques can be classified into two main categories: block-based and feature-based. Block-based techniques essentially compare blocks in an efficient manner and provide invariance to some transformations. The simplest approach to detect a copy-move forgery is to use an exhaustive search as pointed in [1]. In CMF the duplicate area can be of any shape and location, searching all possible image locations and sizes would be computationally infeasible. The technique of [2] reduces the time complexity of the PCA-based approach by using a discrete wavelet transform (DWT), but again does not address geometrical transformations. In [3], a technique based on the Fourier-Mellin Transform, which is invariant to small rotation and resizing of the copied regions as well, is proposed. However, this technique fails when the rotation and/or resizing is significant. Markov features in DCT and DWT domain are used to detect forgery in [4]. They extract the original Markov features from the transition probability matrices in DCT domain to capture the inter-block correlation between block DCT coefficients. Then the support vector machine (SVM) is exploited to classify the authentic and spliced images using the final dimensionality reduced feature vector. The authors in [5] improve the detection efficiency by using the Fast Walsh-Hadamard Transform (FWHT) and Multi-Hop Jump (MHJ) algorithm. Although block-based approaches seem effective to detect duplicated regions, the accuracy of these kind of methods are still unsatisfactory while performing on the rotated and scaled objects [6]. To overcome this issue, a different category of approaches in CMFD try to emphasize the use of feature matching for detecting forged regions in images.

In pattern recognition, the feature-based techniques usually are applied to two images: a target and a test image. In the case of CMFD, the feature-based techniques are applied to one image only. The key-points extracted in that region will be quite similar to the original ones; therefore, a matching between key-points can be used to discover which part was copied and which geometric transformation was applied [7]. Recently, feature-based CMFD techniques have been spurred, as forgeries have become more convincing with various transformations. In [8, 9], a scale invariant feature transform (SIFT) technique [10], which invariant to various geometrical transformations, is used to extract the features. Forgery decision is performed while a number of SIFT features are matched. In [11], Speeded-Up Robust Features (SURF) features [12] is extracted instead of SIFT. However, the detection result is hardly improved since the transformation invariance of SURF is little more than SIFT [13]. Transform-invariant features are obtained from the MPEG-7 image signature tools in [6]. Such CMFD approach obtain a feature matching accuracy in excess of 90 % across postprocessing operations and are able to detect the cloned regions with a high true positive rate and lower false positive rate. Recently, ORB features are used in [14]. Forgery decision is made by matching the orientated FAST key points and ORB features which extracted in the image. The FAST method is based on the SVM technique [15, 16]. Dense-field techniques is used in [17] to especially deal with the occlusive forgeries in which pieces of background copied elsewhere the dense-field. Although these feature-based methods are able to detect the forgery manipulated by geometric transformation. The accuracy of CMFD is still unable to be used as evidence. Furthermore, mismatches usually occur in the image regions when changes in intensity is quite similar, such as the forgery in Fig. 1.

In this paper, an effective forensics method is proposed to detect duplicated regions, while these regions are allowed to undergo several geometric changes, as well as some manipulations including JPEG compression, and Gaussian noise addition. The processing time is greatly reduced through the high-speed corner detection (HSCD) technique which is based on machine learning. Furthermore, the proposed method can give reliable estimates of the affine transformation parameters while applying to the geometric transformed region. Moreover, our method is able to handle the problem of lack of feature points while the forgery is perform in the area that textures are almost uniform.

The rest of this paper is organized as follows. Section 2 presents the proposed forensic method for copy-move forgery detection. Section 3 presents the experimental results, while conclusions are finally drawn in Sect. 4.

2   Proposed Algorithm

Although the keypoint-based algorithms are able to locate and extract the key-points, they may suffer the problem of insufficient or even none key-points in the area where the textures are almost uniform [18]. Thus, the keypoint-based CMFD schemes (such as [8, 9, 11, 19]) are hard to detect the duplication in such area. Moreover, many SIFT-based methods can hardly expose the forgery which is mirror transformed. Our method is proposed to overcome the weakness of insufficient key-points. Figure 2 illustrates the flowchart of the proposed scheme, and generally it can be separated into three parts. Firstly, the feature points are detected by HSCD based on machine learning. Afterward, the feature points in the set $X = (x_1, x_2, ..., x_n)$ are then described as $F = (f_1, f_2, ..., f_n)$ using the improved SIFT descriptor. Finally, the feature matching determines whether each pair of two feature points is similar, an effective method is adopted instead directly using nearest neighbor.

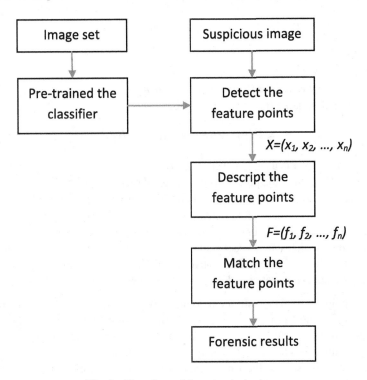

Fig. 2. Flowchart of the proposed scheme

2.1 Key-points Detection

The feature points are detected by using a simple and rapid algorithm HSCD, which is based on the FAST (Features from Accelerated Segment Test) [20]. Most feature detection algorithms work by computing a corner response function (C) across the image. Pixels which exceed a threshold cornerness value (and are locally maximal) are then retained. The algorithm can be illustrated as:

1. For each location on the circle x1. For each pixel $x \in \{1 ... 16\}$ on the circle which centered at p, we denote $S_{p \rightarrow x}$ as the states of x relative to p. The states can be presented as:

$$S_{p \to x} = \begin{cases} d, I_{p \to x} \leq I_p - t & \text{(darker)} \\ s, I_p - t < I_{p \to x} < I_p + t & \text{(similar)} \\ b, I_p + t \leq I_{p \to x} & \text{(brighter)} \end{cases} \tag{1}$$

2. Let P be the set of all pixels in all training images. P is divided into three subsets, P_d, P_s, and P_b, where $P_s = \{p \in P : S_{p \to x} = b\}$ and P_d and P_s are defined similarly.
3. Let K_p be a Boolean variable which is true if P is a corner and false otherwise. The total entropy of K for an arbitrary set of corners Q is:

$$H(Q) = (c + \bar{c}) \log_2 (c + \bar{c}) - c \log_2 c - \bar{c} \log_2 \bar{c}, \tag{2}$$

where $c = |\{i \in Q : K_i \text{ is true}\}| \text{ (number of corners)}$
and $\bar{c} = |\{i \in Q : K_i \text{ is false}\}| \text{ (number of noncorners)}$.
The information gain (H_g) can be presented as:

$$H_g = H(P) - H(P_d) - H(P_s) - H(P_b) \tag{3}$$

4. A given choice of x is used to partition the data into three sets. The variable x yields the most information, the process is then applied recursively on all three subsets. P_b is divided into $P_{b,d}$, $P_{b,s}$, and $P_{b,b}$, P_s is divided into $P_{s,d}$, $P_{s,s}$, and $P_{s,b}$, and so on, where each x is chosen to yield maximum information about the set.
5. While the entropy of a subset is zero, the recursion process terminates. Finally, a decision tree which can correctly classify all corners seen in the training set is created. The decision tree is then converted into C code. A long string of nested if-else statements is generated and be used as a corner detector.

The key-points would be insufficient to meet the forensic need in the area where the textures are almost uniform. We developed a novel key-points distribution algorithm to adapt the forensic scenario. In the algorithm, the input is an ordered list L_s which saves all the key-points extracted from the image. And the output is a list L_o which saves the suppressed key-points. V_s is the value of the strength of detected feature. Let m and r denote the desired number of key-points and the radius of the testing circle, respectively. The details of the algorithm is presented below.

Algorithm 1: key-points distribution algorithm

Input: $L_s = \{p_1, p_2, \ldots, p_n\}$, m $(m<=n)$, $r=10$ *(default)*
Output: $L_o = \{p_1, p_2, \ldots, p_m\}$
Begin:
// Initialize
$q = \lfloor n/m \rfloor$ // q is the number of eliminating key-points in every literation
// Begin of the literation
for $i=1,2,\ldots,m$ do
    select the minimum key-point p_k of V_s // $1 \le k \le n$
    select the maximum key-point p_l of V_s in the area which centered by p_k with radius r
    // $1 \le l \le n$
    insert p_{max} into L_o
    remove the smallest q key-points and the p_l in L_s
// End of the literation
output the result L_o

In the initialization step, the number of eliminating key-points in every literation is calculated, which is composed of the number of total key-points divided by the number of desired output key-points. In the literation, the first selection is the global minimum p_k, and then we find the local maximum point p_l around p_k. Thus, the relative small key-point in where the textures are almost uniform, could be retained. After inserting the local maximum point into the output list L_o, we eliminate the smallest q points to enlarge the retaining chance of the relative large key-points.

Since a key-point with relatively small V_s can be retained in the proposed strategy. The key-points, which extracted by our improved strategy, become more uniformly distributed throughout an image. We demonstrate the extraction results by using (Fig. 3a) and without using (Fig. 3b) the proposed key-points distribution strategy. Note that the key-points of the former (Fig. 3a) are much better distributed throughout entire image.

(a)   (b)

Fig. 3. Detected key-points results of using (a) and without using (b) the key-points distribution strategy. In which the green spots denote the key-points.

2.2 Improved SIFT Description

For a good feature descriptor, two criteria should be considered in describing the extracted feature points [21]. The first criterion is distinctiveness. The extracted feature should contains enough information to distinguish the key-points. The second criterion is robustness which means that the extracted feature should be robust to photometric and geometric deformations. SIFT technique, which combines a scale invariant region detector and a descriptor based on the gradient distribution in the corresponding regions, has been widely used for image retrieval and object recognition. However, it's neither mirror reflection invariant nor completely invariant to the viewpoint change. Recently, an improved SIFT descriptor is proposed in [22]. The descriptor uses a circular region instead of a rectangular region, for the circular region has better rotational invariance. Our proposed descriptor is similar to [22], but is optimized to make it more adapt to CMFD.

An elliptical neighboring region around the interest point is normalized to a circular one. The histogram of dominant gradient orientations in the normalized circular neighboring region around the point are computed. The second moment matrix is used to estimate the elliptical neighborhood of a key point. Given a key-point p, the second moment matrix μ of p is defined as:

$$\mu\left(x, M_l, M_i\right) = \begin{pmatrix} \mu_{11} & \mu_{12} \\ \mu_{21} & \mu_{22} \end{pmatrix} = g\left(x, M_l\right) * \left(\nabla L\left(x, M_i\right) \nabla L\left(x, M_i\right)^T\right) \tag{4}$$

$$\nabla L\left(x, M_i\right) = \left(\frac{L_x\left(x, M_i\right)}{L_y\left(x, M_i\right)}\right) \tag{5}$$

where M_l and M_i is a symmetric positive definite matrix corresponding to the local scale and integration scale, respectively; and $g(x, M)$ is the non-uniform Gaussian kernel:

$$g(x, M) = \frac{1}{2\pi\sqrt{detM}} exp\left(-\frac{x^T M^{-1} x}{2}\right) \tag{6}$$

where $x \in R^2$, and M is a symmetric positive definite covariance matrix corresponding to the scale. $L(x, M)$ is the affine Gaussian scale-space representation for an image $I(x)$, and it can be generated by a convolution with a non-uniform Gaussian kernel $g(x, M)$:

$$L(x, M) = g(x, M) * I(x) \tag{7}$$

We use a practical iterative procedure which is proposed in [23] to adapt the covariance matrix. The elliptical region is normalized to a circular one by using the ellipse parameters from the point's second moment matrix. The pixel in the elliptical region is transformed to a normalized frame using the formulas (8–9):

$$N = \mu\left(x, M_l, M_i\right) \tag{8}$$

$$x' = N^{1/2} x \tag{9}$$

Given the normalized circular neighboring region $I'(x)$ of an interest point, the affine scale space representation L' with the scale σ of the point, can be generated by convolution with the Gaussian kernel $g(x, \sigma)$:

$$g(x, \sigma) = \frac{1}{2\pi\sigma^2} exp(-\frac{x^T x}{2\sigma^2}) \tag{10}$$

$$L'(x, \sigma) = g(x, \sigma) * I'(x) \tag{11}$$

The main direction of the elliptical region is determined based on the normalized frame. The magnitude $m(x, y)$ and orientation $\theta(x, y)$ of the image gradient are computed in by Pixel-Value Differencing (PVD):

$$m(x, y) = \left(\begin{array}{c} \left(\bar{L}(x + 1, y) - \bar{L}(x - 1, y)\right)^2 \\ +\left(\bar{L}(x, y + 1) - \bar{L}(x, y - 1)\right)^2 \end{array} \right)^{1/2} \tag{12}$$

$$\theta(x, y) = \tan^{-1} \left(\frac{\left(\bar{L}(x, y + 1) - \bar{L}(x, y - 1)\right)}{\left(\bar{L}(x + 1, y) - \bar{L}(x - 1, y)\right)} \right) \tag{13}$$

2.3   Key-point Matching and Forgery Detection

After describing the key-points, the descriptive vectors for each key-points are generated. Given a test image I, a set of key-points $X = (x_1, x_2, ..., x_n)$ with their corresponding descriptors $F = (f_1, f_2, ..., f_n)$ is extracted. For each key-point x_i in the image I, the Euclidian distance of all the other $(n-1)$ key-points are calculated. Then the nearest neighbor with the minimum Euclidean distance is the best candidate key-point of x_i. Once we have applied the key-point matching procedure, a set of matched key-points are procured. Agglomerative hierarchical clustering (AHC) [24] technique is performed on spatial locations (i.e., coordinates) of the matched key-points to detect possible duplicated regions. The matching algorithm is presented follow:

(1) Assigning each key-point to a cluster.
(2) Computing all the reciprocal spatial distances among clusters.
(3) Identifying the closest pair of clusters;
(4) Merging the closest pair clusters into one cluster;
(5) Repeating the steps of (3) and (4) until there are no clusters unmerged;
(6) Eliminating the clusters which do not contain more than three matched key-points;

After the matching procedure, if there is more than one cluster remaining, the suspicious image can be classified as tempered.

3   Experimental Result

In this section, we present the results of the proposed copy-move forgery detection approach. For this purpose an experimental version of the proposed method was implemented in Matlab2012b. The algorithm is coded in MATLAB 2012b on a machine equipped with Intel i7 3.1 GHz CPU with 8 GB DDR3RAM.

3.1   Settings for Forgery Detection

All images used in the experiment were in a dataset named NISL-FIM which consists of 878 images: 439 are tampered images and 439 are originals. The NISL-FIM dataset are composed of images with different contents coming from CoMoFoD [25] and laboratory collection. The image resolution varies from 400 * 300 to 4000 * 3000 pixels. In our experiments, 300 copy-move forgery images were selected to test by the proposed method. The size of forged patch covers, on the average, 10 % of the whole image. The threshold λ is set to 0.7. Support Vector Machine (SVM) is an optimal and efficient classifier which is commonly used for machine learning systems. Because our work only focuses on feature extraction rather than the design of classifier, we utilize the SVM-light as the classifier in our experiment and a non-linear kernel is chosen. 700 images (includes tampered and original images) are randomly selected as training data, the remaining 178 images are used as test cases. The most significant advantages of our method is that the processing time is decrease greatly.

To measure the detection performance, True Positive Rate (TPR) and False Positive Rate (FPR) were used. They can be represented as:

$$TPR = \frac{TP}{(TP + FN)} \tag{14}$$

$$FPR = \frac{FP}{(FP + FN)} \tag{15}$$

where TP and TN are the number of the true detection of forged images and original images, respectively. FP and FN are the number of the wrong detection of original images and forged images, respectively.

3.2   Visual Test on Duplicated Regions

A number of images subjected to various image transformations are described below. These transformations are representatives of the most frequent manipulations in applying CMF. The types and ranges of the transformations that applied in our experiments are listed in the Table 1.

Detection results are presented in Fig. 4. As can be seen, the proposed method is able to detect the duplicated region accurately.

Table 1. The types and ranges of the transformations

Transformation types	Ranges
Translation	1/10 to 9/10 of largest spatial dimension of the image
Rotation or flipping	rotated with the angle from 0 to 360 degree
Scaling	scaled up/down with the factor from 0.1 to 2.0
Illumination change	the intensities modulated from 70 % to 130 % of their original values
Gaussian blurring	blurred by Gaussian kernels of sizes 3 * 3, 5 * 5 or 7 * 7

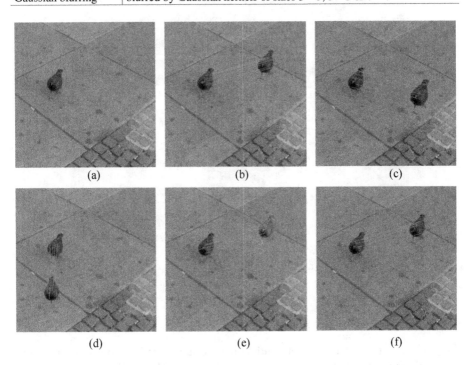

Fig. 4. CMFD results to various image transformations. (a) is the original image; (b) is the detection result of translation; (c) is the detection result of scaling; (d) is the detection result of rotation; (e) is the detection result of Illumination change; (f) is the detection result of blurring.

3.3 Forgery Detection in Uniform Image Regions

Many keypoint-based CMFD approaches suffer from the problem of insufficient or even none key-points in the area where the textures are almost uniform [18]. As shown in the second column of Fig. 1(b), the forensic task is a great challenge to the CMFD procedures. By using the proposed key-points distribution algorithm, the key-points, which are extracted from detection procedure, are much better distributed throughout entire image. Figure 5 demonstrates the detection results.

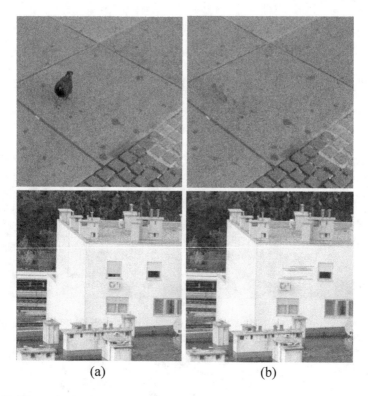

(a)   (b)

Fig. 5. CMFD results in almost uniform image regions. (a) is the original image. (b) is the detection result.

3.4 Forgery Detection in Multiple Cloning

In some cases, it may happen that multiple regions are copied and pasted once within the same image in order to make the forgery difficult to detect. Such an operation is known as multiple cloning and often attempts to obscure the regularity of the copied regions by changing their relative arrangement upon pasting. As such, a single geometric transform may prove to be insufficient in detecting all the copied regions. It would be challenge to some key-point based methods. As is presented in Fig. 6, the proposed method can detect the multiple cloning very well, even the forged car has been rotated to increase the difficulty of CMFD.

(a)   (b)

Fig. 6. Example of CMFD in multiple cloning tampering. (a) is the original image. (b) is the detection result.

All the experiments are based on the forgery image dataset NISL-FIM. The TPR and FPR of the forgery detection for multiple kinds of transformations are shown in Table 2.

Table 2. TPR and FPR of the forgery detection for different kind transformation.

Transformation	TPR %	FPR %
Translation	97.33	8.91
Rotation/mirror transforming	94.80	9.25
Scaling	93.88	8.92
Illumination change	94.64	8.55
Gaussian blurring	94.32	8.83
Multiple cloning	95.21	9.34

3.5   Comparison with Other Methods

To evaluate the proposed approach comprehensively, we make a comparison between the proposed approach and some state-of-the-art CMFD methods. Table 3 shows the overall performance of all the forgery detection methods. For comparison, P. Kakar and N. Sudha [6], Pan et al. [8] and Popescu [2] CMFD methods were implemented and applied to the same forgery image set.

Table 3. Overall performance (on weighted average) for each method.

Methods	TPR %	FPR %
Our method	93.84	8.83
Kakar and N. Sudha [6]	90.21	8.65
Pan et al. [8]	88.66	10.31
Popescu [2]	75.49	14.81

The results indicate that our copy-move forgery detection method have considerably higher performance. As presented in Table 2, our proposed method obtains the highest

TPR. The approach [6] performs well, the FPR is relative low while the TPR is over 90 %. Since they match features by selecting pairs of likely matching features and then performing clustering in a modified spatial domain. However, the processing time is relative high due to the usage of MPEG-7 image signature tools. The approach [8] is the first SIFT based CMFD method. But they have not considered the multiple cloning issue, and hard to detect the mirror transformed forgery. Block-based method [2] practically fail to detect forgery regions where extreme rotation and/or scaling are applied. This is basically due to the incapacity of such methods to properly deal with cases where a geometrical transformation, which is not pure translation, is applied to the duplicated regions [9]. It is notice that, all the other experiment methods are hard to detect the images with the extremely similar scene except ours, such as pure sky, floor, etc.

4 Conclusion

Many keypoint-based methods (either based on SIFT or SURF) may be hard to locate the matched key-points in such tampering. We have proposed an automatic and robust duplication image regions detection method to support image CMFD based on high-speed corner detection technique and improved SIFT descriptor. Machine learning technique is used to detect feature points which greatly decreasing the processing time compare to other feather detectors. The experimental results show that the proposed method can accurately detect the duplicated regions. Furthermore, the proposed method improves the invariance to mirror transformation and rotation by using an improved descriptor. In our future work, we will investigate the use of our technique in detecting regions which have undergone nonaffine transformations.

Acknowledgment. This work is supported in part by the National Natural Science Foundation of China (NO. 61232016, U1405254, 61173141, 61173142, 61173136, 61373133, 51503084); the Fundamental Research Funds for the Central Universities (NO. JUSRP11534); the Priority Academic Program Development of Jiangsu Higher Education Institutions (PAPD); Jiangsu Collaborative Innovation Center on Atmospheric Environment and Equipment Technology (CICAEET).

References

1. Fridrich, J., Soukal, B.D., Lukáš, A.J.: Detection of copy-move forgery in digital images. In: Proceedings of Digital Forensic Research Workshop, Cleveland, OH (2003)
2. Popescu, A.C., Farid, H.: Exposing digital forgeries by detecting traces of resampling. IEEE Trans. Sig. Process. **53**, 758–767 (2005)
3. Bayram, S., Sencar, H.T., Memon, N.: An efficient and robust method for detecting copy-move forgery. In: IEEE International Conference on Acoustics, Speech and Signal Processing, ICASSP 2009, Taipei, Taiwan, pp. 1053–1056 (2009)
4. He, Z., Lu, W., Sun, W., Huang, J.: Digital image splicing detection based on Markov features in DCT and DWT domain. Pattern Recogn. **45**(12), 4292–4299 (2012)
5. Yang, B., Sun, X., Chen, X., Zhang, J., Li, X.: An efficient forensic method for copy-move forgery detection based on DWT-FWHT. Radioengineering **22**, 1098–1105 (2013)

6. Kakar, P., Sudha, N.: Exposing postprocessed copy-paste forgeries through transform-invariant features. IEEE Trans. Inf. Forensics Secur. **7**, 1018–1028 (2012)
7. Amerini, I., Barni, M., Caldelli, R., Costanzo, A.: Counter-forensics of SIFT-based copy-move detection by means of keypoint classification. EURASIP J. Image Video Process. **2013**, 1–17 (2013)
8. Pan, X., Lyu, S.: Region duplication detection using image feature matching. IEEE Trans. Inf. Forensics Secur. **5**, 857–867 (2010)
9. Amerini, I., Ballan, L., Caldelli, R., Del Bimbo, A., Serra, G.: A SIFT-Based forensic method for copy-move attack detection and transformation recovery. IEEE Trans. Inf. Forensics Secur. **6**, 1099–1110 (2011)
10. Lowe, D.: Distinctive image features from scale-invariant keypoints. Int. J. Comput. Vis. **60**, 91–110 (2004)
11. Neamtu, C., Barca, C., Achimescu, E., Gavriloaia, B.: Exposing copy-move image tampering using forensic method based on SURF. In: 2013 International Conference on Electronics, Computers and Artificial Intelligence (ECAI), pp. 1–4 (2013)
12. Bay, H., Ess, A., Tuytelaars, T., Van Gool, L.: Speeded-up robust features (SURF). Comput. Vis. Image Underst. **110**, 346–359 (2008)
13. Luo, J., Oubong, G.: A comparison of SIFT, PCA-SIFT and SURF. Int. J. Image Process. **3**, 143–152 (2009)
14. Zhu, Y., Shen, X., Chen, H.: Copy-move forgery detection based on scaled ORB. Multimedia Tools Appl. **75**(6), 3221–3233 (2016)
15. Gu, B., Sheng, V.S., Tay, K.Y., Romano, W., Li, S.: Incremental support vector learning for ordinal regression. IEEE Trans. Neural Netw. Learn. Syst. **26**, 1403–1416 (2015)
16. Gu, B., Sheng, V.S.: A robust regularization path algorithm for ν-support vector classification. IEEE Trans. Neural Netw. Learn. Syst. **PP**, 1–8 (2016)
17. Cozzolino, D., Poggi, G., Verdoliva, L.: Efficient dense-field copy-move forgery detection. IEEE Trans. Inf. Forensics Secur. **10**, 2284–2297 (2015)
18. Guo, J.-M., Liu, Y.-F., Wu, Z.-J.: Duplication forgery detection using improved DAISY descriptor. Expert Syst. Appl. **40**, 707–714 (2013)
19. Shivakumar, B.L., Baboo, S.: Detection of region duplication forgery in digital images using SURF. Int. J. Comput. Sci. Issues **8**, 199–205 (2011)
20. Rosten, E., Porter, R., Drummond, T.: Faster and better: a machine learning approach to corner detection. IEEE Trans. Pattern Anal. Mach. Intell. **32**, 105–119 (2010)
21. Li, C., Ma, L.: A new framework for feature descriptor based on SIFT. Pattern Recogn. Lett. **30**, 544–557 (2009)
22. Liao, K., Liu, G., Hui, Y.: An improvement to the SIFT descriptor for image representation and matching. Pattern Recogn. Lett. **34**, 1211–1220 (2013)
23. Lindeberg, T., Gårding, J.: Shape-adapted smoothing in estimation of 3-D shape cues from affine deformations of local 2-D brightness structure. Image Vis. Comput. **15**, 415–434 (1997)
24. Friedman, J., Hastie, T., Tibshirani, R.: The elements of statistical learning[M]. Springer, Berlin (2001). Springer series in statistics
25. Tralic, D., Zupancic, I., Grgic, S., Grgic, M.: CoMoFoD—new database for copy-move forgery detection. In: 2013 55th International Symposium on ELMAR, pp. 49–54 (2013)

Analysis of Topic Evolution on News Comments Based on Word Vectors

Lin Jianghao[1], Zhou Yongmei[1,2(✉)], Yang Aimin[1,2], and Chen Jin[3]

[1] Laboratory for Language Engineering and Computing,
Guangdong University of Foreign Studies, Guangzhou 510006, China
yongmeizhou@qq.com
[2] Cisco School of Informatics, Guangdong University of Foreign Studies,
Guangzhou 510420, China
[3] International College, Guangdong University of Foreign Studies,
Guangzhou 510420, China

Abstract. The analysis of topic evolution mainly refers to the mining of topic content which evolves as the time goes on. With the assumption that topic content may be embodied by key words, this article adopted word2vec for the training of 750,000 pieces of news and micro-blog texts and thus established the model of word vector. Then, the text information flow was applied into the model and all word vectors by time series were acquired. Finally, the word vectors were clustered by K-means before the key words were drawn and the analysis of topic evolution was visualized. By comparing the effect of the model of word vector on drawing topic with those of LDA or PLSA topic models, the results showed that the former is superior to the latter two models. Besides, to collect abundant and varied data will facilitate the training of the model of word vector with better generalization ability and the investigation on real-time analysis of topic evolution.

Keywords: Topic evolution · Word2vec · LDA · PLSA · K-means

1 Introduction

Topic evolution analysis is of importance in both spheres of text analysis and network public opinion monitoring and management (Chen et al. 2004; Wang 2012). It not only refers to the rapid processing for, and automatic summarizing of massive complicated texts, but can also analyze the topic content which evolves as the time goes on. Topic content is easily to be evolved variously in news comment which is direct expression from netizens to the news event based on their personal experience and social cognition. For instance, the main topic in the news from IFENG. COM - "Hunan: Protest by Doctors Forced to Kneel Down for Corpse" was about the condemnation of family members' making trouble out of nothing and evolved into topics like unreasonable charges of hospital and deterioration of doctor ethics. This evolution process is likely to stimulate the diversified development of events and provoke stronger social public opinion. In turn, it is significant to do the research into the analysis of topic content evolved in Internet news events.

© Springer International Publishing AG 2016
X. Sun et al. (Eds.): ICCCS 2016, Part II, LNCS 10040, pp. 464–475, 2016.
DOI: 10.1007/978-3-319-48674-1_41

TDT (topic detection and tracking) is a method initially used in topic detection and tracking (Allan et al. 1998). Currently, such pivotal methods as text clustering (Han et al. 2012; Zhang et al. 2014; Sakaki et al. 2010; Zhou et al. 2015a,b), theme model based on PLSA(Xing et al. 2005) and LDA(Chen et al. 2015; Lin and Huang 2014; Cao et al. 2014; AlSumait et al. 2008; Keane et al. 2015; Chu and Li 2011), multi-keyword ranked (Fu et al. 2015; Gu et al. 2015; Xia et al. 2015) etc. are adopted by the analysis of topic evolution. Based on wavelet transform, Han et al. (2012) proposed algorithm WKSC by improving K_SC, which can significantly reduce the complexity of clustering time, and be applied to the model analysis of a large number of high dimensional hot topics. Zhang and Liu (2013) automatically mined the hot key words according to the title of the article and the key words in turn was used as clues to cluster the topics. Zhou (2015a) improved the weight calculation method to effectively extract the topic key words with strong resolution and used the BIC value as the basis of the topic in the clustering process to foster the accuracy of clustering. Zhou (2015b) realized the analysis of the focus of network topic content and used the key words and sentences to express the focus of transfer.

Based on the topic analysis research via theme model and PLSA model, Xing et al. (2005) put forward CPLSA which analyzed through the core interpreting data of the text (such as: authors, publishers and publishing time etc.), and determined whether the theme of the two texts is the same and the levels of the dependence on interpreting data. In order to modify LDA model, He et al. (2015) initially set the document weight via LDA output "document-topic" matrix, with an aim of reducing the document weight of broad topics, and then computed the degree of topic association via Jensen - Shannon horizontal distance. In view of the principle of LDA, Lin and Huang (2014) established space model of network emergency topics via the idea of discrete time topic model, and analyzed the evolution path of topic via social network analysis method according to the degrees of association between feature words.

According to the method of text clustering or topic analysis of theme model, the processing modes on text stream mainly include: (1) obtain the content of the text topic, as well as the relationships of levels, inclusion and separation between topics and sub-topics, directly through the clustering analysis of massive topic texts or the construction of topic model; (2) obtain the evolution pattern on the time series based on the time characteristics and continuous input of text stream. These methods could effectively identify and track the topic with similar content, which is widely applied to topic detection and tracking (TDT). However, the direct analysis methods of massive topic text focus mainly on the analysis of static massive text. They have such drawbacks as the ineffective analysis of the developmental trend of the topics, especially that of incremental network texts from micro blog or news comment, and also lack of tracking ability for topics. In addition, the analysis based on characteristics of the time concentrates on the developmental trend, more on the heat levels, breadth and other indicators of the topic. It pays not enough attention on the content. As a consequence, this article made use of keywords set to represent topic (Chu and Li 2011). First, the short texts of comment was input into the model in the way of text stream, and then the word vectors were extracted based on word2vec, which contain the semantic context information and the lexical mapping to a multidimensional space. Next, the space position of word vectors were used to cluster, extract topic content and analyze the evolution pattern of topic content from the aspect of time. Finally, the effects of mainstream theme models like PLSA and LDA on topic evolution analysis were compared with that of method based on word vectors proposed by the article. The results revealed that the effect of the latter, which could be used to characterize the evolution patterns of the topic content and developmental trend effectively, is more effective than the former two methods. Besides, there is no need to train the vector model again only if a large number of corpus is used to train the word vector model and the text stream is input directly to get word vectors, which is beneficial to the analysis of real topic evolution.

2   An Overview of Topic Evolution Based on Word Vectors

This article uses the topic extraction method as shown in Fig. 1. Firstly, the model parameters of word2vec were set up, the data set Data_w2v was used as the training set and input into the word2vec for training, and the word2vec model was saved as M_w2v; Then, the set of collected news comment was pre-processed, segmented and filtered, and the word frequency was calculated and obtained wordlist T_t; The wordlist T_t was computed in M_w2v model and the word vector table T_w2v_t was obtained; Finally, K-means was used to cluster the word vector table T_w2vt to obtain the topic set.

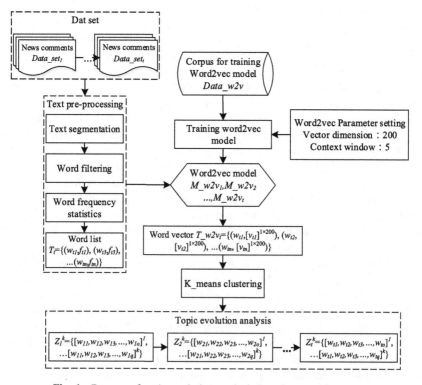

Fig. 1. Process of topic evolution analysis based on word vectors

The topic can be defined by a vector, and the units of the vector are a set of semantically related words and the semantically weights are associated with the topic (Chu and Li 2011). Therefore, we used a set of key words to represent the topic. Then the topic set can be represented as $Z_t^k = \{[w_{t1}, w_{t2}, w_{t3}, ..., w_{to}]^1, [w_{t1}, w_{t2}, w_{t3}, ..., w_{tp}]^2, ... [w_{t1}, w_{t2}, w_{t3}, ..., w_{tq}]^k\}$, where k is the number of topics, and $[w_{t1}, w_{t2}, w_{t3}, ..., w_{tm}]$ are m key words of a topic in time t. The final output of the model in time t is k topics. The algorithm can be described as follows:

Algorithm 1. Topic extraction algorithm of news comments based on word2vec

Input: corpus *Data_set_t*, corpus *Data_w2v*

Output: Z_t^k

Step 1: initialize the parameters of word2vec model, set the word vector to 200 dimension, the window of the context is 5. Used *Data_w2v* to train the word2vec model M_w2v;

Step 2: text preprocessing: word segmentation, filter stop words, and word frequency statistics. If word frequency $f >= a$, added to the word list, and ranked the word list by frequency from high to low. Finally, we gained the word list $T_t = \{(w_{t1}, f_{t1}), (w_{t2}, f_{t2}), (w_{t3}, f_{t3}), ...(w_{tm}, f_{tm})\}$;

Step 3: Gain the word vector of each words in word list T_t by input to word2vec model M_w2v. Then word vector list $T\_w2v_t = \{(w_{t1}, [v_{t1}]^{1 \times 200}), (w_{t2}, [v_{t2}]^{1 \times 200}), ...(w_{tm}, [v_{tm}]^{1 \times 200})\}$;

Step 4: Clustered T_w2v_t by using K_means cluster;

Step 5: Extracted key words of every clustering center as the key words of every topic as Z_t^k;

End: Output Z_t^k.

The output Z_t^k refers to topics in the time window t. Via analysis the topic changes in time sequence, we can realize the analysis of topic evolution.

3 Topic Extraction Method

3.1 The Acquisition of Word Vector

When using the machine-learning algorithm to complete the task of natural language processing, the primary work is the mathematical representation of the character symbols and the word vector is usually used to represent a word. The traditional method of word vector is One-hot Representation, with the size of the dictionary as the length of the vector and establishing the word vector, of which the word is located in 1 and the other is 0. Although this method is quite simple, it is easy to generate the curse of dimensionality, and it also ignores the correlation between words and words. To obtain the word vector (distributed representation), the article trained the neural network with large amounts of data. The basic tenet is that each word was represented into a k - dimensional real vector through training and to get more deep representing features of text data, the context depth was set up. This expression method is better than

One-hot Representation because it not only contains the potential semantic relations between words, but also avoids the curse of dimensionality.

The article used open source tool of word vector, i.e., word2vec[1] to calculate word vector. Word2vec is a tool to represent the real value vector of a single word by using deep learning method (Zhang et al. 2015). Its core structure is mainly based on two models: CBOW (Bags-of-Words Continuous) and Skip-gram model, of which the latter was selected by the article, as shown in Fig. 2. The basic philosophy of CBOW model is similar to that of neural network probabilistic language model (Netword Language Model Neural, NNLM), both of which use the context $w_{t-k}, \ldots w_{t-1}, w_{t+1}, \ldots, w_{t+k}$ of the current word w_t to predict the probability $p(w_t | w_{t-k}, \ldots w_{t-1}, w_{t+1}, \ldots, w_{t+k})$ of the current word w_t. CBOW model is different from NNLM model in that it removes the most time-consuming nonlinear hidden layer and enables all words of the input layer to share the mapping layer. As shown in Fig. 2, CBOW model uses the surrounding word of the word w_t as input and then do the weighted processing before outputting the word w_t.

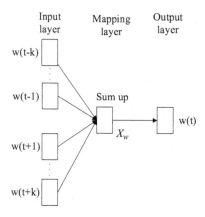

Fig. 2. The structure of continuous bag of words

Word2vec takes into account the context information of the current word and the word vectors contain a variety of semantic and grammatical relations. The training corpus in the article was downloaded from the whole network news data (SogouCA) in Sogou labs, which were taken randomly from 25 million pieces of news with regard to 18 channels of domestic, international, sports, social and entertainment news data etc. Considering that the news data is very formal but the news comments may pop up some the network words, the article collected automatically a total of 500 thousand micro-blog texts from Sina and Tencent micro-blog platform. A corpus of a total of 750 thousand texts from Sogou and micro-blog were used as the training data set of *Data_w2v* of word2vec. A total of 750 thousand Sogou corpus and micro-blog corpus are used as the training data set of Data_w2v word2vec. CBOW was selected as the training model and *M_w2v* was finally obtained.

---

[1] https://code.google.com/p/word2vec/.

3.2 Topics Extraction Based on K-means

Due to the adoption of the keywords set to represent a topic, the issue of topic extraction could be converted into that of word clustering through the process of clustering all words of the corpus into K clusters to extract the concentrated topics and contents in corpus K. Each word vector $V_w = \{v_1, v_2, \ldots v_{200}\}$ can be obtained when each word in the corpus is calculated via model M_w2v after pre-processing the data set, i.e., $Data\_set_t$. The clustering training data could be represented as $= \{V_w^{(1)}, V_w^{(2)}, \ldots V_w^{(n)}\}, V_w^{(i)} \in R^{200}$, and the sample could be clustered into k clusters via K-means. The clustering process of K-means is as follows.

Algorithm 2. K-means cluster algorithm
Input: $V = \{V_w^{(1)}, V_w^{(2)}, \ldots V_w^{(n)}\}, V_w^{(i)} \in R^{200}$
Output: Z^k
Step 1: Selected K cluster centroids $(\mu_1, \mu_2, \ldots, \mu_k \in R^{200})$ randomly; it means the number of topic is k;
Selected a word as the center word of a topic randomly;
Step 2: Calculate each word vector $V_w = \{v_1, v_2, \ldots v_{200}\}$ belong to which category by formula (1)

$$c^{(i)} := \arg\min_j \left\| x^{(i)} - \mu_j \right\|^2 \quad (1)$$

Recalculate cluster centroid of jth category by formula (2)

$$\mu_j := \frac{\sum_{i=1}^{n} \{c^{(i)} = j\} x^{(i)}}{\sum_{i=1}^{n} \{c^{(i)} = j\}} \quad (2)$$

Step 3: The step2 is repeated until the algorithm converges. Then output K clusters;
Step 4: Choose words of each clusters that are close the cluster centroid as topic words. The distances between words and cluster centroids should be less than b;
End: Output Z^k.

The K value of K-means algorithm is very important. We determined the optimal K value when algorithm reach the highest F value. Because of the instability of K-means, we taken the average value of repeated cluster experiments as the final result.

4 The Evaluation Method of Topic Extraction

Due to the use of keywords to represent a topic, the evaluation of the effect of topic extraction can be converted into the evaluation of the accuracy of topic word extraction. In order to examine whether the proposed method of topic extraction is effective, the word frequency of the corpus was first measured and sequenced to obtain the wordlist. Then the topic words under different topics was selected manually based on the wordlist and formed a standard topic set $Zstd_t^k$. To evaluate the extraction results, the recall R, precision P and micro-average $F1$ of the extraction results of the topic words were mainly assessed.

Recall R can be calculated by formula (3):

$$R = \frac{\text{the number of topic words that match the corresponding topic extract by model}}{\text{the total number of topic words}}$$

$$(3)$$

Precision P can be calculated by formula (4):

$$P = \frac{\text{the number of topic words that match the corresponding topic extract by model}}{\text{the total number of topic words extract by model}}$$

$$(4)$$

Then the micro-average $F1$ can be calculated as:

$$F1 = \frac{2 * P * R}{P + R} \tag{5}$$

In order to further examine the analysis method of topic evolution based on word vectors, the article compared the analysis effect of topic evolution via theme models PLSA and LDA in the same corpus. Initially, the calculating results of corpus frequency was saved as "document-word frequency" matrix M_t; Then, the "theme-word" matrix $[M_{word-topic}]_{m \times k} = P(w|z)_{m \times k}$ was obtained via computing $PLSA(M_t)$ and LDA (M_t); Finally, $[M_{word-topic}]_{m \times k}$ was sequenced column by column to obtain the key words with higher probability in each sub-topic z_t^j and also $Z_t^k = \{[w_{t1}, w_{t2}, w_{t3}, ..., w_{to}]^1,$ $[w_{t1}, w_{t2}, w_{t3}, ..., w_{tp}]^2, ...[w_{t1}, w_{t2}, w_{t3}, ..., w_{tq}]^k\}$. The recall ratio R, accuracy ratio P and micro average $F1$ of the extraction results of the topic words under three algorithms were mainly compared.

5   Experimental Results and Analysis

5.1   Experimental Data

The experiment collected 5871 pieces of comments from the August 22nd, 2014 news from IFENG. COM – "Hunan: Protest by Doctors Forced to Kneel Down for Corpse". Figure 3 shows the distribution of the number of comments as time goes on, with the curve increasing before decreasing and its trend flattening gradually which is accordance with the developmental trend of the network public opinions. The article selected the comments during the period between 7 a.m. to 11 a.m. on 22nd as the subjects of the evolved analysis of group emotion. On the one hand, 4464 pieces of comments were produced in these four hours, accounting for 76 % of the total number of the comments; on the other hand, the number of comments in each period of time is more than 500 pieces, with more obvious characteristics of topics.

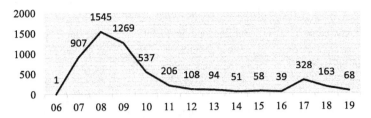

Fig. 3. Distribution of "Comments-Time"

5.2   Comparison of Topic Extraction Results

According to the sequence of time, the interval of time was set as one hour. Then, the data set of news comments was classified as *DS7, DS8, DS9, DS10*. The data was segmented by removing the stop words and useless words and formed the wordlist T_7, T_8, T_9, T_{10}. Finally, the wordlist is input into model M_w2v to obtain word vector list T_w2v_7, T_w2v_8, T_w2v_9, T_w2v_{10}. K-means was used to cluster the word vector list to obtain the final topic words. When extracting topics by PLSA and LDA, the co-occurrence "document-word" matrix *M7, M8, M9, M10* was obtained according to the computing of the word frequency. The matrix was input into LDA and PLSA to calculate and obtain the topic word. Some of the topic words are shown in Table 1.

It can be seen in Table 1 that the sub-topic "to blame the unreasonableness of families" is the core theme of the news in the topic evolution. Other sub-topics have also been embodied in the process of evolution. The topic analysis based on word vector clustering can effectively grasp the key words of the topic. According to the experimental results and the observation of data, most of the comments are driven by the experience of a netizen himself/herself or with family members to the hospital to see a doctor. These comments include not only their own experience or the subconscious of the industry but also the experience of their friends. The comments are related to the life experience of the Internet netizens. Their experience establish the cognition of the medical news events and once reading the relevant news, they are stimulated immediately and are likely to express their own opinions via Internet. There exist strong uncertainties in these "stimulation-reflection" phenomena. This is the difficulty for the analysis of topic evolution and also the core of the analysis of public opinion evolution.

Figure 4 analyzes the ratio and recall based on word vectors and the topic evolution of news comments of the theme model. The accuracy of topic extraction based on word vector in Fig. 4 (a) is slightly better than that based on LDA and PLSA methods, of which the average accuracy of the topic evolution analysis for text sect is 70.75 % (word2vec), 64.25 %(LDA) and 65 %(PLSA) respectively, suggesting the theme model LDA outperforms PLSA. As regard to the recall, the method based on word vector is significantly preferable to the theme model because LDA and PLSA have certain requirements on the clear degrees of corpus theme and the distinguishing ability of theme from words, which are more susceptible to the corpus. The word vector is obtained based on a large amount of training data. The syntactic and semantic relations between words are included in the model of word vector, which can better adapt to the

Table 1. Sample topic words

Corpus	Topic name	Sample topic words of manual tagging	Top 5 topic words extracted by clustering
DS7	to blame the unreasonableness of families	misconduct, make trouble out of nothing, dignity, right, kneel	misconduct, dignity, right protection, make trouble out of nothing, kneel
	terrible attitude of doctors	attitude, scoundrel, bureaucratic, terrible, duplicity	scoundrel, bureaucratic, eat, terrible, attitude
DS8	to blame the unreasonableness of families	right protection, make trouble, bully, unruliness, damn	trouble, bully, damn, kneel, make trouble
	mismatched medicine and unreasonable charges	medical fee, profit, rebate, extortionate price, expensive	fee, extortionate price, rebate, drug, profit
	the deterioration of medical ethics	atmosphere, money tree, angel, responsibility, conscience	moral, angel, hypocritically, responsibility, conscience
	terrible attitude of doctors	grumpy, ferocious, enemy, abuse, roar	Haughty, abuse, insult, patient, grumpy
DS9	to blame the unreasonableness of families	families, kneel, make trouble, emergency department, dead	attitude, murderer, cause, kneel, make trouble
	the deterioration of medical ethics	money-oriented, image, bully, medical ethics, responsibility	medical ethics, image, bully, doctor's overall, disgust
DS10	to blame the unreasonableness of families	medical trouble, check, kneel, HUNAN, YUEYANG	check, kneel, unreasonable, respect, HUNAN
	terrible attitude of doctors	rethink, doctor, service, scoundrel, sympathy	weaker, loudly, scoundrel, sympathy, doctor
	the deterioration of medical ethics	image, usury, medical ethics, first aid, illegal earning	earn money, medical ethics, first aid, atmosphere, illegal earning

changes of the corpus. Figure 5 is the micro-average *F1* of the topic evolution analysis which suggests that the use of word vectors can get better micro-average. Consequently, a more suitable model of word2vec for the analysis of theme evolution could be obtained via using word vectors to collect and train massive and multi-theme Internet documents.

5.3   Visualization of Topic Evolution

According to the analysis results of the topic evolution in Table 1, the distances between the words and the cluster centers were sequenced. The results show that the

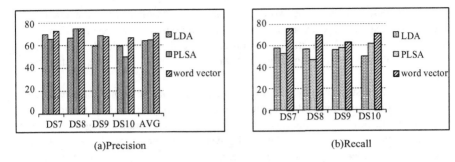

Fig. 4. *P* and *R* of topic exaction

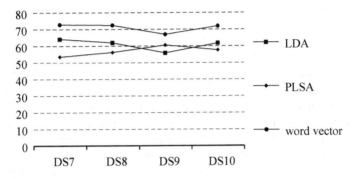

Fig. 5. *F1* of topic exaction (100 %)

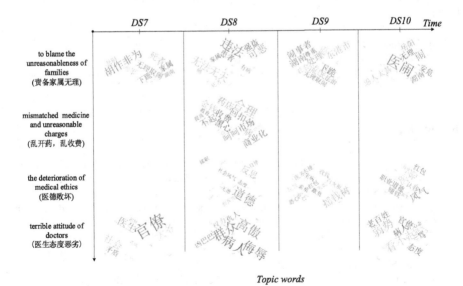

Fig. 6. The visualized results of topic evolution

closer the distance between the words, the larger the word display; the greater the distance, the smaller the word is, in other words, the smaller the contribution of the word to the theme. As shown in Fig. 6, in order to express conveniently, the results of the topic evolution were visualized and the output results of the system were summarized.

Through the visual display, the evolution pattern of the topic content in news comments as time goes by could be perceived directly and the focus of the topic from netizens could be analyzed. This is conductive to the targeted monitoring and guidance of public opinions, especially for the local government who is enabled to investigate quickly, draw detailed conclusions and disclose on the Internet to prevent the deteriorating development of the events.

6 Conclusion

This article made use of substantial multi-theme corpus to train and obtain word vector model of word2vec. The texts of news comments were input constantly as text streams into the model to obtain the vectors of all words one the time sequences. Via clustering based on K-means, the evolution of topic content was obtained and process of evolution was visualized. The experiment compared the effect of PLSA and LDA on the analysis of topic evolution and found that the proposed method based on word vector is more effective. Experiments have compared the performance of PLSA and LDA on this task, and found that the method based on word vector has a better performance. As a result, the topic evolution could be analyzed constantly by using complex and massive Internet text information and locating the words to high-dimension space which contains the lexical, syntactic and semantic information. Further research may investigate the topic evolution pattern via the document vectors, based on the method of deep learning.

Acknowledgment. Supported by The National Social Science Funding Project of China (12BYY045); The Twelfth Five-Year Plan for Philosophy and Social Sciences Project of GuangZhou (15Q16); The Philosophy and Social Sciences Project of GuangDong (GD15YTS01).

References

Chen, H., Wang, F., Zeng, D.: Intelligence and security informatics for homeland security: information, communication, and transportation. IEEE Trans. Intell. Transp. Syst. **5**(4), 329–341 (2004)

Wang, F.: Decision service and academic analytics for development of S&T based on open source intelligence and big data. Bull. Chin. Acad. Sci. **27**(5), 527–537 (2012)

Allan, J., Papka, R., Lavrenko, V.: On-line new event detection and tracking. In: Proceedings of the 21st Annual International Conference on Research and Development in Information Retrieval (SIGIR), pp. 37–45. ACM (1998)

Han, Z., Chen, N., Le, J.J., Duan, D., Sun, J.: An efficient and effective clustering algorithm for time series of hot topics. Chin. J. Comput. **35**(11), 2337–2347 (2012)

Zhang, S., Liu, Z.: Study on clustering method for internet public opinion hotspot topic. J. Chin. Comput. Syst. **34**(3), 471–474 (2013)

Sakaki, T., Okazaki, M., Matsuo, Y.: Earthquake shakes twitter users: real-time event detection by social sensors. In: Proceedings of the Nineteenth International World Wide Web Conference Series (WWW), pp. 851–860. ACM (2010)

Zhou, H., Liu, J., Wang, X.: Retrospective topic identification model for short text information flow. J. Chin. Inf. Process. **29**(1), 111–117 (2015a)

Zhou, Y., Liu, X., Youtian, D., Guan, X., Liu, J.: A method for Identifying the evolutionary focuses of online social topics. Chin. J. Comput. **38**(2), 261–271 (2015b)

Xing, E.P., Yan, R., Hauptmann, A.G.: Mining associated text and images with dual-wing harmoniums. In: Proceedings of the 21st Conference on Uncertainty in Artificial Intelligence (UAI), pp. 633–641 (2005)

Lin, J., Zhou, Y., Yang, A., Chen, Y., Chen, X.: Analysis of public emotion evolution based on probabilistic latent semantic analysis. J. Comput. Appl. **35**(10), 2747–2751 (2015). 2756

He, J., Chen, X., Min, D., Jiang, H.: Topic evolution analysis based on improved online LDA model. J. Cent. S. Univ. (Sci. Technol.) **2**, 547–553 (2015)

Lin, P., Huang, W.: Topic evolution analysis of internet emergency based on LDA model. Inf. Sci. **32**(10), 20–23 (2014)

Cao, J., Wang, H., Xia, Y., Qiao, F., Zhang, X.: Bi-path evolution model for online topic model based on LDA. Acta Automatica Sin. **40**(12), 2877–2886 (2014)

Alsumait, L., Barbará, D., Domeniconi, C.: On-line LDA: adaptive topic models for mining text streams with applications to topic detection and tracking. In: Proceedings of the 8th IEEE International Conference on Data Mining (ICDM), pp. 3–12. IEEE (2008)

Keane, N., Yee, C., Zhou, L.: Using topic modeling and similarity thresholds to detect events. In: Proceedings of the 3rd Workshop on EVENTS at the NAACL-HLT, pp. 34–42 (2015)

Chu, K., Li, F.: LDA model-based news topic evolution. Comput. Appl. Softw. **28**(4), 4–7 (2011)

Zhangjie, F., Xingming, S., Qi, L., Lu, Z., Jiangang, S.: Achieving efficient cloud search services: multi-keyword ranked search over encrypted cloud data supporting parallel computing. IEICE Trans. Commun. **E98-B**(1), 190–200 (2015)

Bin, G., Sheng, V.S., Tay, K.Y., Romano, W., Li, S.: Incremental support vector learning for ordinal regression. IEEE Trans. Neural Netw. Learn. Syst. **26**(7), 1403–1416 (2015)

Xia, Z., Wang, X., Sun, X., Wang, Q.: A secure and dynamic multi-keyword ranked search scheme over encrypted cloud data. IEEE Trans. Parallel Distrib. Syst. **27**(2), 340–352 (2015)

Zhang, D., Xua, H., Sua, Z., Xua, Y.: Chinese comments sentiment classification based on word2vec and SVM^{perf}. Expert Syst. Appl. **42**(4), 1857–1863 (2015)

A Secure JPEG Image Retrieval Method in Cloud Environment

Wei Han, Yanyan Xu[✉], and Jiaying Gong

State Key Laboratory of Information Engineering in Surveying,
Maping and Remote Sensing, Wuhan University, Wuhan 430079, Hubei, China
xuyy@whu.edu.cn

Abstract. In order to protect data privacy, image with sensitive or private information needs to be encrypted before being outsourced to the cloud. However, this lead to difficulties in image retrieval. A secure JPEG image retrieval method is proposed in this paper. Image is encrypted on DCT (Discrete Cosine Transform) domain by scrambling encryption, and the encrypted image is outsourced to the server, then the DC difference histogram and LBP (Local Binary Patterns) among the image blocks are extracted as image feature vectors by the server. Both the image confidentiality and retrieval accuracy are guaranteed in the proposed method with less computational complexity and communication cost. Experimental results prove that the proposed scheme has good encryption security and can achieve better retrieval performance.

Keywords: Compressed domain · JPEG secure image retrieval · DC difference · LBP · Cloud environment

1 Introduction

With the rapid development of cloud computing, massive images are tend to be stored in cloud. Reports show that cloud services specifically designed for image storage and sharing are among the largest growing internet services today [1]. Additionally, how to search and share such large amount of data efficiently becomes another challenging issues. Content-based image retrieval (CBIR), which involves extraction of visual features from image and search in the visual feature space for similar images, has grown rapidly in recent years.

However, it also brings cloud security problems. In order to prevent data leakage, image with sensitive information needs to be encrypted before being outsourced to the cloud, but this may lead to many problems such as image retrieval problem. If users want to retrieve images from cloud service providers (CSP), CSP needs to decrypt it first to make retrieval be operated on plaintext, which will make user's private

---

Fund projects: the National Natural Science Foundation of China (41571426, 61232016), U1405254, PAPD fund, and LIESMARS Special Research Funding

X. Sun et al. (Eds.): ICCCS 2016, Part II, LNCS 10040, pp. 476–486, 2016.
DOI: 10.1007/978-3-319-48674-1_42

information being exposed to CSP, break privacy and hence is not desired. Therefore it is both desirable and necessary to develop technologies of secure image retrieval over encrypted domain.

Many methods of secure image retrieval are proposed in recent years. Lu et al. [2] proposed three methods to solve the problem of image retrieval in the encrypted domain, including bit-plane randomization, random projection and random unary encoding. Although these methods are effective, its security is not very good; Karthik et al. [3] put forward a transparent privacy preserving hashing method whose retrieval accuracy is low due to missing space-frequency information; Hsu et al. [4] proposed a retrieval method based on homomorphic encryption which has better security and better retrieval performance, but this method is not practical because homomorphic encryption will cause serious ciphertext expansion and laborious computing [5]. In addition, there are a common shortcoming of the image retrieval method mentioned above, that is, image features must be extracted after fully decoding JPEG stream, which will inevitably increase computational complexity.

In order to solve these above problems, a secure JPEG image retrieval method is proposed in this paper, which encrypts image in the transform domain [6] with less redundant information and better security; a random encryption method is used in partially decoded image to reduce ciphertext expansion; inter block LBP features and DC coefficient difference histogram features are combined to improve retrieval accuracy. Experimental results show that the proposed scheme has good encryption security and can achieve better retrieval performance.

The organization of this paper is as follows: Sect. 2 proposes our scheme. Section 3 provides experimental results and a performance analysis, and Sect. 4 presents conclusions.

2   Secure JPEG Image Retrieval Method in Cloud Environment

JPEG is a commonly standard to compress digital color images, which was adopted by ISO as still image coding standard. JPEG compression is based on the DCT transform. The results of a 64-element DCT transform are 1 DC coefficient and 63 AC coefficients, where DC coefficient represents average brightness of the image block, and AC coefficients contain texture information of the image. These 64 results are quantized and written in a zig-zag order as follows, with the DC coefficient followed by AC coefficients of increasing frequency. After implementing differential coding for DC coefficients and entropy encoding for AC coefficients, JPEG stream is finally formed.

In this paper, image is encrypted on the transform domain by scrambling encryption: DCT coefficients obtained by partially decoding JPEG stream are scrambled, and then DC differential histogram and LBP (Local Binary Patterns) of inter-blocks are extracted as image feature vectors. DC coefficient reflects the average gray of the block, adjacent block DC coefficient difference reflects the overall color differences between each image block, therefore in a certain extent, it can reflect color distribution of original image, and inter-block LBP is the local image texture descriptor which can retain the texture information of the image space. Consequently, combining these two features, we can retrieve images similar to the target image in the whole color structure or in the texture [7].

The proposed secure image retrieval model in cloud environment is shown in Fig. 1:

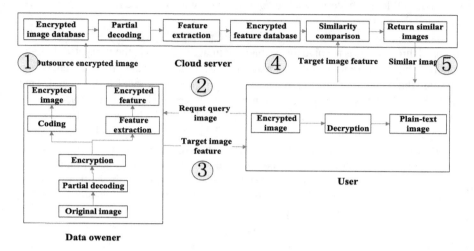

Fig. 1. Secure image retrieval model in cloud environment

There are three entities in image retrieval mode in cloud environment: data owners, cloud servers and users [8]. Data owner encrypts the original image, then uploads it to the server and provides user with the necessary retrieval information; cloud server stores encrypted image, extracts its feature, perform similarity comparison, and return image when user requests; users send queries, decrypt the similar images returned by servers and get target images. Retrieval process is given as below:

(1) Data owner encrypts image and outsources the encrypted image to cloud server, cloud server extracts features of the encrypted image stored in them;
(2) User sends query to data owner, requests necessary information of the target image, including the feature of the target image and the decryption key;
(3) The data owner verifies the validity of the user's identity, then returns the feature vector of the target image and decryption key to the user;
(4) The user sends the feature vector of target image to the server;
(5) The cloud server compares similarity of the feature vectors stored in it with features of the target image, and returns the most similar image to the user;
(6) The user uses the key to decrypt the encrypted image returned by the cloud server, and finally get the similar image of the target image.

2.1 Image Encryption and Feature Extraction

In this paper, we encrypt Y channel coefficients and other channel coefficients separately [9]. The random scrambling method is used to encrypt the DCT coefficients of Y channel in each block unit, AES encryption method is used to encrypt coefficients in Cb and Cr channels. Given the key is k, encryption method is E(), Coeff are DCT coefficient matrix of the 3 color channels, then encryption process can be expressed as:

$$E = E(Coeff, k) \tag{1}$$

Image feature extraction is the most important part of image retrieval. After encrypted image is uploaded to cloud server, image features can be extracted directly by cloud server as follows:

The cloud server will partially decode the encrypted JPEG stream to get DCT coefficients, and these coefficients are sorted in absolute value in descending order, then the mean value of the top 3 coefficients is computed. DC coefficient difference histogram is generated according to these mean value. Since the value of DC coefficients is generally between −1024 to 1024, then the range of coefficient difference is between −2048 and 2048 [10]. Therefore, the histogram can be divided into 12 bins, the value of each bin is defined as $\pm(2^m)$, m = (0, 1, 2, ..., 11), then DC differential histogram vector can be obtained by calculating the frequency of the fall in each bin [11]:

$$V = \left(V_0, V_1, V_2, \ldots, V_m\right)$$

Where

$$V_i = \begin{cases} the \; number \; of \; local \; blocks \; of \; D = 0 \;,\; i = 0 \\ the \; number \; of \; local \; blocks \; of \; D = 1 \;,\; i = 1 \\ the \; number \; of \; local \; blocks \; of \; D \in [2,3] \;,\; i = 2 \\ \qquad\qquad \cdots \\ the \; number \; of \; local \; blocks \; of \; D \in [1024, 2048] \;,\; i = 11 \end{cases}$$

D represents the absolute value of DC coefficient difference of the adjacent blocks.

V_0 is the number of local blocks whose difference absolute value is 0, V_1 refers to the number of local blocks whose difference absolute value is 1, V_2 represents the number of local blocks whose difference absolute value is in [2, 3], ..., V_m denotes the number of local blocks whose difference absolute value is between [1024, 2048]. Then the histogram can be normalized and compared. Three channels' histograms can be integrated together with different weights.

LBP descriptor represents the local texture of image and reflects the relationship between neighboring pixels. LBP can be expressed as:

$$LBP(P, R) = \sum_{p=0}^{p-1} s\left(g_p - g_c\right) \times 2^p \tag{2}$$

$$s(x) = \begin{cases} 1, x \geq 0 \\ 0, x < 0 \end{cases} \tag{3}$$

Where P is a sampling points, R is radius of a circle centered at center point. g_p is the gray value of the adjacent points, g_c is the gray value of center point, s(x) is a comparison function.

To improve retrieval precision, inter-bolck LBP feature is extracted in this paper. Block LBP is an extension of traditional LBP, which places each local block as a pixel in the traditional LBP. We sort local block coefficients according to the absolute value in descending order, take the average of the top three coefficients as a representative of the local block, and then calculate the LBP of that block and make comparison with the one of the center block, the block is noted 1 if the value of sub-block larger than (or equal to) center block, otherwise noted 0, then binary image is formed, and then scan the binary string into 10001111 from the upper left corner of the center block in a clockwise direction, LBP value between blocks is obtained by converting binary string into decimal number, as shown in Fig. 2, the LBP value of the center block is $1 + 16 + 32 + 64 + 128 = 241$.

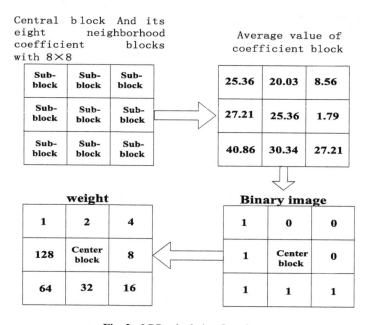

Fig. 2. LBP calculation flowchart

By calculating the LBP value of each block of the image in turn, and calculating the histogram and then normalization, we can get the block LBP feature histogram containing the spatial texture information of the image.

2.2 Similarity Comparison

After getting the index of the target image sent by the user, cloud server compares them with the encrypted image feature database and then calculates the Manhattan distance [12, 13] between them as the measure of similarity between images, the smaller the distance between features, the more similar the image [14], the importance of image feature is determined by weights given to the distance feature.

Suppose the distance between DC coefficient difference histogram is denoted by D_{diff} (X, Y), the distance between inter-block LBP feature is denoted by $D_{texture}$ (X, Y), α and β are the weights, Dis (X, Y) denotes the distance between image features, as shown in formulas (4)–(6):

$$Dis(X, Y) = \alpha * D_{diff}(X, Y) + \beta * D_{textture}(X, Y) \tag{4}$$

$$D_{diff}(X, Y) = \sum_{i=1}^{m} \left| X_{diff}(i) - Y_{diff}(i) \right| \tag{5}$$

$$D_{texture}(X, Y) = \sum_{j=1}^{n} \left| X_{texture}(j) - Y_{texture}(j) \right| \tag{6}$$

Where X and Y, respectively, represent image feature vector of the target image and the database, containing X_{diff}, Y_{diff}, $X_{texture}$, $Y_{texture}$, here X_{diff} (i) and Y_{diff} (i) represent the i-th component of image difference histogram of the target image and the database respectively, $X_{texture}$ (j) and $Y_{texture}$ (j), respectively, represent the j-th component of image block LBP feature of the target image and the database, m and n respectively represent the dimension of the feature vector.

Cloud server sorts the returned images according to the size of the total distance Dis (X, Y), and finally image with minimum distance is returned to the user.

Users get the similar image returned by cloud server, and partially decode the JPEG stream to obtain DCT coefficients encrypted by data owers, and then decrypt the coefficients using key k1, k2, k3 obtained from the data owers to get DCT coefficients of the plaintext, performing inverse DCT transform of the plaintext DCT coefficients can get the plaintext similar images.

3   Experimental Results and Analysis

Experiments were conducted on Corel image database, which includes 1000 images and is divided into 10 categories, and it is a commonly used database in image retrieval evaluation [15].

We compare the proposed method with other methods in terms of computation cost, security strength, search accuracy and computational complexity [16]. computational cost analysis include the mutual interaction rounds and computational complexity; image security is evaluated by measuring PSNR of cipher-image and cryptographic security; Image retrieval accuracy and efficiency can be evaluated by precision-recall curve (P-R curve) [17].

3.1   Computational Cost

Compared with other methods, the proposed method mainly has the following advantages: feature extraction is based on JPEG image partially decoded rather than fully decoded which can reduce the calculation and storage cost; random scrambling encryption is used to improve encryption speed without causing ciphertext expansion problem compared to homomorphic encryption method [4]; features can be extracted through the encrypted JPEG code stream by the cloud server directly, which can reduce the interaction between the data owner and the cloud server. Table 1 is the comparison results of several secure image retrieval methods in ciphertext size and expansion factor.

Table 1. Ciphertext extension of secret image

Methods	Ciphertext size (KB)/expansion factor
Paillier	32005/241.8
Bitplane randomization	159/1.2
Random projection	462/3.5
Randomized unary encoding	457/3.5
Proposed method	132/1.0

In summary, the method proposed in this paper has lower computational cost in image retrieval than that of other methods.

3.2 Security

(1) Perceptual security. We use PSNR to measure visual security of image encryption, encrypted image with smaller PSNR is more indistinguishable and its perceptual security is better [18]. Images randomly selected from the Corel database are encrypted, its encrypted effects and PSNR value is shown in Fig. 3:

PSNR=6.878   PSNR=5.589

Fig. 3. Visual impression of encryption image

As Fig. 3 shows, images encrypted with the proposed method have low PSNR value and one cannot get any useful information [19] from them, so it can be concluded that the encryption method proposed in this paper can ensure the visual security of image.

Encryption experiments are performed with 10 images which are randomly selected from 10 categories, and encrypted image quality is shown in Table 2:

Table 2. Encrypted image quality table

Image	Encrypted image quality(PSNR)
African	7.9955
Beaches	10.9162
Buildings	5.8660
Buses	7.0190
Dinosaurs	5.8326
Elephant	8.9273
Flowers	5.8296
Horse	6.9996
Mountains	8.7873
Food	7.7069
Average	7.5880

From Table 2 we can see that PSNR values of the vast majority of encrypted image are below 10, which means its information leakage is very limited and perceptual security of the proposed method is good.

(2) Cryptographic Security. This paper uses random scrambling method to encrypt image in transform domain, in order to ensure image's cryptographic security and defense KPA (Known PlainText Attack), random generation of new scrambling matrix at each time of encryption is needed.

For Corel database images, the presented method in this paper needs to generate 1536 random matrices with size of 8 * 8 and 2 random matrices with size of 384 * 256 (or 256 * 384), on the contrary, if people want to completely decrypt images then they need to decrypt these random matrices, while the exhaustive approach is difficult and costly, hence, in this point of view, the encryption algorithm is relatively safe.

3.3 Retrieval Accuracy and Validity

The most important criterion to measure performance of image retrieval system is recall and precision. Denote recall as R and precision as P as follows:

$$R = \frac{M}{N}, \quad P = \frac{M}{S} \tag{7}$$

Here, S denotes the number of retrieved images, M denotes the number of relevant images among retrieved images, N denotes the number of relevant images in the database.

Lu [2] selected 10 % of the images in the database as the target images to implement the experiment, this paper calculates the average P-R curve in the same retrieval conditions, then the results of the proposed method are compared with the methods in literature [2–4], P-R curve comparison is shown in Fig. 4.

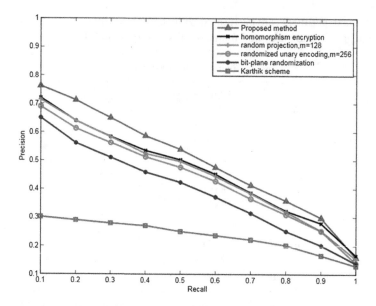

Fig. 4. Comparison of PR curves of several methods

From Fig. 4 we can see that the method proposed in this paper obtains a better average retrieval accuracy than other three methods presented by Lu [2], transparent privacy preserving hashing method proposed by Karthik [3], and homomorphic encryption methods proposed by Hsu [4].

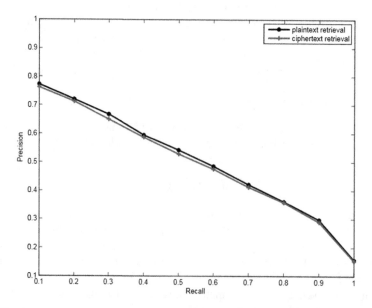

Fig. 5. Comparison of P-R curves of plain text retrieval and cipher text retrieval

Then we calculate the average retrieval P-R curve of plaintext and ciphertext and then compare the two results in Fig. 5:

It can be seen that the average P-R curves of the ciphertext retrieval results almost coincide with the plaintext retrieval results, that is, the proposed method does not cause too much accuracy loss because of encryption, so retrieval accuracy is guaranteed.

From above comparison we can see that this method is effective and accurate for the image retrieval, and it is suitable for the secure retrieval of the JPEG encryption image in the cloud environment.

4   Conclusions

This paper presents a secure JPEG image retrieval method under cloud environment, where a lightweight encryption method – random scrambling encryption is used to reduce the computational complexity, DC difference histogram and inter-block LBP is used to achieve better retrieval performance. Further work is to improve the security and retrieval accuracy further.

References

1. Smeulders, A.W.M., Worring, M., Santini, S., et al.: Content-based image retrieval at the end of the early years. Pattern Anal. Mach. Intell. IEEE Trans. **22**(12), 1349–1380 (2000)
2. Wu, M., Swaminathan, A., Varna, A.L., et al.: Secure image retrieval through feature protection. In: Proceedings of ICASSP, pp. 1533–1536 (2009)
3. Karthik, K., Kashyap, S.: Transparent hashing in the encrypted domain for privacy preserving image retrieval. Signal. Image Video Process. **7**(4), 647–664 (2013)
4. Hsu, C.Y., Lu, C.S., Pei, S.C.: Image feature extraction in encrypted domain with privacy-preserving sift. IEEE Trans. Image Process. **21**(11), 4593–4607 (2012)
5. Yagisawa, M.: Fully Homomorphic Encryption without bootstrapping (2015). https://www.lap-publishing.com/
6. Li, J., Li, X., Yang, B., Sun, X.: Segmentation-based image copy-move forgery detection scheme. IEEE Trans. Inf. Forensics Secur. **10**(3), 507–518 (2015)
7. Lin, C.H., Chen, R.T., Chan, Y.K.: A smart content-based image retrieval system based on color and texture feature. Image Vis. Comput. **27**(11), 658–665 (2009)
8. Rane, S., Boufounos, P., Vetro, A.: Quantized embeddings: an efficient and universal nearest neighbor method for cloud-based image retrieval. Appl. Digit. Image Process. XXXVI **8856**(3), 537 (2013)
9. Chen, B., Shu, H., Coatrieux, G., Chen, G., Sun, X., Coatrieux, J.-L.: Color image analysis by quaternion-type moments. J. Math. Imaging Vis. **51**(1), 124–144 (2015)
10. Chen, C.C., Wen, C.H., Su, C.H.: Systems and methods for randomly accessing compressed images, US, US 8107754 B2 (2012)
11. Schaefer, G., Edmundson, D.: DC Stream Based JPEG Compressed Domain Image Retrieval, pp. 318–327. Springer, Heidelberg (2012)
12. Gao, Y., Zhang, B.: Sobel-LBP. In: Proceedings of ICIP, pp. 2144–2147 (2008)
13. Zheng, Y., Jeon, B., Danhua, X., Jonathan Wu, Q.M., Zhang, H.: Image segmentation by generalized hierarchical fuzzy C-means algorithm. J. Intell. Fuzzy Syst. **28**(2), 961–973 (2015)

14. Wang, J.: Study and Implement on Large-Scalable Face Image Fast Retrieval. University of Science and Technology of China (2014)
15. Bibin, D., Punitha, P.: Image classification using artificial neural networks: an experimental study on corel database. Int. J. Mach. Intell. **3**(4), 225 (2011)
16. Yan, T.W., Garcia-Molina, H.: The SIFT information dissemination system. ACM Trans. Database Syst. **24**(4), 529–565 (1999)
17. Piwowarski, B., Dupret, G.: Evaluation in (XML) information retrieval: expected precision-recall with user modelling (EPRUM). In: Proceedings of ACM SIGIR, pp. 260–267 (2006)
18. Liu, F., Yan, W.Q.: Visual Cryptography for Image Processing and Security. Springer International Publishing, Cham (2014)
19. Guan, L.N.: Research on Image Joint Compression - Encryption Algorithm based on SPIHT Coding. Hainan University (2014)

Photon-Counting Double-Random-Phase Image Authentication in the Fresnel Domain

Faliu Yi[(✉)]

School of Computer and Software,
Nanjing University of Information Science and Technology,
Nanjing, China
yifaliu@hotmail.com

Abstract. In this paper, we propose a method for image authentication using photon counting and double random phase encryption technique in the Fresnel domain. Recently, it was reported that a better avalanche effect can be achieved for double random phase encoding (DRPE) in the Fresnel domain than that in the Fourier domain in bit units. Moreover, it was verified that photon counting technique can enhance the security of DRPE algorithm. Therefore, DRPE in the Fresnel domain combining with photon counting scheme is much safer for image authentication. In this study, an image is first encrypted by DRPE in the Fresnel domain. Then, a photon-limited encrypted image is produced by using photon counting method. Finally, the decrypted image which can not be easily visualized and recognized under a limited number of photon is authenticated with a statistical nonlinear correlation algorithm. Experimental results verify the feasibility of the proposed method.

Keywords: Information security · Image authentication · Photon counting · Double random phase encryption · Statistical nonlinear correlation

1 Introduction

Double random phase encryption (DRPE) algorithm, as a promising information security approach that owes advantages such as multiple-dimensional and parallel processing, has been widely studied in the field of image encryption, information hiding, and watermarking [1–11] since it was proposed by Refregier and Javidi in 1995 [1]. In a DRPE system, the input image is modulated by two statistically independent random phase masks while one mask is employed in the input image plane and the other is placed in the Fourier domain. The authors in [1] have shown that the encrypted image resulted from DRPE is stationary white noise which means there is no relationship among any pair of pixel points in the encrypted image. The DRPE can not only be implemented in the Fourier domain, but can also be done in the Fresnel domain [12] and fractional Fourier domain [13] which are involved in more secret keys.

Even though the DRPE system is extensively used for information security, it was also reported that the DRPE algorithm is vulnerable to some attack methods such as chosen-cipher text attack and known-plaintext attack under some given conditions due to the linear characteristic maintained in these DRPE systems [14–18]. In order to

© Springer International Publishing AG 2016
X. Sun et al. (Eds.): ICCCS 2016, Part II, LNCS 10040, pp. 487–497, 2016.
DOI: 10.1007/978-3-319-48674-1_43

improve the deficiency of the DRPE system, many enhanced methods were presented [19–23]. In [24, 25], the amplitude information in encrypted image is eliminated and only partial phase information which is randomly chosen from encrypted image is kept for image decryption. In [26, 27], the authors have applied photon-counting technique [28] to DRPE systems for image authentication while the decrypted image is sparsely distributed and cannot be visually recognized under a few photon number. In [21], a multispectral photon-counting technique is successfully employed to the DRPE system for color image authentication where the encrypted color image with limited number of non-zero pixel points is beneficial to data transmission on Internet. The decrypted images having limited pixel information in [21, 24–27] cannot be easily recognized with naked eyes but can be successfully verified with a statistical nonlinear correlation algorithm [29, 30]. However, all previous methods based on DRPE are conducted in the Fourier domain. Recently, it was experimentally demonstrated in [31] that the DRPE in the Fresnel domain can achieve better avalanche effect than that in the Fourier domain in bit units. Therefore, authentication algorithm based on DRPE in the Fresnel domain will be much safer than that in the Fourier domain in the view of cryptography since avalanche effect is an attractive property of block ciphers.

In this study, we propose a photon-counting double-random-phase image authentication algorithm in the Fresnel domain. Firstly, the input primary image is encrypted with DRPE method in the Fresnel domain and the amplitude part of the resulting image is photon counted using photon-counting technique. Then, the corresponding phase information at locations with nonzero amplitude value in the photo-counted amplitude image is retained and used for decryption in DRPE in the Fresnel domain. Finally, the decrypted image which cannot be visually verified under a limited number of photon is authenticated with a statistical nonlinear correlation scheme [29, 30]. Experimental results illustrate the feasibility of the proposed approach for image authentication with varied number of photon.

This paper is organized as follows: in Sect. 2, the concept of DRPE in the Fresnel domain is explained. In Sect. 3, we describe the photon counting technique. In Sect. 4, we present the procedure for our image authentication algorithm. In Sect. 5, we give the simulation results, and we conclude the paper in Sect. 6.

2   Double Random Phase Encoding

For a DRPE system in the Fourier domain [1], the primary image is first modulated by a random phase mask in the input image plane. Then, the resulted image is further modulated by another random phase mask in the Fourier domain. The encrypted image is stationary white noise and all of the pixel values are statically independent which means the pixel values from one part in the encrypted image cannot be predicted using pixel values from any other part of the encrypted image. After DRPE was proposed in the Fourier domain, many other version of DRPE system were also presented [12, 13]. The authors in [12] proposed a DRPE system in the Fresnel domain and illustrated that much higher security can be obtained for information encryption using DRPE in the Fresnel domain than that in the Fourier domain. Recently, the authors in [31] analyzed the DREP system both in the Fresnel and Fourier domain in the view of cryptography

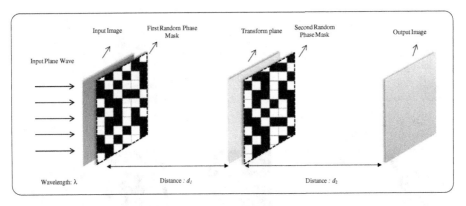

Fig. 1. Schematic diagram of DRPE in the Fresnel domain

and experimentally showed that the DRPE in the Fresnel domain has good avalanche effect and is also better than that in the Fourier domain. Therefore, the proposed image authentication algorithm using DRPE in the Fresnel domain can definitely have better performance in terms of security.

Figure 1 shows the schematic diagram of a DRPE system in the Fresnel domain. As it is shown in Fig. 1, the input image $f(x,y)$ is first modulated using a random phase mask with the same size as the input image where x and y are the pixel locations. This process is the same as that for DRPE in the Fourier domain. Then, the modulated image is Fresnel-propagated at a distance d_1 under a plane wave with a wavelength of λ. Next, the resulted image from previous step is further modulated using another random phase mask of the same size as the input image at the distance of d_1 under the Fresnel plane. Finally, the encrypted image $e(x,y)$ is produced by Fresnel-propagating the resulted image at the previous step for a distance d_2. For the DRPE in the Fresnel domain, the two random phase masks can be expressed as $exp(j2\pi n(x,y))$ and $exp(j2\pi n(\mu,v))$ where $n(x,y)$ and $n(\mu,v)$ are uniformly distributed on the interval [0, 1]. Therefore, each point value in the two random phase masks is located randomly on the interval [0, 2π]. The entire process of DRPE in the Fresnel domain can also be mathematically expressed as follows [1, 21]:

$$e(x,y) = FrT_\lambda\{FrT_\lambda\{f(x,y)\exp(j2\pi n(x,y)); d_1\}\exp(j2\pi n(\mu,v)); d_2\} \qquad (1)$$

where FrT_λ means Fresnel propagation under wavelength λ. The encrypted image $e(x, y)$ is a complex-valued image with amplitude part denoted as $|e(x,y)|$ and phase part expressed as $phase(e(x,y))$. Different from DRPE in the Fourier domain where only two random phase masks are considered as encryption keys, the wavelength λ and two distance values d_1 and d_2 used for Fresnel propagation are also viewed as encryption keys for DRPE in the Fresnel domain. As image decryption for DRPE in the Fresnel domain, the same setup as Fig. 1 can be used in the reverse direction while the input image is the complex conjugate of the encrypted image $e(x, y)$ [12].

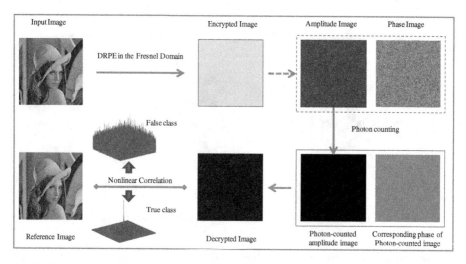

Fig. 2. Flow chart of photon-counting double-random-phase image authentication algorithm in the Fresnel domain

3 Photon Counting Technique

Photon counting technique is specially designed for imaging object under photon-starved conditions or situations where only a limited number of photon can reach the captured sensors [21, 28]. Photon counting technique has been successfully used for 3D imaging and recognition at a low light level [32–35]. The photon-counted image is simulated by allowing only a limited number of incident photons to the captured image scene while assuming that the probability of counting photons at any arbitrary pixel in an acquired image follows a Poisson distribution [21]. In this assumption, the simulated photon-counted image is similar with that captured by using a photon counting imaging device. Therefore, a photon-limited image can be generated by controlling the number of photons in the entire scene. The probability of counting l (x, y) photons at pixel location (x, y) is Poisson distributed and modeled as following equation [21].

$$Poisson(l(x,y);\ \lambda(x,y)) = \frac{[\lambda(x,y)]^{l(x,y)} e^{-\lambda(x,y)}}{l(x,y)!} \qquad (2)$$

where $\lambda(x, y)$ is the Poisson parameter at pixel location (x, y) and it is measured as follows [21]:

$$\lambda(x,y) = \bar{f}(x,y) \times N_p \qquad (3)$$

where N_p is the expected number of photons in the image and $\bar{f}(x, y)$ is the normalized irradiance at image pixel location (x, y) that is represented as follows [21]:

$$\bar{f}(x,y) = f(x,y) \Big/ \sum_{x=1}^{M} \sum_{y=1}^{N} f(x,y) \qquad (4)$$

where $f(x, y)$ is the image at pixel point (x, y), M and N are the total number of points in the image in the horizontal and vertical directions, respectively. Then, the photon-counted image $f_{ph}(x,y)$ derived from image $f(x, y)$ is expressed as following equation.

$$f_{ph}(x,y) = Poissrnd(\lambda(x,y)) = \bar{f}(x,y) \times N_p \qquad (5)$$

where function $Poissrnd()$ is to generate random numbers from a Poisson distribution with Poisson parameter $\bar{f}(x,y) \times N_p$. Therefore, a photon-counted image as obtained from photon counting imaging device can be simulated from an input image using previous equations under any number of photons.

4 Procedures of the Image Authentication Algorithm

In this proposed image authentication algorithm, the input image $I(x,y)$ is first encrypted using the DRPE in the Fresnel domain and thus the encrypted image $E(x,y)$ is a complex-valued image. Therefore, the encrypted image $E(x,y)$ can be divided into an amplitude image $E_{Amp}(x,y)$ and a phase image $E_{Pha}(x,y)$. Then, the photon-counting technique is applied to the amplitude image $E_{Amp}(x,y)$ under the number of photon N_p and the resulted photon-counted image is denoted as $E'_{pc}(x,y)$. Here, the photon-counted image $E'_{pc}(x,y)$ is sparsely distributed where many pixel points would have zero value under a limited number of photon. Consequently, it is beneficial to data compression, transmission, and storage. However, only keeping the amplitude and discarding the phase information will make the decryption in DRPE impossible. As a result, the phase information in $E_{Pha}(x,y)$ for those pixels with non-zero amplitude value in photon-counted image $E'_{pc}(x,y)$ are preserved and used for image decryption, and the resulted phase image is represented as $E'_{pha}(x,y)$. It can be noted that both $E'_{pc}(x,y)$ and $E'_{pha}(x,y)$ are sparsely distributed and can be combined as a complex-valued image $E'(x,y)$. For image decryption, the complex conjugate of $E'(x,y)$ is used as input in the reverse direction of image encryption in DPRE in the Fresnel domain. Since the encrypted image is sparely distributed and have missed some information, the decrypted image is not totally the same as the original input image and will be shown as a noisy image when the photon number is small. That is, the decrypted image will not be visually recognized under a limited number of photons. Therefore, the proposed algorithm is not for image visualization and only used for image authentication. On the other hand, the decrypted image unrecognized with naked eyes can safeguard DRPE from unauthorized attacks and improve its security. Fortunately, the decrypted image that is not visually distinguished from its counterpart can be verified with a statistical nonlinear correlation algorithm [21]. The statistical nonlinear correlation algorithm is mathematically defined as following equation [21, 29].

$$NC(x, y) = \Im^{-1}\left\{|\Im[D(x,y)]\Im[R(x,y)]|^k \times exp[i(\phi(\Im[D(x,y)]) - \phi(\Im[R(x,y)]))]\right\}$$

(6)

Where $D(x,y)$ is the decrypted image from DRPE in the Fresnel domain using encrypted complex-valued image $E'(x,y)$, $R(x,y)$ is a reference image, $\Im$ and $\Im^{-1}$ mean Fourier and inverse Fourier transform, respectively, $\phi(\Im[D(x,y)])$ and $\phi(\Im[R(x,y)])$ represent the phase part of $\Im[D(x,y)]$ and $\Im[R(x,y)]$, respectively, and the parameter k defines the strength of the applied nonlinearity. When $k = 0$, Eq. (6) becomes a phase extractor and it is a linear correlation approach when $k = 1$. Different value of parameter k will result in the nonlinear correlation equation having different value. A good parameter k should produce a nonlinear correlation plane in Eq. (6) with sharp and high peak at the center for true class image while it generates a while noise correlation plane for false class image. The appropriate value for parameter k used in the statistical nonlinear correlation is usually measured by evaluating the peak-to-correlation energy or discrimination-ratio metrics [21, 26, 27]. In this paper, we would set $k = 0.3$ for the following simulations while the 0.3 is verified to be a reasonable value for nonlinear correlation authentication in [21, 26, 27, 33]. Finally, an image would be verified as true class image if the output nonlinear correlation plane has sharp and high peak. Otherwise, it will be considered as a false class image. The whole flow chart of our proposed image authentication algorithm is shown in Fig. 2.

5   Simulation Results

In this section, we will show that our proposed algorithm can successfully achieve image authentication using photon-counting double-random-phase technique in the Fresnel domain. One "true class" grayscale image and one "false class" grayscale image as shown in Fig. 3 are used to illustrate our method. The size of the image is 512×512 and the quantization level is 256. All the simulations are conducted on a 64-bits window 7 OS computer consisting of an Intel Core i5-2500 k processor of 3.3 GHz while the RAM is 6 GB. Total 10 "true class" and 10 "false class" images are tested with proposed authentication approach, and we only show the result of a pair of image in this paper because all "true class" images produce similar results and all "false class" images have similar authentication output.

At the first step, the input image is encrypted by DRPE in the Fresnel domain with wavelength $\lambda = 0.5145$ μm, $d_1 = 100000$ μm, and $d_2 = 1000000$ μm. Since the encrypted image is a complex-valued image, the amplitude part and phase part of one of the encrypted images is shown in Fig. 4. It can be found from Fig. 4 that both the amplitude and phase image are stationary white noise and there are no relationship among these pixel points. Then, the amplitude image of the encrypted image is photon-counted under the photon number N_p. Definitely, different photon number N_p would result in different photon-counted image. For a successful image authentication in our proposed method, the fewer the photon number is, the better because it will make the encrypted image much sparser and this is beneficial to data storage and transmission. Some of the photon-counted images with varied number of photon based on

Fig. 3. Grayscale images (a) a true class image (b) a false class image

Fig. 4. Encrypted image with DRPE in the Fresnel domain (a) amplitude part of encrypted image (b) phase part of encrypted image

amplitude image in Fig. 4(a) are given in Fig. 5(a)–(c). It is noted from Fig. 5(a)–(c) that the smaller the photon number N_p is, the more zero points would be resulted in the photon-counted image. Also, the corresponding phase images with phase information preserved for those pixels having non-zeros amplitude value in photon-counted image are shown in Fig. 5(d)–(f).

For image decryption in DRPE in the Fresnel domain, the same keys are used as that in the encryption process. The decrypted images from varied photon number are given in Fig. 6 by using the encrypted image including amplitude and phase information as shown in Fig. 5. It is noted from Fig. 6 that the decrypted images cannot be visually recognized when the photon number is less than 10^5.

Even though the decrypted images cannot be well distinguished with naked eyes in a low light level, it can be authenticated with a statistical nonlinear correlation algorithm as described in Sect. 4. The nonlinear correlation planes for both "true class" and "false class" image are shown in Fig. 7. It is found from Fig. 7 that the "true class" image has a sharp and high peak in the nonlinear correlation plane when the number of photon is equal or greater than a threshold value 10^4. On the other hand, all of the nonlinear correlation planes look like noisy images for the "false class" image, even in

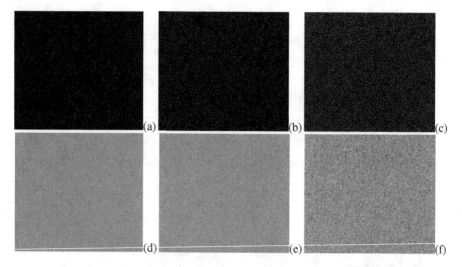

Fig. 5. Photon-counted images (a)–(c) Photon-counted amplitude image under photon number equal $10^3, 10^4$ and 10^5, respectively. (d)–(f) corresponding phase images of (a)–(c)

Fig. 6. Decrypted images (a) under photon number 10^3 (b) under photon number 10^4 (c) under photon number 10^5

the case when a high photon number is given. In addition, the maximum values in the nonlinear correlation planes for both 'true class' and 'false class' image under varied photon number are illustrated in Fig. 8 and it can be considered as quantitative evaluation of the proposed algorithm. Here, all the maximum nonlinear correlation values are normalized based on correlation planes obtained under the same photon number. Obviously, the "true class" image can be distinguished from the "false class" image by evaluating the normalized maximum value in the correlation plane when the number of photon is equal or greater than 10^4. Therefore, it is verified that our proposed algorithm using photon-counting double-random-phase in the Fresnel domain can successfully achieve image authentication.

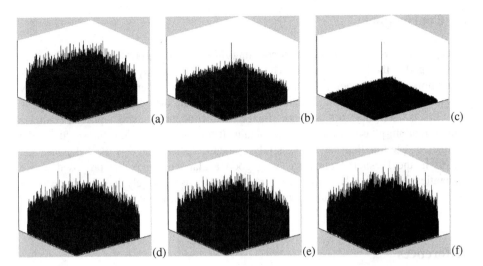

Fig. 7. Nonlinear correlation planes (a)–(c) for true class image under photon number equal to 10^3, 10^4, and 10^5. (d)–(f) for false class image under photon number equal to 10^3, 10^4, and 10^5.

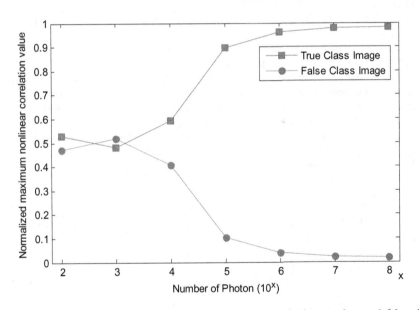

Fig. 8. Normalized maximum nonlinear correlation value for both true class and false class image with varied number of photons.

6 Conclusions

In this paper, we propose a photon-counting double-random-phase image authentication method in the Fresnel domain. The DRPE makes the encrypted image as stationary white noise and the photon counting technique converts the encrypted to be sparsely distributed that is beneficial to data storage and transmission. Simulation results show that it is feasible to achieve image authentication using photon-counting double-random-phase in the Fresnel domain. It also shows that the threshold for the number of photon that can successfully authenticate an image is 10^4. Because the DRPE in the Fresnel domain has very good avalanche effect, the proposed image authentication system based on the Fresnel domain is definitely has the same merit which can enhance the security of system in the view of cryptography.

References

1. Refregier, P., Javidi, B.: Optical image encryption based on input plane and Fourier plane random encoding. Opt. Lett. **20**(7), 767–769 (1995)
2. Zhang, S., Karim, M.A.: Color image encryption using double random phase encoding. Microwave Opt. Technol. Lett. **21**(5), 318–323 (1999)
3. He, M.Z., Cai, L.Z., Liu, Q., et al.: Multiple image encryption and watermarking by random phase matching. Opt. Commun. **247**(1), 29–37 (2005)
4. Yao-yao, C., Xin, Z., Yong-liang, X., et al.: An improved watermarking method based on double random phase encoding technique. Opt. Laser Technol. **42**(4), 617–623 (2010)
5. Sheng, Y., Xin, Z., Alam, M.S., et al.: Information hiding based on double random-phase encoding and public-key cryptography. Opt. Express **17**(5), 3270–3284 (2009)
6. Zhou, X., Chen, J.G.: Information hiding based on double-random phase encoding technology. J. Mod. Opt. **53**(12), 1777–1783 (2006)
7. Zhang, Y., Wang, B., Dong, Z.: Enhancement of image hiding by exchanging two phase masks. J. Opt. A: Pure Appl. Opt. **11**(12), 125406 (2009)
8. Lee, J., Yi, F., Saifullah, R., et al.: Graphics processing unit–accelerated double random phase encoding for fast image encryption. Opt. Eng. **53**(11), 112308 (2014)
9. Li, J., Li, X., Yang, B., et al.: Segmentation-based Image Copy-move Forgery Detection Scheme. IEEE Trans. Inf. Forensics Secur. **10**(3), 507–518 (2015)
10. Chen, B., Shu, H., Coatrieux, G., et al.: Color image analysis by quaternion-type moments. J. Math. Imaging Vis. **51**(1), 124–144 (2015)
11. Zheng, Y., Jeon, B., Xu, D., et al.: Image segmentation by generalized hierarchical fuzzy C-means algorithm. J. Intell. Fuzzy Syst. **28**(2), 961–973 (2015)
12. Situ, G., Zhang, J.: Double random-phase encoding in the Fresnel domain. Opt. Lett. **29**(14), 1584–1586 (2004)
13. Unnikrishnan, G., Joseph, J., Singh, K.: Optical encryption by double-random phase encoding in the fractional Fourier domain. Opt. Lett. **25**(12), 887–889 (2000)
14. Situ, G., Gopinathan, U., Monaghan, D.S., et al.: Cryptanalysis of optical security systems with significant output images. Appl. Opt. **46**(22), 5257–5262 (2007)
15. Peng, X., Zhang, P., Wei, H., et al.: Known-plaintext attack on optical encryption based on double random phase keys. Opt. Lett. **31**(8), 1044–1046 (2006)

16. Peng, X., Wei, H., Zhang, P.: Chosen-plaintext attack on lensless double-random phase encoding in the Fresnel domain. Opt. Lett. **31**(22), 3261–3263 (2006)
17. Carnicer, A., Montes-Usategui, M., Arcos, S., et al.: Vulnerability to chosen-cyphertext attacks of optical encryption schemes based on double random phase keys. Opt. Lett. **30**(13), 1644–1646 (2005)
18. Qin, W., Peng, X.: Vulnerability to known-plaintext attack of optical encryption schemes based on two fractional Fourier transform order keys and double random phase keys. J. Opt. A: Pure Appl. Opt. **11**(7), 075402 (2009)
19. Frauel, Y., Castro, A., Naughton, T.J., et al.: Resistance of the double random phase encryption against various attacks. Opt. Express **15**(16), 10253–10265 (2007)
20. Cheng, X.C., Cai, L.Z., Wang, Y.R., et al.: Security enhancement of double-random phase encryption by amplitude modulation. Opt. Lett. **33**(14), 1575–1577 (2008)
21. Yi, F., Moon, I., Lee, Y.H.: A multispectral photon-counting double random phase encoding scheme for image authentication. Sensors **14**(5), 8877–8894 (2014)
22. Hennelly, B., Sheridan, J.T.: Optical image encryption by random shifting in fractional Fourier domains. Opt. Lett. **28**(4), 269–271 (2003)
23. Liu, Z., Li, S., Liu, W., et al.: Image encryption algorithm by using fractional Fourier transform and pixel scrambling operation based on double random phase encoding. Opt. Lasers Eng. **51**(1), 8–14 (2013)
24. Chen, W., Chen, X.: Double random phase encoding using phase reservation and compression. J. Opt. **16**(2), 025402 (2014)
25. Zheng, J., Li, X.: Image authentication using only partial phase information from a double-random-phase-encrypted image in the fresnel domain. J. Opt. Soc. Korea **19**(3), 241–247 (2015)
26. Pérez-Cabré, E., Cho, M., Javidi, B.: Information authentication using photon-counting double-random-phase encrypted images. Opt. Lett. **36**(1), 22–24 (2011)
27. Pérez-Cabré, E., Abril, H.C., Millán, M.S., et al.: Photon-counting double-random-phase encoding for secure image verification and retrieval. J. Opt. **14**(9), 094001 (2012)
28. Becker, W.: Advanced Time-Correlated Single Photon Counting Techniques. Springer, Heidelberg (2005)
29. Javidi, B.: Nonlinear joint power spectrum based optical correlation. Appl. Opt. **28**(12), 2358–2367 (1989)
30. Cho, M., Javidi, B.: Three-dimensional photon counting double-random-phase encryption. Opt. Lett. **38**(17), 3198–3201 (2013)
31. Moon, I., Yi, F., Lee, Y.H., et al.: Avalanche and bit independence characteristics of double random phase encoding in the Fourier and Fresnel domains. JOSA A **31**(5), 1104–1111 (2014)
32. Tavakoli, B., Javidi, B., Watson, E.: Three dimensional visualization by photon counting computational integral imaging. Opt. Express **16**(7), 4426–4436 (2008)
33. Yeom, S., Javidi, B., Watson, E.: Three-dimensional distortion-tolerant object recognition using photon-counting integral imaging. Opt. Express **15**(4), 1513–1533 (2007)
34. Moon, I., Muniraj, I., Javidi, B.: 3D visualization at low light levels using multispectral photon counting integral imaging. J. Disp. Technol. **9**(1), 51–55 (2013)
35. Aloni, D., Stern, A., Javidi, B.: Three-dimensional photon counting integral imaging reconstruction using penalized maximum likelihood expectation maximization. Opt. Express **19**(20), 19681–19687 (2011)

New Conjugate Gradient Algorithms Based on New Conjugacy Condition

Gonglin Yuan[1](✉) and Gaohui Peng[2]

[1] College of Mathematics and Information Science,
Guangxi Colleges and Universities Key Laboratory of Mathematics
and Its Applications, Guangxi University,
Nanning 530004, Guangxi, People's Republic of China
[2] College of Mathematics and Information Science,
North China University of Water Resources and Electric Power,
Zhengzhou 450011, Henan, People's Republic of China
{gonglin.yuan,gaohui.peng}@springer.com
http://www.springer.com/lncs

Abstract. The nonlinear conjugate gradient (CG) algorithm is one of the most effective line search algorithms for optimization problems due to its simplicity and low memory requirements, particularly for large-scale problems. However, the results of the new conjugacy conditions are very limited. In this paper, we will propose a new conjugacy condition and two CG formulas. Global convergence is achieved for these algorithms, and numerical results are reported for Benchmark problems.

Keywords: Optimization · Convergence · Conjugacy condition · Conjugate gradient algorithm

1 Introduction

The Benchmark problems have wildly applied in engineer fields and they are often used to evaluate the performance of any evolutionary algorithms [24]. However the continuously optimization algorithms are not further studied to solve these problems. In this paper, we will propose the CG algorithms for solving them. Generally, the Benchmark problems can be converted to the following unconstrained optimization problem

$$\min_{x \in \Re^n} f(x), \tag{1}$$

where $f: \Re^n \to \Re$ is continuously differentiable. The iteration formula of CG algorithm for (1) is designed by

$$x_{k+1} = x_k + \alpha_k d_k, \ k = 1, 2, \cdots \tag{2}$$

where x_k is the kth iterate point, $\alpha_k > 0$ is the called steplength, and d_k is the so-called search direction designed by

$$d_k = \begin{cases} -g_k + \beta_k d_{k-1}, & \text{if } k \geq 2 \\ -g_k, & \text{if } k = 1, \end{cases} \tag{3}$$

© Springer International Publishing AG 2016
X. Sun et al. (Eds.): ICCCS 2016, Part II, LNCS 10040, pp. 498–509, 2016.
DOI: 10.1007/978-3-319-48674-1_44

where $\beta_k \in \Re$ is a scalar that determines the different conjugate gradient algorithms (see [4,6,7,17,19–21], among others) and g_k is the gradient of $f(x)$ at point x_k. Many problems can convert to the optimization models (1) (see [13–16] in detail). There are many well-known formulas for β_k and the earlier three formulas listed as follows

$$\beta_k^{FR} = \frac{g_k^T g_k}{\|g_{k-1}\|^2}, \quad \beta_k^{HS} = \frac{g_k^T (g_k - g_{k-1})}{(g_k - g_{k-1})^T d_{k-1}}, \quad \beta_k^{PRP} = \frac{g_k^T (g_k - g_{k-1})}{\|g_{k-1}\|^2}, \quad (4)$$

where FR, PRP, HS denote the abbreviated names of the authors, g_{k-1} is the gradient $\nabla f(x_{k-1})$ of $f(x)$ at points x_{k-1}, $\|.\|$ denotes the Euclidean norm of vectors and we also denote $f(x_k)$ by f_k in this paper. Although these algorithms are equivalent (see [5,33], among others) in the linear case, their behaviors for general objective functions may be considerably different. For general functions, Zoutendjk [37] proved the global convergence of the FR algorithm with exact line search. Although one would be satisfied with its global convergence, the FR algorithm performs considerably worse than the PRP(HS) algorithm in real computations. Powell [23] analyzed a major numerical drawback of the FR algorithm, namely, if a small step is generated away from the solution point, the subsequent steps may also be very short. On the other hand, in practical computations, the PRP algorithm and the HS algorithm are generally believed to be the most efficient conjugate gradient algorithms because these algorithms essentially perform a restart if a bad direction occurs. However, Powell [22] provided a counter example to show that there exist nonconvex functions on which the PRP algorithm does not converge globally, even when the exact line search is used. He suggested that β_k should not be less than zero, which is very important to ensure global convergence (see [5,23]). Considering this suggestion, Gilbert and Nocedal [9] proved that the modified PRP algorithm $\beta_k^+ = \max\{0, \beta_k^{PRP}\}$ is globally convergent with the WWP line search under the assumption of sufficient descent conditions. Based on [28], Yuan [29] presented a modified PRP algorithm $\beta_k^{MPRP} = \beta_k^{PRP} - \min\{\beta_k^{PRP}, \frac{\mu\|y_k\|^2}{\|g_k\|^4} g_{k+1}^T d_k\}$, where $\mu > \frac{1}{4}$ is a constant and $y_k = g_{k+1} - g_k$. This formula has the sufficient descent property $d_k^T g_k \leq -(1 - \frac{1}{4\mu})\|g_k\|^2$ without any other conditions. To obtain the global convergence of the PRP algorithm for non-convex problems, Grippo and Luidi [8] proposed a new line search algorithm. Over the past few years, substantial effort has been dedicated to finding new formulas for conjugate algorithms such that they have not only a global convergence property for general functions but also good numerical performance (see [5,9]). Recently, some promising results on the nonlinear conjugate gradient algorithm (see [1,3,10–12,25,26,30–32,34,36], among others) have been presented.

Dai and Liao [2] recently used a new conjugacy condition and proposed two new algorithms. Interestingly, one of their algorithms is not only globally convergent for general functions but also performs better than the HS and PRP algorithms. Based on their algorithm, Li, Tang and Wei [18] presented another conjugacy condition and new nonlinear conjugate algorithms. Based on the paper [35], Yabe and Takano [27] also presented a new conjugacy condition and several

CG formulas. However, studies and achievements regarding new conjugacy conditions are very limited compared with the normal conjugacy condition. Thus, we can conclude that finding other new conjugacy conditions is an interesting line of work that can enrich the fields of CG theory and optimization. Motivated by this idea, we established a new conjugacy condition and proposed two new CG formulas for β_k. The main attributes of this algorithm are as follows. • A new conjugacy condition is introduced. • Two new CG formulas are presented. • Global convergence of the given CG algorithms is established. • Numerical results show that this algorithm is competitive with other similar algorithms for given problems.

This paper is organized as follows, the next section states the new conjugacy condition and new nonlinear conjugate gradient algorithms. The global convergence of the given algorithms is established in Sect. 3. Numerical results are reported in Sect. 4, and one conclusion is presented in the last section.

2   New Conjugacy Condition and Related Conjugate Gradient Algorithms

This section will state a new conjugacy condition and related conjugate gradient algorithms. First, we will present a new quasi-Newton equation that is based on the concept of Wei, Yao, and Liu [26], and then we derive our new conjugacy condition by using this new quasi-Newton equation.

To ensure that the scalar $\beta_k \geq 0$ of the conjugate gradient, Wei, Yao and Liu [26] presented a modified formula defined by

$$\beta_k = \frac{g_k^T\left(g_k - \frac{\|g_k\|}{\|g_{k-1}\|}g_{k-1}\right)}{\|g_{k-1}\|^2}. \tag{5}$$

It is easy to obtain

$$\frac{g_k^T\left(g_k - \frac{\|g_k\|}{\|g_{k-1}\|}g_{k-1}\right)}{\|g_{k-1}\|^2} \geq \frac{\|g_k\|^2 - \frac{\|g_k\|\|g_k\|}{\|g_{k-1}\|}\|g_{k-1}\|}{\|g_{k-1}\|^2} = 0.$$

The convergent results are established, and numerical experiments show that this algorithm is competitive with other similar algorithms. If we let $y_{k-1}^m = g_k - \frac{\|g_k\|}{\|g_{k-1}\|}g_{k-1}$ and replace y_{k-1} by y_{k-1}^m in the quasi-Newton update formula, it is not difficult to obtain

$$B_k y_{k-1}^m = s_{k-1}. \tag{6}$$

Then, we present the modified conjugacy condition as follows:

$$d_k^T y_{k-1}^m = 0. \tag{7}$$

By the secant condition of quasi-Newton algorithms and the search direction d_k, we have

$$H_k y_{k-1}^m = s_{k-1}, \ d_k = -H_k g_k. \tag{8}$$

By (8), we obtain that

$$d_k^T y_{k-1}^m = -(H_k g_k)^T y_{k-1}^m = -g_k^T (H_k y_{k-1}^m) = -g_k^T s_{k-1}. \tag{9}$$

Taking this relation, we replace the conjugacy condition by the following condition

$$d_k^T y_{k-1}^m = -t g_k^T s_{k-1}, \tag{10}$$

where $t > 0$ is also a scalar. If $t = 0$, (10) reduces to (7). However, if $t = 1$, (10) reduces to (9). To ensure that the search direction d_k satisfies this condition, by (3) and (10), we obtain

$$-g_k^T y_{k-1}^m + \beta_k d_{k-1}^T y_{k-1}^m = -t g_k^T s_{k-1}.$$

Then, we deduce that a new conjugate gradient formula is given as follows

$$\beta_k^{new1} = \frac{g_k^T (y_{k-1}^m - t s_{k-1})}{d_{k-1}^T y_{k-1}^m}. \tag{11}$$

Similarly, to obtain the global convergence for general functions, we propose another new formula defined by

$$\beta_k^{new2} = \max\{\frac{g_k^T y_{k-1}^m}{d_{k-1}^T y_{k-1}^m}, 0\} - t \frac{g_k^T s_{k-1}}{d_{k-1}^T y_{k-1}^m}. \tag{12}$$

Let $t = 1$ in (11); then,

$$\beta_k^{new1} = \frac{g_k^T y_{k-1}^m - g_k^T s_{k-1}}{d_{k-1}^T y_{k-1}^m}.$$

Here and in the following sections, we will concentrate on conjugate gradient algorithms with (11) and (12).

3   Global Convergence for General Functions

This section will present the global convergence of the algorithms (11) and (12). First, we prove the global convergence of the conjugate gradient algorithm with (11) for uniformly convex functions. Second, we show that the conjugate gradient algorithm with (12) is globally convergent for general functions. Now, we present our conjugate gradient algorithm as follows, and we call it Algorithm 1.

Algorithm 1 (New conjugate gradient algorithm).
Step 1: Choose an initial point $x_1 \in \Re^n$, $0 < \delta < \sigma < 1$, $\varepsilon \in (0,1)$. Set $d_1 = -g_1 = -\nabla f(x_1)$, $k := 1$.
Step 2: If $\|g_k\| \leq \varepsilon$, then stop; Otherwise, go to the next step.
Step 3: Compute the step size α_k by the following strong Wolfe line search: find α_k such that

$$f(x_k + \alpha_k d_k) - f_k \leq \delta \alpha_k g_k^T d_k \tag{13}$$

and

$$|g(x_k + \alpha_k d_k)^T d_k| \le -\sigma g_k^T d_k. \tag{14}$$

Step 4: Let $x_{k+1} = x_k + \alpha_k d_k$. If $\|g_{k+1}\| \le \varepsilon$, then stop.
Step 5: Calculate the search direction

$$d_{k+1} = -g_{k+1} + \beta_k d_k, \tag{15}$$

where β_k follows (11) or (12).
Step 6: Set $k := k + 1$, and go to Step 3.

The following two properties play important roles in our convergent analysis. We say that the descent condition holds if for each search direction d_k :

$$g_k^T d_k < 0, \ \forall k \ge 1, \tag{16}$$

and we say that the sufficient descent condition holds if there exists a constant $c > 0$ such that for each search direction d_k :

$$g_k^T d_k < -c\|g_k\|^2, \ \forall k \ge 1, \tag{17}$$

To obtain the global convergence of nonlinear conjugate gradient algorithms, basic assumptions on the objective function are needed.
Assumption A. The level set $\Omega = \{x \mid f(x) \le f(x_1)\}$ is bounded, namely, there exists a constant $b > 0$ satisfying

$$\|x\| \le b, \ \forall x \in \Omega. \tag{18}$$

Assumption B. In some neighborhood N of $\overline{co}\Omega$, f is continuously differentiable, and its gradient is globally Lipschitz continuous, namely, there exists a constant $L > 0$ such that

$$\|g(x) - g(y)\| \le L\|x - y\|, \ \forall x, y \in N, \tag{19}$$

where $\overline{co}\Omega$ is the closed convex hull of Ω.

It is well known that the convex closure of a bounded set in $\Re^n$ is still bounded. Then, this together with Assumption A implies that $\overline{co}\Omega$ is a bounded convex subset in $\Re^n$. Thus, Assumption B holds for any function f that satisfies Assumption A and has a locally Lipschitz gradient g. Moreover, by (18) and (19), we deduce that there exists a constant $\lambda > 0$ satisfying

$$\|g(x)\| \le \lambda, \forall x \in \Omega. \tag{20}$$

We state two lemmas that are very important for our convergent results as follows.

Lemma 1 *(Lemma 5.3 in [18]). Suppose that Assumptions A and B and the descent condition hold. Consider Algorithm 1; then, we have either*

$$\lim_{k \to \infty} \inf \|g_k\| = 0 \tag{21}$$

or

$$\sum_{k=1}^{\infty} \frac{\|g_k\|^4}{\|d_k\|^2} < \infty. \tag{22}$$

Lemma 2 *(Corollary 5.1 in [18]). Suppose that Assumptions A and B and the descent condition hold. Consider Algorithm 1; if*

$$\sum_{k \geq 1} \frac{1}{\|d_k\|^2} = \infty \tag{23}$$

then we obtain (21).

Similar to [18], it is easy to obtain the following lemma. For completeness, we provide the detailed proof here.

Lemma 3. *Consider Algorithm 1, where β_k is calculated by (12) in (15). Let Assumptions A and B and the sufficient descent condition (17) hold. Suppose that there exists a constant $\epsilon_0 > 0$ satisfying*

$$\|g_k\| \geq \epsilon_0, \ \forall k \geq 1. \tag{24}$$

Then, we have $d_k \neq 0$ and

$$\sum_{k \geq 2} \|u_k - u_{k-1}\|^2 < \infty,$$

where $u_k = \frac{d_k}{\|d_k\|}$.

Proof. Note that $d_k \neq 0$; otherwise, (17) is false. Then, u_k is well-defined. By (24) and Lemma 2, we have

$$\sum_{k \geq 1} \frac{1}{\|d_k\|^2} < \infty. \tag{25}$$

Let $\beta_k^{new2} = b_1 + b_2$, where $b_1 = \max\{\frac{g_k^T y_{k-1}^m}{d_{k-1}^T y_{k-1}^m}, 0\}$ and $b_2 = -\frac{t g_k^T s_{k-1}}{d_{k-1}^T y_{k-1}^m}$. Define

$$e_k = \frac{v_k}{\|d_k\|} \ \text{and} \ \delta_k = b_1 \frac{\|d_{k-1}\|}{\|d_k\|}, \tag{26}$$

where $v_k = -g_k + b_2 d_{k-1}$. By (15), for $k \geq 2$, we obtain

$$u_k = e_k + \delta_k u_{k-1}. \tag{27}$$

Considering $\|u_k\| = \|u_{k-1}\| = 1$ and (27), we know that

$$\|e_k\| = \|u_k - \delta_k u_{k-1}\| = \|\delta_k u_k - u_{k-1}\|. \tag{28}$$

Moreover, by $\delta_k \geq 0$, the triangle inequality and (28), we have

$$\|u_k - u_{k-1}\| \leq \|(1 + \delta_k)u_k - (1 + \delta_k)u_{k-1}\| \leq \|u_k - \delta_k u_{k-1}\| + \|\delta_k u_k - u_{k-1}\| = 2\|e_k\|.$$

By the definition of y_{k-1}^m and the strong Wolfe condition (14), we obtain

$$
\begin{aligned}
d_{k-1}^T y_{k-1}^m &= \frac{d_{k-1}^T g_k \|g_{k-1}\| - \|g_k\| d_{k-1}^T g_{k-1}}{\|g_{k-1}\|} \\
&= \frac{d_{k-1}^T g_k \|g_{k-1}\| - d_{k-1}^T g_{k-1}\|g_{k-1}\| + d_{k-1}^T g_{k-1}\|g_{k-1}\| - \|g_k\| d_{k-1}^T g_{k-1}}{\|g_{k-1}\|} \\
&= \frac{d_{k-1}^T (g_k - g_{k-1})\|g_{k-1}\| + d_{k-1}^T g_{k-1}(\|g_{k-1}\| - \|g_k\|)}{\|g_{k-1}\|} \\
&= d_{k-1}^T y_{k-1} + \frac{d_{k-1}^T g_{k-1}(\|g_{k-1}\| - \|g_k\|)}{\|g_{k-1}\|} \\
&= d_{k-1}^T y_{k-1} + + \frac{-d_{k-1}^T g_{k-1}(\|g_k - g_{k-}\|)}{\|g_{k-1}\|} \\
&\geq d_{k-1}^T y_{k-1} \geq -(1-\sigma)g_{k-1}^T d_{k-1}.
\end{aligned}
\tag{29}
$$

This relation (29) together with the sufficient descent condition indicate that

$$
\left| \frac{g_k^T d_{k-1}}{d_{k-1}^T y_{k-1}^m} \right| \leq \frac{\sigma}{1-\sigma}.
\tag{30}
$$

Therefore, by the definition of v_k, (30), (20) and (18), we have

$$
\|v_k\| \leq \|g_k\| + t\left| \frac{g_k^T s_{k-1}}{d_{k-1}^T y_{k-1}^m} \right| \|d_{k-1}\| = \|g_k\| + t\left| \frac{g_k^T d_{k-1}}{d_{k-1}^T y_{k-1}^m} \right| \|s_{k-1}\| \leq \lambda + \frac{t\sigma b}{1-\sigma}.
\tag{31}
$$

Let $C_0 = \lambda + \frac{t\sigma b}{1-\sigma}$; it follows from the definition of e_k and (25) that

$$
\sum_{k \geq 2} \|u_k - u_{k-1}\|^2 \leq 4\sum_{k \geq 2}\|e_k\|^2 = 4\sum_{k \geq 2}\frac{\|v_k\|^2}{\|d_k\|^2} \leq 4\sum_{k \geq 2}\frac{C_0^2}{\|d_k\|^2} < \infty.
$$

Thus, we conclude the result of this lemma. The proof is complete.

Recall the following property that was given by Dai and Liao [2].

Property (P). There exist constant $p > 1$ and $\xi > 0$ such that $|\beta_k| \leq p (\forall k \geq 1)$ and

$$
\|s_{k-1}\| \leq \xi \Rightarrow |\beta_k| \leq \frac{1}{p}, \forall k \geq 1.
$$

The following lemma shows that our formula (12) possesses this property.

Lemma 4. *Suppose that the conditions of Lemma 3 hold. Then, the formula β_k^{new2} satisfies property (P) for all $t \geq 0$.*

Proof. By (29), the sufficient condition (17) and (24), we have

$$
d_{k-1}^T y_{k-1}^m \geq -(1-\sigma)g_{k-1}^T d_{k-1} \geq c(1-\sigma)\|g_{k-1}\|^2 \geq c(1-\sigma)\epsilon_0.
\tag{32}
$$

By (18), (19) and (20), we obtain

$$
|g_k^T y_{k-1}^m| = |g_k^T (g_k^T - \frac{\|g_k\|}{\|g_{k-1}\|} g_{k-1})|
$$

$$
\le \|g_k\| \| \frac{g_k\|g_{k-1}\| - g_{k-1}\|g_{k-1}\| + g_{k-1}\|g_{k-1}\| - \|g_k\|g_{k-1}}{\|g_{k-1}\|} \|
$$

$$
\le \|g_k\| \frac{\|g_{k-1}\|\|g_k - g_{k-1}\| + \|g_{k-1}\|\|g_{k-1} - g_k\|}{\|g_{k-1}\|} \|
$$

$$
= 2\|g_k\|\|g_k - g_{k-1}\|
$$

$$
\le 2\lambda L \|s_{k-1}\|. \tag{33}
$$

The inequality (33) together with (12) and (32) indicate that for all $t \ge 0$

$$
|\beta_k^{new2}| \le |\frac{g_k^T y_{k-1}^m}{d_{k-1}^T y_{k-1}^m}| + t|\frac{g_k^T s_{k-1}}{d_{k-1}^T y_{k-1}^m}|
$$

$$
\le \frac{2L\lambda \|s_{k-1}\|}{c(1-\sigma)\epsilon_0^2} + t \frac{\lambda \|s_{k-1}\|}{c(1-\sigma)\epsilon_0^2}
$$

$$
= \frac{(2L+t)\lambda}{c(1-\sigma)\epsilon_0^2} \|s_{k-1}\|.
$$

Considering (18) and letting $p = \max\{2, \frac{(2L+t)b\lambda}{c(1-\sigma)\epsilon_0^2}\}$ and $\xi = \frac{c(1-\sigma)\epsilon_0^2}{p\lambda(2L+t)}$, it follows from (33) and the definitions of p and ξ that $p > 1$,

$$
|\beta_k^{new2}| \le b
$$

and

$$
|\beta_k^{new2}| \le \frac{(2L+t)\lambda}{c(1-\sigma)\epsilon_0^2} \|s_{k-1}\| \le \frac{(2L+t)\lambda}{c(1-\sigma)\epsilon_0^2} \xi = \frac{1}{b}.
$$

This completes the proof.

Making use of Lemma 4, we can prove the following lemma.

Lemma 5 *(Lemma 3.5 in [2]). Consider Algorithm 1, where β_k is calculated by (12) in (15). Let Assumptions A and B and the sufficient descent condition (17) hold. Then, if (24) holds, there exists $\xi > 0$ such that, for any $\Delta \in N^*$ and any index k_0, there is an index $k > k_0$ satisfying*

$$
|\kappa_{k,\Delta}^\xi| > \frac{\Delta}{2},
$$

where $|\kappa_{k,\Delta}^\xi|$ is the number of elements in $\kappa_{k,\Delta}^\xi = \{i \in N^* : k \le i \le k + \Delta + 1, \|s_{k-1}\| > \xi\}, N^*$ is the set of positive integers, and Δ is a positive integer.

Based on Lemmas 3 and 5, we establish the global convergence theorem of conjugate gradient algorithms with (12). Similar to Theorem 3.6 of [2], it is not difficult to obtain this result; hence, we state it as follows but omit the proof.

Theorem 1. *Consider Algorithm 1, where β_k is calculated by (12) in (15). Let Assumptions A and B and the sufficient descent condition (17) hold. Then, we have (21).*

4 Numerical Results

This section reports the results from some numerical experiments. We test Algorithm 1 with the strong Wolfe-Powell line search on these problems and compare its performance with the ones of the Dai-Liao [2] algorithm, the Li-Tang-Wei [18] algorithm, and the Yabe and Takano [27] algorithm. We will test the following Benchmark problems using these algorithms:

Table 1. Definition of the benchmark problems together with their features

Functions	Definition	Multimodal?	Separable?	Regular?
Sphere	$f_{Sph}(x) = \sum_{i=1}^{P} x_i^2$ $x_i \in [-5.12, 5.12]$, $x^* = (0, 0, \cdots, 0)$, $f_{Sph}(x^*) = 0$.	No	Yes	N/a
Schwefel's	$f_{SchDS}(x) = \sum_{i=1}^{P}(\sum_{j=1}^{i} x_j)^2$ $x_i \in [-65.536, 65.536]$, $x^* =$ $(0, 0, \cdots, 0)$, $f_{SchDS}(x^*) = 0$.	No	No	N/a
Rastrigin	$f_{Ras}(x) = 10p + \sum_{i=1}^{P}(x_i^2 - 10\cos(2\pi x_i))$ $x_i \in [-5.12, 5.12]$, $x^* = (0, 0, \cdots, 0)$, $f_{Ras}(x^*) = 0$.	Yes	Yes	N/a
Schwefel	$f_{Sch}(x) = 418.9829p + \sum_{i=1}^{P} x_i \sin\sqrt{|x_i|}$ $x_i \in [-512.03, 511.97]$, $x^* =$ $(-420.9678, -420.9678, \cdots, -420.9678)$, $f_{Sch}(x^*) =$ 0.	Yes	Yes	N/a
Griewank	$f_{Gri}(x) = 1 + \sum_{i=1}^{P}\frac{x_i^2}{4000} - \prod_{i=1}^{P}\cos\frac{x_i}{i}$ $x_i \in [-600, 600]$, $x^* = (0, 0, \cdots, 0)$, $f_{Gri}(x^*) = 0$.	Yes	No	Yes

The above Benchmark problems in Table 1 about the choice of tested problems for an algorithm can be found at: http://www.cs.cmu.edu/afs/cs/project/jair/pub/volume24/ortizboyer05a-html/node6.html.

In this paper, we will use these Benchmark problems to perform experiments using the algorithms. All codes were written in MATLAB 7.6.0 and run on a PC with a Core 2 Duo CPU, E7500 @2.93 GHz and 2.00 GB memory and Windows XP operating system. For the dimension, we do not fix it as $p == 30$, namely, it can be larger than 30, where the details regarding the dimensions can be found in Table 2. The following *Himmeblau* stop rule is used: If $|f(x_k)| > e_1$, let $stop1 = \frac{|f(x_k) - f(x_{k+1})|}{|f(x_k)|}$; Otherwise, let $stop1 = |f(x_k) - f(x_{k+1})|$. For each problem, if $\|g(x)\| < \varepsilon$ or $stop1 < e_2$ is satisfied, the program will be stopped, where $e_1 = e_2 = \epsilon = 10^{-4}$.

Because the line search cannot always ensure the descent condition $d_k^T g_k < 0$, an uphill search direction may occur in the numerical experiments. In this case, the line search rule may fail. To avoid this case, the stepsize α_k will be accepted if the search number is more than ten in the line search. We also stop the program if the iteration number is more than five thousand, and the corresponding algorithm is considered to be failed. The columns of Table 2 have the following meanings: NI: the total number of iterations for all the test problems with all the dimensions and all the initial point; NFG: the number of function and gradient evaluations for all the test problems with all the dimensions and all the initial point; x_0 : the initial point;

$x_{Sph10} = (-3, -3, \cdots, -3); \ x_{Sph20} = (3, 3, \cdots, 3); \ x_{Sph30} = (-3, 0, -3, 0, \cdots);$
$x_{Sph40} = (3, 0, 3, 0, \cdots); \ x_{SchDS10} = (-0.001, -0.001, \cdots, -0.001); \ x_{SchDS20} =$
$(0.0001, 0.0001, \cdots, 0.0001); \ x_{SchDS30} = (-0.001, 0, -0.001, 0, \cdots); \ x_{SchDS40} =$
$(0.0001, 0, 0.0001, 0, \cdots); \ x_{Ras10} = x_{Sch10} = (-0.01, -0.01, \cdots, -0.01);$
$x_{Ras20} = x_{Sch20} = (0.01, 0.01, \cdots, 0.01); \ x_{Ras30} = x_{Sch30} =$
$(-0.01, 0, -0.01, 0, \cdots); \ x_{Ras40} = x_{Sch40} = (0.01, 0, 0.01, 0, \cdots); \ x_{Gri10} =$
$(-20, -20, \cdots, -20); x_{Gri20} = (30, 30, \cdots, 30); \ x_{Gri30} = (-20, 0, -20, 0, \cdots);$
$x_{Gri40} = (30, 0, 30, 0, \cdots).$ For functions Schwefel and Griewank with all the
dimensions specified 30, 3000 and 10000; the dimensions of Sphere function were
30, 3000, 30000; the other two functions with all the dimensions specified 30, 50
and 100. In Table 2, the parameters are chosen as follows: **DL1:** Dai-Liao's [2]
formula 1 with strong Wolfe rule, where $\delta = 0.0001$, $\sigma = 0.1$. **DL2:** Dai-Liao's [2]
formula 2 with strong Wolfe rule, where $\delta = 0.0001$, $\sigma = 0.1$. **LTW1:** Li-Tang-
Wei's [18] formula 1 with strong Wolfe rule, where $\delta = 0.0001$, $\sigma = 0.1$. **LTW2:**
Li-Tang-Wei's [18] formula 2 with strong Wolfe rule, where $\delta = 0.0001$, $\sigma = 0.1$.
YT1: Yabe and Takano's [27] formula 1 with strong Wolfe rule, where $\delta =$
0.0001, $\sigma = 0.1$, $\rho = 5$, $u_{k-1} = (2, 2, \cdots, 2)$. **YT2:** Yabe and Takano's [27]
formula 2 with strong Wolfe rule, where $\delta = 0.0001$, $\sigma = 0.1$, $\rho = 5$, $u_{k-1} =$
$(2, 2, \cdots, 2)$. **NEW1:** the proposed formulas (11) with strong Wolfe rule, where
$\delta = 0.0001$, $\sigma = 0.1$. **NEW2:** the proposed formulas (12) with strong Wolfe rule,
where $\delta = 0.0001$, $\sigma = 0.1$.

Table 2. The line search is used by the strong Wolfe rule for different parameter t.

t	DL1	DL2	LTW1	LTW2	YT1	YT2	NEW1	NEW2
	NI/NFG	NI/NFG	NI/NFG	NI/NFG	NI/NFG	NI/NFG	NI/NFG	NI/NFG
0.5	176/480	176/480	192/513	178/500	173/475	137/489	178/446	185/440
1	181/500	178/509	183/508	180/506	177/496	174/514	227/816	186/432
5	182/529	182/529	183/533	183/535	182/541	181/526	182/570	185/550

For these Benchmark problems, it is not difficult to see that all four of these
algorithms are effective from the above three tables. Moreover, these numerical
results indicate that the parameter t does not obviously influence the results as
the dimension increases. Compared with the other three algorithms, the proposed algorithm is competitive. Overall, these four new conjugacy conditions
and related conjugate gradient algorithms are interesting for these test problems. Thus, we hope that these new conjugacy conditions be further considered.

Acknowledgments. This work is supported by China NSF (Grant No. 11261006
and 11161003), the Guangxi Science Fund for Distinguished Young Scholars (No.
2015GXNSFGA139001), Guangxi Higher Education Institutions (No. YB2014389),
NSFC No. 61232016, NSFC No. U1405254, and PAPD issue of Jangsu advantages
discipline.

References

1. Dai, Y.: A nonmonotone conjugate gradient algorithm for unconstrained optimization. J. Syst. Sci. Complex. **15**, 139–145 (2002)
2. Dai, Y., Liao, L.: New conjugacy conditions and related nonlinear conjugate methods. Appl. Math. Optim. **43**, 87–101 (2001)
3. Dai, Z.F., Tian, B.S.: Global convergence of some modified PRP nonlinear conjugate gradient methods. Optim. Let. **5**, 1–16 (2010)
4. Dai, Y., Yuan, Y.: A nonlinear conjugate gradient with a strong global convergence properties. SIAM J. Optim. **10**, 177–182 (2000)
5. Dai, Y., Yuan, Y.: Nonlinear Conjugate Gradient Methods. Shanghai Scientific and Technical Publishers, Shanghai (1998)
6. Fletcher, R.: Practical Method of Optimization: Unconstrained Optimization, vol. 1, 2nd edn. Wiley, New York (1997)
7. Fletcher, R., Reeves, C.: Function minimization by conjugate gradients. Comput. J. **7**, 149–154 (1964)
8. Grippo, L., Luidi, S.: A globally convergent version of the Polak-Ribière gradient method. Math. Program. **78**, 375–391 (1997)
9. Gibert, J.C., Nocedal, J.: Global convergence properties of conugate gradient methods for optimization. SIAM J. Optim. **2**, 21–42 (1992)
10. Hager, W.W., Zhang, H.: A new conjugate gradient method with guaranteed descent and an efficient line search. SIAM J. Optim. **16**, 170–192 (2005)
11. Hager, W.W., Zhang, H.: Algorithm 851: $CG_D ESCENT$, a conjugate gradient method with guaranteed descent. ACM Trans. Math. Softw. **32**, 113–137 (2006)
12. Hager, W.W., Zhang, H.: A survey of nonlinear conjugate gradient methods. Pacif. J. Optim. **2**, 35–58 (2006)
13. Li, J., Li, X., Yang, B., Sun, X.: Segmentation-based image copy-move forgery detection scheme. IEEE Trans. Inf. Forensics Secur. **10**, 507–518 (2015)
14. Gu, B., Sheng, V.S., Tay, K.Y., Romano, W., Li, S.: Incremental support vector learning for ordinal regression. IEEE Trans. Neural Netw. Learning Syst. **26**, 1403–1416 (2015). doi:10.1109/TNNLS.2014.2342533
15. Xia, Z., Wang, X., Sun, X., Wang, Q.: A secure and dynamic multi-keyword ranked search scheme over encrypted cloud data. IEEE Trans. Parallel Distrib. Syst. **27**, 340–352 (2015). doi:10.1109/TPDS.2015.2401003
16. Pan, Z., Zhang, Y., Kwong, S.: Efficient motion and disparity estimation optimization for low complexity multiview video coding. IEEE Trans. Broadcast. (2015). doi:10.1109/TBC.2015.2419824
17. Hestenes, M.R., Stiefel, E.: Method of conjugate gradient for solving linear equations. J. Res. Nat. Bur. Stand. **49**, 409–436 (1952)
18. Li, G., Tang, C., Wei, Z.: New conjugacy condition and related new conjugate gradient methods for unconstrained optimization problems. J. Comput. Appl. Math. **202**, 532–539 (2007)
19. Liu, Y., Storey, C.: Effcient generalized conjugate gradient algorithms, Part 1: theory. J. Optim. Theor. Appl. **69**, 17–41 (1992)
20. Polak, E., Ribiere, G.: Note sur la xonvergence de directions conjugees Rev. Francaise informat Recherche Operatinelle, 3e Annee, vol. 16, pp. 35–43 (1969)
21. Polyak, B.T.: The conjugate gradient method in extreme problems. USSR Comput. Math. Math. Phys. **9**, 94–112 (1969)
22. Powell, M.J.D.: Nonconvex minimization calculations and the conjugate gradient method. In: Griffiths, D.F. (ed.) Numerical Analysis. Lecture Notes in Mathematics, vol. 1066, pp. 122–141. Spinger, Heidelberg (1984)

23. Powell, M.J.D.: Convergence properties of algorithm for nonlinearoptimization. SIAM Rev. **28**, 487–500 (1986)
24. Siva Sathya, S., Radhika, M.V.: Convergence of nomadic genetic algorithm on benchmark mathematical functions. Appl. Soft Comput. **13**, 2759–2766 (2013)
25. Wei, Z., Li, G., Qi, L.: New nonlinear conjugate gradient formulas for large-scale unconstrained optimization problems. Appl. Math. Comput. **179**, 407–430 (2006)
26. Wei, Z., Yao, S., Liu, L.: The convergence properties of some new conjugate gradient methods. Appl. Math. Comput. **183**, 1341–1350 (2006)
27. Yabe, H., Takano, M.: Global convergence properties of nonlinear conjugate gradient methods with modified secant condition. Comput. Optim. Appl. **28**, 203–225 (2004)
28. Yu, G.H.: Nonlinear self-scaling conjugate gradient methods for large-scale optimization problems. Doctor's Degree thesis, Sun Yat-Sen University (2007)
29. Yuan, G.L.: Modified nonlinear conjugate gradient methods with sufficient descent property for large-scale optimization problems. Optim. Lett. **3**, 11–21 (2009)
30. Yuan, Y.X.: Analysis on the conjugate gradient method. Optim. Methods Softw. **2**, 19–29 (1993)
31. Yuan, G.L., Lu, X.W.: A modified PRP conjugate gradient method. Ann. Oper. Res. **166**, 73–90 (2009)
32. Yuan, G.L., Lu, X.W., Wei, Z.X.: A conjugate gradient method with descent direction for unconstrained optimization. J. Comput. Appl. Math. **233**, 519–530 (2009)
33. Yuan, Y.X., Sun, W.Y.: Theory and Methods of Optimization. Science Press of China, Beijing (1999)
34. Yuan, G.L., Wei, Z.X., Zhao, Q.M.: A modified Polak-Ribière-Polyak conjugate gradient algorithm for large-scale optimization problems. IIE Trans. **46**, 397–413 (2014)
35. Zhang, J.Z., Deng, N.Y., Chen, L.H.: New quasi-Newton equation and related methods for unconstrained optimization. J. Optim. Theory Appl. **102**, 147–167 (1999)
36. Zhang, L., Zhou, W., Li, D.: A descent modified Polak-Ribière-Polyak conjugate method and its global convergence. IMA J. Num. Anal. **26**, 629–649 (2006)
37. Zoutendijk, G.: Nonlinear programming computational methods. In: Abadie, J. (ed.) Integer and Nonlinear Programming, pp. 37–86. North Holland, Amsterdam (1970)

LS-SVM-Based Prediction Model of Tread Wear Optimized by PSO-GA-LM

Sha Hua[✉], Jiabin Yuan, and Weijie Ding

College of Computer Science and Technology,
Nanjing University of Aeronautics and Astronautics, Nanjing, China
{huasha,jbyuan,dingweijie}@nuaa.edu.cn

Abstract. The wheel wear is a dynamic phenomenon that varies with many mechanical and geometrical factors. Accurately estimating wheel wear is a vital issue in wheel maintance. This paper presents a nature-inspired metaheuristic regression method for precisely predicting wheel status that combines least squares support vector machine (LS-SVM) with a novel PSO-GA-LM algorithm. The PSO-GA-LM algorithm integrates Particle Swarm Optimization (PSO), Genetic Algorithm (GA) and Logistic Map (LM). The method is used to optimize the hyper-parameters of the LS-SVM model. The proposed model was constructed with datasets of the tread wear derived from Taiyuan North Locomotive Depot. Analytical results show that the novel optimized prediction model is superior to others in predicting tread wear with lower RMSE (0.037MPa), MAE (0.027MPa) and MAPE (0.0008 %).

Keywords: LS-SVM · Hyper-parameters optimization · PSO-GA-LM algorithm · Tread wear

1 Introduction

Higher safety requirements have been put forward for the rapid development of rail transport in China. As the mainly key and worn components of the train, the wheels closely contact to the security of train running. The locomotive's development towards high-speed and overloading will accelerate the abrasion of the wheels, and the repair costs will increase greatly as well. Therefore, the prediction of the wheel wear will help take precautions against risks in advance, ensure the operating safety and serve to maintenance advice. Furthermore, the prediction will accelerate the repair of locomotive from time/running kilometers based to condition based.

A number of domestic and foreign scholars devoted themselves to wheel wear prediction. Fires etc. built a prediction model based on the Multi Body Dynamics, and concluded that the wheel wear model in direct proportion to the law force is the best [1]. Dirks etc. described the differences between Wear and Relative centrifugal force (RCF) prediction models. They found that the adjustments of the models have a significant influence on RCF prediction [2]. Based on FAST-SIM algorithm and Zobory tread wear model, DING etc. simulated the wheel

© Springer International Publishing AG 2016
X. Sun et al. (Eds.): ICCCS 2016, Part II, LNCS 10040, pp. 510–521, 2016.
DOI: 10.1007/978-3-319-48674-1_45

wear of heavy haul freight car [3]. To conclude, most of the wheel wear prediction models are based on Multi Body Dynamics, Vehicle Track coupling Dynamics and dynamics simulation, but few data mining methods have been applied to this field.

There are several types of SVM: v-SVM [4–6], LS-SVM and so on. The least squares support vector machine (LS-SVM) proposed by Suykens in 1999 based on SVM [7] simplified the training process by replacing the inequality constraints with equality ones. The Finite Element Method (FEM) uses the LS-SVM to establish a map between the units, with which the risk of experience will be reduced [8]. Also, it has been widely applied to biological, medical science, architecture and so on [9–12]. However, the performance of LS-SVM is affected by the selection of hyper-parameters, which directly impact the fitting and generalization performance. There are two kinds of approaches to determine the hyper-parameters, one is based on the empirical value, and the other depends on modern heuristic algorithms. Guo etc. combined practicle swarm optimization (PSO) with LS-SVM and applied it to binary classifications [13]. Pai etc. optimized the hyper-parameters with Simulated Annealing (SA) algorithm to predict electrical load [14]. Ma etc. established incident degradation model with LS-SVM and accurately forecast development tendency [15]. Zhong etc. proposed Coupled Simulated Annealing (CSA) algorithm to predict wheel tread wear [16]. With Bayesian inference to select hyper-parameters, the nonlinear prediction model of the engine service life was set up [17].

In this study, PSO-GA-LM algorithm is proposed to optimize hyper-parameters of LS-SVM prediction model. The datasets of tread wear is used to evaluate the performance of proposed model. To demonstrate its efficacy, the model is compared with LS-SVM based on other approaches. Prediction performance is evaluated in terms of Root-mean-square error (RMSE), Mean-absolute error (MAE) and Mean-absolute-percentage error (MAPE).

The rest of this paper is organized as follows: the LS-SVM principles is introduced in Sect. 2, then a novel hyper-parameters selection method is proposed, and experiments are presented in the fourth part. Finally, the conclusion is presented in Sect. 5.

2   LS-SVM Principles

LS-SVM intelligent approach [7] considers the problem which approximates a given dataset $(x_1, y_1), (x_2, y_2), \cdots, (x_N, y_N)$ with the following function:

$$y = f(x) = \langle w, \varphi(x) \rangle + b \tag{1}$$

where $\langle \bullet, \bullet \rangle$ is dot product, and $\varphi(x)$ is a nonlinear function, the weight vector w and bias term b are unknown parameters.

Based on the statistical learning theory, Eq. (1) transforms into follows:

$$min \quad J(w, e) = \frac{1}{2} \|w\|^2 + \frac{1}{2} \gamma \sum_{k=1}^{N} e_k^2 \tag{2}$$

$$s.t \quad y_k = \langle w, \varphi(x_k) \rangle + b + e_k, k = 1, 2, .., N$$

where $\|w\|$ is used to control the complexity of the model, γ is regularization parameter (also called penalty parameter, $\gamma \geq 0$), and e_k is the regression error for N training objects.

The Lagrange function Eq. (3) is used to simplify the calculation of Eq. (2)

$$L(w, b, e, \alpha) = J(w, e) - \sum_{k=1}^{N} \alpha_k \{\langle w, \varphi(x) \rangle + b + e_k - y_k\} \tag{3}$$

where α_k is the Lagrange multiplier. The solution of Eq. (3) is determined by partial derivation of w, b, e_k, α_k:

$$\begin{cases} \frac{\partial L}{\partial w} = 0 \\ \frac{\partial L}{\partial b} = 0 \\ \frac{\partial L}{\partial e_k} = 0 \\ \frac{\partial L}{\partial \alpha_k} = 0 \end{cases} \rightarrow \begin{cases} w = \sum_{k=1}^{N} \alpha_k \varphi_k(x_k) \\ \sum_{k=1}^{N} \alpha_k = 0 \\ \alpha_k = \gamma e_k, \quad k = 1, 2, .., N \\ \langle w, \varphi(x) \rangle + b + e_k - y_k = 0, \quad k = 1, 2, .., N \end{cases} \tag{4}$$

By defining $\mathbf{1}_N = [1; 1; \ldots; 1]$, $Y = [y_1; y_2; \ldots; y_N]$, $\alpha = [\alpha_1; \alpha_2; \ldots; \alpha_N]$, and eliminating w and e, the following linear equation can be obtained:

$$\begin{bmatrix} 0 & \mathbf{1}_N^T \\ \mathbf{1}_N & \Omega + \gamma^{-1} I_N \end{bmatrix} \begin{bmatrix} b \\ \alpha \end{bmatrix} = \begin{bmatrix} 0 \\ Y \end{bmatrix} \tag{5}$$

where I_N is $N \times N$ identity matrix, and Ω is $N \times N$ symmetric matrix which is also called Kernel matrix. The regularization parameter γ is related to the fitting precision and generalization ability. Each element of the Kernel matrix is called Kernel function which follows the Mercer condition, and is defined as

$$\Omega_{i,j} = K(x_i, x_j) = \varphi(x_i)^T \times \varphi(x_j), \ i, j = 1, 2, .., N \tag{6}$$

By Eq. (5), the parameters b and α can be got to help establish the prediction function of unmodeled input sample x

$$y = \sum_{k=1}^{N} \alpha_k \times K(x, x_k) + b \tag{7}$$

In Eq. (7), the Kernel function $K(x, x_k)$ is related to the new input sample x and the modeled sample x_k.

There are several kernel functions, such as linear, polynomial, spline, and radial basis function (RBF), among which the RBF is the most widely used one for its wonderful regression ability. The RBF is formulated as:

$$K(x, x_k) = exp(-\|x - x_k\|^2 / 2\delta^2) \tag{8}$$

where σ denotes the width of the RBF.

3   Hyper-parameters Optimized Algorithm

3.1   The PSO Algorithm

Particle Swarm Optimization (PSO) firstly introduced by Kennedy and Eberhart is an evolutionary optimization algorithm based on group theory, and is widely applied to function optimization, neural network training, pattern classification, fuzzy control system and other engineering fields.

In the standard PSO model, there are N particles in a D-dimensional space, each particle is denoted as $X_i = (x_{i1}, x_{i2}, ..., x_{iD}), i = 1, 2, ..., N$. The velocity of every particle in each dimension is denoted as $v_i = (v_{i1}, v_{i2}, ..., v_{iD})$. PSO initialize a group of random particles, and then find the optimal solution through iterations.

The velocity and position of particle i in dimension d at $(t + 1)$ iteration are updated by the following equations:

$$v_{id}^{t+1} = wv_{id}^{t} + c_1r_1\left(pBest_{id}^{t} - x_{id}^{t}\right) + c_2r_2\left(gBest_{id}^{t} - x_{id}^{t}\right) \tag{9}$$

$$x_{id}^{t+1} = x_{id}^{t} + v_{id}^{t} \tag{10}$$

where r_1, r_2 are random numbers distributed uniformly in the interval $[0, 1]$ and c_1, c_2 are acceleration constants which belong to $[0, 4]$. The previous step velocity term, v_{di}^{t}, is affected by the constant inertia weight w.

3.2   PSO-GA-LM Algorithm

There are two key factors to determine the optimized hyper-parameters using PSO: one is how to update the particles' velocity, and the other is the method to renewal the particles' position.

The first key factor is solved by bringing in compressibility factor k. In KPSO proposed by CLERC MIN [18], Eq. (11) is imported to update the velocity. The compressibility factor k can assure the convergence of the PSO.

$$v_{id}^{t+1} = k[wv_{id}^{t} + c_1r_1\left(pBest_{id}^{t} - x_{id}^{k}\right) + c_2r_2\left(gBest_{id}^{t} - x_{id}^{t}\right)] \tag{11}$$

where $k = \dfrac{2}{\left|2-\varphi-\sqrt{\varphi^2-4\varphi}\right|}$, $\varphi = c_1 + c_2$. The compressibility factor k can assure the convergence of the PSO.

Genetic Algorithm (GA) and the Logistic Map (LM) are introduced to work out the second factor. Genetic algorithm (GA) is a search heuristic that mimics the process of natural selection. GA may have a tendency to converge towards the local optimum or even a arbitrary point rather than the global optimum of the problem. Nonetheless, the best qualities will be propagated to the next generation. Logistic Map (LM), a polynomial map of degree 2, is one of the Chaos Map. The relative simplicity of the logistic map makes it a widely used point of entry into the consideration of the concept of chaos. The map is complex and similar to random, but it has a delicate internal regularity.

To overcome the drawbacks of local convergence in PSO and GA, N_{local} are introduced here to measure the particle's situation. N_{local} represents the local optimum status. Simultaneously, a new variable T is used to record the frequency of the occurrence of the continuous same fitness value. With the effect of N_{local} and T, there will be two circumstances as follows:

- When $T \leq N_{local}$, GA will be applied. The particles will be sorted according to the fitness value first, and then the top ten particles will be chosen to mutate. And the bottom ten particles will be replaced by the new ones, generated by the mutations of top ten particles.
- When $T > N_{local}$, we assume the process has been trapped into the local optimum. In this situation, LM is used to regenerate the particles so that the process can escape the local optimum in a certain probability.

With the position update method, the pseudocode of the proposed algorithm is shown in Algorithm 1.

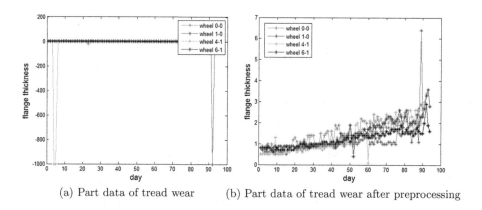

(a) Part data of tread wear   (b) Part data of tread wear after preprocessing

Fig. 1. Dataset of tread wear

4   Numerical Experiments

4.1   Experimental Datasets

The data of the wheel profile used in this paper are collected from train of SS4-0997 type in Taiyuan North Locomotive Depot. Figure 1(a) shows the part original data of tread wear while (b) is the data with outlier removing.

4.2   Phase Space Reconstruction

As the wheel is tested every 3 days, the data in this paper can be considered as a set of one-dimensional time series. C-C method proposed by Kim in 1999

Algorithm 1. PSO-GA-LM
___
Initialization:
for all $particl_i \in particles$ **do**
   $initialize\ velocity\ v_i\ and\ position\ x_i$
   $evaluate\ particle_i\ and\ set\ pBest \leftarrow fit(x_i)$
end for
$exetime \leftarrow 1, gBest_{exetime} \leftarrow min\{pBest_i\}, flag \leftarrow 0$
Iteration:
for all $exetime \in [2, M]$ **do**
  for all $particl_i \in particles$ **do**
    $update\ the\ velocity\ and\ position\ with\ Eq.(11)$
    $evaluate\ particl_i$
    if $fit(X_i) \leq fit(pBest_i)$ **then**
      $pBest_i \leftarrow fit(x_i)$
    end if
  end for
  $gBest_{exetime} \leftarrow min(pBest)$
  if $flag == 1$ **then**
    $break$
  end if
  if $gBest_{exetime} == gBest_{exetime-1}$ **then**
    $T \leftarrow T + 1$
  end if
  if $T \leq N_{local}$ **then**
    $choose\ top10\ and\ bottom10\ particles$
    $cross\ mutation\ with\ GA$
  else
    if $T > N_{local}$ **then**
      $regenerate\ the\ initial\ population\ with\ Logistic\ Map$
      $T \leftarrow 0$
    else
      $flag \leftarrow 1$
    end if
  end if
end for
___

[18] is used to reconstruct the phase space. It firstly defines correlation integral, then constructs a statistical variable $S_1(m, N, r, t)$, where m, N, r are determined by the conclusion of the BDS (Brock-Dechert-Scheinkman) statistics. Statistical conclusion $S_2(m, N, r, t) \sim t$ is used to estimate the optimal time delay (τ_d) and embedding window length (τ_w) in the end.

Figure 2 shows the results of C-C method applying on the data of tread wear. The first subplot shows the mean of $S_2(m, N, r, t)$ (marked as $\overline{S_2}$). The mean of ΔS_2 ($\Delta S_2 = max\{S_2(m, N, r_j, t)\} - min\{S_2(m, N, r_j, t)\}$) is presented in the second subplot. The first minimal value of $\overline{\Delta S_2(t)}$ is the first local maximum of time series, which is also called the optimal time delay (τ_d). The third subplot displays $S_{2cor}(S_{2corr} = \overline{\Delta S_2} + |\overline{S_2}|)$. The global minimum of S_{2cor} is the time window length of the time series (τ_w). The relationship between τ_d and τ_w is $\tau_w = (m-1) \times \tau_d$, where m is the embedding dimension.

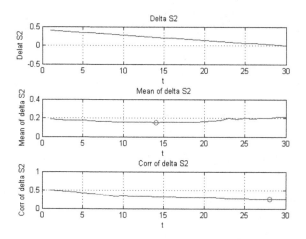

Fig. 2. Results of phase reconstruct

As shown in Fig. 2, the time delay (τ_d) of the tread wear in is 14, and the embedding window length (τ_w) is 28, so the embedding dimension (m) is 3. The data is reconstructed as:

$$\left\{ \left(X_1, \mathrm{x}\left(t_{2+(m-1)\tau}\right)\right), \left(X_2, \mathrm{x}\left(t_{3+(m-1)\tau}\right)\right), \ldots, \left(X_{m-1}, \mathrm{x}\left(t_n\right)\right) \right\}$$

where $X_i = \left(x\left(t_i\right), x\left(t_{i+\tau}\right), \ldots, x\left(t_{i+(m-1)\tau}\right)\right)$ is the input data and $x(t_{i+1+(m-1)\tau})$ is the output. The number of the datasets after reconstruction is 286, and the dimension of the input data is 3.

According to the phase space reconstruction theory, we obtain

$$x\left(t_{i+1+(m-1)\tau}\right) = f\left(X_i\right) \tag{12}$$

where the model $f(.)$ is built by LS-SVM theory.

4.3   The Prediction Model of Tread Wear

Accurate solutions for predicting the train situation with the reconstructed data require the optimization of regularization parameter γ and kernel bandwidth σ. We propose the PSO-GA-LM algorithm integrating PSO, GA and LM to optimize the LS-SVM parameters and minimize the prediction error.

Figure 3, a flowchart of model building and evaluation, shows that the proposed PSO-GA-LM algorithm can be used as a subroutine to optimize the structure parameters. The steps to build the prediction model is as follows:

Step 1 Data collection. The datasets of tread wear are collected from Nanjing Tych.co. Detail information can be got from Sect. 4.1.

Step 2 Phase space reconstruction. C-C method is used to calculate embedding dimension and delay time. Section 4.2 has shown that the time delay (τ_d) is 14, and the embedding dimension (m) is 3. Then the datasets are divided into two groups, one of which is used to train the prediction model, and the rest is used to test it.

Step 3 Set up prediction model. Because of the choice of Gaussian radial basis function, regularization parameter γ and kernel bandwidth σ must be determined to build the LS-SVM prediction model. The proposed PSO-GA-LM algorithm is used in this step to confirm the hyper-parameters, and Eq. (13) describes the fitness function of the prediction model. More details of the proposed algorithm are shown in the Sect. 3.2.

$$ fitness = RMSE = \sqrt{\frac{1}{n}\sum_{i=1}^{n}\left(y_{prediction} - y_{actual}\right)^2} \qquad (13) $$

Step 4 With the LS-SVM prediction model, the tread wear can be predicted.

4.4   Results and Comparison

The performance of the proposed optimized prediction model is validated in terms of Root-mean-square error (RMSE), Mean-absolute error (MAE), and Mean-absolute-percentage error (MAPE). And the mathematical calculations are as Eqs. (14)–(16):

$$ \text{RMSE} = \sqrt{\frac{1}{n}\sum_{i=1}^{n}(y - y')^2} \qquad (14) $$

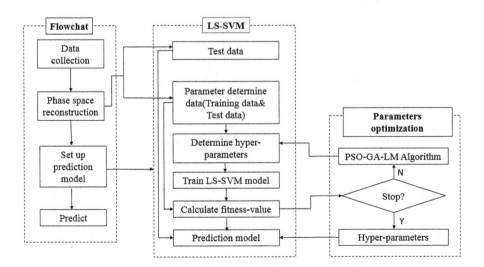

Fig. 3. Flowchart of the prediction model

$$\mathrm{MAE} = \frac{1}{n} \sum_{i=1}^{n} |y - y'| \tag{15}$$

$$\mathrm{MAPE} = \frac{1}{n} \sum_{i=1}^{n} \left| \frac{y - y'}{y} \right| \tag{16}$$

where y' represents the predicted value, y represents the actual value, and n is the number of data samples.

RMSE is computed to find the square root of the prediction values compared to actual values and work out the square root of the summation value. MAE measures the average error between the forecasts and the actual values. MAPE is a statistical measure used to evaluate the performance of prediction model, which is effective for identifying the relative differences.

The experiments were implemented with MATLAB (R2014a, the Math-Works Inc., USA) and a LS-SVM toolbox for MATLAB (LS-SVM v1.7, Suykens,Leuven, Belgium) under Windows 7.

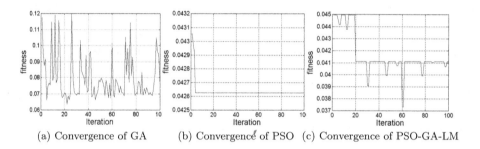

(a) Convergence of GA   (b) Convergence of PSO   (c) Convergence of PSO-GA-LM

Fig. 4. Convergence of different optimized methods

Figure 4 shows the convergence curves of different models, where xlabel represents the fitness value while ylabel is the iteration times. The convergence curve of GA optimized model shown in Fig. 4(a) is disorderly and unsystematic while the curve of PSO optimized model in Fig. 4(b) has been trapped into local optimum (0.043) prematurely. The convergence curve of our proposed model is shown in Fig. 4(c). While the iteration process has been trapped in a local optimum, the PSO-GA-LM method prevents it from stopping further search for the optimal solution.

The predicted data of different models are shown in Fig. 5(a) and apparently the curve in blue which represents the proposed model fits the actual data (curve in red) well. Table 1 shows detailed information of the actual and predictive data with different optimized models.

PSO, GA, PSO-GA-LM are used to confirm the applicability and efficiency of the proposed model in predicting tread wear. The iteration is 100 in all methods. Table 2 shows performance of the prediction model optimized by different methods. Obviously, the proposed model has a MAE lower than 0.027 MPa and a

Table 1. Results of the prediction model with different optimized methods.

Actual data	PSO+GA+LM	GA	PSO	Actual data	PSO+GA+LM	GA	PSO
1.78	1.77	1.79	1.70	2.15	2.12	2.18	2.12
1.88	1.79	1.80	1.72	2.13	2.14	2.21	2.14
1.91	1.86	1.88	1.80	2.13	2.11	2.16	2.10
1.91	1.88	1.91	1.83	2.13	2.12	2.18	2.12
1.91	1.88	1.91	1.83	2.16	2.13	2.19	2.13
1.95	1.94	1.92	1.84	2.14	2.15	2.21	2.15
1.94	1.93	1.96	1.87	2.14	2.15	2.20	2.15
1.96	1.92	1.96	1.88	2.16	2.15	2.20	2.15
1.95	1.93	1.97	1.89	2.16	2.16	2.21	2.17
1.98	1.96	1.97	1.89	2.18	2.17	2.22	2.18
1.96	1.96	2.00	1.92	2.17	2.19	2.24	2.20
1.94	1.95	1.99	1.91	2.19	2.18	2.22	2.18
1.95	1.94	1.98	1.90	2.10	2.19	2.23	2.20
1.95	1.95	2.00	1.92	2.14	2.12	2.16	2.12
1.96	1.96	2.01	1.93	2.17	2.17	2.22	2.18
1.98	1.97	2.02	1.94	2.18	2.21	2.25	2.22
1.98	2.00	2.06	1.98	2.20	2.20	2.25	2.21

Table 2. Performance of the prediction model optimized by different methods.

Performance index	Training set (POS)	Training set (GA)	Training set (PSO+GA+LM)	Testing set (POS)	Testing set (GA)	Testing set (PSO+GA+LM)
RMSE (MPa)	0.308	0.293	0.288	0.043	0.063	0.037
MAE (MPa)	0.099	0.084	0.082	0.043	0.054	0.027
MAPE (%)	0.0070	0.0055	0.0055	0.0140	0.0504	0.0008

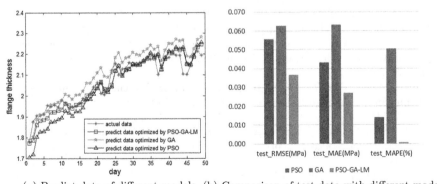

(a) Predict data of different models (b) Comparison of test data with different models

Fig. 5. Results of different optimized methods (Color figure online)

lower RMSE (0.037 MPa) compared to GA (0.063 MPa) and PSO (0.043 MPa). In the term of MAPE, the proposed model obtains 0.008 %, which is the lowest in the models we compared. To conclude, the proposed model outperforms all other models (GA, PSO) in terms of RMSE, MAE and MAPE. Figure 5(b) is a comprehensive comparison of performance measures for the proposed model and other approaches.

5   Conclusion and Future Work

A novel PSO-GA-LM hyper-parameters selection algorithm for LS-SVM prediction model is proposed to escape the local optimum by introducing a new variable T. Analysis of the results of the reconstructed data applied to the prediction model was given in the end. The results show that the proposed algorithm has a good performance in the prediction of tread wear. In addition, the model can help the train shooter foresee the status of the train, and help determine whether it is necessary to repair in this period.

However, the proposed algorithm still has one or two units time delay and a little pat of the data has slight errors. So in the future we will extend the present study and take more newly published prediction models into consideration to improve the accuracy of predict data.

Acknowledgments. This work was supported by Funding of National Natural Science Foundation of China (Grant No. 61571226), Jiangsu Program for the transformation of scientific and technological achievements (BA2015051).

References

1. Fries, R.H., Dvila, C.G.: Analytical methods for wheel and rail wear prediction. Veh. Syst. Dyn. **15**(15), 112–125 (1986)
2. Enblom, R., Dirks, B.: Prediction model for wheel profile wear and rolling contact fatigue. Wear **271**(1), 210–217 (2011)
3. Ding, J.J., Sun, S.L., Fu, L.I., Huang, Y.H.: Simulation of wheelwear for heavy haul freight car. J. Traffic Transp. Eng. **11**(4), 56–60 (2011)
4. Gu, B., Sheng, V.S.: A robust regularization path algorithm for -support vector classification. In: IEEE Transactions on Neural Networks and Learning Systems, pp. 1–8 (2016)
5. Gu, B., Sheng, V.S., Tay, K.Y., Romano, W., Li, S.: Incremental support vector learning for ordinal regression. IEEE Trans. Neural Netw. Learn. Syst. **26**(7), 1403–1416 (2014)
6. Gu, B., Sun, X., Sheng, V.S.: Structural minimax probability machine. In: IEEE Transactions on Neural Networks and Learning Systems, pp. 1–11 (2016)
7. Suykens, J.A.K., Vandewalle, J.: Least squares support vector machine classifiers. Neural Process. Lett. **9**(3), 293–300 (1999)
8. Chun, Y.: LSSVM based constitutive model of geomaterial used in element analysis. J. Hebei Univ. Eng. (Natural Science Edition) **30**(3), 26–29 (2013)

9. Chou, J.S., Ngo, N.T., Pham, A.D., Ngo, N.T.: Shear strength prediction in reinforced concrete deep beams using nature-inspired metaheuristic support vector regression. J. Comput. Civil Eng. **39**(8), 945–949 (2015)

10. Czarnecki, W.M., Podlewska, S., Bojarski, A.J.: Robust optimization of SVM hyperparameters in the classification of bioactive compounds. J. Cheminformatics **7**(1), 1–15 (2015)

11. Lou, I., Xie, Z., Ung, W.K., Kai, M.M.: Integrating support vector regression with particle swarm optimization for numerical modeling for algal blooms of freshwater. Appl. Math. Model. **39**(19), 5907–5916 (2015)

12. Geng, L.Y., Zhang, T.W., Zhao, P.: Forecast of railway freight volumes based on LS-SVM with grey correlation analysis. J. China Railway Soc. **34**(3), 1–6 (2012)

13. Guo, X.C., Yang, J.H., Wu, C.G., Wang, C.Y., Liang, Y.C.: A novel LS-SVMS hyper-parameter selection based on particle swarm optimization. Neurocomputing **71**(16–18), 3211–3215 (2008)

14. Gupta, A.R., Ingle, V.R., Gaikwad, M.A.: LS-SVM parameter optimization using genetic algorithm to improve fault classification of power transformer. Int. J. Eng. Res. Appl. **2**(4), 1806–1809 (2012)

15. Ma, X.J., Ren, S.H., Zuo, H.F., Wen, Z.H.: Prediction method of aero-enginelife on wing based on LS-SVM algorithm and performance reliability. J. Traffic Transp. Eng. **15**(3), 92–100 (2015)

16. Zhong, L., Cheng, L., Gong, J.: Prediction of wheel tread wear volume based on least squares support vector machine optimized by coupled simulated annealing. Appl. Res. Comput. **32**(2), 397–402 (2015)

17. Wang, Y., Zuo, H., Cai, J., Rong, X.: Forecasting model of engine life on wing based on LS-SVM and Bayesian inference. J. Nanjing Univ. Sci. Technol. **37**(6), 955–960 (2013)

18. Clerc, M.: The swarm and the queen: towards a deterministic and adaptive particle swarm optimization. In: Proceedings of the 1999 Congress on Evolutionary Computation, CEC 1999 (1999)

A Hybrid Firefly Algorithm for Continuous Optimization Problems

Wenjun Wang[1], Hui Wang[2,3(✉)], Hui Sun[2,3], Xiang Yu[2,3],
Jia Zhao[2,3], Yun Wang[2,3], Yunhui Zhang[2], Jinyong Zheng[2],
Yueping Lu[2], Qianya Chen[2], Chuanbo Han[2], and Haoping Xie[2]

[1] School of Business Administration,
Nanchang Institute of Technology, Nanchang 330099, China
[2] School of Information Engineering,
Nanchang Institute of Technology, Nanchang 330099, China
huiwang@whu.edu.cn
[3] Jiangxi Province Key Laboratory of Water Information Cooperative Sensing
and Intelligent Processing, Nanchang 330099, China

Abstract. The search behavior of firefly algorithm (FA) is determined by the attractions among fireflies. In the standard FA and its most modifications, worse fireflies can move toward other better ones, while better fireflies seldom move to other positions. To enhance the search of better fireflies, this paper presents a hybrid firefly algorithm (HFA), Which employs a local search operator inspired by differential evolution (DE). Moreover, the control parameters are dynamically adjusted during the search process. Experiments are conducted on thirteen continuous optimization problems. Computational results show that HFA achieves better solutions than the standard FA and three other improved FA variants.

Keywords: Firefly algorithm (FA) · Differential evolution · Local search · Continuous optimization

1 Introduction

Firefly algorithm (FA) is a recently developed swarm intelligence algorithm [1]. It mimics the social behavior of fireflies based on the flashing and attraction of fireflies. In FA, each firefly represents a candidate solution, and its brightness is associated with the objective function for a given problem. The attraction between among fireflies is based on the differences of brightness. It means that a less brighter firefly can move to a brighter one by the attraction. During the search process, fireflies move to new positions through the attraction, and find new candidate solutions.

Since the introduction of FA, it has attraction much attention. Many researchers have proposed different FA variants and used FA to solve various real-world optimization problems [2–5]. In [6], Fister et al. proposed a memetic FA (MFA) to solve combinatorial optimization problems, in which the parameter α is dynamically decreased. This is helpful to increase the convergence. It has been pointed out that if α is reduced too fast, the premature convergence may occur. The attractiveness β is

© Springer International Publishing AG 2016
X. Sun et al. (Eds.): ICCCS 2016, Part II, LNCS 10040, pp. 522–531, 2016.
DOI: 10.1007/978-3-319-48674-1_46

limited between 0.2 and 1.0. Moreover, the parameter α is multiplied by the length of the search range for the given problem. Simulation results show that MFA achieves much better solutions than the standard FA on some classical benchmark functions. On the basis of MFA, Wang et al. [7] proposed a new FA variant called RaFA, which employs two strategies: random attraction and Cauchy mutation. The first one aims to reduce the number of attractions and computational time complexity. The second one focuses on enhancing the global search ability. Though the random attraction can accelerate the convergence, it runs a risk of falling into local minima. The Cauchy mutation conducted on the global best firefly may help trapped fireflies escape from the local optima. Computational results show that RaFA outperforms the standard FA and MFA in terms of the solution accuracy and convergence speed. Based on MFA and random attraction, Wang et al. [8] introduced a neighborhood search strategy, which consists of one local and two global neighborhood search operators. Experimental results show that NSRaFA performs better than MFA and RaFA. Like other stochastic search algorithms, the performance of FA is also sensitive to its control parameters. To select the best settings of the control parameters, some researchers have proposed different strategies. In [9], twelve chaotic maps were used to update the light absorption coefficient γ and the attractiveness coefficient β. Results show that the proposed chaotic FA (CFA) can find better solutions than the standard FA on two benchmark functions. Yu et al. [10] designed a variable step size FA (VSSF), in which the parameter α is not fixed, but changed with increasing of iterations. Simulation results show that VSSFA performs better than the standard FA on sixteen benchmark functions. However, most of these functions are low-dimensional. In our further experiments, VSSFA is not suitable for solving high-dimensional functions, such as $D \geq 30$, where D is the dimensional size. In [11], Wang et al. investigated the relations between the control parameters (α and β) and the convergence characteristics. The literature concluded that the parameter α should tend to zero when FA is convergent. The β maybe changed to suit for the search.

In FA, the movement of fireflies is determined by the attractions, which are associated with the brightness of fireflies. Darker fireflies can move to brighter ones because of the attraction. It means that a darker (worse) firefly will have more chances of moving to other new positions then a brighter (better) one. This may not be suitable for the search. If both the darker (worse) and brighter (better) fireflies have the same chance of moving to new positions. The brighter firefly may find more accurate solutions than the darker one. Under this case, we propose a hybrid FA called HFA, which employs a local search operator inspired differential evolution (DE). It is hopeful that the DE based local search can help the brighter fireflies find better candidate solutions. Moreover, the HFA uses the same parameter control strategies with MFA. To verify the performance of HFA, there are thirteen benchmark functions used in the experiments. Computational results show that HFA can find more accurate solutions than the standard FA, MFA, VSSFA, and CFA on the majority of test functions.

The rest paper is organized as follows. The standard FA is briefly described in Sect. 2. In Sect. 3, the proposed approach HFA is introduced. Experimental results and discussions are given in Sect. 4. Finally, the summary and future work are presented in Sect. 5.

2 Firefly Algorithm

The idea of FA is inspired by the social behavior of fireflies. On clear summer nights, there can be seen many fireflies give off flashes of light. There are about 2,000 kinds of fireflies in the world. Each species of firefly has a special flicker code to attract mates of the same species. The FA developed by Yang is based on the attraction of fireflies. To model the FA, Yang proposed three assumptions as follows [12]:

(1) all fireflies are unisex;

(2) the attractiveness of a firefly is proportional to its brightness. For any two different fireflies, the less brighter one will move towards the brighter one, and their attractiveness and brightness decrease with increasing of their distance;

(3) the brightness of a firefly is affected or determined by the landscape of the objective function for a given problem.

In FA, the light intensity I can be approximated as [12]:

$$I(r) = I_0 e^{-\gamma r^2}, \tag{1}$$

where I_0 is the original light intensity, and γ is the light absorption coefficient.

As the attractiveness is proportional to the light intensity, the attractiveness β of a firefly can be defined by [12]:

$$\beta(r) = \beta_0 e^{-\gamma r^2}, \tag{2}$$

where β_0 is the attractiveness at $r = 0$. For two fireflies X_i and X_j, their distance $r_{i,j}$ can be calculated by [12]:

$$r_{i,j} = \|X_i - X_j\| = \sqrt{\sum_{d=1}^{D} (x_{i,d} - x_{j,d})^2}, \tag{3}$$

where D is the problem size.

For two fireflies X_i and X_j, if firefly X_j is brighter than firefly X_i, firefly X_i will be attracted by the firefly X_j. Due to the attraction, firefly X_i will move towards as firefly X_j follows [12]:

$$x_{i,d}(t+1) = x_{i,d}(t) + \beta_0 e^{-\gamma r_{i,j}^2} \big(x_{j,d}(t) - x_{i,d}(t)\big) + \alpha \varepsilon_{i,d}(t), \tag{4}$$

where $x_{i,d}$ and $x_{j,d}$ are the dth dimensions of X_i and X_j, respectively, α is a random value with the range of [0,1], $\varepsilon_{i,d}$ is a Gaussian random number for the dth dimension, and t indicates the generation index.

3   Proposed Approach

As mentioned before, the movement of fireflies is determined by the attractions among fireflies. In the standard FA, less brighter fireflies will move towards other brighter ones. For two fireflies X_i and X_j, if firefly X_j is brighter than firefly X_i, X_i will move towards X_j by the attraction. However, the brighter (better) X_j has not any search operation (except for random walk). If brighter X_j moves can move to other positions, it may provide more chances of finding better candidate solutions than moving X_i. Under this case, we propose a hybrid FA (HFA), which uses the DE scheme to search the neighborhood of the brighter fireflies in the population.

DE is an effective meta-heuristic for global optimization [13]. In this work, we embed DE into FA. Assume that X_j is the jth firefly in the population, where $j = 1,2...,$ N, and N is the population size. First, a mutant firefly V_j is generated based on the brighter firefly X_j:

$$v_{j,d}(t) = x_{j1,d}(t) + F \cdot \left(x_{j2,d}(t) - x_{j3,d}(t)\right), \tag{5}$$

where $d = 1,2,...,D$, $j1, j2$, and $j3$ are mutually different random integers between 1 and N. The parameter F is called scale factor, which controls the amplification of the difference vector.

Second, a crossover operator is conducted on X_j and V_j, and a new candidate solution U_j is generated as follows:

$$u_{j,d}(t) = \begin{cases} v_{j,d}(t), & if\ rand_d \leq CR \vee d = l \\ x_{j,d}(t), & otherwise \end{cases}, \tag{6}$$

where $d = 1,2,...,D$, the parameter $CR \in (0, 1)$ is called crossover rate, $rand_d$ is a random value between 0 and 1, and $l \in \{1,2,...,D\}$ is a random index.

Third, a selection operator is employed to select the better one between X_j and U_j as the new X_j entering the next generation. Without loss of generality, this paper only considers minimization problems. The selection process can be presented as follows:

$$X_j(t+1) = \begin{cases} U_j(t), & if\ f\left(U_j(t)\right) \leq f\left(X_j(t)\right) \\ X_j(t), & otherwise \end{cases}, \tag{7}$$

In HFA, the parameters α and β use the same strategies as MFA, and they are updated by [6]:

$$\alpha(t+1) = \left(\frac{1}{9000}\right)^{\frac{1}{t}} \alpha(t). \tag{8}$$

$$\beta = \beta_{min} + (\beta_0 - \beta_{min})e^{-\gamma r_{i,j}^2}. \tag{9}$$

where β_{min} is the lower bound of the attractiveness β.

The main steps of the proposed HFA are presented in Algorithm 1, where N is the population size, and FEs is the number of fitness evaluations, and Max_FEs is the maximum number of fitness evaluations.

Algorithm 1: Proposed HFA

```
1:   Begin
2:       Randomly initialize all fireflies in the population;
3:       FEs=N;
4:       while FEs <= MaxFEs do
5:           Update the parameter α according to Eq. (8);
6:           for i=1 to N do
7:               for j=1 to i do
8:                   if firefly j is better than firefly i then
9:                       Update the parameter β according to Eq. (9);
10:                      Generate a new firefly according to Eq. (4);
11:                      Evaluate the new solution;
12:                      FEs++:
13:                  end if
14:                  else
15:                      Generate a mutant Vⱼ based on Xⱼ according to Eq. (5);
16:                      Generate Uⱼ according to Eq. (6);
17:                      Evaluate Uⱼ;
18:                      FEs++;
19:                      Conduct the selection according to Eq. (7);
20:                  end else
21:              end for
22:          end for
23:      end while
24: End
```

---

4 Experiments

4.1 Test Problems

To test the performance of HFA, thirteen benchmark functions are used in the experiments [14, 15]. All functions are minimization problems, and their dimensions are set to 30. The detailed descriptions of these functions are described as follows.

$$f_1(x) = \sum_{i=1}^{D} x_i^2$$

where $x_i \in [-100, 100]$, and the global optimum is 0.

$$f_2(x) = \sum_{i=1}^{D} |x_i| + \prod_{i=1}^{D} x_i$$

where $x_i \in [-10, 10]$, and the global optimum is 0.

$$f_3(x) = \sum_{i=1}^{D} \left(\sum_{j=1}^{i} x_j \right)^2$$

where $x_i \in [-100, 100]$, and the global optimum is 0.

$$f_4(x) = \max_i (|x_i|, 1 \leq i \leq D)$$

where $x_i \in [-100, 100]$, and the global optimum is 0.

$$f_5(x) = \sum_{i=1}^{D-1} \left[100(x_i^2 - x_{i+1})^2 + (x_i - 1)^2 \right]$$

where $x_i \in [-30, 30]$, and the global optimum is 0.

$$f_6(x) = \sum_{i=1}^{D} (\lfloor x_i + 0.5 \rfloor)^2$$

where $x_i \in [-100, 100]$, and the global optimum is 0.

(7) Quartic with noise

$$f_7(x) = \sum_{i=1}^{D} i x_i^4 + rand[0, 1)$$

where $x_i \in [-1.28, 1.28]$, and the global optimum is 0.

$$f_8(x) = \sum_{i=1}^{D} -x_i \sin\left(\sqrt{|x_i|}\right)$$

where $x_i \in [-500, 500]$, and the global optimum is -12569.5.

$$f_9(x) = \sum_{i-1}^{D} \left[x_i^2 - 10 \cos(2\pi x_i) + 10 \right]$$

where $x_i \in [-5.12, 5.12]$, and the global optimum is 0.

$$f_{10}(x) = -20 \exp\left(-0.2 \sqrt{\frac{1}{D} \sum_{i=1}^{D} x_i^2} \right) - \exp\left(\frac{1}{D} \sum_{i=1}^{D} \cos(2\pi x_i) \right) + 20 + e$$

where $x_i \in [-32, 32]$, and the global optimum is 0.

$$f_{11}(x) = \frac{1}{4000} \sum_{i=1}^{D} x_i^2 - \prod_{i=1}^{D} \cos\left(\frac{x_i}{\sqrt{i}}\right) + 1$$

where $x_i \in [-600, 600]$, and the global optimum is 0.

$$f_{12}(x) = 0.1\{\sin^2(3\pi x_1) + \sum_{i=1}^{D-1}(x_i - 1)^2[1 + \sin^2(3\pi x_{i+1})]$$
$$+ (x_D - 1)^2[1 + \sin^2(2\pi x_D)]\} + \sum_{i=1}^{D} u(x_i, 10, 100, 4)$$

where $x_i \in [-50, 50]$, and the global optimum is 0.

$$f_{13}(x) = \frac{\pi}{D}\{10\sin^2(3\pi y_1) + \sum_{i=1}^{D-1}(y_i - 1)^2[1 + \sin^2(3\pi y_{i+1})]$$
$$+ (y_D - 1)^2[1 + \sin^2(2\pi x_D)]\} + \sum_{i=1}^{D} u(x_i, 5, 100, 4)$$

where $x_i \in [-50, 50]$, and the global optimum is 0.

4.2   Comparisons of HFA with Other FA Variants

In this section, we compare the proposed HFA with the standard FA, VSSFA [10], MFA [6], and CFA [9] on the test suite. For the sake of fair comparisons, the same parameter settings are listed as follows. The population size N and Max_FEs are set to 20 and 5.0E + 05, respectively. For MFA and HFA, the initial α, β_{min}, β_0, and γ are set to 0.2, 0.2, 1.0, and 1.0, respectively. For other parameters in HFA, $F = 0.5$ and $CR = 0.9$ are used. In the standard FA, α, β_0, and γ are set to 0.2, 1.0 and $1/\Gamma^2$, where Γ is the length of the search range for a given problem. For VSSFA and CFA, we use the same parameter settings as suggested in the their literature [9, 10]. For each test function, each algorithm is run 30 trials and the mean best fitness values are recorded.

Table 1 presents the mean best fitness values achieved by the standard FA, VSSFA, MFA, CFA, and HFA. The best results among five FA variants are shown in bold.

Table 1. Comparison results of HFA with FA, VSSFA, MFA, and CFA.

Functions	FA	VSSFA	MFA	CFA	HFA
	Mean	Mean	Mean	Mean	Mean
f_1	5.14E − 02	5.84E + 04	1.56E − 05	3.27E − 06	**1.85E − 08**
f_2	1.07E + 00	1.13E + 02	1.85E − 03	8.06E − 04	**8.96E − 05**
f_3	1.26E − 01	1.16E + 05	5.89E − 05	1.24E − 05	**2.80E − 07**
f_4	9.98E − 02	8.18E + 01	1.73E − 03	8.98E−04	**2.78E − 04**
f_5	3.41E + 01	2.16E + 08	2.29E + 01	2.06E + 01	**1.06E − 03**
f_6	5.24E + 03	5.48E + 04	**0.00E + 00**	**0.00E + 00**	**0.00E + 00**
f_7	7.55E − 02	4.43E + 01	1.30E − 01	9.03E − 02	**1.36E − 03**
f_8	9.16E + 03	1.07E + 04	4.94E + 03	4.36E + 03	**3.85E + 03**
f_9	4.95E + 01	3.12E + 02	6.47E + 01	5.27E + 01	**4.67E + 01**
f_{10}	1.21E + 01	2.03E + 01	4.23E − 04	4.02E − 04	**5.79E − 05**
f_{11}	2.13E − 02	5.47E + 02	9.86E − 03	7.91E − 06	**8.53E − 08**
f_{12}	6.24E + 00	3.99E + 08	5.04E − 08	8.28E − 09	**9.47E − 11**
f_{13}	5.11E + 01	8.12E + 08	6.06E − 07	1.69E − 07	**7.62E − 10**

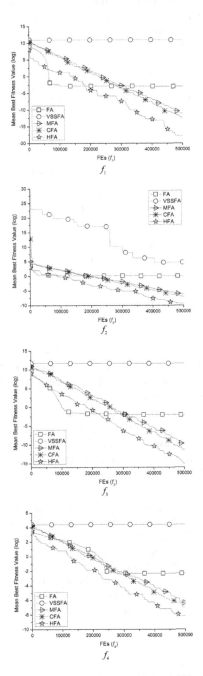

Fig. 1. The convergences curves of FA, VSSFA, MFA, CFA, and HFA.

From the results, HFA achieves better solutions than the standard FA and VSSFA on all test functions. MFA, CFA, and HFA can converge to the global optimum on f_6. For the rest of twelve functions, HFA outperforms MFA and CFA. Figure 1 shows the convergence curves of the five FA variants on four selected functions. As seen, HFA converges faster than the other four algorithms.

Table 2 presents the results achieved by the Friedman test. It can be seen that HFA achieves the best mean rank (the smallest value). CFA obtains the second best rank, while VSSFA takes the worst rank. Results show that HFA is the best algorithm among the five FA variants.

Table 2. Results achieved by the friedman test.

Algorithms	Mean Rank
HFA	**1.08**
CFA	2.15
MFA	3.08
FA	3.69
VSSFA	5.00

5   Conclusions

In the standard FA, the movement of fireflies is determined by the attractions, which are associated with the brightness of fireflies. Less brighter fireflies can move towards brighter ones because of the attraction. It means that a less brighter firefly will have more chances of moving to other new positions then a brighter one. This may not be suitable for the search. In this paper, we present a hybrid FA (HFA) variant, in which the DE scheme is utilized to enhance the search of brighter fireflies. In addition, HFA uses the parameter control method as suggested in MFA. Experiments are conducted on thirteen benchmark functions. Computational results show that HFA achieves more accurate solutions than the standard FA, VSSFA, MFA, and CFA.

Acknowledgement. This work is supported by the Priority Academic Program Development of Jiangsu Higher Education Institutions (PAPD), Jiangsu Collaborative Innovation Center on Atmospheric Environment and Equipment Technology (CICAEET), the Humanity and Social Science Foundation of Ministry of Education of China (No. 13YJCZH174), the National Natural Science Foundation of China (Nos. 61305150, 61261039, and 61461032), the Science and Technology Plan Project of Jiangxi Provincial Education Department (No. GJJ151099), the Natural Science Foundation of Jiangxi Province (No. 20142BAB217020), and the Student Research Training Program of Nanchang Institute of Technology (No.53).

References

1. Yang, X.S.: Nature-Inspired Metaheuristic Algorithms. Luniver Press, Beckington (2008)
2. Fister, I., Yang, X.S., Brest, J.: A comprehensive review of firefly algorithms. Swarm Evolu. Comput. **13**, 34–46 (2013)
3. Chandrasekaran, K., Simon, S.P., Padhy, N.P.: Binary real coded firefly algorithm for solving unit commitment problem. Inf. Sci. **249**, 67–84 (2013)
4. Gandomi, A.H., Yang, X.S., Alavi, A.H.: Mixed variable structural optimization using firefly algorithm. Comput. Struct. **89**(23–24), 2325–2336 (2013)
5. Marichelvam, M.K., Prabaharan, T., Yang, X.S.: A discrete firefly algorithm for the multi-objective hybrid flowshop scheduling problems. IEEE Trans. Evol. Comput. **18**(2), 301–305 (2014)
6. Fister Jr., I., Yang, X.S., Fister, I., Brest, J., Memetic Firefly Algorithm for Combinatorial Optimization, arXiv preprint arXiv:1204.5165 (2012)
7. Wang, H., Wang, W.J., Sun, H., Rahnamayan, S.: Firefly algorithm with random attraction. Int. J. Bio-Inspired Comput. **8**(1), 33–41 (2016)
8. Wang, H., Cui, Z.H., Sun, H., Rahnamayan, S., Yang, X.S.: Randomly attracted firefly algorithm with neighborhood search and dynamic parameter adjustment mechanism. Soft. Comput. (2016). doi:10.1007/s00500-016-2116-z. in press
9. Gandomi, A.H., Yang, X.S., Talatahari, S., Alavi, A.H.: Firefly algorithm with chaos. Commun. Nonlinear Sci. Numer. Simul. **18**(1), 89–98 (2013)
10. Yu, S.H., Zhu, S.L., Ma, Y., Mao, D.M.: A variable step size firefly algorithm for numerical optimization. Appl. Math. Comput. **263**, 214–220 (2015)
11. Wang, H., Zhou, X.Y., Sun, H., Yu, X., Zhao, J., Zhang, H., Cui, L.Z.: Firefly algorithm with adaptive control parameters. Soft. Comput. (2016). doi:10.1007/s00500-016-2104-3. in press
12. Yang, X.S.: Engineering Optimization: An Introduction with Metaheuristic Applications. Wiley, Hoboken (2010)
13. Storn, R., Price, K.: Differential evolution–a simple and efficient heuristic for global optimization over continuous spaces. J. Global Optim. **11**, 341–359 (1997)
14. Wang, H., Wu, Z.J., Rahnamayan, S., Liu, Y., Ventresca, M.: Enhancing particle swarm optimization using generalized opposition-based learning. Inf. Sci. **181**(20), 4699–4714 (2011)
15. Wang, H., Rahnamayan, S., Sun, H., Omran, M.G.H.: Gaussian Bare-Bones Differential Evolution. IEEE Trans. Cybern. **43**(2), 634–647 (2013)

A Particle Swarm Optimization with an Improved Updating Strategy

Zheng Fu[1], Haidong Hu[2], Chuangye Wang[3], and Hao Gao[1(✉)]

[1] The Institute of Advanced Technology,
Nanjing University of Posts and Telecommunications,
Nanjing, China
tsgaohao@gmail.com
[2] Beijing Institute of Control Engineering, Beijing, China
[3] State Grid Guzhen Electric Power Company, Bengbu, China

Abstract. In this paper, we introduce a novel pbest updating strategy to improve the achievement of the original particle swarm algorithm (PSO). First, we set a threshold for using our proposed updating strategy for pbest. Then if the algorithm reaches the condition of using this threshold, we select a pbest with an excellent performance in the population to search in a local valuable region for improving the precise search of particles. Meanwhile, we also select a pbest with a worse performance to search in the entire solution space for improving the global search ability of particles. By comparing with the traditional PSO and its variants on benchmark functions, the PSO algorithm with a novel pbest updating strategy (PPSO) performs much better than the other compared algorithms.

Keywords: Particle swarm optimization · Exploration search ability · Exploitation search ability · Convergence rate

1 Introduction

In recent years, a particle-swarm-optimization (PSO) [1, 2], which is an Evolutionary Computation algorithm, has attracted many researchers to develop. Compared with other population-based algorithms, the PSO algorithm simulates social behavior among individuals (or particles) search through a multidimensional potential solution space, where each particle represents a point at the intersection of all search dimensions. By now, PSO has been widely used to solving complex optimization problems, such as industrial processing [3], pattern recognition [4], fuzzy system control [5], and so on [6].

Compared to other EAs, PSO uses new concepts of individual experience and population experience, which is called as pbest and gbest separately. Then it shows more efficient and fast convergence rate which means it finds an acceptable result more quickly. But it also has a problem of premature convergence, which means it should have little opportunity to jump out of a local optimum. Ling et al. [7] present a PSO with a wavelet mutation (HWPSO). Inspired by the property of wavelet theory, at the beginning of iterations, the proposed HWPSO searches the solution space more thoroughly, and it is more likely to make a local search for a better solution in the last stage

© Springer International Publishing AG 2016
X. Sun et al. (Eds.): ICCCS 2016, Part II, LNCS 10040, pp. 532–540, 2016.
DOI: 10.1007/978-3-319-48674-1_47

of iterations. A novel paradigm of PSO with natural and simpler forms, called naïve PSO is presented in [8]. In this algorithm, the updating equation of PSO is difference with the traditional PSO and the improve PSO shows more favorable performance over the standard PSO. Although many improved PSO algorithms have been proposed in the last years, new strategies also need do further research for enhancing the traditional PSO achievements.

In this paper, we introduce a new pbest updating strategy into the traditional PSO. During iterations, we should check the diversity of the population in each dimension. When it reaches a defined threshold, we think particles have converged to a small region. Then we should use a global search operator for enhancing its global search ability to conquer the premature. Furthermore, if we enable some particles to jump out of the local optimum during iteration, it means these particles should terminate their current searching which means the jump operation interrupt the processing of their learning search ability from the gbest and pbest. For remedying losses of the convergence rate by using the global search operator, we adopt a local search operator by randomly selecting a pbest with good performance to search its local region, which is between the pbest and gbest. By using this two operator, particles should not only have more power global search ability but also can make precise search.

The rest of this paper is organized as follows. In Sect. 2, the original PSO is introduced. The proposed algorithm is described in Sect. 3. In Sect. 4, numerical studies are presented. Finally, conclusions and future work are provided in Sect. 5.

2   Particle Swarm Optimization

Inspired by a model of social interactions between independent birds or fishes seeking for food, PSO is a population-based algorithm to achieve the goal of optimization. Each individual called particle in PSO search the solution space with a velocity which is adjusted according to its own searching experience (called pbest) and the experience of the entire population (called gbest). The particle updates its new velocity as well as the position of the i th dimension as follows:

$$
\begin{aligned}
v_{id}(t+1) = wv_{id}(t) + c_1 rand_1 * \left(p_{pid} - x_{id}(t)\right) \\
+ c_2 rand_2 * \left(p_{gd} - x_{id}(t)\right)
\end{aligned}
\tag{1}
$$

$$
x_{id}(t+1) = x_{id}(t) + v_{id}(t+1)
\tag{2}
$$

where, c_1 and c_2 are positive constants and represent the acceleration coefficients, and $rand_1$, $rand_2$ are two random variables within [0, 1]. v_{id} is the velocity of individual i on dimension d. x_{id} is i's current position on dimension d. p_{pid} is the location of the best problem solution vector found by i, and p_{gd} is the location of the best particle among all the particles in the population on dimension d. w is the inertia weight that ensures convergence of the PSO algorithm. Generally, a maximum velocity (V_{max}) for each modulus of the velocity vector of the particles is defined in order to control excessive roaming of particles outside the user defined search space. Whenever a v_{id} exceeds the defined limit, its velocity is set to V_{max}.

3 PSO with a Novel Pbest Updating Strategy

Since the traditional PSO is guaranteed to converge, then the tendency of the best individual is to dominate the whole swarm. Finally, the whole individual is almost same. This problem has also been referred to in the literature as the premature convergence problem. Researchers have present many methods to conquer the problem. In this paper, since the pbest components could lead a particle to search in a new region, we use a new pbest updating strategy to enhance the PSO's global search ability. First, we define a threshold to check whether the swarm converges to a small region. Second, once the algorithm finds the premature, we use a global search operator to randomly select a pbest with a worse achievement for enhancing the global search ability of the individual. Although global updating operation may increase the diversity of population, its random nature also likely to destroy good experience of individual and therefore we use another pbest updating operation to preserve a better experience in population. The details of this strategy are listed as below.

The diversity of population on dimension j is formulated as:

$$diversity(d) = abs(sum(x(:,d)))/\mathbf{dim} \tag{3}$$

in which dim represents the total dimension of problems.

Once the diversity of the population on dimension d reaches the defined threshold *thresh*, we random select a pbest with worse achievement which means the achievement of pbest is ranked in the last half of the total population to use a global updating strategy.

$$pbest(r1,d) = rand * (i\_r - i\_l) + i\_l \tag{4}$$

in which $r1$ represents a random particle which achievement is ranked the last half percent of population. i_r and i_l represent the lower and upper limitation of the search space respectively.

Since the global updating strategy of pbest should destroy the experiences of individual, we also use a local pbest search operator to enhance its precise search ability. The region between pbest and gbest has been proven as a valuable space in [9]. Thus we make the pbest $r2$ with a better achievements which means the achievement of pbest is ranked in the first half of the total population, to search in the local valuable space. Then the algorithm should have more chances to update in this valuable local region. In Fig. 2, the $r2$ is tagged as a cross.

$$pbest1 = gbest + randn * (gbest - pbest(r2,:)); \tag{5}$$

The main steps of the PPSO algorithm are listed as follows (Fig. 1):

Begin
Initialize the population: $t=0$, random initialize $x_i(t)$, $thresh=x\max/10$, and evaluate $f(x_i(t))$
while (termination condition $==$ false)
do
   for (i = 1 to population size S)
  if $f(X_i(t))<f(pbest_i)$
      $pbest_i=X_i(t)$
        end if
          if $f(X_i(t))<f(gbest)$
      $gbest=X_i(t)$
    end if
    Update particles using Eq. (1) and (2)
    $diversity(j)=abs\big(sum(x(:,j))\big)/\dim$
    for (d=1 to dimension size)
    if $diversity(j)<thresh(j)$
    random select a pbest which achievement is ranked in the last half of the total population;
    $pbest(r1,j)=rand*(i\_r-i\_l)+i\_l$
    for j=1:5
    random select a pbest which achievement is ranked in the first half of the total population;
    $pbest1=gbest+randn*\big(gbest-pbest(r2,:)\big)$;
    evaluate $f(pbest1)$; if it is better than $f(pbest(r2))$ and $f(gbest)$, update them separately.
    end for
    $thresh(j)=thresh(j)/5$
    end if
    end for
  end do
end

Fig. 1. Pseudo code for the PPSO algorithm.

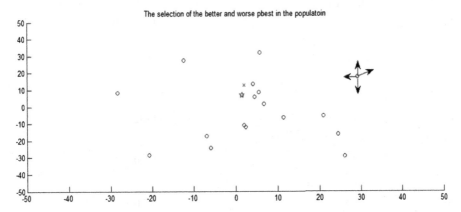

Fig. 2. The illustration of the selection of the better pbests in the population

4 Performance Evaluation

4.1 Experimental Setup

To test the performance of our algorithm, 13 benchmark functions [10, 11] are listed in Table 1. Under the same maximum function evaluations (FEs), they are used for comparison with the standard PSO [1], NPSO [6], HWPSO [7] and PPSO algorithms. The parameters of the compared algorithms are same with their own papers, which achieved the best results. The boundary of the search space and the global solution X^* are listed in Table 1. The population size of our compared algorithms is all set as 20. The value of *thresh* is set as 0.01. Furthermore, we used the same set of initial random populations to evaluate different algorithms. The max iterations for each algorithm on 20 and 40 dimensions are set as 2000 and 4000 iteration separately. According to this, the Fes are set as 40000 and 80000. Each algorithm is repeated 50 times on the benchmark functions [12].

Table 1. Benchmark test functions

F.	Formula	Range	X_{max}	f_{min}	X^*
f_1	$\sum_{i=1}^{n} x_i^2$	$[-100,100]$	100	0	0
f_2	$\sum_{i=1}^{n-1}\left[100\left(x_{i+1}-x_i^2\right)^2+(x_i-1)^2\right]$	$[-100,100]$	100	0	0
f_3	$\sum_{i=1}^{n} i*x_i^2$	$[-100,100]$	100	0	0
f_4	$\sum_{i=1}^{n}\left(\lfloor x_i+0.5\rfloor\right)^2$	$[-100, 100]$	100	0	0
f_5	$\sum_{i=1}^{n}|x_i|+\prod_{i=1}^{n}|x_i|$	$[-10, 10]$	100	0	0
f_6	$\sum_{i=1}^{n}(x_i)^2+\prod_{i=1}^{n}(x_i)^2$	$[-10, 10]$	10	0	0
f_7	$\sum_{i=1}^{n}\max|x_i|$	$[-100, 100]$	100	0	0
f_8	$\sum_{i=1}^{n}\left(x_i^2-10\cos(2\pi x_i)+10\right)$	$[-5.12, 5.12]$	5.12	0	0
f_9	$1+\frac{1}{4000}\sum_{i=1}^{n}x_i^2-\prod_{i=1}^{n}\cos\left(\frac{x_i}{\sqrt{i}}\right)$	$[-600, 600]$	600	0	0
f_{10}	$-20\exp\left(-0.2\sqrt{\frac{1}{n}\sum_{i=1}^{n}x_i^2}\right)-\exp\left(\frac{1}{n}\sum_{i=1}^{n}\cos 2\pi x_i\right)+20+e$	$[-32, 32]$	100	0	0
f_{11}	$\pi/n\{10\sin^2(\pi y_1)$ $+\sum_{i=1}^{n-1}(y_i-1)^2*\left[1+10\sin^2(\pi y_{i+1})\right]+(y_n-1)^2\}$	$[-50,50]$	50	0	0
f_{12}	$0.1\{\sin^2(3\pi x_1)+\sum_{i=1}^{n-1}(x_i-1)^2*\left[1+\sin^2(\pi x_{i+1})\right]$ $+(x_n-1)^2[1+\sin^2(2\pi x_n)]\}$	$[-50,50]$	50	0	0

4.2   Testing PPSO on Unimodal Functions

The performance of the total algorithms on unimodal functions $f_1 \sim f_7$ are shown in Tables 2 and 3.

Table 2. Comparison between different PSO algorithms

Alg.	f_1		f_2		f_3		f_4	
	Dim = 20	40	20	40	20	40	20	40
	G = 2000	4000	2000	4000	2000	4000	2000	4000
PSO	1.78e-16	3.43e-11	102.72	103.12	3.88e-16	1.06e-9	0	0.333
	(5.8e-16)	(8.4e-11)	(153.2)	(91.34)	(1.4e-15)	(2.71e-9)	(0)	(0.596)
NPSO	6.5e-12	7.8e-4	45.299	164.62	5.37e-13	1.86e-4	38.866	382
	(3.5e-11)	(0.0042)	(45.66)	(81.466)	(1.45e-12)	(9.8e-4)	(77.32)	(319.74)
HWPSO	**1.75e-11**	7.3e-8	66.14	**113.48**	6.68e-11	1.4e-6	0	0.3
	(4.5e-11)	(1.23e-7)	(109.3)	**(88.22)**	(1.49e-10)	(1.88e-6)	(0)	(0.526)
PPSO	**1.43e-25**	**9.28e-24**	**1.99**	**0.873**	**1.1e-17**	**9.26e-13**	**0**	**0**
	(7.6e-25)	**(4.99e-23)**	**(4.667)**	**(4.6991)**	**(4.16e-17)**	**(4.599e-12)**	**(0)**	**(0)**

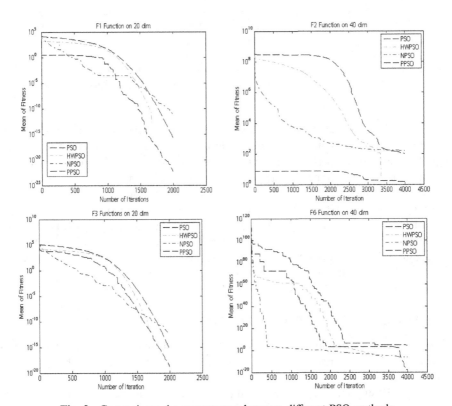

Fig. 3. Comparisons the convergence between different PSO methods

Table 3. Comparison between different PSO algorithms

Alg.	f_5		f_6		f_7		f_8	
	Dim = 20	40	20	40	20	40	20	40
	G = 2000	4000	2000	4000	2000	4000	2000	4000
PSO	2.42e-9	43.29	1.05e-5	32139	0.589	17.013	20.73	71.54
	(7.5e-9)	(209.67)	(5.6e-5)	(64408)	(0.394)	(2.794)	(4.399)	(15.67)
NPSO	1.26e-8	0.115	1.9e-13	4.93e-7	16.42	31.403	22.14	53.396
	(3.6e-8)	(36.108)	(4.7e-13)	(1.288e-6)	(5.346)	(5.508)	(6.688)	(11.137)
HWPSO	0.0617	22.084	1.76e-10	**7.36e-7**	0.515	4.503	20.1	73.595
	(0.15)	(0.0584)	(3.78e-10)	**(9.93e-7)**	(0.195)	(0.6395)	(7.618)	(17.762)
PPSO	**2.48e-11**	**3.98e-4**	**1.92e-25**	**3.49e-19**	**2.04e-9**	**1.04e-4**	**5.51**	**2.388**
	(1.02e-10)	**(0.0021)**	**(7.28e-25)**	**(7.43e-19)**	**(1.1e-8)**	**(5.58e-4)**	**(2.343)**	**(8.935)**

Table 4. Comparison between different PSO algorithms

Alg.	f_9		f_{10}		f_{11}		f_{12}	
	Dim = 20	40	20	40	20	40	20	40
	G = 2000	4000	3000	4000	1000	2000	3000	4000
PSO	0.0319	0.0137	9.29e-9	0.153	0.0156	0.6558	94.73	1222
	(0.0292)	(0.016)	(2.5e-8)	(0.4619)	(0.0467)	(2.686)	(79.35)	(367.54)
NPSO	0.0599	0.2446	2.8266	8.0423	1.1561	4.001	666.34	2122
	(0.0857)	(0.3534)	(1.444)	(2.198)	(3.3965)	(8.2734)	(307.489)	(424.75)
HWPSO	0.0341	0.0111	8.73e-7	**0.1876**	7.14e-14	0.0104	3.73e-10	479.969
	(0.0289)	(0.0124)	(9.27e-7)	**(0.484)**	(2.4e-13)	(0.0264)	(1.89e-9)	(356.34)
PPSO	**0.0025**	**3.29e-4**	**7.16e-15**	**5.51e-13**	**8.88e-23**	**8.219e-19**	**1.15e-23**	**2.166e-30**
	(0.0101)	**(0.0018)**	**(1.57e-14)**	**(2.88e-12)**	**(4.8e-22)**	**(4.43e-18)**	**(6.06e-23)**	**(1.15e-29)**

Sphere function maybe is the mostly used as the benchmark function in the comparison of Evolutionary Algorithms. From the results shown in Table 2, our algorithm gets the best performance. It mainly depend on the pbest has more chances to search in the local region nearby the gbest. Then the PPSO can get more precise results than the other algorithms. f_2 is the Rosenbrock algorithm. Due to a saddle point, the other algorithms cannot get acceptable results. But our algorithm significantly outperforms them. The differences between the compared algorithms on the total unimodal functions suggest that our strategy used in the PPSO is very suit for a local search.

Figure 3 shows the convergence of the compared algorithms. It also proven that our algorithm is most suitable for solving the unimodal functions.

4.3 Testing PPSO on Multimodal Functions

Comparing with the unimodal functions, multimodal functions $f_8 - f_{12}$ have many local optima. In this comparison, we mainly investigate the global search ability of the compared algorithm.

f_8 is the Rastrigin problem, which is the most used multimodal functions. From the results shown in Table 3, it is easy to find our algorithm gets the most acceptable results. It mainly attributes the pbest updating strategy enables particles have more opportunities to search in the entire solution space. Then the PPSO algorithm shows a power global search ability. The results on the other multimodal functions also prove our algorithm shows the best performance among the compared algorithm. f_{12} is Montalvo functions, which has approximately 10^n local minima and n is the dimension of the function. From Table 4, our algorithm gets the best results on this function. Moreover, when the dimension of f_{12} is increasing to 40, all of the compared algorithms, except our algorithm, have been trapped in the local optima. The new pbest updating strategy helps our algorithm to have more opportunities to jump out of the local optima, which is the main reason that our algorithm shows more power global search ability.

5 Conclusion

In this paper, we introduce a new particle swarm algorithm with new pbest updating strategy to improve its global search ability. The first strategy used in the pbest updating equation helps particles have more opportunity to search in the entire search space. The second strategy makes pbest to make the selected pbest to make a precise search nearby a valuable region. Experimental results validate the powerful capability of our approach compared with the other PSO algorithms. The use of the PPSO in the complex real-world problems merits further research in our future work.

Acknowledgment. The authors acknowledge support from the National Nature Science Foundation of China (No. 61203196, 61571236, 61502245), and China Postdoctoral Science Foundation (No. 2014M551632).

References

1. Kennedy, J., Eberhart, R.C.: Particle swarm optimization. In: Proceeding IEEE International Conference Neural Network, pp. 1942–1948 (1995)
2. Kennedy, J., Mendes, R.: Population structure and particle swarm structure. In: IEEE Congress on Evolutionary Computation, pp. 1671–1676 (2002)
3. Sun, J., Palade, V., Wu, X.J., Fang, W.: Solving the power economic dispatch problem with generator constraints by random drift particle swarm optimization. IEEE Trans. Ind. Inf. **10**, 222–232 (2014)
4. Gao, H., Xu, W.B., Sun, J., Tang, Y.L.: Multilevel thresholding for image segmentation through an improved quantum-behaved particle swarm algorithm, vol. 59, pp. 934–946 (2010)
5. Chan, K.Y., Dillon, T.S., Kwong, C.K.: Modeling of a liquid epoxy molding process using a particle swarm optimization-base fuzzy regression approach. IEEE Trans. Ind. Inf. **7**, 148–158 (2011)
6. Shen, K., Zhao, D., Mei, J., Tolbert, L.M.: Elimination of harmonics in a modular multilevel convert using particle swarm optimization-based staircase modulation strategy. IEEE Trans. Indus. Electr. **61**, 5311–5322 (2014)

7. Ling, S.H., Iu, H.H.C., Chan, K.Y., et al.: Hybrid particle swarm optimization with wavelet mutation and its industrial applications. IEEE Trans. Syst. Man Cybern. Part B **38**, 743–763 (2008)

8. Jin, Q., Liang, Z.J.: A naïve particle swarm optimization. In: IEEE Congress Evolutionary Computation, pp. 1–8 (2012)

9. Gao, H., Kwong, S., Yang, J.J., Cao, J.J.: Particle swarm optimization based on intermediate disturbance strategy algorithm and its application in multi-threshold image segmentation. Inf. Sci. **250**, 82–112 (2013)

10. Yao, X., Liu, Y.: Evolutionary Programming Made Faster. IEEE Trans. Evol. Comput. **3**, 82–102 (1999)

11. Ali, M.M., Khompatraporn, C., Zabinsky, Z.B.: A numerical evaluation of several stochastic algorithms on selected continuous global optimization test problems. J. Global Optim. **31**, 635–672 (2005)

12. van den Bergh, F., Engelbrecht, A.P.: A study of particle swarm optimization particle trajectories. Inf. Sci. **176**, 937–971 (2006)

A Manifold Learning Algorithm
Based on Incremental Tangent Space Alignment

Chao Tan[(✉)] and Genlin Ji

School of Computer Science and Technology,
Nanjing Normal University, Nanjing, China
{chtan,glji}@njnu.edu.cn

Abstract. Manifold learning is developed to find the observed data's
low dimension embeddings in high dimensional data space. As a type
of effective nonlinear dimension reduction method, it has been widely
applied to data mining, pattern recognition and machine learning. However, most existing manifold learning algorithms work in a "batch"
mode and cannot effectively process data collected sequentially (or data
streams). In order to explore the intrinsic low dimensional manifold structures in data streams on-line or incrementally, in this paper we propose a
new manifold Learning algorithm based on Incremental Tangent Space
Alignment, *LITSA* for short. By constructing data points' local tangent spaces to preserve local coordinates incrementally, we can accurately obtain the low dimensional global coordinates. Experiments on
both synthetic and real datasets show that the proposed algorithm can
achieve a more accurate low-dimensional representation of the data than
state-of-the-art incremental algorithms.

Keywords: Nonlinear dimension reduction · Manifold learning · Incremental tangent space

1 Introduction

Dimension reduction is a prerequisite for many tasks in data mining, pattern
recognition and machine learning. Accordingly, developing effective methods for
dimension reduction has been a hot research topic in recent years.

Specifically, manifold learning, a type of effective nonlinear dimension reduction method, aims to discover the low dimensional smooth manifold structure of
observed high-dimensional data. In the past decade, a number of manifold learning algorithms are developed, including Isometric feature mapping (Isomap) [1],
Laplacian eigenmaps algorithm [2], locally linear embedding (LLE) [3], Local
Tangent Space Alignment (LTSA) [4] and so on. All these algorithms operated
in a "batch" mode, i.e., the whole set of data must be collected before running
the algorithm, which makes it ineffective to deal with data collected sequentially (or data streams). In reality, however, many applications need to handle
realtime data streams where data are collected in turn. Therefore, incremental

© Springer International Publishing AG 2016
X. Sun et al. (Eds.): ICCCS 2016, Part II, LNCS 10040, pp. 541–552, 2016.
DOI: 10.1007/978-3-319-48674-1_48

manifold learning methods being able to continuously and efficiently update the manifold constructed on new-coming data and existing data without repeatedly computing the whole data set are required. Meanwhile, the incremental learning algorithms can be used to visualize the data manifold's changing process, which provides a great help to understand the feature of data structure.

In this paper we propose a new incremental manifold learning algorithm called *LITSA*, which finds the local principal components of the sample points by incremental PCA. *LITSA* is not subject to the size of sample points' covariance matrix, thus solving the large-scale matrix eigen decomposition problem in LTSA. In this method, in order to obtain its coordinates in a low dimension space, we construct the tangent space of each data sample in high dimension space incrementally. To avoid reconstructing the eigenspace repeatedly, we construct the local tangent space matrix incrementally in the light of the sample points' covariance matrix. Thus, the proposed algorithm can update the manifold structure directly via computing the eigenvectors of local tangent space matrix constructed on the basis of existing samples and newly-arrived data samples. The experimental results on both synthetic and real-world datasets show that the proposed algorithm can achieve a more accurate low-dimensional representation of the original data efficiently.

2 Related Work

The idea of existing incremental manifold learning algorithms can be roughly summed up into two categories.

The first one is based on the hypothesis that existing results are entirely correct, so the the new samples can be efficiently dealt with. These algorithms can efficiently deal with the new data. However, existing data often can not accurately reflect the intrinsic manifold structure. Especially in the case of non-uniform sampling, these algorithms may not provide low dimensional embedding of high-dimensional data correctly.

Algorithms in the second class will update the training data set's embedding coordinates when embedding the other samples. So they can better reflect the dataset's characteristics. By contrast, these methods can give more reliable results.

Existing typical incremental manifold learning algorithms include the incremental Isomap algorithm (IIsomap) [5], the incremental version of Laplacian eigenmaps (ILE) [6], the incremental LLE algorithm (ILLE) [7], and the incremental LTSA algorithm (ILTSA) [8]. Another incremental manifold learning algorithm via LTSA by Liu et al. [9] proposed a modified LTSA algorithm and an incremental eigen-decomposition problem with increasing matrix size.

The core idea of the IIsomap algorithm is to efficiently update the geodesic distances and re-estimate the eigenvectors, using the previous computation results. There exists the problem of disconnected neighborhood graphs when the data are undersampled or unevenly distributed, new points may change the current neighborhoods and local distribution of the manifold, the continuity of the neighborhood matrix is not guaranteed. The addition of a new sample can delete critical edges in the graph and subsequently change the geodesic distances dramatically. In this case, short-circuit or cavitation phenomenon will happen. The algorithm of ILE is traditionally performed in a batch mode. It introduces a locally linear reconstruction mechanism to add new adjacent information and revise the existing samples' low-dimensional embedding results. The sub-manifold method involved needs to solve a $(k + 1) \times (k + 1)$ eigenvector problem and the overall time complexity of solving the eigenvector problem is $O((k + 1)^3)$. ILLE algorithm evaluated the mapping results of the new samples and re-calculated the projections of original samples. This algorithm assumed that the eigenvalues of the cost matrix remained the same when a new data point arrived and the incremental learning problem of LLE was tackled by solving a $d \times d$ minimization problem, where d was the dimensionality of the low-dimensional embedding space. In ILTSA the previous work of incremental algorithms mostly adopted iterative methods of whole process which need abundant repetitive computation, because one does not know what part of a iterative optimization problem has to be recomputed. The problem in method [9] is similar to ILTSA that the alignment matrix has to be reconstructed to include the new point, which is not very practical for large datasets. The other limitation of existing incremental methods is that there is no guarantee on the approximation error, so these approaches suffer from unpredicted approximation error [10]. Similar problems also exist in other incremental methods such as ILLE algorithm, the error in process of dimension reduction will become larger, because the eigenvalues of new cost matrix M_{new} in this algorithm have not been updated. As the number of new samples increases, the difference value between the first d smallest eigenvalues of the original cost matrix M will become larger, hence a larger error [11].

Given a set of N data points $\{x_i | i = 1, 2, \cdots, N\}$, Local Tangent Space Alignment (LTSA) assumes that the data points are sampled from a high dimensional manifold, i.e. located in a m-dimensional manifold $\mathbb{R}^m$. It maps x_i to the d-dimensional representation τ_i and reserves the local geometry information of x_i as much as possible, where $d < m$. Local geometry information of x_i is defined as the manifold constructed by its k nearest neighbor points to generate tangent space of x_i. All the data points in tangent spaces are then aligned to give their global coordinates in the low dimension manifold. Though LTSA can effectively evaluate a dataset's global mapping coordinates that reflects the data set's low-dimensional manifolds structure, it has two shortcomings: On the one hand, the size of the covariance matrix used for eigen decomposition in LTSA is equal to the number of samples, so it is inefficient to handle large datasets; On the other hand, it cannot deal with new sample point effectively for the high time complexity, so it is difficult for incremental learning.

Min et al. [12] proved that the local tangent space of a sample can be represented by the eigenvectors of the covariance matrix constructed by the samples in its neighborhood. The matrix's eigenvectors can be computed by local principal component analysis method. Therefore the problem of computing the sample points' projection coordinates in the low dimensional space can be transformed into solving the local principal component analysis problem.

Recently, a number of semi-supervised feature extraction algorithms [13–16] have come out, which combine semi-supervised techniques with local discriminant analysis approaches. While they have lost considerations of incremental learning on dynamic manifold, which has become a hot topic in big data stream nowadays.

The algorithm proposed in this paper can overcome these shortcomings. It finds the local principal components of the sample points by incremental PCA [17,18], which is not subject to the size of sample points' covariance matrix, thus solving the large-scale matrix eigen decomposition problem in LTSA. In addition, by taking the adaptive factor into account, our algorithm is able to deal with new arrived sample points effectively.

3   Manifold Learning Algorithm Based on Incremental Tangent Space Alignment

3.1   Update New Covariance Matrix After Inserting New Point

Firstly, we construct new local tangent spaces for existing sample points and newly arrived one. Given a set of data points $X = [x_1, \cdots, x_N]$ sampled from non-linear manifold $\mathbb{R}^m$, they will be mapped from m dimension space to d dimension space. Suppose $X_i = [x_{i_1}, \cdots, x_{i_k}]$ as a matrix containing k nearest neighbours of x_i (in Euclidean distance). Traditional PCA searches for vectors c, T and matrix U to project X_i to low dimension manifold $\mathbb{R}^d$. In order to get the optimal solution, we minimize the reconstruct error: $\min \|E\| = \min_{c,U,T} \|X - (ce^T + UT)\|_F$, in which c is the mean value of X, indicated as: Xe/N. Matrix $U \in \mathbb{R}^{m \times d}$ is a set of orthonormal basis of affine subspace, singular value decomposition in linear condition can be used to solve this problem. While in nonlinear conditions, especially in realtime environment, situation is more complicated. Local linear array must be used in realization to solve incremental non-linear mapping problem.

When a new point arrives, denoted by x_{new}, we prepare to update the local information of the new point from eigenvectors of existing points. Suppose the eigenspace of existing N samples has already been constructed, with k-neighbor points of each point. The new point's coordinate X_{new} is projected into existing eigenspace through following form: $w_i = u_i^T(X_{new} - \overline{X}_N), i = 1, 2, \cdots, N$,where u_i is the ith eigenvector in eigenspace which consists of N sample points, $\overline{X}_N$ is mean of the N samples, w_i is the ith coefficient of the new point in the eigenspace.

Then we can reconstruct the new point's coordinate based on these coefficients: $X_{new} = w_i u_i + \overline{X}_N$. To solve incremental nonlinear mapping problem, the first step is to estimate mean value and construct the sample points' covariance matrix, thereby to determine the sample points' eigenvectors in eigenspace.

Let M_N be the mean value of the existing N samples in m dimension space. In this paper we propose a novel formulation M_{new} in order to describe the geometric information of the existing sample points' covariance matrix after inserting the new point:

$$M_{new} = \alpha M_N + (1 - \alpha)x_{new}e^T, \tag{1}$$

where α is an adaptive factor controlling how exited samples influence the estimation of M_{new}'s value, e denotes the identity vector. How to choose α is based on the incremental environment: if the samples in current environment update fast, α is set to be small; if slow, α has larger value. We set $(1 - \alpha)$ as the *learning rate* which depends on the nature of data sets in realtime practice and requires a $trial - and - error$ procedure to determine, while it is impractical for "on-line" applications [19]. This process lies on the measurement of observed data samples X_{new}. From [20] we know the sample mean is an efficient estimate of mean distribution. The use of samples' mean value M_N also inspires us to divide the learning rate by $\frac{1}{N}$ here. So we set $(1 - \alpha) = \frac{1}{N}$ as sample mean. Although $\alpha = \frac{N-1}{N}$ added on M_N is close to 1 when N is large enough, it is very important for fast convergence with primary samples. If the estimate does not converge well at the beginning, it is harder to be pulled back later when N is large. We can also know that the estimate of M_{new} has a fairly low error variance and high statistical efficiency through experiments in subsequent section.

Traditional PCA (Principle Component Analysis) computes the eigensolutions by solving the SVD (Singular Value Decomposition) of the covariance matrix: $C = \frac{1}{N}\sum_{i=1}^{N}(x_i - \bar{x})^T(x_i - \bar{x})$. The corresponding expression in matrix form can be written as: $C = (X_i - \bar{x}_i\,e^T)^T(X_i - \bar{x}_i\,e^T)$. Compute C's eigenvectors corresponding to d first eigenvalues which span a subspace of d dimension. We only need to save M_{new} and existing covariance matrix C_n because existed samples can be discarded during recursive updating process, thereby the algorithm's complexity can be greatly decreased. Similarly we can obtain the iterative estimation of covariance matrix given as below:

$$C_n = \alpha C_{n-1} + (1 - \alpha)(X_n - \overline{X}_n)^T(X_n - \overline{X}_n) \tag{2}$$

After substituting α with $\frac{N-1}{N}$ and inserting new sample x_{new}, we get the updating form C_{new} for C as follows, where X_{new} is the matrix form of $x_{new}e^T$.

$$C_{new} = \frac{N-1}{N}C + \frac{1}{N}(X_{new} - M_{new})^T(X_{new} - M_{new}) \tag{3}$$

According to PCA, the optimal solution of $C = (X_i - \bar{x}_i\,e^T)^T(X_i - \bar{x}_i\,e^T)$ is given by SVD of $(X_i - \bar{x}_i\,e^T)$. Let $\lambda_i(i = 1, \cdots, d)$ be the d first eigenvalues of C, v_i as the corresponding eigenvectors, so: $C \approx U_{Nd}\Lambda_{dd}U_{Nd}^T = \sum_{i=1}^{d}\lambda_i v_i v_i^T$, where the column vectors U_{Nd} are the eigenvectors v_i of C, and diagonal matrix Λ_{dd} is comprised of $C's$ eigenvalues λ_i.

Now we can get the incremental C_{new} in matrix form and its expression model:

$$C_{new} = \frac{N-1}{N} U \Lambda U^T + \frac{1}{N}(X_{new} - M_{new})^T (X_{new} - M_{new}) \qquad (4)$$

To facilitate the calculation, the above formula can be written as:

$$C_{new} = \frac{N-1}{N} \sum_{i=1}^{d} \lambda_i v_i v_i^T + \frac{1}{N}(X_{new} - M_{new})^T (X_{new} - M_{new}) \qquad (5)$$

where:

$$X_{new} - M_{new} = x_{new}e^T - \frac{N-1}{N} \bar{x_i}\, e^T - \frac{1}{N} x_{new}e^T = \frac{N-1}{N}(x_{new} - \bar{x_i})e^T \quad (6)$$

3.2   Construct the Local Tangent Space in Incremental Form

For the updating of all the points' embedding coordinates in low dimensional space by an incremental way, we proceed in the following steps.

Firstly, we perform eigen-decomposition for C_{new} and obtain its first d eigenvalues λ_i and eigenvectors v_i, $i = 1, 2, ..., d$. Then we construct $d + 1$ vectors based on v_i and λ_i: $A = [y_1, y_2, \cdots, y_{d+1}]$ of $k \times (d + 1)$ size, where: $y_i = v_i\sqrt{\frac{N-1}{N}\lambda_i}, i = 1, \cdots, d, y_{d+1} = \sqrt{\frac{1}{N}}(X_{new} - M_{new})^T$. It can satisfy the condition of $C_{new} = AA^T$, which indicates the local tangent space matrix of neighbour points of the new sample including itself.

Secondly, an inner-product matrix B of $k \times k$ size can be formulated as: $B = AA^T$, much smaller than C_{new}. The advantage of this approach is that we can construct local tangent space matrix incrementally instead of recomputing the new covariance matrix C_{new}. The matrix B is the orthogonal projector onto the subspace spanned by the columns of A. So the local coordinates of new point x_{new} in the incremental subspace can be obtained by computing the d first singular vectors of A [21], equivalently the d eigenvectors $u_1, \cdots, u_d$ corresponding to the d smallest eigenvalues of B. Set the eigenvectors and eigenvalues of B as: $\{v_n^i\}$ and $\{\lambda_n^i\}$, we have: $Bv_n^i = \lambda_n^i v_n^i, i = 1, 2, ..., k$. Then, $A^T Av_n^i = \lambda_n^i v_n^i$, multiplied by A on both sides: $AA^T Av_n^i = \lambda_n^i Av_n^i$. Let $u_n^i = Av_n^i$, then: $AA^T u_n^i = \lambda_n^i u_n^i$, i.e.: $C_{new} u_n^i = \lambda_n^i u_n^i$. So we have C_{new}'s eigenvectors: $u_n^i = Av_n^i$.

With eigenvectors of the covariance matrix in incremental form, new sample point x_{new}'s local coordinate can be calculated by formulation Eq. (7):

$$x_{new} = w_i u_i + \bar{X}_N = \sqrt{\lambda_n^i} u_n^i + \bar{X}_N = \sqrt{\lambda_n^i} Av_n^i + \bar{X}_N \qquad (7)$$

3.3   Compute the Low Dimensional Global Coordinates

Now we consider the incremental updating situation. The local coordinates of new sample point in Eq. (7) can be represented in following matrix form:

$$X_{new} = WU + \overline{X}_N, \qquad (8)$$

where the low-rank matrix WU is the d-dimensional optimal approximation of original coordinates, U is orthonormal and W has k column vectors: $U = [u_1, \cdots, u_d]$, $W = [w_1, \cdots, w_k]$. $\overline{X}_N$ is the mean of X_N.

Since the structure of global coordinates is linear in low dimensional feature space, the new sample point's local coordinate can be approximated by Eq. (8). Then we can construct global coordinates according to the local coordinates:

$$Y_i = \frac{1}{k} Y_i e e^T + L_i(WU + \overline{X}_N) + E_i, i = 1, ..., N. \tag{9}$$

Y_i denotes the global coordinates in low dimensional space, L_i and E_i denote local affine transformation matrix and reconstruction error respectively after inserting new data point. So,

$$E_i = Y_i(I - \frac{1}{k} e e^T) - L_i(WU + \bar{X}_N) \tag{10}$$

To minimize the reconstruction error we can describe Eq. (10) as: $\min_{Y_i, L_i} Y_i(I - \frac{1}{k} e e^T) - L_i(WU + \bar{X}_N)$, then:

$$L_i = Y_i(I - \frac{1}{k} e e^T)(WU + \bar{X}_N)^\dagger \tag{11}$$

where: $(WU + \bar{X}_N)^\dagger = ((WU + \bar{X}_N)^T(WU + \bar{X}_N))^{-1}(WU + \bar{X}_N)^T$ is pseudo-inverse of $(WU + \bar{X}_N)$. So:

$$E_i = Y_i(I - \frac{1}{k} e e^T)(I - (WU + \bar{X})^\dagger(WU + \bar{X})) \tag{12}$$

Suppose $H_i = (I - \frac{1}{k} e e^T)(I - (WU + \overline{X})^\dagger(WU + \overline{X}))$, to determine Y_i uniquely $Y_i Y_i^T = I_d$ is the constraint condition. Let $Y = [Y_1, \cdots, Y_N]$ and S_i be the 0-1 selection matrix such that $YS_i = Y_i$, we have:

$$||E_i||_F^2 = ||Y_i H_i||_F^2 = ||YSH||_F^2 = Tr(H^T S^T Y^T YSH) = Tr(H^T S^T SH) \tag{13}$$

Then we minimize the reconstruction error: $\min ||E_i||_F^2 = \min Tr(H^T S^T SH)$, Y in Eq. (13) is constituted with d eigenvectors corresponding to the 2nd to $d + 1^{st}$ smallest eigenvalues of matrix D: $D = H^T S^T SH$, where $S = [S_1, \cdots, S_N]$ and $H = diag(H_1, \cdots, H_N)$.

In order to solve the eigenvalues and eigenvectors of D locally and linearly, we can construct U_i based on eigenvectors $u_1, ..., u_d$ of B: $U_i = [e/\sqrt{k}, u_1, \cdots, u_d]$, then, $H_i = I - U_i U_i^T$. After new data points arrive, we update incremental alignment matrix: $D(I_i, I_i) \leftarrow D(I_i, I_i) + I - U_i U_i^T$, then compute the 2nd to the $(d + 1)^{th}$ smallest eigenvalues and the corresponding eigenvectors $[t_2, \cdots, t_{d+1}]$ of D, which correspond to the optimal low dimensional global coordinates of data points.

4   Implementation of LITSA

Given a dataset with N m-dimensional points $X = [x_1, \cdots, x_N]$ sampled from manifold $\mathbb{R}^m$ and a new point x_n which will be inserted into X. The proposed algorithm projects these points into low dimensional space, provides d-dimensional $(d < m)$ coordinates $y_1, ..., y_N$ and the new point's low dimensional mapped point y_n in an incremental way.

Step 1. Update new covariance matrix.

- Determine k nearest neighbours of each point x_i (Euclidean distance) and compose the matrix X_i, $i = 1, ..., N$;
- Construct the covariance matrix C_n in Eq. (2) iteratively, which represents the incremental tangent space of each data point;
- Construct matrix A and B;
- Compute the eigenvectors $u_1, ..., u_d$ corresponding to the d smallest eigenvalues of B;
- Set $U_i = [e/\sqrt{k}, u_1, \cdots, u_d]$.

Step 2. Construct alignment matrix in incremental form.

Set $I_i = \{i_1, \cdots, i_k\}$ as k nearest neighborhood's index set of data point x_i, compute alignment matrix in incremental form:

Initialize $D \leftarrow 0$;
for $i = 1 \rightarrow N$ **do**
    $D(I_i, I_i) \leftarrow D(I_i, I_i) + I - U_i U_i^T$
end for

Step 3. Obtain the low dimensional coordinates.

Make eigen-decomposition of matrix D, compute the 2nd to the $(d+1)^{th}$ smallest eigenvalues and the corresponding eigenvectors $[t_2, \cdots, t_{d+1}]$ which correspond to the optimal low dimensional global coordinates $y_1, ..., y_N$ of each point in original dataset including the new point's low dimensional coordinate y_n.

5   Experiments

5.1   Experiments on Olivetti-Faces

In this section we will apply LTSA and the proposed algorithm LITSA to process *Olivetti-faces* dataset[1] which contains 400 face images with 64×64 pixels. Some samples are shown in Fig. 1(a). One image of them is randomly selected for testing, while the rest ones serve as training samples. Figure 1(b) shows the dimension reduction results of training samples by LTSA.

---

[1] Available from website: http://www.cs.toronto.edu/~roweis/data.html.

The horizontal axis represents the face expression changing from unhappy to happy and the vertical axis denotes the face images from without glasses to wearing glasses. The testing images shown in Fig. 1(a) are projected to the low-dimensional space accurately according to their characteristics, because images with similar expressions and characteristics have clustered together. This experiment intuitively shows the effectiveness of LITSA as manifold learning dimension reduction algorithm, which accurately detects and preserves the intrinsic structure of original high dimensional data sets.

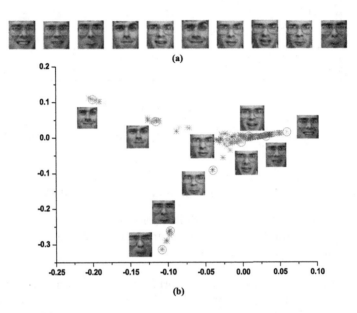

Fig. 1. (a) Some test images, (b) The unfolding results of the *Olivetti-faces* dataset by LITSA

Dimension reduction is often used as a preprocess step of classification in many machine learning. So dimension reduction always plays an important role in such classification tasks. In this section we display classification effect after dimensional reduction by several incremental algorithms on *Olivetti-faces* dataset, where 40 facial images including 5 images of each individual are randomly selected for testing and the rest ones for training. The experiment is repeated for 10 times. After reducing the dataset to different dimensions, we classify them using k-Nearest Neighbors classifier (k-NN, the nearest neighbors number k is set to be 5). From the classification accuracy rates shown in Fig. 2 we can observe that our algorithm LITSA well detects the intrinsic structure information of the input manifold and achieves better classification precision than other incremental algorithms. It indicates that our algorithm has played a positive role to the subsequent classification learning, has vital significance in many applications such as pattern recognition, image processing and so on.

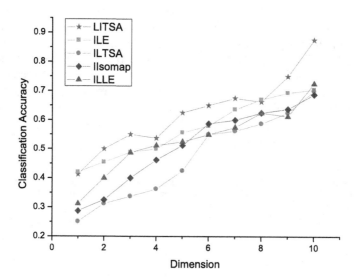

Fig. 2. Accuracy results of kNN classification after dimensional reduction on 10 dimensions

5.2 Local Reconstruction Performance on Rendered Face

In this section we consider the experimental results on Rendered face dataset [1]. This dataset contains 698 facial sculpture images with 64×64 pixels. The facial images have two groups of pose parameters which are up to down and left to right.

We compare the reconstruction performance between the proposed algorithm LITSA and other incremental algorithms on Rendered face dataset. To recover these implicit parameters we use matrix P to represent pose parameters. By making affine transformation on the dimensional reduction projection results T by these algorithms mentioned above, we can get the affine transformation expression: $Y = ce^T + LT$. Define the following expression: $||P - Y||_F^2 = \min_{c,L} ||P - (ce^T + LT)||_F^2$. Then the relevant reconstruction error can be measured by: $error = \frac{||P - Y||_F^2}{||P||_F^2}$.

Various reconstruction error computed by IIsomap, ILTSA, ILLE, ILE and LITSA along with neighborhood size k are shown in Table 1, in which LITSA keep the minimum reconstruction error. Reconstruction error of IIsomap after reducing dimensions already exceed the comparison range of other algorithms, which indicates that our method has leading position and superiority among these algorithms with reconstruction error in small area.

To sum up, the algorithm LITSA has showed obvious superiority both in intuitive and mathematical sense, through the experiments of this section on local reconstruction performance and reconstruction error measure.

Table 1. Reconstruction error computed by IIsomap, ILTSA, ILLE, ILE and LITSA

k	$IIsomap$	$ILTSA$	$ILLE$	ILE	$LITSA$
8	0.79	0.0358	0.0088	0.0091	0.0084
9	0.69	0.0352	0.0233	0.0096	0.0087
10	0.58	0.0387	0.0170	0.0096	0.0090
11	0.49	0.0397	0.0230	0.0098	0.0091
12	0.39	0.0381	0.0264	0.0102	0.0093
13	0.26	0.0373	0.0235	0.0105	0.0096
14	0.22	0.0373	0.0191	0.0107	0.0095
15	0.18	0.0385	0.0178	0.0111	0.0096
16	0.19	0.0393	0.0195	0.0116	0.0102
17	0.20	0.0398	0.0210	0.0120	0.0108

6   Conclusion

This paper proposes a new incremental manifold learning algorithm named LITSA based on incremental tangent space construction. Compared with LTSA algorithm and other incremental manifold learning methods, the innovation of this algorithm can be concluded as three aspects: (1) A novel formulation M_{new} is proposed in order to insert the new point's geometric information into existing sample points' covariance matrix. (2) We construct the incremental expression of C_{new} by inserting $(X_{new} - M_{new})$. (3) Inspired by the idea of literature [15], after constructing smaller size inner product matrix $B = AA^T$, we can immediately obtain the local coordinates of dataset inserted with new sample point by computing the eigenvectors and eigenvalues of matrix B. Extensive experiments have been performed in order to evaluate our algorithm's performance both on artificial and actual datasets, demonstrating its ability of dimension reduction effect and recognition accuracy on large scale datasets.

Acknowledgements. This work is supported by National Natural Science Foundation of China under Grants No. 41471371 and the Natural Science Foundation of Jiangsu Higher Education Institutions of China under Grant No. 15KJB520022.

References

1. Tenenbaum, J., Silva, V., Langford, J.: A global geometric framework for nonlinear dimensionality reduction. Science **290**, 2319–2323 (2000)
2. Belkin, M., Niyogi, P.: Laplacian eigenmaps for dimensionality reduction and data representation. Neural Comput. **15**(6), 1373–1396 (2003)
3. Roweis, S.T., Saul, L.K.: Nonlinear dimensionality reduction by locally linear embedding. Science **290**, 2323–2326 (2000)
4. Zhang, Z.Y., Zha, H.Y.: Principal manifolds and nonlinear dimensionality reduction via tangent space alignment. SIAM J. Sci. Comput. **26**, 313–338 (2004)

5. Law, M.H.C., Jain, A.K.: Incremental nonlinear dimensionality reduction by manifold learning. IEEE Trans. Pattern Anal. Mach. Intell. **28**, 377–391 (2006)
6. Jia, P., Yin, J., et al.: Incremental Laplacian eigenmaps by preserving adjacent information between data points. Pattern Recogn. Lett. **30**, 1457–1463 (2009)
7. Kouropteva, O., Okun, O., et al.: Incremental locally linear embedding. Pattern Recogn. **38**, 1764–1767 (2005)
8. Abdel-Mannan, O., Ben Hamza, A., et al.: Incremental line tangent space alignment algorithm. In: Proceedings of Canadian Conference on Electrical and Computer Engineering (CCECE), pp. 1329–1332. IEEE (2007)
9. Liu, X., Yin, J., Feng, Z., Dong, J.: Incremental manifold learning via tangent space alignment. In: Schwenker, F., Marinai, S. (eds.) ANNPR 2006. LNCS, vol. 4087, pp. 107–121. Springer, Heidelberg (2006). doi:10.1007/11829898_10
10. Zhao, D.F., Yang, L.: Incremental isometric embedding of high-dimensional data using connected neighborhood graphs. IEEE Trans. Pattern Anal. Mach. Intell. **31**, 86–98 (2009)
11. Abdel-Mannan, O., Ben Hamza, A., et al.: Incremental Hessian locally linear embedding algorithm. In: Proceedings of 9th International Symposium on Signal Processing and Its Applications (ISSPA), pp. 1–4. IEEE (2007)
12. Min, W.L., Lu, L., He, X.F.: Locality pursuit embedding. Pattern Recogn. **37**(4), 781–788 (2004)
13. Ling, G, Han, P., et al.: Face recognition via semi-supervised discriminant local analysis. In: Proceedings of International Conference on Signal and Image Processing Applications (ICSIPA), pp. 292–297. IEEE (2015)
14. Li, B., Du, J., Zhang, X.: Feature extraction using maximum nonparametric margin projection. Neurocomputing **188**, 225–232 (2016)
15. Han, P., Yin, O., Ling, G.: Semi-supervised generic descriptor in face recognition. In: Proceedings of International Colloquium on Signal Processing and Its Applications (CSPA), pp. 21–25. IEEE (2015)
16. Xu, Y., Huang, H., et al.: Semi-supervised local fisher discriminant analysis for speaker verification. Adv. Inf. Sci. Serv. Sci. **6**, 1–11 (2014)
17. Artac, M., Jogan, M., Leonardis, A.: Incremental PCA for on-line visual learning and recognition. In: Proceedings of International Conference on Pattern Recognition (ICPR), pp. 781–784. IEEE (2002)
18. Zhao, H., Yuen, P.C., Kwok, J.T.: A novel incremental principal component analysis and its application for face recognition. IEEE Trans. Syst. **36**(4), 873–886 (2006)
19. Li, Y.M.: On incremental and robust subspace learning. Pattern Recogn. **37**(7), 1509–1518 (2004)
20. Weng, J.Y., Zhang, Y.L., Hwang, W.S.: Candid covariance-free incremental principal component analysis. IEEE Trans. Pattern Anal. Mach. Intell. **25**(8), 1034–1040 (2003)
21. Golub, G.H., Van Loan, C.F.: Matrix Computations. Johns Hopkins University Press, Baltimore (2012)

Learning Based K-Dependence
Bayesian Classifiers

Limin Wang[1]([✉]), Yuanxiang Xie[2]([✉]), Huisi Zhou[2], Yiming Wang[2],
and Jiangshan Guo[2]

[1] Key Laboratory of Symbolic Computation and Knowledge Engineering of Ministry
of Education, Jilin University, ChangChun 130012, China
wanglim@jlu.edu.cn
[2] College of Computer Science and Technology,
Jilin University, ChangChun 130012, China
xieyx2113@mails.jlu.edu.cn

Abstract. In this paper, we introduce a new mining algorithm to
improve the classification accuracy rates aiming at the deficiency of the
typical K-Dependence Bayes (KDB) model which ignores the topology
changing as the result of inputing of test instances. Under this condition,
we put forward an algorithm called Base K-Dependence Bayes (B-KDB)
which consists of a Label-based K-Dependence Bayes (L-KDB) algorithm
and a Instance-based K-Dependence Bayes (I-KDB) algorithm. The
I-KDB algorithm is used to build I-KDB model by instances to be tested
and it can deal with the problem of test instances topology keep on
changing. However I-KDB model is extraordinarily sensitive to data and
it may suffer from overfitting and the effect of noisy instances, therefore L-KDB algorithm is designed as complement. After combing these
two algorithms into B-KDB, we built B-KDB model and tested the performance against the KDB model in classification accuracy, precision,
sensitivity-specificity analysis with 10-fold cross validation on 55 real
benchmark datasets from University of California Irvine (UCI) machine
learning repository. The experimental result, which shows the classification accuracy of our model twice as much as KDB, indicates our algorithm efficient and proves our idea of improving the KDB algorithm
classification accuracy feasible.

Keywords: Bayesian Network · Base K-Dependence Bayes algorithm ·
Denial-validity attribute

1 Introduction

Bayesian Networks (BN) [1], based on the Bayesian Rule, an important branch in
Data mining, is a probabilistic graphical model [2] (a type of statistical model)
that represents a set of random variables and their conditional dependencies

---

Y. Wang and J. Guo—These authors contributed equally to this work.

X. Sun et al. (Eds.): ICCCS 2016, Part II, LNCS 10040, pp. 553–566, 2016.
DOI: 10.1007/978-3-319-48674-1_49

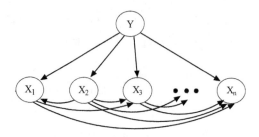

Fig. 1. Bayesian Network (BN)

via a Directed Acyclic Graph (DAG) [3]. In DAG, a node X_i represents a random variable while arcs represent conditional dependencies. A node which is not connected represents that the variable is conditionally independent with others. Bayesian network can be used as a classifier that determines the probability distribution $P(Y|X)$, in which Y denotes class variable label and X represents a set of attributes $X = \{X_1, X_2, X_3, \ldots, X_n\}$, predicts the class variable label with the highest conditional probability. Each node is associated with probability function that takes, as input, a particular set of values for the node's parent variables, and gives (as output) the probability (or probability distribution, if applicable) of the variable represented by the node. Figure 1 graphically shows an example of Bayesian network. The Bayesian network estimates above probability using Eq. 1, the posterior probability formula.

$$P(Y|X_1, X_2, X_3, \ldots, X_n) = \frac{P(Y, X_1, X_2, X_3, \ldots, X_n)}{P(X_1, X_2, X_3, \ldots, X_n)} \tag{1}$$

After deformation, we get the following Eqs. 2 and 3.

$$P(Y|X_1, X_2, X_3, \ldots, X_n) \propto P(Y, X_1, X_2, X_3, \ldots, X_n) \tag{2}$$

$$P(Y, X_1, X_2, X_3, \ldots, X_n) = P(Y)P(X_1|Y)P(X_2|X_1, Y) \ldots P(X_n|X_1, X_2, X_3, \ldots, X_{n-1}, Y) \tag{3}$$

Unfortunately, it has proved that a general BN is a NP-hard [4] problem so its hard to apply Bayes Network into real life to deal 5 with practical problems. In order to avoid the intractable complexity for Bayesian network, Naïve Bayes (NB) algorithm [5] and other improved Naïve Bayes algorithms are proposed such as K-Dependence Bayes Network [6], Tree augmented Naïve Bayes [6], Average One Dependence Estimation [7] and so on.

In NB, each attribute node X_i only has the class node Y but no more attribute nodes as its parent, which means independency among attributes. The topology structure for Naïve Bayes is as Fig. 2. According to the topology structure and Bayesian formula, the posterior probability formula as Eq. 4.

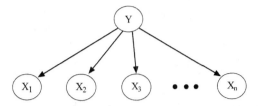

Fig. 2. Naïve Bayes

$$P(C|X) = \frac{P(X|C)P(C)}{P(X)} \quad\quad \text{among} \quad X = \{x_1, x_2, x_3, \ldots, x_n\}$$

$$P(X|C) = P(x_1, x_2, x_3, \ldots, x_n|C) \Rightarrow P(X|C) = P(x_1|C)P(x_2|C)P(x_3|C)\ldots P(x_n|C) \quad (4)$$

$$P(C|X) \propto P(C)\textstyle\prod_{i=1}^{n} P(x_i|C)$$

The strict constraint for each attribute node in Naïve Bayes neglects the conditional dependencies among attribute nodes which may harm the classification accuracy. Amongst all the improved NB algorithms, K-Dependence Bayesian algorithm proposed by Merhan Sahami [8] is the most effective one which allows each attribute X_i to h parent nodes whose maxnum is k, while capturing much of the computational efficiency of the Naïve Bayesian Model. As a result, compared with NB, KDB is more worthy to be trusted in conditional independence assumption. However KDB model is constructed only once using datasets in large quantities to train and no matter how the input-test instances is tested, the topology structure remains unchanged unless we rebuild the topology structure. Thus classification performance in KDB is not ideal. Moreover, since class label depends more on the Denial-validity attribute (D-V attributes) which is defined in the next section, choosing the highest value for Condition Mutual Information (CMI) [9] as a parent cannot perform so well.

In the rest of the paper, we will analyze the disadvantage of KDB and its causes and propose our improved algorithm. Section 2 will list out relevant notions used in our algorithm. Section 3 shows the algorithm of KDB and its core idea. Section 4 gives our final Base K-Dependence Bayes (B-KDB) classifier. Section 6 will list the experiments and results and the comparison with the KDB algorithm on 55 datasets from the UCI [10] machine learning repository. The last section will give conclusions.

2 Relevant Notions and Computing Methods

To present our contribution, we introduce some relevant notions below. Based on information theory from Shanon [8], we redefine the following four formulas and propose a new definition to clarify our algorithm better.

Definition 1. *The mutual information (MI) $I(x_i, Y)$ of x_i and value Y is a measure of the Variables mutual dependence and is defined as follows:*

$$I(x, Y) = \sum_{y \in Y} I(x, y) = \sum_{y \in Y} P(x, y) \log \frac{P(x, y)}{P(x)P(y)} \tag{5}$$

Definition 2. *The mutual information (MI) $I(X_i, y)$ of X_i and value y is a measure of the Variables mutual dependence and is defined as follows:*

$$I(X_i, y) = \sum_{x \in X_i} I(x, y) = \sum_{x \in X_i} P(x, y) \log \frac{P(x, y)}{P(x)P(y)} \tag{6}$$

Definition 3. *Conditional mutual information (CMI) $I(X_i, X_j | y)$ is defined as follows:*

$$I(X_i, X_j | y) = \sum_{x_i, x_j} P(x_i, x_j, y) \log \frac{P(x_i, x_j, y)}{P(x_i | y)P(x_j | y)} \tag{7}$$

Definition 4. *Conditional mutual information (CMI) $I(x_i; y_i | Y)$ is defined as follows:*

$$I(x_i, x_j | Y) = \sum_{y} P(x_i, x_j, y) \log \frac{P(x_i, x_j, y)}{P(x_i | y)P(x_j | y)} \tag{8}$$

Definition 5. *Denial-validity attribute (D-V attributes) is chose as the valid attribute which can estimate the value of the class attribute y if $I(x_i, yy)$ is the minimum value in all $I(x_k, yy)$, x_k represents any attribute node.*

3   K-Dependence Bayes

The disadvantage of NB is that it makes a conditional attribute independence assumption, while it is rarely true in the real-world application. The KDB can weak the condition independence assumption by allowing attributes have extra parents besides the class attribute. Beyond that, it successfully avoids the intractable complexity for BN.

The KDB algorithm is as follows:

(1) Compute MI, $I(X_i; Y)$ for each non-class attribute X_i, where Y represent class attribute, then sort the result in descending order and save the corresponding X_i into an vector $V[n]$, where n represents the number of non-class attribute X.
(2) Compute class CMI $I(X_i, X_j | Y)$ for each pair of attributes X_i and X_j, where $i! = j$.
(3) Construct the Bayesian network (BN) started by setting the class node Y as root.
(4) Set $i = 0$.
(5) Loop until i equal to $n - 1$.
     a. Add node X_i to BN representing $V[i]$.

    b. Add an arc from Y to X_i.

    c. Add $m = min(|n|; k)$ arcs from m distinct attributes X_j in $A[n]$ with the highest value for $I(X_i, X_j|Y)$.

    d. $i = i + 1$.

(6) Compute the conditional probability tables inferred by the structure of BN by using counts from DB, and output BN.

    Supposing that $X = \{X_1; X_2; X_3; X_4; X_5\}, I(X_1; Y) > I(X_2; Y) > I(X_3; Y) > I(X_4; Y) > I(X_5; Y)$. An example of KDB classifier ($K = 2$) shows in Fig. 3, where X is a set of training instance, Y denotes the class attribute, and an arc from X_i to $X_i (i < j)$ means that X_i is a parent of X_j.

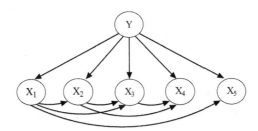

Fig. 3. K-Dependence Bayesian classifier (KDB)

4   Base K-Dependence Bayesian Classifier

4.1   Instance-Based K-Dependence Bayes

In real world, an attribute X_i which affects class label Y are sometimes multiple while attribute label X_i may have a variety of values $x(i, j)$. And the set $x(i, 1), x(i, 2), ..., x(i, n)$ is in large quantity. KDB considers mostly the dependence of attribute labels and the class attribute label while it thinks little of the dependence among attribute values and the class attribute value in each instance. Similar to the proposal of KDB which takes the relationship among attribute labels into consideration, we consider situations that attributes have different relationship when having different values worthy to pay attention to.

    There is an example with four attributes sexual, muscular, height and well-featured and class label good-looking. For a male, the relationship between his sexual and muscular has a great influence on the value of class label good-looking. As for a female, the couple of sexual and muscular affects the class label value weakly.

    Therefore to make full use of the relationship among values of attributes, we construct an Instance-based K-Dependence Bayes model (I-KDB) with the class label and attribute values of instances in training data where each instance has the same attribute values as each in testing data. Since the model constructing is targeted, its prediction performance is highly improved.

The I-KDB algorithm shows as follows:

Input: a database of pre-classified instances, DB, and the K value for the maximum allowable degree of attribute dependence.

Output: a I-KDB classifiers with conditional probability tables determined from the input data.

(1) Compute MI, $I(x_i|Y)$ for each non-class attribute value $x_i \in X$, where Y represent class attributes, then sort the result in descending order and save the corresponding x_i into an vector $V[n]$, where n represents the number of non-class attribute value x_i.

(2) Compute class CMI $I(x_i, x_j|Y)$ for each pair of attributes value x_i and x_j, where $i! = j$.

(3) Construct the Bayesian network (BN) started by setting the class node Y as root.

(4) Set $i = 0$.

(5) Loop until i equal to $n - 1$.
    a. Add node x_i to BN representing $V[i]$.
    b. Add an arc from Y to X_i.
    c. Add $m = min(|n|, k)$ arcs from m distinct attributes x_j in $A[n]$ with highest value for $I(x_i, xj|Y)$.
    d. $i = i + 1$.

(6) Compute the conditional probability tables inferred by the structure of BN.

The topology structure is as Fig. 4 shows, in which each $x(i, j) \in X_i$ represents a possible value of X_i and Y is the class label.

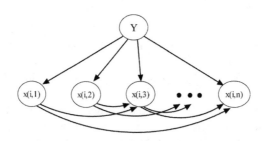

Fig. 4. Instance-based K-Dependence Bayesian (I-KDB)

However, there is a possible existing of overfitting, which means the model cannot be used in a widen area and noisy contradictory instances may lead to accuracy decrease. Besides not all instances in 55 datasets in experiment is made full use, therefore we construct another algorithm below to make up for this deficiency.

4.2   Label-Based K-Dependence Bayes

With the variety of class labels, constructing one model in KDB to estimate the probability of the class label is rarely true. Similar to I-KDBs using values of attributes when constructing model, we construct a Label-based K-Dependence Bayes (L-KDB) model which formalizes the results calculated from all topology structures which regards each value of class labels as a class attribute node. Additionally, we regard a D-V attribute as a more credible attribute. Assume that X_i is the non-class attribute and y is value of the class attribute.

The I-KDB algorithm is as follows:

Input: a database of pre-classified instances, DB, and the K value for the maximum allowable degree of attribute dependence.

Output: a L-KDB classifiers with conditional probability tables determined from the input data.

(1) Compute MI $I(X_i; X_j; y)$ between each non-class attribute and the value of class attribute, then sort the result in descending order and save the corresponding X_i into an vector $V[n]$, where n represents the number of non-class attribute X.

(2) Compute class CMI $I(X_i; X_j; y)$ for each pair of attributes X_i and X_j, where $i! = j$.

(3) Construct the Bayesian network (BN) started by setting the class node y as root.

(4) Set $i = 0$.

(5) Loop until i equal to $n - 1$.

    a. add node X_i to BN representing V[i].

    b. Add an arc from y to X_i.

    c. Add $m = min(|n|, k)$ arcs from m distinct attributes X_j in $A[n]$ with highest value for $I(X_i; X_j; y)$.

    d. $i = i + 1$;

(6) Compute the conditional probability tables inferred by the structure of BN by using counts from DB, and output BN.

(7) if not all the structure based on a y have been built, then go back to the step 2.

(8) Compute and update the conditional probability tables using the standard normalization.

Specific to each class attribute value, constructing topology structures can efficiently lower the probability loss. The topology structures show as follows:

There may be differences between structures constructed for different class attribute labels. For instance, in Fig. 5(a) parents of X_n are X_2 and X_3, while in Fig. 5(b) are X_1 and X_2. We compute the conditional probability tables inferred by each topology structure and get the result using standard function notation, then calculate the value of y_i (y_i is a value of Y) and select the highest as the final result.

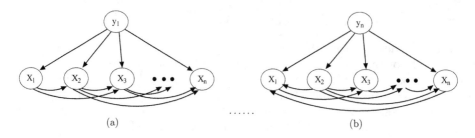

Fig. 5. Label-based K-Dependence Bayesian classifier (L-KDB)

5   Model Merging Algorithm

To combine these two complementary algorithm, an Averaged-Best strategy is achieved which is a math method resembling the Mean Function. Innovatively it attaches more attention to the result which has a higher probability. The A-B Strategy is defined as follows. For each y_i, we calculate the average value and select a model which has the highest value of y_i and then add the two values. Then we standard-normalize the result for each y_i. Supposing that there are two classification models A and B, the probabilities of class attribute value $Y = \{y_1, y_2, y_3\}$ are as follows: According to A-B strategy, for each class attribute value. Add the averaged value of A and B to the bigger one and then normalize the result. In the example above, the final probability is A-B $(y_1, y_2, y_3) = 34.6\%, 42.3\%, 23.1\%$. And y_2 is selected. When using the mean function, the final probability is $(y_1, y_2, y_3) = 40\%, 40\%, 40\%$. The probability of y_1 is the same as y_2 and we cannot select a unique y. Compared with Mean Function, A-B strategy improves the proportion of incredible probability (Table 1).

Table 1. Instance

	y_1	y_2	y_3
A	50%	10%	40%
B	30%	70%	0%

6   Experiments and Results

Aiming at promoting the KDB algorithm, we conduct our experiments with 10-fold cross validation method on 55 real benchmark datasets from UCI machine learning repository to compare the class probability estimation performance of I-KDB, L-KDB and B-KDB with KDB model in terms of three indexes including 0–1 loss, bias and variance. 0–1 loss is used to measure degree of inaccuracy. Bias

Table 2. 55 datasets.

Name	INS	ATT	Class	Name	INS	ATT	Class
anneal	898	38	6	lymphography	148	18	4
audio	226	69	24	new-thyroid	215	5	3
autos	205	25	7	nursery	12960	8	5
balance-scale	625	4	3	optdigits	5620	64	10
breast-cancer-w	699	9	2	page-blocks	5473	10	5
car	1728	6	4	pima-ind-diabetes	768	8	2
chess	551	39	2	poker-hand	1025010	10	10
connect-4	67557	42	3	promoters	106	57	2
contact-lenses	24	4	3	satellite	6435	36	6
contraceptive-mc	1473	9	3	seer-mdl	18962	13	2
credit-a	690	15	2	segment	2310	19	7
crx	690	15	2	shuttle	58000	9	7
cylinder-bands	540	39	2	sick	3772	29	2
dermatology	366	34	6	sign	12546	8	3
dis	3772	29	2	soybean	683	35	19
german	1000	20	2	spambase	4601	57	2
glass-id	214	9	3	splice-c4.5	3177	60	3
heart	270	13	2	syncon	600	60	6
heart-disease-c	303	13	2	thyroid	9169	29	20
hepatitis	155	19	2	tic-tac-toe	958	9	2
horse-colic	368	21	2	vehicle	846	18	4
hungarian	294	13	2	vowel	990	13	11
hypo	3772	29	4	wall-following	5456	24	4
hypothyroid	3163	25	2	waveform	100000	21	3
iris	150	4	3	waveform-5000	5000	40	3
kr-vs.-kp	3196	36	2	wine	178	13	3
labor	57	16	2	zoo	101	16	7
lung-cancer	32	56	3				

and Variance is considered to measure the classifier accuracy and stability. There is no wonder that accuracy is an important index when measuring an algorithm. In the real world, an algorithm may be applied in various domains and we want its accuracy fluctuates in a definitive range. Consequently stability also plays an important role. 0–1 loss, Bias and Variance measures degree of inaccuracy in different angels and the classifier performs better when their values are lower. Besides there is a limit to data size when testing Bias and Variance, in which only some bigger datasets are able for testing.

Table 3. Experimental results of variance.

Name	KDB	AODE	B-KDB	L-KDB	I-KDB
anneal	0.0089	0.0089	0.0067	0.0078	0.0078
audio	0.3230	0.2035	0.2434	0.2124	0.3009
autos	0.2049	0.2049	0.1951	0.1707	0.2244
balance-scale	0.2928	0.2976	0.2960	0.2912	0.2928
breast-cancer-w	0.0744	0.0358	0.0701	0.0916	0.0758
car	0.0382	0.0816	0.0318	0.0347	0.0550
chess	0.0998	0.0998	0.0780	0.0690	0.0944
connect-4	0.2283	0.2420	0.2160	0.2258	0.2228
contact-lenses	0.2500	0.3750	0.4167	0.3750	0.4167
contraceptive-mc	0.5003	0.4942	0.4922	0.4881	0.4969
credit-a	0.1464	0.1391	0.1507	0.1623	0.1565
crx	0.1565	0.1348	0.1478	0.1638	0.1580
cylinder-bands	0.2259	0.1889	0.2204	0.2463	0.2315
dermatology	0.0656	0.0164	0.0246	0.0137	0.0301
dis	0.0138	0.0130	0.0119	0.0125	0.0125
german	0.2890	0.2480	0.2650	0.2870	0.2590
glass-id	0.2196	0.2523	0.2290	0.2056	0.2383
heart	0.2111	0.1704	0.2037	0.2185	0.2037
heart-disease-c	0.2244	0.2013	0.2145	0.2211	0.2079
hepatitis	0.1871	0.1806	0.1677	0.1806	0.1677
horse-colic	0.2446	0.2011	0.2011	0.2228	0.2500
hungarian	0.1803	0.1667	0.1803	0.1769	0.1803
hypo	0.0114	0.0095	0.0109	0.0125	0.0114
hypothyroid	0.0107	0.0136	0.0101	0.0098	0.0130
iris	0.0867	0.0867	0.0733	0.0800	0.0733
kr-vs-kp	0.0416	0.0842	0.0363	0.0457	0.0419
labor	0.0351	0.0526	0.0351	0.0351	0.0702
lung-cancer	0.5938	0.5000	0.5625	0.5625	0.5625
lymphography	0.2365	0.1689	0.1486	0.1486	0.1622
new-thyroid	0.0698	0.0465	0.0605	0.0605	0.0605
nursery	0.0289	0.0730	0.0529	0.0567	0.0547
optdigits	0.0372	0.0311	0.0304	0.0228	0.0391
page-blocks	0.0391	0.0338	0.0316	0.0312	0.0340
pima-ind-diabetes	0.2448	0.2383	0.2383	0.2448	0.2435
poker-hand	0.1961	0.4812	0.0711	0.0723	0.0709
promoters	0.2547	0.1321	0.3302	0.2547	0.3491
satellite	0.1080	0.1148	0.1131	0.1040	0.1299
seer-mdl	0.2165	0.2280	0.2407	0.2506	0.2429
segment	0.0472	0.0342	0.0359	0.0377	0.0476
shuttle	0.0009	0.0008	0.0007	0.0005	0.0012
sick	0.0223	0.0273	0.0231	0.0223	0.0255
sign	0.2539	0.2821	0.2288	0.2379	0.2478
soybean	0.0556	0.0469	0.0571	0.0571	0.0630
spambase	0.0635	0.0672	0.0622	0.0617	0.0752
splice-c4.5	0.0941	0.0365	0.0642	0.0806	0.0790
syncon	0.0133	0.0100	0.0183	0.0150	0.0217
thyroid	0.0706	0.0701	0.0593	0.0559	0.0657
tic-tac-toe	0.2035	0.2651	0.2370	0.2015	0.2714
vehicle	0.2943	0.2896	0.2861	0.2943	0.3132
vowel	0.1818	0.1495	0.1626	0.1556	0.2202
wall-following	0.0401	0.0370	0.0297	0.0368	0.0321
waveform	0.0256	0.0180	0.0189	0.0183	0.0199
waveform-5000	0.2000	0.1462	0.1718	0.1812	0.1844
wine	0.0225	0.0225	0.0393	0.0337	0.0562
zoo	0.0495	0.0297	0.0099	0.0099	0.0297

Table 4. Win/draw/loss record (W/D/L) comparison results of zero-one loss on all datasets.

	KDB	AODE	B-KDB	L-KDB
AODE	28\21\15			
B-KDB	31\26\7	23\19\22		
L-KDB	27\27\10	24\20\20	14\33\17	
I-KDB	20\24\20	14\20\20	0\30\34	10\26\28

Table 5. B-KDB L-KDB I-KDB 0–1 loss W/D/L between bigger and smaller datasets.

	B-KDB			L-KDB			I-KDB		
	W	D	L	W	D	L	W	D	L
Bigger	15	7	2	13	7	4	9	6	9
Smaller	16	19	5	14	20	6	11	18	11
Sum	31	26	7	27	27	10	20	24	20

Furthermore in order to measure the difference on performance on each classifier, a win/draw/loss (W/D/L) record below concisely showing the results is presented for each pair of competitors X and Y with respect to a kind of way for measuring performance. The three numbers together indicates the number of datasets in which X beats, ties with or loses to Y according to the experimental results. When the outcome of a one-tailed binomial sign test is greater than 0.05, we consider the difference significant. Generally when $W > L$, we consider X performs better than Y.

We tested our final B-KDB on 55 datasets from the UCI machine learning repository which has a wide range of domains and data characteristics. Table 2 contains characteristics of each datasets, including the amounts of instances, classes and attributes.

Table 3 shows the averaged 0–1 loss, tested by 10-fold cross-validation to measure estimation accuracy of the proposed algorithm using 55 datasets. We give out the comparison among our B-KDB, L-KDB, I-KDB and KDB, AODE. We can see that the accuracy of our final B-KDB is higher than KDB signally with 31 superior datasets and 7 inferior datasets, which is preliminary expected. Focusing on the comparison between L-KDB and KDB, we observe that the improvement is obvious with 27 superiors and 10 inferiors. With the supplement of I-KDB, the improvement becomes more prominent. Moreover, Fig. 6 presents a more intuitive comparison between results of B-KDB and KDB in which a row and a line respectively represents the number of datasets and the value of 0–1 loss. Its obvious that our B-KDB presents a more stabilized result which means our classifier may behave better when adding new data. Thus its able to avoid the presence of overfitting. Possessing this advantage, B-KDB is more likely to fit a wide range of instances (Table 4).

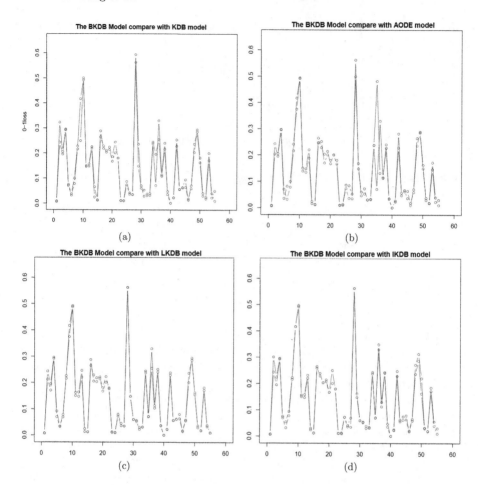

Fig. 6. 0–1 loss comparison between B-KDB and KDB

Besides, we picked out bigger datasets, each with more than 1000 instances, and then make a comparison among our B-KDB, L-KDB and KDB. As Table 5 shows, for bigger datasets, B-KDB has a significant improvement from KDB with 15 wins, 7 draws and 2 loss. And for L-KDB, it also improves a lot with 13 wins, 7 draws and 4 loss. As for smaller ones, B-KDB and L-KDB has a less significant outcome each with 16 wins, 19 draws, 5 losses and 14 wins, 20 draws, 6 losses. Its shows B-KDB has greater efficiency on bigger datasets. After improving, our B-KDB makes up the shortcoming of KDB in smaller datasets. Improving performance in bigger and smaller datasets at the same time makes our B-KDB improves a lot from KDB. The result indicates that we can get a more credible dependency with bigger datasets.

Bias is a way of measuring accuracy. However only some bigger datasets is able to be tested. To explain the results more specifically, here we also divide

Table 6. B-KDB Variance Bias W/D/L.

	Variance	Bias
	KDB	KDB
B-KDB	5 \ 6 \ 3	9 \ 3 \ 2

Table 7. B-KDB Variance and Bias W/D/L between bigger and smaller datasets.

	Variance			Bias		
	W	D	L	W	D	L
Bigger	4	4	1	6	3	0
Smaller	1	2	2	3	0	2
Sum	5	6	3	9	3	2

these selected bigger datasets into a bigger one and a smaller one. From results on Bias in Table 6, we may see that accuracy of our B-KDB has a modest increase than KDB. However, our B-KDB outperforms KDB especially in bigger datasets from Table 7. And the performance distinction on smaller datasets is unconspicuous. For smaller datasets here are ones selected from those who are already bigger ones, how our classifier works on these smaller datasets seems not like that essential. As for Variance, its to measure how sensitive is the classifier to data. Table 5 shows that our B-KDB outperforms much KDB which indicates a proper complexity of dependency and degree of fitting.

7   Conclusions

In modern world, classification acts as an important role in many domains thus how to improve its accuracy is eagerly required. Based on the classical KDB algorithm, we proposed a new Base K-Dependence Bayes (B-KDB) algorithm to amend the static model into a dynamic one in order to have a wider range when fitting data. After experimentally investigating the class probability estimation performance of B-KDB in terms of 0–1 loss, we find its higher accuracy and better stability. To make its performance better than KDB, we construct a model for each class attribute value in L-KDB, coalesced with L-KDB into a L-KDB model. We innovatively trust the rejective dependency instead of the credible dependency in KDB which provides a more restrictive way. Compared with KDB, B-KDB has the advantages bellow:

1. Classification accuracy doubles;
2. High anti-noise property. Its able to present an excellent performance facing high-noise data;
3. No overfitting. B-KDB can give an accurate classification predict for new-added data.

With the optimized performance, the application of B-KDB is likely to improve medical diagnostic accuracy which brings convenience for medical stuffs and patients.

References

1. Bielza, C., Larranaga, P.: Discrete Bayesian network classifiers: a survey. ACM Comput. Surv. **47**, 1–43 (2014)
2. Sloin, A., Wiesel, A.: Proper quaternion Gaussian graphical models. IEEE. Trans. Signal Process. **62**, 5487–5496 (2014)
3. Cheng, J., Greiner, R., Kelly, J., Bell, D., Liu, W.: Learning Bayesian networks from data: an information-theory based approach. Artif. Intell. **137**, 43–90 (2002)
4. Cooper, G.F.: The computational complexity of probabilistic inference using Bayesian belief networks. Artif. Intell. **42**, 393–405 (1990)
5. Minsky, M.: Steps toward artificial intelligence. Proc. IRE **49**, 8–30 (1961)
6. Friedman, N., Geiger, D., Goldszmidt, M.: Bayesian network classifiers. Mach. Learn. **29**, 131–163 (1997)
7. Webb, G.I., Boughton, J., Wang, Z.: Not so Naïve Bayes: aggregating one-dependence estimators. Mach. Learn. **58**, 5–24 (2005)
8. Sahami, M.: Learning limited dependence Bayesian classifiers. In: Proceedings of the Second International Conference on Knowledge Discovery and Data Mining (KDD 1996), Portland, OR, USA, pp. 335–338, 2–4 August 1996
9. Zhang, H., Sheng, S.: Learning weighted Naïve Bayes with accurate ranking. In: The 4th IEEE International Conference on Data Ming. IEEE Computer Society, Chicago (2004)
10. Asuncion, A., Newman, D.J.: UCI Machine Learning Repository. University of California, Department of Information and Computer Science, Irvine, CA (2007). http://www.ics.uci.edu/mlearn/MLRepository.html

Scale Invariant Kernelized Correlation Filter Based on Gaussian Output

Xiangbo Su, Baochang Zhang$^{(\boxtimes)}$, Linlin Yang, Zhigang Li, and Yun Yang

School of Automation Science and Electrical Engineering,
Beihang University, Beijing, China
bczhang@buaa.edu.cn

Abstract. Kernelized Correlation Filter (KCF) is one of state-of-the-art trackers. However, KCF suffers from the drifting problem due to inaccurate localization caused by the scale variation and wrong candidate selection. In this paper, we propose a new method, named Scale Invariant KCF (SIKCF), which estimates an accurate scale and models the distribution of correlation response to address the template drifting problem. The features of SIKCF consist in: (1) A scale estimation method is used to find an accurate candidate. (2) The correlation response of the target image is reasonably considered to follow a Gaussian distribution, which is used to select the better candidate in tracking procedure. Extensive experiments on the commonly used tracking benchmark show that the proposed method significantly improves the performance of KCF, and achieves a better performance than state-of-the-art trackers.

Keywords: Tracking · Correlation filters · Scale invariant

1 Introduction

Visual object tracking is one of the most important problem in numerous applications of computer vision, including robotics, video surveillance, and intelligent vehicles [1]. The problem involves estimating the states of the target object in subsequent image frames, with initial state (position and size) given. Despite many works have solved object tracking problem in simple scenes, online object tracking in complex scenarios remains a great challenge due to significant variations in appearance, such as occlusion, illumination variation, motion blur, etc. [1–4]. As the appearances of object and background are ordinarily dynamic and variable, the conventional data association and temporal filters [23] relying on motion modeling typically fail.

Most recently, the KCF tracker, which works by learning a kernelized discriminative classifier of the target appearance and uses a specific model namely circulant matrices for translations, has shown excellent tracking performance [5,8–10]. The KCF experimentally outperforms many other state-of-the-art trackers while maintaining running at high speed. Despite the performance of the KCF is extremely competitive, it is still prone to drift in long-term tracking,

© Springer International Publishing AG 2016
X. Sun et al. (Eds.): ICCCS 2016, Part II, LNCS 10040, pp. 567–577, 2016.
DOI: 10.1007/978-3-319-48674-1_50

due to the scale variation of target and wrong candidate selection. The fixed-size search window would introduce noises into the KCF when scale variations exist, which would lead to inaccurate localization. Moreover, the KCF persistently execute its incremental learning mechanism without filtrating candidates when updating the model of target, which might introduce even more noises to the filter and eventually leads to drift the tracker away [16,19]. In this paper, we have tackled the problem of inaccurate localization caused by scale variation and template drift to achieve stable long-term tracking and robustness to appearance variation.

Our approach builds on two significant observations as mentioned above, which correspond to two main crux to improve the performance of tracking: (i) estimating the accurate scale of a target and (ii) avoiding from template drift in long-term tracking. For scale estimation, the proposed tracker learns a separated 1-dimensional correlation filter. For training the scale filter, we construct a scale feature pyramid as input, and detect the optimal scale of the target from corresponding response output. When a new scale is estimated, a new image patch of target with accurate scale is cropped, which can be used to update the translation filter and to predict the position more accurately in the next frame.

For solving the problem of drift, we propose a coarse and fine tuning method based on Gaussian distributed output. Data typically lies on specific distributions, i.e., faces are considered to be from subspace [17,18]. As long as the optimal solution resides on the data domain, the constraints derived from the data structure can bring robustness to the variations [11–13]. We propose an assumption that the maximum correlation response should comply with Gaussian distribution when the target is tracked precisely in each frame. As we know, it can be considered as well-tracked when a sample are highly correlated with the ideal model, with the result that the maximal correlation outputs distribute around the mean value in a comparatively great probability. This could be confirmed through observation in practice. Different with existing works which use fixed threshold of correlation output to detect the failure case, we develop a Gaussian constraint method to reduce noisy samples, which take full advantage of the manifold structure of video data. As the variations between two successive frames are commonly small, the response values hardly fall into intervals far from the mean value. Hence, the wrong candidates are detected by determine whether the correlation response comply with a Gaussian distribution. If not, it is reasonable to believe that the tracker drift in current frame. Then the coarse and fine tuning is executed to detect the accurate translation of the target around.

Figure 1 shows the proposed approach, which mainly innovates at learning robust and scale invariant kernelized correlation filters for long-term object tracking. The Gaussian prior constraint and scale estimation are interrelated and interact on each other, which could reduce noisy samples and achieve accurate tracking without drifting. By incorporating the constraint and scale estimation, our tracker has shown to be stable and scale-invariant in long-term tracking. Experimentally, we show that our proposed algorithm outperforms state-of-the-art trackers on a benchmark dataset of 51 sequences, while maintaining computational efficient.

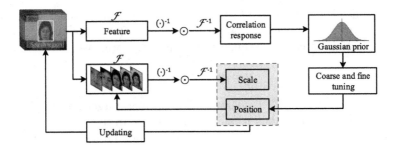

Fig. 1. A scheme of the proposed SIKCF for object tracking.

2   Related Work: Kernelized Correlation Filter

KCF starts from the kernel ridge regression method [9], which is formulated as:

$$
\min_{w,\xi} \quad \sum_i \xi_i^2
$$
$$
subject\ to\ \ y_i - \boldsymbol{w}^T\boldsymbol{\phi}(x_i) = \xi_i\ \ \forall i;\quad ||w|| \le B \tag{P1}
$$

Here, x_i is a $M \times N$-sized image. $\phi(.)$ is a non-linear transformation. $\phi(x_i)$ (later ϕ_i) and y_i are the input and output of the filter respectively. ξ_i is a slack variable. B is a small constant. According to the Lagrangian method, the objective corresponding to P1 is rewritten as:

$$
\mathcal{L}_p = \sum_{i=1}^{M \times N} \xi_i^2 + \sum_{i=1}^{M \times N} \beta_i \left[y_i - \boldsymbol{w}^T\phi_i - \xi_i\right] + \lambda(||\boldsymbol{w}||^2 - B^2) \tag{1}
$$

where λ is a regularization parameter ($\lambda \ge 0$). From Eq. 1, we have:

$$
\boldsymbol{\alpha} = (K + \lambda \boldsymbol{I})^{-1}\boldsymbol{y},
$$
$$
\boldsymbol{w} = \sum_i \alpha_i \phi_i. \tag{2}
$$

The matrix K with elements $K_{ij} = K(x_i, x_j) = \phi(x_i)^T \phi(x_j)$. Taking advantage of the circulant matrix [8], circulant matrix K can be obtained with circulant inputs and the FFT of $\boldsymbol{\alpha}$ denoted by $\mathcal{F}(\boldsymbol{\alpha})$ is calculated by:

$$
\mathcal{F}(\boldsymbol{\alpha}) = \frac{\mathcal{F}(y)}{\mathcal{F}(k^{xx}) + \lambda}, \tag{3}
$$

where $\mathcal{F}$ denotes the discrete Fourier operator, and k^{xx} is the first row of the circulant matrix K. In tracking, all candidate patches that are cyclic shifts of test patch z are evaluated by:

$$
\mathcal{F}(z) = \mathcal{F}(k^{z\hat{x}}) \odot \mathcal{F}(\boldsymbol{\alpha}), \tag{4}
$$

where $\odot$ is the element-wise product and $\hat{x}$ means the learned target appearance model of x. Here $\hat{x}$ is calculated by Eq. 6a [19] and $\mathcal{F}(z)$ is the output response for all the testing patches in frequency domain. Then we have:

$$\hat{y} = \max(\mathcal{F}^{-1}(z)), \qquad (5)$$

where $\mathcal{F}^{-1}$ is the inverse FFT operator. The optimal target position is the one with the maximal value among $\hat{y}$ calculated by Eq. 5. In the tth frame, the target appearance model and correlation filter are then updated with a learning rate η as:

$$\begin{cases} \hat{x}^t = (1 - \eta)\hat{x}^{t-1} + \eta x^t, & (6a) \\ \mathcal{F}(\alpha^t) = (1 - \eta)\mathcal{F}(\alpha^{t-1}) + \eta\mathcal{F}(\alpha). & (6b) \end{cases}$$

We use HOG features to learn the translation filter. As an input for the filter, feature map of x_i is extracted from the target region. The position of the target in a new frame is estimated by compute the maximum correlation response $\hat{y}$ using Eqs. 4 and 5. Then the filter is updated using Eq. 6. The following subsection describes how the coarse and fine tuning works based on gaussian constraints.

3   SIKCF

For the purpose of developing an online object tracker that is robust to appearance variation without drift, we divide the task into two parts. The first part is target detection, which locates the target precisely by coarse and fine tuning with gaussian constraints based on KCF. The second part is scale estimation which is achieved by learning a 1-dimensional correlation filter. By this strategy, we can achieve our purpose while still maintaining computational efficient.

3.1   Coarse and Fine Tuning Based on Gaussian Constraints

Since the appearance of a target would alter over time, the tracker might gradually drift and finally fail to track the object. Existing works use fixed threshold for correlation outputs to detect the failure case and take measure to re-detect the target. That might be not adaptable to all cases since the performance is partly determined by the threshold. We propose an assumption that the maximum correlation response should comply with Gaussian distribution when the target is tracked precisely in each frame, which partly results from the manifold structure of data in videos or image sequences. This could be confirmed through observation in practice.

We argue that the maximal response value between the well-tracked sample and the filter belongs to a Gaussian distribution:

$$\hat{y}^t \sim \mathcal{N}(\mu^t, \sigma^{t^2}) \qquad (7)$$

where μ^t and σ^t are the mean and variance of the Gaussian distribution respectively in current frame, which are calculated from all the previous frames. Then a sample is accepted when satisfying the following equation:

$$\left| \frac{\hat{y}^t - \mu^t}{\sigma^t} \right| < \mathcal{T}_g \tag{8}$$

where $\mathcal{T}_g = 1.6$ is empirically set to a constant.

We propose a coarse and fine tuning method to precisely localize the target. If the maximal correlation response is out of the Gaussian distribution, the tracking is considered as drifting, which would activate the coarse and fine tuning process. The coarse tuning is implemented by sampling a set of candidate patches in a local region, instead of searching over the whole image extensively. We first generate sets of n_r different transformations in each of n_t directions around the last location (x_{t-1}, y_{t-1}) within a radius, resulting in a set of $n_r * n_t$ candidate patches centered around the target:

$$Z = \{z_1, z_2, \ldots, z_{n_r * n_t}\}. \tag{9}$$

Our purpose is to find the optimal patch where the target would appear with the maximum probability. Hence, the maximal correlation response of each patch is obtained by:

$$\begin{cases} r_i = \max(\mathcal{F}^{-1}(\mathcal{F}(z_i))), \\ \mathcal{F}(z_i) = \mathcal{F}(k^{z_i \hat{x}}) \odot \mathcal{F}(\alpha). \end{cases} \tag{10}$$

Then the optimal candidate is selected by:

$$\hat{z} = \operatorname*{argmax}_{i=1}^{n_r * n_t} (z_i). \tag{11}$$

Given the optimal patch $\hat{z}$, the fine-tuning step is executed to find the location of the object precisely as shown in Eq. (4).

The first 20 frames are empirically treat as initialization process, which make the mean and variance value comparatively stable and reliable. By the coarse and fine tuning based on Gaussian output, the wrong candidates can be filtered out, which reduces the noises for learning both the translation and scale filer.

3.2   Scale Estimation

In our approach, the position of a target is detected by the translation filter as mentioned above, and the scale variation is estimated by learning a separate 1-dimensional correlation filter. Considering that scale variation between two consecutive frames is ordinarily smaller than translation, in a new frame, we first detect the location of target by the kernelized correlation filter based on Gaussian output. During tracking, we construct a scale feature pyramid as input for training the scale filter, which consists of features extracted from image patches of various sizes around the estimated position. We consider a target;

Algorithm 1 - The SIKCF algorithm for object tracking

1: Initial target bounding box $b_0 = (x_0, y_0, s_0)$.
2: **repeat**
3:     Crop out the search windows according to $(x_{n-1}, y_{n-1}, s_{n-1})$, and extract the HOG features.
4:     Update the maximum correlation response $\hat{y}$ using Eqs. 4 and 5 and record the maximal correlation response as y_n.
5:     **if** the frame $n \leq 20$ **then**
6:         The position (x_n, y_n) is obtained according to the maximal correlation response.
7:     **else**
8:         Compute the mean μ and variance σ^2 using $\{y_1, y_2, \ldots, y_{n-1}\}$.
9:         **if** $\left|\frac{\hat{y}-\mu}{\sigma}\right| > T_g$ **then**
10:             Crop out a set of candidate patches $Z = \{z_1, z_2, \ldots, z_{n_r * n_t}\}$ with scale s_{n-1} around (x_{n-1}, y_{n-1}).
11:             **Coarse searching step:**
                Detect the optimal patch $\hat{z}$ with maximal response using Eqs. 10 and 11
12:             **Fine searching step:**
                Locate the position (x_n, y_n) precisely from patch $\hat{z}$ using Eq. 4.
                Update y_n by the maximum correlation response.
13:         **end if**
14:     **end if**
15:     **Scale estimation step:**
        Construct the scale pyramid around (x_n, y_n) and estimate the optimal scale s_n by scale filer using Eq. 13.
16:     Update translation filter and scale filter using Eq. 6.
17: **until** End of the video sequence.

---

whose size is $P \times Q$ in current frame. Let N_s be the size of scale filter. For each $k \in \{a^n | n = [-\frac{N_s-1}{2}], [-\frac{N_s-3}{2}], \ldots, [\frac{N_s-1}{2}]\}$, we crop an image patch J_s of size $kP \times kQ$. Here, a donates scale factor. Therefore, N_s image patches with different scale centered around the target are cropped as:

$$J = \{J_1, J_2, \ldots, J_{N_s}\}. \tag{12}$$

As in Eq. 10, let r_i denote the maximal correlation response of each patch J_i. Then the scale that the target most probably appears with is obtained by:

$$\hat{J} = \underset{i=1}{\overset{N_s}{\arg\max}}(J_i). \tag{13}$$

Correspondingly, the scale filter is updated separately by Eq. 6. Each new estimated scale provides a new image patch that can be used to update the translation filter and to predict the position more accurately in the next frame. To sum up, Algorithm 1 recaps the complete method.

4   Experiments

We evaluate our tracker on a commonly used benchmark [6] that contains 51 sequences, with comparisons to state-of-the-art methods. The selection of Gaussian kernel and most parameters is based on [9]: $\lambda = 10^{-4}$, $\rho = 0.1$. We set the searching window for translation estimation to 1.5 times of the target size. The size of scale space is $N_s = 33$ and the scale factor a is set to 1.02. For parameters of coarse tuning, we empirically set $n_r = 5$, $n_t = 16$. The experiments are implemented with the same parameter values for all sequences.

When KCF tracker performs well, the maximal correlation response of the target approximately follows a Gaussian distribution. As shown in Fig. 2a, when KCF fails to track a target, the histogram of response output obviously becomes irregular. Figure 2b shows that in our proposed SIKCF, the output is constrained to comply with a Gaussian distribution, meanwhile the tracking performance is significantly improved. The detailed comparisons between KCF and SIKCF on these sequences can be seen in Fig. 4.

We report the experimental results on the benchmark of 51 sequences using the distance precision and overlap success rate by the area-under-curve(AUC). If the distance between a predicted target center and the labeled ground truth is within a threshold, the target is considered to be correctly tracked in current frame. Similarly, if the overlap between a predicted target region and the ground truth is larger than a threshold, the tracking on current frame is thought to be successful. The precision and success curves show the percentage of frames where the target is correctly or successfully tracked within the given threshold. We compare our proposed SIKCF with 10 state-of-the-art trackers of top rank.

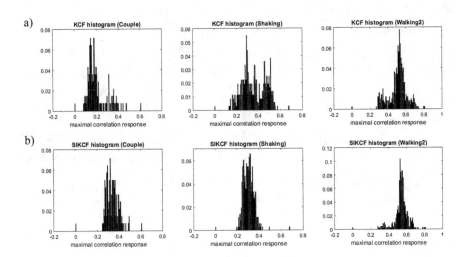

Fig. 2. Illustration of KCF and the proposed SIKCF on three sequences. The correlation response outputs in SIKCF are constrained to follow a Gaussian distribution, meanwhile SIKCF improves the performance of KCF on these sequences.

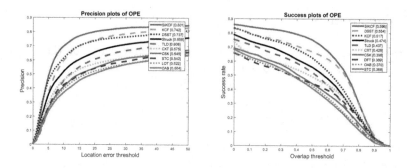

Fig. 3. Success and precision plots according to the online tracking benchmark [6]

As show in Fig. 3, the proposed SIKCF algorithm perform well against the existing trackers in terms of distance precision (DP) and overlap success (OS). Among these existing trackers, the KCF achieves the best result in precision, with DP (threshold = 20 pixels) of 74.2 %; the DSST, one of latest variants of KCF, achieves the best result in success with OS (AUC) of 55.4 %. Our SIKCF reports the results with DP of 80.1 % and OS of 59.6 %. From the experimental results, it can be seen that the proposed SIKCF achieves significantly higher performance than the KCF, and outperforms state-of-the-art trackers.

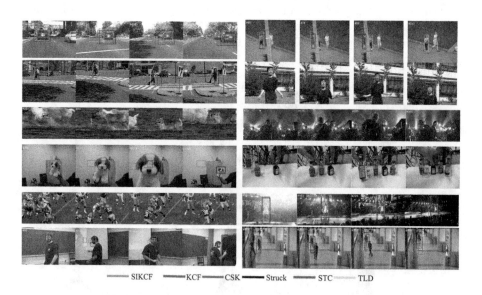

Fig. 4. Illustration of some key frames on 12 challenging sequences (from top to down and left to right: *Car4, Couple, Deer, Dog1, Football, Freeman1, Jogging-1, Jumping, Shaking, Liquor, Singer1, Walking2*).

We compare our proposed SIKCF with other five state-of-the-art trackers on 12 challenging sequences, and illustrate the tracking results from some key frames in Fig. 4. The KCF tracker drifts when the targets move fast (Deer, Jumping), while SIKCF, STC and TLD perform well. When the targets undergo heavy occlusions (Football, Jogging-1, Liquor), the SIKCF tracks well while other trackers fail to track the target successfully. Moreover, the KCF can not handle background clutter (Couple, Shaking) as well as significant deformation (Freeman1), but SIKCF improves the performance of KCF. The TLD tracker is able to estimate scale variation, but fail to perform well than SIKCF when there is background clutter or illumination variation (Car4, Singer1, Dog1). Overall, our proposed SIKCF perform well on all the 12 challenging sequences, both in scale and position estimation.

In Matlab on an Intel I5 3.20 GHZ (4 cores) CPU with 8GB RAM, the KCF achieves high frame rate to 185 frames per second (fps), while the SIKCF achieves 42 fps. Without losing the real-time performance, the proposed SIKCF significantly improves the performance of KCF by about 6 % on the distance precision and 8 % on overlap success.

5   Conclusion

In this paper, we propose a stable and robust algorithm for visual object tracking. Our approach learns discriminative correlation filters separately for translation and scale of the target. Estimation for translation is achieved by correlation output constraint to Gaussian distribution based on correlation filter tracking. By coarse and fine tuning, we can precisely estimate the location of target. The optimal scale of target is obtained by learning a 1-dimensional correlation filer, where scale feature pyramid is extracted as the input. Experimentally, we show that the proposed algorithm remarkably improves the performance of KCF, and outperforms the state-of-the-art trackers while still maintaining computational efficient.

Acknowledgements. This work was supported in part by the Natural Science Foundation of China under Contract 61272052, 61473086, 61672079, 61601466, in part by PAPD, in part by CICAEET, and in part by the National Basic Research Program of China under Grant 2015CB352501. The work of B. Zhang was supported by the Program for New Century Excellent Talents University within the Ministry of Education, China, and Beijing Municipal Science & Technology Commission Z161100001616005. Baochang Zhang is corresponding author.

References

1. Yilmaz, A., Javed, O., Shah, M.: Object tracking: a survey. ACM Comput. Survey **38**(4), 13 (2006)
2. Yao, R., Shi, Q., Shen, C., Zhang, Y., Hengel, A.V.: Part-based visual tracking with online latent structural learning. In: Proceedings of the IEEE Conference on Computer Vision and Pattern Recognition(CVPR), pp. 25–27. IEEE (2013)

3. Adam, A., Rivlin, E., Shimshoni, I.: Robust fragments-based tracking using the integral histogram. In: Proceedings of the IEEE Conference on Computer Vision and Pattern Recognition (CVPR), pp. 798–805. IEEE (2006)
4. Ross, D.A., Lim, J., Lin, R.S., Yang, M.H.: Incremental learning for robust visual tracking. Int. J. Comput. Vis. **77**(1–3), 125–141 (2008)
5. Zhang, K., Zhang, L., Yang, M., Zhang, D.: Fast tracking via spatio-temporal context learning. In: Proceedings of European Conference on Computer Vision (ECCV), pp. 127–141. IEEE (2014)
6. Wu, Y., Lim, J., Yang, M.-H.: Online object tracking: a benchmark. In: Proceedings of the IEEE Conference on Computer Vision and Pattern Recognition (CVPR), pp. 2411–2418. IEEE (2013)
7. Han, Z., Jiao, J., Zhang, B., Ye, Q., Liu, J.: Visual object tracking via sample-based adaptive sparse representation. Pattern Recogn. **44**(9), 2170–2183 (2011)
8. Henriques, J.F., Caseiro, R., Martins, P., Batista, J.: Exploiting the circulant structure of tracking-by-detection with kernels. In: Proceedings of European Conference on Computer Vision (ECCV), pp. 702–715. IEEE (2012)
9. Henriques, J.F., Caseiro, R., Martins, P., Batista, J.: High speed tracking with kernelized correlation filters. IEEE Trans. Pattern Anal. Mach. Intell. **37**(3), 583–596 (2015)
10. Danelljan, M., Hager, G., Khan, F.S., Felsberg, M.: Accurate scale estimation for robust visual tracking. In: Proceedings of British Machine Vision Conference (BMVC). BMVA Press, 1–5 September 2014
11. Zhang, B., Perina, A., Li, Z., Murino, V., Liu, J., Ji, R.: Bounding multiple gaussians uncertainty with application to object tracking. Int. J. Comput. Vis., pp. 1–16 (2016)
12. Kalal, Z., Mikolajczyk, K., Matas, J.: Tracking-learning-detection. IEEE Trans. Pattern Anal. Mach. Intell. **34**(7), 1409–1422 (2012)
13. Cabanes, G., Bennani, Y.: Learning topological constraints in self-organizing map. In: Wong, K.W., Mendis, B.S.U., Bouzerdoum, A. (eds.) ICONIP 2010. LNCS, vol. 6444, pp. 367–374. Springer, Heidelberg (2010). doi:10.1007/978-3-642-17534-3_45
14. Bishop, C.M.: Pattern Recognition and Machine Learning. Elsevier, New York (2006)
15. Gu, B., Sheng, V.S., Tay, K.Y., Romano, W., Li, S.: Incremental support vector learning for ordinal regression. IEEE Trans. Neural Netw. Learn. Syst. **26**(7), 1403–1416 (2015)
16. Zhang, B., Li, Z., Perina, A., Del Bue, A., Murino, V.: Adaptive local movement modelling (ALMM) for object tracking. In: IEEE Transactions on Circuits and Systems for Video Technology, in press
17. Wright, J., Yang, A.Y., Ganesh, A., Sastry, S.S., Ma, Y.: Robust face recognition via sparse representation. IEEE Trans. Pattern Anal. Mach. Intell. **31**(2), 210–227 (2009)
18. Zhang, B., Perina, A., Murino, V., Del Bue, A.: Sparse representation classification with manifold constraints transfer. In: Proceedings of the IEEE Conference on Computer Vision and Pattern Recognition (CVPR), pp. 4557–4565 (2015)
19. Ma, C., Yang, X., Zhang, C., Yang, M.-H.: Long-term correlation tracking. In: Proceedings of the IEEE Conference on Computer Vision and Pattern Recognition (CVPR), pp. 5388–5396 (2015)
20. Ren, Y., Shen, J., Wang, J., Han, J., Lee, S.: Mutual verifiable provable data auditing in public cloud storage. J. Internet Technol. **16**(2), 317–323 (2015)

21. Ma, T., Zhou, J., Tang, M., Tian, Y., Al-Dhelaan, A., Al-Rodhaan, M., Lee, S.: Social network and tag sources based augmenting collaborative recommender system. In: IEICE transactions on Information and Systems, vol. E98-D, no. 4, pp. 902–910, April 2015
22. Li, J., Li, X., Yang, B., Sun, X.: Segmentation-based image copy-move forgery detection scheme. IEEE Trans. Inf. Forensics Secur. **10**(3), 507–518 (2015)
23. Nummiaro, K., Koller-Meier, E.: An adaptive color-based particle filter. Image Vis. Comput. **21**(1), 99–110 (2003)

A Novel Selective Ensemble Learning Based on K-means and Negative Correlation

Liu Liu$^{(\boxtimes)}$, Baosheng Wang$^{(\boxtimes)}$, Bo Yu$^{(\boxtimes)}$, and Qiuxi Zhong$^{(\boxtimes)}$

College of Computer, National University of Defense Technology,
Changsha 410073, China
{hotmailliuliu,hotmailwbs,
BoYUnudt,Qiuxizhong}@163.com

Abstract. Selective ensemble learning has drawn high attention for improving the diversity of the ensemble learning. However, the performance is limited by the conflicts and redundancies among its child classifiers. In order to solve these problems, we put forward a novel method called KNIA. The method mainly makes use of K-means algorithm, which is used in the integration algorithm as an effective measure to choose the representative classifiers. Then, negative correlation theory is used to select the diversity of classifiers derived from the representative classifiers. Compared with the classical selective learning, our algorithm which is inverse growth process can improve the generalization ability in the condition of ensuring the accuracy. The extensive experiments demonstrate that the robustness and precision of the proposed method outperforms four classical algorithms from multiple UCI data sets.

Keywords: Ensemble learning · K-means · Negative correlation · Neural network

1 Introduction

With the development of machine learning, various methods are put forward continually [1–3]. Since Hansen and Salamon proposed neural network ensemble learning [4], ensemble learning has become an important branch of machine learning. It is also considered as the first of the four directions in machine learning by Dietterich [5]. Although many researchers have proposed different methods [6–8] to improve the conventional algorithms on good generalization ability and the diversity, but these can still lead to huge computational overhead for most users.

Usually ensemble learning is defined as, using different algorithms to solve the same problem, and using a strategy to integrate the separate solutions to achieve a joint decision [9]. The ensemble learning can be divided into two categories. One is only a method as the basic algorithm [10], such as Random-Forest algorithm [11], EENCL [12], GA-SVMs [13]. And the other is a variety of methods as the base, such as ensemble diversity measures. Ensemble learning is to diversity advantage into better learning accuracy, but the diversity maybe lead to significant time and space complexity. Selective ensemble learning method [14] was presented to give a solution to the problem. "Selective ensemble" concept was first introduced by Zhou [15], and had

© Springer International Publishing AG 2016
X. Sun et al. (Eds.): ICCCS 2016, Part II, LNCS 10040, pp. 578–588, 2016.
DOI: 10.1007/978-3-319-48674-1_51

theoretical and experimental demonstration. Due to selective ensemble learning makes the weak learning algorithm combined with a strong learning algorithm, it has been a strong focus on the international academic community. But the difficulty lies in how to choose the algorithm by eliminating redundancy algorithm to reduce the computational complexity, and how to enhance the integration of diversity through the selection algorithm.

In the remainder of this article, the related knowledge to selective ensemble learning is introduced in Sect. 2. In Sect. 3, a novel selective ensemble learning (KNIA) is described, which has dynamic adaptability. This algorithm uses k-means to generate the representative classifiers, and then applies a negative correlation to select the derived algorithms. Different from traditional methods, this new method trains and chooses new algorithms by incremental learning, rather than training and testing all the algorithms. KNIA algorithm has more accuracy than other classical algorithms. This novel approach will significantly reduce the number of training and enhance the algorithm's adaptability and diversity. In Sect. 4, there are three experiments to show our algorithm has higher performance than other classical algorithms. To the impartiality of the experimental results, our experiments adopted the five experimental data from UCI. Finally, we summarize this paper and outline some future researches.

2 Related Work

Compared with other ensemble learning algorithms, the goal of the selective ensemble algorithm is to choose a subset from a large library of classifiers. The selective algorithm excludes the redundant classifiers to construct a streamlined ensemble learning. Thereby, it is able to reduce the storage space, and the computational complexity of ensemble learning approach. In the other words, the diversity and the quality among basal classifiers are important factors for improving the selective ensemble learning performance [16]. According to the characteristics of the current mainstream selective ensemble learning methods, it can be divided into three categories: according to the correlation about the subset of algorithms, according to the data set processing method, and according to the classification algorithm optimization. Correlation between the underlying algorithms generally can be divided into clustering algorithm based on distance metric and negative correlation algorithm utilizing the output of difference. Clustering is one of the unsupervised learning for analyzing data relationship. Clustering has the ability to divide similar data into the same class. This classification ability is based on some features, such as Euclidean distance. Negative correlation algorithm will be described in the following sections.

Using of processing data sets to design ensemble learning generally has two ways, one is the data set using different sampling methods, such as Bagging [17], Boosting [18, 19], AdaBoost [20]; the other is a set of data to extract its own characteristics, for example wrap, Attribute Bagging [21], FS-PP-EROS method [22]. The former tries to extract the dataset from different aspects as different training sets. So we can train up the different characteristics of methods with the different training sets. Difference between the two is to use different strategies to choose the training sets. The latter focuses on the choice of properties. However, the former produces different training sets that are obtained by random sampling.

The selective ensemble algorithm is optimized by coordinating the relationship between sub-algorithms. At present the Optimization method mainly makes use of the genetic algorithm, such as GASEN [23], PSO optimization algorithm [24]. GASEN assigns initial weights to all classifiers and employs genetic algorithm to evolve the weights. Through the evolved weights, it chooses some classifiers combined into the ensemble.

Selective ensemble algorithm apart from the three categories: Kappa Pruning [25], Stacked Generalization [26], mixtures-of-experts [27] and so on. However, these algorithms have a common drawback that will end once the learning algorithm to form a fixed pattern, not suitable for incremental learning, thus reducing the generalization ability of the model. To solve this problem, a novel method will be introduced which has adaptive and incremental capacity in the next section.

3   Algorithm Description

3.1   Selective Ensemble Learning

Construction of selective ensemble learning is divided into three parts: the first part is to determine the sampling methods of data collection, the second part is to choose an appropriate set of algorithms, and the third part is how to integrate independent algorithms to generate the final decision. To simplify the description of selective ensemble learning, M1 represents the sampling method, M2 represents the selection strategy which is used to choose the algorithms with diversity, and M3 stands for the final joint algorithm. M2 generally chooses the representative algorithms which have the minimum generalization error to constitute the ensemble learning, $E = Agrmin_{S_{i \in S}}(e(S_i))$. Where S is the space-based classifier, s_i represents an optional sub-base algorithm space, e denotes an error subspace. Assume that dataset space for training set D and validation set $\underline{D}$, M1 uses the i-th sampling subset $D_i = \{(x_i, y_i) | M1(D) \in D\}$. If M2 uses a classic clustering algorithm, it can be described as selective integration algorithm:

Step 1: The data set in the proportion is divided into a training set D and validation set $\underline{D}$. D_i is the subset of D, which is sampled by Bootstrap method;

Step 2: S uses the training set D_i to train each algorithm, then the validation set D tests the performance of classifier s_i and their output matrix set $O = \{o_1, o_2, \cdots, o_n\}$ are recorded;

Step 3: M2 is a clustering process, which is as follows:

Input: It output $O = \{o_1, o_2, \cdots, o_n\}$ of each individual classifier is input of clustering algorithm;

Output: The plurality of $\{s_1, s_2, s_3, \cdots\}$ are the output of M2;

Processing: Let o_{ih}^l and o_{ih}^j is the output of the algorithm l and j on the h-th sample of the training set D_i. d denotes the differences between $o_{ih}^l = \{y_1, y_2, \cdots, y_n\}$ and

$o_{ih}^j = \{z_1, z_2, \cdots, z_n\}$, the distance function is $d\left(o_{ih}^l, o_{ih}^j\right) =$ $\sqrt{(y_1 - z_1)^2 + (y_2 - z_2)^2 + \cdots + (y_n - z_n)^2}$. If $d(o_{ih}^l, o_{ih}^j)$, l and j will be classified as same category. After completion of the first classification, the various types of center will be updated, and then continue the previous procedure. Until the final point of the center of the sample does not change, then the algorithm ends;

Step 4: Each subclass will adopt the algorithm with the smallest generalization error for a representative algorithms.

Step 5: Using the weights of the algorithm joint. Weight method is to give a certain weight $w_i(\sum_{i=k} w_i = 1)$ to each individual algorithm, and joint decision-making $\sum_{i=k} w_i d_i$.

From the above process, we can know that the traditional methods only choose the child algorithms which have the minimum classification error, without taking into account the relationship between algorithms. But some child algorithms have the positive correlation is that weaken the advantage of the ensemble learning. In the following section, we will introduce a novel algorithm, which reflects the process of selecting the child algorithms with complementary relationship.

3.2 KNIA Algorithm

The purpose of selective ensemble algorithm is to choose the appropriate classifiers instead of the whole algorithm library. ZHOU [15] has proved that many could be better than all. Based on the previous theory, the selective adaptive algorithm can be used instead of the traditional method. Our method does not need training all classifiers, compared with conventional selective ensemble algorithm. The novel algorithm uses an incremental strategy to build an adaptive architecture. K-means produces farther algorithms. And the negative correlation theory is used to select child-classifiers which are derived. If the result cannot achieve the intended effect, a number of new algorithms are constructed, which screened through a negative correlation theory. If the updating achieves the desired effect, the end of the algorithm; if the effect is increased, but the algorithm is not suitable for the expectations, then the algorithm returns to the previous step; if the effect is the same or deteriorated after the addition, then the newly added methods are deleted, and new classifiers are selected. Before the novel algorithm is described, some relevant affirmed must be explained. Suppose there are k representative classifiers, which are to derive the sub-algorithms. Assume that the set $S_{init} = \{c_1, c_2, c_3, \cdots, c_q\}$ represents the initial set of classifiers. Train$(x, y) = \{(x_i, y_i), i \in 1, 2, \cdots, N\}$ and $D = \{(x_i, y_i), i \in m\}$ represent the training data set and the validation data set, $T_1, T_2, T_3, \cdots \in Train(x, y)$ indicates the sample training set. Bagging sampling method is used [24], when the sampling frequency is enough large, there are approximately 36.8% of the data will not be drawn. Then the data is not drawn as the verification data.

Negative correlation [28, 29]: the relationship between child interaction classifiers is by a penalty term θ_i to the performance. If $e_i(N)$ represents the algorithm i at the N-th training error function, you can get the following error expression:

$$E_i(d) = \frac{1}{N}\sum\nolimits_{d=1}^{N} e_i(d) = \frac{1}{N}\sum\nolimits_{d=1}^{N}(F_i(d) - y(d))^2 + \frac{1}{N}\sum\nolimits_{d=1}^{N}\gamma p_i(d)$$

Wherein $p_i(d) = (F_i(d) - F(d))\sum_{i \neq j}(F_j(d) - F(d))$. When $\gamma = 0$ the penalty term is zero, which represents the sub algorithms are an independent. When $\gamma = 1$ calculating $\frac{\partial E_i(d)}{\partial F_i(d)} = F(d) - y(d)$. While similar definition, error function integrated algorithm can be expressed as $E_{en}(n) = \frac{1}{2}\left(\frac{1}{N}\sum_{i=1}^{N}F_i(d) - y(d)\right)$, then $\frac{\partial E_{en}(n)}{\partial F_i(d)} = \frac{1}{M}(F(d) - y(d))$, so as to get the following formula $\frac{\partial E_{en}(n)}{\partial F_i(d)} \propto \frac{\partial E_i(n)}{\partial F_i(d)}$. This indicates that ensemble learning error is passed ultimately by each individual sub algorithm, in order to obtain better accuracy. The ensemble learning uses a negative correlation to select the diversity of sub-classifiers [30].

The description of the novel algorithm is as follows:

Step 1:   Initializing the set has q algorithms (S_{init}), wherein d << n
Step 2:   Using k- means K, different algorithms ($S_{en} = \{c_1, c_2, \cdots, c_k\}$, $K = |S_{en}|$) are obtained from S_{init}. The process refers to the third step of the last section;
Step 3:   Each of the classifier derives M child classifiers, so there are K * M child classifiers. The child classifiers are trained by the samples which are collected by Bagging method
Step 4:   K * M classifiers are processed by a negative correlation method. It excludes the algorithms which does not meet the requirements and holds h child classifiers. $S_{en} = S_{en} + S' = \{c_1, c_2, \cdots, c_K, c_{K+1}, \cdots, c_{K+h}\}$, $K = |S_{en}| + h$, $h \leq |S_{en}|$;
Step 5:   If the updating S_{en} reaches the maximum precision, then stopping. Otherwise, it goes on to step 2;
Step 6:   Finally, the classifiers are connected by the majority voting method

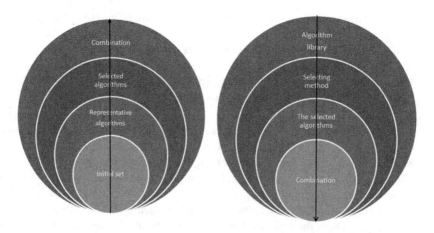

Fig. 1. Comparison chart of the process of the algorithms

We can easily get the novel algorithm's time complexity is O (n1 * m + NktT), wherein the n1 refers to the total number of application of the algorithm, T denotes iteration about our method and O(Nkt) stands for the complexity of k-mean. And the previous algorithm time complexity is O(n * m + nkt), where n represents the size of library, k denotes the numbers of clusters and t is iteration about k-mean. n1 and N are far less than n. And T is a fixed number. Therefore, the complexity of our method is less than the previous algorithms, when the n is very large.

Can be seen from the Fig. 1, our algorithm with adaptive is inverse growth process, which compares with the original algorithm. Algorithms growth process is the direction of arrow along a straight line. The original algorithm is to reach equilibrium by training an algorithm library. However, KNIA is along the opposite view. It incrementally chooses new classifiers with negative correlation to achieve the result of optimization. KNIA uses the K-means algorithm to generate the father algorithms, rather than generating the candidate classifiers directly. This has the advantage that the different fathers have a greater probability of producing the diversity of children. By calculating the negative correlation, the algorithms can be selected with the appropriate subset of difference. KNIA is a derived method can improve the adaptive ability, and strengthen generalization ability. And only a limited number of training algorithms can achieve the desired effect.

4 Experiment

4.1 Comparison of Various Models

One main objective of the experiment is to compare the performance difference between BPNN, Random-Forest method, Decision-Tree method, BPEnsemble and our algorithm. Five data sets from UCI are used in the experiment, which are Wine data set, Breast_Cancer dataset, Vote dataset, Chronic_Kidney dataset, and Phishing_Web_sites_Features dataset. Wine dataset records three kinds of Italian wine ingredients, and it contains 178 samples. And each sample contains 13 different ingredients and a given sample label. Breast-cancer dataset contains 569 various health indicators, including 30 findings parameters and a result label. Vote dataset is the devoting information of the U.S. congress, and it contains 435 examples and 16 properties. Chronic_Kidney_disease dataset is about the chronic kidney disease, which was collected from the hospital nearly 2 months of period. This dataset includes 400 instances and 25 attributes. Phishing_Websites_Features dataset is the latest data set about phishing websites, which contains11055 examples. There are 30 features and a result label in every example (Fig. 2).

BPNN refers to the feed-forward neural network, which has 10 neurons. BPEnsemble is an ensemble learning method using BPNN as a sub algorithm. It contains 100 BPNN, and each BPNN adopts eight neurons. Random-Forest uses the Boostrap sampling method, meanwhile it contains 500 randomly Decision-Tree. KNIA initial state integrates 5 BPNN, 10 Decision-Tree, 5 support vector machine (SVM) and 1 extreme learning machine. To evaluate the performance of all the training methods

Table 1. Experiment results

Data set	BPNN	Decision-Tree	Random-Forest	BPEnsemble	KNIA
Wine	0.9438	0.9326	0.9888	0.9663	1
Bcancer	0.9420	0.9420	0.9560	0.9855	0.9888
Vote	0.9471	0.9632	0.9632	0.9524	0.9643
Cdisease	0.9524	1	1	0.9762	1
PWsites	0.8751	0.8878	0.9367	0.9647	0.9763

described above, we use the five data sets to train the methods. The results are shown in Table 1. Observing the table of results, we notice that:

(1) When the ensemble algorithms only are considering, KNIA outperforms BPEnsemble and Random_Forest in four of all five data sets. And it can find that the Random-Forest and BPEnsemble algorithms with the integrated nature are better than the other two algorithms. This shows that ensemble learning method has the natural advantages, which can integrate the advantages of large classifiers.

(2) The results show that the accuracy of our new method is improved by an average of 5.38%, 5.38%, 1.694% and 1.686% compared respectively with other methods. Although the performance of the new algorithms and the best algorithms is similar or equal in some data set, our algorithm is always better than the worst algorithm. This shows that our algorithm has very good generalization ability.

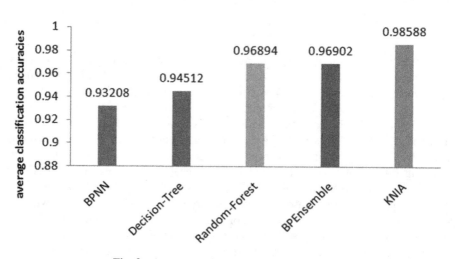

Fig. 2. Average performance of five algorithms

(3) Compared with other algorithm integration algorithm, we found that the result of the integration algorithm is significantly affected by selection. And the experimental results show that the new algorithm has a negative correlation is better than all integration or random selection, because the negative correlation property is able to eliminate and mitigate the mutual exclusion.

4.2   The Impact on the Number of Neurons

In order to prove the superiority of the new method from several aspects, the KNIA integrates the BPNN algorithm in this part. Neuron was a very important parameter for most neural networks, so there were two experiments to be carried out for different neurons. One was to compare the use of different neurons in the new methods, the other was the comparison of BPEnsemble and KNIA using different neurons. The first part of the experiment was aimed at KNIA, and it was assumed that the number of neurons was the same in the neural network sub algorithm, and the second was to compare the KNIA with different neurons (Fig. 3):

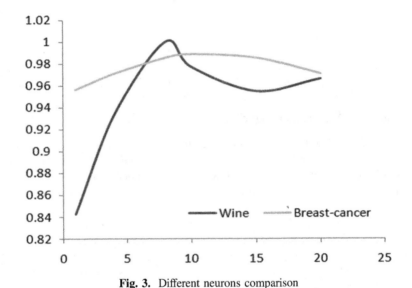

Fig. 3. Different neurons comparison

We used the method with 1, 4, 8, 10, 15 and 20 neurons. The result shows that the test result has a close relationship with the neurons. Not the more neurons the better, nor is it good for different data to use the same. For Wine and Breast-cancer, KNIA method can get the best effect by using 8 and 10 neurons respectively (Fig. 4).

As can be seen from the above, KNIA and BPEnsemble have similar curves, but the KNIA method is better than the BPEnsemble method. This shows that even though the two methods use the BP as the integrated sub algorithm, but the different integration methods have different effects. Secondly, the performance of the algorithm is related to the number of neurons, and it is very important to select the appropriate number of neurons. The reason of this phenomenon is that too many neurons can lead to over fitting of training, but too few of neurons can lead to the network's ability to classify.

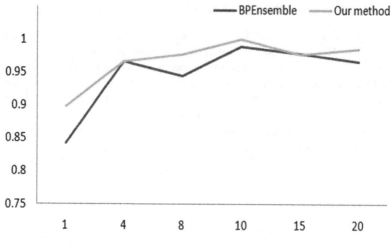

Fig. 4. KNIA and BPEnsemble comparison

4.3   Effect of Classification Algorithm K-means

In the KNIA method, K-means method is used to divide a subset of data, so different K maybe have an important impact on the results. To confirm this, this experiment constructed six different KNIA methods which corresponded to six different k on the data set Wine. The results are as follows:

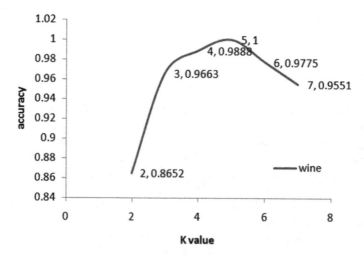

Fig. 5. The effect of K value

Figure 5 shows that the number of K-means clustering has a significant effect on performance. When K is five, the algorithm is close to maximum performance. When K is 2, it shows the worst performance. The reason is that too few of the clusters cannot achieve the purpose of training sufficient number of algorithms, so that the negative correlation theory is not enough to choose a different algorithm. And too many of the different data sets training a large number of method sets, may have a greater probability to obtain a conflict with each other or have a repeat of the method sets, which is not conducive to improve the performance of the integrated algorithm.

5 Conclusion

In this paper, KNIA method is employed to create the heterogeneous ensemble learning. It mainly uses K-means method to construct derived classifiers. And negative correlation theory is used to select the weights with different properties. KNIA method effectively raises the differences between the selected weights. Meanwhile the new algorithm with adaptive algorithm significantly reduces the time complexity. The experiments show that KNIA algorithm compared with other classical algorithms improves 3.54% on average. And we prove that its superiority has universality from different angles. Although there are more than ten thousand records in Phishing_Websites data set, it cannot achieve the level of big data. This may be not sufficient to show the advantages and disadvantages of the algorithm. There is a disadvantage of the novel method is that the advantages of sub-algorithms are not reasonably utilized in the joint phase. So KNIA algorithm still needs us to continue to in-depth study.

Acknowledgment. The author is grateful to Baosheng Wang and Bo Yu for the guidance and advice, and thanks to the support of the project. The work was supported by Science Foundation of China under (NSFC) Grant No. 61472437 and No. 61303264.

References

1. Gu, B., Sheng, V.S., Tay, K.Y., Romano, X., Li, S.: Incremental support vector learning for ordinal regression. IEEE Trans. Neural Netw. Learn. Syst. **26**(7), 1403–1416 (2015)
2. Gu, B., Sheng, V.S.: A robust regularization path algorithm for -support vector classification. IEEE Trans. Neural Netw. Learn. Syst. (2016). doi:10.1109/TNNLS.2016.2527796
3. Gu, B., Sun, X., Sheng, V.S.: Structural minimax probability machine. IEEE Trans. Neural Netw. Learn. Syst. (2016). doi:10.1109/TNNLS.2016.2544779
4. Hansen, L.K., Salamon, P.: Neural network ensemble. IEEE Trans. Pattern Anal. Mach. Intell. **12**(10), 993–1001 (1990)
5. Dietterich, T.G.: Machine learning research: four current directions. AI Mag. **18**(4), 97–136 (1977)
6. Liu, X., Wang, L., Huang, G.B., et al.: Multiple kernel extreme learning machine. Neurocomputing **149**, 253–264 (2015)
7. Yao, W., Chen, X.Q., Zhao, Y.: Efficient resources provisioning based on load forecasting in cloud. IEEE Trans. Neural Netw. Learn. Syst. **23**(2), 247–259 (2012)
8. Tang, J., Cao, Y., Xiao, J., et al.: Predication of plasma concentration of remifentanil based on Elman neural network. J. Central South Univ. **20**, 3187–3192 (2013)
9. Krogh, P.S.A.: Learning with ensembles: how over-fitting can be useful. In: Proceedings of the 1995 Conference, vol. 8, p. 190 (1996)

10. Liu, J., Chen, H., Cai, B., et al.: State estimation of connected vehicles using a nonlinear ensemble filter. J. Central South Univ. **22**, 2406–2415 (2015)
11. Breiman, L.: Random forests. Mach. Learn. **45**(1), 5–32 (2001)
12. Liu, Y., Yao, X., Higuchi, T.: Evolutionary ensembles with negative correlation learning. IEEE Trans. Evol. Comput. **4**(4), 380–387 (2000)
13. Tao, H., Ma, X., Qiao, M.: Subspace selective ensemble algorithm based on feature clustering. J. Comput. **8**(2), 509–516 (2013)
14. Cheng, X., Guo, H.: The technology of selective multiple classifiers ensemble based on kernel clustering. In: Second International Symposium on Intelligent Information Technology Application, IITA 2008, vol. 2, pp. 146–150. IEEE (2008)
15. Zhou, Z.H., Wu, J., Tang, W.: Ensembling neural networks: many could be better than all. Artif. Intell. **137**(1), 239–263 (2002)
16. Breiman, L.: Bagging predictors. Mach. Learn. **24**(2), 123–140 (1996)
17. Efron, B., Tibshirani, R.J.: An Introduction to the Bootstrap. CRC Press, Boca Raton (1994)
18. Freund, Y.: Boosting a weak learning algorithm by majority. Inf. Comput. **121**(2), 256–285 (1995)
19. Freund, Y., Schapire, R.E.: A decision-theoretic generalization of on-line learning and an application to boosting. J. Comput. Syst. Sci. **55**(1), 119–139 (1997)
20. Bryll, R., Gutierrez-Osuna, R., Quek, F.: Attribute bagging: improving accuracy of classifier ensembles by using random feature subsets. Pattern Recogn. **36**(6), 1291–1302 (2003)
21. Hu, Q., Yu, D., Xie, Z., et al.: EROS: ensemble rough subspaces. Pattern Recogn. **40**(12), 3728–3739 (2007)
22. Thompson, S.: Pruning boosted classifiers with a real valued genetic algorithm. Knowl.-Based Syst. **12**(5), 277–284 (1999)
23. Fu, Q., Hu, S.X., Zhao, S.Y.: A PSO-based approach for neural network ensemble. J. Zhejiang Univ. (Eng. Sci.) **38**(12), 1596–1600 (2004)
24. Margineantu, D.D., Dietterich, T.G.: Pruning adaptive boosting. ICML **97**, 211–218 (1997)
25. Ting, K.M., Witten, I.H.: Issues in stacked generalization. J. Artif. Intell. Res. (JAIR) **10**, 271–289 (1999)
26. Jordan, M.I., Jacobs, R.A.: Hierarchical mixtures of experts and the EM algorithm. Neural Comput. **6**(2), 181–214 (1994)
27. Breiman, L.: Bagging predictors. Mach. Learn. **24**(2), 123–140 (1996)
28. Liu, Y., Yao, X.: Ensemble learning via negative correlation. Neural Netw. **12**(10), 1399–1404 (1999)
29. Minku, F.L., Inoue, H., Yao, X.: Negative correlation in incremental learning. Nat. Comput. **8**(2), 289–320 (2009)
30. Liu, Y., Yao, X.: Simultaneous training of negatively correlated neural networks in an ensemble. IEEE Trans. Syst. Man Cybern. B Cybern. **29**(6), 716–725 (1999)

Real-Time Aircraft Noise Detection Based on Large-Scale Noise Data

Weijie Ding[(✉)], Jiabin Yuan, and Sha Hua

College of Computer Science and Technology,
Nanjing University of Aeronautics and Astronautics, Nanjing, China
{dingweijie,jbyuan,huasha}@nuaa.edu.cn

Abstract. With the development of Internet of Things, aircraft noise monitoring system can be more accurate and real-time by laying large-scale monitoring devices on monitoring areas. In this paper, we present a real-time aircraft noise detection algorithm based on large-scale noise data. The spatial characteristics of the distribution of noises are discussed firstly as the premise of analyzing the differences of aircraft noises and other kinds of noises. Then we propose a way to represent the tendency surface of noise propagation and attenuation, and the unit tendency increment in one direction is defined. Finally the aircraft noise is detected by comparing threshold with the maximum sum of tendencies that all points direct to the estimated aircraft position. The noise data of the experiment is got by the monitors lay around a large domestic airport and the experiment shows that the algorithm can detect aircraft even it is 1000 m away from the monitoring area and the trace of the aircraft can be reappeared roughly.

Keywords: Aircraft noise detection · Real-time detection · Noise monitoring · Noise attenuation tendency

1 Introduction

With the rapid development of civil aviation industry, the problem of aircraft noise pollution is increasingly severe which is in an urgent need to be solved. And the airport noise monitoring system plays a very important role in it. However, the airport noise monitoring systems being used now usually put only one or a few monitors at one area, e.g. a village or a school and their surroundings. The average noise for an hour or one day is used to describe the noise of that area, which loses much data and weakens the aircraft noises. With the development of Internet of things, the devices become cheaper and the noise data can be saved at the servers through Zigbee and 3G for further processing, which is possible to figure out the problems and have a more detailed description of noise distribution in the monitoring area.

Recently, plenty of works on the new airport noise monitoring system have been put forward. In terms of the layout and its optimization, DING etc.

© Springer International Publishing AG 2016
X. Sun et al. (Eds.): ICCCS 2016, Part II, LNCS 10040, pp. 589–600, 2016.
DOI: 10.1007/978-3-319-48674-1_52

established the minimum vertex cover model and employed the improved greedy algorithm to minimize the number of vertices [1] and DING etc. brought out an optimization algorithm based on gray dynamic neural network model in 2012 [2]. A node deploy optimization algorithm based on Swarm theory is presented in 2014 [3], and in 2015 an improved grid-enabled airport noise monitoring method and a generic grid node layout method are proposed [4]. In order to fill the missing data and predict noise value, algorithms based on shadowed C-Means [5], Hybrid Ensemble Learning [6] and STARMA models [7] have been studied. Besides, Gu etc. proposed an ATNSOA-Apriori algorithm to improve the validity of the monitoring data sets and lower the number of traversing database [8].

In terms of aircraft noise detection, a simple way is to apply thresholds to sound level time history. When noise level reaches a value over the threshold for longer than an established time threshold, an aircraft noise event is detected [9], but it cannot handle noise data in real-time and can be easily effected by other noises. Some researchers used pattern recognition and machine learning technologies to detect [10–12] and classify the aircraft noises, including MFCC [13], PLP [14] and SVM [15] methods, which are based on audio recordings and gathered by acoustic measurements like microphones. But it is quite expensive and wasteful to deploy acoustic measurements at all monitoring places with the need of long and real time monitoring, that kind of accurate audio data is not necessary while one or a few data per second per node is enough.

In this paper, dozens of monitors are widely lay on the monitoring area and real-time noise data is sent to the server, and the monitoring area is divided into grids to simply the detection of aircraft noise. Based on which, a spatial method with large-scale monitors is proposed to detect the aircraft noise. Through expounding the propagation attenuation and superposition of noise, spatial characteristics of the distribution of noise are analyzed and some conclusions are summed up. Then, we propose a way to describe the tendency surface of noise distribution and the sum of unit tendencies which directs to the same position can be represented as the probability of the existence of aircraft at that position. The experiment shows that it works well for the aircraft noise detection even the aircraft is 1000 m away from the monitoring area, and the trace of the aircraft can be reappeared roughly.

The rest of this paper is organized as follows: Sect. 2 describes the spatial characteristics of distribution of noise with some conclusions. Section 3 describes in detail our proposed tendency surface of noise distribution and aircraft noise detection algorithm. The experiment is presented in Sect. 4. Finally, some concluding remarks are given in Sect. 5.

2   Spatial Characteristics of Distribution of Noise

The distribution of noise value presents a certain space characteristics because of the propagation attenuation of noise. However, it is almost impossible to analysis the propagation of noise theoretically, which is affected by many aspects. Geometric divergence (A_{div}), atmospheric absorption (A_{atm}), ground effect (A_{gr}), barrier effect (A_{bar}) and miscellaneous effects (A_{misc}) all have a big or small influence on attenuation intension of noise [16]. The formula of propagation attenuation of noise is as follows:

$$L(r) = L(r_0) - (A_{div} + A_{atm} + A_{gr} + A_{bar} + A_{misc}) \tag{1}$$

where $L(\cdot)$ represents the value of sound pressure level, and r is the distance from noise monitor to noise source, while r_0 and $L(r_0)$ is already known at reference position but $L(r)$ needs to be calculated at target position.

On actually laying monitoring devices, the devices are put in open area and 3 to 5 m above the ground to eliminate barrier and ground effect. To simplify the formula and get a brief look at the propagation attenuation, the attenuations caused by geometric divergence and atmospheric absorption are chosen, which are the most important effects in short and long distances, respectively. Suppose the noise source is point noise source, so the formula is as follows:

$$\begin{aligned} L(r) &= L(r_0) - (A_{div} + A_{atm}) \\ A_{div} &= 20\log\frac{r}{r_0} \\ A_{atm} &= \alpha(r - r_0)/1000 \end{aligned} \tag{2}$$

where α is sound attenuation coefficient, which is closely related to the temperature and humidity, along with the change of the acoustic frequence. The more accurate algorithm is introduced in [16]. Suppose the sound attenuation coefficient $\alpha = 5.0$(with $20°C$, 10% relative humidity and $1000\,Hz$) and the reference position $r_0 = 1$, the relationship between attenuation and distance is shown in Table 1. Because the geometric divergence is of log level, the noise value attenuates rapidly at close range, and becomes slow over long distance, but the atmospheric absorption becomes obvious gradually. When the noise source is at 10 m away, the noise value will decrease 20 dB, and 40 dB at 100 m.

Table 1. Noise attenuation of distance

Distance(m)	1	2	5	10	20	50	100	200	500	1000	2000	5000
$\Delta L(dB)$	0.0	6.0	14	20.0	26.0	34.0	40.1	46.2	54.5	61.0	68.0	79.0

Usually, the noise at one position are superposed by many noises, and the total noise value is as Eq. (3).

$$L = 10\log(\sum_{i=1}^{n} 10^{0.1*L_i}) \tag{3}$$

Suppose the background noise is superposed by many small noises, when a big noise propagates here, they superposes to be the total noise. So two noise values are taken as an example, the value of the larger one is L_1, the lower one is L_2

Table 2. Superposition of two noises

$L_1 - L_2(dB)$	0	1	2	3	4	5	6	7	8	9	10	20
$L - L_1(dB)$		3.0	2.5	2.1	1.8	1.5	1.2	1.0	0.8	0.6	0.5	0.4	0.04

and the total noise value is L. The changes of superposition of two noises are shown in Table 2.

If the propagating noise is greater than the background noise, the total noise value changes less than 3 dB compared to the propagating noise and the background noise is almost covered. If $L_1 - L_2 > 6 dB$, the change is negligible because of the noise error. Thus, the big noise can almost represent the total noise value and there is always a dominant noise event for one monitor point.

Table 3. Noise value of common noise events

Noise event	Noise Value(dB)
Normal talk	40–60
Street environmental noise	60–70
Noisy office	70–80
Car	80–100
Motorcycle	95–120
Aircraft	120–140

According to Tables 1, 2 and 3, if the background noise is 60 dB, the car and aircraft noise can propagate about 200 m and 2000 m, respectively (suppose the change of noise value is observable when the change is over 1 dB, which means the superposed one is greater or within less than 6 dB). With the discussion of the propagation attenuation and superposition of noise above, some conclusions of the spatial characteristics of noise distribution are summed up:

1. The greater the intensity of sound source is, the larger the range of influence is. Every 6 dB increment of noise source doubles the radius of influence, which tells the difference between big noise sources and normal noise sources, e.g. noises caused by aircraft and car, respectively. Aircraft noise can influence about 2 km, which is almost 10 times greater than car noise.
2. It will have a higher nose intensity and bigger noise attenuation tendency if the distance to the source becomes shorter. And it helps us to estimate the position of aircraft noise, which is either (a) close to the position of greatest noise value, (b) outside the monitoring area but effects the monitoring area or (c) just doesn't exist.
3. The noise value got from the monitor can almost present the biggest noise event. That makes the noise data got from the monitors meaningful. Because

the noise data can represent the biggest noise event at that position, and the neighbouring positions are possibly affected by the same noise event, the correlation of these points can be analyzed and has reality meaning.

3   Methodology

3.1   Attenuation Tendency of Noise Distribution

Obviously, the noise surface is continuous and derivable. At every position, there is a tendency surface $g(x, y) = ax + by + c$, representing the rising or falling tendency of noise in all directions, which fits the characteristics of noise propagation attenuation. And the local maximum points represent the possible sound sources.

In order to calculate the tendency surface, the correlation between the point and its neighbouring points should be considered. Suppose the monitoring area is divided into $M \times N$ grids, $Z = \begin{bmatrix} z_{11} & z_{12} & \cdots & z_{1n} \\ z_{21} & z_{22} & \cdots & z_{2n} \\ \vdots & \vdots & \ddots & \vdots \\ z_{m1} & z_{m2} & \cdots & z_{mn} \end{bmatrix}$, where z_{ij} represents the noise value at $point(i, j), 1 \leq i \leq m, 1 \leq j \leq n$. Because of the spatial characteristics of distribution of noise, for $point(i, j)$, its noise value z_{ij} is primary caused by one noise source. As the noise propagates, it influences other points as well. Thus besides $point(i, j)$, the neighbouring points are affected by that noise source possibly, and have positive relationships to the noise value z_{ij}.

Let $X_{ij} = \begin{bmatrix} x_1 & x_2 & \cdots & x_t \\ y_1 & y_2 & \cdots & y_t \end{bmatrix}^T$ be the matrix of the coordinates of the target point and its neighbouring points, where t is the number of points. While $Z_{ij} = [z_1, z_2, \ldots, z_t]^T$ represents the corresponding noise values and $W_{ij} = [w_1, w_2, \ldots, w_t]^T$ represents the correlation coefficients of points used as weights, where the correlation coefficients of the target point is 1 and others are all in $[0, 1]$. If a point is closer to the target point, that point is more likely to be influenced by the same noise source and the weight might be higher.

However, with increasing the number of points, the accuracy of the tendency will eventually decrease. As the point is too far away from the target point, the relationship between a neighbouring point and the target point will be unstable and hard to estimate, and wrong weights may cause great error. So when choosing the neighbouring points, its correlation coefficients should be greater than a certain threshold. In this paper, most recent 10 times of noise data is used by Pearson Correlation Coefficient, the number of neighbouring points is in $[4, 8]$ and the threshold is set as 0.6.

The following situation describes the best circumstance of the tendency surface function $g(x, y) = ax + by + c$, where a, b, c are 3 variables. Let $P_{ij} = \begin{bmatrix} X_{ij}, & \underbrace{1, 1, \cdots 1}_{t} \end{bmatrix}^T$, $\beta = [a, b, c]^T$, and the equation becomes $P_{ij} \times \beta = Z_{ij}$, which has no solution generally because of the complex noise influences and noise errors. In this paper, an improved Least Square Method is used to minimize the weighted Sum of Squares for Error (SSE) to estimate the variables. Because the correlation coefficients of points are different, the errors will have the corresponding weights as W_{ij}. Let $diag\,(W_{ij}) = \begin{bmatrix} w_1 & 0 & \cdots & 0 \\ 0 & w_2 & \cdots & 0 \\ \vdots & \vdots & \ddots & \vdots \\ 0 & 0 & \cdots & w_t \end{bmatrix}$ and the formula of the weighted SSE and the estimates are as follows.

$$SSE\,(\beta) = \|diag\,(W_{ij}) \times (P_{ij} \times \beta - Z_{ij})\|^2 \tag{4}$$

$$\hat{\beta} = argmin\,(SSE\,(\beta)) = \left(P_{ij}{}^T \times diag(W_{ij})^2 \times P_{ij} \right)^{-1} \times P_{ij}{}^T \times diag(W_{ij})^2 \times Z_{ij} \tag{5}$$

The estimate is $\hat{\beta} = \begin{bmatrix} \hat{a}, \hat{b}, \hat{c} \end{bmatrix}^T$ and the tendency surface function becomes $g\,(x, y) = \hat{a}x + \hat{b}y + \hat{c}$. After the variables are determined, the unit tendency at (x_i, y_j) directing to $(x_i + \Delta x, y_j + \Delta y)$ is defined in Eq. (6), which means the rising or falling of unit tendency in one direction and is used in the aircraft noise detection in Sect. 3.2.

$$g\,(\Delta x, \Delta y) = \frac{g\,(x_i + \Delta x, y_j + \Delta y) - g\,(x_i, y_j)}{\sqrt{(x_i + \Delta x - x_i)^2 + (y_j + \Delta y - y_j)^2}} = \frac{\hat{a}\Delta x + \hat{b}\Delta y + \hat{c}}{\sqrt{\Delta x^2 + \Delta y^2}} \tag{6}$$

3.2   Aircraft Noise Detection

The distances between monitors are about 200 to 300 m, which means that most of the noise sources are too far to be detected and the rest sound sources only influence one or a few monitors. While the aircraft noise affects a large area of monitors and other noises will be covered.

If there is an aircraft nearby, for one point which is mainly affected by the aircraft noise, its noise tendency should be positive by directing to the aircraft, and its unit tendency in that direction should be the maximum compared with other directions theoretically. When the tendencies of all points directing to the aircraft point are added up, the value can be regarded as the possibility of the existence of aircraft noise, and the aircraft noise is detected if the sum is greater than the threshold. The sum of all tendencies that directs to one position is shown in Eq. (7). And we assume that the aircraft will not be on the top of the point in case the denominator is zero.

$$S\,(x, y) = \sum_{i=1, j=1}^{m, n} g_{ij}\,(x - x_i, y - y_j) = \sum_{i=1, j=1}^{m, n} \frac{\hat{a_{ij}}\,(x - x_i) + \hat{b_{ij}}\,(y - y_j) + \hat{c_{ij}}}{\sqrt{(x - x_i)^2 + (y - y_j)^2}} \tag{7}$$

A simulation experiment shown in Fig. 1 illustrates the sum of tendencies. For simplicity, the number of surrounding points are 4 and all the weights are set

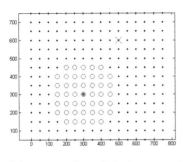

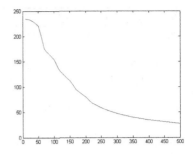

(a) propagation of single source   (b) sum of tendencies along with distance

Fig. 1. A simulation experiment of noise propagation attenuation

to be 1. Figure 1(a) shows the propagation of a single point noise source with 100 dB at 1 m reference position and the background noise is 60 db. The circle in Fig. 1(a) is the position clearly affected by the noise source, while the dots are not (total noise − background noise > 1 dB), and the 'X' label is the position that the unit tendencies of all points direct to. Figure 1(b) shows the sum of tendencies changes along with distance to the noise source. The x-axis is the distance between the position 'X' to the position of real noise source and the y-axis is the sum of tendencies. We can see from the figure that the sum attenuates along with the distance and the maximum position is at the position of noise source.

In order to check the existence of aircraft, the maximum sum of tendencies should be figured out. Eq. (8) defines the estimate value of the aircraft position, and Eq. (9) compares the maximum value with the threshold to identify the existence of aircraft noise.

$$[\hat{x}, \hat{y}] = argmax\,(\mathrm{S}\,(x, y)) \tag{8}$$

$$MaxVal = \mathrm{S}\,(\hat{x}, \hat{y}) > threshold \tag{9}$$

The Nelder-Mead algorithm is a simplex algorithm for nonlinear unconstrained optimization. It attempts to minimize a scalar-valued nonlinear function of n ($n = 2$ in this paper) real variables using only function values, without any derivative information (explicit or implicit) [17]. In this paper, The Nelder-Mead algorithm with specific optimizations is used to calculate the maximum of $S(\hat{x}, \hat{y})$. Four scalar parameters must be specified to define a complete Nelder-Mead method: coefficients of reflection(ρ), expansion(χ), contraction(γ) and shrinkage(σ). These parameters should satisfy $\rho > 0$, $\chi > \rho$, $0 < \gamma < 1$ and $0 < \sigma < 1$. And the nearly universal choices used in the standard Nelder-Mead algorithm are $\rho = 1$, $\chi = 2$, $\gamma = \frac{1}{2}$ and $\sigma = \frac{1}{2}$[17]. In this algorithm, three points form a region, reflection or expansion means updating the region, while contraction or shrinkage means the maximum point is in the region and they converge. The specific method is shown in Algorithm 1. For one time, and the algorithm terminates with following situations:

Algorithm 1. Aircraft Noise Detection

Require: $MaxIterations$, $Threshold$, ρ, χ, γ, σ

  $i = 1$

  if Aircraft noise wasnt́ detected at previous time **then**

    Choose the point of biggest noise value and its left and upper one as X_1, X_2, X_3

  else

    Choose the previous timeś target position and its left and upper one as X_1, X_2, X_3

  end if

  while $i < MaxIterations$ **do**

    $i = i + 1$

    Order 3 vertices to satisfy $f_1 = -S(x_1) \leq f_2 = -S(x_2) \leq f_3 = -S(X_3)$

    if X_1, X_2, X_3 are too far away from the monitoring area **then**

      return False

    end if

    if X_1, X_2, X_3 are too close with each other **then**

      return $S(X_1) \geq Threshold$

    end if

    Calculate reflection point $X_r = \overline{X} + \rho(\overline{X} - X_3), \overline{X} = \frac{X_1 + X_2}{2}$ and $f_r = -S(X_r)$

    if $f_1 \leq f_r < f_2$ **then**

      $X_3 = X_r$, **Continue**

    end if

    if $f_r < f_1$ **then**

      Calculate expansion point $X_e = \overline{X} + \chi(X_r - \overline{X})$ and $f_e = -S(x_e)$

      if $f_e \leq f_r$ **then**

        $X_3 = X_e$, **Continue**

      else

        $X_3 = X_r$, **Continue**

      end if

    end if

    Calculate outside contraction $X_c = \overline{X} + \gamma(X_r - \overline{X})$, $f_c = -S(X_c)$

    Calculate inside contraction $X_{cc} = \overline{X} - \gamma(\overline{X} - X_3)$, $f_{cc} = -S(X_{cc})$

    if $f_c \leq f_r < f_3$ **then**

      $X_3 = X_c$, **Continue**

    end if

    if $f_{cc} \leq f_3$ **then**

      $X_3 = X_{cc}$, **Continue**

    end if

    Shrink option $X_2 = X_1 + \sigma(X_2 - X_1), X_3 = X_1 + \sigma(X_3 - X_1)$, **Continue**

  end while

  return $S(X_1) \geq Threshold$

---

1. Three points have converged as the maximum position is found.
2. The estimate position is too far from the monitoring area, which means there is no aircraft noise.
3. It exceeds the maximum iterations and points haven't converged.

4   Experiments

The noise data used in this paper is got by the monitors lay on the south of a large domestic airport, and stored at cloud servers for further research. There are totally 100 monitors in the region of about 4 km × 4 km area. When the region is divided into grids, the grid data is interpolated or predicted by noise data as initialization operation. The algorithm we proposed is based on the grid data.

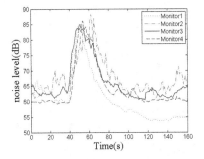

Fig. 2. Noise level with time

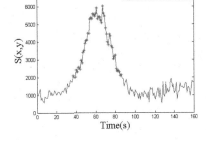

Fig. 3. Sum of tendencies with time

Figures 2 and 3 share the same time line from 2014-11-18 14:50:40 to 2014-11-18 14:53:20, which sustains 160 s, and an aircraft flew over during that time. Figure 2 shows the exact values of 4 monitors changing with time. The monitors are located at different positions. We can discover from the figure that the average background noise is about 55–65 dB at different positions. As is shown in Fig. 2, the curves of noise values can be divided into three parts. In normal

Fig. 4. Reappearance of trace of the aircraft

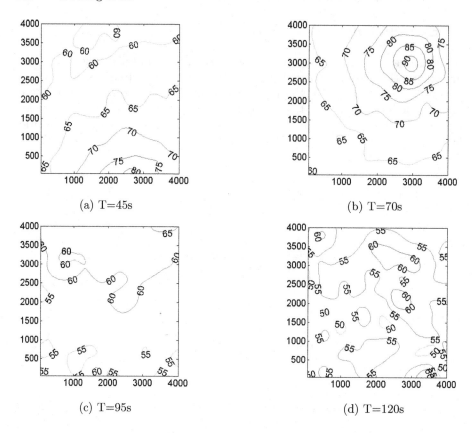

(a) T=45s

(b) T=70s

(c) T=95s

(d) T=120s

Fig. 5. Contour maps at different times.

situation, the curves are irregular and the noise data is fluctuant at average level. When the aircraft comes, all curves get risen distinctly and come to the top with some time interval and then come down to the background noise. It describes the process of an aircraft flying over. At 3rd stage, the aircraft has flown away and curves become irregular as usual. At the macroscopic level, the time series of noise data of all monitors repeats that three stage, and the parts of significant growth of noise data are caused by aircraft noise.

Figure 3 shows the $S(\hat{x}, \hat{y})$ of the monitoring area changes along with the time. The asterisk means the aircraft is detected. In analyizing the sum of tendencies, it can be contrasted with Fig. 3. The sum of tendencies is irregular and in low intensity when there are no aircraft noises. But it enlarges along with the increase of the noise data which can be speculated that the aircraft is flying over the monitoring area.

If there are no aircraft noises, the monitoring area is affected by lots of noise sources of different types, e.g. noises caused by cars and trucks and people's talks, which can only influence one or a few surrounding monitors. The tendency surfaces of the monitoring points are disordered, and the sum of tendencies directing to one position will not be very large. Because aircraft noise is much larger than normal noises, when an aircraft is flying over, a vary large range will be affected by aircraft noise and other kinds of noises will be covered, the noise values at different positions also change corresponding to the distances to the aircraft. Therefore the noise surface of the monitoring area becomes smooth and the sum of tendencies directing to the aircraft enlarges conspicuously.

Figure 4 shows the trace of aircraft more specifically, the white spots are the estimate pos itions of the aircraft. The monitoring area is in the center of the figure. But in Fig. 5, when $T = 45\,s$, the contour map can merely figure out the aircraft existence, which is possibly at the south of monitoring area. When $T = 70\,s$, the aircraft is in the monitoring area apparently. And when $T = 95\,s$, the aircraft is at the north of the monitoring area but it is hard to find through the contour map. When $T = 120\,s$, the monitoring area becomes chaotic. And the aircraft can be detected even it is 1000 m away from the monitoring area.

Some villages are on the south of the airport, and a university lays on the west. So the surrounding areas are necessary to be monitored, and the detection of aircraft can provide the basis for the noise pollution. When it is contrasted with the airline data, flights can be contrasted with the noise distribution and noise pollution, which will help the airline company and airport reduce noise pollution. Besides, the detection of aircraft and the trace can help analyze the real-time distribution of aircraft noise for further study.

5 Conclusion

The algorithm provided in the paper can detect the aircraft noise well with large-scale noise data, as the sum of tendencies of aircraft time is quite larger than that of normal time. Moreover, the algorithm can estimate the location of the aircraft as well, which is impossible for other detecting methods. By connecting the point of each time, the trace of the flight can also been known. Besides, the threshold of aircraft detection is set manually in this paper, but in further research, it can be more intelligent and self-adapting on the basis of historical data.

Acknowledgments. This work is supported by the National Nature Science Foundation of China (61139002Ding2012Automatic). We would like to thank Bojia Duan and Xingfang Zhao for their constructive comments that improved the quality of this paper.

References

1. Ding, W.T., Tao, X.U., Yang, G.Q.: Locating of airport noise monitoring points based on minimum vertex cover model of single aircraft noise event. Noise Vib. Control **32**(3), 166–170 (2012)
2. Ding, J.L., Yang, Z.H.: Optimization the layout of airport noise monitoring points based on gray dynamic neural network model. Adv. Mater. Res. **459**, 615–619 (2012)

3. Jianli, D., Delong, Z., Rong, C.: Airport noise monitoring point layout optimization method based on the swarm theory. Comput. Digit. Eng. **05**, 743–746 (2014)
4. Xiao, X., Gong, Z., Zhang, Y.: Research on simulation analysis of airport noise monitoring nodes grid-enabled layout. Comput. Technol. Dev. **09**, 12–16 (2015)
5. Wang, L., Bin, G., He, J., Chen, H.: Application of shadowed c-means in time series prediction of airport noise. Int. J. Adv. Comput. Technol. **5**(9), 597–605 (2013)
6. Xu, T., Yang, Q., Lv, Z.: A prediction method of airport noise based on hybrid ensemble learning. Sens. Transducers **171**(5), 162–168 (2014)
7. Wang, S.B., Wang, J.D., Chen, H.Y.: STARMA-network model of space-time series prediction. Appl. Res. Comput. **08**, 2315–2319 (2014)
8. Gu, F., Xu, T., Lv, Z.: Mining association rules from airport noise value among multiple monitoring points. Sens. Transducers **167**(3), 43–49 (2014)
9. Asensio, C., Ruiz, M., Recuero, M.: Real-time aircraft noise likeness detector. Appl. Acoust. **71**(6), 539–545 (2010)
10. Zheng, Y., Jeon, B., Xu, D., Wu, Q.M., Zhang, H.: Image segmentation by generalized hierarchical fuzzy C-means algorithm. J. Intell. Fuzzy Syst. **28**(2), 961–973 (2015)
11. Pan, Z., Zhang, Y., Kwong, S.: Efficient motion and disparity estimation optimization for low complexity multiview video coding. IEEE Trans. Broadcast. **61**(2), 166–176 (2015)
12. Li, B.Y.J., Li, X., Sun, X.: Segmentation-based image copy-move forgery detection scheme. IEEE Trans. Inf. Forensics Secur. **10**(3), 507–518 (2015)
13. Jianli, D., Yong, Y.: Noise detection algorithm based on modified-MFCC method. J. Convergence Inf. Technol. **7**(19), 390–397 (2012)
14. Ding, J.L., Yang, Y.: Automatic recognition of aircraft noise with PLP method. Appl. Mech. Mater. **160**, 145–149 (2012)
15. Jianli, D., Yong, Y.: Aircraft noise detection based on SVM optimized with genetic algorithm. J. Convergence Inf. Technol. **8**(10), 422–428 (2013)
16. Schreiber, L., Beckenbauer, T.: Sound propagation outdoors. In: Müller, G., Moser, M. (eds.) Handbook of Engineering Acoustics, pp. 125–135. Springer, Heidelberg (2013)
17. Lagarias, J.C., Reeds, J.A., Wright, M.H., Wright, P.E.: Convergence properties of the nelder-mead simplex method in low dimensions. Siam J. Optim. **9**(1), 112–147 (1998)

Chinese Sentiment Analysis Using Bidirectional LSTM with Word Embedding

Zheng Xiao[(⊠)] and PiJun Liang

College of Information Science and Engineering, Hunan University, Hunan, China
{zxiao,pjliang}@hnu.edu.cn

Abstract. Long Short-Term Memory network have been successfully applied to sequence modeling task and obtained great achievements. However, Chinese text contains richer syntactic and semantic information and has strong intrinsic dependency between words and phrases. In this paper, we propose Bidirectional Long Short-Term Memory (BLSTM) with word embedding for Chinese sentiment analysis. BLSTM can learn past and future information and capture stronger dependency relationship. Word embedding mainly extract words' feature from raw characters input and carry important syntactic and semantic information. Experimental results show that our model achieves 91.46 % accuracy for sentiment analysis task.

Keywords: Chinese sentiment analysis · BLSTM · Word embedding

1 Introduction

The rapidly increase and popularity of Chinese social networking platform(such as Weibo, Wei-chat etc.), online-shopping platform (such as Taobao) and the user amount lead to the explosively increasing amount of user generated text available on the Internet, organizing the vast amount of unstructured text data into structured information has become vital important. Data mining or more specifically, text mining techniques are used to extract knowledge from this type of user generated text content. Sentiment analysis is performed to extract the opinion and subjectivity knowledge from online text, formalize this knowledge discovered and analyze it for specific use [1].

Sentiment Analysis can be considered as a classification task. There are three main classification levels in sentient analysis: document-level [2], sentence-level [2,3], and aspect-level [4] sentiment analysis. Document-level sentiment analysis aims to classify an opinion document as expressing a positive or negative opinion or sentiment. It considers the whole document a basic information unit (based on one topic). Sentence-level aims to classify sentiment expressed in each sentence. Aspect-level sentiment analysis aims to classify the sentiment with respect to the specific aspect of entities. This paper will mainly focus on sentence-level sentiment analysis.

© Springer International Publishing AG 2016
X. Sun et al. (Eds.): ICCCS 2016, Part II, LNCS 10040, pp. 601–610, 2016.
DOI: 10.1007/978-3-319-48674-1_53

Using machine learning method to solve classification problem, there are many researchers and relative paper, they mainly focus on features selected and constructed [5–7]. For Chinese sentiment analysis task, Some syntactic cues like part-of-speech (POS), Chinese word segmentation (CWS), Lexicon and their contextual counterparts are commonly used for sentiment analysis problem [8–10]. Many statistical methods have been researched for Chinese text sentiment analysis, including Maximum Entropy model [11], Hidden Markov Model [12], Condition Random Field (CRF) [13], and so on.

Although sentiment analysis researches have been done for many years, it is still a great challenging task, especially for Chinese text. In above method, there are many drawbacks for sentiment analysis classification task. First, they heavily rely on the performances POS, CWS, and emotion words. Second, selecting effective features is critical to achieved great results. In addition, establishing the feature template for statistical methods requires abundant experience, and it is difficult for new researchers to build a successful classification model.

Recently, deep learning (DL) [14] methods has been successful applied to Natural Language Processing (NLP), such as, machine translation, POS, Question answering [15,16], and deep learning models have also been effective in tackling sentiment analysis problem [17–19]. Graves et al. [19] proposed long short-term memory (LSTM) neural network for sequences modeling task. And Socher et al. [17,18] used tree-structured long short-term memory networks to improve semantic representations. That recurrent neural networks are able to retain memory between training examples, allows it to capture relations between words. And it is more promising to apply recurrent neural networks to solve sentiment analysis problem because its variants LSTM having the ability to capture long short-term dependencies [20]. Although there are many researches about sentiment analysis, they are mainly focused on English text. Due to the difference of English and Chinese, Chinese has richer information than English. Chinese is quite different with English in grammatical structure also. That means Chinese focuses more in context. Therefore, putting English sentiment analysis methods and models into Chinese will lead to different result.

In this paper, we introduce bidirectional LSTM model and show its superiority for sentiment analysis problem. Bidirectional long short-term memory networks are able to incorporate contextual information from both past and future inputs. And word embedding can capture semantic relationship between words. Our model relies on neither the feature selected nor Chinese word segment, it can learn from large raw text corpus automatically. We evaluate our model on the online-shopping reviews and Weibo data show that our proposed architecture achieves superior performance.

2 Recurrent Neural Network

2.1 Overview

A recurrent neural network (RNN) is able to process a sequence of arbitrary length by recursively applying a transition function to its internal hidden states for each symbol of the input sequence. The activation of the hidden states at time step t is computed as a function $\mathcal{H}$ of the current input symbol x_t and the previous hidden states h_{t-1}:

$$h_t = \mathcal{H}(Wx_t + Uh_{t-1}) \tag{1}$$

Where $\mathcal{H}$ is common to use state-to-state transition function, usually a logistic sigmoid function or hyperbolic tangent function. W is the input-to-hidden weight matrix, U is the state-to-state recurrent weight matrix.

2.2 Long Short-Term Memory

Difficulties of training an RNN to capture long-term dependencies during training and components of the gradient vector can grow or decay exponentially over long sequences [22,23]. Hochreiter et al. [20] propose LSTM architecture addresses this problem of learning long-term dependencies by introducing a memory cell that is able to preserve state over long periods of time. There are several variants of LSM [24,25]

Figure 1 illustrates a single LSTM memory cell, which consists of a memory cell c_t, an input gate i_t, a forget gate f_t and an output gate o_t. For the LSTM, $\mathcal{H}$ is implemented by the following block functions:

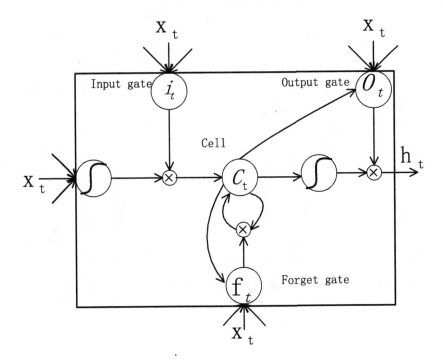

Fig. 1. A single LSTM cell [25]

$$i_t = \sigma(W^{xi}x_t + W^{hi}h_{t-1} + W^{ci}c_{t-1} + b^i) \tag{2}$$

$$f_t = \sigma(W^{xf}x_t + W^{hf}h_{t-1} + W^{cf}c_{t-1} + b^f) \tag{3}$$

$$c_t = f_t \odot c_{t-1} + i_t \odot tanh(W^{xc}x_t + W^{hc}h_{t-1} + b^c) \tag{4}$$

$$o_t = \sigma(W^{xo}x_t + W^{ho}h_{t-1} + W^{co}c_t + b^o) \tag{5}$$

$$h_t = o_t \odot tanh(c_t) \tag{6}$$

Where $x = (x_1, x_2, ..., x_T)$ is the input feature sequence, σ is the logistic function. The symbol $\odot$ represent the element-wise operation, W is the weight matrix and the superscript indicates it is the matrix between two different gates.

3   Model

Now we describe how to use a bidirectional long short-term network to build sentiment analysis model. Figure 2 illustrate BLSTM model for Chinese sentiment analysis.

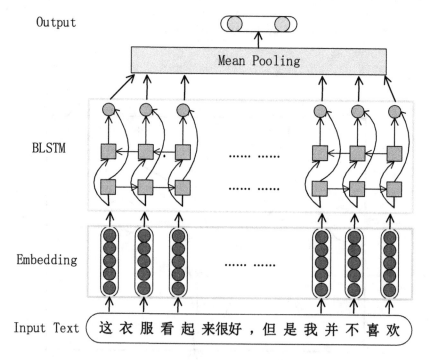

Fig. 2. BLSTM with word embedding sentiment analysis model

Word embedding map the words or phrases from the vocabulary to the vectors of real number in a low-dimensional space than the vocabulary size and it also plays a vital important role for NLP task, since distributed representation or word embedding can carry import syntactic and semantic information [26,27]. And word embedding shows superior performance for Chinese text too [28]. This word embedding layer mainly extracts word feature from raw Chinese characters.

One shortcoming of conventional RNNs is that they are only able to make use of previous context. However, that Chinese has dependency relation with context leads to the result that we need to utilize not only past previous information but also future information. A Bidirectional LSTM consists of two LSTMs that are run in parallel: one on the input sequence and the other on the reverse of the input sequence. At each time step, the hidden state of the Bidirectional LSTM is the concatenation of the forward and backward hidden states. This setup allows the hidden state to capture both past and future information [21].

Figure 3 illustrated a BRNN computes the forward hidden sequence $\overrightarrow{h}$, the backward hidden sequence $\overleftarrow{h}$ and the output sequence y by iterating the backward layer from $t = T$ to 1, the forward layer from $t = 1$ to T and then updating the output layer:

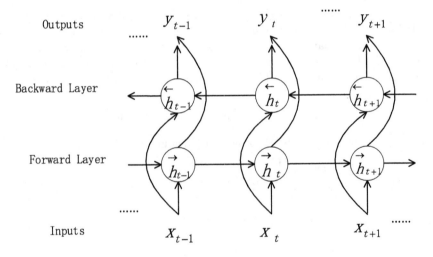

Fig. 3. Bidirectional recurrent neural network

$$\overrightarrow{h}_t = \mathcal{H}(W_{x\overrightarrow{h}}x_t + W_{\overrightarrow{h}\overrightarrow{h}}\overrightarrow{h}_{t-1} + b_{\overrightarrow{h}}) \tag{7}$$

$$\overleftarrow{h}_t = \mathcal{H}(W_{x\overleftarrow{h}}x_t + W_{\overleftarrow{h}\overleftarrow{h}}\overleftarrow{h}_{t-1} + b_{\overleftarrow{h}}) \tag{8}$$

$$y_t = W_{\overrightarrow{h}y}\overrightarrow{h}_t + W_{\overleftarrow{h}y}\overleftarrow{h}_t + b_y \tag{9}$$

Where $y = (y_1, y_2, ..., y_T)$ is the BLSTM sequence output.

In sentiment analysis model, the BLSTM input is the word embedding and $\mathcal{H}$ is the LSTM block transition function. And we wish to predict sentiment label $\tilde{c}$ from some discrete of class $\mathcal{C}$ (in this paper, $\mathcal{C}$ is the binary sentiment label set: positive or negative). Given the input sequence sample $x = (x_1, x_2, ..., x_T)$, and $y = (y_1, y_2, ..., y_T)$ for the BLSTM output. $z = \frac{1}{T} \sum_i y_i$ is the average over all the timesteps results of the y. $\widetilde{c}$ is predicted by softmax classifier that takes the BLSTM average output z as input:

$$\widetilde{p}_\theta(c|\{x\}_i) = softmax(W^z z + b^z) \tag{10}$$

$$\widetilde{c}_i = argmax\widetilde{p}_\theta(c|\{x\}_i) \tag{11}$$

4   Experiments

We evaluate our model on online-shopping product reviews and Weibo data, all these reviews and data has been tagged by their author as positive and negative. This corpus consists of 13000 reviews, which has 7000 positive comments and we shuffled the positive and negative data. We use the standard train/dev/test splits 9100/950/2950 for sentiment predict task.

In comparing our LSTM/BLSTM model against for Chinese sentiment analysis, we used CRF-based model as baseline. And the CRF-based feature template used the model proposed by Li et al. [13].

In order to get the best performance of BLSTM architecture, we control the BLSTM and LSTM architecture model by varying their number of hidden units. Specifically, for two layers LSTM/BLSTM, the number of parameters are kept the small, the forward and backward transition function are share for BLSTM. Table 1 gives the number of hidden units included in LSTM and BLSTM.

Table 1. LSTM architecture and hidden units

LSTM variant	Hidden units
LSTM	200
2-layer LSTM	128
BLSTM	100
2-layer BLSTM	64

We used back-propagation through time (BPTT) method [29] and AdaGrad [30] with learning rate of 0.8 and minibatch size of 20 to train our model. We use the development set to tune the hyperparameters for our model, and use dropout regularized technology [31] to against overfitting. The experiment result with baseline are summarized in the Table 2.

According to the experiment, we found the best performances for Chinese text sentiment analysis which are obtained by the LSTM and BLSTM architecture topology relatively, In order to investigate the performance of word embedding, we compare the pre-random initial and pre-train word embedding initial using word2vec [25], these embedding had 200-dimensional and were tuned during training epoch. We are summarized our result for BLSTM and LSTM model on sentiment analysis in Fig. 4.

Table 2. The result of the sentiment analysis with different method

Model	Accuracy
CRF-based	88.34 %
LSTM	87.49 %
2-layer LSTM	87.00 %
BLSTM	91.46 %
2-layer BLSTM	90.28 %

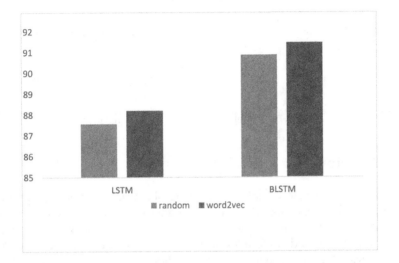

Fig. 4. BLSTM sentiment analysis accuracy with different initial ways

From the Fig. 4, we found that the pre-train word embedding initial with well-tuned during training epoch can obtain better performance. Because using pre-train word embedding initial can easily train and tune the hyperparameters, and pre-train word embedding initial have been captured the syntactic and semantic information during training. For pre-random initial word embedding, it is difficult to tune weights and capture dependency between words and phrases than pre-word2vec.

We investigate the effect of sentence length on the performance of the LSTM and BLSTM model for sentiment analysis. In Fig. 5, we show the relationship between accuracy with sentence length, we can find bidirectional long short-term memory network obtain better performance than long short-term memory network, and the LSTM get the best performance with sentence length 10, BLSTM with sentence 20. Because BLSTM can learn previous and feature information and can capture more stronger dependency between words and phrases than LSTM. The result demonstrated that the sentence length limits the performance of the BLSTM/ LSTM on sentiment analysis task as well.

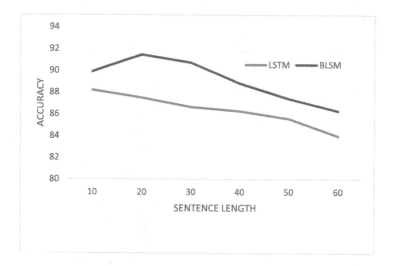

Fig. 5. The effect of the sentence length

5 Conclusion

In this paper, we propose bidirectional long short-term memory network for Chinese text sentiment analysis, and this model take raw characters as input. Word embedding can learned context and syntactic and semantic information during train model, and these information is important for Chinese text sentiment analysis task. The experiment results show it superior performance. Our results suggest that it is promising to use bidirectional long short-term memory network for Chinese text process.

Acknowledgment. The authors thank the anonymous reviewers for their valuable comments and suggestions. The research was partially funded by the National Science Foundation of China (Grant No. 61370095, 61502165), the Open Foundation of Jiangsu Engineering Center of Network Monitoring No. KJR1541, CICAEET fund and PAPD fund, the Scientific Research Fund of Hunan Provincial Education Department (Grant No. 14C0680), and Hunan Normal University of Youth Science Foundation (Grant No. 11404).

References

1. Liu, B.: Sentiment analysis and subjectivity. In: Handbook of Natural Language Processing, pp. 627–666 (2010)
2. Balahur, A., Steinberger, R., Kabadjov, M.: Sentiment analysis in the news. Infrared Phys. Technol. **65**, 94–102 (2014)
3. Long, J., Yu. M., Zhou, M., et al.: Target-dependent twitter sentiment classification. In: Proceedings of the 49th Annual Meeting of the Association for Computational Linguistics: Human Language Technologies (2011)

4. Pak, A., Paroubek, P.: Twitter as a corpus for sentiment analysis and opinion mining. In: Proceedings of International Conference on Language Resources and Evaluation (LREc), vol. 10 (2010)
5. Wen, X., Shao, L., Xue, Y., Fang, W.: A rapid learning algorithm for vehicle classification. Inf. Sci. **295**(1), 395–406 (2015)
6. Chen, B., Shu, H., Coatrieux, G., Chen, G., Sun, X., Coatrieux, J.-L.: Color image analysis by quaternion-type moments. J. Math. Imag. Vis. **51**(1), 124–144 (2015)
7. Bin, G., Sheng, V.S., Wang, Z., Ho, D., Osman, S., Li, S.: Incremental learning for - support vector regression. Neural Netw. **67**, 140–150 (2015)
8. Cui, A., Zhang, H., Liu, Y., Zhang, M., Ma, S.: Lexicon-based sentiment analysis on topical chinese microblog messages. In: Li, J., Qi, G., Zhao, D., Nejdl, W., Zheng, H.-T. (eds.) Semantic Web and Web Science, pp. 333–344. Springer, New York (2013)
9. Yuan, B., Liu, Y., Li, H.: Sentiment classification in Chinese microblogs: lexicon-based and learning-based approaches. In: International Proceedings of Economics Development and Research, vol. 68, p. 1 (2013)
10. Wang, D., Li, F.: Sentiment analysis of Chinese microblogs based on layered features. In: Loo, C.K., Yap, K.S., Wong, K.W., Teoh, A., Huang, K. (eds.) ICONIP 2014. LNCS, vol. 8835, pp. 361–368. Springer, Heidelberg (2014). doi:10.1007/978-3-319-12640-1_44
11. Lee, H.Y., Renganathan, H.: Chinese sentiment analysis using maximum entropy. In: Sentiment Analysis Where AI Meets Psychology (SAAIP), vol. 89 (2011)
12. Liu, L., Luo, D., Liu, M., et al.: A self-adaptive hidden Markov model for emotion classification in Chinese microblogs. Math. Prob. Eng. **2015**, 1–8 (2015). doi:10.1155/2015/987189. Article ID 987189
13. Li, J., Hovy, E.H.: Sentiment analysis on the people's daily. In: EMNLP, pp. 467–476 (2014)
14. Bengio, Y., LeCun, Y., Hinton, G.: Deep learning. Nature **521**, 436–444 (2015)
15. Bengio, S., Vinyals, O., Jaitly, N., et al.: Scheduled sampling for sequence prediction with recurrent neural networks. In: Advances in Neural Information Processing Systems, pp. 1171–1179 (2015)
16. Wang, D., Nyberg, E.: A long short-term memory model for answer sentence selection in question answering. In: ACL, July 2015
17. Socher, R., Perelygin, A., Wu, J.Y., et al.: Recursive deep models for semantic compositionality over a sentiment treebank. In: Proceedings of the Conference on Empirical Methods in Natural Language Processing (EMNLP), pp. 1631–1642 (2013)
18. Tai, K.S., Socher, R., Manning, C.D.: Improved semantic representations from tree-structured long short-term memory networks. arXiv preprint arXiv:1503.00075 (2015)
19. Graves, A.: Supervised sequence labelling. In: Graves, A. (ed.) Supervised Sequence Labelling with Recurrent Neural Networks. SCI, vol. 385, pp. 5–13. Springer, Heidelberg (2012)
20. Hochreiter, S., Schmidhuber, J.: Long short-term memory. Neural Comput. **9**(8), 1735–1780 (1997)
21. Graves, A., Jaitly, N., Mohamed, A.-R.: Hybrid speech recognition with dee bidirectional LSTM. In: IEEE Workshop on Automatic Speech Recognition and Understanding (ASRU), pp. 273–278 (2013)
22. Hochreiter, S.: The vanishing gradient problem during learning recurrent neural nets, problem solutions. Int. J. Uncertainty Fuzziness Knowl. Based Syst. **6**(02), 107–116 (1998)

23. Bengio, Y., Simard, P., Frasconi, P.: Learning long-term dependencies with gradient descent is difficult. IEEE Trans. Neural Netw. **5**(2), 157–166 (1994)
24. Gers, F.A., Schraudolph, N.N., Schmidhuber, J.: Learning precise timing with LSTM recurrent networks. J. Mach. Learn. Res. **3**, 115–143 (2003)
25. Zaremba, W., Sutskever, I.: Learning to execute. arXiv preprint arXiv:1410.4615 (2014)
26. Mikolov, T., Sutskever, I., Chen, K., Corrado, G.S., Dean, J.: Distributed representations of words and phrases and their compositionality. In: Proceedings of NIPS, pp. 3111–3119 (2013)
27. Mikolov, T., Yih, W., Zweig, G.: Linguistic regularities in continuous space word representations. In: Proceedings of HLT-NAACL, pp. 746–751 (2013)
28. Liu, X., Duh, K., Matsumoto, Y., et al.: Learning character representations for Chinese word segmentation. In: NIPS Workshop on Modern Machine Learning and Natural Language Processing (2014)
29. Williams, R.J., Zipser, D.: Gradient-based learning algorithms for recurrent networks, their computational complexity. In: Back-Propagation: Theory, Architectures and Applications, pp. 433–486 (1995)
30. Duchi, J., Hazan, E., Singer, Y.: Adaptive subgradient methods for online learning, stochastic optimization. J. Mach. Learn. Res. **12**, 2121–2159 (2011)
31. Hinton, G.E., Srivastava, N., Krizhevsky, A., Sutskever, I., Salakhutdinov, R.R.: Improving neural networks by preventing co-adaptation of feature detectors. arXiv preprint arXiv:1207.0580 (2012)

Domain Adaptation with Active Learning for Named Entity Recognition

Huiyu Sun[✉], Ralph Grishman, and Yingchao Wang

Department of Computer Science, New York University,
New York, NY 10012, USA
{hs2879,yw1978}@nyu.edu, grishman@cs.nyu.edu

Abstract. One of the dominant problems facing Named Entity Recognition is that when a system trained on one domain is applied to a different domain, a substantial drop in performance is frequently observed. In this paper, we apply active learning strategies to domain adaptation for named entity recognition systems and show that adaptive learning combining the source and target domains is more effective than non-adaptive learning directly from the target domain. Active learning aims to minimize labeling effort by selecting the most informative instances to label. We investigate several sample selection techniques such as Maximum Entropy and Smallest Margin and apply them to the ACE corpus. Our results show that the labeling cost can be reduced by over 92 % without degrading the performance.

Keywords: Named entity recognition · Active learning · Domain adaptation

1 Introduction

Named entity recognition (NER) is the task of identifying mentions of names in text and classify them into pre-defined categories such as persons, organizations and locations. In traditional supervised approaches, training a NER system on a new domain uses whatever labeled data is provided. This requires costly human labeling of large quantities of data, and is often a bottleneck in building a supervised model for a new domain. By contrast, Active learning selects the most informative data for labeling, aiming to achieve a high accuracy with as little labeling effort as possible.

An active learner starts out with a small set of labeled data, it then selects a number of informative samples from a large pool of unlabeled data, these samples are labeled and added to the dataset, and the process is repeated many times until some stopping criterion is met. A popular sampling strategy is to use uncertainty sampling where the least certain samples are selected and added to the training dataset. Domain adaptation assumes that the source and target domains are inherently similar to each other, although this is not always the case. Therefore we also consider non-adaptive active learning: where the training data

© Springer International Publishing AG 2016
X. Sun et al. (Eds.): ICCCS 2016, Part II, LNCS 10040, pp. 611–622, 2016.
DOI: 10.1007/978-3-319-48674-1_54

from the source domain are not used in the active learning process. Instead, we build the training dataset from scratch, gradually adding samples from the target domain to it.

The remainder of this paper is organized as follows. Section 2 discusses related works on NER, active learning, and domain adaptation. Section 3 gives the pre-processing pipeline including our NER system. Section 4 gives the active learning algorithm and introduces different sampling strategies. Section 5 provides our experimental settings. Section 6 presents the experimental results, comparing the effect of sampling methods, batch sizes, etc. Section 7 presents potential future research areas. Section 8 concludes with a summary of our findings.

2 Related Works

Shen et al. 2004 [2] proposed a multi-criteria-based active learning approach to NER. They selected samples for labeling according to the following criteria: informativeness, representativeness and diversity. Becker et al., 2005 [3] used a committee-based active learning methods for bootstrapping a statistical NER system. They used the KL-divergence metric to quantify the degree of deviation between classifiers in a committee and found that the averaged KL-divergence performs the best with a 23.5 % reduction in annotation cost to reach an F-score of 69 %. Sun et al. 2011 [30] proposed a cross-domain bootstrapping algorithm for NER domain adaptation. They first generalized lexical features of the source domain with word clusters, then selected target domain instances based on multiple criteria. Without using annotated data from the target domain they were able to improve the source model's performance by 7 %.

Zhu et al. 2008 [4] presented a new uncertainty sampling technique for active learning, called sampling by uncertainty and density (SUD), in which a k-Nearest-Neighbor-based density measure is adopted to determine whether an unlabeled example is an outlier. Zhu et al. 2010 [14] found that many uncertainty sampling methods such as maximum entropy often fail by selecting outliers. They proposed two techniques to solve the outlier problem; sampling by uncertainty and density (SUD) and density-based re-ranking.

Xiao et al. 2013 [6] investigated domain adaptation for sequence labeling tasks, and used distributed representation learning to learn a log-bilinear language adaptation model. Rai et al. 2013 [7], Chiticariu et al. 2013 [8] and Li et al. 2012 [9] investigated various aspects of domain adaptation and active learning and applied it to applications such as NER, text classification and WSD. Settles et al. 2008 [5] presented an analysis of active learning strategies for sequential labeling tasks. They also proposed a new sampling strategy called information density (ID), where the informativeness of a sample is weighted by its average similarity to all other sequences in the unlabeled set.

3 Pre-processing and Our NER System

We use the CoNLL03 (Tjong et al. 2003 [25]) corpus as the source domain. It classifies named entities (NE) into the following types: organization, location, person, and miscellaneous. The target domain we chose is ACE05 (NIST, 2005), a collection of broadcast news, conversations, and reports. ACE05 classifies NEs into the following types: organization, location, person, geo-political entity, facility, weapon, and vehicle. ACE05 is already annotated. Therefore, we will remove the annotations where necessary to simulate a domain of un-annotated data. The pre-processing pipeline used to assist the active learning process is shown in Fig. 1.

First we tokenize the ACE05 corpus, matching the different tags between ACE and CoNLL so that the tag set remains unchanged. In the case of a domain that is completely different from CoNLL such as a biomedical corpus, we need to use non-adaptive active learning: a small set of labeled data from the target domain make up the entirety of the training data, without using any from CoNLL03. We also use ACE05 as the target domain for non-adaptive active learning in order to compare results with adaptive active learning.

The tokenized ACE05 corpus is then tagged for Part-of-speech (POS). We trained a bi-gram POS tagger using the Hidden Markov Model and used the Viterbi decoding algorithm to find the optimal tag sequence. The training data are drawn from the Wall Street Journal (WSJ) corpus. Then unknown words rules and Transformation-based Learning rules are applied to improve performance. Our POS tagger has an accuracy of 96.6 % scored on the WSJ test set.

Next, we trained a Noun chunk tagger using the Maximum Entropy model and applied it to the POS tagged ACE corpus. The training data are drawn from the WSJ corpus. Our Noun chunk tagger has an F-measure of 94 % scored on the WSJ test set. The results from the POS and Noun chunk tagged ACE05 corpus is first merged together consisting of the token, its POS tag, and its Noun chunk tag. This is later used for active learning.

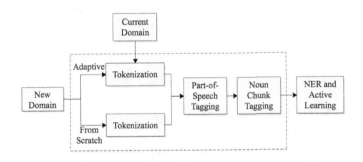

Fig. 1. The pre-processing pipeline for NER active learning.

We trained a NER tagger on the CoNLL03 corpus using the Maximum Entropy (MaxEnt) model. Here we introduce the features used to train the MaxEnt model. First, a list of local features is listed in Table 1. The shape features is a regular expression transformation in which each character of a word is substituted with X if it is capitalized, with x if it is lower case, with d if it is a

Table 1. Local features. w_i indicates the current word, p_i indicates the current POS tag, c_i indicates the current noun chunk tag, and n_i indicates the current NE tag.

Token features	$w_i, w_{i-1}, w_{i-2}, w_{i+1}, w_{i+2}$
	p_i, p_{i+1}, p_{i+2}
	n_{i-1}
Conjunction features	$w_{i-1} + w_i, w_i + w_{i+1}$
	$p_{i-1} + p_i, p_i + p_{i+1}, p_{i-1} + p_i + p_{i+1}$
	$c_{i-1} + c_i$
	$s_{i-1} + s_i, s_i + s_{i+1}, s_{i-1} + s_i + s_{i+1}$
Disjunction features	$n_{i-1} + w_i, n_{i-1} + p_{i-1} + p_i, n_{i-1} + c_{i-1} + c_i, n_{i-1} + s_i$
	$s_i + w_{i-1}, s_i + w_{i+1}$
	$p_i + w_{i+1}$
Word shape features	$s_i, s_{i-1}, s_{i-2}, s_{i+1}$

digit, and with the character itself otherwise. Additionally, sequences of two or more characters x is substituted with x* to form another set of shape features.

Next, external features are added. Wikipedia gazetteers containing pages of persons, locations, organizations and their redirect pages are used as features. Then, we used Brown's words clustering features. Brown's algorithm (Brown et al. 1992 [11]) is a hierarchical clustering algorithm that clusters words with a higher mutual information of bigrams. The output paths of a word can be encoded with a bit sequence. Brown clusters were prepared by the authors of (Turian et al. 2010 [12]). We used prefixes of the length of 5, 10, 15, and 20 of such encodings as features.

Our NER tagger uses MaxEnt with Generalized Iterative Scaling (GIS), which improves the estimation of the parameters at each iteration. We used 100 iterations with the cutoff frequency of 4. Our tagger achieves a F-measure of 91 % on the CoNLL03 development dataset, and a F-measure of 87.4 % scored on the CoNLL03 test dataset.

4   Active Learning

In this section, we introduce the active learning algorithms we used to adapt our NER tagger to ACE05. The active learning algorithm is shown in Algorithm 1. In traditional approaches, additional training data is selected using the random sampling strategy from the target domain. However, to minimize the amount of human labeling effort required to adapt our system, we employ active learning strategies with uncertainty sampling [13]: choosing for labeling the example for which the model's current predictions are least certain. We compare and use two uncertainty sampling methods: Maximum Entropy and Smallest Margin.

The uncertainty sampling based on Entropy is expressed as follows:

$$S(x) = \sum_{y \in Y} P(y|x) \log P(y|x) \tag{1}$$

where x is an unlabeled example, $P(y|x)$ is the a posteriori probability of the output class $y \in Y = y_1, y_2, ..., y_k$ given the input x, i.e. the predicted probability of class y given input x. $S(\cdot)$ is the uncertainty measurement function based on the entropy estimation of the classifier's posterior distribution. This method picks examples whose prediction vector displays the greatest entropy.

An alternative is to pick examples with the Smallest Margin: the difference between the largest two predicted probabilities in the prediction vector. It is expressed as follows:

$$S(x) = |P(y_1|x) - P(y_2|x)| \tag{2}$$

where $P(y_1|x)$ is the a posteriori probability of its most likely class y_1, and $P(y_2|x)$ is the posterior of its second most likely class y_2. We take the absolute value so as to ensure that $S(x)$ acts as a maximizer for use with Algorithm 1. $S(\cdot)$ is the uncertainty measurement function based on the posterior's two most likely labeling. With uncertainty sampling, the computational cost of picking a sample from N candidates is: $O(NDK)$ where D is the number of predictors and K is the number of categories.

Algorithm 1. Active learning algorithm

1: $L \leftarrow$ the set of labeled training data;
2: $U \leftarrow$ the set of unlabeled target domain data;
3: $N \leftarrow$ NER system;
4: $S \leftarrow$ sampling strategy;
5: $B \leftarrow$ batch size;
6: **repeat**
7:     train(L, N);   ▷ train classifier on the current L using N
8:     **for** $b = 1$ to B **do**
9:         $x_b^* = argmax_{x \in U} S(x)$;   ▷ apply sampling strategy to unlabeled data
10:         $L = L \cup (x_b^*, label(x_b^*))$;   ▷ label selected examples and add to L
11:         $U = U - x_b^*$;   ▷ remove selected examples from U
12:     **end for**
13: **until** the predefined stopping criterion is met

---

5 Experimental Setting

In this section, we describe the experimental setup used to apply the different uncertainty sampling methods. Any examples selected by active learning from ACE05 first go through the pre-processing pipeline where it is tagged for POS and Noun chunks. Then the correct NE tag is supplied and the examples are added to the training data.

5.1   Adaptive vs. Non-adaptive Uncertainty Sampling

When adapting from CoNLL03 to ACE05, we first mapped different types of NE tags between CoNLL and ACE. Adaptive sampling means that the training data from CoNLL03 is combined with labeled examples from ACE05 to form the training dataset. We trained our NER system on the available training data from CoNLL03 and applied it to the un-annotated examples on ACE05. Examples for which our system's current predictions are least certain are selected and removed from ACE05, and are labeled and added to our training data set. The process is repeated many times until we reach a stopping criterion.

However, in many cases, the target domain is completely different from the source domain and therefore training data from the source are mostly useless. In our case, this is true if the target domain is, for example, a biomedical corpus. We would have to apply non-adaptive uncertainty sampling. We also use the ACE05 corpus as the target domain for non-adaptive learning, so that the results can be compared to adaptive learning. But since ACE05 has many similarities with CoNLL03, the results are therefore more optimistic than if we had used a biomedical corpus.

For non-adaptive learning, we start with a small portion of labeled examples of ACE05 as the training data. This is used to train a model using our NER system. The model is then applied to the un-annotated examples on ACE05. Examples for which our system's current predictions are least certain about are selected and removed from ACE05, and are labeled and added to our training data set. To compare adaptive and non-adaptive uncertainty sampling, we employed the same format for both CoNLL03 and ACE05 training data: each line of the CoNLL03 training data consists of the token, its POS tag, its Noun chunk tag, and its NE tag. And we used the pre-processing pipeline on the ACE05 corpus so that it also has POS tags and Noun chunk tags.

5.2   Iterations, Context and Batch Size

Each iteration of active learning selects a batch size of a certain number from the un-annotated pool. We ran many sampling iterations, and for moderate to large batch sizes (1000 tokens plus), we were able to include as much of the ACE05 corpus data as possible. However, for small batch sizes such as 100, it will take more than 1000 iterations to include one third of the ACE05 data. That would take several days and be totally impractical to implement. Therefore, we tried to run as many as 100 iterations in most cases to make different results comparable.

For active learning in NER, it is not reasonable to select a single word without context for labeling. Even if we request the label of a single word, the labeling part, such as an oracle, would have to make the additional effort to refer to the context of the word. Therefore, in our active learning process, when a word is selected by the sampling strategy, we additionally select the sentence context that the word is in for labeling.

Another factor to consider is the batch size: the number of examples selected for labeling in each iteration. Selecting too few examples will make the learning process much longer. On the other hand, selecting too many examples means that a big portion of the unlabeled corpus will need to be labeled, which is not ideal. In the next section, we investigate these factors against our sampling strategy.

6   Experimental Result

In this section, we compare the results from different active learning and uncertainty sampling strategies. We investigate the effect of varying the batch size of uncertainty sampling strategies, compare adaptive active learning with non-adaptive active learning and discuss our results.

6.1   Sampling Methods

We introduced two uncertainty sampling methods in the previous section: maximum entropy and smallest margin. We also include the random selection strategy where random words and their context are selected from ACE05 for labeling. Another method is the sequential selection method: samples from ACE are selected in sequence according to their position in the text document. We compare the performance of these four methods here. The default batch size we used is 1000 words, and default starting ACE05 corpus size for non-adaptive active learning is the first 1000 words. Figure 2 shows the active learning curve for each of the four different sampling methods. It plots the number of learned examples in thousands (Data size) against the F-measure for a number of uncertainty sampling iterations. We choose a default batch size of 40, which equates to roughly 1000 words taking into account each word's context that needs to be labeled and added to the training data.

For adaptive active learning using CoNLL03 as the training data, our NER system gets an initial F-measure of 62.96 % on ACE05 which is our baseline. As expected, the two uncertainty sampling methods achieve a much higher F-measure compared to random and sequential. Comparing entropy with margin, for the first 1 % of ACE (3100 words) learned, they achieve similar F-measure increase of 10.39 % and 10.34 % respectively. But as more examples are learned, margin clearly achieves a higher performance: for the first 10 % of ACE(31000 words) learned, the F-measure increase for margin, entropy, random and sequential are respectively 26.07, 25.49, 18.90 and 12.63, where margin beats random and sequential by over 7 % and also beats entropy by 0.58 %. For this reason, in the next sections, we use smallest margin as the default sampling method.

Now we compare the four different sampling strategies for non-adaptive active learning. By default, we start with the first 1000 words of the ACE05 corpus as the starting training data. The results are shown in Fig. 2. The starting training data gets a F-measure of 37.99 % on ACE05, much less compared to adaptive learning. Once again, uncertainty sampling methods perform better than random and sequential sampling.

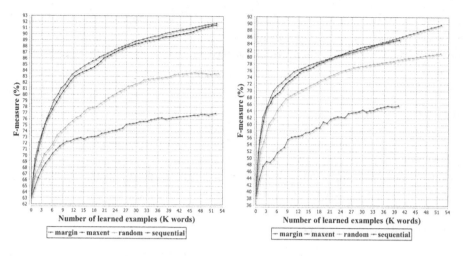

Fig. 2. Adaptive (*left*) and non-adaptive (*right*) active learning curves for different sampling methods.

We note that for both adaptive and non-adaptive learning, random sampling does much better than sequential sampling: a F-measure of 6.27 % and 13.58 % higher than sequential for adaptive and non-adaptive respectively when 10 % of ACE has been learned. Although each run of random sampling produces different results, a similar conclusion is found in many runs. This is because firstly, sequential annotation, and in particular, annotating documents in their entirety, is likely to repeatedly tag the same names. Secondly, we found that the distribution of the most informative examples favors the final two thirds of the corpus: there are a larger number of informative examples in the middle 1/3 and later 1/3 of the corpus compared to the first 1/3. This is not a problem for random sampling, but for sequential sampling, it means that a large number of NEs selected will not be as informative and hence provide little help.

6.2   Batch Size Variations

The default batch size used in previous sections is 1000 words. Now we investigate the effect that different batch sizes have on the F-measure. First, we focus on adaptive active learning. The smallest batch size possible is 1 word, which in context means an average of 25 words are selected for labeling. This is too small for us to consider since it will take too long to learn a decent amount of examples. The smallest batch size we consider is 4 words, equaling 100 words taking context into account. We first computed the F-measures for each iteration of sampling with batch sizes of 100, 500 and compared it to the default batch size of 1000. This is shown in Fig. 3.

For batch size of 100, we did over 100 iterations, learning roughly 3.7 % of the ACE corpus. We found that the smaller the batch size, the better the performance: batch size of 100, 500 and 1000 gets a F-measure increase of 21.54,

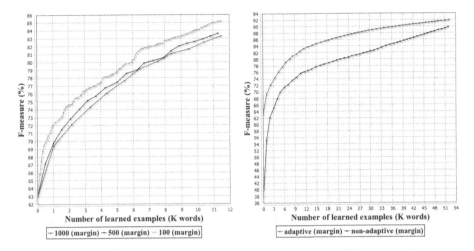

Fig. 3. Adaptive active learning curves for different batch sizes for the smallest margin sampling method (*left*), and adaptive vs. non-adaptive learning curves for batch size of 1000 (*right*).

20.65, and 20.32 respectively after learning 3.7 % of the corpus; for batch size of 100, a over 1 % performance increase over the other two. However, although a higher F-measure is achieved, learning using smaller batch sizes does result in a much longer training time. Therefore, if the intended task has no time constraint or can be accomplished with only a small number of learned examples, a batch size as small as possible is preferred. We compared different batch sizes for non-adaptive active learning and found the same results.

6.3   Discussion

We first compare the results from adaptive and non-adaptive uncertainty samplings. Figure 3 shows the result when using smallest margin sampling with batch size of 1000 for adaptive, and starting size of 1000 for non-adaptive. The baseline F-measure for adaptive is 62.96 %, and for non-adaptive is 37.99 %. It is clear that at all iterations, adaptive learning achieves a much higher performance than non-adaptive learning. This is apparent for the first 40 iterations, and for later iterations, the F-measure gap narrows but adaptive still outperforms non-adaptive. This proves the usefulness of domain adaptation as long as the tag set remains unchanged.

In terms of labelling reduction, non-adaptive active learning using the smallest margin sampling strategy achieves a F-measure of over 87 % after 44k words from ACE05 are labeled and learned. This means that labeling 14.12 % of the corpus using active learning gets the same performance as supervised learning. In this case, we have reduced the labeling effort by 85.88 %. The labelling effort is further reduced using adaptive active learning: we achieved a F-measure of over 87 % labelling just 23k words from ACE05, equaling 7.38 % of the entire corpus. In this case, we have reduced the labelling effort by 92.62 % using active learning while achieving the same performance as supervised method.

7   Future Work

We compared two uncertainty sampling methods for active learning: maximum entropy and smallest margin. There are other methods that we didn't investigate, such as the density measure method. Many researches, such as [14], found that uncertainty sampling often produce noisy outputs and selects outliers. Many improvements have been made on fix various aspect of uncertainty sampling, such as the sampling by uncertainty and density (SUD) method. In future work, we wish to investigate other uncertainty sampling methods and improvements. Apart from the uncertainty sampling methods themselves, there are various other ways to improve the effectiveness of active learning. Adding other criteria such as word representativeness, informativeness, and diversity was investigated by [2]. In the future, we also wish to investigate these and potentially other criteria. On another note, we used the ACE05 corpus as the target domain. In future works, we wish to employ a much more different domain such as a biomedical domain and investigate the challenges of non-adaptive active learning on the domain. Finally, in future works, we want to investigate active learning on different areas of NLP such as relation and event extraction.

8   Conclusion

In this paper, we addressed the learning knowledge bottleneck problem for Named Entity Recognition of a new domain using active learning with uncertainty sampling. We employed two uncertainty sampling methods: maximum entropy and smallest margin; and showed that uncertainty sampling is far more effective in reducing the number of labeled examples compared to traditional sampling methods such as random and sequential. We found that among adaptive uncertainty sampling, the smallest margin method performs better than the maximum entropy method for our chosen domains. We also compared between adaptive and non-adaptive active learning and showed that adaptive active learning is far more effective for our target domain. Additionally, we showed that smaller batch sizes (such as 100) gets a higher F-measure compared to larger batch sizes (500 and 1000). In general, the smaller the batch size, the better the performance; but in many applications, we can make compromise between speed and performance, allowing different sampling optimizations based on specific tasks. Finally, we showed that adaptive active learning can reduce the labeling effort by 92.6 % applied to the ACE05 corpus, and at the same time, achieve the same F-measure as supervised method. The labelling effort can be further reduced for even smaller batch sizes.

References

1. Jurafsky, D., Martin, J.H.: Speech and Language Processing: An introduction to Natural Language Processing, Computational Linguistics, and Speech Recognition, 2nd edn. Prentice-Hall, Upper Saddle River (2009)
2. Shen, D., Zhang, J., Su, J., Zhou, G., Tan, C.: Multi-criteria-based active learning for named entity recognition. In: Proceedings of the 42nd Annual Meeting on Association for Computational Linguistics, ACL 2004 (2004)
3. Becker, M., Hachey, B., Alex, B., Grove, C.: Optimising selective sampling for bootstrapping named entity recognition. In: Proceedings of the Workshop on Learning with Multiple Views, 22nd ICML, Bonn, Germany (2005)
4. Zhu, J., Wang, H., Yao, T., Tsou, B.K.: Active learning with sampling by uncertainty and density for word sense disambiguation and text classification. In: Proceedings of the 22nd International Conference on Computational Linguistics (Coling 2008), Manchester, pp. 1137–1144, August 2008
5. Settles, B., Craven, M.: An analysis of active learning strategies for sequence labeling tasks. In: Proceedings of the 2008 Conference on Empirical Methods in Natural Language Processing, pp. 1070–1079, Honolulu, October 2008
6. Xiao, M., Guo, Y.: Domain adaptation for sequence labeling tasks with a probabilistic language adaptation. In: Proceedings of the 30th International Conference on Machine Learning, Atlanta, Georgia, USA (2013)
7. Rai, P., Saha, A., Daume III., H., Venkatasubramanian, S.: Domain adaptation meets active learning. In: Proceedings of the NAACL HLT 2010 Workshop on Active Learning for Natural Language Processing, Los Angeles, California, pp. 27–32, June 2010
8. Chiticariu, L., Krishnamurthy, R., Li, Y., Reiss, F., Vaithyanathan, S.: Domain adaptation of rule-based annotators for named-entity recognition tasks. In: Proceedings of the 2010 Conference on Empirical Methods in Natural Language Processing, MIT, Massachusetts, USA, pp. 1002–1012, 9–11 October 2010
9. Li, L., Jin, X., Pan, S.J., Sun, J.: Multi-domain active learning for text classification. In: KDD 2012, Beijing, China, 12–16 August 2012
10. Walker, C., Strassel, S., Medero, J., Maeda, K.: ACE 2005 Multilingual Training Corpus. Linguistic Data Consortium, Philadelphia (2006)
11. Brown, P.F., Pietra, V.J.D., Desouza, P.V., Lai, J.C., Mercer, R.L.: Class-based n-gram models of natural language. Comput. Linguist. **18**, 467–479 (1992)
12. Turian, J., Ratinov, L., Bengio, Y.: Word representations: a simple and general method for semi-supervised learning. In: Proceedings of the 48th Annual Meeting of the Association for Computational Linguistics, ACL 2010, Stroudsburg, PA, USA, pp. 384–394 (2010)
13. Schein, A.I., Ungar, L.H.: Active learning for logistic regression: an evaluation. Mach. Learn. **68**, 235–265 (2007)
14. Zhu, J., Wang, H., Tsou, B.K., Ma, M.: Active learning with sampling by uncertainty and density for data annotations. IEEE Trans. Audio Speech Lang. Process. **18**(6), 1323–1331 (2010)
15. Xia, Z., Wang, X., Sun, X., Wang, Q.: A secure and dynamic multi-keyword ranked search scheme over encrypted cloud data. IEEE Trans. Parallel Distrib. Syst. **27**(2), 340–352 (2015)
16. Fu, Z., Ren, K., Shu, J., Sun, X., Huang, F.: Enabling personalized search over encrypted outsourced data with efficiency improvement. IEEE Trans. Parallel Distrib. Syst. (2015)

17. Fu, Z., Sun, X., Liu, Q., Zhou, L., Shu, J.: Achieving efficient cloud search services: multi-keyword ranked search over encrypted cloud data supporting parallel computing. IEICE Trans. Commun. **E98-B**(1), 190–200 (2015)

18. Xia, Z., Wang, X., Sun, X., Liu, Q., Xiong, N.: Steganalysis of LSB matching using differences between nonadjacent pixels. Multimedia Tools Appl. **75**(4), 1947–1962 (2016)

19. Tkachenko, M., Simanovsky, A.: Named entity recognition: exploring features. In: Proceedings of KONVENS 2012 (Main Track: Oral Presentations), Vienna, 20 September 2012

20. He, Y., Grishman, R.: ICE: rapid information extraction customization for NLP novices. In: Proceedings of NAACL-HLT 2015, Denver, Colorado, pp. 31–35, May 31–June 5 2015

21. Chen, B., Shu, H., Coatrieux, G., Chen, G., Sun, X., Coatrieux, J.: Color image analysis by quaternion-type moments. J. Math. Imag. Vis. **51**(1), 124–144 (2015)

22. Fu, L., Grishman, R.: An efficient active learning framework for new relation types. In: International Joint Conference on Natural Language Processing, Nagoya, Japan, October 2013

23. Cao, K., Li, X., Fan, M., Grishman, R.: Improving event detection with active learning. In: Proceedings of Recent Advances in Natural Language Processing (RANLP) (2015)

24. Nguyen, T., Plank, B., Grishman, R.: Semantic representations for domain adaptation: a case study on the tree Kernel-based method for relation extraction. In: Proceedings of 53rd Annual Meeting Association for Computational Linguistics (ACL) (2015)

25. Tjong, E.F., Meulder, F.D.: Introduction to the CoNLL-2003 shared task: language-independent named entity recognition. In: Proceedings of the Seventh Conference on Natural Language Learning at HLT-NAACL, CONLL 2003, vol. 4, pp. 142–147 (2003)

26. Xia, Z., Wang, X., Sun, X., Wang, B.: Steganalysis of least significant bit matching using multi-order differences. Secur. Commun. Netw. **7**(8), 1283–1291 (2014)

27. Sun, H., Mcintosh, S.: Big data mobile services for New York city taxi riders and drivers. In: 2016 IEEE International Conference on Mobile Services, San Francisco (to appear)

28. Li, J., Li, X., Yang, B., Sun, X.: Segmentation-based image copy-move forgery detection scheme. IEEE Trans. Inf. Forensics Secur. **10**(3), 507–518 (2015)

29. Gu, B., Sun, X., Sheng, V.S.: Structural minimax probability machine. IEEE Trans. Neural Netw. Learn. Syst. (2016)

30. Sun, A., Grishman, R.: Cross-domain bootstrapping for named entity recognition. In: Proceedings of SIGIR 2011 Workshop on Entity-Oriented Search (EOS) (2015)

31. Sun, H., Grishman, R., Wang, Y.: Active learning based named entity recognition and its application in natural language coverless information hiding. J. Internet Technol. (to appear)

An Empirical Study and Comparison for Tweet Sentiment Analysis

Leiming Yan[1,2(✉)] and Hao Tao[3]

[1] Jiangsu Engineering Center of Network Monitoring of Nanjing
University Information Science Technology, Nanjing, China
yan_leiming@163.com
[2] School of Computer and Software,
Nanjing University of Information Science and Technology, Nanjing, China
[3] Faculty of Computer Science, University of New Brunswick,
Fredericton, Canada
htao@unb.ca

Abstract. Tweet sentiment analysis has been an effective and valuable technique in the sentiment analysis domain. We conduct a systematic and thorough empirical study on traditional machine learning algorithms and two deep learning approaches for tweet sentiment analysis, and expect to provide a guideline for choosing which efficient classification algorithms. Based on our experiments, we found that the Support Vector Machine and the Random Forest work better statistically than other methods. Although deep learning approaches have achieved many successes in image and voice processing, simple RNN and LSTM networks do not outweigh SVM and RF in our experiments. Moreover, for the tweet feature selection, the combination of bi-grams, SentiWordNet and Stop words removal shows more effectiveness in accuracy improving.

Keywords: Sentiment analysis · Classification · Deep learning · Machine learning

1 Introduction

Sentiment analysis is called opinion mining as well, as the name implies. This technique aims at analyzing people's opinions, attitudes and emotions based on source materials [1]. It is a difficult but useful task. With the significant increase of social media, more and more people and companies pay attention to the information in reviews, forum discussions and social networks, and use opinions in these media if they need to make decisions. However, extracting and analyzing opinions from texts is a challenge. Users in social media use different languages and have different cultures. So they have their own judgment standards. Moreover, while an opinion word means positive in some contexts, it may be considered negative in different context. In order to overcome these challenges and limitations, effective approaches for accurate sentiment analysis system will be needed.

The increase of user-generated tweets has produced a wealth of messages. However, although there is a lot of useful information hidden in tweets, it is very difficult to

© Springer International Publishing AG 2016
X. Sun et al. (Eds.): ICCCS 2016, Part II, LNCS 10040, pp. 623–632, 2016.
DOI: 10.1007/978-3-319-48674-1_55

classify the sentiment of tweets automatically. Sentiment analysis over tweets faces some unique challenges that are caused by short and messy texts of tweets. The content length limitation and abnormal structures are the primary problem for solving. Positive, negative and neutral are the three common classes for tweet classification. A variety of machine learning algorithms have been studied for this purpose. However, there is a lack of a systematic study on the machine learning methods for tweet sentiment analysis. Which classification algorithms are most suitable for tweet sentiment analysis? Are those traditional methods based on Bag of Words (BoW) not effective than those deep learning approaches based on Word Embedding?

The motivation of this paper is that we would like to conduct a systematic and thorough empirical study on the machine learning algorithms for tweet sentiment analysis, and expect to provide a guideline for applying machine learning algorithms for tweet sentiment analysis. For this topic, we will choose different data sets, use some different text features to evaluate different machine learning methods and two popular deep learning approaches, RNN and LSTM.

2 Related Work

Researchers have been working on different aspects of sentiment analysis and proposed a variety of algorithms and techniques. Generally, there are two popular types of approaches for sentiment analysis: BoW-based methods and Word Embedding-based methods.

Liu et al. [1] suggested a sentiment analysis framework based on machine learning algorithm and BoW features. Go et al. [2] presented machine learning algorithms to automatically classify the sentiment of Twitter messages with distant supervision. In order to prove that pre-processing steps are necessary, they used noisy labels of Twitter messages like emoticons. After training three machine learning algorithms: Naive Bayes, Maximum Entropy and Support Vector Machine, they found using tweets with emoticons for distant supervised learning was feasible. SVM maybe have the most wide range of application and can be trained incrementally or used as regression tool also [3, 4]. Adaboost is another powerful classification algorithm, has been applied in many domain, such as vehicle image classification [5].

In Nature Language Processing (NLP) and text classification, POS tagging is a widely used method [6]. In general, POS tagging is to determine and distinguish syntactic meaning of words in a sentence by specific tags, such as adjective, adverb, verb, and so on. N-grams mode with a size 2 (n = 2) is bi-grams. It is to predict the next word based on the previous word, and it also determines the double words combination, such as "very good" and "so bad". SentiWordNet [7] is a lexical resource to determine each word in a sentence in three sentiment scores: positivity, negativity and objectivity according to speech of words for sentiment classification and opinion mining. Using stop words removal is a good way to discriminate them in the pre-processing. Stop words mean the words will not be considered by classifiers, because they are extremely common and not sentiment words, such as "a", "an", "above", "below", etc.

On the other hand, classifiers based on deep neural networks have shown powerful ability for text classification with the advantage of inherently taking into account the ordering of the words by using word vectors.

Mikolov et al. [8] introduced word vector training algorithm and a RNN based language model with applications to speech recognition. After that, some framework based on LSTM are proposed [9–11], which improve the performance of RNN obviously. Ray et al. [12] suggested a deep RNN model to obtain more better results.

However, there is few works about comparing the traditional classifiers based on BoW features and the deep learning classifiers based on word embedding. In this paper, we will conduct the comparison task and find what kinds of approaches are more efficient for sentiment analysis.

3   Methodology

3.1   Baseline Machine Learning Methods

We attempt to explore some traditional machine learning classification algorithms for sentiment analysis.

We select five different and widely used machine learning algorithms as baselines for a systematic comparison: Naive Bayes (NB), Linear Support Vector Machines (SVMs), Maximum Entropy (MaxEnt), Random Forest (RF), and Adaptive Boosting (Ada-Boost).

Naive Bayes is an algorithm which is widely used for classification problems, which is based on the so-called conditional independence assumption.

Random forest is an algorithm that learns a model of multiple decision trees for classification. That is, a set of decision trees are trained and used to classify instances in random forest. There are two main parameters in random forest algorithm: the number of decision trees t and the number of attributes used for branching.

AdaBoost is the abbreviation of "Adaptive Boosting". It is also an ensemble learning algorithm, in which a set of weak classifiers are built through multiple iterations. In the AdaBoost algorithm, each instance in the training set has a weight.

Linear SVMs perform well in most of linear separable dataset, are also the popular classifiers for sentiment analysis.

These methods usually classify tweets based on Bag of Word feature space. In the simple Bow representation of a tweet, the tweet is represented as a vector in which the words emerging in the tweet are mapped to 1.

Feature Extraction. To improve the performance of machine learning algorithms, appropriate features based on Bag of Word (BoW) must be selected in sentiment analysis. Preprocessing methods play an important role to deal with features, such as n-grams mode and part-of-speech (POS) tagging. In order to provide a systematic empirical study on machine learning algorithms for tweets sentiment analysis, we chose 4 most popular and widely used pre-processing methods: part-of-speech tagging (POS), bi-grams, Sentiment WordNet (SentiWordNet) and stop words removal, and made 6 combinations based on these methods. The purpose of using these combinations is that we try to figure out whether these pre-processing methods are useful for improving classification performance. The 6 feature combinations are shown below:

1. PBSeSt: POS + bi-grams + SentiWordNet + Stop words removal
2. PBSt: POS + bi-grams + Stop words removal
3. BSeSt: bi-grams + SentiWordNet + Stop words removal
4. PSt: POS + Stop words removal
5. St: Stop words removal
6. None: not use any pre-processing method

3.2 Deep Learning Approaches

A efficient deep learning classification framework normally consists of a deep network and word embedding.

The representations based on Bow lose the word order and much of the sematic meaning. So more recent works focus on representing the word and document as a distributed vector which retaining as much sematic information as possible. Word embedding is such a feature representation method. Take the Word2Vec as a word embedding example, it is trained by unsupervised method and then transform a word into a fixed length vector according to the context.

We choose simple RNN and LSTM to evaluate their performance for sentiment analysis on our bench dataset.

RNN. Recurrent Neural networks (RNNs) have been a very competitive classifier for Natural Language Processing. Simple RNN (SRNN) has the basic structure of RNN models, which has basically three layers: input layer X, hidden layer H and output layer Y. The input layer represents the input sequence, where each node is represented as a fix-length vector. For text, word vectors can be produced by word embedding algorithms such as Word2Vec. The output layer Y represents the predict sequence of input sequence.

Predictions are made sequentially, that means in a deep RNN, the previous hidden layer is fed into the next hidden layer; the results from previous predictions can inform future predictions. RNN is seen as a network with memory.

LSTM. Long short-term memory (LSTM) models are a special kind of recurrent neural network, which has been proposed as a state-of-the-art method for speech recognition. LSTMs add additional factors, like gates in electric circuit, to a traditional RNN. Using these factors, LSTM network can control the previous memories matters to some extent. Moreover, LSTM attempts to avoid gradient vanishing by these gates.

LSTM has been widely used for text recognition, speech recognition, and time series prediction problems, etc.

4 Data Sets

For sentiment analysis over Twitter, a number of benchmark datasets have been released in the last few years, and they are available online. Furthermore, we prefer to select the datasets that have been widely used in the Twitter sentiment analysis experiments in literatures. Saif et al. [13] introduced eight publicly available and manually annotated evaluation datasets for Twitter sentiment analysis. Based on their descriptions, we selected 2 datasets for our experiments from their eight datasets, which are Stanford Twitter Sentiment Gold dataset (STS-Gold), and Sanders Twitter Dataset (Sanders). In addition, we also collected tweets from the Twitter API. The tweets were all about video games.

The datasets we used in the experiments are described as follow:

Sanders. The Sanders Twitter dataset we used contains 3,090 tweets with three sentiments polarities: positive, negative and neutral. We ignored the irrelevant tweets. Specifically, all the tweets are constructed based on four different topics: Apple, Microsoft, Twitter and Google. They were all manually annotated which resulted in 2,123 neutral, 460 positive and 507 negative tweets.

STS-Gold. The Stanford Twitter Sentiment Gold dataset (STS-Gold) was built by Saif et al. [13] based on original Stanford Twitter corpus. This dataset contains 2,034 tweets with two types of sentiment polarities: negative (number 0) and positive (number 4). There are 1,402 tweets labeled as 0 and 632 tweets labeled as 4.

GameTweet. The GameTweet was constructed by searching topics of games like the Game dataset from twitter. There are 12,780 tweets in this dataset, and all of them were annotated by hands, including positive 3952, neutral 915 and negative 7913.

5 Experiment Results

5.1 Evaluating Traditional Machine Learning Algorithms

We first evaluate the traditional machine learning methods with Bag of Word (BoW) feature space.

In our experiments, we test 5 machine learning algorithms for each feature combinations using 10 times of 5-fold cross-validation. All prediction accuracy and variance of accuracy in the Table 1 are the mean accuracy and mean variance of 10 rounds.

From the results described in the Table 1, all accuracy numbers in bold type are the best in one feature combination and one dataset. As mentioned in Sect. 3.1, we have 6 feature combinations and test 3 datasets. In terms of accuracy, there are two machine learning algorithms that perform better on all datasets and all feature combinations. Linear Support Vector Machine (SVM) totally provided the most outstanding accuracy, Random Forest (RF) preformed the best in all times for GameTweet dataset. Besides, AdaBoost shows better prediction accuracy for all of dataset. We will evaluate these three algorithms further by optimizing algorithm parameters in next section.

Especially, all machine learning algorithms are most stable based on STS-Gold dataset, because the STS-Gold dataset just has two sentiment labels: 0 (negative) and

Table 1. Accuracy of 5 classifiers and 6 feature combinations

Features	Algorithms	GameTweet	Sanders	STS-gold
PBSeSt	NB	0.566 ± 0.012	0.661 ± 0.014	0.834 ± 0.017
	SVM	0.775 ± 0.009	0.771 ± 0.012	0.859 ± 0.015
	MaxEnt	0.752 ± 0.013	0.743 ± 0.012	0.776 ± 0.022
	RF	0.783 ± 0.007	0.732 ± 0.012	0.797 ± 0.022
	AdaBoost	0.747 ± 0.011	0.694 ± 0.019	0.547 ± 0.066
PBSt	NB	0.552 ± 0.010	0.658 ± 0.016	0.831 ± 0.018
	SVM	0.774 ± 0.008	**0.769** ± 0.011	**0.853** ± 0.014
	MaxEnt	0.754 ± 0.010	0.740 ± 0.014	0.770 ± 0.024
	RF	**0.781** ± 0.012	0.731 ± 0.010	0.799 ± 0.019
	AdaBoost	0.753 ± 0.011	0.698 ± 0.015	0.518 ± 0.031
BSeSt	NB	0.566 ± 0.013	0.662 ± 0.016	0.835 ± 0.017
	SVM	0.775 ± 0.010	**0.771** ± 0.011	**0.861** ± 0.011
	MaxEnt	0.752 ± 0.010	0.742 ± 0.015	0.776 ± 0.020
	RF	**0.782** ± 0.009	0.732 ± 0.014	0.803 ± 0.016
	AdaBoost	0.748 ± 0.010	0.691 ± 0.015	0.498 ± 0.068
Pst	NB	0.585 ± 0.011	0.683 ± 0.014	0.844 ± 0.015
	SVM	0.768 ± 0.010	**0.775** ± 0.011	**0.856** ± 0.012
	MaxEnt	0.741 ± 0.010	0.709 ± 0.019	0.767 ± 0.018
	RF	**0.784** ± 0.009	0.747 ± 0.017	0.819 ± 0.016
	AdaBoost	0.749 ± 0.011	0.693 ± 0.017	0.486 ± 0.043
St	NB	0.586 ± 0.011	0.683 ± 0.014	0.844 ± 0.014
	SVM	0.771 ± 0.009	**0.773** ± 0.013	**0.854** ± 0.014
	MaxEnt	0.741 ± 0.010	0.707 ± 0.019	0.764 ± 0.021
	RF	**0.786** ± 0.010	0.746 ± 0.010	0.821 ± 0.018
	AdaBoost	0.750 ± 0.011	0.692 ± 0.015	0.488 ± 0.035
None	NB	0.609 ± 0.012	0.630 ± 0.013	0.808 ± 0.020
	SVM	0.774 ± 0.008	**0.731** ± 0.013	**0.829** ± 0.014
	MaxEnt	0.741 ± 0.012	0.708 ± 0.016	0.763 ± 0.024
	RF	**0.778** ± 0.009	0.654 ± 0.016	0.793 ± 0.013
	AdaBoost	0.752 ± 0.010	0.606 ± 0.019	0.477 ± 0.051

4 (positive), that is, the five algorithms are good at classifying the binary data rather than other datasets.

We try to figure out which feature combination is valuable for machine learning classifier.

According to Table 1, stop words removal gives an obvious improvement for the prediction accuracy. Among PSt (part-of-speech + stop words removal) and St tested, adding POS features individually did not give any obvious extra help for sentiment classification. However, BSeSt (bi-grams + SentiWordNet + Stop words removal) is the feature combination which provides the best performance among all features tested. In other words, POS feature is only beneficial when using the bi-grams.

Parameters Optimization. Since the Linear SVM and Random Forest (RF) are the top 2 better classification algorithms, we further evaluate these two methods by optimizing their parameters.

We test Linear SVM by different C value and RF by different decision tree estimators with feature combinations PBSeSt, St and None.

According to Fig. 1, the SVM shows more stable than RF, and SVM obtains the better accuracy when using the feature PBSeSt (POS + bi-grams + SentiWordNet +

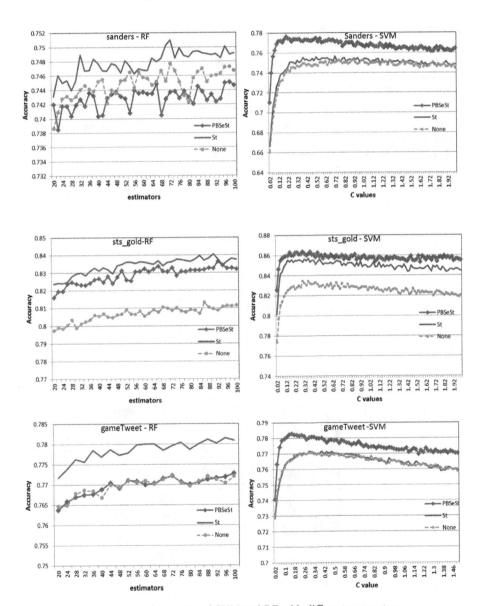

Fig. 1. The Accuracy of SVM and RF with different parameters

Stop words removal), while the RF classifier achieves better performance using St than using PBSeSt.

5.2   Evaluating Deep Learning Approaches

First, we use Word2Vec algorithm to train a word embedding model by 150 MB tweets data. Using this model, each word in tweet dataset could be transformed into a vector with 200 dimensions.

The LSTM was trained using rmsprop optimizer, which works better than annealed optimizer in our experiment. Activation function is set as *tanh*, which perform better than *ReLU*. Dropout layer is necessary as a regularizer, its rate is set 0.5. The hidden layer dimension is 200.

Simply adding multiple RNN or LSTM layer, one layer is fed as input to the next, has not obtain better performance than one layer network in our experiments, which inspires us that should design more sophisticate model structure to improve the classification performance of sentiment analysis.

Optimal performance is obtained after 10–15 training epochs.

According to Table 2 and Fig. 2, the LSTM easily attains higher accuracy than simple RNN.

Table 2. Accuracy of SRNN, LSTM and Linear SVM

Dataset	SRNN	LSTM	SVM	RF
Sanders	0.6952	0.6997	0.7764	0.7510
STS_Gold	0.7643	0.8398	0.8637	0.8404
GameTweet	0.7187	0.7497	0.7829	0.7815

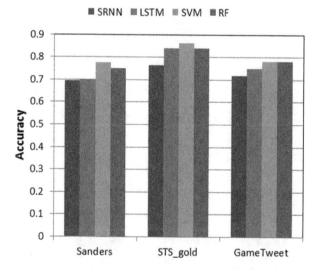

Fig. 2. Accuracy comparison among 4 algorithms

Overall, the deep network methods, such as Simple RNN and LSTM, do not outweigh SVM classifier in our experiments.

Our results show that RNN and LSTM based on Word2Vec do not perform better than traditional machine learning algorithms based on BoW features. One reason could be that the length of tweet for RNN and LSTM is still too long to memory the word sequences. Paragraph vectors seem helpful to handle this situation.

6 Conclusions

In our study, we carried out a systematic and thorough empirical study on the machine learning algorithms for tweet sentiment analysis. Through our experiments, we systematically compared 5 machine learning algorithms and 2 deep learning approaches, and investigated the performance and effectiveness of these algorithms combined with some features or word embedding. We found that the Support Vector Machine (SVM) and the Random Forest (RF) are the two algorithms that are most effective and provide the best performance based on the experimental results.

We also noticed that part-of-speech (POS) tagging cannot affect the performance of sentiment classification if using it individually. We concluded that the combination of bi-grams + SentiWordNet + Stop words removal is the most effective pfeature combination in the problem of tweet sentiment classification based on our experimental study.

Secondly, we also studied RNN and LSTM networks. Although deep learning approaches have achieved many successes in image and voice processing, simple RNN and LSTM networks do not outweigh SVM and RF in our experiments.

Acknowledgements. This work is supported by the NSFC (61272421, 41271410), the Priority Academic Program Development of Jiangsu Higher Education Institutions (PAPD)

References

1. Liu, B.: Opinion mining and sentiment analysis. In: Liu, B. (ed.) Web data mining: exploring hyperlinks, contents, and usage data. Data-Centric Systems and Applications, pp. 459–526. Springer, Heidelberg (2011)
2. Go, A., Bhayani, R., Huang, L.: Twitter sentiment classification using distant supervision. In: Cs224n Project Report, Stanford, vol. 1, p. 12 (2009)
3. Gu, B., Sheng, V.S.: A Robust regularization path algorithm for v-support vector classification. IEEE Trans. Neural Netw. Learn. Syst. (2016). doi:10.1109/TNNLS.2016.2527796
4. Bin, Gu, Sheng, V.S., Wang, Z., Ho, D., Osman, S., Li, S.: Incremental learning for v-support vector regression. Neural Netw. **67**, 140–150 (2015)
5. Wen, X., Shao, L., Xue, Y., Fang, W.: A rapid learning algorithm for vehicle classification. Inf. Sci. **295**(1), 395–406 (2015)
6. Ravi, K., Ravi, V.: A survey on opinion mining and sentiment analysis: tasks, approaches and applications. Knowl. Based Syst. **89.C**, 14–46 (2015)

7. Baccianella, S., Esuli, A., Sebastiani, F.: SentiWordNet 3.0: an enhanced lexical resource for sentiment analysis and opinion mining. In: International Conference on Language Resources and Evaluation, LREC 2010, 17–23 May 2010, Valletta, Malta, pp. 83–90 (2010)
8. Mikolov, T, et al.: Recurrent neural network based language model. In: INTERSPEECH 2010, Conference of the International Speech Communication Association, Makuhari, Chiba, Japan, September 2010, pp. 1045–1048
9. Cheng, J., et al.: Exploring sentiment parsing of microblogging texts for opinion polling on chinese public figures. Appl. Intell. **45**(2), 1–14 (2016)
10. Sundermeyer, M., Schlüter, R., Ney, H.: LSTM neural networks for language modeling. In: Interspeech, pp. 601–608 (2012)
11. Wang, X., et al.: Predicting polarities of tweets by composing word embeddings with long short-term memory. In: Meeting of the Association for Computational Linguistics and the, International Joint Conference on Natural Language Processing (2015)
12. Anupama, R., Rajeswar, S., Chaudhury, S.: A hypothesize-and-verify framework for text recognition using deep recurrent neural networks. In: International Conference on Document Analysis and Recognition IEEE Computer Society, pp. 936–940 (2015)
13. Saif, H., et al.: Evaluation datasets for twitter sentiment analysis. a survey and a new dataset, the STS-Gold. In: Workshop: Emotion and Sentiment in Social and Expressive Media: Approaches and Perspectives From Ai (2013)

Author Index

Author Index

Printed in the United States
By Bookmasters